DEVELOPMENTAL
PSYCHOLOGY

DEVELO

PSYC

PMENTAL
HOLOGY

Robert M. Liebert
STATE UNIVERSITY OF NEW YORK AT STONY BROOK

Rita Wicks Poulos
STATE UNIVERSITY OF NEW YORK AT STONY BROOK

Gloria D. Strauss
BROOKLYN COLLEGE

PRENTICE-HALL, INC.
Englewood Cliffs, New Jersey

Library of Congress Cataloging in Publication Data

LIEBERT, ROBERT M.
    Developmental psychology.

    Bibliography: p.
    1. Developmental psychology.   I. Poulos, Rita Wicks,
joint author.   II. Strauss, Gloria D., joint author.
III. Title.
BF713.L53   155.2   73-19508
ISBN   0-13-208223-3

DEVELOPMENTAL PSYCHOLOGY
Robert M. Liebert, Rita Wicks Poulos, Gloria D. Strauss

© 1974 by Prentice-Hall, Inc.
Englewood Cliffs, New Jersey

PRINTED IN THE UNITED STATES OF AMERICA

10   9   8   7   6   5   4   3

PRENTICE-HALL INTERNATIONAL, INC., *London*
PRENTICE-HALL OF AUSTRALIA, PTY. LTD., *Sydney*
PRENTICE-HALL OF CANADA, LTD., *Toronto*
PRENTICE-HALL OF INDIA PRIVATE LIMITED, *New Delhi*
PRENTICE-HALL OF JAPAN, INC., *Tokyo*

CONTENTS

II

METHODS OF
DEVELOPMENTAL RESEARCH 21

III

EARLY GROWTH
AND DEVELOPMENT 47

VI

PERCEPTUAL DEVELOPMENT   171

VII

COGNITIVE DEVELOPMENT   207

XV

BEHAVIOR PROBLEMS
OF CHILDHOOD   515

SELECTIONS

PREFACE

WHEN THIS BOOK WAS CONCEIVED a number of years ago there were far fewer texts devoted to developmental psychology than there are today. The field, as well as the volumes that introduce it to the undergraduate, has proliferated enormously in the interim, and this growth has altered appreciably the specific content and emphasis of the book that finally emerged. At the same time, though, our basic goals have not changed.

We believe that a student's first introduction to developmental psychology should provide a broad survey of what is known about human development in all of its aspects and also present at least a few in-depth contacts with the major issues and disputes that characterize the field. Equally important, the reader should become truly conversant with most of the fundamental ideas and terms used by developmentalists. This familiarity can only be achieved by repeated contact with such basic concepts as intelligence, learning, and maturation in various complementary lights, as they are applied to a number of different substantive issues. We have tried to include such planned repetition throughout the book, capitalizing on the advantages of a process-oriented, topical treatment of development as opposed to a chronological one.

To achieve the breadth they desire, teachers usually have had to rely on a "basic" text, individual reprints or readings books, and an occasional specialized monograph—integrating them as best they could. But, as students and faculty are increasingly aware, the costs of such a multi-book approach have become prohibitive. More important, when a general introduction comes from one printed source, research articles from a second volume, and specialized or extended topical discussions from a third, the beginning student is often at a loss to find any "flow" in the multitude of materials appearing in diverse styles and formats.

Our aim in writing *Developmental Psychology* has been to combine the advantages of the basic text–readings–extended discussion approach with the benefits of a single, coherent presentation. Thus, reprinted selections from the related professional literature and extended discussions of various socially and theoretically important issues (appearing in shaded print) have been included. We have tried to weave these materials into our basic text presentation so as to optimize the degree to which they are understandable —and meaningful.

Within this framework, most of the usual content areas of child and developmental psychology has been surveyed. We also have emphasized some relatively less typical aspects of the field that are among the most exciting for the future: the influence of ethology on the study of human development, learning approaches to remediation, language acquisition as viewed from contemporary psycholinguistic theory, and attention to the developmental problems of the socially disadvantaged, retarded, and disturbed. In these treatments, as elsewhere in the book, we have tried to emphasize the underlying continuities—from normal to abnormal; from theory to research to practical application; and from childhood and adolescence through senior citizenry and the problems of old age.

In preparing this volume we received invaluable help from many people, not all of whom can be named here. Those who provided formal reviews are acknowledged elsewhere. In addition, special thanks are due William Anderson, Angela Edwards, and Robert S. Siegler, who drafted sections of text for us, Ann DiSanza and Joyce Sprafkin, who provided help with the indexes, and Patricia Donagher for untiring research and secretarial assistance throughout the final stages of writing and production.

ROBERT M. LIEBERT

RITA WICKS POULOS

GLORIA D. STRAUSS

State University of New York at Stony Brook
Stony Brook, New York

ACKNOWLEDGMENT

We are greatly indebted to those who reviewed the manuscript during its preparation; without their thoughtful input this book would be less complete, less accurate, and less interesting. Responsibility for any problems that remain rests solely with the authors.

JUSTIN ARONFREED, *University of Pennsylvania*

ROBERT BORNSTEIN, *Miami University*

TERRY T. FAW, *University of California at Los Angeles*

PATRICIA KEITH-SPIEGEL, *California State University at Northridge*

FRANK B. MCMAHON, *University of Southern Illinois at Edwardsville*

HENRY L. MORELAND, *Florida Junior College*

WILLIAM ROHWER, *University of California at Berkeley*

ALETHA H. STEIN, *Temple University*

RICHARD G. WARGA, *Bucks County Community College*

F. L. WHALEY, *The Pennsylvania State University*

GROVER WHITEHURST, *State University of New York at Stony Brook*

JOACHIM F. WOHLWILL, *The Pennsylvania State University*

JOHN W. YOUNG, *Florida Junior College*

DEVELOPMENTAL PSYCHOLOGY

SOME DEVELOPMENTAL VIEWPOINTS

FROM CONCEPTION TO DEATH, each of us is continually changing because of certain inevitable processes of development. Some of the most overtly dramatic changes are physical; others, equally significant, are less apparent to the eye and more subtle to describe. The child who used to blush in social situations, to commit various faux pas, and to struggle with his arithmetic often becomes a socially skilled, poised adult with abilities that sometimes amaze those who "knew him when."

The fact that such changes occur is sufficient reason to be interested in them, but students of human development can claim more than the general right to pursue the intriguing and the unknown. Our growing understanding of the psychology of development already has provided us with valuable information about the basic psychological processes involved in perception, thought, learning, and socialization. This permits not only a better understanding of children's growth but also a better grasp of adolescent and adult behavior. Through an understanding of basic processes, we can hope to learn how development may go awry and to create treatment programs that will remedy deficiencies or prevent the occurrence of similar difficulties for other children and adults. There is also the other side of the coin. Some individuals seem to develop especially well, displaying unusual levels of success, competence, and interpersonal sensitivity in adulthood. Understanding how *they* got that way can be socially useful in guiding child-rearing practices.

In this book we present a general introduction to the study of human psychological development. There is, though, such an abundance of findings and viewpoints that complete coverage of the relevant literature would result in a truly encyclopedic presentation. Our approach, instead, has been to emphasize those processes and problems which are most central to contemporary developmental psychology and most likely to be of interest to the reader.

In addition to the "basic" presentation, we have included two features which will permit a close-up exploration of some particularly significant issues. First, a number of selections from the writings of prominent developmental psychologists are reprinted here in order to provide direct exposure to the language and approach found in the professional literature. Second, a few topics are examined in relatively greater detail, through extended discussions, so that the reader may obtain an in-depth familiarity with the facts, methods, and disputes which surround these issues of scientific and social importance. Before proceeding, however, we must say a word about our subject matter and about the various theories and research methods which have characterized the study of human behavior.

HISTORICAL BACKGROUND

Most of our present views about psychological development are relatively recent innovations. Medieval writers thought of the child as an "ill-formed adult at the edges of society" (Kessen, 1965), a notion that is reflected in the art of this period. (See Figure 1-1.) According to one analysis of medieval society,

> . . . the idea of childhood did not exist; this is not to suggest that children were neglected, forsaken, or despised. The idea of childhood is not to be confused with affection for children: it corresponds to an awareness of the particular nature of childhood, that particular nature which distinguishes

FIGURE I-1

Erasmus Quellin's "Portrait of a Boy with a Dog," painted in the seventeenth century, shows that little distinction was made between childhood and adulthood, for the child is depicted simply as a miniature adult. From the Museum of Fine Arts, Antwerp. SCALA New York/Florence.

Norman Rockwell's "Boy with Dog," painted in 1958, clearly captures the special mood of childhood that only emerged more recently. Rockwell illustration reproduced by permission of and copyrighted by Brown & Bigelow, St. Paul, Minnesota. Courtesy Mr. M. W. Eichers.

the child from the adult, even the young adult. In medieval society this awareness was lacking. That is why, as soon as the child could live without the constant solicitude of his mother, his nanny, or his cradle-rocker, he belonged to adult society. [Ariès, 1962, p. 128.]

Born in seventeenth- and eighteenth-century philosophy, the idea of childhood as a special period, in which youngsters were seen to have unique psychological, educational, and physical needs, came to hold sway. Philippe Ariès writes of the times: ". . . fondness for childhood and its special nature no longer found expression in amusement and coddling, but in psychological interest and moral solicitude. The child was no longer regarded as amusing or agreeable, but as in need of help and guidance. [It

3

was realized that] in order to correct the behavior of children people must first understand them" (1962, p. 133). At first it was hoped that philosophy would provide this understanding, but by the middle of the nineteenth century a new approach to understanding childhood had emerged: abstract speculation about the child's "nature" was replaced by empirical efforts to record and study the behavior and development of the young. This was the dawn of contemporary developmental psychology. The impetus for the new science came from many sources, but evolutionary biology and its founder, Charles Darwin, played a unique role.

> . . . with the publication of Darwin's *Descent of man,* in 1871, the child became a unique part of the scientific endeavor. . . . For nearly half a century after Darwin's shattering of the mirror, the child became the best natural laboratory for the study of evolution, and the idea of *development* dominated the science of man [Later workers] built child psychology with Darwin's bricks. [Kessen, 1965, p. 6.]

To illustrate the marriage of evolutionary theory and development, we can turn to Darwin's diary of his own infant son—kept for the purpose of observing the "natural development of the lad and comparing it with what was known of the development of other animal species." Here is one of Darwin's early observations:

> When nearly four months old, and perhaps much earlier, there could be no doubt, from the manner in which the blood gushed into his whole face and scalp, that he easily got into a violent passion. . . . When eleven months old, if a wrong plaything was given him, he would push it away and beat it; I presume that the beating was an instinctive sign of anger, like the snapping of the jaws by a young crocodile just out of the egg, and not that he imagined he could hurt the plaything. . . . [Quoted in Kessen, 1965, p. 121.]

Darwin did much to generate the nineteenth century's pervasive interest in development of all sorts, but developmental psychology had a founder more uniquely its own. G. Stanley Hall shared Darwin's general viewpoint but he focused it in a particular way. Hall devised objective methods as a substitute for casual observation and studied groups of children over an appreciable age range. As a psychologist, he soon turned to children for the study of such traditional topics as perception, memory, and learning. Meanwhile, Alfred Binet had begun to distinguish between intellectually normal and subnormal children in France, and Sigmund Freud had startled the world with his suggestion that the experiences of early childhood seemed to account for behavior in adulthood. There was clearly much to be learned and expansion was in order.

By the 1920s developmental psychology had come into the public eye as the bearer of solutions to practical problems. John Watson, the father of behaviorism, had begun to write and lecture on psychology and child-rearing practices. His impact, along with that of Freud, Binet, Hall, and many others, was felt in the emergence of clinics established for the purpose of assessing children and advising parents. In turn, this interest led to an enormous research investment in child development. Short-term studies were set up in numerous university-based nursery schools, and long-range (or *longitudinal*) projects were established at such places as Berkeley and Yale in the United States and in several principal European cities. The Fels Research Institute was established in 1929 at Yellow Springs, Ohio, to trace human growth and development from birth through maturity. Many significant contributions which contemporary developmental psychology has inherited from these pioneering efforts appear throughout this book.

But the descriptive information which these trends produced was not alluring enough to continue attracting researchers. While the field of psychology as a whole continued to grow, developmental research waned sharply. In 1938 approximately five hundred publications concerned with children's development appeared; in 1949 that number had shrunk in half (Stevenson, 1968).

Then, at the beginning of the 1950s, developmental psychology was revitalized. Many factors—a prospering economy and the research funds that came with it, a large new generation of youngsters, the establishment of various government agencies—contributed to this rise, but chief among them was the fact that developmental psychologists had adopted a new approach to their subject. No longer concerned primarily with description for its own sake, their interest had turned to a concern with the processes that underlie the development of behavior.

THE CONCEPT OF DEVELOPMENT

Development refers to a process of change in growth and capability over time, as a function of both maturation and interaction with the environment. Harold Stevenson, a prominent developmental psychologist and former director of the University of Minnesota's Child Development Institute, has put it this way:

> Developmental psychology is concerned with the study of changes in be-
> havior throughout the life span. Although, logically, equal emphasis should
> be placed on development during all stages of life, so far most research has
> dealt primarily with infants, children, and adolescents. Because of this
> emphasis the term "developmental psychology" is often used interchange-
> ably with the older terms "child psychology," "adolescent psychology," and
> "genetic * psychology." . . . Underlying all the terms, however, is a con-
> cern with the emergence of behavior in the human being. [Stevenson, 1968,
> p. 136.]

Using this broad definition, our discussion will be guided by more precise guidelines derived from the theoretical disputes, problem areas, and
research questions which have influenced developmental psychologists. As
with any area of study, the concept of development is defined in part by
these dimensions. Thus, the brief list of issues considered below serves
to introduce a number of interrelated themes which will recur regularly
throughout this book.

Chronological versus Functional Analyses

One possible way to explore development is through a simple chronology.
We might attempt to describe the child as completely as possible during
his intrauterine existence (i.e., in the womb of his mother before birth),
proceed to a similarly detailed description of the first weeks or months
of life, then on to early childhood, middle childhood, and so on. Studying
changes in behavior over time often provides a valuable descriptive account
of the progress of development. Chronological data also have an important,
practical value, for they provide norms against which individuals can be
measured. When we say, for example, that a particular child is retarded
or precocious, a comparison with other children is always implied. It is
from chronological studies that information as to what constitutes a "normal" rate and course of development is derived (cf. Langer, 1969).

The value of such descriptive chronological data is illustrated in Figure
I–2, which pictures the growth of early motor development disclosed by
Mary Shirley's (1933) observation of twenty-five children. Information of
the sort presented in this illustration may be useful to parents, physicians,
and psychologists in determining whether a child's progress is sufficiently

---

* The term *genetic,* in this context, refers to the psychology of the origins or *ontogenesis*
of behavior, and not to the study of heredity.

FIGURE 1–2

The sequence of motor development during the first fifteen months of life, illustrating the utility of a chronological approach for providing normative information. Adapted from Shirley, M. M. The First Two Years: A Study of Twenty-Five Babies, Volume II. University of Minnesota Press, Minneapolis. © 1933, 1961, University of Minnesota. By permission.

unusual to warrant further diagnosis or perhaps even special treatment.*

Although a chronological strategy seems to be ideal for observing and exploring development, in fact, it has a number of limitations. In the first place, a chronological account may lead us to overlook basic processes underlying development. We must not, in other words, forget that developmental changes occur *over* time, but none occur merely *because* of time. Then, too, many factors in development are largely independent of time and the child's age. Hereditary determinants of behavior, for example, may run the entire gamut of the individual's life, and it is helpful to inspect them in this context. Similarly, questions that at first appear to be chronological (how does a child's willingness to share with others change as he grows older?) may be best answered in terms of learning processes which operate at all ages. Thus, although we shall have a number of occasions to focus upon chronological trends in development as the child grows, the major orientation of this book is toward analyzing the processes that underlie change rather than toward describing the changes themselves.

Biological versus Environmental Determinants of Behavior

Of all the issues and disputes which appear in the study of development, perhaps none has been as pervasive as the debate regarding the relative contributions of biological and environmental influences to behavior. The problem has been discussed as the *heredity-environment* issue, the *nature-nurture* controversy, and by many other names. Although the question underlying this dichotomy appears to be quite simple (i.e., "How much of the individual's behavior is contributed by his biological and genetic makeup and how much by social and environmental influences?"), the apparent simplicity is deceptive.

As Anastasi (1958) has noted in a careful analysis, the questions "Which one?" and "How much?" naïvely overlook the fact that an individual's hereditary endowment and the environment to which he is exposed must *interact* in order to produce behavior. Because both heredity and environment make an absolutely necessary contribution to behavior, questions which presume that these factors simply differ in quantity or importance,

---

* Of course, caution must be exercised lest one become unnecessarily concerned about minor individual differences between a given child and the norms. A parent may be justifiably concerned if his or her child cannot walk alone at thirty months of age, but concern would not be appropriate if the child is only one or two months "behind" the published averages.

like two bank accounts, are not likely to be fruitful. Instead, we ultimately must ask *how* (i.e., in what manner) biological and social influences combine for various types of behavior.

Continuity versus Discontinuity in Development

Two types of behavioral change often are identified in the study of human development, those that are gradual or *continuous* and those that are sudden or *discontinuous*.

To understand the nature of this distinction, consider the following example suggested by the work of Jean Piaget (whose theory of cognitive development will be discussed in detail in a later chapter). An experimenter begins by showing a four-year-old child two short, wide glass beakers, each containing the same quantity of milk. The youngster is asked whether both beakers have an equal amount of fluid, and agrees that they do. Then, while the child watches, the experimenter pours the entire contents of one of these beakers into a third beaker—a tall, thin one. When the child is asked to compare the two beakers that now contain milk, he often will say that the tall, thin beaker has more milk in it than the untouched short, wide one. In contrast, older children, like adults, will immediately point out that the two beakers in question must have the same amount of milk, for the volume of the two original beakers was equal at the beginning and no liquid was lost or gained by pouring the contents from one container into another.

How and why does this transition in handling the problem occur? Is there a qualitative change or *discontinuity* from one mode of thinking to another as the child grows older, or would the change, if we were able to watch it more closely, appear to be a gradual, *continuous* process of growing sophistication? The former viewpoint leads to the suggestion that development proceeds in a series of relatively discrete *stages;* it thus compels the theorist to try to identify them and analyze their components. As we shall see, this is the conclusion which, with some qualifications, Piaget has reached in examining the child's *intellectual* development. Likewise, other stage theorists have argued that many aspects of human *emotional* and *social* development proceed in a relatively discontinuous, stagewise fashion.

Other theorists, though, have emphasized the possibility that development may only seem discontinuous: observers who compare children of different ages may be unable to detect gradual changes as they occur, and thus may mistakenly take large or dramatic shifts as evidence of discontinuity. Even if the same children are observed over time, the frequency and nature of the observations can play an important role in determining whether developmental changes will seem gradual or relatively abrupt.

The continuity-discontinuity issue involves much more than measurement. Major questions revolve around the processes through which change occurs. Stage theorists often insist that universal, biologically based factors play a prominent role in development; relatively uniform structural changes, they argue, occur in the psychological processes of almost all children and give rise to relatively discontinuous changes in behavior.

In contrast, theorists who emphasize continuities often assume that social and experiential factors underlie many developmental changes. Children, they point out, must *learn* to behave as they do; the learning is likely to be a gradual, continuous process that will vary from one child to another depending upon individual differences in socioeconomic, ethnic, and cultural background.

Although it should be emphasized that all theorists agree that there are both continuities and discontinuities in development, differences in emphasis and vantage point are of sufficient importance to have implications for almost every substantive topic raised in this book.

THE ROLE OF THEORY

Even in our brief discussion thus far, it has been impossible to avoid the word "theory." What functions do theories serve in the investigation of development? The answers are many.

Theories always serve an explanatory-descriptive role, providing a basis for organizing and condensing facts which are already known. They also should enable us to predict future events. To do so, a theory must be *testable* and thus potentially *capable of being refuted* or falsified. It must lead to the derivation of specific hypotheses or predictions which can be confirmed or disconfirmed publicly. Related to this predictive function is the manner in which theories guide research into areas that might not otherwise attract interest or that might otherwise seem too complicated to be handled. Like a prospector's map of secret treasure, they lead us to expect substantial yields in areas that would otherwise seem to have little promise.

On the other hand, theories also may turn research away from phenomena that, from the standpoint of other theories, are generally believed to be critical. For example, it is widely held that a child's early toilet-training experiences play a vital role in his later social development. However, several learning theory approaches to behavior suggest that these early experiences have little or no important bearing on, say, the behavior of an adolescent. Adherents to the latter view will be guided by their theory to *not* seek, and perhaps eschew, information about lavatory practices in early childhood which might otherwise occupy their research or clinical efforts.

Although many developmental investigations have been conducted without the impetus of an elaborate theoretical basis, it is almost impossible to investigate any phenomenon without some initial or tentative ideas about its nature or relationship with other phenomena. We thus shall have occasion to discuss many theories throughout this book. Their importance and a general introduction to them, is suggested in Selection 1.

SELECTION 1

THE IMPACT OF THEORIES OF CHILD DEVELOPMENT

Bettye M. Caldwell and Julius B. Richmond

. . . Probably each major theory which left any mark on the history of ideas had to be attuned to its era—a little bit, but not too far, ahead of its time. Thus intellectual prerevolutionary France was receptive to Rousseau's challenge of the doctrine of innate depravity with his assertion that the child is inherently good until corrupted by society. In postrevolutionary America, when rigid self-discipline and industry were required to subdue the frontier, theories which stressed obedience, discipline, and submission to adult authority found acceptance.

In every era there are two kinds of "experts" about child behavior—those who publish and those who do not. Every parent has his or her theory about

Reprinted from Caldwell, Bettye M., and Julius B. Richmond. The impact of theories of child development. *Children,* **9**, 1962, 73–78. Reproduced by permission of Bettye M. Caldwell.

how children develop. This theory may remain at the level of proverbs or cultural maxims ("Spare the rod and spoil the child"), may involve broad generalizations lacking behavioral referents ("Just give them love and security"), or may propose precise hypotheses about genetic influence on behavior or the relative efficacy of reward or punishment for inducing learning.

These implicit theories are important determinants of parental action and reaction. For example, "a spare the rod" theory makes it unnecessary for the parent to make a fresh decision about how to handle a particular type of behavior each time it occurs; it also insulates the parent from guilt about behaving punitively toward his child.

Twentieth Century Theories

During the twentieth century, three theoretical systems about child development have made major inroads into the personal learning theories of American parents: the behavioristic (or social learning); the maturational; and the psychoanalytic.

Social Learning Theories

While the work of several theorists could be cast into the framework of social learning theory, John B. Watson had the greatest influence in this direction. Watson's concept of infancy was essentially a Lockean *tabula rasa*—an amorphous bit of behavior potential to be shaped by the learning opportunities experienced by the infant. His psychological theories appeared at a time in the history of ideas when most complex types of emotional experience were attributed to the expression of instincts.

Convinced as he was that emotions were acquired throughout the learning process, Watson used naive subjects, infants, to test his hypothesis. He designed and executed a number of ingenious experiments which demonstrated that many fears could be acquired and subsequently eliminated through conditioning. From these experiments he concluded that most forms of complex behavior were the result of concatenations of reflexes and simple response systems associated through conditioning.

Such a view of the child places an awesome degree of power into the hands of parents and other "teachers." A completely malleable infant bespeaks an omnipotent training agent. Watson wasted no time in extrapolating from the laboratory to home and school and in communicating his ideas directly to parents. His widely read publications had considerable influence on recom-

mendations made to parents about child care. The 1928 edition of *Infant Care*, always the best statement of current professional ideas, relied heavily upon Watsonian suggestions about shaping behavior, such as developing habits of regularity, dependability, independence, and self-reliance.

Watson attempted to put to pasture many sacred cows of child development literature, including mother love and the importance of encouraging emotional dependency between parents and children. His language was too pungent to escape caricature. Witness this example:

> There is a sensible way of treating children. Treat them as though they were young adults. Let your behavior always be objective and kindly firm. Never hug and kiss them, never let them sit in your lap. If you must, kiss them once on the forehead when they say good night. Shake hands with them in the morning. Give them a pat on the head if they have made an extraordinarily good job of a difficult task. Try it out. In a week's time you will find how easy it is to be perfectly objective with your child and at the same time kindly. You will be utterly ashamed of the mawkish, sentimental way you have been handling it (Watson, 1928).

Unfortunately publishers have no standard code for reporting whether an author wrote a particular passage with tongue in cheek. Therefore, an author must expect to be taken literally and to live with the implications of his words as written. In recent years Watson and his theories of conditioning have been felled by the impact of just such statements as the above. The reactions of his critics have ranged from vilification to mere ridicule, and feeling still runs high. Several modern theorists, however, notably Skinner (1953), Miller and Dollard (1953), and Rotter (1954), have significantly advanced social learning theory and have extended our knowledge about the limits of external manipulation and control of infant and child behavior.

Maturational Theory

This system is represented by the writings of Arnold Gesell (1940; 1943; 1946; 1956). A prolific and at times poetic writer, Gesell also recognized the journalistic principle that one picture is worth a thousand words and copiously illustrated his books with pictorial samples of child behavior. Although perhaps referred to more often for his methods of developmental diagnosis and cinema-analysis and for the norms of behavioral development which he and his students accumulated over the years, Gesell was nonetheless an important formulator of a theory of child behavior.

Gesell's theory of development is relatively simple yet, in some ways, more global than other more complex theories. The key concept is that of *maturation* or growth. It is a theory of intrinsic development, of an infant's maturation proceeding from both the human and the individual nature of the infant.

Implicit in the concept of maturation is self-regulation of growth. Gesell urged recognition of this principle in every aspect of development from the establishment of infant feeding schedules to the acquisition of moral values. Acceptance of the principle by parents calls for a certain considerateness, an "alert liberalism," to use Gesell's phrase. Infants, as well as older children, are entitled to certain courtesies, to being regarded as "people." A passionate regard for the individual was, Gesell maintained, crucial to a truly democratic orientation to life.

A corollary of this stress on the importance of the individual is the concept of individual differences. Yet, paradoxically, it is here that Gesell seems to have been most generally misinterpreted and, indeed, almost to have courted misinterpretation. This stems from the organization of most of his books in terms of ages and stages of behavior. Indeed, the books' typography—the capitalization of each age period as though personified—conduces to such misinterpretation. For example:

> THREE is a kind of coming-of-age.
> . . . You can bargain with THREE and he can wait his turn. . . . FOUR (and half past) tends to go out of bounds. . . . FIVE is a SUPER-THREE with a socialized pride in clothes and accomplishments, a lover of praise (Gesell and Ilg, 1943).

About this approach, Gesell and Ilg say:

> We regard the formal concept of chronological age and the functional concept of maturity level as indispensable both for practical common sense and for the science of child development. In the guidance of children it is absolutely necessary to consider the age values of behavior and the behavior values of age. The reader is warned, in advance, however, that *the age norms are not set up as standards and are designed only for orientation and interpretive purposes.* . . . The prevalence and significance of individual variations are recognized at every turn (1943).

Perhaps these occasional warnings do not carry enough weight to counterbalance the continued stress on ages and stages in development throughout childhood and adolescence.

With respect to the timing of the maximum impact of the three major theories we are discussing, Gesell followed Watson and preceded Freud. Nevertheless, many of Gesell's most popular publications came out during the period of popularization of psychoanalytic thought. Gesell did not seem to be a man for polemics, however, and he seldom bothered to take notice of other points of view. His books deal largely with the presentation of his own material. He quotes other researchers only when their studies relate to his interests. In the four Gesell books reviewed for this article, there are only two references to Freud. Gesell was more concerned with developmental congruences than interpersonal conflicts, with eye-hand coordination and prehension than emotional cathexes. Even in the volume *Youth* (Gesell, 1956), "sex" is indexed in terms of "differences" and not of preoccupations and problems.

Watson is quoted once in these four Gesell works, but anonymously as "a distinguished behaviorist" and the source of the quote is not in the reference list. However, in isolated articles, Gesell occasionally opposed certain points important in behavioristic doctrine, as he did when he suggested (1929) that the conditioned reflex theory promised too much and threatened too much, and that maturation protected the infant from certain chance conditionings.

In reflecting on the impact of Gesell's work one must not overlook the influence of distribution.

Until the appearance of the amazing Spock volume (1946), Gesell's writings were probably more widely disseminated than any other full-length book on child development. Furthermore, Gesell, like Watson, was persuaded of the obligation to present child development material directly for parental consumption. Knowledge about infants and young children, he said, "must extend into the homes of the people; for the household is the 'cultural workshop' where human relationships are first formed."

Psychoanalytic Approach

The theoretical formulations of psychoanalysis and the body of empirical data collected to test the hypotheses have provided perhaps the most significant and pervasive influence on child-development theories and child-rearing practices in recent decades. By clinically reconstructing the life history of the adult or child through therapeutic efforts, psychoanalysts have developed theoretical formulations concerning the meaning of interaction of the infant or young child with his environment. It is understandable that, in a scientific era, a theory explaining the development in all its subtleties (unconscious and conscious) would capture widespread attention.

The complexities of psychoanalytic theory are difficult to distill into a few paragraphs. Unlike the maturation theory, psychoanalytic theory has undergone many revisions and is continuously modified. Classical (or Freudian) psychoanalysis and the neo-Freudian formulations differ in many respects.

Psychoanalysis is generally referred to as a biological theory of personality; yet the biological drives are manifested entirely in a social context. From the standpoint of the developing child, this context is mainly the family group. Unless basic drives (instincts) are gratified during early interactions with the parents—primarily the mother—the child moves forward from infancy with some degree of fixation at this earlier stage and somewhat impaired in adaptability. Or, if gratification at succeeding stages of development is insufficient, the child falls back on earlier patterns of behavior (regression) for gratification.

The concepts of fixation and regression are based on a sequence of stages in development. Thus personality development progresses from oral to anal stages in early life and then to a sequence of genital stages—oedipal, latent, adolescent, and mature. Experiences during each period are conceived of as affecting character traits of later life.

During the "oral period" in infancy, for example, it is thought the child develops feelings about accepting things and the mother's manner of giving them. Erikson (1950) has postulated that from the totality of experiences in this period, the individual develops a basic sense of trust in people—or else a lack of trust which hampers his ensuing development. During the period of acquisition of bowel and bladder control when the child must integrate contradictory impulses of retention and elimination, traits related to orderliness, punctuality, and thrift are thought to develop.

The awareness of genital differences and feelings brings with it even more complex integrative tasks. Personality begins to take shape in more recognizable form, and characteristic modes of dealing with adaptive problems (mech-

anisms of defense) become evident. The relationship of the individual's later feelings and character traits to earlier experiences suggests that manipulation of these experiences in a "healthy" direction may favorably influence later development. This assumes agreement on a desirable mature model toward which to strive. Chronic failure of the parents to provide for the gratification of the basic drives is likely to result in permanent personality distortions remediable only through a kind of regrowth process via the therapeutic relationship.

These formulations have been theoretically enticing and have provided many hypotheses for investigation by workers in the field of child development as well as for child-care workers in various disciplines interested in the prevention of emotional disorders. Many psychoanalytic concepts have been embraced as guides to child rearing by parents concerned with raising "emotionally healthy" children. However, a review of the experimental literature indicates that no specific relationships between early experiences and later development can be established at the present time.

There is growing recognition among psychoanalytic investigators that the application of knowledge gained from psychoanalysis in preventive efforts must be approached cautiously. The objective of psychoanalytic investigation as stated by Erikson (1950) a decade ago remains valid:

> Psychoanalysis today is implementing the study of the ego, the core of the individual. It is shifting its emphasis from the concentrated study of the conditions which blunt and distort the individual ego to the study of the ego's roots in social organizations. This we

try to understand not in order to offer a rash cure to a rashly diagnosed society, but in order to first complete the blueprint of our method.

To pursue these objectives, psychoanalytic research workers are departing from the predominant use of reconstructive interview or play techniques to the greater use of direct observation of development (as indicated by the current interest in research in mother-infant interaction), experimental approaches (animal and human), and cross-cultural studies. Also, more intensive and objective studies of psychoanalytically oriented interviews are being developed.

Implications for Today

The fact that different theories can flourish contemporaneously validates Knapp's observation (1960) that man is a "recalcitrant and reluctant experimental subject." Yet these theories of child development are not contradictory or mutually exclusive. All are concerned with learning, with the interaction of organism and environment. They all highlight different facets of behavior and use different conceptual systems. And, undoubtedly, they are all a little bit right.

From all of them one can infer that parents wield an awesome degree of power in shaping the lives of their children. Even maturational theory, with its emphasis upon the growth integrity of the young organism, its inherent potential for healthy development, implies that the parent can inhibit or distort this growth potential. With greater awareness of the implications of their

caretaking activities, some parents have shown signs of what might be loosely termed a midcentury parental neurosis: an over-determination to seek suggestions for child rearing as insurance of healthy development for their children.

Professional workers in the field of child care (pediatricians and other health workers, psychologists, and child welfare workers) have not been immune to these pressures. They have sometimes advocated as universally desirable such programs as "natural childbirth," rooming-in of the newborn with the mother at the hospital, breast feeding, and permissive or self-regulating patterns of child care. To their credit, psychoanalysts have not been in the forefront of these movements. Rather, these movements have often represented misinterpretation or premature application of psychoanalytic principles. Recently they have been placed in a more appropriate perspective, as doctrinaire approaches to "prevention" have been given up in favor of the more traditionally eclectic orientation of child-care professions—except perhaps by social work which has remained heavily committed to psychoanalytic theory.

Guidance in child rearing will probably become increasingly professionalized in the United States in the years to come. The child-care professions, therefore, must face up to the challenge of providing services for parents even with incomplete knowledge. If these services are to be provided for families, adequate professional personnel must be made available. The specific professions to provide this personnel, the appropriate distribution, and the organization of services are issues with which we as a nation have not yet come to terms. The current ferment about the "new pediatrics" and concern with the directions in which this profession should move educationally and in practice suggests the need for planning constructively for all kinds of child-care services.

Since the launching of Sputnik in 1957, we have awakened to our responsibilities to fulfill our potentialities as a democratic nation. The resultant emphasis on academic achievement has the same over-determined emphasis which other child-rearing formulae have had in previous years. While we must strive for full intellectual development of our children, this need not be at the expense of their social and emotional growth. If it is, we may inhibit the learning we seek to foster.

Implications for Future Theories

What thoughts can now be projected about the child development theories of the future? Undoubtedly they will continue to be prevalent both at the scientific level and as part of each individual's general philosophy. The individual theories will change only as rapidly as cultural changes occur, and presumably those cultural changes will be at least in part a function of the rapidity of scientific change. However, we will make a few predictions about the characteristics of heuristic child development theories of the future:

1. Extrapolation from research data will not be so extreme.

The science of behavior has matured into a more conservative, slightly subdued stage. Professionals in the field have themselves matured somewhat.

Also the interdisciplinary origin of many of the reasonably stable parts of child development knowledge is conducive to conservatism.

The young Watson, with little knowledge of genetics and its constitutional limitations upon adaptability of the organism, could assert that he could take any four healthy infants and make them whatever type of adult he wished. The somewhat provincial Freud, unaware of the nascent body of data from cultural anthropology, could assume that the memories and fantasies of individuals from a fairly narrow sociocultural context represented universal attributes. Today's theorists are no longer permitted the luxury of being uninformed about work in any area of knowledge which might limit the predictions from a given theoretical system. With greater availability of information which might make predictions hazardous, the theories themselves will become more cautious about specific predictions.

2. Future theories of child behavior will be concerned with a broader time spectrum.

The view of the child as a miniature adult is outmoded. But in its place has come with too much finality a view of the child almost as an eternal child. The child *is* a future adult, as he is a future adolescent and a future senescent. The 6-month-old baby who experiences a certain type of mothering will presumably carry some residual of that experience with him at age 3 or 13. Since each type of later experience may modify the nature of the residual, such differences need to be fully explored. Useful child development theories of the future will be concerned with predictions which span wide segments of the developmental curve, not just one narrow section.

3. Future theories of child behavior will be related to broader aspects of social theory and philosophy.

A point already stressed in this paper is that each enduring or influential child development theory is related to powerful currents of social history. Within the past few decades even the seemingly remote physical sciences have had to face such a relationship. There is now less talk about a separation of science from values. Certainly in the field of child development no such separation is possible. We rear children to fit into a particular culture, on the basic premise that the culture is somehow "good" or at least acceptable.

The past two decades have seen considerable sniping at Watson for the naïveté of his theories, with an occasional implication that he was heartless and cruel for denouncing mother love and the child-rearing practices of most parents. Such criticism fails to recognize that Watson was far more explicit than most theorists about the behavioral attributes he wished to foster. He concludes one of his books (Watson, 1928) with a formal apologia to critics who have taken him to task for having no "ideals" for bringing up children, commenting perceptively that different programs of care fit different civilizations. Then he describes briefly the kind of child he had in mind when making his child-rearing suggestions, the kind he considered best adapted to the changing America of the late twenties:

We have tried to sketch in the foregoing chapters a child as free as possible of sensitivities to people and one who, almost from birth, is relatively independent of the family situation. . . . Above all, we have tried to create a problem-solving child. We believe that a problem-solving technique (which can be trained) plus boundless absorption in activity (which can also be trained) are behavioristic factors which have worked in many civilizations of the past and which, so far as we can judge, will work equally well in most types of civilizations that are likely to confront us in the future (Watson, 1928).

Undoubtedly, many persons would not agree with Watson's goals, but it is to his credit that he attempted to relate his theory to the social milieu.

4. Future theories of child development will not attempt to answer (or predict) everything about child development for all time. They will modestly relate themselves to one sociocultural group—until something is proven to have universal relevance—and for a finite scientific era.

New discoveries can outmode existing theories overnight. For example, future research on behavioral genetics might drastically modify many of the assumptions underlying research on the effects of specific parent practices on child behavior. Any heuristic theory will be quick to incorporate new data, thus building a more stately theoretical structure. Victor Hugo's tribute to the power of an idea whose time has come might well apply in reverse here, for nothing is more effete than a theory that has outlived its time.

THE CENTRAL IMPORTANCE OF METHOD AND RESEARCH EVIDENCE

In this book we have sought to exemplify and explain the research strategies and sources of evidence which bear on various phases and aspects of development. Although some of the findings may surprise the reader (or run counter to "intuition"), others may seem so obvious that formal investigation appears unnecessary. But it is necessary. In *Tactics of Scientific Research,* Murray Sidman (1960) made the point this way:

> Sometimes, when a commonly observed type of behavior is demonstrated in the laboratory, we hear the remarks, "So what! Everybody knows people behave like that . . ." Such a statement assumes beforehand that common observation is an adequate substitute for controlled observation. The two may, at times, be in agreement, but there is no predicting this before experimental studies are undertaken. Everyday observation of human behavior is notoriously unreliable. In our impressions and interpretations of behavior as it goes on around us, we tend to overlook many properties of the behavior and of its controlling variables. We read into our descriptions of behavior much that is not actually there, and assume on too little evidence that two or more types of behavior are the same simply because they look the same. The very language of our everyday discourse often serves to obscure the critical data. [p. 29.]

Everyone "knows," for example, that a child will be more likely to do something for which he has been rewarded than to do something which has not previously brought positive consequences. Nonetheless, it was only after much basic laboratory research on the timing and scheduling of rewards that such remarkable and practical accomplishments as successfully teaching language to psychotic children who had never spoken before (e.g., Lövaas, Berberich, Perloff, and Schaeffer, 1966) or producing effective automated "teaching machines" (Skinner, 1968) became possible.

In developmental psychology many "obvious" facts have been cast into serious doubt by systematic investigation. For example, it is widely held that a child's interpersonal aggressive behavior may be reduced by observing symbolic aggression through movies, television programs, and children's stories. This notion, often referred to as the *catharsis hypothesis,* suggests that aggressive tendencies may be "drained off" by the vicarious experience of observing violence. However, as we shall see, a number of carefully designed experiments with children and adolescents have shown that observing aggression may actually *increase,* rather than decrease, an observer's willingness to aggress against other people.

Research is not simply the scientist's version of casual observation. Instead, it is a very special class of activity in which a systematic effort is made to obtain and evaluate information about one or more phenomena according to a set of explicit rules. It is to the various ways in which developmental psychologists have undertaken this task that the next chapter is devoted.

II

METHODS OF DEVELOPMENTAL RESEARCH

IN CHAPTER I we considered the nature of development and examined some of the issues surrounding the concept. The present chapter is devoted to the methods used in developmental research and to an exploration of the strengths and weaknesses they possess. Each is illustrated by one or more actual examples from contemporary developmental psychology. Regardless of the specific method used, though, any developmental investigation may be categorized according to whether it involves a *longitudinal* or a *cross-sectional* vantage point.

LONGITUDINAL VERSUS CROSS-SECTIONAL APPROACHES

In a *longitudinal study,* the same individuals are observed at different points in their lives and changes in their characteristics are noted over time. For example, in order to study the development of language longitudinally, one group of investigators systematically recorded the verbalizations and language productions of three children for almost two years (Brown, Cazden & Bellugi-Klima, 1969).

On the other hand, in a *cross-sectional* study, development is explored by observing different individuals of varying ages, usually at approximately the same point in calendar time. One such investigation of language development involved the observation for a brief period of a relatively large number of children of three different ages (Liebert, Odom, Hill, & Huff, 1969). There are advantages and disadvantages to both approaches, and selection between them often depends upon the investigator's purpose.

The Logic of Longitudinal Research

As the name implies, the longitudinal approach involves a "lengthwise" or running temporal account of the development of one or more persons. Perhaps the greatest advantage of longitudinal studies is that they permit the investigator to measure individual rates of change directly, over time, and thus to actually "see" growth occurring. The method is also indispensable for studying questions which involve documenting the stability (or identifying the instability) of various aspects of behavior. The only way to answer the question of whether a child's intelligence or aggressiveness or dependency remains relatively constant from early childhood to adolescence to the adult years is to measure the same child repeatedly across an appreciable span of time. Finally, if certain critical events which occur early in life do not immediately affect the child's functioning but instead influence his later behavior, the longitudinal approach is the best method of identifying them.*

---

* At first blush, an alternative method for tracing this process is to acquire information *retrospectively* by asking about the person's early development or experiences and applying this information to his present behavior as an adolescent or adult. However, gathering retrospective information is still an attempt to paint a time-span or longitudinal picture. Additionally, as we shall have occasion to mention later, the retrospective method recently has been called into very serious question because the reports of both parents and subjects themselves may be so inaccurate as to render them useless or misleading.

Despite its advantages, the longitudinal approach also has a number of drawbacks. These, along with the values of the method, are reviewed in Selection 2 by Nancy Bayley, who was closely involved with one of the most significant longitudinal investigations of intelligence.

SELECTION 2

RESEARCH IN CHILD DEVELOPMENT: A LONGITUDINAL PERSPECTIVE

Nancy Bayley

The longitudinal method of research in child development has had a history of early optimistic espousal followed by vehement rejection on the part of many investigators, only to be reconsidered more recently as essential for gaining an understanding of the nature of many developmental processes. With this current renewed interest in the method, it seems appropriate to review both the values and the difficulties of this form of research, to try to find ways to circumvent these difficulties, and thus to enhance the values that may be derived from the study of the same individuals over time.

Longitudinal studies were among the first carefully documented records of child growth and behavior. And like other methods of research they have gone through a process of methodological improvement. So far as I know, the earliest longitudinal study to be reported is that of Buffon in 1837, in which he gives heights of one child, measured repeatedly over a period of 17 years from 1759 to 1776. Then

Reprinted from Bayley, Nancy. Research in child development: A longitudinal perspective. *Merrill-Palmer Quarterly,* **11**, 1965, 184–190. Reproduced by permission.

there was a series of biographies of infants, in which the scientist observed and recorded behaviors of a single child (usually his own or a close relative) at frequent intervals over periods of one to three years. Included among these biographies are the well-known publications of Tiedemann (1863), Perez (1878), Preyer (1882), Shinn (1907), Moore and Mrs. W. S. Hall in 1896, and Pestalozzi (1899). In all of these individual case reports there was clear evidence of the age-related processes of development. In the very young infant the changes were often evident from one day to the next. In the older child the changes were more gradual. But again at adolescence physical growth, at least, was accelerated for a period, after which growth rates gradually diminished.

Clearly, the next logical step would be to go on from measuring one or two children in one's own family to measuring a larger number of children, and thus to obtain more general information about growth rates and processes. The first of these larger studies, concerned with physical growth, were carried out at Harvard University (Dearborn and Rothney, 1941). The first of the Harvard growth studies, reported by the physiologist Bowditch in 1872, gives the average heights of twelve males and twelve females, measured annually over a period of 25 years. Another physiologist, Porter (1922) in the second Harvard growth study secured monthly heights and weights of a large number of Boston school children over a period of nine years, between 1910 and 1920. Baldwin at Iowa published in 1921 a series of individual curves of several body dimensions and of lung capacity of school children.

From these and other similar studies much of value was learned about the nature of growth in individual children. Also, Baldwin added to his studies the variable of rates of maturing, as observed from measures of X-rays of the carpal bones.

The next most obvious step was to include in the longitudinal studies measures of still other aspects of growth. During the 1920's, with the establishment of a number of child research centers, many interdisciplinary longitudinal growth studies were initiated. The most frequent types of data collected, in addition to body dimensions and skeletal maturing, were measures of intelligence (thanks to Binet, I.Q.'s and mental ages were available). Social and emotional behaviors, and a variety of physiological functions were also included in a number of the studies. Information about socioeconomic status and ethnic background was usually included in all studies for purposes of both classification and comparison.

Populations to be studied varied in size from twenty or so to several thousand. Their starting ages varied from the prematures and normal neonates of Gesell, to the 17-year-olds included among Terman's sample of gifted children. The intervals between measures ranged from a few days or weeks to an occasional retesting after lapses of five or ten years or even longer. The longitudinal span, so far as the age of the subject was concerned, might be a year or eighteen years, or possibly a lifetime. There was some effort to obtain a "normal" sample by selecting an entire first grade in a school, or a "random" subsample of a community or of hospital births. There was also in some studies selection of a special population, such as prematurely born persons, or "gifted" children selected on the basis of I.Q.'s.

The investigators used the best measuring instruments and procedures available. They were careful to set up and follow carefully defined and described procedures for conducting the tests and measurements.

With the data coming in from these carefully measured poulations, the investigators set out to answer a variety of questions about the individual processes of growth and the interrelations between the various aspects of growth. But their questions proliferated like the flood of the sorcerer's apprentice. They got many answers to their questions, but no answer ever seemed to be complete. Each effort seemed to terminate in a whole array of new questions which themselves often called for new techniques, new instruments, or new samples of populations.

However, this tends to be the nature of practically all research. Each new set of verified, or even potentially verifiable, facts points the way to other possible knowledge and opens up new fields to explore. This kind of continually expanding range of questions for investigation can be exhilarating and sometimes discouraging. But then there is another phenomenon related to the rate of progress in gaining information in a field or method. Although the first fruits of a new method yield a big harvest of the easy-to-find answers, the returns tend gradually to be reduced, until a period is reached when nothing new of any significance can be learned. What is needed at this point is some new breakthrough—some different and better instruments or procedures, or an entirely new perspective.

This was the impasse in which longitudinal research found itself in the 1940's and 1950's, and many people put the blame on the longitudinal method itself. However, the discontent with the method was not entirely the result of slow returns in new information. The years of experience with such programs had revealed many difficulties in carrying out the intended projects and many limitations on the extent to which generalizations from the data are possible.

Some of the criticisms leveled at longitudinal studies are concerned with the same problems inherent in most research, but perhaps intensified. Others are peculiar to the method itself. Some criticisms are more devastating to certain types of data; other data may be relatively immune. The criticisms loomed so large that people began to shy away from such research as too difficult, too wasteful, and impossible to conduct with adequate controls. Still, after all of these criticisms were leveled and longitudinal studies were denounced and rejected, it remained evident that certain important theories could not be tested and certain burning questions could not be answered except by careful observation, measurement, and documentation of the same individuals over time as they grew.

In the interests of knowledge and science, then, let us look at these criticisms and see what can be done about them.

The horrible example of the longitudinal study described by its critics is one in which the investigators rushed into a long-term project with no research design: they just started measuring everything they could think of in the hope of finding some significant relations. This I consider to be an irresponsible criticism, usually made by young persons who forget that many of the hypotheses to be tested thirty or forty years ago have long since been proved (or disproved) and are now in the textbooks as common knowledge. Also, these earlier hypotheses were not formulated in the words of the current ritual, which gives at least a semblance of scientific exactitude. What the earlier investigators did was to ask questions that were relevant for testing accepted beliefs, partially verified theories, or even sometimes mere hunches. There is nothing the matter with this procedure in its proper place. When a field of investigation is new, it is necessary to be more exploratory, to make a crude map of the territory in order to get one's bearings, before an exact and detailed map is possible.

The critics also held that longitudinal researchers did not select their cases with care but took a readily available, and often atypical, sample because it was willing and at hand. It might be a captive, institutional population, a clinically biased sample seeking help, or the children of cooperative highly educated parents who understood the "scientific" reasons for the study. But this criticism can be made of many "cross-sectional" studies in which the typical population might, for example, be composed of college sophomores. The captive school population such as that used in the third and best known Harvard Growth Study is probably one of the most representative of a broad general sample to be found among many studies, both longitudinal and other.

In all of the longitudinal samples —but even more so if the sample is carefully selected as generally representative—there is the bugaboo of maintaining sample constancy. This is one of the real limitations of longitudinal research. It is impossible to test every child at every scheduled testing on every item to be tested. Children get sick (one case of measles on the projected testing date could ruin a rigid research design); they become upset and a measure must be omitted; they refuse to comply on some items. Families go on vacation and take the study subject out of town at just the wrong time, or mother forgets the appointment and takes the child shopping; families move away permanently, or refuse to cooperate further in the study, and thus diminish the size of the sample for the older ages. These are certainly problems to be concerned about. If they cannot be eliminated, they can at least be acknowledged and designated as limitations on the general applicability of the findings of the study. Sometimes if the original sample is large enough, it is possible to select, for a given age-span, a subsample which meets certain criteria of representativeness.

In the matter of sampling, after the sample is selected, perhaps most important for the investigator who conducts a longitudinal study is the need to find ways to keep the subjects motivated and willing to continue to participate. This requires consideration of the subjects as persons, with rights, needs, and values which are not to be violated. Care must be taken to keep records confidential, to maintain a friendly interest in each person, to make adjustments to his preferences and needs whenever these do not defeat the goals of the study, to avoid causing hardship or distress, and whenever appropriate to give some return in the form of information about the study or the value of the subject's contribution to it.

Whether or not the sample is constant, the very fact that the children are tested so many times changes the nature of the behaviors tested. Familiarity with the situation makes a difference. Test-wise children make better scores than the naive children on whom the tests were standardized. The answers to specific test items may be learned through repeated tests—often the very repetitions which are needed to measure growth in intelligence. Or the children grow bored with the same old TAT pictures. But if, in order to avoid familiarity and boredom, you change the test, then how do you evaluate the children's responses? How comparable are the different but similar tests you use? These questions call for such devices as including cross-sectional studies on some aspects of the data. And they often require some specialized statistical procedures.

The problem about the testing instrument doesn't stop here. In the lapse of time during which the study is in process new and better tests are devised. The investigator is faced with the decision whether to stay with the old test and maintain constancy of instrument, or to change to the new and get a more adequate measure. For example, do we measure growth in intelligence by staying with the 1916 Stanford-Binet with which we started, or by changing to the 1937 and then the 1960 revision because they are more up-to-date and have more top at the upper levels? Or do we change to a still different test that has been constructed to measure identified factors of intelligence and thus permit more adequate analyses of mental growth? Or can we add new tests without dropping the old ones, and without overburdening the time and tolerance of the subjects?

If the investigators should get carried away with enthusiasm for new tests, or the potentialities of adding new dimensions of investigation to enrich the already-full program, the study can easily flounder. Not only are they asking too much of their subjects, but they are also overloading the staff who do the testing.

The problem of staff time is often crucial. In growth studies the children keep on having birthdays. The predetermined schedule of testings must be met, if the cells of the design are to be filled, and at the correct retest intervals. Too much data to collect and to analyze, too many cases to test, often means that there is not time left for analysis and writing up of the data already obtained. Files and files of undigested data accumulate and grow out-of-date for their possible significance. Time may be wasted collecting data that, if studied, could have been dropped from the program if it turned out to be value-less. Furthermore, a schedule of continuous data analysis, writing, and publishing not only serves to help weed out useless and unreliable material, it makes for continued productivity of research findings, and maintains staff morale at a high level.

Staff continuity is another real problem in long-term studies. For one thing, it is a large factor in maintaining the cooperation of the sample. When the same persons stay with the study and see the children repeatedly as they grow, bonds of friendship and loyalty are established. A child or an adult will often be more willing to return for measures if he is asked by a person he knows and trusts, and to whom he finds it hard to say "No", than if asked through an impersonal letter or by a complete stranger.

A long-term study may also fall apart with a change in the principal investigators. Such a change characteristically brings investigators with a new set of values, skills, and interests. Much material that had been laboriously collected by one person with certain well-considered goals, may seem to the new investigator to be of little value or outside the range of his skills and interests. Old tests are dropped and new ones instituted, thus producing new discontinuities. It may be that the useful returns of a long-term growth study are in direct proportion to the term of participation of the key persons on the staff. Changes are, of course, inevitable. But they may be buffered, when they can be anticipated, by cooperative programs, with gradual shifts in personnel.

The passage of time is accompanied by many changes that bother the longitudinal researchers. If, as in the Berkeley studies, the entire sample, all approximately the same age, is collected at one time, and then followed, one cannot know whether certain changes are inherent in the subjects under study —or whether they are the result of certain environmental factors, all encountered by the subjects at about the same age. War, depression, changing cultures, and technological advances all make considerable impacts. What are the differential effects on two-year-olds of parents with depression-caused worries and insecurities, of T.V. or no T.V., of the shifting climate of the baby-experts' advice from strict-diet, let-him-cry, no-pampering schedules to permissive, cuddling "enriching" loving care? On the other hand, as in some studies, one might eliminate this chronological problem by adding from five to ten newborn infants each year, and then making comparisons according to age of the child and not the calendar year. But then one must wait five years or so to get a large enough sample at any one age for statistical purposes. Over this time, staff, measuring procedures and test instruments may change, making it impossible ever to get enough children for study who are the same age measured in the same way on the same instrument. Furthermore, such a procedure might only obscure significant environmental changes, and introduce uncontrolled variables that would mask significant developmental processes.

No wonder there are impatient people who cannot tolerate all of these problems, even when they are reduced with careful planning and, when irreducible, are at least spelled out as limiting conditions. Also, the impatient find the necessarily long wait for results intolerable. One solution that is offered,

recurrently, is only a partial solution. This is the short-term longitudinal study, which is a combination of cross-sectional and longitudinal methods, hopefully to be completed in from three to five years' time. Typically, on this method the design calls for the selection of equal numbers of children at each of five or more ages, and the retesting of all children at predetermined intervals, e.g., at intervals of one year for a period of five years.

There is much to be said in favor of such a research design. It will at least reduce the magnitude of many of the problems we have just listed. The shorter the elapsed time of data collection the less will be the attrition of the sample, and the greater the ease of maintaining the same staff and measuring instruments and procedures. Annual increments can still be studied, and the effects of different life experiences can be cancelled out or measured and statistically controlled. As Warner Schaie has recently pointed out (1964), the research can be so designed that data can be collected concurrently for both longitudinal and cross-sectional as well as age-specific comparisons. For example, the growth rates of children between successive one-year intervals can be compared for children born in 1956 and children born in 1960 or 1964. Eight-year-olds tested for the first time can be compared with eight-year-olds tested for the second, third, or fourth time. In addition, one can get quickly (at least once a year) measures on cross-sectional samples of children of different ages all measured at the same time. With these combinations it should be possible to untangle some of the nagging problems of the effects on test scores of differing life experience and of different testwiseness, and thus to estimate the amount of change due to the growth process itself.

This is all good, so far as it goes. But it still cannot give answers to many of the problems we ask of a long-term study of the same individuals. It cannot tell us such things as how long the effects of experiences in infancy will last, or how early we can predict a child's adult height or I.Q., or the degree of persistence into adulthood of characteristic response tendencies evidenced in infancy.

The Logic of the Cross-sectional Approach

The cross-sectional approach, with its focus upon the behavior of a number of individuals at the same point in time, introduces a major cost savings into developmental research and also eliminates or "controls for" the environmental and cultural changes mentioned in Selection 2, that may contaminate longitudinal studies. But this approach, as Bayley implies, has its weaknesses.

Perhaps the most significant weakness of cross-sectional studies is that reported age-related differences between subjects may in fact be the result of spurious differences between the groups. Suppose, in a cross-sectional study of language development, involving both six- and seven-year-old children, that the older subjects did not display greater linguistic competence than the younger ones. The failure to obtain such a difference—which might be interpreted as a lack of growth during that period—could have resulted simply from differences in the intelligence, social background, or environments of the two groups. It would not be surprising, for instance, to learn that seven-year-old children from so-called disadvantaged homes performed no better on language tasks than six-year-olds reared in middle-class urban surroundings.

This example is, in fact, an extreme case; researchers usually attempt, often with considerable care and shrewdness, to assign subjects in such a manner that the groups do not differ initially on any *relevant variables* that would contaminate the study. But to equate groups on *all* variables is an impossible task, for in the last analysis each child is different from every other child. Thus, the possibility always remains that some important and potentially misleading contamination existed. Finally, as Bayley suggested, cross-sectional studies reveal little or nothing about the durability or stability of behavior.

From the foregoing discussion we see, then, that both the cross-sectional and longitudinal approaches may make important but somewhat different contributions to the study of development. Greatest knowledge accrues when they are used in a complementary way in addressing a particular problem or issue.

THREE METHODS OF DEVELOPMENTAL RESEARCH

In addition to its cross-sectional or longitudinal character, every developmental investigation can be characterized in terms of whether its underlying strategy involves the *experimental, correlational,* or *case study* approach. Although all of these methods involve *observation* of one sort or another, they differ in crucial ways.

The experimental method involves the explicit manipulation of various treatments, circumstances, or events to which the child is exposed; it thereby permits strong inferences as to causal relationships between these manipulations and subsequent behavior. The correlational method explores the relationship between two or more events or variables but, although it provides a relatively large informational yield, does not typically permit causal inferences to be drawn directly. The case study method involves systematic description of the behavior of a single individual, thus providing a depth of information not otherwise typically available but severely limiting what can be inferred about children generally, inasmuch as any one child may be too unique to tell us what most children are like.

The Experimental Method

A Cross-sectional Example of Experimental Research. The experimental method can be illustrated by tracing a specific study, that of Coates and Hartup (1969). The point of departure for Coates and Hartup's research was an earlier finding that children's learning of an adult's behavior was greater if they had been asked to describe out loud—i.e., to verbalize—each act as it was observed than if they had been permitted to watch the adult's actions passively. Coates and Hartup wanted to examine the relationship between chronological age and the influence of such verbalizations on observational learning by young children. In their study children of two age groups, four-year-olds and seven-year-olds, observed a film of an adult's performance on some novel tasks. Before watching this film, though, the children received one of three sets of instructions. Only two need concern us here: in the *induced verbalization* condition, the children were given specific labels to use in describing the model's actions as they occurred; in the *passive observation* condition, they were given no instructions regarding verbal descriptions.

Coates and Hartup, like most investigators, were guided by an initial set of theoretical possibilities. Specifically, they believed that younger children do not spontaneously produce relevant verbalizations in solving problems, whereas older children do produce and employ such verbalizations. Further, the investigators felt that if younger children were helped to produce relevant descriptions or labels, their learning would be improved.

On the basis of these hypotheses, the following predictions were made: (1) seven-year-olds in the *passive observation* condition will show greater observational learning than four-year-olds in the *passive observation* condition; (2) four-year-olds will show greater observational learning in the *induced verbalization* condition than in the *passive observation* condition; and (3) there will be little difference in observational learning in the *induced verbalization* and *passive observation* conditions among the seven-year-olds, for they presumably produce relevant verbalizations spontaneously.

So far in this example, the investigators have taken a finding from earlier studies and combined it with theory to generate the three predictions or *experimental hypotheses* stated above. At this point, though, the three predictions are still untested. They are no more than ideas, but the ideas are well formulated as general propositions that can be tested in a *controlled situation*. The controlled situation not only must meet the requirements of the propositions under test but also must exclude or minimize the effect of other factors not hypothesized to be relevant. What are these requirements in the present example? First, a situation must be created in which children have an equal opportunity to be exposed to novel behaviors and are either asked or not asked to verbalize a description of what they see. Their recall (learning) under these two conditions must then be compared. Second, the subjects must differ in age in the manner prescribed by the hypotheses. Finally, precise measurement of the *variables of interest* (in this case, the children's reproduction of the model's actions) must be possible.

To meet these requirements, children in the Coates and Hartup experiment were brought individually to a mobile research laboratory by an adult experimenter who there introduced them to a second adult. They were told that they were going to watch a movie, after which they would go into another room of the laboratory and "be asked to show what the man in the movie did" (1969, p. 558). Additionally, one of the adults demonstrated two novel behaviors (turning around and marching in place) which illustrated the type of things the child would subsequently see. To provide an adequate test of the experimental hypotheses the film had to display a fairly large number of behaviors which met the dual criteria of being both novel and readily subject to imitation and verbal representation. The production met these qualifications admirably.

> A 7-minute color film . . . was prepared that depicted the behavior of a 25-year-old male model. The model displayed 20 critical behaviors. In order of presentation, these were: has his hands over his eyes; puts his hands behind his back; builds a tower of blocks in a unique way; puts a toy on top of the tower; walks backward four steps from the tower; puts a baton in front of him on the floor; kneels down on one knee behind the baton; fires a pop gun at the tower; takes down the tower of blocks in a unique way; sits on a Bobo clown; hits the clown in the nose; hits the clown with a mallet; throws a ball at the clown; tosses a Hoola Hoop around the clown; drags the clown with the hoop to a corner of the room; walks backward four steps from the bean bag target; throws a bean bag between his legs at the bean bag target; walks backward four steps from the target; squats down with his back to the target; walks across the room whirling the Hoola Hoop over his arm. [1969, p. 558.]

All of the children who participated in this experiment saw the live demonstration and film described above, but the type of instruction they received before the observational period varied.

In the *induced verbalization* condition, the experimenter indicated that he would describe what the actor was doing while the film was being shown and that the child should repeat his statements. A short practice session then ensued in which the child was asked to imitate a verbal description of the other adult's turning and marching. In the *passive observation* group, no verbalization instructions were given. Thus the condition or manipulation which the experimenter created, the *independent variable,* was the type of instruction.

A *dependent variable* is a measurable aspect of the subject's behavior which changes as the independent variable changes. The term derives from the fact that these measures *depend upon* or are controlled by the experimental manipulations (which are *in*dependent in the sense that the experimenter can change them at will). In the Coates and Hartup experiment, the major dependent variable was the number of behaviors in the film which were correctly reproduced by the child. This measure was obtained by taking the subjects, after they had watched the movie, into another room that contained all of the objects with which the filmed model had played. The child was then asked to demonstrate what the man in the movie had done. He was first asked to show what the man did before playing with the toys, then what the man did with the blocks, and so on.

A portion of the results of this experiment are shown in Figure II–1.

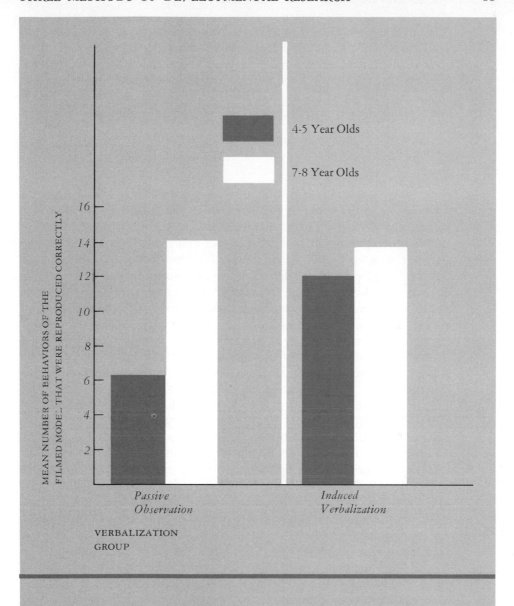

FIGURE II−1

A portion of the results of Coates and Hartup's experiment. Data from Coates and Hartup, 1969.

The three experimental predictions considered here (see p. 31) received clear support. Of particular importance, the study demonstrates that asking young children to verbalize what they have seen can produce or *cause* improvements in learning, since this factor was manipulated directly as part of the experiment (cf. Neale and Liebert, 1973). In correlational research, direct manipulations are not used and thus we can rarely be as confident about cause and effect.

The Correlational Method

Correlation, as the name implies, deals with the co- or joint relationship between two or more factors or variables. The method involves questions of the general form: "Do variable X and variable Y go together or vary together in some way?" Questions of this type frequently are asked in developmental psychology: Is the child's performance in school related to the socioeconomic status of his family? Is there a relationship between late toilet training and compulsiveness in adulthood? Is the frequency of dating behavior during adolescence related to later marital success and happiness?

A characteristic feature of the correlational method is the fact that all subjects are observed under identical conditions. Rather than manipulating the events or experiences to which the child is exposed, the investigator measures phenomena that already exist. In studying the correlation between variables, researchers often compute a correlation coefficient. One commonly used coefficient, designated by the symbol *r,*[*] indicates both the direction and the magnitude of the relationship. It may range from +1.00 to −1.00.

The *direction* is shown by the sign of the coefficient. A positive sign means that high scores on X tend to be associated with high scores on Y, and low scores on X tend to go with low scores on Y. For example, a positive correlation is regularly found between a child's age and his height; the older a child is, the taller he is likely to be. Conversely, a negative sign means that high scores on X tend to be associated with low scores on Y and low scores on X with high scores on Y. Age and the quickness of reflexes are usually found to be negatively correlated; as people grow older, their reflexes become slower.

The *magnitude* or strength of a correlation is indicated by the absolute

---

[*] There are several types of correlation coefficients of which *r*, the Pearson product-moment correlation coefficient, is only one. Our comments on correlational techniques also apply to the other types.

value of the coefficient (disregarding sign). Correlation coefficients of $+.60$ and $-.60$ are equivalent with respect to how strongly the variables under consideration are related. The strongest relationship is indicated when $r = +1.00$ or $r = -1.00$; in both cases, the two variables are perfectly correlated so that either can be determined from the other with perfect accuracy. As the coefficient decreases in absolute value, the magnitude of the relationship becomes weaker, and the ability to estimate one variable from the other decreases. A coefficient of 0.00 indicates that the variables are unrelated, in which case knowledge of one does not tell us anything at all about the other.

A word of caution should be introduced here. Because correlation coefficients range in absolute value from 0.00 to 1.00 it is tempting to view them as percentages (i.e., to assume that a correlation of .60 means a "60 percent" correlation). From this faulty assumption one may be tempted to conclude that a correlation of .50 is twice as large as one of .25. This is an error. The appropriate rule of thumb is to compare squared correlation coefficients to get an idea of the relative strengths of each. Thus, in a sense, a correlation of .80 is approximately *four* times as large as a correlation of .40 (i.e., $.80^2 = .64$ and $.40^2 = .16$; .64 is four times .16).

EXTENDED DISCUSSION

A COMPARISON OF THE EXPERIMENTAL AND CORRELATIONAL METHODS

The critical issue that distinguishes experimental and correlational research is whether or not we can infer a causal relationship between (or among) the variables under investigation. With an experimental design, a cause-and-effect relationship is always implied; that is, the independent variable can be said to lead to a change in the dependent variable. Correlational findings, on the other hand, reveal relationships between (or among) variables without *necessarily* implying causality—although some causal relationship may underlie the findings. For example, there is a positive correlation between the amount of ice cream eaten by children in a particular city on summer days and the number of children who drown on those days. But drownings do not cause an increase in ice cream consumption nor, contrary to popular opinion, does eating ice cream markedly increase the likelihood of cramps and subsequent drowning. Rather, it is a third variable—temperature—that is causally related to both of the other variables. Warmer weather makes it more likely that children will both be swimming (and drowning) *and* eating ice cream.

It is, unfortunately, easy to misconstrue some developmental studies as experimental when they are really correlational in character. To illustrate this point, consider the following hypothetical example. A school psychologist notices that the mothers of many of the children who have been referred to him with behavior problems seem particularly impatient in dealing with their children. To check on this observation he conducts a systematic investigation. Specifically, twelve problem children and twelve children with no reported school difficulties are asked to work with their mothers on a standardized task which requires an interaction between mother and child. Two independent raters are asked to observe the mothers during the sessions and evaluate their interaction with their children on a seven-point scale (1 = very patient, 7 = very impatient). The raters agree almost perfectly. For each mother and child, the psychologist now has reliable information both as to whether the child is considered a school problem or not and a reliable rating of patience for the mother. Note that the investigator made no attempt to influence the mother's interaction with her child; he merely measured this behavior as it occurred. When the psychologist in our example proceeds to analyze his findings, he might begin by arranging them in a manner such as that shown in Table II–1. Then he might compute the average ratings of the mothers for both the problem and no-problem children (6 and 4, respectively, in our example) and compare them with a statistical test. Finally, he might reasonably describe his results by saying: "As predicted, mothers of problem children were found to be less patient in parent-child interactions than were those of children with no reported behavioral difficulties in the school situation."

When the results are described this way, it might be tempting to conclude that the ability of some children to get along with their peers, to please their teachers, and otherwise to avoid being labeled "problems" is partially caused by the patience of their mothers, just as the inability of other children in these areas results from maternal impatience. To draw this conclusion may be erroneous, however, for it treats the study as if it involved an experimental manipulation, which it did not. In fact, the study does not necessarily indicate that a mother's impatience can lead to problems for her child.

It is possible that the impatience of the mothers and the problems of their children "go together" because children who are uncooperative or

TABLE II–1

DATA FROM A HYPOTHETICAL CORRELATIONAL STUDY
COMPARING THE RATED PATIENCE OF MOTHERS
WITH PROBLEM CHILDREN AND CHILDREN WITH
NO REPORTED SCHOOL PROBLEMS

PROBLEM CHILDREN		CHILDREN WITH NO REPORTED PROBLEMS	
Family	Ratings of Mother	Family	Ratings of Mother
A	7	M	5
B	6	N	2
C	6	O	1
D	7	P	7
E	4	Q	4
F	7	R	3
G	7	S	6
H	7	T	5
I	6	U	3
J	7	V	2
K	5	W	6
L	3	X	4
TOTAL	72		48
AVERAGE	6.0		4.0

unruly have an adverse effect on their parents' interactions with them—
that is to say, "problem" children may produce impatient parents. Or it may
be that some third variable, such as the social class or health of the families
involved, is influencing the ratings of both the mothers and the children.
The so-called problem children and their mothers may suffer poor health
due to diets low in nutrition, whereas the mothers and children in the other
group may enjoy the good health provided by adequate nutrition. This un-
observed variable, poor health, might account for both the child's unruliness
and the mother's impatience. Because the investigator merely obtained
measures for each mother-child pair without experimental intervention,
he has no solid basis for distinguishing among these alternatives; because

he did not create or manipulate the behavior of the mothers, he cannot infer any causal relationships. He may, however, predict the occurrence of one of the variables from the presence of the other, as they vary together.

In a sense, then, correlational research compromises the control which is provided by the experimental method for the sake of economically making a broad inspection of a particular problem. By measuring existing characteristics of the subject, it also often permits the naturalness of the situation to remain; the very absence of control may bring the investigation closer to "real life" than is typically possible with experimental investigations. Behavior is almost always *multiply determined* (i.e., it is caused by a number of variables operating at the same time and in conjunction with one another), and the correlational approach easily can take this fact into account by studying the relationships among many variables. Although the experimental approach also can deal with multiple determinants of behavior by manipulating a number of different independent variables at once, it is rare in practice for a single experiment to employ more than three or four independent variables, and many experiments have only one.

A Cross-sectional Example of Correlational Research. One application of the correlational approach which exemplifies many of the advantages of the method is found in a report by Katkovsky, Crandall, and Good (1967). These investigators were interested in a variable which has come increasingly to the fore in recent psychological research. The variable in question, referred to as "internal-external control of reinforcements," concerns the degree to which persons believe that they, rather than something or someone else, are responsible for—and therefore can control—the rewards which they obtain in various life situations.

"Internal control" was of particular interest to these developmental psychologists because of two previous findings. First, an extensive report sponsored by the United States Office of Education (Coleman, Campbell, Hobson, McPartland, Mood, Weinfeld, and York, 1966) * showed that the school achievement of children from minority group backgrounds was more closely related to a measure of internal-external control than to any

---

* The volume's official title is *Equality of Educational Opportunity,* but it is often referred to as the "Coleman Report."

of the numerous other variables included in the study (e.g., the children's attitudes, school and family characteristics, teachers, and the like). Second, an earlier investigation suggested that beliefs in internal control become established in early childhood and appear to remain fairly constant through the years of public education—i.e., grades 3–12 (Crandall, Katkovsky, and Crandall, 1965). Taken together, these considerations suggest the importance of determining the correlates of a belief in internal control during childhood.

Specifically, Katkovsky, Crandall, and Good suggested (among other things) that:

> The extent to which parents are positively or negatively reinforcing . . . may have a significant bearing on the child's beliefs in internal versus external control. When the reinforcements [that is, consequences] which follow his behavior are negative, the child may deny his responsibility for them in order to defend himself against the threat of punishment, insecurity, or inadequacy feelings. When the reinforcements are positive, however, he may maximize the link between his behavior and the outcome. Thus, the more positive the parent's reactions to his child's achievement behaviors, the more the child is likely to develop a belief in internal control of reinforcements; and the more negative the parent's reactions, the more a belief in external control will be fostered. [1967, p. 766–777.]

In order to determine whether this and other relationships held, the investigators performed two correlational studies, one of which we shall consider here. The studies were based on data from families participating in a major study which the Fels Research Institute has been conducting for more than forty years. For the purpose of this research, forty-one children between the ages of six and twelve were administered orally a questionnaire, the Intellectual Achievement Responsibility Questionnaire (IAR), which was designed to measure children's belief or lack of belief in their ability to control their outcomes. The questionnaire contained thirty-six so-called *forced-choice* items, each of which presents either a positive or a negative achievement situation and two contrasting explanations for the outcome. Two of the actual items used, one positive and the other negative, appear below.

> When you do well on a test at school, is it more likely to be (a) because you studied hard, or (b) because the teacher gave an easy test?

> When you find it hard to work arithmetic problems at school, is it usually (a) because the teacher gave hard problems, or (b) because you haven't tried hard enough to work them?

Information regarding the parents came from behavior rating scales based on the observations of a professional home visitor who spent between three and four hours in the home, noting particularly the interactions between mother and child.*

The investigators' expectation, then, was this: The children whose parents most often used approval should tend to have the strongest beliefs in internal control—i.e., that they controlled their own fate—while those whose parents most often used negative criticism should tend to believe that their outcomes and rewards usually were determined by chance or external circumstances. Analysis showed just such a relationship; the correlation between parental use of approval and the children's belief in internal control was +.57, which is statistically significant and, in fact, impressively high.† This relationship, along with other data in the original report, provides correlational support for the proposition outlined previously.

It is easy to see how this pattern of evidence might, in turn, guide a longitudinal *experimental* study designed to foster beliefs in internal control. For example, parents of one group of children might be instructed to reward achievement efforts while parents of a comparable group would not. If the former youngsters showed greater long-term increments than the latter on the internal control measure and on measures of school achievement, then the hypothesis of Katkovsky *et al.* would be supported further.

The Case Study Method

Systematic biographies of children from birth or early childhood constituted the earliest source of data for developmental psychology. Such longitudinal case studies are still employed for some purposes in the investigation of developmental processes.

---

* Parent ratings for this study were based on home visits when the children were approximately six years old, but the larger Fels study has provided longitudinal data by conducting these visits to participant families on a continuous semiannual basis.

† In most psychological research the likelihood that the findings were due to unknown chance factors, rather than to a "real" relationship, is determined statistically. Traditionally, a result (either a difference between means or a correlation) is considered statistically significant, and therefore admissable as evidence, if the odds are no more than five in one hundred that the finding would have occurred by chance. This level of significance, called the ".05 level," is commonly written "$p < .05$." A "$p < .01$" finding would be even less likely— i.e., only one chance in a hundred—to have occurred simply by chance. The correlation of +.57 obtained in the research of Crandall *et al.* is significant at $p < .001$, meaning that a relationship of this strength would occur by chance less than one time in a thousand.

Case studies are often used *didactically,* to provide a prototypical example of some form of behavior or behavioral development. To illustrate both the remarkable verbal ability of children of very high intelligence and the continuity and growth of this ability over time, Munn (1946) presented the following poem, written by a seven-year-old girl with an IQ of 188:

> *Oh, Master of fire! Oh, Lord of air,*
> *Oh, God of waters, hear my prayer!*
> *Oh, Lord of ground and of stirring trees,*
> *Oh, God of man and of pleasant breeze,*
> *Dear Father, let me happy be—*
> *As happy as a growing tree!* [p. 418]

Noting that "follow-up studies of children whose IQs were very high when first determined have shown that, in most instances, the promise of early childhood has been fulfilled," he then reports a story written by the same child at twelve:

Now, behold, there was once an Untutored Child of Nature whose abode was in the wildest wilds of Africa, whose name was Itchy-galoop. And he lived in primitive bliss and ate mangosteens and fried pig, and his drink was the limpid waters of the brook. And he wore a neat but not gaudy garment of leaves, and used no hair tonic.

And it came to pass that a Missionary came unto those wilds and when he beheld Itchy-galoop with his incumbrous garments he was aghast and said unto him:

"Untutored Child of Nature, the way thou goest thou wilt inevitably end up in perdition, so come to my tent and be baptized tomorrow at nine A.M."

And Itchy-galoop was awed by the majestic and noble aspect of the Missionary's nose, and consented.

And the Missionary was glad, and said unto him: "I will now proceed to civilize thee." So he got out his second-best pair of pants and a violet shirt and arrayed Itchy-galoop therein.

And it come to pass that when Itchy-galoop had learned to read, the Missionary presented him with a book of the science of medicine and hygiene. And Itchy-galoop looked therein and was dismayed. He saw plainly that it was a miracle he had survived so long, and began industriously to study.

And he boiled the limpid water of the brook before he quaffed thereof, and partook no more of fried pig which is hard to digest, and washed his mangosteens before he ate of them. And he thumped his chest doubtfully and felt of his pulse, and foresaw that he was dying of tuberculosis and heart disease. And he said, "Yea, it is a certainty that I have every disease in this book from appendicitis on." So he took unto a folding couch that the Missionary had brought and groaned when he thought he ought to.

And when he had survived for a week in this precarious state he awoke one morning with a feeling of unaccountable happiness. And he said unto himself, "This is verily the light-heartedness before the end," and felt his pulse. And suddenly it came to him that the sky was blue and that he was feeling better than ever in his life before. A great conviction dawned on him and he arose and went in search of the Missionary and said to him with menacing aspect, "Get out of here on the double-quick, and if you come into my vision perambulating around in this vicinity again I will immediately examine into the contents of your cranium with my primeval stone hatchet."

And Itchy-galoop stood on a high hill and when the speck of Missionary had faded into the distance he took the book and wrapped his trousers around it and threw it far out into the sea. And he sighed with happiness and went and ate some mangosteens without washing them. [Munn, 1946, p. 418.]

The author of this lovely fable, Munn reports, grew up to become "a writer of poetry and fiction which ranks with that of the greatest writers" (p. 418).

With these examples Munn has illustrated (1) a qualitative difference between the abilities of people with superior and average IQs, and (2) the persistence of achievement in high IQ individuals as they mature. Case study material in this instance clearly serves the purpose of painting a vivid picture of the phenomena which it is intended to exemplify.

Case studies are also especially helpful when circumstances preclude the use of other methods. Investigations of the development of the so-called "feral children"—human infants who, lost or abandoned by their parents, spent the early years of their lives in the wilderness—have been approached in such a manner (Davis, 1947). Obviously, there are constraints on the experimenter who wishes to study the development of children subsequent to years of social isolation. He cannot in good conscience set up the relevant experimental study because it would involve a comparison between two groups of children, one consisting of children reared normally, and a second consisting of children who are banished to the wilderness to fend for themselves or to be reared by wild animals. Nor does he have the opportunity to employ the usual correlational techniques, for there are too few such individuals for any statistical study to be meaningful. The researcher's only alternative is to wait for the discovery of such a child and to fit the pieces of the child's life together into a case study.

The case study method, however, does have some serious drawbacks which the experimental and correlational study methods do not have. First, the investigator can never be entirely certain that he knows all the relevant facts, especially if they have been provided by untrained observers, as is the case with reports of feral children. Second, there is often no individual or group introduced for purposes of comparison. The reader could better understand the contribution of IQ to literacy if Munn had compared the six-line poem written by a child of superior intelligence with a six-line poem composed by a child of the same age but with average intelligence. The author of a case study thus depends upon certain rough-and-ready assumptions by the reader, who will inevitably make his own comparisons. As far as it goes, there is nothing wrong with this; one does not need much experience with children to recognize that the poem reprinted above is beyond the capacity of most seven-year-olds. But how much beyond? Our guesses based on the seven-year-olds we have known cannot provide this information. In sum, the case study method can provide certain gross discriminations in some clear-cut cases, but for finer discriminations we need comparisons which the case study method does not provide.

Finally, it is difficult to draw inferences that extend to people in general from observations of a single individual. The child studied may be quite unlike most other individuals and therefore may not represent the population adequately. In contrast to the experimental and correlation approaches, which try to meet the requirement of representativeness by randomly selecting a whole sample of subjects from the population about which inferences are to be made, the case study, focusing on one or only a few individuals, makes no such claims of representativeness.

Single-subject Experimental Designs. The case study method most often involves the nonmanipulative observation of a single individual, and in this sense it may be contrasted with other research methods in which the behavior of many different individuals or groups of individuals is explored. It is possible, however, to employ the experimental method with a single subject and to demonstrate the controlling influence of certain environmental events upon behavior.

The logic of the single-subject experimental design involves careful measurement of some aspect of the subject's behavior during a given time period (i.e., as a *base-line* or control procedure), the introduction of some environmental modification or treatment during the next (*experimental*) time period, a return to the conditions which prevailed during the control period, and finally a second introduction of the experimental manipulation. The intent of this procedure, sometimes referred to as an *ABAB* design, is straightforward. If behavior changes from *A,* the control period, to *B,* the experimental period, reverses again when the experimentally manipulated conditions are reversed (i.e., returned to *A*), and "re-reverses" when *B* is again introduced, then there is little doubt that it is the manipulation, and not chance or uncontrolled factors, which has produced the change.

The *ABAB* single-subject design may be illustrated by a study conducted by Tate and Baroff (1966) in which methods of reducing the self-injurious behavior of a nine-year-old boy, Sam, were investigated. The lad, who had been diagnosed as psychotic, engaged in a range of self-injurious behaviors including "banging his head forcefully against floors, walls, and other hard objects, slapping his face with his hands, punching his face and head with his fists, hitting his shoulder with his chin, and kicking himself." The investigators also reported that such acts were "a frequent form of behavior observed under a wide variety of situations."

Despite his self-injurious behavior, Sam was not entirely asocial. In fact, it was noted that ". . . he obviously enjoyed and sought bodily contact with others. He would cling to people and try to wrap their arms around him, climb into their laps and mold himself to their contours." It was this observation that gave rise to the experimental treatment. Specifically, the investigators decided to punish Sam's self-injurious outbursts by the immediate withdrawal of physical contact. Their hope, of course, was that this contingent "time-out" from human contact would reduce the frequency of the behaviors which produced it.

The study was run for twenty days and involved a daily walk around the campus for Sam, with two adult experimenters who talked to him and held his hands continuously. During the control days, Sam was simply ignored when he engaged in self-injurious behavior. During the experimental days, the adults responded to any self-injurious actions by immediately jerking their hands away from Sam and maintaining this time-out until three seconds after the last self-injurious act. The results of the systematic reversal of these procedures, shown in Figure II–2, illustrate the dramatic effects of contingent punishment for reducing undesirable behavior in this case. It is clear that these changes resulted from the punishment rather than chance or accident, for the self-injury disappeared, reappeared, and diminished again according to the manipulation. Moreover, the "side effects" of the punishment procedure appear to be positive rather than negative. Tate and Baroff note that:

> On control days Sam typically whined, cried, hesitated often in his walk, and seemed unresponsive to the environment in general. His behavior on

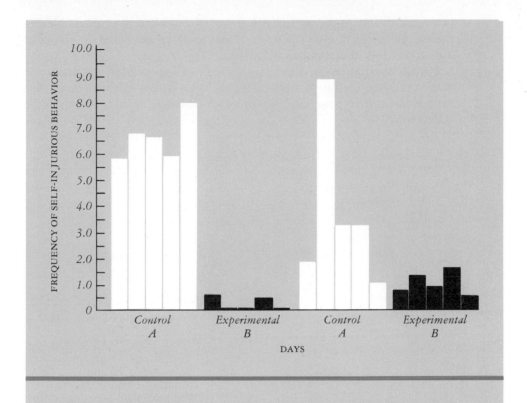

FIGURE II-2

Effects of the contingent punishment procedure in Tate and Baroff's study, illustrating experimental effects within a single-subject design. (The individual bars are data for each day of the experiment.) Adapted from Tate and Baroff, 1966, by permission.

experimental days was completely different—he appeared to attend more to environmental stimuli. . . . There was no crying or whining, and he often smiled. [1966, p. 283.]

The Tate and Baroff study shows that the single-subject design can serve as a well-controlled experiment and can demonstrate convincing causal relationships. Rather than illustrating the complexity of an individual case, the design can be used to demonstrate a principle of behavior through the systematic treatment of one individual under controlled conditions. Nevertheless, as with all case studies, caution must be exercised in drawing inferences about the population at large.

Further applications of this procedure, as well as each of the others we have considered in this chapter, will become apparent as we consider the various substantive issues and topics to which the remainder of this book is devoted.

III

EARLY GROWTH AND DEVELOPMENT

THE COURSE OF MAN'S DEVELOPMENT is influenced by the hereditary endowment of his species. As *Homo sapiens,* all human beings share certain attributes; they walk upright on two feet, they are able to manipulate their environments with a high degree of manual dexterity, and they possess a large, well-convoluted cerebrum. Some of these characteristics are present at birth and others develop later. In other species, we know that the familiar cycle of egg, larvae, cocoon, and butterfly is a genetically determined metamorphosis. One may wonder, as many researchers have, whether analogous stages of physical development, although more subtle, also exist for humans. But even though all human beings share many attributes that emerge in the course of development, each individual also possesses unique characteristics, many of which appear to be inherited.

Thus, inherited *intraspecies* differences may determine much of the behavior which each of us exhibits.

An overview of early growth and abilities—both physical and psychological—can serve as a useful starting point for tracing and understanding the development of human behavior; further amplification of some of the processes which we shall touch on here will be provided in later chapters. Our discussion begins with conception and those factors in development that are virtually universal in man.

CONCEPTION AND FORMATION OF THE ZYGOTE

All humans begin their unique path of development at the moment of conception when the female reproductive cell, the *ovum,* and its male counterpart, the *spermatozoan,* join to produce the *zygote* or fertilized egg. Like all cells of the human body, the reproductive cells contain *chromosomes,* each of which has thousands of *genes.* The genes, which are segments of deoxyribonucleic acid (DNA), bear the genetic information which is passed on from one generation to the next.*

The exact structure and number of chromosomes are distinct and characteristic for each species, with the number ranging from as few as two to as many as 127 pairs (Sinnott, Dunn, and Dobzhansky, 1958). Virtually all human cells contain twenty-three pairs of chromosomes, twenty-two of which—the autosomes—are common to both sexes and one pair of which —the sex chromosomes—differs sharply in males and females. Figure III–1 depicts the chromosomal complements for each sex. Note that the sex chromosomes in females are alike; they are called X chromosomes. Males, on the other hand, have one X and one Y chromosome, the latter carrying less genetic information and being smaller and lighter.

An exception to the uniform number of chromosomes in each cell occurs in the reproductive cells or *gametes.* In these cells the count is reduced by one-half as a result of a special type of cell division, *meiosis.* During maturation of the gametes, the chromosomes of each pair migrate toward opposite walls of the cell. The cell then divides forming reproductive

---

* Analysis of the DNA molecule by Watson and Crick in their 1953 Nobel Prize winning efforts has opened the way to further understanding of genetic transmission. Specifically, a coiled ladderlike arrangement of pairs of chemical structures, forming a double helix, permits DNA molecules to simply "unzip," divide, and then reproduce in a mirror-image fashion. The discovery itself was a magnificent drama, which has been recorded in a candid but confessedly personal history written by Watson (1968).

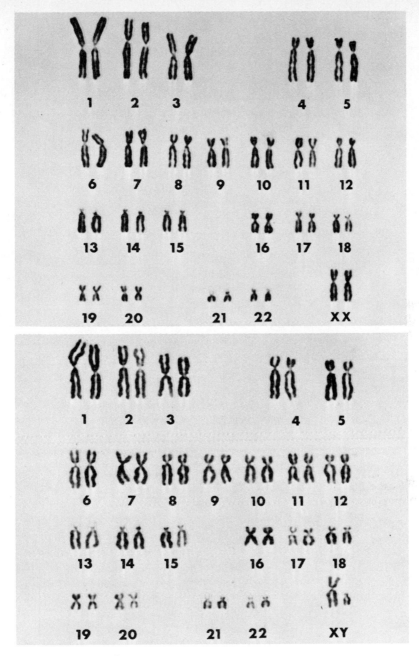

FIGURE III—1

The twenty-three pairs of chromosomes in females and males. Courtesy of M. M. Grumbach, University of California, San Francisco.

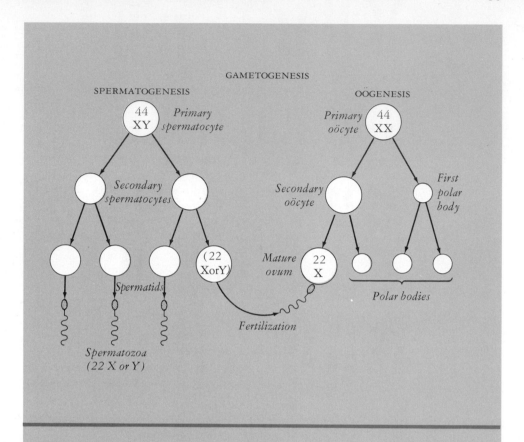

FIGURE III—2

The meiotic sequence in males and females. The process of spermato-genesis results in the formation of four sperm cells (left); oögenesis re-sults in the formation of one ovum and three polar bodies (right). From William F. Evans, Anatomy and Physiology: The Basic Principles *© 1971. Reprinted by permission of Prentice-Hall, Inc., Englewood Cliffs, New Jersey.*

cells, each with twenty-three *single* chromosomes; these are the ova or the spermatazoa, which join to produce the zygote. Figure III–2 provides a diagram of this process, which is called spermatogenesis and oögenesis for males and females respectively.

When conception occurs, the father and mother each contribute half of the normal complement of chromosomes to the zygote. If we consider only two chance factors, the manner in which the chromosomes sort out in meiosis and the manner in which sperm and ovum unite, there are millions of possible chromosomal combinations. Because the effects of environmental interaction and of genetic mechanisms not yet discussed create even more diversity, it is not surprising that we see enormous variability among human beings.

Sex Determination

Each parent contributes one sex chromosome to the offspring. Mothers pass on only an X chromosome for they themselves carry no Y chromosomes. Fathers, on the other hand, may contribute either an X or Y chromosome. The sex of the newly formed human being depends on whether an X-chromosome sperm or a Y-chromosome sperm unites with the ovum. A female zygote is produced when the twenty-third pair of chromosomes are both X chromosomes, whereas a male zygote results from a pair with one X and Y.

Theoretically, there should be an equal chance of the zygote's being male or female, inasmuch as one half of the sperm cells contain the X and one half contain the Y chromosome. In fact, more males apparently are conceived, for the ratio of male to female births is 106:100 (in the United States) even though a larger proportion of males die during uterine development. It has been speculated that more Y-chromosome spermatozoa penetrate the ova because their light weight enables them to reach the female gametes more quickly than the X-chromosome spermatozoa. The greater vulnerability of males to death and abnormality both preceding and after birth has been attributed to the relative lack of genes in the Y chromosomes.

Formation of Twins

The integrity of the organism once it is formed typically is maintained throughout the reproductive process, so that a single fertilization results in a single birth. Occasionally, however, during the first two weeks after conception, the zygote will divide into two cell masses. When such a division occurs, two individuals of the same sex and with identical genetic endowments are formed. Children from such a mating are referred to as *monozygotic* (true identical twins), because they both derive from a single zygote. Multiple births also can occur as the result of a different process in which two different ova and two different spermatazoa unite at approximately the same time. In this case the two individuals that result are referred to as *dizygotic* twins because they develop from two different zygotes. Dizygotic (or fraternal) twins need not be of the same sex and may be as genetically different as two different siblings conceived of the same parents at different times. But regardless of whether fertilization results in the conception of a single individual or of monozygotic or dizygotic twins, the development of the zygotes proceeds in approximately the same way.

PRENATAL DEVELOPMENT

Fertilization takes place in the Fallopian tube leading from the ovary; the fertilized ovum then journeys downward and becomes implanted on the uterus wall, a process which takes approximately seven days. During this time, rapid cell multiplication, by the process of *mitosis,* has already begun so that several dozen cells exist by the time the migration is complete. In mitosis, the total number of chromosomes in a cell doubles by splitting lengthwise before cell division, resulting in two identical cells (Figure III–3). Within the rapidly forming cellular mass a cavity appears; the outer layer of cells then develops into the placenta and other supporting tissues. Cells lining the inside of the cavity are destined to be the *embryo.*

It is during the next two to eight weeks, known as the period of the embryo, that the multiplying cellular mass undergoes differentiation. Three layers of cells form: the *ectoderm* is the basis for the formation of skin, sense organs, and the nervous system; the *mesoderm* further differentiates into the muscles, blood, and circulatory system; and the *endoderm* gives rise to the digestive system and other internal organs and glands. By two months the embryo is about one inch long and roughly resembles a human being (see Figure III–4). Limbs are relatively well developed with fingers or toes; the face, ears, eyes, and mouth are clearly visible; the heart beats; and the nervous system shows the beginnings of a response capability.

The embryonic period is marked by a high mortality rate; probably about

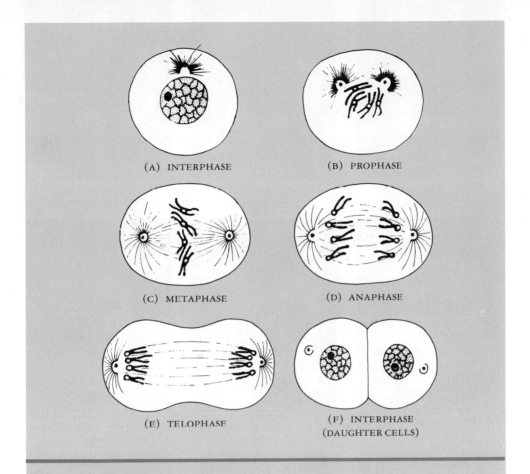

(A) INTERPHASE

(B) PROPHASE

(C) METAPHASE

(D) ANAPHASE

(E) TELOPHASE

(F) INTERPHASE
(DAUGHTER CELLS)

FIGURE III–3

Diagram representing mitosis in a cell with four chromosomes. From William F. Evans, Anatomy and Physiology: The Basic Principles © *1971. Reprinted by permission of Prentice-Hall, Inc., Englewood Cliffs, New Jersey*

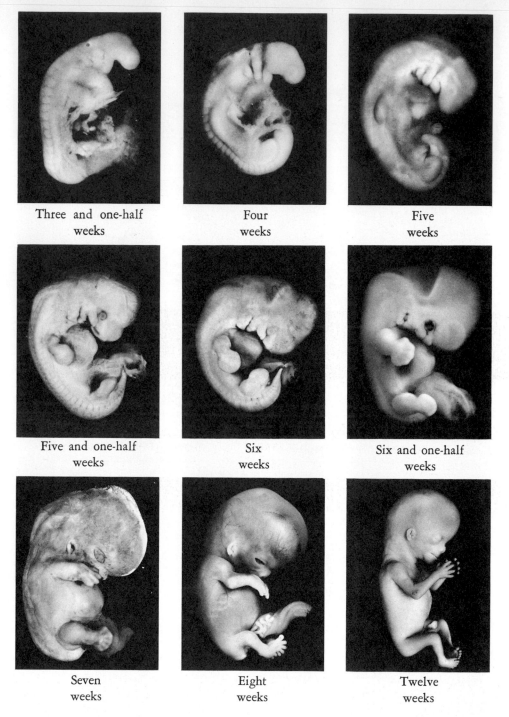

Three and one-half
weeks

Four
weeks

Five
weeks

Five and one-half
weeks

Six
weeks

Six and one-half
weeks

Seven
weeks

Eight
weeks

Twelve
weeks

opposite: FIGURE III–4

Development in the womb during the first three months of life. Courtesy of A. S. Romer.

---

30 percent of all embryos are spontaneously aborted. Chromosomal abnormality exists in 3–4 percent of the fertilized ova but in only 0.25 percent of newborns, an indication that many abnormal embryos are aborted (Tanner, 1970). The embryo also appears particularly sensitive to a variety of conditions. If the mother contracts rubella (German measles) during the first three months (trimester) of pregnancy, the infant often will be intellectually retarded and/or will suffer from physical abnormalities such as eye cataracts or deafness. If, however, she becomes ill with this disease during the second or third trimester of pregnancy, the infant typically will not suffer from such defects. Experimental evidence from animal studies (Nelson, Asling, and Evans, 1952) and correlational data involving human infants who were born retarded (Knobloch and Pasamanick, 1958) indicate that deficiencies in the mother's dietary intake during the earlier period also may have a considerably greater effect on the young than the same deficiencies would have if they occurred later in the process of prenatal development.

Growth and Behavior of the Fetus

From the beginning of the third month to birth, the developing organism is referred to as the *fetus*. Considerable knowledge of both the physical characteristics and the behavior of the fetus has been obtained from three different sources. First, fetuses sometimes must be operatively removed from the uterus for therapeutic reasons. Although it has not yet been possible to maintain the lives of very young fetuses outside of the womb until they mature, under well-controlled circumstances they can remain alive long enough to permit recording of both their spontaneous behavior and their reactions to certain forms of electrical and mechanical stimulation

(Landreth, 1967). Second, studies can be made of premature infants (born between the sixth and eighth month after conception) which presumably reflect their behavioral capacities while in the uterus. Finally, measures of the behavior of the living fetus in the uterus may be obtained, either through the systematic reports of mothers or through the use of specialized instruments capable both of recording the behavior of the fetus and of stimulating this behavior. From these sources, researchers have been able to gain enough information to paint a reasonably complete picture of prenatal development.

Characteristics of the Fetus

The rate of growth reaches its peak during the early fetal period and then declines. Except for the differentiation of such parts as hair, nails, and external sex organs, development in the fetal period is characterized primarily by further genesis of existing structures, changes in body proportion, and increases in function. From the earliest beginnings of movement and responsive behavior in the second trimester—spontaneous movement can be felt by the mother at about sixteen weeks—to the time of birth, there is a fairly steady overall increase in activity.

In addition to quantitative change, there are some interesting qualitative changes. Kicking appears to decrease and squirming to increase as the fetus approaches birth (Newberry, 1941), and head movements show a particularly striking increase in the third trimester (Watson and Lowrey, 1954). It appears that maternal fatigue stimulates fetal activity (Schmeidler, 1941), as does the mother's cigarette smoking (Sontag and Wallace, 1935). Such increased activity, particularly when it is related to maternal stress, is associated with low birth weights and certain gastrointestinal problems at birth (Sontag, 1940; Sontag, Reynolds, and Torbet, 1944).

Reflexes, automatic and apparently innate responses, develop over an extended period and tend to appear as they become important for survival. All of the reflexes that are important for life in the uterus appear by about the fifth month (Landreth, 1967), and "advance preparation" begins during the last trimester for those functions that will be vital during the infant's postnatal existence (e.g., swallowing, urinating, muscular movements of the gastrointestinal tract). Other reflexive responses, such as the pupillary reflex, do not appear to be present in the twenty-eight-week-old premature infant. The organism at this age will, however, respond with body movements when shown a very intense light.

BIRTH

Approximately 270 days after conception, the human fetus is sufficiently developed to enter the outside world. Biological preparation for *parturition,* the technical term for birth, begins with *lightening.* Toward the end of gestation, the head of the fetus turns down so that birth occurs with head first. In turn, the fetus' movement into this position relieves ("lightens") the pressure against the mother's abdomen so that she can breathe more freely. *Labor,* the process by which the fetus is expelled from its mother's womb, occurs within a few hours to a few weeks after lightening. The normal length of labor varies widely, being related to such factors as the age of the mother and the number of prior deliveries. Although the causal relationships are difficult to identify, very long labor is related to certain types of deficiencies in the physical condition of the neonate (Prechtl, 1963).

The happening of birth, as dramatic as it is, frequently has been assigned immense psychological importance. Usually it is seen as a traumatic thrust of the child from a serene and warmly protective environment into a confusing and cold world. Although it is impossible to know the psychological experiences of the newborn, we can assess birth as a biological event. We know, for instance, that for a small number of infants difficult birth (c.g., when the placenta is entangled or when instruments are required) can result in impairment or death. Even in the usual course of events some change and upheaval occurs—as in the respiratory and circulatory systems. At the same time, for at least some systems, birth is an "incident without much significance in a steadily maturing and changing program of events" (Tanner, 1970, p. 92). For example, at about the thirty-fourth week of pregnancy there begins a gradual decrease in fetal hemoglobin and an increase in the "adult" form of this blood substance. These changes in blood chemistry are not influenced by birth itself. Nor does the maturation of the nervous system, as detailed by EEG recordings * and motor responses, appear to be altered by birth.

THE NEONATE

Appearance

The newborn human infant,† or *neonate,* is a creature approximately twenty inches in length and usually weighing between six and nine pounds. Its appearance and posture shortly after birth are captured in Figure III—6 (see p. 72), a photograph taken soon after birth.

The neonate's skin is thin and dry, and takes on a striking red and wrinkled appearance when the infant cries. In other physical aspects, the baby has a "standard" appearance which later will give way to the particular physical features which will characterize it in later life. Virtually all newborns appear to have flat noses, high foreheads, receding jaws (according to one upset mother, "no chin at all!"), and blue eyes. But these features will all swiftly mature and change, as will the behavioral capabilities of the young organism.

Physical Condition: The Apgar Score. Since the middle 1950s, one widely used method of assessing the medical condition of the infant at birth has involved the use of what is called the Apgar score, a name derived from that of its originator. The measure is simply a rating by the pediatrician, within one minute after the infant's birth, of heart rate, respiratory efficiency, reflex irritability, muscle tone, and color. Each of these five dimensions is scored as 0, 1, or 2, with the larger numbers indicating the more superior condition of medical health. Thus, an Apgar score of 10 reflects an infant with a steady heartbeat, lusty cry, and well-developed reflexes.

---

* The EEG, or electroencephalogram, is a tracing, plotted against time, of the frequency and potential (voltage) of electrical currents emitted by the brain.

† Interestingly, the term *infant* derives from the Latin word *infans,* meaning "not speaking."

PREMATURITY AND ITS CONSEQUENCES

The child who is born prematurely is, not surprisingly, subject to many more deficiencies and debilities in its later development than an infant who spends the full term of gestation in its mother's uterus. The consequences of prematurity have become increasingly important from a practical, social viewpoint as recent medical advances have assured the survival of an increasing number of premature infants. These strides have been truly remarkable; one estimate, for example, is that mortality among premature infants was reduced by 55 percent in the United States between 1933 and 1955 (Caputo and Mandell, 1970). And as more prematures have come to survive, understanding of their deficiencies has grown.

In most studies, infant maturity is measured by body weight at the time of birth; thus, although other criteria such as gestational age in weeks may be more useful for some purposes (cf. Caputo & Mandell, 1970), our discussion is based almost entirely on the birthweight criterion.

Birthweight and Intelligence. One of the most important longitudinal studies of the relationship between birthweight and later intelligence, initiated at Johns Hopkins University during the early 1950s, is the Baltimore Study. This investigation followed the intellectual development of almost one thousand infants, including a premature group (less than 3.3 pounds at birth) and a normal weight group, through their twelfth year of life. The study utilized sophisticated controls for a variety of factors, such as social class, race, and season and hospital of birth. Measures of intelligence taken at forty weeks of age, three to five years, six to seven years, eight to ten years, and twelve to thirteen years showed that the low weight individuals did significantly less well than did the normal weight ones. There were also differences in the degree of impairment within the so-called premature group as a function of birthweight; heavier infants within the low birthweight class were less likely to show impairment than are those of very low birthweight.

Other evidence of this relationship is found in three studies of twins (Babson, Kangas, Young, and Bramhall, 1964; Churchill, 1965; Willerman and Churchill, 1967), all suggesting that the twin with the higher birthweight tends to have the higher IQ during middle childhood. (One of the advantages of the twin study method for assessing the relationship between birthweight and intelligence is that other variables, such as socioeconomic status, parental education, gestational age, and the like, are automatically controlled.)

The Baltimore study was also interested in determining whether children who had been low birthweight infants were more likely to be in special or below grade level school classes than were controls. It was found that while 75 percent of the control group was in an appropriate grade, only 45 percent of the smaller prematures had achieved regular school placement by the age of twelve (Wiener, 1968; Caputo and Mandell, 1970). Similarly, it has been reported that, among black high school students, "dropouts" tend to have had the lowest birthweight, "slow learners" next, and normal school performers the highest birthweight.

Physical Defects. Many studies have shown that low birthweight is associated with an increased likelihood of physical defects and impairments, both at birth and through later life. More than half of the low birthweight children in one sample had at least one physical or neurological impairment, including 37 percent with visual defects and 12 percent with hearing defects (Drillien, 1961). Interestingly, the incidence of defects was positively related to the year of birth; that is, children born more recently were more likely to display them. This finding presumably is a result of the increased survival rate of very low birthweight babies in recent years.

Neurological damage also has been found to be associated with low birthweight (De Hirsch, Jansky, and Langford, 1966; Lubchenco, Horner, Reed, Hix, Metcalf, Cohig, Elliott, and Bourg, 1963; Wiener, Rider, Oppel, Fischer, and Harper, 1965). These findings include evidence of strabismus (a condition in which both eyes cannot be focused on the same point, so that the individual appears to be "cross-eyed"), abnormal EEG recordings, and spastic movement. As with other findings already mentioned, physical defects appear to be associated with very low birthweight, rather than with relatively "heavy" prematures (Robinson and Robinson, 1965).

Adjustment and Social Behavior. A relationship between low birthweight and later adjustment difficulties or problems in social behavior has been established in many correlational studies (Caputo and Mandell, 1970). Caution is needed, however, in interpreting this finding. Consider, for example, a study of Pasamanick, Rogers, and Lilienfeld (1956), in which the frequency of referrals to the Baltimore Board of Education for deviant behavior was significantly higher for low birthweight children than for matched control children. But when only premature children who were born *without pregnancy complications* are considered, this difference disappears. Thus, the underlying factor may be pregnancy complications or events associated with them. Likewise, Robinson and Robinson (1965) reported that neither low birthweight nor very low birthweight children differed from controls in terms of teacher behavior ratings when corrections were made for social class.*

Despite difficulties in identifying *causal* relationships, very low birthweight is clearly associated with at least some difficulties in later life. Because the incidence of survival for premature infants has gone up dramatically with advances in medical and health technology, it is becoming even more important to improve psychological and educational technology to prevent or ameliorate deficiencies.

Reflexes

The neonate's behavior may be characterized in terms of various reflexes, which are made to particular forms of stimulation. Virtually all of them appear to have biological significance or to have had such importance at an earlier point in man's evolution.

Among the reflexes which are clearly adaptive for the infant in its new environment are those involving *breathing, blinking, coughing* or *sneezing* in response to an irritant, and three reflexes, *rooting, sucking,* and *swallowing,* which are related to feeding. The rooting reflex manifests itself in the fact that stimulation to the cheek of the neonate will cause it to turn its head and mouth toward the direction of that stimulation.

At least four other reflexes exist which appear to have no obvious func-

---

* Social class and birth weight are themselves related.

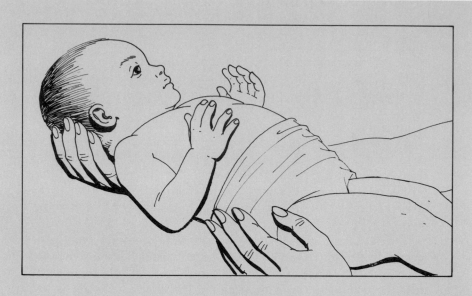
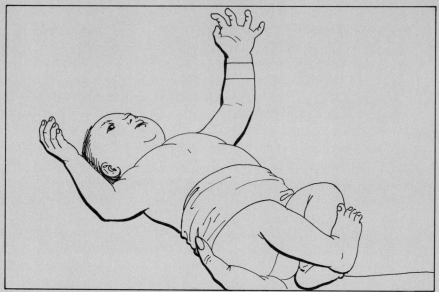

FIGURE III-5

An illustration of the Mōro reflex in a nine-day-old infant.

tional significance, although it has been speculated that they may have been adaptive in man's past evolutionary life. The palmar or *grasp reflex* can be seen in the infant's tendency to firmly grasp a rod or finger that is placed in its palm, sometimes with enough strength to actually suspend its own weight. The plantar or *Babinski reflex* appears as a fanning out of the toes upon stimulation of the sole of the foot. The *swimming reflex,* as the name implies, consists of swimminglike movements of the arms and legs which an infant makes when placed in water. Finally, the *Moro reflex* is manifested in the infant's response to loss of support or intense stimulation such as a loud noise. As can be seen in Figure III–5, it consists of arching the back, throwing back the head, and extending the arms outward from the body. All four of these reflexes disappear within the first year of life. They are, nevertheless, important in that they can signify whether development is proceeding in a typical or atypical fashion.

Early Behavioral Repertoire

Much of the young infant's activity involves generalized movements of many parts of the body. When crying occurs, the entire organism, including arms and legs, appears to be involved; this diffuse or mass activity involving seemingly irrelevant movement can be elicited by a variety of stimuli. One explanation for this behavior, which decreases during the first year of life, is a lack of inhibitory mechanisms in the immature nervous system (Wolff, 1966).

Other behaviors are more precise and specific and tend to be related to particular stimuli. Movements of the eyelids (both "spontaneously" and in response to various types of stimulation) as well as of the eyes themselves in visually tracking an object can be observed very shortly after birth. Movements of the lips, mouth, and head in response to tactile stimulation, such as gentle stroking, can be observed in most infants within a few days after birth. For many babies, grimaces (wrinkling of the forehead, twisting of the mouth and lips) will be produced when unpleasant solutions of salt water or quinine are introduced into the mouth.

The newborn infant immediately begins to interact with his environment and displays a rapid growth in its behavioral repertoire. For example, Shirley (1933), studying the development of visual ability, found that more than half of a sample of twenty-five infants could: (1) follow a light with their eyes by the end of the first week after birth; (2) fix their eyes visually on an object by three weeks of age; and (3) visually follow a horizontally moving object by nine weeks.

AN OVERVIEW OF INFANT RESEARCH

The behavior of the very young human has enjoyed two periods of peak interest in developmental psychology, one in the 1920s and 1930s and the current one which began in the 1960s. The former was concerned primarily with the neonate as a novel organism, a concern reflected in such questions as whether (or to what extent) the infant could see, hear, smell, or be conditioned by the environment. Although more recent investigations have extended these findings considerably, present concerns and approaches are not identical to those of the past. In the following Selection, an overview of the points of view which emerged in the 1960s is presented as they were outlined and discussed by William Kessen; we shall return to many of them in later chapters.

SELECTION 3

RESEARCH IN THE PSYCHOLOGICAL DEVELOPMENT OF INFANTS: AN OVERVIEW

William Kessen

The infant has not always been treated kindly by American psychologists. Although almost all theories . . . celebrate the importance of infant behavior, and claim that the baby is striking proof of the validity of their views, systematic empirical study of the child in his crucial first year has been an on-again, off-again affair. And for a number of reasons, not the least of which is the difficulty of seeing young children in the large numbers that we have at our command in studying the pre-school child or the adolescent. Once a child leaves the hospital after the lying-in period, he is not again easily available for research until he appears in nursery school. It may also be that the infant is so clearly one of us—in that he is human, and so clearly and incomprehensibly different, in that he is a baby—that we have, on occasion, escaped our frustration by constructing theoretical babies instead of observing real ones.

Happily, these disabilities no longer block research. There is evidence, and not only in the United States, that psychologists are studying the infant more closely than ever before. Merely to call the names of investigators and

Reprinted from Kessen, W. Research in the psychological development of infants: An overview. *Merrill-Palmer Quarterly,* **9**, 1963, 83–94. Reproduced by permission.

refer to some of their findings would consume many pages. This is not to say, by the way, that the theoretical or constructed child has disappeared. Far from it! Behind each empirical investigation, there is a model, and this model colors and sometimes dominates the interpretation that is given the empirical protocols.

I would like to be able to present a neat, clear (even if artificial) dichotomy or trichotomy of theoretical positions concerning infancy—I recall with some nostalgia our antique friend "maturation *versus* learning"—but the current situation in the psychological study of infancy does not accept such simple classification. It is only a modest exaggeration to say that a recitation of theoretical subtleties would approach the complexity of a recitation of research findings. In the face of this kind of variety, I cannot hope to lay out a complete or even a fair summary of current research and thought about the behavior of the infant. Rather, I will present for your comment, review, and evaluation, a short set of propositions about babies and studies of babies; under each of these loose-jointed statements, we can examine a part of the research and speculation that has appeared over the last several years.

The first proposition or summary statement that I will propose is that *a comparative psychology of infancy can be anticipated*. Harlow's well-known work (1958) on affectional systems in the monkey, though incomplete, is as stimulating a body of research as has been done on animal development over the last decade. Less widely known, but of at least equal theoretical impact, are T. C. Schneirla's (1959) speculations about approach and avoidance and their relation to stimulus intensity. Hess (1959), among others, has presented

data and commentary on the phenomena of imprinting. Seymour Levine (1957) has contributed a number of papers on the effect of infantile stress on later behavior. These names only begin a list of the researchers who are working on developmental problems with infra-human animals.

Two general comments are warranted here. The animal work which is now going on in developmental psychology is not "dry-as-dust" laboratory demonstration. Moreover, little of this work leads to procedures routinely applicable to children, in the way that some current studies of reinforcement are; nor is the current animal work aimed at elaboration of the obvious. The psychologists studying animal development are in advance of their colleagues in human developmental studies, not only in regard to novel empirical techniques, but more important, in their willingness to take an intellectual chance or risk a speculation. The second note to be appended to the work with animals is the classical one, namely, the possibility of experimental manipulation of more than a trivial sort. We have only seen the beginning of work with animals, and particularly with primates, that will permit us to examine experimentally propositions that would otherwise remain available only to limited observational examination. Studies of the relation of infant to parent, for example, can be investigated along all relevant dimensions only by the use of animals. This is not to say that once we have found the rhesus we can abandon the human being, but the thoughtfulness and energy of investigators currently working in animal research will have no small impact on current research in the psychology of development.

But let me put aside the allure of

precision and control possible with animal work and confine the rest of my general propositions to those about human behavior.

The first proposition about children to be considered, and perhaps the most obvious, is that *infants are various*—young children are different from one another. I may see a straw man when I speak against the notion that human infants at birth, like well-made cigarettes, cannot be distinguished from one another; but there is still abroad in psychology—at least in the academical variety—the feeling that children at birth are, by and large, pretty much undifferentiated protoplasm or no more than merely randomly varying beings. Whatever the present state is of the pure, undifferentiated position in the sociology of knowledge, evidence is accumulating that parents and nurses were right all along—stable differences in behavior can be detected in the first days of life. Hammond (1957) has shown the stability of physical growth patterns. Richmond and his colleagues at Syracuse [Richmond and Lustman, 1955] have reported psychophysiological stabilities in the newborn. Thomas, Chess, Birch, and Hertzig (1960), although they have published only preliminary reports, have stated that on nine variables—among them, reactivity and irritability—they have found stability in children followed longitudinally over a period of two years. There are some suggestions in Bell's work (1960), and there are some findings in our work on newborns at Yale [Kessen, Williams, and Williams, 1961], which tend to support a strong generalization that stable individual differences in a large number of behaviors —sucking, general movement, reactivity—exist very early in life. Yet, impressive as it is, the work on the

assessment of individual differences among human infants has not, like some of the animal work, been "built out" from novel observations and speculations. Rather, it has come largely from the essential and tedious work of constructing adequate response measures. These advances in technology or method are clear and welcome, but they leave open two larger questions about individual differences.

First, what is the long-range stability or relevance of these differences? It is good to know that the newborn shows stable differences in activity level from his colleague in the next crib, but the importance of this observation is markedly reduced if the difference does not show up in some form later. Among the investigators, other than the Birch group, who have done some interesting speculative work on this score, is the French psychologist Stambak (1956). She has segregated two groups of infants—hypertonic and hypotonic—and has discussed the relation of this tendency to be active or quiet to such important developmental changes as onset of walking. In addition, the Czech group (Papoušek, 1961) is investigating the stability of the infant's behavior during conditioning over the first six months of life. Such studies are provocative curtain-raisers on the intricate question of behavioral stability in infancy.

There is a second question about which we have very little evidence. How are these early behavioral variations related to variations in the environment? How do different combinations of infant and caretaker mesh together? We can tag babies as active or quiet; we can make this discrimination in the first five or ten days of life. We can suspect, too, that some mothers like active babies and some mothers like quiet babies. What do you get when you combine an active baby with a mother who wanted a quiet one or a quiet baby with a mother who wanted an active one? We have very little to go on here, not only because of the obvious technical difficulties of longitudinal studies of this kind, and not only because of the fluidity of our ideas about what is important in the home, but also because, until recently, we have not had reliable ways of describing the young child's environment. The technical advance in the methods of describing newborn behavior have not been matched by methods for describing the home. But here, again, there is promise. Schaefer, Bell, and Bayley (1959) have proposed a parent attitude scale. The important interview work of Sears *et al.* (1957) provides a framework for the description of parents' behavior. Rheingold (1960) has recently specified some of the dimensions of variation between home and institution. These papers point the way toward the time when a genuine analysis can be made of the interaction between mother and child. The word "genuine" reflects the hope that this analysis will not be a contaminated one; that we can make assessments of the status of the newborn, independent of observing the mother, and make assessment of the mother, independent of observing the child.

The next summary proposition that I want to suggest warrants detailed examination. I submit that *the young infant is not incompetent* or, by André-Thomas' (1954) catching phrase, "the neonate is not a neophyte."

We have passed the time, not so very long ago, when the newborn was considered to be sensorily bereft (*e.g.,* Preyer's contention that children are born deaf), but the notion of newborn incompetence persists. It has perhaps its strongest statement in the work of the psychoanalysts, especially Spitz (1959), who maintains the existence of a non-differentiated phase in early life, where the newborn does not code inputs at all. In this view of the infant, by no means limited to psychoanalysts, both the baby's sensory capacities and his response capacities are held to be severely limited. The trend of recent research is clearly against this conception of the child. Research on newborn behavior over the last five years has invariably added to the newborn's list of abilities. Peiper (1956) in his encyclopedic treatment, André-Thomas (1954) and his colleagues in Paris, Madame Ste. Anne-Desgassies, and Prechtl (1958) are among the workers who have discussed the extended sensory and response range of the newborn in some detail. Gorman and his associates [Gorman, Cogan, and Gellis, 1959] have recently found in a study of acuity that the newborn has visual resolving powers which are not markedly inferior to those of the older child. From the research available on the competence of the newborn, let me present three studies in some detail as illustrative and somewhat representative of this newer view of the newborn.

The first study, by Blauvelt [Blauvelt and McKenna, 1960], deals with the precision of at least one response the newborn makes. Following up earlier work of Prechtl on head-turning, Blauvelt has studied the baby's response to a very simple stimulation, in which the experimenter moves her fingers from the tragus of the baby's ear—the baby lying on its back in the crib—toward the baby's mouth and then away again in a flat elliptical course. It turns out that the baby tracks this movement by turning his head at a speed and to a position that will reduce the distance between his mouth and the stimulating finger. He tracks this movement without special tuition; it is, if you like, built-in. The infant can pick up approaching stimulation and reduce the distance to it very quickly; he can "find" the approaching breast or bottle. What is impressive about this response is the precision of it. This is not the response of a wild newborn, flailing around uselessly and without direction; this is an organism making a precise and exact tracking response. It is a limited skill, to be sure, and certainly not widely generalizable to other activities, but it illustrates the responding precision of some newborn.

The second study illustrative of newborn competence may be one of the most important empirical research products of the last decade in infancy work. Bronshtein, Antonova, Kamenetskaya, Luppova, and Sytova (1958) have described a technique for assessing the limits of sensory differentiation in the infant that promises a precision in psychophysical description that has heretofore been possible only for the much older child. Briefly, the procedure is this. You permit or induce the child to suck, and record his rhythmic response. If, during sucking, you sound a brief tone, say of 512 cycles/sec., the baby stops sucking. When the tone stops, the baby begins to suck again. To a second stimulation of the same tone, he will stop sucking. This sequence can be repeated four or five times for sounds and then when you sound your 512-cycle tone he goes on sucking without interruption. He has adapted to that sound. If, however, you now present a different tone, say one of 1,024 cycles, he will stop sucking. If he continues to suck on the application of the second stimulus, this is presumptive evidence

that he cannot discriminate the two stimuli. If he does stop sucking on the second stimulus, if it "undoes the adaptation," then there is evidence that he can discriminate these two stimuli. If this technique is as sensitive as the Russians suggest, we will be able to find out more about the sensory capacities of the young infant than we can find out about the sensory capacities of young five- or six-year-olds. Bronshtein presents data to indicate that the infant makes clearly differential responses to variations in pitch, light intensity, and other stimulus changes. Lipsitt, at Brown, has adapted this technique to a study of olfactory stimulation and has found that not only is sucking inhibited and adapted in this fashion but so also is movement. Just as the Blauvelt study illustrates the possible response flexibility of the newborn, so the Bronshtein and Lipsitt studies indicate the remarkable amount of stimulus coding the newborn is capable of. The world of the infant is not a vast confusing "blob."

Consider yet a third study. In our work at Yale [Kessen and Leutzendorff, 1963], we have found that if you put a nipple in a baby's mouth, he will stop general movement at once, and when you take it out he will start moving again. This effect appears in the absence of nutrient; the nipple does not supply food—it only provides an opportunity to suck. And, this inhibition of movement takes place in the fourth or third or second, or even first day of life. The child is able to deal with a complex and vitally important input— namely, nipple or sucking—by a very regular response. Nor, apparently, does he have to learn either how to suck or how to quiet. There is of course the argument that he learned the responses *in utero,* but we have hardly advanced beyond Hippocrates' statement of that argument 2,500 years ago.

These studies suggest that the newborn has far greater capacities for sensory discrimination than could have been guessed a decade ago, and though less impressive, the evidence is beginning to indicate that he has surprising response competencies as well. But the evidence for newborn resourcefulness poses a peculiar paradox. To put the question very bluntly, if the human newborn is so capable, why does he not learn more? If he is so capable, why is he so stupid? These questions form the bridge to my next general proposition, one which seems so insecure that I have phrased it in the form of yet another question.

There is early adaptation, but is there early learning? The conflict represented in this question can be expressed simply enough. On the one hand the behavior of baby seems to change over the first few days of life. There are many examples, let me cite just one.

Peiper maintains that there are three techniques of infantile sucking. One of them is the response that most mammals use to get milk out of a breast; it is a lapping response that involves pressing the nipple against the roof of the mouth with the tongue and squeezing milk out of it. Another one is to reduce pressure inside the mouth so as to pull the milk in by a discrepancy in pressure. This is the way most babies suck from bottles. And the third, fairly infrequent technique—confined to bottle-fed babies for obvious reasons—is to bite hard at the back of the nipple and squirt milk into the mouth. This variation is interesting because babies apparently come to use one of these different patterns very quickly. They

learn, if "learn" is appropriate, the kind of sucking to use.

The difficulty with calling this kind of change "learning" arises from our failure to demonstrate early learning in a controlled setting. If the newborn is capable of this natural learning it should be possible for a psychologist to teach him something in a systematic learning study. And yet the evidence, controlled evidence for newborn learning, hardly exists. There is research by Marquis (1931), recently replicated in the USSR, showing that the baby adapts to a feeding rhythm, but the evidence does not support the conclusion that learning according to the usual theoretical models takes place in the period of early infancy. The Russians, with their strong demand for environmental control of behavior, have tried a large number of times to condition young infants. Sometimes they are successful; oftentimes they are not. Russian studies do not report conditioning in children under eight or nine days of age, and most conditioning studies indicate that it may take weeks or even months to condition an infant child in the Pavlovian mode (Dashkovskaya, 1953). How do we interpret this curious discrepancy between the fact that the human baby seems to adapt his sucking style and to his feeding routines on the one hand, and the difficulty that all investigators have had in demonstrating newborn learning on the other? [1]

The following three options seem available to us: First, in spite of my statements about newborn competence, there may be genuine neurological incapacity in the newborn. There is no

---

[1] The argument for early adaptation by the infant can probably be made much more forcefully, but a natural history of the first months of life remains to be written.

such thing as early learning, in the usual sense, because the child is not complete. A case for this position can be made. There are data on myelinization, on changes in pattern of EEG, on developments of vision and prehension, on the appearance of smiling—to take the most obvious case—all of which can be used to bolster the view that the young infant is a neurologically deficient organism. Under this reading, how do we account for the changes in behavior that do take place? Perhaps by maintaining that the caretaker becomes more competent. This would be a case of training the parent to adapt more effectively to the child rather than teaching the child to adapt to his environment. And to the data from Bronshtein and Lipsitt on the ability of the young infant to make sensory discriminations, we would have to say, "True, infants can make sensory discriminations, but there is no associative coding; there is a deficiency in the hooking of links together."

The second answer, and the one I think that would be given by the learning analysts (Gewirtz, 1961), is that nobody has tackled the problem of early learning. In particular, holders of this position would maintain that the procedures of classical conditioning as used by the Russians are the wrong tactics. What we should do if we want to demonstrate early learning is to use instrumental techniques; that is, to make some effective reinforcement contingent on the occurrence of some response of the infant. For example, let the baby turn his head and then give him something to suck on. This is a testable propositon and it is being tested.

I would like to suggest a third possibility—an unpopular one. In brief,

there may be experiential effects that are not learning. To put it another way, not all adaptation of the infant represents either classical conditioning or instrumental learning. I think it is inappropriate to maintain that all changes in behavior that can be related to the child's contact with the environment are the result of reinforcement contingencies. Of course, the instrumental learning position can be made to fit them, but it seems to me that such a forced fit results in theoretical vagueness and a weakening of the instrumental position.

Perhaps in pulling apart the problem of behavioral change in early infancy to exaggerate the variation among options, I have only shown that the resolution of the problem will require revisions in method, new knowledge of infantile neurophysiology, and a reworking of contemporary learning theory.

But consider now another interesting problem which illuminates some theoretical disagreements among students of infancy. Two theoretical positions have occupied this field—the psychoanalytic and the learning-theoretical. Justice can be done to neither in a summary presentation; Rapaport (1959) and Wolff (1960) present the psychoanalytic presuppositions in detail and with force; Gewirtz (1961) has prepared a closely reasoned argument for a learning analysis.[2] Now, there is a new entrant into the field of theories of mother attachment. John Bowlby in a series of recent papers (1958) has bor-

---

[2] It should be noted in passing that a learning analysis is both stronger and in a better position for compromise with other views by virtue of a retreat from the drive-reduction interpretation of reinforcement and by recent animal studies which show stable secondary reinforcement effects.

rowed from the investigators of instinct in animals, a notion that sounds very much like imprinting and has suggested that the child's responses of sucking, clinging, and following lead to mother-attachment. Just sucking, and just clinging, and just following on the part of the child, without obvious reinforcement or redistribution of cathexis, will result in a union between child and mother; much as the chick will imprint on a blinking light. Not only does Bowlby discuss what ties the child to his mother—namely, these three responses—but he also discusses what links the mother to the child. Not only does the child become attached to the mother because of sucking, clinging, and following, but the mother is drawn or attached—Bowlby does not use the word "imprinting"—to the child by the child's smiling and crying. Smiling and crying are held to be congenital or innate releases of maternal behavior.

It is difficult to evaluate this position and I am hard pressed to invent a satisfactory test for it. Perhaps we must call on animal research to work out the implications of Bowlby's assertions. But the main value of this new view will probably be the value of all theories of development—that they jog thinking, they make people run a study just to see what happens. Certainly Bowlby's ideas have had that effect. His own research with Robertson on separation [Robertson and Bowlby, 1952], the work done by Schaffer [Schaffer and Callendar, 1959] on hospitalization of young children, and an unpublished study by Ainsworth (1961) have demonstrated the provocative effect of these speculations. One of the achievements of the work done by Ainsworth, in Uganda, is that, instead of discussing mother attachment as a unitary notion,

she has, in these longitudinal field observations of the child between four weeks of age and fourteen months, described some ten or twelve indexes of the child's attachment to the mother, and in this way has made possible a more subtle analysis of the relation than we have had heretofore.

It is interesting to note, as an adjunct to the problem of mother-attachment, that something very curious indeed seems to happen to children near the middle of the first year. Ambrose's (1961) results on smiling indicate that at 17–25 weeks, general social smiling begins to decay and the child begins to smile only at its caretakers. Schaffer's work indicates that children who are hospitalized before they are 28 weeks old, accept hospital routines and separation easily; children hospitalized after 28 weeks-of-age show striking symptom patterns of distress and refusal to accept normal hospital care. Ainsworth finds that almost all of her criteria of mother attachment begin to show transition in the period from 17 to 30 weeks, with much of the change occurring in the narrow band between 25 and 28 weeks. Somewhere in the middle of the first year, the child appears to shift from being attached to human beings at large to being attached to one, or two, or three human beings.

The Ainsworth study is comparable in its impact to Rheingold's (1956) study of caretaking in institutionalized infants—both of these studies represent the payoff for the theoretical positions underlying them. The psychology of infancy undoubtedly profits from being in a state of theoretical dis-equilibrium, and the diversity of ideas about the nature of the child's attachment to his mother will almost certainly be productive of important empirical advances.

Consider one last generalization about infancy. It is one where contention, compromise, and reciprocation among theoretical positions has already resulted in general agreement. *The infant is active, and the relation of infant and caretaker is reciprocal.*

It is on this issue that the psychologist's view of the child has changed most dramatically in recent years. The model of the child which was drawn from Pavlov through Watson, and supported by the development of learning psychology in the United States, was of a recipient organism—a reactive one. Behavior at any particular time is the function of the current stimulating environment. This remains technically a sound view, but the effect of it on the psychology of the infant was to diminish our appreciation of how complicated and subtle is the child.

Not only can the child be usefully seen as active, rather than merely as reactive, but it may also be useful to think of even the infant as a problem-solver. Certainly the child, like the adult, can be seen as encountering problems in his environment. At least from the age of six months, the child's behavior can be discussed in terms of discrepancy, goal-seeking, means to an end, and so on. One student of children has not deviated from this view of the active searching child. Piaget and his students have seen the child, especially the infant, as being in a constant exchange with the environment, meeting its demands, and what American investigators somehow forgot, making its own demands on that environment.

The shift in point-of-view—to set the antithesis sharply—has been from the child who is a passive receptacle, into which learning and maturation pour knowledge and skills and affects until he is full, to the child as a complex, competent organism who, by acting on the environment and being acted on in turn, develops more elaborated and balanced ways of dealing with discrepancy, conflict, and disequilibrium. This shift, I believe, is of incalculable implication and seems to have been accepted to some degree by almost all students of children. Bowlby emphasizes the control by the child in crying and smiling; psychoanalytic theory makes more space for autonomous ego functions; child psychologists dedicated to a learning analysis speak of the child as active; and I suspect Piaget thinks of how he knew it all the time. But this shift only sets the problem for the psychology of the infant; questions abound. What is a "problem" for the infant? What is an environmental discrepancy for the newborn, for the six-

---

opposite: FIGURE III–6

The appearance of the neonate shortly after birth. From LIFE Science Library, Growth, *by J. M. Tanner, G. R. Taylor, and the Editors of Time-Life Books. Photo by Lennart Nilsson. Copyright © 1965 Time Inc.*

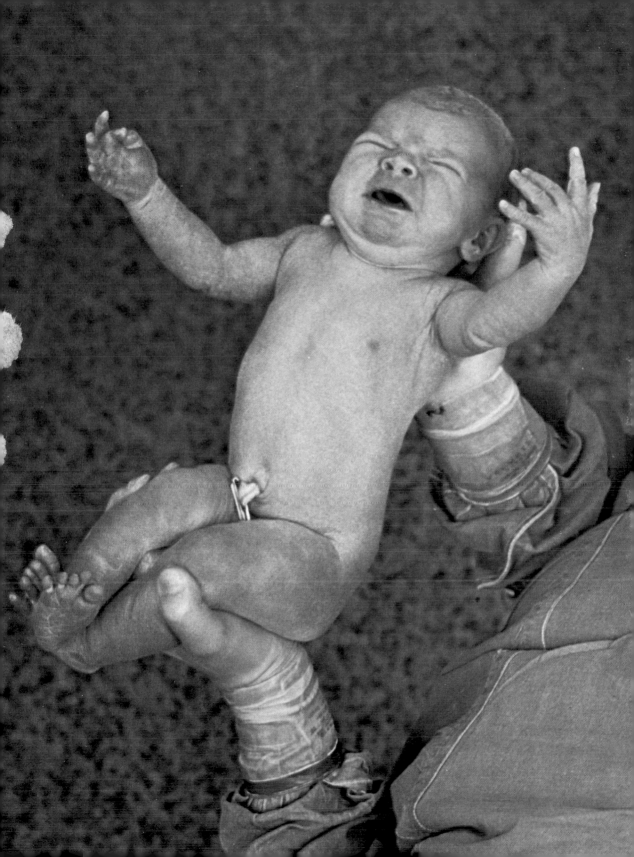

month old, for a walker? Do Piaget's speculations about assimilation, accommodation, and equilibrium have more than a metaphorical value? Can child psychologists follow the lead of psychologists of cognition in adults, who use computer analogies? Can we build a theory of cognitive development without the use of terms like reinforcement, drive, or dissonance resolution?

Only one thing seems certain. We are better equipped, with attitude and technique, to make a systematic and meaningful analysis of infant behavior than ever before. The current psychology of infant behavior, by and large, is managing to steer skillfully between the Scylla of "Oh, Oh, look what the baby did!" and the Charybdis of "But the theory says thus and so." We are engaging in hot, theoretical debate, but more and more the debate refers back to the child—back to the theory-illuminated facts.

The five propositions raised by Kessen not only have proven relevant to the study of the infant per se, but also have contributed more widely to developmental psychology. In later chapters we shall see, for example, how new knowledge of the neonate's visual capability has helped revive the nature-nurture controversy in perception. Similarly, the exciting contribution being made by the comparative approach will become more evident. For the present, however, we will turn to an examination of the physical growth which underlies the remarkable advances the infant makes within a relatively short time after birth. This will be followed by a general description of early perceptual-motor development.

PATTERNS OF PHYSICAL GROWTH

The physical development of the child has long been a source of fascination for parents, biologists, and psychologists. As even casual observation reveals, the first two or three years of life are a period of very rapid growth for the human organism. The question for researchers has been twofold: (1) to identify general principles which can adequately characterize and summarize growth; and (2) to collect normative data regarding the development of particular body parts and functions.

Major Periods of Growth

Viewed in its larger perspective, bodily growth occurs through approximately the first twenty years of life in humans. It is generally felt to be fruitful to divide this overall growth period into three major subdivisions—infancy and early childhood (up to about the fifth year of life), middle and late childhood (up to about age twelve) and adolescence (up to about age twenty). Generally, growth is more rapid and more likely to show spurts during both the infancy-early childhood period and the adolescent period than during middle childhood.

Systems of Growth

Different parts of the body show somewhat different growth patterns relative to the age of the child. Various organ systems or tissues and their growth curves are represented in Figure III–7. The *body size* category, which includes the skeleton, muscles, and internal organs, shows more rapid growth during the infancy-early childhood period and the adolescent period than during middle childhood. The *lymphatic system* (thymus, lymph nodes, and intestinal lymphoid mass) reaches an adult level by seven years of age and is even larger during preadolescence before it declines. Similarly, the *neural system* (head, brain, spinal cord) is almost fully developed by the age of six. In contrast, the *reproductive organs* grow very slowly until adolescence, at which point they undergo rapid growth.

General Principles

It has often been noted that early development proceeds *cephalocaudally*—that is, from the cephalic or head region to the caudal or tail region. Thus, as seen in Figure III–8, the appearance of the fetus is remarkably top-heavy and the neonate's less so; not until middle adolescence are the proportions of adulthood fully apparent. The functioning of the organism appears in keeping with this direction of physical growth. Infants are able to lift their heads within the first weeks of life but cannot stand until the end of the first year.

A second general principle of development is that growth proceeds from the proximal or center axis of the body to the extremities or more distal regions. Not surprisingly, the *proximodistal* pattern of physical growth is also reflected in the youngster's behavioral competence. The infant moves his entire upper body in order to orient his hands when grasping an object, and only later becomes able to move his arms and hands independently. It is even later before the infant can execute relatively refined movements of his fingers.

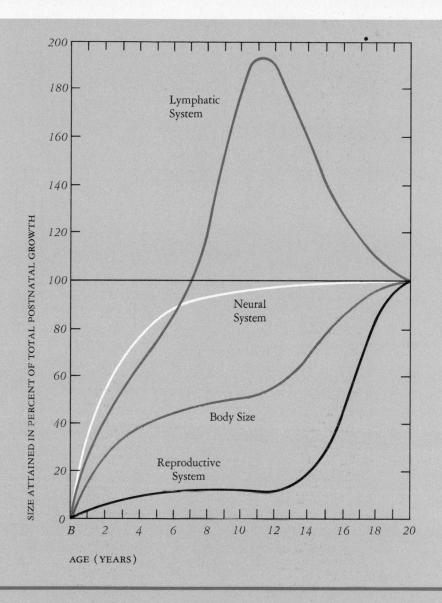

SIZE ATTAINED IN PERCENT OF TOTAL POSTNATAL GROWTH

Lymphatic
System

Neural
System

Body Size

Reproductive
System

AGE (YEARS)

FIGURE III—7

*Varying patterns of development for the four systems of growth.
Adapted from J. M. Tanner, Physical growth. In P. H. Mussen, ed.,*
Carmichael's Manual of Child Psychology, 3rd ed., Vol. 1 Copyright
1970, reproduced by permission of John Wiley & Sons, Inc.

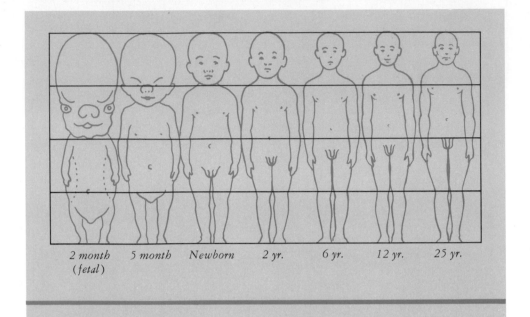

2 month   5 month   Newborn   2 yr.   6 yr.   12 yr.   25 yr.
(fetal)

FIGURE III–8

Changes in body form associated with age. Adapted from C. M. Jackson, Some aspects of form and growth. In W. J. Robbins et al., Growth. New Haven: Yale University Press, 1929, p. 118, by permission.

Rate of Physical Growth

One of the most intriguing facets of body growth is that there are large individual differences in the *rate* at which growth occurs. This fact has potentially important implications for the development of social behavior.

Tanner (1963) has suggested that each individual displays a biologically determined natural growth curve. Evidence for such an argument comes from a number of different sources. First, the correlation between an individual's body length when he is two years old and in adulthood is approximately .80. Second, Tanner notes that when children have been impeded from normal growth for a period of time, they appear to "catch up" or make up for the loss when the impeding factor is removed.

The most striking and perhaps most fundamental characteristic of the growth of an animal is that it is self-stabilizing, or, to take another analogy, "target-seeking." Children, no less than rockets, have their trajectories, governed by the control systems of their genetical constitution and powered by energy absorbed from the natural environment. Deflect the child from its natural growth trajectory by acute malnutrition or a sudden lack of a hormone and a restoring force develops so that as soon as the missing food or hormone is supplied again the child catches up towards its original curve. When it gets there, it slows down to adjust its path onto the old trajectory once more. [Tanner, 1963, p. 818.]

The evidence for such predetermined growth patterns is illustrated in the case cited by Tanner of a boy suffering from hypothyroidism. (Hypothyroidism is a deficiency in the activity of the thyroid gland, which decreases the amount of thyroxine, a growth-regulating hormone produced by the gland.) The lad's growth virtually ceased from the age of eight to the age of twelve, although, as seen in Figure III–9, he showed a rate of growth that was almost exactly average until then. When appropriate treatment was given for the glandular condition, growth not only resumed but showed an unusually rapid acceleration so that he quickly "caught up" with the growth rate which would have been predicted from his height at ages one through four.

PERCEPTUAL-MOTOR DEVELOPMENT

As the child grows physically, his ability to manipulate his environment also shows rapid growth. This type of accomplishment, usually referred to as perceptual-motor development, involves many complex perceptual and cognitive processes that will be discussed in later chapters. For now, though, we can begin with a description of this early development and of some of the general principles which characterize it.

Principles and Issues

Two general principles of perceptual-motor development, closely related to one another, are *differentiation* and *hierarchic integration*. The term *differentiation* refers to the fact that the child's physical development is

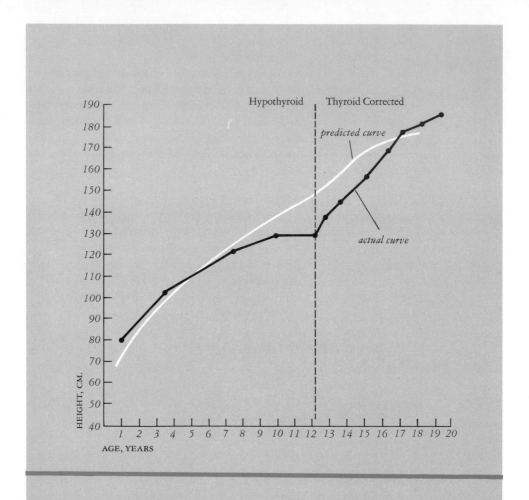

The rate of growth of a boy suffering from hypothyroidism, both before and after treatment. Note how he "caught up" with the normal growth rate. Adapted from J. M. Tanner, The regulation of human growth. Child Development, 1963, 34, 825, figure 5. Copyright 1963 by the Society for Research in Child Development, Inc. Reproduced by permission.

characterized by an increasing degree of control and specificity in its motor functions. The very young infant quickly begins to manifest growing motor coordination; first he shows good control over arm movements, then hand movements, and finally finger movements. Along with this increase in co-ordination comes increasing differentiation in the control which the child exercises over his body. The many individual movements over which the child gains mastery are then "put together" or integrated into more complex and sophisticated patterns of behavior. This process, which Heinz Werner (1948) has called "hierarchic integration," implies that individual parts of the child's new motor competence are integrated into larger and coherent whole units of motor behavior. After gaining greater and greater control over arm, leg, and neck movements (differentiation), the infant will begin to put these differentiated but relatively simple actions together and perform the more complex and integrated act of sitting up by himself (hierarchic integration).

Maturation and Experience. To what extent, though, is the type of development described above simply a function of bodily maturation and to what extent does it rely on experience? The question has continually woven itself into the inquiries of developmental psychologists (see Chapter I). The concept of maturation refers to those changes which primarily represent an unfolding of the nature or the physical capacities of the organism (and the species) that are at least relatively independent of special environmental circumstances, training, or experience. One psychological dictionary defines *maturation* as referring to those changes "that take place more or less inevitably in all normal members of the species so long as they are provided with an environment suitable to the species" (English and English, 1958).

A classical experiment demonstrating maturational processes in motor development was conducted by Carmichael in the late 1920s. Working with the salamander, *Amblystoma,* he divided the animals into a control group and an experimental group. The latter were placed in water containing an anesthetic; the control animals were allowed to develop in fresh water. In time, the control salamanders began to show vigorous movement, whereas those in the anesthetic were immobile. But when the drugged animals were then placed in fresh water, they immediately began to swim. Within half an hour they were indistinguishable from the controls who had been swimming for five days (Carmichael, 1970). Although other similar experiments have not shown such clear effects, this study serves to strengthen belief in built-in processes which operate independently of experience.

A few early investigations (Gesell and Thompson, 1929; McGraw, 1935) addressed to the maturation-experience issue involved training one member of a twin * pair in such motor skills as walking, climbing, or roller skating while the other was not trained. In general, experience before the child was apparently ready (i.e., sufficiently mature) was relatively ineffective; even when it did produce early gains, the previously untrained twin was able to "catch up" very quickly upon the introduction of training when maturationally ready.

The concept of maturation has implications, then, for the training or teaching of children. As the principle of maturational readiness suggests, if a child is not ready to perform a task, trying to teach it to him will be a waste of time and effort. Of course, this does *not* mean that biological readiness assures that the skill will be learned. Optimal achievement is undoubtedly the result of the conjunction of appropriate learning opportunities at the time of maximum readiness.

With these principles in mind, we now can turn—after pausing briefly for one cautionary point—to some of the specific ways in which a child's perceptual-motor skills develop during the early years.

Norms: A Word of Caution. In much of what follows we will be citing norms or averages regarding perceptual-motor development and, in later chapters, will have occasion to mention similar norms regarding intellectual and social skills. Although this procedure helps us to define groups adequately and thus to understand the approximate rate and nature of human development, it cannot be emphasized too strongly that it is unwise to apply it to any one individual case. Williams (1946) has likened the problem to one of determining the average shoe size in an army. Having such information, would, of course, be of enormous value in determining the quantity of leather which we would need to outfit the army in shoes. It would not, however, be of any value whatsoever in helping us to determine the particular sizes which should actually be ordered and made. It would be completely ludicrous to try to outfit the entire group with average-size shoes, which would, in fact, actually be suitable for very few individuals and conceivably might not fit anyone at all.

Development of Manual Skills

The child's ability to manually handle objects in his environment proceeds

---

* Identical twins, who share a common hereditary endowment, were employed in these studies to assure the genetic equivalence of maturation and physical abilities. The twin study methodology will be considered in greater detail in Chapter IV.

through a series of orderly stages which illustrate most of the principles discussed in the preceding section. Halverson (1931; 1936), for example, identified a series of stages in manual development from film records of neonates and infants. These stages, which are shown in Figure III–10, range from simply touching and holding objects (at twenty weeks) to the increasingly sophisticated use of the fingers (twenty-four to thirty-six weeks) and the successful coordination of hand, thumb, and fingers in producing highly precise and effective pincer movements (at fifty-two weeks).

Later changes are equally dramatic. By eighteen months, the child can typically fill a cup with cubes, build a tower from three blocks, and turn

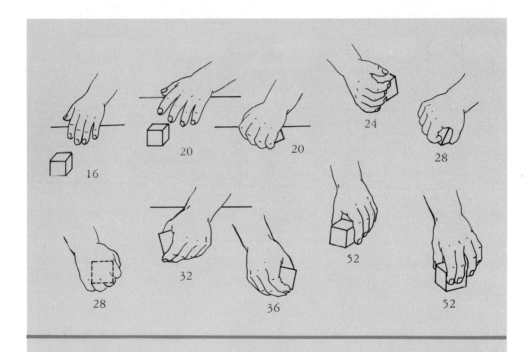

FIGURE III–10

The development of manual skills during the first year of life. The numbers indicate the age of the child in weeks, while the hands illustrate the growth in manual dexterity that occurs. Adapted from H. M. Halverson, 1931. By permission.

TABLE III–1

THE DEVELOPMENT OF HANDEDNESS
DURING THE FIRST FOUR YEARS OF LIFE

16–20 weeks:	Contact unilateral and, in general, tends to be *with left hand*.
24 weeks:	A definite shift to *bilaterality*.
28 weeks:	Shift to unilateral and most often *right hand is used*.
32 weeks:	Shift again to *bilateral*.
36 weeks:	Bilaterality dropping out and unilaterality coming in. Behavior usually characterized "right or left." *Left predominates in the majority*.
40–44 weeks:	Same type of behavior, unilateral, "right or left," but now *right predominates in the majority*.
48 weeks:	In some a *temporary, and in many a last shift, to use of left hand*—as well as use of right—either used unilaterally.
52–56 weeks:	Shift to clear unilateral dominance of *right hand*.
80 weeks:	Shift from rather clearcut unilateral behavior to *marked, inter-changeable confusion. Much bilateral, and use of non-dominant hand*.
2 years:	Relatively clearcut unilateral use of *right hand*.
2½–3½ years:	Marked shift to *bilaterality*.
4 years:	Unilateral, *right-handed* behavior predominates.

Source: Gesell and Ames, 1947. By permission.

the pages of a book (Landreth, 1967). Through early childhood these accomplishments continue to advance; a four-year-old typically can fold paper diagonally and produce simple figures like a cross; at five years, the youngster can usually

> . . . pluck a dozen pellets one by one and drop them deftly into a bottle in about 20 seconds, typically with a preferred hand. . . [The five-year-old] wields a crayon with greater assurance and definitiveness. He draws a rec-

TABLE III—2

SOME MILESTONE ACCOMPLISHMENTS DURING THE FIRST TWO YEARS

AGE (MONTHS)	ACCOMPLISHMENT	AGE (MONTHS)	ACCOMPLISHMENT
3	*Can support its own head when in prone position*	10	*Can creep; pull self to a standing position*
4	*Can shake a rattle; head is self-supported*	12	*Can walk when held by one hand; seat self on floor*
6	*Can sit, stand when held, and reach effectively*	18	*Can walk by self, although with a "stiff" gait; crawl down stairs backward*
8	*Can stand holding on and grasp with thumb opposition*	24	*Runs; climbs up and down stairs, can alternate rapidly between sitting and standing*

Source: Adapted from Lenneberg, E. H. *Biological foundations of language.* New York: John Wiley & Sons, Inc., 1967. Copyright 1967, reproduced by permission of John Wiley & Sons, Inc.

ognizable man. . . . He has difficulty with the obliques required in the copying of a diamond, but he is quite equal to copying a square and a triangle. [Gesell, Halverson, Thompson, Ilg, Castner, Ames, and Amatruda, 1940, p. 53.]

The Appearance of Laterality (Handedness). The synonymous terms *laterality* and *handedness* refer to the fact that, with very rare exceptions, adults show a clear preference for the use of one hand over the other. Although the preference is not absolutely consistent across activities (i.e., some people may write with their right hand but eat with their left), there is a remarkable consistency across cultures. Between 90 and 95 percent of the adult population all over the world show a preference for using the right hand in most activities.

The difference in preference for one hand over the other appears in the latter part of the first year of life. At that time at least 15 percent of the population display preference for the left hand. The percentage becomes smaller as individuals reach adulthood and some shift to right-handedness. Several other interesting facts are associated with laterality. One is that some other primates (e.g., rhesus monkeys) are about equally likely to be left- or right-handed in their manual preferences. Relatively few individuals are truly ambidextrous, in the sense that they are equally comfortable in using either hand.

The development of handedness is not, however, an immediate all-or-none event in the developmental process. It involves a complex transition and shifting from bilaterality (using either hand) through the first three to four years of life (Gesell and Ames, 1947). The shifts themselves are shown in Table III–1, based on data collected and recorded on film by Gesell and Ames in a complete longitudinal study of seven cases and supplemented with cross-sectional data from well over one hundred other infants and young children.

Integrated Motor Acts: Some Milestones

Through the first two years of life the child's increasing physical growth and competence is reflected in a variety of milestone activities. As the reader may recall from Figure I–2 in Chapter I, Shirley (1933) observed a regular growth associated with age in the development of skills related to crawling, climbing, and walking. Other age-exemplary accomplishments related to motor development are shown in Table III—2 (p. 83).

Although many of the biological changes discussed above characterize the entire human species, some, such as rate of maturing, reveal wide individual differences among persons. These differences appear to be determined, in part, by the child's unique hereditary endowment. It is to genetic determinants of behavior and development that we turn our attention in the next chapter.

IV

GENETIC DETERMINANTS OF BEHAVIOR

THAT A PERSON'S PHYSICAL CHARACTERISTICS and social dispositions can be passed on "through the blood" from one generation to another is an ancient idea. It was not until quite recently, though, that the fundamentals of genetic transmission were carefully investigated or adequately established. It is to these mechanisms and principles, and to the investigations they have inspired, that the present chapter is devoted. We will first consider the hereditary determinants of individual characteristics, then turn to some of the major research methods and issues of interest to developmental psychologists, and finally address the problem of the inheritance of behavioral dispositions.

MENDELIAN PRINCIPLES OF INHERITANCE

Much of our present understanding of human heredity comes to us from Gregor Mendel, an obscure nineteenth-century monk. From his original publication in 1865 until 1900, Mendel's ideas were not popular with most experts of the day. But, as with many extremely important notions, they were later rediscovered almost simultaneously by others—in this case, the Dutch biologist Hugo de Vries, the German botanist Karl Correns, and the Austrian Erich Tschermak.

Working with common garden peas, Mendel first identified overt characteristics in which the plants differed and then mated dissimilar ones. For example, he carefully cross-fertilized smooth-seeded and wrinkle-seeded plants to see how this selective breeding would affect the next generation. When the resulting pods were ripe, there was no evidence of the wrinkledness; rather, all the offspring displayed smooth seeds. When these second-generation plants were allowed to self-fertilize, however, the resulting third generation had both smooth and wrinkled seeds, in the ratio of 3:1. A similar pattern of result was found for several other characteristics, as can be seen in Table IV–1. Mendel's self-appointed task was thus to explain why some characteristics disappeared in the second generation only to reappear in the third generation in one-fourth of the plants.

To do so, he assumed that each of the parent plants contained two hereditary factors that were different forms of the particular characteristic. These factors, later called *genes,* separated in the germ cells (see Chapter III, pp. 48–50); the second generation, therefore, received two genes influencing the characteristic, only one of which was contributed by each parent. Mendel also proposed that when dissimilar forms of the characteristic were transmitted to the offspring (a so-called *heterozygous* gene pair), one, which he labeled *dominant,* always displayed itself over the other, which was called *recessive.* On the other hand, when the same form was transmitted by both parents (i.e., when the gene pair is *homozygous*), it was necessarily displayed. Thus, the dominant form was overtly manifested in the offspring if it was transmitted by both parents or if it was passed on by only one parent, whereas the recessive form appeared only if it was contributed by both parents.

It is obvious, then, that a form not overtly displayed may still be present, to be passed on to future offspring. The distinction can thus be made between *genotype,* the entire genetic endowment, and *phenotype,* the outward

TABLE IV–1

PHENOTYPIC RESULTS OF MENDEL'S EXPERIMENTS WITH
SEVEN CHARACTERISTICS OF THE PEA PLANT

| FIRST GENERATION | SECOND GENERA-TION | THIRD GENERATION | | |
		Same as Second Generation	Displayed Other Form	Ratio
Smooth vs. wrinkled seeds	smooth	5474	1850	2.96:1
Yellow vs. green seeds	yellow	6022	2001	3.01:1
Violet vs. white flowers	violet	705	224	3.15:1
Inflated vs. constricted pods	inflated	882	229	2.95:1
Green vs. yellow pods	green	428	152	2.82.1
Axial vs. terminal flower position	axial	651	207	3.14:1
Tall vs. dwarf stem length	tall	787	277	2.84:1

Source: Mendel, 1865.

manifestation of the genes. Figure IV–1, which shows the inheritance of brown-blue eye color in humans, demonstrates this difference as well as representing exactly Mendel's findings. Note that, paralleling the plant examples in Table IV–1, only the dominant form (brown) appears in the second generation, but that both brown and the recessive form (blue) are displayed in the third generation in the ratio 3:1.

OTHER GENETIC MECHANISMS

So far, some of Mendel's principles have been applied to examples of hereditary mechanisms involving the influence of a single gene contributed by each parent. Among the other human characteristics inherited *monogenically* are straight versus curly hair, and such abnormalities as excessively

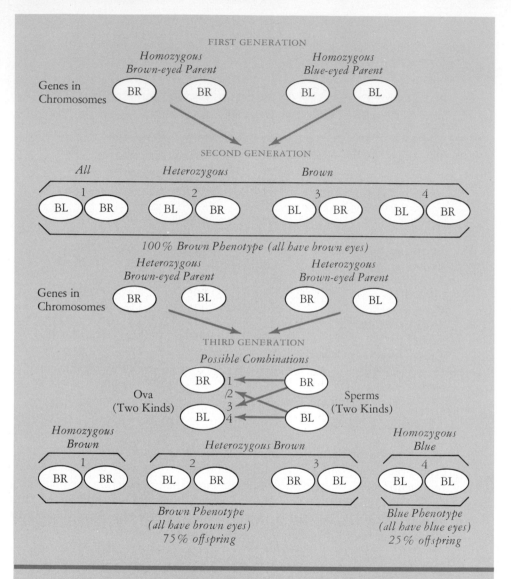

FIRST GENERATION

Homozygous
Brown-eyed Parent

Homozygous
Blue-eyed Parent

Genes in
Chromosomes

BR   BR   BL   BL

SECOND GENERATION

All   *Heterozygous*   *Brown*

1   2   3   4

BL   BR   BL   BR   BL   BR   BL   BR

100% Brown Phenotype (all have brown eyes)

Heterozygous
Brown-eyed Parent

Heterozygous
Brown-eyed Parent

Genes in
Chromosomes

BR   BL   BR   BL

THIRD GENERATION

Possible Combinations

BR 1   BR
    /2
Ova   3   Sperms
(Two Kinds) 4   BL   (Two Kinds)
BL

Homozygous
Brown

Heterozygous Brown

Homozygous
Blue

1   2   3   4

BR   BR   BL   BR   BR   BL   BL   BL

Brown Phenotype
(all have brown eyes)
75% offspring

Blue Phenotype
(all have blue eyes)
25% offspring

FIGURE IV—1

Inheritance of brown-blue eye color in humans assuming brown-eyed
and blue-eyed homozygous parents in the first generation. Brown is
dominant and blue is recessive.

short fingers and toes (brachydactyl), albinism, sickle cell anemia, and a type of mental deficiency known as phenylketonuria. But many other mechanisms operate to determine individual heredity. A gene may exhibit only partial dominance. Likewise, a characteristic may be carried on the sex chromosomes, so that it will affect female and male offspring differently, and one gene may reduce or increase the effects of others. Irregularities in the chromosomes themselves also may occur, or genes may spontaneously change (mutate), thereby producing new characteristics.

Further, some traits are transmitted by *polygene* inheritance, which means that many genes influence a characteristic in an additive way, so that the attribute tends to vary continuously. In the case of intelligence, for example, individuals are not only extremely bright or dull; rather, they fall into the entire range between these extremes. Polygene inheritance is of great importance in man, partly determining, besides intelligence, such characteristics as height, weight, skin color, and perhaps more importantly to the psychologist, temperament.

Unfortunately, though, much is still not known. Whereas tracing single gene inheritance can often be accomplished by noting the pattern of ratios in which an attribute appears, identifying many genes involves more complicated statistical analyses. It is also difficult to delineate characteristics controlled by many genes, for such characteristics do not fall into all-or-none categories. Finally, attributes determined by multiple genes are particularly susceptible to influence from the environment (Davis, 1970).

DETERMINING GENETIC INFLUENCE ON HUMAN BEHAVIOR

Understanding genetic mechanisms that influence development is, however, not the only aspect of heredity of interest to psychologists. An additional question concerns the degree to which physical structure, temperament, and intelligence might be genetically determined. When a child is very similar in intelligence or sociability to one or both of his biological parents, it is commonly inferred that he has inherited these characteristics. But a youngster with very bright parents may himself appear to be quite bright because his parents provide a relatively rich environment rather than because of the genetic contribution that they have made to his endowment. Argument and intuition alone do not enable us to discriminate between these two alternatives. Instead, a research strategy in which either heredity or environment is varied while the other is held constant is needed if we are to sort out the effects of genetic and environmental determinants of behavior. We will turn now to examine some of the methods of *behavior genetics,* a field of research that focuses on determining the influence of genetics on behavior.

Animal Studies

In animal research, one of the approaches to behavior genetics involves examining and comparing the behavior of genetically pure strains. If the behavior of one strain differs markedly from that of another, some genetic influence is suggested.

Perhaps an even more common method is to selectively breed animals. In investigating principles governing learning, for example, experimenters quickly recognized that some rats learned much faster than others to find their way to the feeder of a maze, a complex of unfamiliar corridors. One investigator (Thompson, 1954) then interbred maze "bright" animals and maze "dull" ones separately for six succeeding generations. As seen in Figure IV–2, the difference in learning ability between the two groups steadily increased as selective breeding continued. Eventually, in the sixth generation, the maze "dull" strain made 100 percent more errors than the maze "bright" strain.

Although animal studies do not provide firm evidence for the inheritance of human attributes, they do demonstrate its possibility. At the same time, the kinds of investigations just described require selective breeding and tight environmental control—both of which are forbidden with humans for ethical reasons. So other methods have been devised.

Pedigree Analysis

In pedigree analysis, the investigator identifies a representative or *index case* of the characteristic or disorder of interest. He then studies the family history, examining each relative of the index case, including both *lineal* or direct descendants and *collateral* relatives such as siblings, aunts, and uncles. If this information is sufficiently accurate and complete, a Mendelian pattern might be successfully identified.

One of the most interesting pedigree analyses was published by Henry Goddard in 1912, concerning the two distinct family lines of Martin Kallikak. As a Revolutionary War soldier, Kallikak reputedly had an affair with a feeble-minded tavern girl which eventually resulted in 480

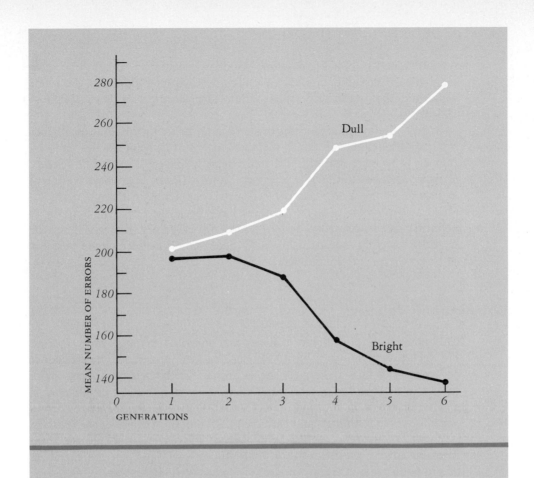

FIGURE IV–2

Errors in maze learning for successive generations of selectively bred "bright" and "dull" strains of rats. From Jensen, A. R. How much can we boost IQ and scholastic achievement? Harvard Educational Review, 39, *Winter 1969, p. 49. Copyright 1969 by the President and Fellows of Harvard College.*

descendants. Another line of 496 descendants was produced as the consequence of his later marriage into presumably better stock. Interviews of all family members or persons who knew them revealed a striking difference between the two lines, with Kallikak's first liaison resulting in more mental deficiency, immorality, alcoholism, and criminality. The difference was attributed to hereditary factors. Goddard concluded that he had separated the effects of nature and nurture (McClearn, 1963), and the study supported the passing of many compulsory sterilization laws (McNeil, 1966).

In fact, the investigation was contaminated by many weaknesses, including inability to locate all family members, death of some of the descendants, refusals to be interviewed, and the unreliability of verbal reports of friends. Further, the possibility that the two family lines experienced different environments evidently was not seriously considered. Although more sophisticated modern pedigree analyses have been successful in helping to delineate some Mendelian patterns, most investigators have given up the hope that such an approach can help determine whether complex aspects of behavior are transmitted genetically.

Consanguinity Studies

Closely related to pedigree analyses are so-called *consanguinity studies.* For such investigations information must be obtained about the frequency or degree to which a characteristic is present in the relatives of an index case, as well as in the general population. The characteristic presumably is genetic in origin if it occurs more frequently among first-degree relatives (such as parents, siblings, and children) than among second-degree relatives (such as grandparents, aunts, or nephews). Moreover, it should be more frequent among the latter group than among randomly selected members of the population at large who are unrelated to the index case. Using such an analysis, Lennox, Gibbs, and Gibbs (1940) found that whereas only 10 percent of the population at large showed occasional abnormalities in brain wave patterns (EEG), some 60 percent of the nonepileptic relatives of epileptic patients displayed them.

However, for behavioral analysis, this method, too, has its interpretive pitfalls. Rosenthal (1970) notes:

> Although such studies are well worth undertaking for their own sake, the inference of a genetic basis must be held in abeyance until it can be shown that the association between incidence and consanguinity cannot be explained on some other basis. We might conceivably find a similar association . . . where environmental factors may be of overriding importance. [p. 37.]

A third approach, the so-called *twin study method,* overcomes some of the difficulties inherent in both pedigree and consanguinity studies.

Twin Study Method

Approximately 1.2 percent of all births are multiple, producing two children.* About two-thirds of the twin pairs are *dizygotic* (cf. Chapter III) and the members are no more like each other genotypically than are siblings born months or years apart. On the other hand, the small remaining group of *monozygotic* twins, who develop from the same union of ovum and sperm, are genetically identical. The degree to which monozygotic twins are more alike on a characteristic than dizygotic twins (or siblings) provides a basis for determining the influence of genetic endowment. Customarily, comparisons are made only among children who have been reared together, so that the environment is held reasonably constant.

The similarity or *concordance* of pairs of individuals, on measures such as IQ or personality tests, usually is assessed in such studies. Dissimilarities between twins on these measures are instances of *discordance.* The question can then be asked: Is there greater concordance among monozygotic twins on a particular measure than among same-sexed dizygotic twins reared together? For a variety of characteristics and behaviors, as shown in Figure IV–3, the answer appears to be yes.

That monozygotic twins are physically more alike than dizygotic twins is suggested in both Figures IV–3 and IV–4. Nevertheless, Sydow and Rinne (1958) have presented an interesting example of monozygotic twins who were remarkably *un*equal in blood values and size at birth; one twin, as is illustrated dramatically in Figure IV–5, was more than twice the birth weight of the other.

This example serves to dispute the assumption frequently made in twin studies that adequate discrimination can be made between same-sexed monozygotic and dizygotic twins on the basis of physical appearance.† The task is not as easy as it may appear and there are numerous instances in the early literature of dizygotic twins labeled monozygotic because their appearance was similar. Today, information about blood group, serum protein, and other physical measures has made discrimination easier. In one study (Gottesman, 1963), which will be considered in detail later, the combined criteria of blood typing on nine blood groups, fingerprint ridge count,

---

* This figure is probably increasing slightly in Western societies since the advent of the use of ovulation-inducing drugs which appear to increase the frequency of multiple births (Lerner, 1968).

† If twins are of different sex, we know they are dizygotic.

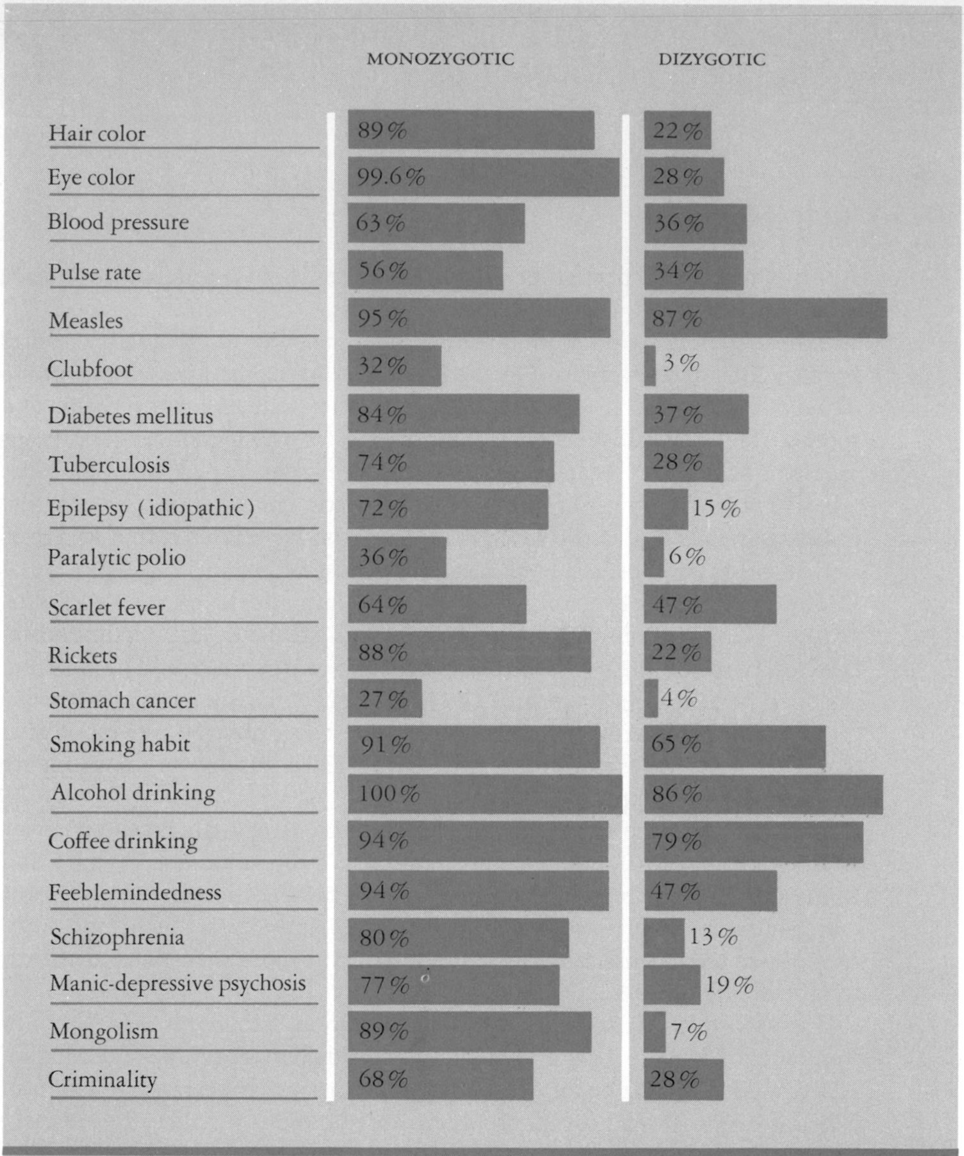

	MONOZYGOTIC	DIZYGOTIC
Hair color	89%	22%
Eye color	99.6%	28%
Blood pressure	63%	36%
Pulse rate	56%	34%
Measles	95%	87%
Clubfoot	32%	3%
Diabetes mellitus	84%	37%
Tuberculosis	74%	28%
Epilepsy (idiopathic)	72%	15%
Paralytic polio	36%	6%
Scarlet fever	64%	47%
Rickets	88%	22%
Stomach cancer	27%	4%
Smoking habit	91%	65%
Alcohol drinking	100%	86%
Coffee drinking	94%	79%
Feeblemindedness	94%	47%
Schizophrenia	80%	13%
Manic-depressive psychosis	77%	19%
Mongolism	89%	7%
Criminality	68%	28%

FIGURE IV–3

Percentage of concordance or similarity between dizygotic twins and monozygotic twins for a variety of characteristics and diseases. Reprinted with permission of Macmillan Publishing Co., Inc. from Genetics *by M. W. Strickberger. Copyright © Monroe W. Strickberger 1968.*

FIGURE IV–4

Photographs of a pair of monozygotic twins taken at ages 5, 20, 55, and 86 years. From F. J. Kallmann and L. F. Jarvik. Individual differences in constitution and genetic background. In J. E. Birren, ed., Handbook of Aging and the Individual, *p. 241. Copyright © 1959 The University of Chicago Press. Courtesy Dr. John Rainer.*

height and weight, and judgments by geneticists, psychologists, and artists were used. We can be fairly certain that monozygotic and dizygotic twins had been distinguished; the probability of a chance likeness on all of these characteristics, if the twins were actually dizygotic, is about one in two hundred. Further, skin grafting, although more difficult to use, is the best method to test the relationship between twins, for only monozygotic twins will accept grafts from each other (Lerner, 1968).

Another assumption often made in twin studies is that the environments of both kinds of twins, reared together, do not substantially differ. Although being reared together does minimize overall environmental differ-

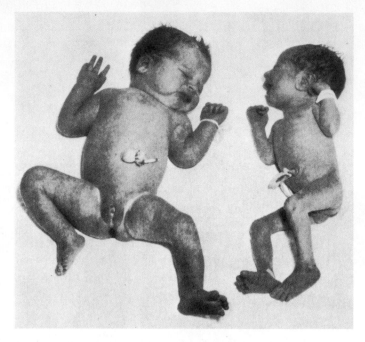

FIGURE IV-5

Monozygotic twins may not be physically identical. Source: von Sydow and Rinne, 1958. Reproduced by permission of Acta Paediatrica Scandinavica.

ences *between the members* of a twin pair, monozygotic twins nevertheless have more common experiences than dizygotic twins. Only fraternal twins can differ on sex, and members of different-sexed pairs undoubtedly are treated less alike than same-sexed pairs. Monozygotic twins are also more likely to have the same friends, to dress alike, and to share in such activities as studying or attending sports events than even same-sexed dizygotic twins (Smith, 1965). Perhaps these differences have only a minor influence, but this limitation of the twin study should be kept in mind.

Adoptee or Foster Family Method

An adopted or foster child shares the same environment with his adopted family, but has no genetic relationship to it; any resemblance between the child and his foster parents, therefore, must be attributed to environmental factors. On the other hand, any resemblance between the child and his biological parents must be due to genetic factors. The degree to which the child resembles his foster parents compared to his biological parents thus offers a method of weighing the influence of heredity and environment. The most severe limitation of this procedure involves the possibility of selected placement. Because of the presumed desirability of placing a child into a compatible home, "bright" children, for example, may be adopted by the more intelligent families and less capable children may be placed into homes with less intelligent families.

We can now turn to some of the substantive aspects of behavior and development in which genetics have been implicated. Any one investigation mentioned may combine the methods discussed in the preceding pages or variations of them in order to obtain maximal information.

INHERITANCE OF PHYSICAL CHARACTERISTICS

Perhaps the most obvious way in which children tend to resemble their biological parents is in physical appearance. Interestingly, the similarity between parents and children in some physical characteristics tends to be greater during childhood and adolescence than during the first year of life. Bayley (1954) has reported correlations between size of parents and their children at six months of age and at various subsequent times. Some of these data are summarized in Table IV–2; they show that the height of the child is related to that of his parents and that this relationship tends to be stronger for same-sexed than for opposite-sexed comparisons—that is, male children more closely resemble their fathers, female children their mothers.

Impressive relationships are found when one compares twins. For example, Newman, Freeman, and Holzinger (1937) found a correlation of .94 between the heights of monozygotic twins, but correlations of only .58 and .50, respectively, for dizygotic twins and siblings of different ages.

Of greater social importance is whether abilities and social behaviors may be based, entirely or in part, on individual genetic endowment. We shall consider three separate areas of research on this topic: intelligence and mental retardation, abnormal behavior (specifically, schizophrenia), and variations in personality and social behavior within the normal range.

TABLE IV-2

CORRELATIONS BETWEEN HEIGHT OF PARENTS AND
THEIR CHILDREN AS THEY BECOME OLDER

	BOYS		GIRLS	
AGE	Father	Mother	Father	Mother
6 Mo.	.25	.27	.42	.47
1 Yr.	.30	.31	.36	.67
5	.52	.30	.24	.70
10	.60	.37	.24	.72
15	.42	.71	.43	.68
18	.52	.44	.64	.52

Source: Adapted from Bayley, 1954.

HEREDITY OF INTELLIGENCE

It is extremely difficult to arrive at a totally satisfactory definition of intelligence. Whether the term should designate the ability to learn, rate of learning, the ceiling upon what can be learned, or yet some other human capacity is still undecided. In a later chapter this topic will be discussed in detail, but for the present purposes intelligence simply will refer to performance on a variety of tasks or tests which presumably tap mental ability.

Correlational Studies of Human Intelligence

The notion that human intelligence is at least in part genetically determined is perhaps a little distasteful to members of a society that cherishes the belief that "all men are created equal." Nevertheless, both animal studies and a great deal of research involving humans show that considerable intellectual variation among individuals can be traced to genetic endowment.

Sir Francis Galton (1822–1911) was among the first to study the possibility that intelligence might be inherited. Influenced by the work of Charles Darwin, his half cousin, he argued that eminent men tend to be related to one another. As evidence, he presented the genealogies of the families of prominent men in the fields of law, science, art, and the military, which indicated that greatness ran in certain families. Although Galton set up a proposition that would later be tested repeatedly, the pedigree analysis that he employed failed to distinguish between the effects of heredity and environment.

In order to examine the relative roles of these two variables, investigators typically have administered tests of mental ability to individuals who vary in regard to familial relationship. Then correlations are calculated for different degrees of kinship. A summary by Jensen (1969) of over one hundred such studies involving eight countries (e.g., Erlenmeyer-Kimling and Jarvik, 1963; Burt, 1966) appears to provide clear evidence that much of the variability in scores between groups can be attributed to heredity.

The findings, shown in Table IV–3, reveal a substantial correlation between the IQs of biological parents and their children, regardless of whether the offspring have been reared by their true parents or in foster or adopted homes. Correlations for children and their foster parents are a good deal lower. Although correlations for dizygotic twins also are substantial, they only approximate those for siblings. Monozygotic twins, however, show more similar test scores, and the greatest similarity occurs when they are reared together.

Further evidence suggesting the existence of genetic determinants of IQ is supplied by three major studies involving identical twins who were separated early in life and brought up in different homes. In a study by Newman, Freeman, and Holzinger (1937), the Stanford-Binet Scale was administered to nineteen pairs of separated monozygotic twins, revealing an average correlation of .77 between the scores of each member of the pair. A correlation of .86 between the IQ scores of two members of a pair resulted from a study involving fifty-three pairs of monozygotic twins who were also reared apart (Burt, 1966). A corroborative finding was obtained by Shields (1962), with yet a different test of intelligence. The high degree of similarity between IQ scores of twins sharing identical genetic constitutions but having different environments, as indicated by these studies, strongly supports the notion that inheritance, at least in part, plays a role in determining IQ.

TABLE IV-3

CORRELATIONS OF IQ SCORES AS A FUNCTION OF DEGREE OF FAMILY RELATIONSHIP, ILLUSTRATING THE HERITABILITY OF INTELLIGENCE

CORRELATIONS BETWEEN	NUMBER OF STUDIES	OBTAINED MEDIANS
Unrelated Persons		
Children reared apart	4	−.01
Foster parent and child	3	+.20
Children reared together	5	+.24
Collaterals		
Second Cousins	1	+.16
First Cousins	3	+.26
Uncle (or aunt) and nephew (or niece)	1	+.34
Siblings, reared apart	3	+.47
Siblings, reared together	36	+.55
Dizygotic twins, different sex	9	+.49
Dizygotic twins, same sex	11	+.56
Monozygotic twins, reared apart	4	+.75
Monozygotic twins, reared together	14	+.87
Direct Line		
Grandparent and grandchild	3	+.27
Parent (as adult) and child	13	+.50
Parent (as child) and child	1	+.56

Source: Jensen, A. R., How much can we boost IQ and scholastic achievement? *Harvard Educational Review, 39,* 1–123. Copyright 1969 by the President and Fellows of Harvard College.

GENETIC INFLUENCE AND
THE POSSIBILITY OF RAISING IQ

Data reviewed in the foregoing section make it quite clear that an hereditary component of IQ has been identified. But the important practical question remains: What are the implications of these findings for the possibility of increasing a child's IQ? At first blush, it appears that, to the extent that IQ is genetically determined, it is relatively impervious to modification by environmental influences. As will become apparent from the following considerations, *this conclusion is erroneous.*

The Heritability of Developmental Change

McCall (1970) has reported IQ assessments, made at the Fels Research Institute, of 270 children who had been administered intelligence tests every six months from three to six years of age and subsequently once a year through age twelve. The sample included thirty-five parent-child and one hundred sibling pairs, each member of whom had taken the same tests during childhood. In addition, comparable unrelated pairs were included as controls.

With several IQ scores for each subject, not only could the general level of intelligence for each individual be estimated, but the developmental pattern (as represented by a graph of each subject's scores on eight or more tests taken at different ages) could be evaluated. Observation of the developmental patterns revealed that there may be a great deal of fluctuation in an individual's IQ score, at least between the ages of three and twelve years.

Given these intriguing results, the investigator asked the question, "Does the child's genetic inheritance determine the pattern of change that occurs as he grows older or does the environment produce these developmental changes in IQ?" If heredity indeed plays a role in producing developmental trends in IQ, then the closer the familial relationship between two individuals, the more similar their patterns of change will be. Interestingly, the findings indicate that *change patterns are no more similar for related than for unrelated subjects.* Thus, the investigation failed to muster support for the heritability of developmental change. These results are illustrated in Figure IV–6, where each graph represents the developmental patterns of a pair of siblings or unrelated children and each line on each graph

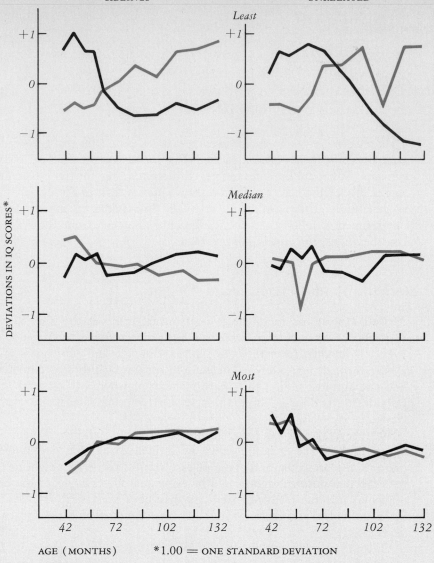

FIGURE IV–6

Trends in IQ *for the least, median, and most similar sibling and control pairs in McCall's study, showing that patterns of* IQ *change do not appear to be genetically determined. Adapted from R. B. McCall, Intelligence quotient pattern over age: Comparisons among siblings and parent-child pairs,* Science, *November 1970, 170, 644-648, figure 6. Copyright 1970 by the American Association for the Advancement of Science.*

represents one member of the pair. Note that there is the same range of similarity for both related and unrelated pairs of subjects.

What does account for developmental changes in IQ? McCall suggests that although general IQ level is set genetically, environmental circumstances may produce sizeable changes in it. The environmental elements that may be shared by siblings, such as the intellectual climate of their family, apparently are not responsible for the change patterns. Rather, experiences which are unique to the individual may account for the fluctuations. Thus, although IQ is genetically based to a certain degree, it is *not* immutable to change by environmental influences.

Correlations versus Means and the Problem of Change

When assessing the possibility for change in IQ, we must also consider the nature of correlational data, which are used in most relevant studies. Correlation indicates the presence of genetic factors by showing that the more genetically similar individuals are, the more their scores vary together. Although this appears to suggest that IQ will not yield to environmental influences, one must consider another kind of data: mean performance scores.

To illustrate, let us view the hypothetical data shown in Table IV–4. In Column I, data from seven monozygotic twin pairs are shown, along with the correlation coefficient (*r*) and the means of the scores. Note that *r* is quite high (actually higher than is usually found), that the overall means of the pairs of twins are quite similar, and that each twin has nearly the same IQ as his mate.

Assume that one member of each pair is now given an intensive training program for increasing intellectual ability, while the other member of the pair is not. If the program succeeded in raising IQ, while the IQ scores of the controls remained unchanged, then a comparison made after the program might be similar to that shown in Column II. Now the overall means are quite different, with most twin pairs no longer very similar in their scores.

But what about the correlation between twins *after* the environmental manipulation? It has, in this example, remained virtually unchanged and still shows an impressively high relationship. The scores of the twins in each pair still "go together" in the sense that the twins in Column I retain their relative standing in Column II regardless of training. (The lowest individual in Column I–A is still the lowest individual in Column II–A.) It is precisely such a phenomenon which is tapped by the correlational approach, and not necessarily the similarity per se between twin and twin

TABLE IV—4

HYPOTHETICAL DATA SHOWING MEANS AND IQ SCORES
OF A SET OF MONOZYGOTIC TWINS BEFORE AND
AFTER SPECIAL TRAINING PROGRAM: AN ILLUSTRATION
OF THE DIFFERENCE BETWEEN MEANS
AND CORRELATIONS

I (BEFORE)			II (AFTER)	
Twin A	Twin B		[Training] Twin A	[No Training] Twin B
80	82		90	82
103	100		112	100
94	94		107	94
105	109		115	109
97	95		108	95
121	116		140	116
68	77		85	77
95.4	96.1	*Means*	108.1	96.1
$r = .98$		*Correlations*	$r = .96$	

or between parent and child. To ask whether the environmental intervention was effective, we must inspect means rather than correlations. *To determine the possibility that IQ scores can be raised, experimental rather than
correlational studies must be undertaken.*

Mental Retardation

When we look to mental retardation, we find the most severe genetic
restrictions of intelligence as well as demonstrations of dramatic etiological
breakthroughs. Although it is beyond the scope of this book to fully discuss
the many genetic abnormalities which have been identified, examples of
a few of the more commonly known ones will be described.

PKU. The biological basis for phenylketonuria is the lack of the enzyme which metabolizes the amino acid phenylalanine to tryosine. Incomplete oxidation results in the production of particular substances which are injurious to the nervous system. The defect, which is transmitted by a single recessive gene, results in retardation in the majority, although not all, of untreated individuals. It has been estimated that PKU is responsible for about 1 percent of all institutional retardates and occurs in one case per twenty thousand live babies.

It is possible to detect PKU within the first two weeks of life with urine or blood tests, and several states of the United States now provide massive screening programs. Early detection is valuable because it has been found that children placed on low phenylalanine diets within the first few years of life often show considerable improvement in intellective abilities. Unfortunately, if the diet restriction is delayed until later, little or no improvement is likely to occur. Thus, the PKU syndrome is an interesting example of how heredity and the external environment conspire to determine behavior. If a child does not have the relevant mutant gene he can, of course, consume quantities of phenylalanine (found in bread, eggs, cheese, fish, and milk) without experiencing difficulties. Similarly, noticeable retardation will not appear in a child who has the genetic component responsible for PKU if he is provided with a low phenylalanine diet. But, children with both the defective gene and a normal diet frequently will become retarded.

Down's Syndrome. Approximately 10–15 percent of the people institutionalized for mental deficiency suffer from Down's Syndrome, also known as mongoloid idiocy. The afflicted show from moderate to severe retardation and are strikingly alike in physical appearance. They frequently have small skulls, chins, and ears; short, broad necks, hands, and feet; flat nasal bridges; sparse hair; a fissured tongue; and, perhaps most recognizable, a fold over the eyelid which appears oriental to westerners and suggested the name "mongolism."

Over the years there was considerable speculation about the etiology of the syndrome, with both genetic and environmental factors being variously suspected. The fact that concordance was almost perfect for monozygotic twins and extremely low for dizygotic twins strongly supported belief in some genetic basis for the disorder (Carter, 1964). Finally, in 1959, with the improvement of cell preparation techniques, it was discovered that mongoloids have a third (extra) number 21 chromosome. In most instances, this condition occurs at meiosis when the two number 21 chromosomes fail to separate in the formation of the germ cells. Thus, the defect is genetic but not inherited. (There is, however, a rare form of mongolism in which the chromosomal aberration is transmitted from generation to generation [Robinson and Robinson, 1965].) Further, there are indications that the error in cell division may arise predominantly in the female, for the mother's age much more than the father's is related to the incidence of mongolism. It is estimated that the risk in a mother from forty to forty-five years of age is fifty-five times greater than in a mother from twenty to twenty-four years of age.

Sex Chromosome Aberrations. Two disorders, Klinefelter's Syndrome and Turner's Syndrome, are representative of a larger group of abnormalities resulting from aberrations of the sex chromosomes.

Klinefelter's Syndrome is the most commonly occurring malady of such origin. Most often, individuals suffering from this defect have an additional X chromosome (XXY), although other variations also occur. Found exclusively in phenotypic males, it is responsible for 1 percent of all institutionalized males. As in Down's Syndrome, there is an apparent error in meiosis, and the mothers of Klinefelter's Syndrome children are older than those in the general population. About 25 percent of the cases have below normal intelligence, and the afflicted also suffer from atypical sexual development and skeletomuscular abnormalities.

Turner's Syndrome, on the other hand, occurs in phenotypic females and is the result of a lack of sex chromosomes. Most frequently there is only a single X chromosome (XO) or a structural defect of one of the Y chromosomes. Mental deficiency occurs in about 20 percent of the cases (Robinson and Robinson, 1965), and appears to involve deficiency in organizing incoming stimulation. Other abnormalities include a lack of ovarian tissue, failure of development of secondary sex characteristics, short stature, and deformity of the neck and forearm. The syndrome does not run in families, is not associated with maternal illness or age, but does occur disproportionately among monozygotic twins (Rosenthal, 1970).

GENETIC DETERMINANTS OF ABNORMAL BEHAVIOR

Another class of behaviors which may have some genetic component is that which is customarily labeled seriously abnormal, deviant, or psychotic.*

---

* It should be noted that the adequacy of these labels and the reliability of their usage has been seriously challenged (e.g., Bandura, 1968; Mischel, 1968). Nonetheless, inasmuch as there are undeniable differences between the behavior of most hospitalized persons who have been diagnosed as schizophrenic and persons who are functioning more or less adequately in occupational and marital roles, the question of genetic determinants of abnormal behavior remains a meaningful one, despite terminological and even major theoretical disputes.

The largest body of research on genetic determinants of abnormal behavior has involved the etiology of the psychosis called schizophrenia.

According to the American Psychiatric Association, schizophrenia "represents a group of psychotic reactions characterized by fundamental disturbances in reality relationships and concept formations, with affective, behavioral and intellectual disturbances in varying degrees and mixtures. The disorders are marked by a strong tendency to retreat from reality, by emotional disharmony, unpredictable disturbances in stream of thought, regressive behavior, and by a tendency to 'deterioration' " (1965, p. 26). Within the general category of schizophrenia, there are several subtypes (e.g., simple, hebephrenic, catatonic, and paranoid), but these differences will not be of concern here.

There has been considerable speculation about schizophrenia, and three main types of theories have been advanced to explain its occurrence. *Monogenic-biochemical* theory proposes that the presence of one particular gene, which determines abnormal metabolic function, leads to schizophrenia. The *diathesis-stress* model postulates that schizophrenia results from the coexistence of a biological constitution with a predisposition to develop the illness and a set of environmental stresses to precipitate it.("Diathesis" means constitutional predisposition toward abnormality.) Such a theory may incorporate models involving either the monogenic or the polygenic inheritance of the disorder. *Life-experience* theory ignores possible genetic determinants of the disorder and is concerned entirely with conditions in the environment that might produce it (Rosenthal, 1970). It is possible, of course, that no one theory is exclusively correct, for the disorder may have more than one etiology.

Empirical Evidence of Genetic Influence on Schizophrenia

Theories that propose a genetic basis for schizophrenia logically predict that the closer the genetic relationship between two individuals, one of whom is schizophrenic, the higher the risk that the other will also obtain the same diagnosis. Considerable evidence has been collected that supports this prediction.

Franz Kallmann, a German psychiatrist who was an early worker in the field, estimated the risk of being labeled a schizophrenic by examining large samples of individuals labeled as such and their relationships to each other. Figure IV–7 summarizes some of his results, which frequently are interpreted as supporting a genetic hypothesis. Several other studies conducted in different countries have reported concurring findings (Fuller and

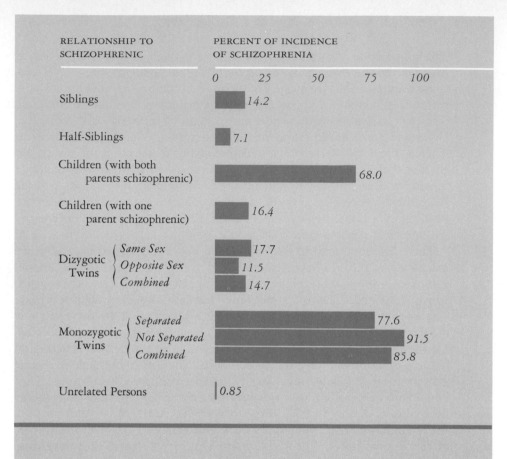

RELATIONSHIP TO SCHIZOPHRENIC	PERCENT OF INCIDENCE OF SCHIZOPHRENIA				
	0	25	50	75	100
Siblings	14.2				
Half-Siblings	7.1				
Children (with both parents schizophrenic)	68.0				
Children (with one parent schizophrenic)	16.4				
Dizygotic Twins — Same Sex	17.7				
Dizygotic Twins — Opposite Sex	11.5				
Dizygotic Twins — Combined	14.7				
Monozygotic Twins — Separated	77.6				
Monozygotic Twins — Not Separated	91.5				
Monozygotic Twins — Combined	85.8				
Unrelated Persons	0.85				

FIGURE IV–7

Schizophrenia among relatives of the schizophrenic. Adapted from Abnormal Psychology and Modern Life by James C. Coleman. Copyright © 1964 by Scott, Foresman, and Company. Reprinted by permission of the publisher.

Thompson, 1960). Overall, it has been shown, for instance, that parents and siblings of schizophrenics have a greater risk of schizophrenia than the general population, that first degree relatives have a greater risk than second degree relatives, and that the risk for third degree relatives is only slightly greater than that for the population at large (Rosenthal, 1970).

Nevertheless, these findings support environmental as well as genetic theories. According to the environmentalist viewpoint, the closer the relationship between individuals, the more they will interact and influence each other's environment. Comparing the risk of monozygotic and dizygotic twins who were reared apart from infancy offers a better method of separating the variables, and the results of such investigations frequently are cited in support of the genetic hypothesis. Actually, though, little reliable data have been collected (cf. Jackson, 1960; Slater, 1968). In regard to the often-cited Kallmann twin studies, which showed a much greater risk for monozygotic than for dizygotic twins even when they were reared separately, Jackson (1960) relevantly points out that Kallmann's "separated" category refers only to separation five years prior to the appearance of the psychosis. Thus:

> Because his [Kallmann's] age group ranged from 15 to 44 years; and because his average age of subjects is stated to be 33 years . . . it is obvious that the twins were not apart during their formative years. Indeed, most remained together well past the usual age for marriage; and even this late in life separation resulted in a significant decrease in concordance for schizophrenia. [p. 40.]

Perhaps the greatest efficiency in separating genetic from environmental variables is achieved through studying children of schizophrenics who have been adopted or reared by foster parents. The investigator selects, as index cases, adoptees who have been categorized as schizophrenic and also chooses a control group of normal adoptees who are similar to the index cases in chronological age, age of transfer, sex, and social class of adoptive parents. Heredity would appear to play a major role in the disorder if there are more disturbed individuals among the biological relatives of the experimental group than among the biological relatives of the control group. The view that social interaction with a schizophrenic leads to schizophrenia would find support if the frequency of the disorder is greater among the adopted relatives of the index group than among the adopted relatives of the control group.

Kety, Rosenthal, Wender, and Schulsinger (1968) employed the adoptee's family method in a study initially involving 5,500 cases of adoption in Denmark. A significantly greater number of disorders—either schizophrenia or a closely associated disturbance—was found among the biological relatives of schizophrenic adoptees than among the control group. What is more, there was no difference in the frequency of disorder that was detected among the adopted relatives of either group. Thus, the findings support an hereditary hypothesis.

The studies discussed above and several others (cf. Heston, 1966; Karlsson, 1966; Rosenthal and Kety, 1968) provide data that genetic factors are involved in schizophrenia. The issue, however, is far from settled. Attempts to determine the possible mode of transmission and the specific influence of genes have not been very successful. In any event, the findings do not imply that schizophrenia is unalterable. Instead, they may pave the way for preventive measures for individuals who appear to have a genetic disposition toward such behavioral problems (Davison and Neale, 1974).

THE HERITABILITY OF PATTERNS OF SOCIAL BEHAVIOR

Although much of the investigation into genetic bases of behavior has focused upon abnormalities and deficiencies, some interesting work is available on the genetic determinants of patterns of more "normal" social behaviors.

Among the best broad-spectrum studies in this regard is one conducted by Gottesman (1963), to which we alluded earlier. He began by enumerating all of the same-sexed twins enrolled in public high schools in the Minneapolis-Saint Paul area, drawing his twin sample from a population of over 31,000 children. Voluntary cooperation of more than half of the twin pairs in this sample was secured. Gottesman legitimately noted that his sample "compares favorably in size with the majority of twin studies reported in the psychological literature. In representativeness, it is superior to the majority" (p. 4). Using sophisticated criteria (see p. 93), Gottesman identified sixty-eight twin pairs—thirty-four monozygotic pairs and thirty-four dizygotic pairs, and compared concordance rates on several scales.

The measures used in the study were derived from three paper-and-pencil tests, a test of intelligence and two personality measures. IQ scores were more closely related for monozygotic than for dizygotic pairs and, more importantly for our present interest, six scales of the twenty-four on the personality tests were found to be more closely related for monozygotic than for dizygotic twins. Overall, Gottesman's results seem to suggest *some* hereditary component on *some* measures of personality. However, the evidence requires a good deal of cautious qualification and has revealed some inexplicable peculiarities. (For example, fraternal twins were *more* alike than identical twins on four of the personality dimensions.) More recent investigations, to which we now turn, have attempted to demonstrate heritability of more restricted dimensions of behavior.

Temperament

Thomas, Chess, and Birch (1970) define temperament by a set of rating scales including such items as level and extent of motor activity, sensitivity to stimuli, and response to new objects. They followed the development of 141 children for over a decade by interviewing the parents periodically— every three months during the first year, every six months during years one to five, and annually after age five. The interviews were structured objectively so that parental statements, such as that their baby "couldn't stand" a new food, had to be restated by the parent in terms of specific step-by-step descriptions. In addition, some home observations were conducted by individuals unfamiliar with the child's behavioral history. From their data, the authors conclude that children show distinct individuality in temperament in the first weeks of life and that these characteristics persist over time. Acknowledging that they do not have evidence that these differences are "inborn," Thomas *et al.* state, nevertheless, that they are inclined toward this view. Support for this hypothesis is forthcoming from studies of newborns which show, for example, individual differences in the intensity of responding to stimuli which are consistent during even the first few days of life (Birns, 1965). (Recall, too, Kessen's remarks on this point in Selection 3.)

Introversion-Extroversion

Several studies suggest that genes play a part in determining introversion-extroversion (Eysenck, 1956; Gottesman, 1966; Partenan, Brunn, and Markkanen, 1966; Scarr, 1969; Vandenberg, 1966, 1967). These terms refer to two opposing styles or approaches to the social environment. An extreme introvert is shy and anxious in novel social situations and always ready to withdraw from people; an extreme extrovert is friendly, at ease among people, and ready to seek out social gatherings. Differences on this dimension may be observed during the first years of life and, moreover, do not change much over time. Friendly infants, for example, tend to become friendly adolescents, whereas unfriendly infants tend to become unfriendly teenagers (Schaefer and Bayley, 1963).

Scarr (1969) gave psychological tests to twenty pairs of female monozygotic and dizygotic twins for whom zygosity had been accurately diagnosed through the use of blood grouping. Monozygotic twins were found to be more similar on measures of introversion-extroversion than were dizygotic twins. In another investigation (Freedman and Keller, 1963), twenty pairs of same-sexed twins, eleven of whom were monozygotic and nine of whom were dizygotic, comprised the sample. Every child was filmed individually in many situations over an eight-month period. At the end of the observation period, the films of one twin in each pair were shown to a group of four judges while the films of the other twin were presented to a comparable group. The judges rated each child's behavior on several dimensions, one of which was social orientation. Comparison of the ratings showed a greater similarity in social behavior between monozygotic twins than between dizygotic twins.

Fortuitously, the films provided a clear record of the development of smiling over the eight-month period. During the first month no social smiles appeared, although the babies usually smiled as they fell asleep after being fed. In the second month, external stimulation such as the sound of a voice or bell initiated smiling; in the next stage, fixation on the mother's face preceded the infants' smiles. Until the age of five months, most infants smiled freely at anyone. They became increasingly discriminating with time, however, and began to smile only at familiar persons. From the age of nine to twelve months not only did the infants fail to smile at strangers, but they displayed fear in the presence of strangers.

Monozygotic twins appeared to be more similar in age at the onset of the various stages in the development of smiling and fear of strangers than did dizygotic twins. For example, at the age of 2 months, 0 days, monozygotic twin brothers, Marty and Chucky, both displayed presocial visual fixation during feeding. Some of the photographs of these brothers are shown in Figure IV–8. They can be contrasted with photographs of Arturo and Felix, dizygotic twins who behaved quite differently from each other at 2 months and 4 days of age. Arturo smiled drowsily with eyes closed when touched by the adult, whereas Felix was alert and sober with eyes open in the same situation.

Although these instances appear to support the genetic hypothesis, other film sequences were difficult to interpret. Nevertheless, the overall pattern of results is provocative. Ample agreement among experimental findings is available to make hypotheses concerning the heritability of normal personality an exciting issue to pursue.

HEREDITY-ENVIRONMENT INTERACTION

As seen in the foregoing discussion, there is considerable evidence suggesting that genetic factors influence a variety of human attributes. We have attempted to point out weaknesses of the methods employed in relevant

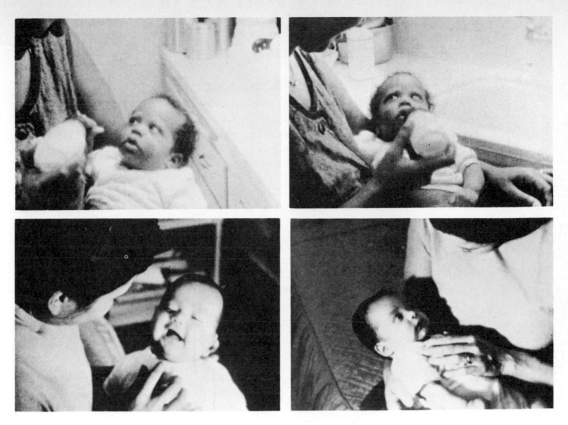

FIGURE IV–8

Photographs illustrating the similarity of staring at age 2 months in monozygotic twins, Marty and Chucky. They may be contrasted with the dissimilarity in social behavior of dizygotic twins, Arturo and Felix, at age 2 months, 4 days. Courtesy Dr. Daniel G. Freedman.

research. Certainly, insofar as the methods and their interpretations have limitations, conclusions must be drawn tentatively. In conceptualizing the roles of heredity and environment in development, it is critical to consider the interaction of these factors. The tendency is, of course, to assume that any characteristic which is known to be controlled by heredity cannot be influenced by the environment. There are many examples that demonstrate the fallaciousness of this assumption. We know, for instance, that temperature of the environment can affect the development of coat color in particular rabbits and the development of the eye in fruit flies, even though these attributes are genetically controlled. More directly related to psychological characteristics, we have seen that special diet can decrease or eliminate the detrimental effects of genetically influenced PKU children. One can also note that, almost invariably, concordance among monozygotic twins decreases when they are reared apart, thereby substantiating the environment-heredity interaction. Similarly, McCall's (p. 101) data suggest that an individual's unique experiences may affect the development of intelligence. Thus, as one writer has put it:

> . . . even a full set of relevant genes does not fixedly determine the corresponding trait. Rather, most genes contribute to determining a *range of potential* for a given trait in an individual, while his past and present environments determine his phenotype (that is, his actual state) within that range. At a molecular level the explanation is now clear: the structure of a gene determines the structure of a corresponding protein, while the interaction of the gene with subtle regulatory mechanisms, which respond to stimuli from the environment, determines the amount of protein made. Hence, the ancient formulation of the question of heredity versus environment (nature versus nurture) in qualitative terms has presented a false dichotomy which has led only to sterile arguments. [Davis, 1970, p. 1280.]

BASIC LEARNING PROCESSES

LEARNING IS ONE CLEAR BASIS for the many changes that occur between infancy and adulthood. Illustrations abound. Only through learning do children acquire vocabularies, bicycle riding skills, and table manners. But they also learn other things; prejudices and preferences, fearfulness and daring, ambition and sloth are all acquired through basic learning processes that have been extensively studied by psychologists.

What is learning? Many useful terms are not easy to define, and learning is one of them. The following general definition does appear at least to capture the important features of the phenomenon.

> Learning is the process by which an activity originates or is changed through reacting to an encountered situation, provided that the characteristics of the change in activity cannot be explained on the basis of native response tendencies, maturation, or temporary states of the organism (e.g., fatigue, drugs, etc.). [Hilgard and Bower, 1966, p. 2.]

In fact, learning is not one single process; rather, there are a number of related processes through which learning occurs. Each of these has been found to play a central role in development.

ASSOCIATIVE LEARNING

At the end of the nineteenth century the Russian physiologist, Ivan Pavlov, began a series of investigations on the digestive processes of dogs. His basic experimental procedure involved introducing a small quantity of food, in the form of meat powder, into the mouths of his subjects and then observing and measuring the flow of various digestive juices. During the course of this work, Pavlov ran into an irritating problem. The dogs often appeared to anticipate the food, so that salivary flow began even before any meat powder had been introduced. When earnest efforts to eliminate this troublesome interference failed, the decision was made to study it systematically.

Beginning with an introspective approach, Pavlov's associates tried to imagine the situation from the dog's point of view. This strategy soon led to quite unfruitful arguments, because they could not agree on what a dog was likely to think or feel. Pavlov then abandoned the introspective approach—and, in fact, banned any discussion of it from the laboratory—and proceeded with a systematic effort to understand the anomalous finding through objective research.

Inasmuch as naïve dogs salivated, apparently without particular training, when meat powder was placed on their tongues, it was reasoned that the response is natural or reflexive. But salivation that came to be elicited by the *sight* of the food had to be acquired or *conditioned* by environmental events—events which could be manipulated experimentally. This reasoning led Pavlov to investigate the manner in which conditioned responses are formed. He presented the sound of a metronome (*conditioned stimulus* or CS) followed in a few seconds by food (*unconditioned stimulus* or UCS). At first, no salivation occurred until the UCS was presented. Then, after a number of presentations, saliva was secreted during the time interval before the meat powder was presented, apparently in response to the CS. This salivation was a learned or *conditioned response* (CR). With such a *classical conditioning* procedure Pavlov taught dogs to salivate to an impressive array of environmental stimuli, including a rotating disk and a light. And his investigations went far beyond merely demonstrating the phenomenon, for he also was interested in the specific circumstances under which conditioned responses were formed, modified, and weakened.

In order to develop a conditioned response, it is necessary to follow the conditioned stimulus repeatedly with the unconditioned stimulus; with repeated presentation the conditioned response develops gradually (Figure V–1a). But conditioning would have few implications for understanding the development of behavior if the particular CS used in training were the only one which could produce the CR. Research has shown, though, that the effects of classical conditioning are not limited in this way. Stimuli

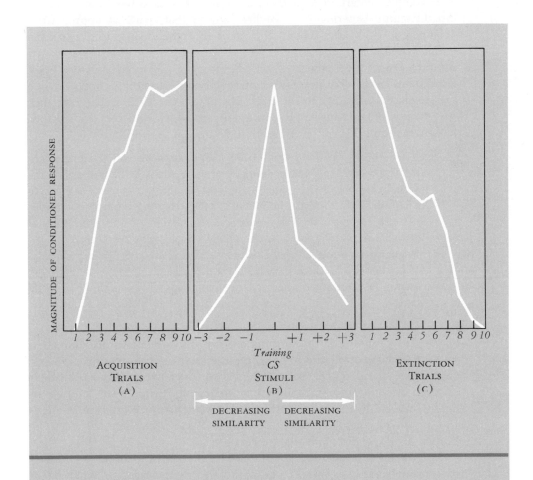

FIGURE V–1

Schematic representation of (a) acquisition, (b) generalization, and (c) extinction of a classically conditioned response.

which are similar to the one used during training also can produce the conditioned response. The greater the similarity between the new stimulus and the original conditioned stimulus, the greater the degree to which they are substitutable. Thus, there is *generalization* after classical conditioning, which forms an orderly relationship referred to as a *generalization gradient* (Figure V–1*b*).

A complementary phenomenon, *discrimination,* also has been observed. An intriguing experiment by Pavlov showed that, with an appropriately arranged situation, the subject will learn to respond only to a particular stimulus and not to other, similar ones. For example, the animal was always reinforced with meat powder, the UCS, after the presentation of one CS— a luminous circle—but never after presentation of an ellipse. Soon the dog was regularly salivating to the circle but not to the ellipse. The task then was made more difficult by presenting ellipses which were less cigar-shaped and more round. When the two stimuli became quite similar:

> . . . not only did the discrimination fail to improve, but it became considerably worse, and finally disappeared altogether. At the same time the whole behaviour of the animal underwent an abrupt change. The hitherto quiet dog began to squeal in its stand, kept wriggling about, tore off with its teeth the apparatus for mechanical stimulation of the skin, and bit through the tubes connecting the animal's room with the observer, a behaviour which never happened before. On being taken to the experimental room the dog now barked violently, which was also contrary to its usual custom; in short it presented all the symptoms of a condition of acute neurosis. On testing the cruder differentiations they were also found to be destroyed. . . . [Pavlov, 1927, p. 291.]

The latter phases of this experiment not only illustrate discrimination training, but are often said to have implications for child-rearing practices. One might speculate, for example, that overeager parents who push their children beyond their capabilities, by requiring early toilet training or nearly impossible academic or athletic achievements, may produce reactions and problems analogous to those which Pavlov encountered when he pushed his dogs' discriminatory powers too far.

And finally, it has been observed that just as responses can be conditioned to neutral stimuli, so they can be eliminated by repeated presentation in the absence of the UCS. This gradual diminution of a conditioned response is called *extinction* (Figure V–1*c*).

Higher-order Conditioning. We have seen that when food and the sound of a metronome are paired, the metronome will come to elicit salivation—a result that may be thought of as *first-order conditioning.* But, Pavlov asked, what happens if the now conditioned metronome sound is paired with presentation of a new neutral stimulus (such as a black square)? The answer was clear: the metronome functioned much as the meat powder had previously, so that the black square eventually elicited salivation although it had never been paired directly with the meat powder. The outcome, which Pavlov referred to as *second-order conditioning,* demonstrates a principle of great importance: conditioning may work through several generations of responses.* Consider, for example, an experiment by Pavlov's colleague, Krylov (cited in Ruch & Zimbardo, 1971) in which an injection which produced nausea and vomiting conditioned the mere sight of the administering needle so that it also produced vomiting. Then the sight of the needle, itself originally neutral, was paired with other stimuli (e.g., alcohol on the skin); soon they, too, elicited nausea. It is plausible that many complex human reactions—positive as well as negative—are developed in this way.

Watson's Influence

One of the first psychologists in the United States to take seriously the proposition that Pavlovian, or classical, conditioning may have implications for the development and modification of human behavior was John Watson, the father of modern behaviorism. Like Pavlov, Watson rejected introspective efforts to understand behavior through an analysis of the processes of the mind, stating that the science of behavior need "never use the terms consciousness, mental states, mind, content, will, imagery, and the like. . . . Certain stimuli lead . . . organisms to make . . . responses. In a system of psychology completely worked out, given the responses the stimuli can be predicted; given the stimuli the responses can be predicted" (1914, pp. 9–10). Moreover, Watson approached the prospect of applying these principles to the development of children's behavior with enthusiasm. He said:

> Give me a dozen healthy infants, well-formed, and my own specified world to bring them up in and I'll guarantee to take any one at random and train him to become any type of specialist I might select—doctor, lawyer, merchant, chief and yes, even beggar-man and thief, regardless of his talents, penchants, tendencies, abilities, vocations, and race of his ancestors. [Watson, 1958, p. 104.]

---

* Third- and fourth-order conditioning has been difficult to show with animals, but there have been some successful demonstrations (e.g., Brogden and Culler, 1935).

No such demonstration occurred. Watson did, however, instigate several studies with young children that illustrate the early application of conditioning procedures. Perhaps the most famous of these studies is the one involving "little Albert," whose case history was published by Watson and Rayner in 1920.

Albert was an eleven-month-old child with no major detectable fears except for an avoidance response to the sound made by striking a steel bar behind him. Assuming that the sound was a UCS which elicited fear, Watson and Rayner tried to show that they could induce or condition the fear of a white rat (a CS) in Albert by systematically pairing exposure to the animal with the sound. After a series of seven such presentations, the rat, which previously had not elicited any fear, produced a fairly sharp avoidance reaction which included crying and attempts to escape from the situation.

In a follow-up study, Mary Cover Jones (1924) showed that fear responses can be partially extinguished by procedures similar to conditioning. Her subject, Peter, was a boy of 2 years and 10 months, who had previously developed a severe fear reaction to furry objects. Jones first arranged for Peter to play, in the presence of a rabbit, with three children who exhibited no fear of the animal. The treatment appeared to be working well when a setback occurred, due to Peter's illness and accidental exposure to a large dog. Jones then decided to treat the boy with a combination of exposure to fearless others and *counter-conditioning;* the latter involved moving the animal progressively closer to Peter while he ate some of his favorite foods. The boy's fear diminished with this treatment until he was able to hold the rabbit and other previously feared objects by himself.

Classical Conditioning in Infancy

The question of whether infants can be conditioned has been of long-standing concern to child psychologists because it suggests that learning operates as a developmental process very early in life. However, until quite recently (as Kessen's article, Selection 3, shows) some psychologists questioned the positive results of early conditioning studies, many of which were inadequately controlled. For example, the use of aversive stimuli, such as electric shock, as the UCS may have resulted in heightened arousal levels in the subjects, which in turn may have created uninterpretable changes in reactivity. In the mid-1950s, the introduction of nonnoxious stimulation, along with improved techniques (Stevenson, 1970), gradually erased most doubt that a variety of responses, such as blinking, crying, heart rate change, head turning, eye movement, fear responses, and sucking, can be classically conditioned during the first few weeks of life (Brackbill and Koltsova, 1967; Fitzgerald and Porges, 1970).

Classical Conditioning in Older Subjects

A question has been raised as to whether there is an increase in the susceptibility to conditioning with increasing age. It has been suggested (e.g., Mateer, 1918) that speed of conditioning increases with age among young children, but reports have not been consistent on this matter and variations in factors such as reward and capability to respond may underlie reported age differences (Reese and Lipsitt, 1970). Thus, any definitive conclusion concerning age trends would be premature at present.

Nevertheless, the substance of some of the conditioning studies with older subjects is instructive with regard to understanding the development of behavior. A considerable amount of research has been conducted by Russian psychologists, who are particularly interested in the role of language as a classically conditioned "second signal system." If, for example, a light has been conditioned to food, the word "light" also may come to signal food (Berlyne, 1970). Such conditioning requires only that a word be associated with the first signal (e.g., the light). In one experiment (conducted by Degtier and cited by Brackbill and Koltsova, 1967), children ranging in age from one-and-one-half to three years were taught conditioned responses to visual and auditory stimuli; for example, the sound of a bell and the word "bell" were used. For the older subjects, the words alone came to elicit the conditioned responses. This study is not unlike ones done in the United States many years ago, in which subjects were trained to contract their pupils when they heard the word "contract." Apparently thinking the word elicited the pupillary responses (Berlyne, 1970).

It appears that many of the meanings which are attached to people and events also are developed through this form of associative learning. The manner in which this may occur during childhood has been demonstrated in a series of experiments by Nunnally and his associates (Nunnally, Duchnowski, and Parker, 1965; Nunnally, Stevens, and Hall, 1965; Parker and Nunnally, 1966). To illustrate the typical findings, we shall consider the work of Nunnally, Duchnowski, and Parker (1965).

Elementary school children were asked first to play a spin-wheel game similar to the situation shown in Figure V–2 in which one of three nonsense syllables (ZOJ, MYV, GYQ) appeared in each of the eighteen possible stopping points on the wheel. Each child was permitted to spin

FIGURE V–2

A child playing the spinning-wheel game used to condition reward value in the research of Nunnally and his associates. Courtesy Dr. Jum C. Nunnally.

the wheel thirty times; one of the syllable stopping points led to a reward (two pennies), one led to no consequences, and one led to a negative outcome (the loss of one penny).

The major purpose of the experiment was to show that the three initially neutral nonsense syllables could take on positive or negative value through pairing them with various outcomes. To show that such conditioning had, in fact, occurred, three measures were employed; we shall consider two of them, a *verbal evaluation* and a *looking box* task.

The verbal evaluation task involved showing the child three stick figures with blank faces. One of the three nonsense syllables previously associated with rewards, punishments, or neutral events was placed below each of the figures. The child was told that each of the syllables was the name of the "boy" with which it was now associated, read a list of pleasant and unpleasant adjectives, and asked to attribute each to one of the boys. For example, the subject was asked "Which is the *friendly* boy?" or "Which is the *mean* boy?"

The "looking box" contained six small windows, with a button beneath each. Pushing a button illuminated a slide in the box which, in turn, showed one of the syllables which had been previously associated with positive, negative, or neutral outcomes. After a short time, the slide went off and the child had to push the same button again to bring it back on. Time spent looking at each syllable was the dependent measure.

All measures suggested that the positive and negative experiences had clearly conditioned positive and negative meaning to the previously neutral stimuli. For example, 4.77 (out of a possible 5) positive evaluations were attributed to the positively conditioned stimulus in the verbal evaluation, .23 positive evaluations to the neutral stimulus, and none to the negative stimulus. Similarly, the looking box data suggest that ". . . pairing of a neutral object with a reward subsequently makes the subject 'want' to look at the formerly neutral object. Since the subjects were told that no pennies would be given regardless of which buttons were pushed, choices should not have been influenced by that factor" (Nunnally Duchnowski, and Parker, 1965, p. 273).

More recently, Nunnally and his associates have turned to naturalistic field settings for further corroboration of their results. Wilson and Nunnally (1971), for example, associated nonsense syllables with various ongoing classroom activities for sixth grade boys and girls by using the syllables as "tickets of permission" to participate in various activities. As in the earlier laboratory results, striking effects were obtained in the real-life classroom situation. For example, initially neutral syllables which were associated with Easter vacation (which occurred during the conditioning period) were later evaluated as about 50 percent more pleasant than those associated with spelling lessons.

The concept of conditioned reward value, illustrated in Nunnally's research, may be applied to the development of a host of social behaviors and attitudes. We already have seen that when previously neutral stimuli are paired with rewarding stimuli or events, they tend to take on positive properties themselves.

The manner in which complex attitudes may be conditioned in just this fashion is illustrated in an experiment performed by Staats and Staats (1958). Their subjects, college students, heard various proper names (such as Tom and Bill) and national names (such as Swedish and Dutch) associated with either positive or negative words (e.g., *gift, sacred,* and *happy* versus *bitter, ugly,* and *failure*). The students were told to try to learn the CS words—i.e., the proper names—by looking at them while pronouncing the auditorily presented UCS adjectives aloud and to themselves. A relatively short period of such conditioning, the purpose of which was not known to the participants, produced dramatic differences in the attitudes that were subsequently expressed when the subjects were asked to indicate how they *felt* about the names. Some of the results, for *Bill* and *Swedish,* are shown in Figure V–3. It is easy to see the possibility that, during the course of development, children acquire attitudes toward school, minority groups, and perhaps even themselves through just this type of associative learning.

The Staats and Staats experiment described above suggests that positive and negative prejudices can be classically conditioned; other evidence suggests that such a process is operative early in life. For example, a series of studies (Edwards and Williams, 1970; Renninger and Williams, 1966) has shown that white children of preschool age already have begun to associate white figures with positive adjectives and black figures with negative ones. In a typical situation, children are shown two full-length drawings of human figures of the same age. The figures are identical except for skin and hair color; one figure ("Caucasian") has blond hair and pinkish skin, while the other ("Negro") has black hair and brown skin (Figure V–4). The picture is presented in the context of a story that includes a question with an evaluative adjective—e.g., "Everyone likes one of these little boys because he is always doing good things for people. Which do you guess is the good little boy?" The white figure is regularly selected over the black one by white children in this situation.

Negative evaluations can be reversed, as well as shaped, by learning procedures. Edwards and Williams (1970) have shown that when a simple reward (pennies) is withdrawn after white children apply negative evaluations to black figures, the children will begin to show more positive evaluations of blacks. These results are not limited to the actual pictures used during retraining; they also generalize to other figures for which reward has not been used. Thus, the investigators write, "the strong tendencies toward customary responses which the children had learned under natural, 'real-life,' conditions, were shown to be amenable to modification by laboratory learning procedures" (pp. 153–164).

The modification referred to by Edwards and Williams was produced by instrumental conditioning, an important learning process to which we next turn our attention.

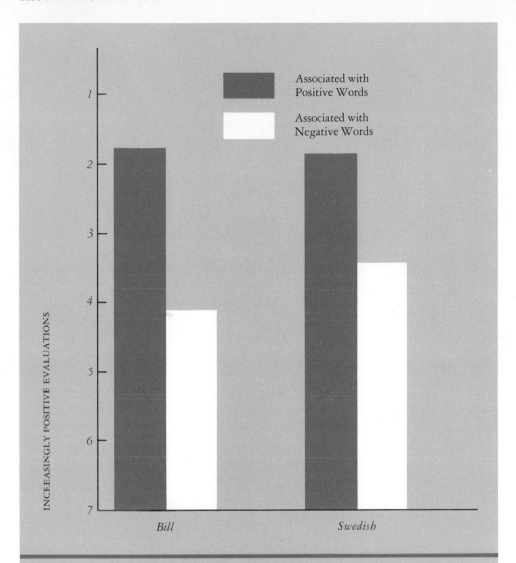

FIGURE V-3

Mean conditioned attitude scores in an experiment by Staats and Staats, showing that attitudes can be classically conditioned. Data from Staats and Staats, 1958.

FIGURE V—4

A picture used by Williams and his associates to assess racial attitudes in preschool children. Courtesy Dr. John E. Williams.

INSTRUMENTAL LEARNING

Unlike associative learning, in which behavior is elicited by some identifiable stimulus, instrumental learning focuses on the consequences (rewards and punishments) which follow behavior. The pioneer investigator in this area was E. L. Thorndike.

In a typical experiment, Thorndike (1898) placed a cat into a slatted cage with food located outside; thus, escape was potentially followed by food reward. The cat had to perform a particular response, such as pulling a cord or pressing a lever, to open the door; by virtue of the creature's high level of activity, sooner or later it "accidentally" performed the act and succeeded in escaping. Thorndike observed that, on subsequent trials, "All the other nonsuccessful impulses will be stamped out and the particular impulse leading to the successful act will be stamped in by the resulting pleasure . . ." (1898, p. 11).

From such observations, he formulated a general law, the *Law of Effect,* applicable to the behavior of all organisms.

> Any act which in a given situation produces satisfaction becomes associated with that situation, so that when the situation recurs the act is more likely than before to recur also. Conversely, any act which in a given situation produces discomfort becomes disassociated from that situation, so that when the situation recurs the act is less likely than before to recur. [Thorndike, 1905, p. 203.]

Although the statement cited above suggests that the strength of the connection between a particular situation and a particular response would be both increased if it were followed by reward (i.e., "satisfaction") and decreased if it were followed by punishment (i.e., "discomfort"), Thorndike later recanted on the latter half of this formulation, concluding that rewards are far more powerful than punishments. We will see that this conclusion also was reached by later researchers, only to be reversed again within the past few years.

Thorndike himself endeavored to apply the law of effect and several other principles derived from his research to a number of practical human problems. He published over five hundred articles and books, among them a fairly complete volume on experimental psychology and several books focusing on educational matters (cf. Joncich, 1962). In one such volume, written for teachers and setting forth his philosophy of educational psychology, he reflected:

> Human nature does not do something for nothing. The satisfyingness and annoyingness of the states of affairs which follow the making of the connection are the chief forces which remodel man's nature. Education makes changes chiefly by rewarding them. The prime law in all human control is to get the man to make the desired response and to be satisfied thereby.
>
> The Law of Effect is the fundamental law of learning and teaching. . . . By it animals are taught their tricks; by it babies learn to smile at the sight of the bottle or the kind attendant, and to manipulate spoon and fork; by it the player at billiards or golf improves his game; by it the man of science preserves those ideas that satisfy him by their promise, and discards futile fancies. It is the great weapon of all who wish—in industry, trade, govern-

ment, religion or education—to change man's responses, either by reinforcing old and adding new ones, or by getting rid of those that are undesirable. [cited in Joncich, 1962, p. 79–80.]

But Thorndike was an exception in his interest in generalizing psychological principles to the practical domain. The application of these principles did not take root in the mainstream of developmental thinking until the law of effect was extended and elaborated in the writings of another pioneering theorist, B. F. Skinner.

Principles of Instrumental Learning

Skinner's work has focused almost exclusively on instrumental learning; in his terminology, instrumentally conditioned acts are designated *operants* (i.e., they operate on the environment) and classically conditioned acts are designated *respondents.* We already have seen that emotions, motor acts, values, and prejudices may be respondents. Examples of operant behavior include doing homework, playing chess, driving a car, and dressing oneself. Completion of any one of these acts results in some consequence. For example, driving a car may result in visiting friends, viewing the countryside, or smashing into another auto. Future behavior is influenced by these outcomes; positive consequences will increase the likelihood of the act's occurring again, whereas negative consequences will decrease the likelihood.

The Nature of Reinforcement. The concept of reinforcement as applied to instrumental learning is intertwined with the concept of need-reduction. All organisms have basic needs or cravings rooted in their biology, such as the need for food, sexual satisfaction, or avoidance of pain. Behavior which results in the reduction of these needs is *positively* reinforced and will gradually increase. Receiving food is a *primary reinforcer* because it reduces a primary need for subsistence. Thus, we might expect that if a hungry child's crying is followed by mother bringing food, the frequency of crying when hungry will go up.

But not all behavior is directly related to basic biological needs. The mother who feeds the child is associated with need reduction; through this process her presence gradually may become a *secondary reinforcer.* Now crying may be reinforced merely by mother's coming to the child. Moreover, many other behaviors, such as babbling or saying "Mama," can be similarly increased by mother's attention. The concept of secondary reinforcement is an important one, as it attempts to explain how new behaviors can be built on the relatively small set of behaviors with which the child is born. Thus, work which earns money, daring which brings a smile from father, and studying which results in an "A" are strengthened because money, father's approval, and social recognition of certain achievements have become reinforcing events. There is no doubt that a vast array of stimuli function as reinforcers for human beings. Because all individuals in a particular culture have virtually identical biological needs and share many similar experiences, we can safely infer that certain objects or events are reinforcing to most of them. On the other hand, only a careful analysis of the individual's past can clearly determine the additional events which serve as effective reinforcers.

Negative Reinforcement. There is another way in which reinforcers operate to strengthen behavior. *Negative reinforcement* consists of the removal of an aversive stimulus. The mechanism frequently has been shown in the laboratory by presenting electric shock to an animal and terminating the shock when the animal performs a predetermined response. The animal learns to complete the act as soon as the shock comes on. In a somewhat different situation, when a prescribed behavior will prevent the shock from coming on at all, the animal soon learns an *avoidance* response. Analogously, a child will run home quickly to reduce his anxiety of the dark outside, or clean his room to avoid parental wrath.

Extinction. Extinction is the weakening of a learned operant due to the lack of reinforcement. If an instrumental response has been strengthened by providing the organism with reinforcement, and if the reinforcement is then withheld, there is soon a decrement in response rate. The mechanism parallels that found in classical conditioning when the CS is presented alone without the UCS after the conditioned response has been acquired. The degree to which an organism resists extinction is an indication of the strength of the conditioned response.

Schedules of Reinforcement

Research has shown that the effects of reinforcement can depend upon the scheduling or patterning with which the reinforcer is given. The most obvious schedule is to give a reinforcer every time the desired behavior is performed. This procedure, referred to as a *continuous reinforcement* (CRF) schedule, rarely parallels the experiences which are found in actual life situations. Investigators thus have been especially interested in the effects of reinforcement which is given on a *partial* or intermittent schedule.

Partial reinforcement may be set up according to a *fixed interval* of time (FI schedule); with this kind of schedule, the subject is reinforced only for the first correct response emitted after a prescribed lapse of time. *Fixed ratio* (FR) schedules, in contrast, are those in which a response is reinforced only after it has occurred for a fixed number of times without consequences, —e.g., a reinforcer after every fourth response. Studies with both animals and humans suggest that FR schedules can be made to produce considerably higher rates of responding than either CRF or FI schedules. Moreover, an experimenter may begin an organism on a particular schedule and slowly decrease the ratio of unreinforced to reinforced responses until the organism is rewarded as infrequently as one response in every thousand.

Reinforcement also may be provided on variable schedules—that is, after a variable time lapse (variable interval or VI) or a variable number of unreinforced responses (variable ratio or VR). The subject therefore never learns exactly when he will be reinforced. His responding usually becomes very steady, with the rate depending upon the length of the time interval or the ratio first employed. The VR schedule is particularly potent for evoking high rates of responding; it is as if the subject knows that the more he responds, the greater his chances of payoff, even though he cannot predict when he will be paid. Variable schedules probably are extremely common in human affairs.

A subtle finding concerns the relation between resistance to extinction and the schedules of reinforcement employed during conditioning. For both nonhuman species and humans, behavior learned under partial reinforcement is more persistent after the termination of reinforcement than behavior learned under a continuous schedule. Although it has been often colorfully noted that the compulsive gambler persists because he is the victim of intermittent reinforcement, the phenomenon also has important, if less dramatic, implications for child-rearing. An example of this effect is provided in an investigation with preschool children in which the correct response consisted of picking up a ball and moving it to a different location (Bijou, 1957). One group of children was given a trinket for each of five consecutive responses (a CRF schedule); the second group was given the same number of reinforcers for five randomly selected responses out of a series of twenty-five trials (a VR schedule). During the extinction phase, when no trinkets were provided, the children trained on the CRF schedule responded less frequently than those exposed to the partial schedule. (See Figure V–5.)

Continuous reinforcement during childhood has potentially dangerous implications for behavior in adulthood. Lundin (1961), for example sug-

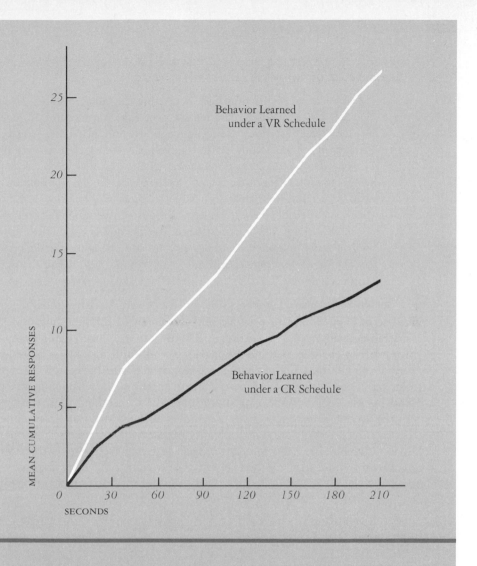

FIGURE V–5

Mean number of responses (cumulative during the 3½-minute extinction period) in Bijou's (1957) experiment. Adapted from S. W. Bijou, Patterns of reinforcement and resistance to extinction in young children. Child Development, 1957, 28, 47-54. Copyright 1957 by the Society for Research in Child Development, Inc. Reproduced by permission.

gests that it may explain why some people break down while others are "like the rock of Gibraltar":

> The application of the principle in training for adult maturity is clear. "Spoiled" or overindulged children are poor risks for later life. In looking into their past histories of reinforcement, we find that those who break down easily or are readily set to aggression were as children too often *regularly* reinforced. Every demand was granted by their acquiescent parents. In youth they may have been so sheltered that failure was unknown to them. As a result these children have never built up a stability of response which would enable them to undergo periods of extinction and still maintain stable activity. The poor resistance to extinction is exemplified in their low frustration tolerance. As adults they are still operating like the rat who was reinforced on a regular schedule. Not only do they exhibit the irregularities of response, but they are easily extinguished or discouraged. [p. 82.]

But there is also the other side of the coin. Variable schedules, by virtue of their ability to produce both high rates of responding and considerable resistance to extinction, probably are responsible for many inappropriate but persistent behavior patterns. A child may begin by requesting a cookie from his mother, a request which she turns down the first time. But the youngster has been reinforced for such behavior in the past and persists, perhaps speaking more loudly and becoming more annoying. If the weary parent now gives in, and continues to do so from time to time on future occasions when nagging becomes intolerable, she has begun to build a durable behavior pattern that may survive even staunch efforts to become more firm. At best it will take a long time to extinguish such harrassment; at worst, quite tyrannical behavior may be taught unwittingly.

Discrimination and Generalization

Instrumental learning is unlike classical conditioning in that particular stimuli do not directly elicit the response; they do, however, come to "set the occasion" for behavior. Consider the behavior typically exhibited by the rat in a Skinner box, a specialized experimental chamber. The animal has little difficulty learning that pressing a bar will result in the delivery of a pellet of food. If reinforcement is then provided only when the bar is pressed in the presence of a light, the animal will soon limit his responding to the time during which the light is on. The light has become a *discriminative stimulus* for the behavior; it enables the rat to discriminate the condition under which reinforcement will occur.

Such stimulus control is at the heart of adaptive functioning, for even behaviors we wish to strengthen in a variety of situations would not be socially desirable in all situations. Eating, for example, is a vital behavior which must be brought under stimulus control; although we want to encourage children to eat meat and vegetables, we do not wish them to attempt to eat string, sticks, or the contents of the bottles in the medicine cabinet.

In the case of the rat whose behavior is under the control of the light, suppose the intensity of the light is varied somewhat. The number of bar presses will now be greater for intensities which closely match that of the training light and will decrease as the intensities are progressively different. In other words, a generalization gradient obtains. This phenomenon, which allows the animal to apply his learned response to somewhat different situations, occurs across many species, including man.

Learning by Successive Approximations

Although principles of reinforcement and scheduling can be employed to establish almost any type of behavior, there is always one basic requirement: the desired behavior must occur before it can be reinforced. Thus, if the initial frequency of the behavior which one wishes to strengthen is near zero, reinforcement alone will not work—at least not very efficiently. When dealing with either extremely complex behaviors or with persons whose behavioral repertoires are very limited (the very young, the retarded, the disturbed), we must *shape* the form of the desired behavior. How is this to be done?

The technique most often used is *successive approximation*. As the name implies, it involves a successively changing reinforcement contingency. At first, a large class of responses which has some relevance for the ultimately desired behavior is reinforced. Then, the contingency is gradually altered so that reinforcement is given only for closer and closer approximations of the desired behavior. Sometimes the shaping contingency will involve narrowing the criteria for reinforcement. In teaching a pigeon to stand in one small corner of its cage, for example, the investigator might begin by rewarding the bird for standing anywhere on the left-hand side of the cage. After a while, the bird will spend most of its time there, so the investigator can now safely narrow the contingency down to one quadrant, one-half of the quadrant, and so on. One such progression illustrating the basic principle of successive approximation is shown in Figure V–6.

A variant of the successive approximation technique involves building

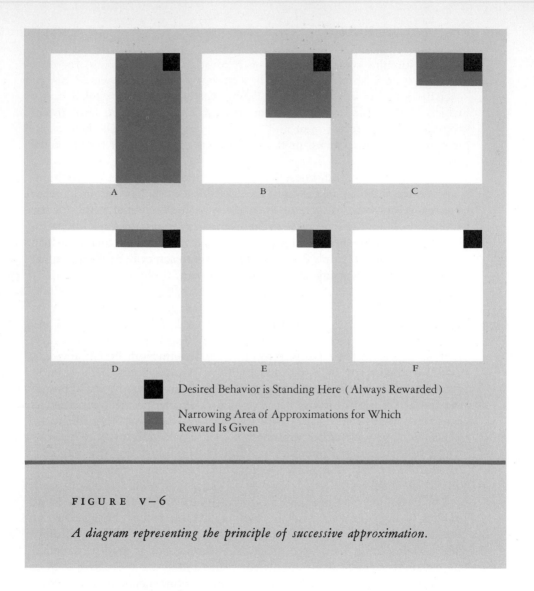

Desired Behavior is Standing Here (Always Rewarded)

Narrowing Area of Approximations for Which Reward Is Given

FIGURE V-6

A diagram representing the principle of successive approximation.

the components of the behavior which is finally desired. For example, in teaching language to a woman who was a mute psychotic, Neale and Liebert (1969) first rewarded imitation of single syllables (e.g., "Buh," "Mmm"), then words (e.g., "Bread," "Milk"), then abbreviated sentences ("Milk, please"), and finally complete sentences ("May I have some bread, please?"). Such a procedure has often been shown to be highly effective. In contrast, if the investigators had waited for the patient to produce a full sentence before issuing any reward, little progress would ever have been made.

THE EFFECTS OF PUNISHMENT

It was noted earlier that, although Thorndike's original statement of the "law of effect" stated that reward and punishment work in equal and opposite ways, he later rescinded a part of this statement and concluded that punishment is relatively ineffective. Likewise, investigations with laboratory animals have shown that punishment may produce a temporary suppression of certain responses, but after the termination of the punishment schedule the punished animals require *more* trials to extinction than those who have not been punished. Thus, in these studies, the total number of trials required for complete cessation of responding (extinction) by punished and nonpunished animals appears to be the same (cf. Estes, 1944).

Obviously, however, punishment does play a prominent role in the practices of many parents, and under some circumstances it can exert a powerful influence on children. In fact, according to one survey (Sears, Maccoby, and Levin, 1957), virtually all parents (98 percent) use punishment at least occasionally. As Parke (1970) has noted, in this instance parents may have been wiser than the "experts," for punishment can be an extremely potent child-rearing technique under some circumstances, although its effects are widely varied.

Reducing the Likelihood of Undesirable Behavior

Whereas reinforcement is most effective in building new patterns of behavior, the effects of punishment are primarily *suppressive;* when punishment "works," it reduces the likelihood of certain noxious or potentially dangerous responses. For this reason, punishment is frequently most effective when it is used in conjunction with reinforcement for an alternative desirable behavior. In this section we shall focus upon recent evidence which outlines the circumstances under which punishment is most and least likely to be an effective means of inhibiting unacceptable behavior by children.

The Timing of Punishment. Perhaps no factor is more important in the naturalistic use of punishment than its timing, relative to an act of transgression. If a child acts in an extremely antisocial way, whether by hitting a younger sibling, stealing, lying, or committing some act of vandalism, some time inevitably will pass before the transgression is detected. Even after detection, an extended waiting period may be present before potential punishment, as in the familiar "Wait till your father comes home!" It is therefore important to determine the relationship between the timing of punishment and its effectiveness.

As a general rule, mild punishment will be maximally effective if it occurs at the outset of a deviant act, or while the act is occurring, and will be much less effective if considerable periods of delay are introduced. There are many theoretical reasons which can explain why this is so, but most involve the following two points.

First, a transgression usually is an instrumental response, producing some positive outcome for the child. Taking forbidden candies or cookies provides the pleasure of eating these treats, and a temper tantrum in a department store may effectively intimidate one's mother into buying a five-dollar notebook. These outcomes are reinforcers for the child, and the longer they are held or savored, the more likely they are to "balance out" the negative experience of punishment.

Second, very late punishment may be confusing in its purpose, at least for very young children. A youngster who seriously breaks some rule subsequently may try to "be good all day" (perhaps to forestall punishment). If he is then punished in the evening for the morning's transgression, the parents have created a situation in which negative consequences follow some very desirable behavior which they would otherwise wish to encourage and reinforce.

Effects of Punishment as a Function of Its Intensity. Another factor that plays an important role in the effectiveness of punishment is its intensity. Research with laboratory animals has shown consistently that very mild levels of punishment usually do *not* permanently eliminate responses; however, moderate punishments often tend to suppress the behaviors which they follow and quite intense punishments are very effective in completely eliminating certain kinds of well-practiced responses (Solomon, 1964).

Although ethical considerations obviously preclude using very intense punishments with human subjects, a few carefully designed studies with children have varied the intensity of a punishing noise (e.g., Parke, 1969; 1970). These investigations clearly mesh both with other laboratory studies and with certain naturalistic investigations: ". . . the overall findings from field and laboratory studies generally support the expectation that high-intensity physical punishment in most circumstances more effectively inhibits the punished behavior than does punishment that is less intense" (Parke, 1970, p. 86).

One particularly striking finding is the manner in which the intensity and timing of punishment interact. Parke (1970) has presented evidence to show that late punishment is less effective than early punishment *only* when the punishment is relatively mild but that children are quite responsive to late punishments of high intensity. This relationship is shown in Figure V–7.

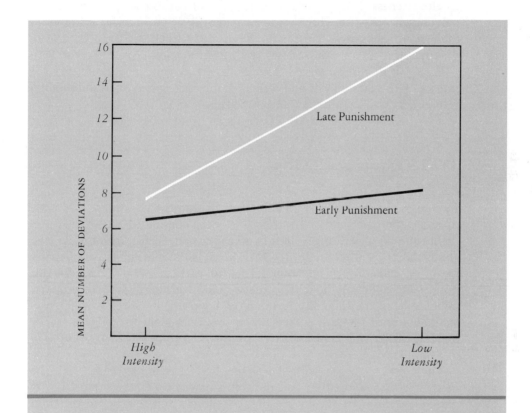

FIGURE V–7

The relationship of intensity and timing of punishment. Adapted from R. D. Parke, The role of punishment in the socialization process. In R. A. Hoppe, G. A. Milton, and E. C. Simmel, eds., Early Experiences and the Process of Socialization *(New York: Academic Press, 1970). By permission of the author and Academic Press.*

Effects of the Parent-Child Relationship. The effectiveness of a particular punishment will depend on many factors. For example, research (Aronfreed, 1968; Parke, 1967; Whiting, 1954) suggests that punishment from an adult who is usually rewarding and nurturant to the child is likely to be more effective than the same punishment from one who is usually cold and distant. What is more, explaining the reason for punishment increases its effectiveness (Parke, 1969). Certain types of consistency also are critical; parents who practice what they preach are likely to be more effective in their reprimands than those who do not (Mischel and Liebert, 1966). Finally, "the parent who follows the administration of punishment with a display of affection directed toward the errant child may counteract the impact of the punishment and will probably strengthen the [undesirable] response as well" (Parke, 1970, p. 103).

OBSERVATIONAL LEARNING

In contrast to classical conditioning and instrumental learning, the study of observational or imitative learning has been considered and studied predominantly as a particularly human phenomenon. Thus Aristotle, writing almost 2300 years ago, suggested that "man is the most imitative of living creatures, and through imitation learns his earliest lessons." Despite this propitious beginning, however, observational learning played a peculiarly minor role in the thinking, research, and writing of developmental psychologists until the early 1940s, when it was brought to the fore briefly in Neal Miller and John Dollard's landmark treatise, *Social learning and imitation* (1941).

These writers began with the assumption that imitativeness, like the desire for money, prestige, and the companionship of others, must be acquired. According to their view, the tendency to imitate arises in the child as a joint function of the operation of instrumental learning and the presence of social conditions which foster its development and maintenance. Thus:

> Imitation is a process by which "matched," or similar, acts are evoked in two people and connected to appropriate cues. It can occur only under conditions which are favorable to learning these acts. If matching, or doing the same as others do, is regularly rewarded, a secondary tendency to match may be developed, and the process of imitation becomes the derived drive of imitativeness. [1941, p. 10.]

Copying and Matched-dependent Behavior

Miller and Dollard identified two types of behavior which might properly be described as imitation. In one of these, so-called *copying,* one individual learns from another by endeavoring simply to reproduce his behaviors faithfully and accurately. Thus, for copying to be successful, the copier must know (or be told) whether his responses are acceptable reproductions. Although Miller and Dollard did not place much research emphasis on copying, they argued that it plays a prominent role in human development, noting that "copying units are established early in the history of each individual, and appear to play a considerable role in all fundamental social learning" (1941, p. 11).

The second type of imitative phenomena of interest to Miller and Dollard was *matched-dependent behavior,* a type of behavior which can be understood in terms of the leader-follower relationship. In the matched-dependent situation it is assumed that the leader or model is able to read certain critical cues in the environment which the follower cannot detect for himself. The follower is therefore *dependent* upon the leader's behavior as a cue to guide his actions. In this situation it is further assumed that the follower begins to imitate the behavior of the leader in order to gain for himself the rewards which the leader has obtained. Miller and Dollard considered matched-dependent behavior the basis for both the learning of imitation and the acquisition of a variety of new behaviors imitatively.

In order to create the matched-dependent situation experimentally, Miller and Dollard conducted a series of imitation studies with young children. A typical experiment involved a specially arranged room containing two chairs with a closed box on each, as shown in Figure V–8, and two sets of children, grouped in pairs. One set of children was told (i.e., given an informative *cue*) in which of the two boxes a piece of candy was to be found. Children in the second set were not informed of the location of the candy. In each pair, then, there was one child who could play the role of "leader" and one who had been cast as a "follower."

After the prospective leader had been told the location of the candy, the prospective follower was brought into the room. The two children were asked to stand at the start position and were told: "You are to find the candy. If you don't find it the first time, you'll get another turn." Because the leader had been told where to look ahead of time, he always found one of the pieces of candy immediately, thereby demonstrating a rewarded response. Then half of the followers, on their turns, found another piece

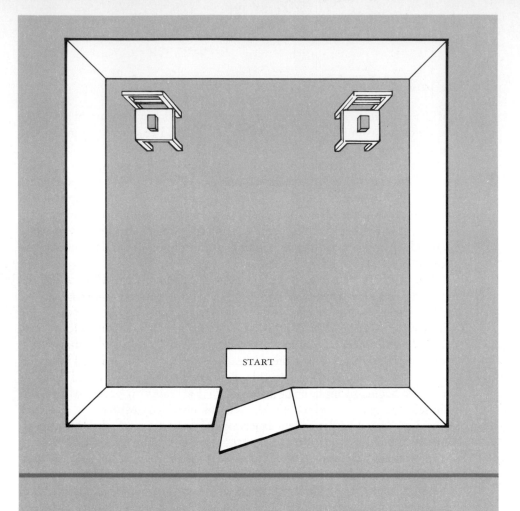

FIGURE V—8

The experimental setup employed by Miller and Dollard in matched-dependent imitation experiments with children. Adapted from Miller and Dollard, 1941, by permission.

of candy (for themselves) under the box which the leader had chosen, while the remaining children found the second piece of candy under the opposite box.

To the extent that the matched-dependent analysis is correct, the first group of "followers" would become imitators while the latter would not.

The outcome, presented in Figure V–9 shows that this is exactly what occurred.

Miller and Dollard argued that their demonstrations of learning to imitate reflected an important aspect of learning in real-life situations:

> . . . individuals are constantly being placed in [such situations]. The young, the stupid, the subordinate, and the unskilled must depend on the older, the brighter, the superordinate, and the skilled. . . . Society . . . is so organized that the situation . . . occurs over and over again. [1941, p. 97.]

As this statement implies, it is likely that many characteristics of the "leader" determine whether he will be imitated. It has been shown that children's imitative behavior is influenced strongly by the degree of *similarity* between the model and the observer. Rosekrans (1967), for example, asked boys in various experimental groups to watch a brief movie in which a peer model played a war-strategy game. In the *high similarity* condition, the peer was dressed just as the subjects (in a boy scout uniform) and was described as being very much like them in interests, skills, and place of residence. In contrast, the *low similarity* model was dressed in street clothes and was described on all dimensions as being very unlike the young observers. After viewing the film, the children were permitted to play the war-strategy game themselves (so that they could spontaneously imitate the behavior of the model) and were then asked to demonstrate all of the model's behaviors which they could remember. Those who had observed a highly similar model were found to show more spontaneous rehearsal of the model's behaviors and to recall more of his behaviors than those in the low similarity condition. As Rosekrans notes, her findings show that perceived similarity to the model may affect not only the performance of imitative responses but also how well the model's behavior is learned. We will have more to say about this second point later.

There appear to be many reasons why characteristics of the model influence imitation. For example, it has been suggested that children infer from a model's characteristics whether imitation will be appropriate or lead them to successful outcomes (Liebert and Allen, 1969; Liebert and Fernandez, 1970). Consider an effort by Smith (1967) to inspire achievement efforts in black high school freshmen through exposure to successful adult blacks. Smith reports that the models (including a teacher, an engineer, a lawyer, and a poetess) were for the most part former slum-dwellers who had overcome extremely adverse circumstances to achieve personal success. This similarity of origin, he feels, made them credible models. It is thus not surprising that the pupils involved showed an increase in their own self-esteem over the course of the project.

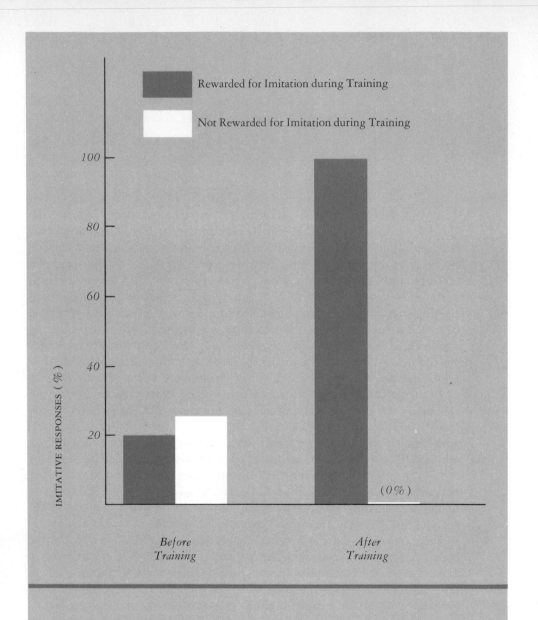

FIGURE V–9

Mean percentage of imitative responses of children exposed to imitative and nonimitative cues in Miller and Dollard's experiment. Adapted from Miller and Dollard, 1941, by permission.

Generalized Imitation

Although Miller and Dollard's analysis has led to some interesting and important findings, their view implies that imitative learning is limited to producing close approximations of the leader's behavior—and then only when the matching response is followed by reward. There are thus many phenomena which cannot be accounted for in terms of matched-dependent analysis. Thus, a second view of the role of imitation in socialization has been put forth. In contrast to Miller and Dollard's emphasis on the learning of relevant (or *discriminative*) cues for reward as a function of observing models, this second view, originally advanced by Donald Baer, James Sherman, and their associates, focuses upon the learning of the more general tendency to imitate others (i.e., *generalized imitation*).

In their first experiment, Baer and Sherman (1964) exposed children to an animated, talking puppet which was dressed as a cowboy and seated on a little chair appearing on a puppet stage. The children observed the puppet engage in four different responses: nodding its head, opening and closing its mouth, pressing a bar located beside its miniature chair, and talking. The subjects were brought into the laboratory, seated in front of the puppet stage, and introduced to the situation as follows.

> "This is Jimmy the puppet. He wants to talk to you. And this (pointing) is your bar. See it's just like Jimmy's bar only bigger (pointing). Do you know how it works?" The usual answer was "No," in which case [the experimenter] demonstrated a bar-press, saying "Now, you try it." . . . Then . . . "You can talk to Jimmy now." [After this introduction] the puppet raised his head and began speaking to the child. He followed a fairly standard line of conversation, starting with greetings, and progressing through expressions of pleasure over the chance to talk with the child to alternating questions about what the child had been doing and colorful stories about what the puppet had been doing. This type of conversation was maintained throughout all the sessions. . . . [1964, p. 39.]

Next, a procedure was instituted to acquaint the child with the bar and to determine the original frequency (i.e., the *operant level*) of bar-pressing before treatment. Specifically, after the puppet and child had talked for a while, the puppet began pressing his bar, alternating between a slow and a fast rate. Neither this procedure nor a brief interlude in which the puppet asked the children to point to their own heads, mouths, and to their own bars produced any appreciable degree of imitative bar-pressing. Likewise, noncontingent reward ("good," "very good," "you're really smart") did not instigate such imitation. In this way, it was demonstrated that generalized imitation—a tendency to imitate everything the puppet did—did not initially characterize the children's behavior.

The next step in the experiment was to establish the imitation of all of the puppet's responses except bar-pressing, by reinforcing imitation of these directly. When the pattern of imitation was well-established, the puppet resumed bar-pressing, as well as continuing his nodding, mouthing, and strange verbalizations. However, while imitation of these latter responses was continuously rewarded, *no reward was ever given for imitating the puppet's bar-pressing.*

The child's bar-pressing was the basic dependent variable of the study. If imitative bar-pressing by the child now increased, it could be attributed only to the direct reinforcement of other imitations and, inasmuch as bar-pressing is very different topographically from rewarded responses, an increase in imitative bar-pressing would show that similarity or imitation per se had become important.

Did such generalized imitation occur? In seven of the eleven children in this experiment it did. Moreover, it was shown, with two of these children, that nonreinforced bar-pressing decreased when reward for imitating the other responses was terminated and increased again when reinforcement for imitating the other responses was reinstated. These findings, based on a shrewd modification of the usual ABA design (see Chapter II), demonstrate the development of a true generalized imitation based on reinforcement.

The procedures devised by Baer and Sherman are potentially useful for more than theoretical purposes. The method appears to be appropriate for teaching those few children who fail to learn to imitate in the normal course of socialization to do so through experimental training procedures. In turn, laboratory-induced generalized imitation may form a basis for the learning of new and important skills, such as language.

In a pioneering study within this framework, Baer, Peterson, and Sherman (1967) employed these procedures in order to produce generalized imitation in three severely and profoundly retarded children between nine and twelve years of age. Although these children were toilet-trained and could feed themselves at the outset of the study, none used any language (except for occasional grunts) and all were practically without imitation. After initial imitation training, a relatively short period (approximately twenty hours) was sufficient to produce meaningful verbalizations such as the subject's own name, "Hi," "Okay," and so on. Modifications of such procedures also have been used in more extensive programs for severely disturbed and autistic children, particularly by Lovaas (1968), whose work will be discussed in a later chapter.

Social Learning and Modeling

The theories of imitation advanced by Miller and Dollard as well as the analysis suggested by Baer, Sherman, and their associates place great emphasis on the manner in which imitation as a *mode of responding* is acquired and maintained. These theories have proven to be both clear and workable in many laboratory experiments and their proponents have appropriately noted a number of ways in which generalized imitation can be directly applied to a variety of life situations. However, these analyses fail to account for the large number of situations in which children appear to learn observationally *without* demonstrating immediate imitative responses.

Virtually every day, children have an opportunity to observe new patterns of behavior as they are exhibited by other children and adults. Thus, for example, the youngster may see her mother combine a variety of ingredients from the cupboard to bake a cake, may observe an older sibling use the telephone, or may overhear a peer reap parental praise for certain self-care activities, such as brushing his teeth. In these situations the observer is not likely to imitate the behaviors immediately. Nevertheless, when environmental circumstances become appropriate or conducive for recalling how another performed in the situation, we often note marked evidence of imitative learning.

The mother in our first example may not be aware, during her own busy culinary activity, how much is being "picked up." Later it may come to her attention dramatically when, entering the kitchen one Sunday morning, she finds that her young daughter has emptied the contents of the sugar package, the laundry detergent, and the orange juice into a large bowl and is stirring them with all the zeal that Mother had earlier displayed in preparing chocolate layer cake.

A comprehensive explanation of imitative learning must, therefore, account for the situation in which a child learns by observation, but does not immediately perform the response. Such a theory has been advanced by Albert Bandura and the late Richard H. Walters.

Specifically, Bandura and Walters have suggested a view of learning by observation in which the *acquisition* or ability to recall responses is distinguished from the *performance* or adoption of these modeled acts. Along with their associates, they have performed a number of ingenious experiments, many of which involved the systematic manipulation of *vicarious consequences*—i.e., outcomes which accrue to the model for his behavior. When these outcomes are positive or desirable in nature, they are called *vicarious reward;* negative or undesirable outcomes are called *vicarious punishment.* In one widely cited study dealing with aggression (Bandura, 1965), modeling cues were provided by showing nursery school children a remarkable five-minute film on the screen of a television console.

> The film began with a scene in which a model walked up to an adult-size plastic Bobo doll and ordered him to clear the way. After glaring for a moment at the noncompliant antagonist the model exhibited four novel aggressive responses each accompanied by a distinctive verbalization.
>
> First, the model laid the Bobo doll on its side, sat on it, and punched it in the nose while remarking, "Pow, right in the nose, boom, boom." The model then raised the doll and pommeled it on the head with a mallet. Each response was accompanied by the verbalization, "Sockeroo . . . stay down." Following the mallet aggression, the model kicked the doll about the room, and these responses were interspersed with the comment, "Fly away." Finally, the model threw rubber balls at the Bobo doll, each strike punctuated with "Bang." This sequence of physically and verbally aggressive behavior was repeated twice. [Bandura, 1965, pp. 590–591.]

The independent variable manipulated in this study involved the consequences which the model received. One group of children saw, in addition to the film segment described above, a final scene in which the model was rewarded generously for assaults upon the clown. Specifically:

> For children in the *model-rewarded* condition, a second adult appeared with an abundant supply of candies and soft drinks. He informed the model that he was a "strong champion" and that his superb aggressive performance clearly deserved a generous treat. He then poured him a large glass of 7-Up, and readily supplied additional energy-building nourishment including chocolate bars, Cracker Jack popcorn, and an assortment of candies. While the model was rapidly consuming the delectable treats, his admirer symbolically reinstated the modeled aggressive responses and engaged in considerable positive social reinforcement. [p. 591, italics added.]

A second group of children watched the film end with a final scene in which the model received punishment for his aggressive behavior. For children in this group

> . . . the reinforcing agent appeared on the scene shaking his finger menacingly and commenting reprovingly, "Hey there, you big bully. You quit picking on that clown. I won't tolerate it." As the model drew back he

tripped and fell, the other adult sat on the model and spanked him with a rolled-up magazine while reminding him of his aggressive behavior. As the model ran off cowering, the agent forewarned him, "If I catch you doing that again, you big bully, I'll give you a hard spanking. You quit acting that way." [p. 591.]

A final group which served as a control group also saw the film, but without any final scene in which the model received consequences for his hostile behavior.

Thereafter, all children were brought individually into an experimental room which contained a plastic Bobo doll, three balls, a mallet, a peg-board, plastic farm animals, and a dollhouse which was equipped with furniture and a miniature doll family. This wide array of toys was provided so that the child would be able to engage either in imitative aggressive responses—i.e., the model's responses—or in alternative nonaggressive and nonimitative forms of behavior. Each child was left alone with this assortment of toys for ten minutes, while his behavior was periodically recorded by judges who watched from behind a one-way vision screen. The frequency of imitative aggressive behavior in this situation constituted the *performance* measure of the study. Not surprisingly, it was found that children who saw the model punished for his untoward actions exhibited far fewer imitative aggressive responses than did those in either of the other two groups. But—and this is the major point of the Bandura and Walters analysis—it would be inappropriate to conclude that because the children in this group did not spontaneously imitate, they had learned nothing.

To demonstrate that learning had occurred in all groups, irrespective of whether it was spontaneously revealed in performance, the experimenter reentered the room well supplied with incentives (colored sticker pictures, sweet fruit juices in an attractive dispenser, and so on) and told the child that, for each act of imitative aggression which he could reproduce, an additional juice treat and sticker would be given. The youngster's ability to reproduce the model's behavior in this situation (i.e., when asked to display what he had learned) constituted the *acquisition* measure. The results provided direct support for distinguishing between two separate aspects of imitative learning, acquisition and performance. As expected, when incentives were specifically offered for demonstrating acquisition of the model's acts, the effects of punishment were wiped out, with all groups showing the same very high level of learning.

This work, as well as a number of successful replications which have followed—e.g., Liebert and Fernandez (1970a), Liebert, Sobol, and Copemann (1972)—has practical implications. Consider, for example, popular entertainment which displays to children the intricate details and planning required for the execution of remarkable acts of larceny or homicide. Widespread showing of these adventures is often justified by the fact that the performers of such felonious acts are inevitably punished. However, even though witnessing punished crimes may be unlikely to lead to spontaneous imitation, Bandura's work shows that punishment does not impede learning of them; later they may be reproduced in "real life," should the environmental contingencies ever unambiguously favor their occurrence.

The Forms and Sequence of Observational Learning

Just as classical conditioning and instrumental learning show generalization (i.e., they extend beyond the situation in which learning originally occurred), observational learning involves more than the recall and exact reproduction of a model's responses. To understand these additional processes, we must distinguish between direct imitative effects and inhibition-disinhibition.

Direct Imitative Effects. We have seen that exposure to a model can lead to relatively exact copying of the exemplary behavior, either immediately or when the environmental conditions are made conducive; this is *direct imitation*. Observing another's behavior also can *reduce* the probability of matching. The child who sees a peer burned by a hot stove, for example, typically will become *less* likely to touch the dangerous appliance than previously; he accepts the exemplar's actions and consequences as a guide for what he should not do. Such an outcome may be thought of as *direct counter-imitation*.

Inhibitory and Disinhibitory Effects. Imitation and counter-imitation do not apply only to behaviors specifically displayed by a model; they may also apply to actions which fall into the same general class as those observed, but which are different in virtually all particulars. A youngster who observes a movie filled with shooting and brawling, for example, may become more likely to yell at or push a younger sibling than if he had not seen exemplary hostilities. In such a case we note that aggressive responses in general have been influenced or *disinhibited*. Similarly, a child who, on the first day of class, sees that the new teacher punishes one of his classmates for disrupting the lesson may subsequently be less likely to turn in his first homework assignment late. Failing to turn in homework and speaking out inappropriately in class, though not identical, fall into a common class of behavior—disobedience to the dictates of the teacher—and thus the second child's general *inhibition* regarding breaking the rules may be traced to the first child's disruption of the class and the negative consequences which it brought him.

Observational learning, then, is a complex process which appears to extend beyond the mere copying of the model's behavior (Davidson and Liebert, 1972). It involves exposure to the responses of others, learning and recalling what one has seen, abstracting classes of behavior, and subsequently accepting the modeled behavior, sometimes after substantial generalization or sophisticated assessment of "what it tells you," as a guide for one's own actions. The sequence itself is presented graphically in Figure V–10 (cf. Liebert, 1972).

A Note on Social Learning

We have seen thus far that each of the three basic types of learning—associative, instrumental, and observational—is implicated in children's social behavior as well as in their acquiring facts and informatoin. Emphasis on the role of such learning processes characterizes a number of "social learning" views of development. These approaches to complex behavior rely heavily on basic learning principles and the relatively more rigorous methods of experimental analysis (e.g., Bandura and Walters, 1963; Miller and Dollard, 1941; Parke, 1972; Rotter, Chance, and Phares, 1972). In later chapters, we shall have occasion to mention and describe the social learning outlook further.

COMPLEX PROCESSES IN LEARNING

Children as well as adults often display a remarkable capacity to process the information to which they are exposed; they can solve whole classes of tasks, retain facts in compacted or coded form, and integrate various bits of old information in an "insightful" way in order to solve new problems. Developmental psychologists have only begun to investigate and understand these complex processes, but what has been disclosed already shows much promise in terms of both furthering our basic understanding of the learning process and suggesting new applications for education.

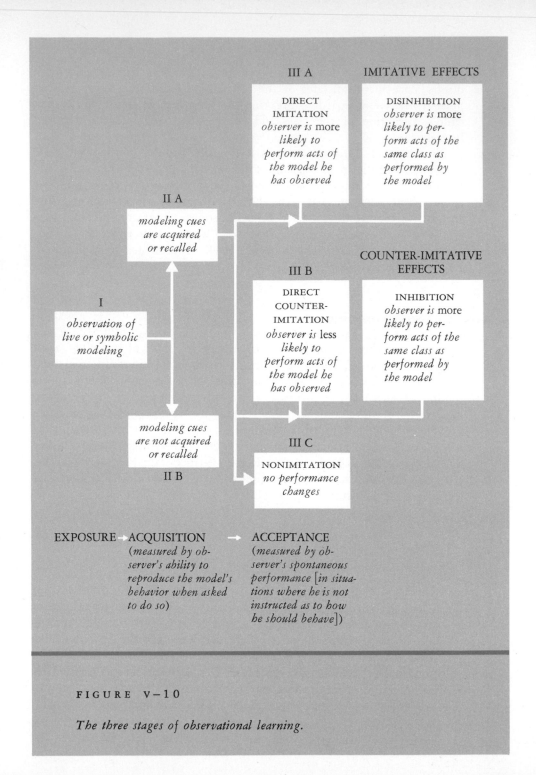

Learning Sets

Trial and Error versus Insight. Finding the solution required by a new problem situation is one important kind of learning. Historically, two types of approaches to problem solving have been recognized: trial and error, and insight. Trial and error, as we have seen already, was first experimentally studied by Thorndike, who placed his subjects (chicks, dogs, and cats) into a box from which they could escape to obtain food only by performing a specific response. According to his observations, complex reasoning was not involved:

> The cat does not look over the situation, much less *think* it over, and then decide what to do. It bursts out at once into the activities which instinct and experience have settled on as suitable reactions to the situation "confinement when hungry with food outside." The one impulse, out of many accidental ones, which leads to pleasure, becomes strengthened thereby, and more and more firmly associated with the sense-impression of that box's interior. . . . Futile impulses are gradually stamped out. The gradual slope of the time curve, then, shows the absence of reasoning. [1898, p. 45.]

But the trying out of behaviors, more or less randomly, or the accidental stumbling on correct solutions is not typical for humans, although it may be found in the very inexperienced. Most instances of trial and error involve some selection of particular acts which have been successful in the past (Berlyne, 1970).

Long ago, Wolfgang Köhler suggested that organisms come to solve problems by discovering relations or principles inherent in the situation. Such apparently insightful behavior was demonstrated in Köhler's studies of apes who were given food placed just beyond their reach. At some point the animals suddenly appeared to realize the solution—using a stick to pull the food toward them. Insight involved, then, an internal restructuring of the situation in terms of the relations of its aspects to each other.

As it turns out, trial and error and insight are not as distinguishable as they once appeared. Insight can be interpreted as the result of previous experiences in somewhat different situations. One psychologist who has taken such a tack in searching for higher mental processes which explain complex learning is Harry F. Harlow. After many years of research, Harlow feels that the key can be found in a single concept, the *learning set*.

His work began with simple discrimination problems, employing both young children and monkeys. For example, in one type of experiment monkeys were permitted to choose one of two objects which had been placed on a board. The correct and incorrect choices always had some distinctive feature, such as color (black versus white) or size (large versus small). If the monkey picked up the item which possessed the correct feature, he found a reward (a peanut or a raisin) underneath. The procedure was repeated many times, with hundreds of different objects placed at various positions on the board in an irregular manner. Initially, the monkeys learned each new problem slowly, by a "fumble and find" process. However, ". . . as a monkey solved problem after problem its behavior changed in a most dramatic way. It learned each new problem with progressively greater efficiency, until eventually the monkey showed perfect insight when faced with this particular kind of situation—it solved the problem in one trial" (Harlow and Harlow, 1949, p. 3).

Research with children showed essentially the same phenomenon. The youngsters made many errors at the beginning, usually of the same type made by the monkeys, but gradually came to solve the class of problems —for example, by always picking the red object—in a single trial. It is this process of progressive "learning to learn" about common features of problems that we have in mind when speaking of learning sets.

Further evidence that a true organizational habit has been established comes from research in which the relevant cue is suddenly reversed; that is, the previously incorrect object is now rewarded while the one that had been correct no longer leads to reward. Such switchovers, called *reversal shifts,* lead to many errors initially. But after extensive experience, the child appears to learn this set as well. We see, after training, perfect performance immediately following the first reversal trial. Even more important, the evidence shows that such sets, once acquired, are retained for long periods of time. When problem types which took weeks to master are reintroduced after a whole year without practice, monkeys will return to top efficiency after a few hours of practice—and sometimes after only a few minutes.

What are the implications of these findings? Harlow and Harlow (1949) have put it this way:

> Suppose we picture mental activity as a continuous structure built up, step by step, by the solution of increasingly difficult problems, from the simplest problem in learning to the most complex one in thinking. At each level the individual tries out various responses to solve each given task. At the lowest level he selects from unlearned responses or previously learned habits. As his experience increases, habits that do not help in the solution drop out and useful habits become established. After solving many problems of a certain kind, he develops organized patterns of responses that meet the demands of this type of situation. These patterns, or learning sets, can also be applied to the solution of still more complex problems. Eventually the indi-

vidual may organize simple sets into more complex patterns or learning sets, which in turn are available for transfer as units to new situations. . . . At the highest level in this progression, the intelligent human adult selects from innumerable, previously acquired learning sets the raw material for thinking. His many years of education in school and outside have been devoted to building up these complex learning sets, and he comes to manipulate them with such ease that he and his observers may lose sight of their origin and development. [p. 5.]

Although it is apparent that learning sets are acquired and used, even by young children, we must still ask what psychological processes underlie or facilitate their formation. One answer may lie in the phenomenon known as verbal mediation.

Verbal Mediation

Many theories of learning postulate some intervening or mediating process between an external stimulus and an overt response. Tracy and Howard Kendler have focused on the role of *verbal mediation* in learning, postulating that the intervening response involves the use of covert language in the development of thought. Consider this example

> . . . in which children ranging in age from two-and-one-half years to about six years were required to choose a 6.1 inch square in preference to a 8.2 inch square. . . . After consistently selecting the smaller square, the children were presented with a pair of much smaller squares (1.4 and 1.9 inches) to determine which they preferred. The youngest children responded on a chance basis—they chose the larger square as often as the smaller one. In other words, there was no transfer between the first and second problems for the younger children. For them, the two problems were separate and distinct. But the older children consistently selected the smaller square. Why this difference? The older children conceptualized the two different tasks as representing a common problem. They frequently verbalized the principle that "the smaller one is correct" when learning the initial problem. This principle was then transferred to the second problem. The experiment illustrates how mediated symbolic reactions can help abstract a common feature from two different problems. [Kendler, 1968, p. 376.]

The Kendlers (Kendler and Kendler, 1962; Kendler, 1963) proposed that discrimination learning cannot adequately be represented by a simple associative habit in which the external stimulus is directly connected to the overt response. Rather, it must be assumed that the external stimulus evokes an internal response—in the above example, the statement that "the smaller one is correct"—which mediates the external response.

To demonstrate the utility of this approach, the Kendlers tested children in a simple discrimination learning task. First, pairs of stimuli which differed on two dimensions were presented. Rewarded each time that they responded to one of these—i.e., the relevant dimension—children learned the solution to the problem. For example, a child was shown two cups. One was black and the other white; one—sometimes the black one, sometimes the white—was large and the other small. Each time he selected the large cup, regardless of whether it was black or white, he received a reward; selecting the small cup never led to reward during training. Thus, the child learned that size was the relevant dimension while color was unimportant, for both black and white cups had been rewarded about half the time. Some subjects were then shifted to reversals: size remained relevant but they now had to pick the *small* cup in order to be correct. Other subjects were shifted to *nonreversals*—i.e., the relevant dimension changed to color so that the *black* cup, for example, had to be chosen regardless of whether it was small or large. (See Figure V–11.)

A simple learning analysis would assume that reversal shifts would be the more difficult task; a response that had been consistently rewarded (large) has to be replaced by a response that had never been rewarded (small). In the nonreversal shift, the newly correct response (black) had been previously rewarded each time the large cup happened to be black. Because it should be easier to strengthen a response which already has been rewarded, nonreversals should be learned more easily than reversals. On the other hand, the mediational hypothesis predicts the opposite outcome. Nonreversals require that the overt response and the mediating response (attending to the dimension, whether size or color) both change; reversal shifts require only that overt responses change. Thus, according to this analysis, organisms effectively using mediation will do better on reversal shift problems. This is exactly what occurs.

> Human adults accomplish a reversal shift much more rapidly than a nonreversal shift . . . whereas rats find a nonreversal shift easier. . . . The explanation for this difference lies in the manner in which rats and humans solve discrimination problems. Rats learn simple habits. Initially they learn to approach black and avoid white. A reversal shift is terribly difficult for them because they have to extinguish completely a habit that has been continuously reinforced and then develop a new habit that has not been previously reinforced. Human adults, on the other hand, find a reversal shift easy to make because they do not simply associate their choice response directly to the relevant stimuli but make instead a mediational implicit response which functions as a cue for their choice. For example, if the correct

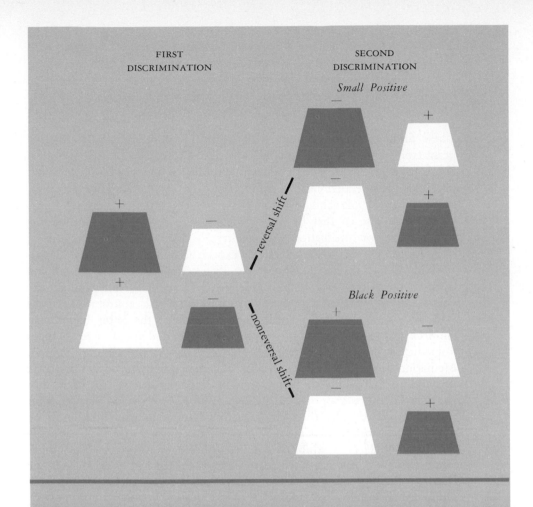

FIRST
DISCRIMINATION

SECOND
DISCRIMINATION

Small Positive

reversal shift

nonreversal shift

Black Positive

FIGURE V—11

Examples of a reversal and a nonreversal shift, where (+) indicates the rewarded and (−) the nonrewarded stimuli. Adapted from H. H. Kendler and T. S. Kendler, Vertical and horizontal processes in problem-solving. Psychological Review, *1962, 69, 1-16. Copyright 1962 by the American Psychological Association. Reproduced by permission.*

stimulus is black, the human generates a symbolic response (e.g., the "darker" or "black but not white") which serves as the cue for the selection of the correct alternative. Since a similar kind of symbolic response is appropriate in a reversal shift, this kind of shift is easy for humans to accomplish.

In a nonreversal shift, however, the human subject must learn an entirely new symbolic response (i.e., from "darker" to "larger" or "smaller"); he therefore finds it more difficult than a reversal shift. [Kendler, 1968, pp. 376–377.]

These findings posed the interesting problem of locating the transition point from simple stimulus-response association to mediation. The Kendlers chose to work with young children in order to investigate mediational processes. In an experiment which typifies their results (Kendler, Kendler, and Learnard, 1962), children from three to ten years of age showed a progressive increase so that by approximately age seven, over half of the subjects employed mediation. (See Figure V–12).

Failure to use mediation effectively can be accounted for by several possibilities. The child may be able to produce verbalizations but not employ them as mediators (*mediational deficiency*). Or he may not produce the verbalizations, even though he is familiar with the appropriate words (*production deficiency*). In an attempt to evaluate the latter hypothesis, children were shown pictures of common objects and asked to recall them immediately or after a short delay (Flavell, Beach, and Chinsky, 1966). Mediation was assessed by observation of their verbalizing or moving their lips and by later asking them how they had gone about the task of memorization. Fifth graders produced more mediators than second graders, who in turn mediated more than kindergartners. Inasmuch as virtually all of the subjects were able to name the items when requested to do so, it appears that the younger ones exhibited a deficiency in production. As the authors point out, they may not have learned to use language as mediators, or alternatively they may not have learned a strategy (verbal coding and rehearsal) for solving the task.

Hypothesis Testing

When position of stimuli is the basis for rewarded outcomes in a discrimination task, subjects of six, eleven, and nineteen years increasingly choose stimuli consistent with this solution, with the older two groups doing only slightly better than the six-year-olds (Odom and Coon, 1966). Nevertheless, differences in performance emerge when the basis for reward is shifted. In such a situation the youngest children persist in choosing stimuli according to their position, while the remaining subjects do not. It is as if the latter groups begin to try out new hypotheses or predictions in order to solve the problem.

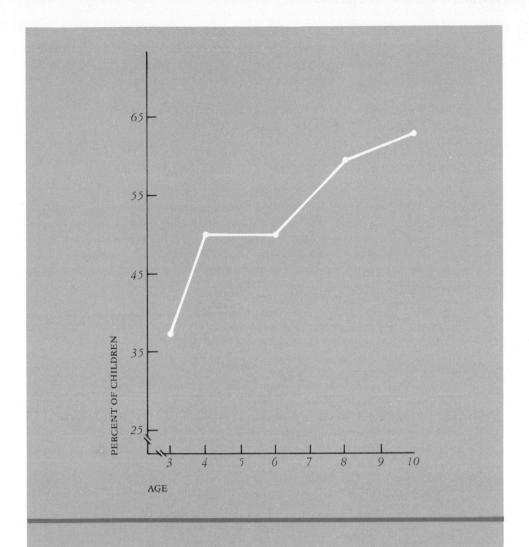

FIGURE V—12

Percentage of children of different ages responding in a mediational manner. Adapted from H. H. Kendler and T. S. Kendler, Vertical and horizontal processes in problem-solving. Psychological Review, *1962, 69, 1-16. Copyright 1962 by the American Psychological Association. Reproduced by permission.*

Marvin Levine, who has addressed himself to hypothesis testing in adults (e.g., Levine, 1966), has more recently focused on children's performance. His work, exemplified in Selection 4, illustrates an ingenious method for exploring problem solving, the most complex of learning processes.

SELECTION 4

THE DEVELOPMENT OF HYPOTHESIS TESTING

Marvin Levine

Let me begin by briefly reviewing the details of discrimination learning. A pair of stimuli are presented and the organism is required to make one of two responses (see Figure 1), usually characterized as a choice between the stimuli themselves or as a response toward the right or the left. If the experiment is done with children the youngster might be asked to push the one he has chosen. Out of sight underneath one of the stimuli is a reward, perhaps an M&M; underneath the other is nothing. Typically, the experimenter follows the rule of placing the reward under the same form (e.g., the triangle) on each trial.

Note that the experimenter could, if he wished, apply the rule that he would always put the reward on the left side. So the reward can be contingent on either one of the positions, (the forms, you will remember, vary randomly from side to side) or it can be contingent on one of the forms. We say,

therefore, that there are two dimensions in this task, a form dimension and a position dimension. Only one of the dimensions is the *revelant* dimension,

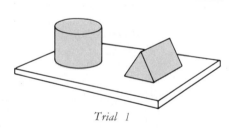

Trial 1

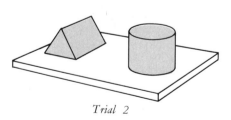

Trial 2

This paper is based upon a talk presented to the Clinical Graduate Program, State University of New York at Stony Brook, 1973. The experiments herein were supported by Research Grant MH–11857 from the National Institute of Mental Health. Reproduced by permission of the author.

FIGURE 1

A typical discrimination learning problem.

the one containing the cue to which reward is tied; the other is *irrelevant*. Consider the typical discrimination procedure referred to above in which food is always under the triangle. Here form is the relevant dimension; position is irrelevant.

Conditioning Theory and Discrimination Learning

For many decades it was assumed that conditioning theory could be applied to this task. To see how this was done, take the case in which the reward is always behind the triangle. According to conditioning theory, every time the child responds to the triangle, pushing the triangle is rewarded and, hence, is strengthened a bit. The child's response to the circle would be an extinction event since no reward ever follows it. Pushing the circle, therefore, would tend to become less likely. Over a series of trials these two processes would gradually accumulate in their effect and soon you would have the characteristic state that we call "learned": the child would always choose the triangle and never the circle.

The presence of an irrelevant dimension—here, position—offers no difficulty to the theory. In the present example, over a series of trials *triangle-and-food* is on the left for half the time and on the right for half the time. In balance, neither position gains; the cues within an irrelevant dimension tend to stay equal in strength throughout the experiment. On the other hand, the cue from the relevant dimension (the triangle, in the example above) is always being strengthened in its ability to evoke the response and, thus, comes to control choice behavior.

This kind of theory has been considered applicable not only to rats and monkeys, but also to children and to adult humans (college students, no less). Indeed, in the decade of the 1950's a serious attempt was made to apply it to the adult human. This is an important sociological fact to which I will return in a moment. First, though, I want to mention an adjustment which was made in the task.

The discrimination shown in Figure 1 is trivial for adults, who usually learn it in one or two trials. A straightforward way to make the task more difficult is to add more dimensions. Figure 2 shows an example of stimuli from what I shall, for the moment, call a five-dimensional task. It contains two forms located in two positions, but the forms can be black or white, large or small, and with a bar above or a bar below the form. Just as the forms in Figure 1 varied randomly with respect to position, each of the various dimensions in Figure 2 varies with respect to all the others. Figure 2, then, portrays a *multi-dimensional* task in which the experimenter picks one of the dimensions to be relevant. Except that there are several irrelevant dimensions, the task is the same as that in Figure 1.

Hypothesis Testing

In the 1950's conditioning theory was applied to adult human performance on this more complex task and, for several years, it appeared that the application was successful. However, by 1960 a change began to creep into theoretical notions. One important reason that the change appeared is worth noting because it is almost unique to the science dealing with the behavior of adult hu-

STIMULI
PRESENTED

TRIAL

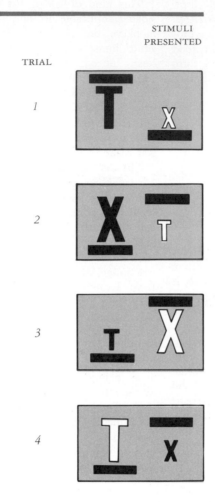

FIGURE 2

A stimulus sequence from a five-di-
mensional discrimination learning task.

mans: The human subject shares many
properties with the human experimenter. The experimenter is like his
subject matter in a sense that does not
hold for any other science. A physicist,

for example, is not like an atom, nor a
physiologist like a kidney. It is even a
little far fetched to say that a biologist
is like a rat. However, the psychologist
is like his (adult human) subject. He
can, in fact, serve as a subject, i.e., have
someone "run" him in these problems.
When he does this, he has access to
processes going on inside himself; he
can get a feeling for what is going on
in this situation in terms of his own experience. When you run yourself in this
task, you realize that a lot of complicated things are going on inside. You
do not feel that the correct response is
gradually being pulled out of you.
Rather you feel that you are searching
for the correct response, first trying out
one thing, and then trying out another.
In a phrase, you seem to be testing
hypotheses. Such experiences motivated
theorists to explore what is now called
Hypothesis (abbreviated H) Theory.

The basic assumption in H Theory is
quite commonsensical. It is that the
subject begins the task with some set of
H's, and samples one. That H dictates
his response. Imagine an adult facing
the problem in Figure 2. Seeing the top
stimulus, he might hypothesize that
large is the solution. According to the
basic assumption, this subject will
choose the left-hand alternative. There
are other details to the early form of
the theory which I am not going to go
into, but the general conception was
that the subject goes through the task
searching for the correct hypothesis.

A hypothesis is viewed as a state of
the learner, so that a subject who believes that X is the solution to the
problem in Figure 2 is in a different
state from one who believes that *large*
is the solution. My own orientation was
that it would be valuable if we could
probe for the hypothesis held by a sub-

ject at any given point in time; I wanted to develop a technique permitting us to say after any trial, "Oh, yes, he thinks X is the solution at this moment." A very obvious probe, which might have occurred to you, is to ask him: "What do you think the solution is now?" While that appears to be a straightforward probe, it was not used —for a number of reasons. Verbal reports were, and to some extent still are, in bad repute. Their validity was suspect; conditioning theorists who were still holding to the older kind of theory would never accept verbal reports as data. Furthermore, I foresaw applying this theory to research with children and even with animals. I sought, therefore, a probe for the H that would be more generally applicable than is a verbal report. What might work?

In practice, an experimental restriction was necessary. I wanted to assume that the subject (either because of his history with some of the problems, or because of some instructions we give) would try only the simple Hs associated with the four stimulus dimensions. That is, at the beginning of a problem he would recognize that the solution could be *large,* or *small,* or *black,* or *white,* or *bar up,* or *bar down,* or *X,* or *T* (for reasons to be mentioned below, *positions* as a dimension will be ignored). He would never think, for example, that "If the experimenter scratches his head I'll press the left side, and when he is not scratching his head I'll press the right side." In practice, the assumption is met by giving the subject careful instructions; we are nice people and he believes us. It is in this restricted situation that we are going to probe for the subject's H. I was no longer trying to prove that subjects tested Hs. There were earlier data

which provided a reasonable foundation for this theory (Bower and Trabasso, 1964; Levine, 1963). I was concerned now with a method for determining which of the eight Hs a subject was holding.

The solution followed from some consideration of the rewards used. You don't have to give a college student a raisin or an M&M for him to learn this task. The words "right" and "wrong" function for him as raisin/no raisin for the monkey. The experimenter also has a third option as an outcome for a trial: he can be silent. Trials on which the experimenter says nothing had been widely used, and came to be called *blank trials.* I began to see that blank trials provide the sought-after H probe. One simple assumption was needed, that during a set of consecutive blank trials the subject, obtaining no feedback, keeps his H and this H dictates his responses during that series. Consider, for example, the stimuli at the center of Figure 3, representing four successive blank trials presented at some point in the problem. Suppose that at the start of this trial series the subject thinks that *black* is the solution to the problem. According to the *blank-trial* assumption just stated, the subject will choose *black* each time, which will be exhibited by three consecutive choices on the left and then one choice on the right. In general, if the assumption is correct, over a series of four blank trials, the H leads to a particular response pattern. What I realized is that you can arrange stimuli so that each possible H leads to a different unique response pattern through the four blank trials.

Each column of Figure 3 shows the response pattern that each of the eight hypotheses will produce. Note that for

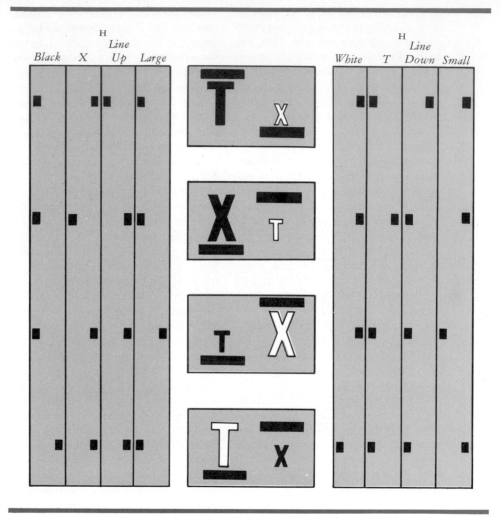

FIGURE 3

A stimulus sequence which permits inference of the eight simple Hs from 3-1 patterns of response.

each of the eight possible hypotheses the subject will generate a different pattern of responses. We can present the four blank trials, look at the pattern of response, and then infer what the hypothesis must be.

This, then, is the probe technique based upon the blank-trial assumption.

How can we test the technique and demonstrate that the response patterns do indeed reflect *H?* One test depends upon the character of the response patterns shown in Figure 3. Note that for each of the eight stipulated hypotheses, each response pattern consists of three responses to one side and one to the other. If the subject shows two responses to each side, or all four responses to one side, the response pattern would not reflect one of the eight simple *H*s associated with the four stimulus dimensions. If the blank-trial assumption or the theory were generally wrong, then the 2–2 and 4–0 patterns should occur as often as the 3–1 patterns. For example, if during these blank trials the subject said to himself, "Well these don't count anyway," and closed his eyes and responded, the hypothesis patterns should occur only fifty percent of the time.

The experiment (Levine, 1966) to evaluate the validity of the blank-trial probe was done as follows: A group of college students were presented with these four-dimensional problems. After each feedback (right-wrong) trial a series of four blank trials was presented. The experimental procedure is schematized in Figure 4. We first determined the percentage of time that these blank-trial patterns were in fact hypothesis (i.e., 3–1) patterns. In this first experiment, the *H* patterns occurred on more than 90 percent of the probes. In a variety of experiments that have been done since, 90–95 percent of these probes have shown hypothesis patterns. The theory, then, passed this first test very nicely.

We also have some intuitive notions about hypothesis testing. When *H*s are disconfirmed, we assume that they are abandoned; when they are confirmed

they tend, we assume, to be retained. These everyday assumptions may be investigated directly. We can look at all those feedback trials where the subjects are told they are correct. In theoretical terms the *H* just preceding that feedback trial has been confirmed. We may now determine whether the subject shows the same *H* following that feed-

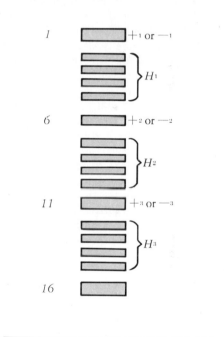

FIGURE 4

Schematization of the blank-trial procedure showing the trials on which the experimenter said right or wrong (+ or −) and the blank trials from which the subject's hypotheses (H_1, H_2, H_3) were inferred after each feedback trial.

back trial. The effects of a "wrong" may be determined in a similar way. We look at all those feedback trials on which the subject was told "wrong" and determine whether the next H is the same as the preceding. Figure 5 shows the results of these tests. The top curve indicates the probability that subjects repeat their hypotheses when there is an intervening "correct." The points represent eight different, independent estimates of that probability. The mean here is .95. It is safe to say that the subject keeps his hypothesis when that hypothesis is confirmed. The lower curve in Figure 5 shows the probability of seeing the same hypothesis when it is *dis*confirmed; on the intervening trial these subjects were told "wrong." The mean is .02. Subjects virtually never keep their H after a wrong. Thus, we again see a confirmation both of the fundamental idea that the subject is testing hypotheses and of the validity of the blank-trial probe. Notice another detail: there is nothing cumulative about the effects of a "right" or a "wrong." A single feedback makes a dramatic difference. The subject either keeps his hypothesis or abandons it in all-or-nothing fashion. Finally, we see that the subject tries a new H after a "wrong," coming up with one of the remaining seven. This means that the subject remembers both the hypothesis he was just holding and that it was disconfirmed. We might imagine a subject whose memory was so terrible that after a "wrong" he forgot what H he had just been holding! He knows he must resample but he doesn't know which of the eight Hs can be eliminated. In such a case the probability of repeating the just-disconfirmed H would not be close to zero but would be one out of eight

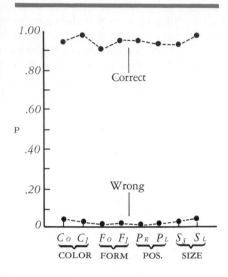

FIGURE 5

The probability that an H *is repeated after the experimenter says correct (top curve) and wrong (bottom curve).*

(.125). He would be just as likely to come up with the just-disconfirmed H as with any of the other seven. I am making specific mention of this memory consideration because it will be important when we look at the children's data.

Studies with Children

Several years later, we started similar experiments with children. In the initial experiment, second graders, fourth graders, sixth graders, and college students were the subjects (Gholson, Levine, and Phillips, 1972). All subjects received the standard pretraining.

They were first told that the solution would be one of eight simple possibilities. They were then given sample problems which exemplified that fact, and which introduced blank trials. These pretraining problems were followed by the standard experimental problems. The same basic tests were made, with some of the same basic results. The three groups of school children showed one of the eight simple *H*s on about 90 percent of the probes and, when told "right," retained the same *H* about 95 percent of the time. In these ways they resembled the adults.

They differed, however, in another way. Recall that adults virtually never keep the same *H* after a *"wrong."* When a child was told "wrong," on the other hand, the probability of his repeating the *H* immediately was about 10 percent, close to the 12.5 percent chance figure that I mentioned above. This value, you will recall, will occur if the subjects forget the *H* that was just disconfirmed. Other researchers using this technique obtained values ranging from 9 percent to 18 percent (Eimas, 1969; Ingalls and Dickerson, 1969). The results seemed to fluctuate around the zero-memory value. It was a puzzling result. I myself couldn't believe that a sixth grader, a ten or eleven year old, would so quickly forget an *H* he had just tried. When we came to look at performance records of individual children, we began to see the explanation. There were a few subjects who, on some problems, showed a stimulus preference that had nothing to do with *H* testing. Some youngsters chose, for example, *large, large, large, . . .* and didn't care whether you told them "right" or "wrong." Presumably they happened to like the large stim-

ulus. These children with a stimulus preference who repeat their *H* after a "wrong" naturally inflated that statistic. If a child doesn't have that mode of responding then he always changes his *H* when it is disconfirmed. The overall 10 percent value, then, had nothing to do with memory. We were just jumbling together two different modes of behaving and trying to talk about some kind of average, which, of course, is misleading.

Whereas adults have a single uniform type of responding, it appeared that children had at least two: stimulus preference and normal *H* testing Wondering whether there were other response styles, we started to look through the protocols.

Consider the most sophisticated style that anyone might show, a mode of testing *H*s that, in this task, always guarantees solution after the third trial. Suppose that the subject, starting out with the *H* "white," chooses the right-hand side of the top stimulus in Figure 2 and is told "wrong." He might say, "Well, it can't be any of these four (on the right); it must be one of these other four." Thus he not only remembers the specific hypothesis that was just disconfirmed, but also recognizes (and remembers) that three others are disconfirmed. Thus, the first feedback permits him to eliminate four *H*s and to narrow his efforts to the remaining four good *H*s. In a similar way, the second feedback trial permits him to eliminate two of these four; the remaining two acceptable *H*s lead to two different responses on the third feedback trial. The response called correct on that third trial, then, defines the solution.

Suppose a subject is being this logical. What will his performance record look like? After his first feedback trial, his H will be one of the four good ones. If he is told wrong on the second feedback trial, his next H will be one of the two good ones, and, if he is told wrong at the third feedback trial, his third H will be the solution. Because he quickly narrows down the number of solutions from 8 to 1, we refer to this H sequence as *Focusing.* The general procedure, then, is to look at a subject's individual protocol and at the sequence of Hs he shows. From that sequence we infer what system he is using on the problem. It is easy enough to spot a child who has a stimulus preference. We look at those problems where he is told "wrong." The child who has a stimulus preference is going to continue to show the same H despite disconfirmations. The top row of Table 1 contains an example of Stimulus Preference: the subject is told "right" (+) on the first trial and "wrong" (−) on the next series of trials, but shows *"large, large, large, large,"* keeping the same H throughout. At the very bottom of Table 1, a manifestation of Focusing is shown.

We saw two other kinds of patterns in children's protocols. Let's first look at Hypothesis Checking, shown in the second row of Table 1. In Hypothesis Checking, it is as though the child imagines a list of the eight Hs, paired by dimension. Thus, at the top of his list might be the words large-small, then white-black, with X-T, and bar up-bar down following. What he does is go through his list trying first both Hs from one dimension, then both from the next, and so on. Our hypothetical subject might first try *large* and if that doesn't work, *small,* and if that doesn't

work he goes to the next dimension. In this case he tries *white* and if that doesn't work, he tries *black,* and so on. The second row of Table 1 contains a representative protocol of Hypothesis Checking for a child who on the Feedback trials was told right, wrong, wrong, wrong. The H sequence shows both cues within a dimension before changing dimensions, a different pattern of Hs from Stimulus Preference and from Focusing.

Finally, we have a fourth system called Dimension Checking (see the third row of Table 1). I will not labor the details of this system. The H pattern shows that the subject changes his dimension each time you tell him he is wrong, but he does not do it in the maximally efficient way. At H_2 he will show us a hypothesis from a new dimension, but it is not necessarily one of the two good ones. Or if it is, and we tell him wrong at Feedback$_3$, a child who is following Dimension Checking will show an H from a third dimension at H_3, but it is not necessarily the solution.

We stipulated these four patterns of Hs just from an informal survey of protocols. It seems to us that we were seeing four kinds of H sequences, referred to as four different *Systems.*

It is evident that these Systems vary in their efficiency. Thus, the Focusing System produces the solution before the fourth feedback trial. The Dimension Checking System, if the child's memory for his performance with this System is good, should require no more than four errors for solution. The Hypothesis Checking System requires no more than eight errors for solution. These three Systems in principle will lead to the solution; collectively they are referred

TABLE 1

THE SYSTEMS, THEIR DEFINITIONS, AND MANIFESTATIONS

SYSTEM	DEFINITION	EXAMPLE OF MANIFESTATION							
		Feedback$_1$	H$_1$	Feedback$_2$	H$_2$	Feedback$_3$	H$_3$	Feedback$_4$	H$_4$
Stimulus Preference	Stays with one *H* even though it is disconfirmed	+	H$_i$ (large)	—	H$_i$ (large)	—	H$_i$ (large)	—	H$_i$ (large)
Hypothesis Checking	Checks all *eight hypotheses* systematically, one dimension at a time	+	H$_i$ (large)	—	opH$_i$ (small)	—	H$_j$ (white)	—	opH$_j$ (black)
Dimension Checking	Checks all *four dimensions* systematically, one dimension at a time	+	H$_i$ (large)	—	H$_j$ (white)	—	H$_k$ (bar down)	—	H$^+$ (T)
Focusing	Eliminates immediately all logically disconfirmed *H*s	+	H$_i$ (large)	—	H$_j$ (white)	—	(H$_k$ = H$^+$) (T)	—	H$^+$ (T)

Note: H$_i$ = an *H* from the ith dimension;
opH$_i$ = the other *H* from the ith dimension;
H$_j$ = an *H* from the jth dimension;
H$^+$ = the solution.

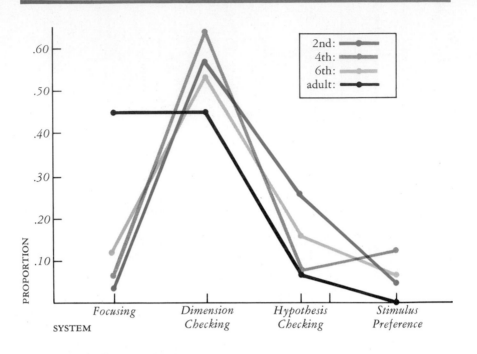

FIGURE 6

The frequency of distributions of the four Systems for each grade, ordered from most to least sophisticated.

to as *strategies*. The fourth System, Stimulus Preference, is characterized as a stereotype; it will never result in a solution unless, of course, it just happens to coincide with the correct *H*. We might remark, in passing, that there are other possible stereotypes. In particular, children might show a Position-Preference System (e.g., always picking the left side) or a Position-Alternation System. They are easily detectable in the protocols since they produce unique response patterns. These are even more primitive than

Stimulus Preference, since they entail response to a dimension specifically excluded by instructions and pretraining. These position stereotypes were omitted from Table 1, because they never appeared in the experiment under discussion.

We have, then, four different Systems. We systematically went through each protocol where children received feedback patterns like that shown in Table 1, and assigned that protocol to one of these four systems. In this way we obtained the frequency with which

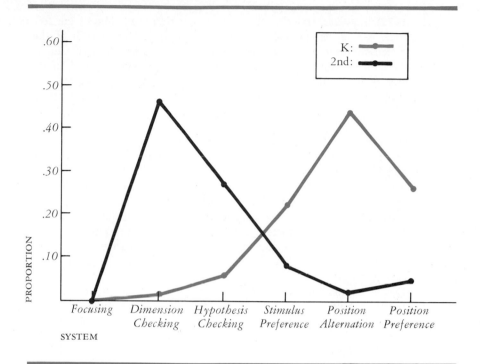

F I G U R E   7

The frequency distributions over the Systems for kindergarten and second-grade subjects.

Stimulus Preference, Hypothesis Checking, and so forth, each occurred. We obtained, in short, the frequency distribution separately for the second, fourth, sixth graders, and adults. These four frequency distributions are shown in Figure 6.

The solid line is the frequency distribution for adults. Focusing is the most frequent System for adults, occurring slightly more often than Dimension Checking. The adult, interestingly, never shows Stimulus Preference; a college student never does that thing that monkeys frequently demonstrate. The dashed lines in Figure 6 show the distributions for the second, fourth, and sixth grades. With these subjects Dimension Checking is the most frequent system; we see very little Focusing. Focusing occurs most frequently with sixth graders, but it is not that much different from the others. In general, these three distributions tend to look alike. It would appear that there are children and there are college students and that they are two different breeds. This is one possibility.

The next experiment (Gholson *et al.*, 1972), however, shows another difference. We ran second-grade and kindergarten children, performing essentially the same experiment and the same analysis. Figure 7 shows the frequency distributions for these two groups; note that the horizontal axis is slightly different from that in Figure 6. The latter contained only the four aforementioned systems, omitting Position-Preference and Position-Alternation stereotypes. It was obvious at the outset, however, that the kindergarten children were showing such patterns. We categorized the present protocols, therefore, into all six Systems. The distribution in Figure 7 for the second-grade children replicates the results of the previous study: Discrimination Checking is again most frequent, and Focusing doesn't occur. A small number of position stereotypes appeared this time, but the results are basically the same as before. The kindergarten children, by contrast, have a different distribution altogether. They are showing primarily those most primitive patterns, the stereotypes.

Furthermore, these youngsters respond to position more than to the characteristics of the stimuli. Most of the protocols showed Position-Alternation, i.e., showed the left-right-left-right pattern at each of the three *H*s (or, to stress the systematic character of this behavior, showed left-right for 16 consecutive responses).

The data collected from these last two experiments suggest, then, three classes of subjects. The youngest show primitive systematic patterns which are not sensitive to the pertinent task information. Their *H*s are from a dimension (position) excluded by instruction, and do not change when *E* says "wrong." Children between the ages of 7 and 11 years tend to show task-relevant approaches, using primarily strategies of intermediate efficiency. College students show no stereotypes; 90 percent of their strategies are of the two most efficient types.

The larger conclusions from this work relate to the contrast between conditioning and hypothesis theory described at the outset. The hypothesis conception not only conformed to our intuitions and made sense of the data, but afforded the basis for new insights into the development of increasingly sophisticated modes of solving complex problems.

VI

PERCEPTUAL DEVELOPMENT

THE STUDY OF PERCEPTUAL PROCESSES was a central aspect of early psychology, which inherited its concern with this issue from the philosophical debate about the way in which man comes to perceive his world. Until relatively recent times the distinction was not made, as it is today, between sensation and perception. *Sensation* refers to stimulation of the sensory apparatus by physical energies from the external and internal environment. *Perception,* on the other hand, is the process of extracting and using information acquired through the sense organs to organize the world. Thus, knowledge of sensation—for example, knowledge about the kinds and degree of stimulation humans can receive—tells us something but not all about perception.

AN OVERVIEW OF SENSATION AND PERCEPTION

Although school children often are taught that man has five senses, there are at least eight energy receptors. In the group of *proprioceptors,* or near senses, belong taste, the cutaneous senses, and smell. The *exteroceptors,* the ear and the eye, receive energy which originates from a distance—sometimes very great distances. Finally, the *interoceptors,* or deep senses, detect changes in body position, balance, and organic states, such as hunger and thirst. When external stimulation is received, it is translated immediately at the receptor site into a code that can be carried by the nervous system. The retina of the eye, although stimulated by light rays, translates them into electrochemical potentials; the Pacinian corpuscles similarly translate pressure on the skin into a neural code (Lowenstein, 1960).

The coded nerve impulses are then transmitted to the brain, where they are acted upon. The brain may act in a relatively simple way, merely relaying the impulses to various response systems, such as the muscles or glands. In many instances, however, intervening brain activity involves selection, reorganization, and modification of sensory inputs (Forgus, 1966). It is also known, although the processes are not completely understood, that parts of the brain cortex can transmit descending impulses which are capable of preventing the ascent of sensory impulses. In addition to such selection, the cortex also can integrate impulses from various senses and, it is postulated, can compare them to previous inputs. These functions are thought to result from and improve with experience; that is, there is increasing ability to select, reorganize, and modify information. It is easy to see, then, how perception may be interrelated with learning and thinking (see Figure VI–1):

> Some percepts are necessary before we can learn since we cannot acquire facts until we have first received them. Obviously a blind person cannot come to perceive or know the color of an object. And who would deny that the tools of thinking and learning depend to a large extent on what the individual has previously learned? . . . But it is also known that the result of thinking modifies future learning and that learning in turn can influence the way we perceive our world. We have only to think of the stereotypes about certain social or ethnic groups . . . to realize the extent to which learning determines the selectivity of perception. It is also established that learning improves perceptual discrimination and selection. . . . [Forgus, 1966, pp. 4–6.]

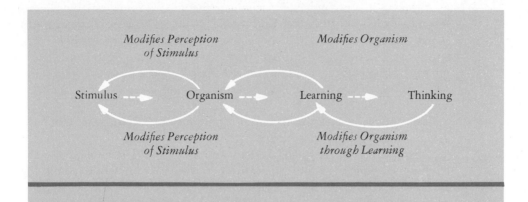

FIGURE VI–1

The interrelationship of perception, learning, and thinking. Adapted from Perception *by R. Forgus. Copyright 1966 McGraw-Hill Book Company. Used with permission of McGraw-Hill Book Company.*

Evidence that perception has occurred is seen in overt responses of the organism; in fact, perception must always be inferred from behavior for there is no direct way of observing it. Thus, whereas most individuals can verbalize what they perceive, identifying responses in the very young, with their poorly developed language and motor systems, has been a difficult task. Nevertheless, increasingly sophisticated methods have provided considerable detail about both early perception and basic sensory ability.

Some Basic Sensory Abilities

Our primary aim in this chapter is to outline human perceptual development; because so much of the relevant research focuses on it, our emphasis is on man's most important sense—vision. First, though, we will sketch briefly some of the other basic sensory abilities as they appear in the human child. In part, the purpose of this summary is to satisfy curiosity about the world of the infant, but it also sets the stage for further exploration of the nature of perceptual development.

Hearing. Although it is not possible to stimulate the unborn fetus visually, we can administer auditory stimulation prenatally. In an early study, Peiper (1925) found that many fetuses responded to a loud sound, an automobile horn, by movement. Similarly, a classic case study (Forbes and Forbes, 1927) reports that an eight-month fetus moved sharply in response to a loud noise while its mother was in the bath, and more recent literature (e.g., Bernard and Sontag [1947]) gives supportive findings.

Early studies of hearing in infants attempted to ascertain sensitivity to gross sounds such as those made by a bell or a tuning fork, but recent investigations have employed better controlled sound stimuli. Although fluidlike substances in the ear of the newborn may somewhat limit the ability to hear in the first few days of life, even very young infants respond to sound with a variety of responses, such as muscle change, breathing disruption, eye blinking, and changes in heart rate and activity level. Less well understood, however, are the specific intensities (or amplitudes, which are measured in decibels) and pitches (or frequencies, which are measured in cycles per second) to which responses are made.

Neonatal heart rate responds to sound between forty and seventy decibels (Pick and Pick, 1970; Steinschneider, 1967), so that conversation, which is in the range of thirty-five to seventy-five decibels, can serve as stimulation for the very young child. Other findings suggest that neonates can discriminate pitch differences of between six hundred and nine hundred cycles per second for the low pitch range (Bridger, 1961; Leventhal and Lipsitt, 1964).

A study of children from ages five to fourteen showed increased sensitivity until the ages of twelve to thirteen years for both sexes and for white and black children (Eagles, Wishik, Doerfler, Melnick, and Levine, as cited by Pick and Pick, 1970). Then, as seen in Figure VI–2, hearing ability decreases progressively through the adult years.

Taste. There have been few investigations of early sensitivity to gustatory stimulation and its development over time. Research has established, however, that the neonate is able to distinguish at least salt, sugar, lemon juice, and quinine (Nemanova, as cited by Pick, 1961), and an early preference for sugar over salt solution has been reported (Pratt, 1954). The neonate relaxes and sucks contentedly when presented with a sweet solution, but reacts to salty, sour, or bitter liquids by grimacing and irregular breathing.

Children's taste buds are more widely distributed on the tongue than adults', but it is not known whether and how this affects relative sensitivity (Pick and Pick, 1970). Interestingly, Korslund and Eppright (1967) found that children with the lowest sensitivity had more enthusiasm and acceptance for food.

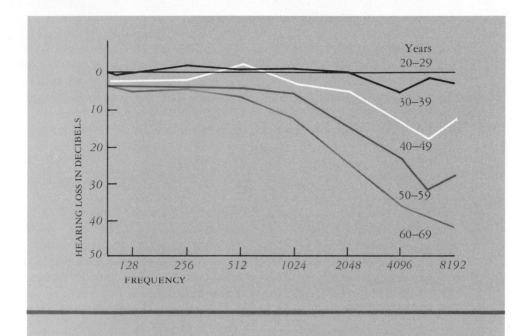

FIGURE VI–2

Audiogram for different age groups, showing hearing loss in higher frequencies as people grow older. Adapted from C. C. Bunch, Age variations in auditory acuity. Archives of Otolaryngology, *1929, 9, 625-636. Copyright 1929, American Medical Association, by permission.*

Cutaneous Senses. Research with prematurely delivered infants has shown that humans are able to respond to tactile stimulation early in life. Prematures respond to touch with fanning of the toes, slight motor responses, and waking from a half-sleep (Saint-Anne Dargassies, 1966). In the neonate, touching various areas of the body produces many of the reflexes discussed in Chapter III, including the Babinski reflex, the grasp reflex, and the rooting reflex. An increase in sensitivity to electric shock has been reported during the first few days of life (Lipsitt and Levy, 1959). Sex differences in sensitivity also appear, with the female being more sensitive; this finding holds for older individuals as well as neonates (Pick and Pick, 1970).

We know that sensitivity to painful stimuli is exhibited early, as shown by withdrawal and crying, but it probably is not well developed. The newborn responds to pinpricks and the number required to cause a reaction decreases over the first few days of life (Sherman and Sherman, 1925). Other developmental studies of localization of touch, with older children and adults, have been conducted by stimulating a point on the skin and requesting the individual, who has his eyes closed, to indicate where he has been touched. In two such experiments (Dunford, 1930; Renshaw, 1930) children performed better than adults. This appears to be a result of the greater reliance adults place upon visual perception, for older subjects are more precise than younger ones when the localization response is given with the eyes open.

Tactual stimulation becomes increasingly important as the young child develops sufficient motor ability to handle objects and navigate his surroundings. He is then able to collect information about the world as he feels the hard floor and soft carpet, the rough stones and the smooth sidewalk, or the round ball and the square block. Under usual circumstances, such perception is the result of the combination of touch and vision. But it is possible to examine the effects of touch only, by asking the individual to perform various tasks as he handles objects that are out of his sight. The ability to recognize objects tactually increases with age as exploration of the objects becomes more systematic (Gliner, 1967).

There is also reason to believe that the sense of touch can be developed more highly when experience and necessity conspire to sharpen it. Thus the blind are better than the sighted in using such cues (Hunter, 1954). Interestingly, blind persons who were sighted until later in life do best of all in tests of tactual perception.

Smell. Recent work with neonates has confirmed and extended earlier studies showing that infants are capable of discriminating odors. In a series of investigations infants were placed on a stabilimeter, which registers activity level, with a pneumograph around the abdomen to measure breathing (Figure VI–3). A cotton swab saturated with an odorant was then placed beneath their nostrils for ten seconds. Results indicated that neonates could discriminate the four odors employed, with repeated presentation of the substances resulting in weaker responses (Lipsitt, Engen, and Kaye, 1963; Engen, Lipsitt, and Kaye, 1963). McCartney (1968) has summarized several European studies showing that sensitivity to odors is well developed by the age of six, continues to improve until middle age, and then declines. Olfactory preferences also exhibit clear-cut changes with age and, as one might expect, smokers for over fifteen years have lower sensitivity than nonsmokers.

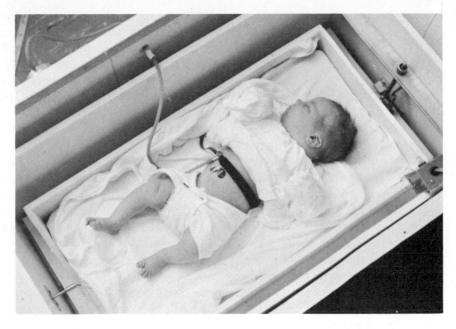

FIGURE VI-3

Neonate in a stabilimeter. Courtesy Dr. Lewis P. Lipsitt.

DEVELOPMENT OF VISUAL PERCEPTION

In many ways, vision may be considered our most important sense modality. Adults report that they value their eyesight more highly than any of their other senses and we use the visual mode to indicate understanding and comprehension that are not in fact related to ocular functions (e.g., "I see what you mean!"). It also has been argued that visual stimulation provides an extremely important source of contact between the infant and his environment:

> . . . when he is both awake and contented the young infant's main pre-occupation is looking—either in exploring the environment or in examining particular parts of it more carefully. No reinforcement is needed for this response other than the presence of sufficiently interesting sights. [Fantz, 1969, p. 48.]

Perhaps for these reasons considerably more work has been accomplished in this area than in any other. For example, visual acuity—the relative ability of individuals to detect both small stimuli and small details of large visual patterns—has been tested in infants through measurements of "opto-kinetic nystagmus," an involuntary lateral movement of the eyes to the presentation of a moving stimulus. The response is elicited when a recognizable striped pattern is rotated above the infant's head. The width of the separation between the stripes in the pattern can be varied to measure visual acuity, inasmuch as the response will occur only if the infant discriminates the striped pattern. Neonates, one day old, possess eyesight approximately equivalent to 20/150 (Dayton, Jones, Aiu, Rawson, Steele, and Rose, 1964). In terms of the Snellen chart used for older individuals, this means that infants see at twenty feet what adults with normal vision see at 150 feet. The disparity is not closed until middle childhood, and visual acuity has been found to increase markedly until ten years of age.

Rudimentary color vision appears to be present shortly after birth. Staples (1937), for example, presented infants with two discs of equal brightness and measured fixation time. Looking behavior was clearly protracted for the colored displays; three-month-olds spent almost twice as much time looking at the colored discs as at the gray ones.

In addition to exploring such basic abilities to see, we also have been able to investigate certain visual perceptual abilities in children that speak to the larger issues of how and when perception develops. Some of these will be discussed in detail.

Visual Constancies

The world would be a far less comfortable place in which to live if we were not able to identify familiar faces and objects. Our ability to recognize the familiar despite changes in distance, position in space, and in the play of light and shadow on surfaces is called *object constancy*. Such constancy stabilizes our perceptions of the world around us, making interactions with the external environment much easier.

Brightness Constancy. Brightness constancy refers to the tendency to perceive the surface brightness of an object as unchanging despite changes in lighting. Sir Isaac Newton observed the phenomenon and wrote about it in 1704. He spread a gray powder in a spot of sunlight on the floor of his chamber and laid a piece of white paper beside it in a shadow. Upon viewing the two objects from a distance great enough so that the character of the objects could not be recognized, he observed the powder to be brighter than the paper. But when the objects were viewed at a distance from which they were recognizable, the paper appeared to be brighter than the powder; that is, when knowledge of their relative brightnesses was allowed to come into play, the effect of the different lightings was eliminated and brightness constancy restored.

The basic sensory information for perceived brightness is probably the amount of light coming to the eye from the object viewed. Thus, under the same lighting conditions, coal is darker than paper. But strangely, even when coal sends more light to the eye than paper, as is the case when the former lies in the bright sun and the latter lies in the shade, it may still appear darker than paper. This is accounted for by the brain correcting the initial sense impression with subsidiary information about the inequality in lighting conditions; removal of this secondary information results in failure of brightness constancy.

Although few studies have been conducted on the development of brightness constancy, Brunswik (1929) discovered that it increased in children between the ages of three and eleven years, followed by a slight decline. Throughout childhood, then, secondary information is used with increasing efficiency.

Size Constancy. The tendency to see an object as a particular size regardless of the distance from which it is viewed is called size constancy. Euclid first noted that the size of the image on the retina greatly influenced the perceived size of the object. Holding distance between the observer and the object constant, larger objects produced larger images on the retina. Nevertheless, retinal image is not solely depended upon for near objects. In a classroom, students across the aisle do not look half the size of those sitting next to you; your own companions do not look like giants nor do friends across the room appear to be dwarfs. Again, the brain supplements the information provided by the retinal image with additional information about relative distances. (At great distances, though, this process of adjustment becomes inadequate; people look no larger than ants when viewed from the air.)

We know that infants, as well as adults, tend to base their perceptions on more information than mere retinal image. The ability to recognize size and/or distance has been observed in neonates of approximately ten to twelve weeks of age. Employing an ingenious technique based on the principles of operant conditioning (see Chapter V), T. G. R. Bower (1966b) trained infants to turn their heads leftward when presented with the training stimulus, a twelve-inch cube held three feet away. As shown in Figure VI–4, a correct response earned a "peek-a-boo" from the experimenter.

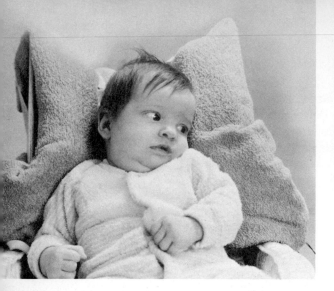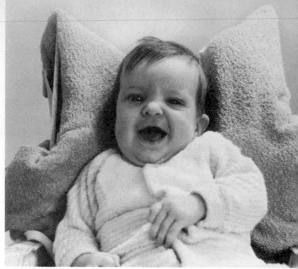

FIGURE VI–4

When the infant responded correctly by turning his head (left) he was reinforced by a "peek-a-boo" from the experimenter. Pleasure at the peek-a-boo (right) was sufficient to keep him responding up to twenty minutes. From T. G. R. Bower, The visual world of infants. Scientific American, *December 1966, p. 87. Photograph by Sol Mednick, by permission.*

After this training was completed, the young subjects' leftward head turns were regularly produced by the presentation of the original cube.

Having thus constructed a medium by which the infant's behavior revealed something of its perceptual world, Bower proceeded to present cubes of various sizes at various distances. He found that the head-turning responses generalized least to the cube that projected the same size retinal image as the training cube but which differed in both size and distance; thus, information other than retinal size was being utilized by the infants. Beyrl (cited in Wohlwill, 1960) has shown that this ability increases with age; that is, children from two to eleven years of age tended to be less likely to underestimate the size of stimuli placed far from them. Interestingly, though, adults tend to *over*estimate the size of distant objects (Wohlwill, 1960). It is as if, having learned that distance "distorts" size, they overcompensate by judging the object larger than its true size.

Shape Constancy. Perceiving a standard shape despite changes in the angle from which an object is observed is called shape constancy. A closed door produces a rectangular image on the retina, a door standing ajar produces a trapezoidal image, and an opened door forms a thin, sticklike configuration of stimulation. But we perceive all three as rectangular (see Figure VI–5).

As with size constancy, constancy of shape appears to increase throughout childhood, followed by a decline at adolescence into adulthood (Wohlwill,

FIGURE VI–5

The door produces a retinal image of different shape in each position. The fact that we continue to perceive it as rectangular despite these variations is an example of shape constancy. Adapted from Gibson, 1950.

1960). And we know that it, too, is present very early in life. Using the same experimental approach as for size constancy, Bower (1966a) has demonstrated it in infants from fifty to sixty days old. Each baby in Bower's experiments learned to turn his head when a particular shape at a particular slant was presented. He was then tested with the same shape at different slants, different shapes at the same slant, and different shapes at different slants. In only the last instance was the projected retinal image the same as for the training stimulus. The infants showed shape constancy by responding most often to the same shape at different slants.

Depth Perception

The manner in which objects at different depths are perceived is related to size-distance perception. Many years ago it was established that perception of depth is almost as accurate in four-year-old youngsters as in adults (Updegraff, 1930), and recent work has explored the question of whether the ability to perceive height and depth is present at birth or soon thereafter. Gibson and Walk provide the following overview of the problem:

> Human infants at the creeping and toddling stage are notoriously prone to falls from more or less high places. They must be kept from going over the brink by side panels on their cribs, gates on their stairways and the vigilance of adults. As their muscular coordination matures they begin to avoid such accidents on their own. Common sense might suggest that the child learns to recognize falling-off places by experience—that is, by falling and hurting himself. But is experience really the teacher? Or is the ability to perceive and avoid a brink part of the child's original endowment? [1960, p. 64.]

To investigate the question, Gibson and Walk developed a special experimental setup, which they referred to as the visual cliff. The "cliff," shown in Figure VI–6, is constructed from a heavy sheet of glass with a platform in the center raised slightly above the surface of the glass. The center platform, covered with a patterned material, is wide enough to hold the baby when it is in creeping position. The "shallow" side of the cliff is created by fastening the same patterned material directly beneath the glass on one side of the platform. The illusion of depth is created on the other side of the platform by placing the material several feet below the glass. The infant's mother stands alternately at either the deep or shallow side and beckons to the child to come to her (Gibson and Walk, 1960; Walk and Gibson, 1961).

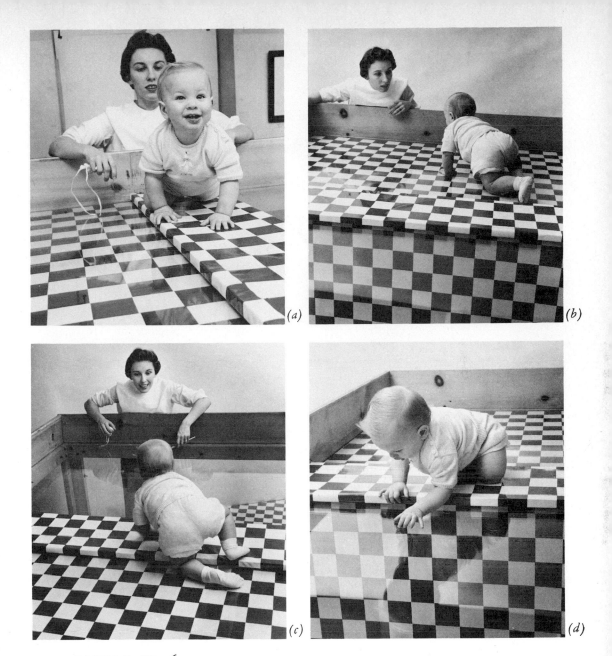

FIGURE VI-6

An infant on the visual cliff (a). He crawls to his mother across the shallow side (b), but refuses to do so on the deep side (c), even though he has tactual evidence (d) that the cliff is solid. From E. J. Gibson and R. D. Walk, The *"visual cliff."* Scientific American, *April 1960, p. 65. Photos by William Vandivert, by permission.*

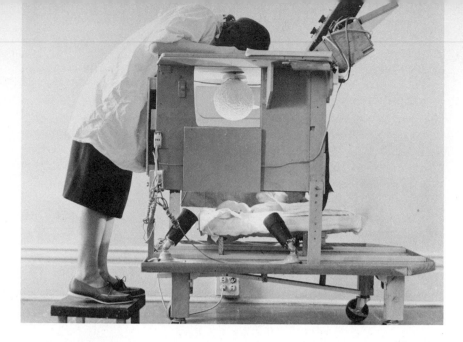

FIGURE VI—7

"Looking chamber" used to test pattern discrimination in human infants. An infant lies on a crib, looking at objects hung from the ceiling, while an observer records the amount of fixation time for each object. From R. L. Fantz, The origin of form perception. Scientific American, May 1961, p. 66. Photograph by David Linton, by permission.

Gibson and Walk began by testing thirty-six infants between 6½ and fourteen months of age. The results of this initial study were quite clear. Twenty-seven of the infants were willing to crawl off the center onto the shallow sides, but only three ventured into the deep area. The investigators note that a number of infants actually crawled *away* from their mothers when called from the cliff side; others cried, presumably because it appeared to them that it was not possible to reach their mothers without crossing the brink.

Form Perception

Another area which has been explored with regard to perceptual development involves various aspects of how form, shape, and pattern are perceived.

Early Form Discrimination: Fantz's Work. The work of Robert Fantz is important in that it took to task an earlier assumption that infants lack the ability to distinguish form. Fantz uses differential attention to stimuli as an indication that a particular pattern is, indeed, being recognized. He began by building a special infant crib, similar to the one shown in Figure VI–7. Above the infant's head was a plain gray ceiling, on which various pairs of target stimuli were placed. An identical pair of figures, such as two triangles, was hung from the ceiling of the "looking chamber" one foot apart and one foot above the infant's head. By means of a special peephole in the top of the apparatus, Fantz could tell how much time the subject spent fixating on each of the triangles. Not surprisingly, looking time was equivalent for these two identical figures. But when a "bull's-eye" and horizontal stripes, such as the pair shown in Figure VI–8, were intro-

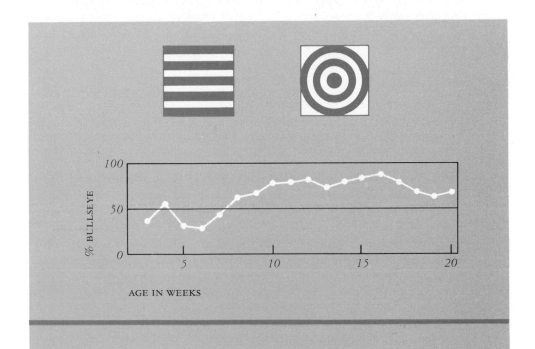

FIGURE VI–8

Infants' visual preference. As the children matured they spent a greater proportion of their time looking at the bull's eye. Unless they actually saw a difference between the two stimuli presented to them, why should they seem to "prefer" one over the other? Adapted and reprinted with permission of author and publisher from Fantz, R. L. Pattern vision in young infants. Psychological Record, *1958, 8, 43–47.*

duced, it was found that infants above the age of eight weeks preferred the bull's-eye to the stripes. Such a finding could be obtained only if the infant could visually discriminate one pattern from the other.

Later the procedure was changed. Under the new rules, only a single stimulus was presented and terminated as soon as the infant looked away. To reduce the likelihood that differences in looking could be accounted for by very early visual experience or learning, babies under five days of age also served as subjects, and were compared with older infants. In addition to the bull's-eye figure, a drawing similar to a human face was included. Some of these results are shown in Figure VI–9, from which it can be seen that the infant appears to attend selectively to certain patterns from just after birth. Further, they indicate that fixation is greater for complex and social rather than simple and nonsocial stimuli. Thus, as Fantz has written:

> The results . . . have already been sufficient to explode both the myth that the young infant is untestable and the myth that there is little to test. It is now difficult to maintain the earlier views that the world of the neonatal infant is a big blooming buzzing confusion. . . . The young infant has a patterned and organized visual world which he explores discriminatingly with the limited means at his command. [1969, pp. 55–56.]

But Fantz's procedure has limitations. The absence of differential fixation does not necessarily indicate that the infant does not discriminate between the two forms; the young subject might be equally attracted to both figures. Nor does the occurrence of differential fixation necessarily reveal the aspects of the stimulus to which the infant is attracted. Other investigators, however, have addressed this question and have discovered interesting changes in what captures the attention of young children.

Changes in Deployment of Attention. In one study that permitted conclusions about early response to contour, infants were placed in head-restraining cribs in which a stimulus display appeared nine inches above their eyes (Salapatek and Kessen, 1966). The beam of marker lights from the visual displays, reflecting on the subjects' corneas, revealed the orientation of the eyes, which was recorded by a camera focused on them. Records were made for both an experimental and a control group. The experimental group was shown a black triangle on a white field; the control group was presented with a circular black field. It was found that control subjects were no more likely to look at one part of the homogeneous field than another, but that the experimental infants tended to gaze at the vertices of the triangle. Many infants fixated on or attended to a single vertex, although they tended to select a different one on each trial. Notably, there was less scanning of

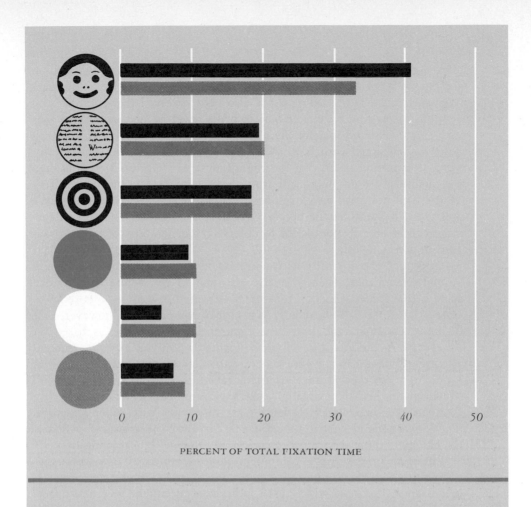

PERCENT OF TOTAL FIXATION TIME

FIGURE VI-9

Fixation time of newborns and older children to patterned and plain discs. Black bars show the results for infants 2-3 months old, gray bars for infants more than 3 months old. Adapted from "Origin of Form Perception," by Robert L. Fantz. Copyright © 1961 by Scientific American, Inc. All rights reserved.

the entire stimulus in the experimental group. The authors concluded that the infants distinguished at least one aspect of form shortly after birth but that, inasmuch as they did not scan the sides of the triangle, they undoubtedly did not perceive the entire figure.

A similar study uncovered a tendency among three-day-olds to fixate on the border between two patches of color—e.g., white and black (Kessen, Salapatek, and Haith, 1965). It has also been observed that infants from seven to twenty-four weeks old tend to make fewer but longer observations of a single item and to refix their gazes on stimuli observed before. Such behavior was noted with both moving and stationary stimuli, and the investigators further noted that the younger infants were less well able than the older ones to sample at will from their visual field (Ames and Silfen, 1965). This primitive visual response, characterized by motoric quiescence and visual fixation, has been called "obligatory attention"; young infants appear to be literally compelled to observe certain objects (Stechler, Bradford, and Levy, 1966).

Aspects of the stimulus itself, such as its contour or complexity, are strong determinants, then, of early attention in the young infant. The same is true for movement. Apparently attraction to such aspects requires little prior experience. Jerome Kagan (1967) has proposed, however, that the most important and persistent determinant of attention is based on familiarity. As the infant develops, he gradually acquires *schemata* (mental pictures or ideas); at any one time a particular schema may be familiar ("older") or emergent. Kagan argues that there are two categories of stimuli to which the child maximally attends: stimuli which reflect emerging schemata and those which violate or are discrepant with older schemata. The former are said to be in the service of "savoring the stimulus," whereas the latter are in the service of "reducing uncertainty" by categorization.

Testing this theory poses a problem of measurement. It is necessary to distinguish between the two different bases of attention. Kagan proposes that fixation, the most widely used indicant of attention, will not suffice. Other measures must be employed. He has chosen smiling and heart deceleration, a measure of attention associated with taking in information.

A typical test of Kagan's hypothesis consists of presenting infants with regular or distorted faces and observing their reactions. In one such study twenty-two infants, four months of age, were shown slides of four different stimuli: a photograph of a man's face (photo regular), a collage of that photo (photo scrambled), a line drawing of a face (schematic regular), and a distorted collage of that drawing (schematic scrambled). These stimuli are reproduced in Figure VI–10. The infants fixated equally on the two regular faces but showed more smiling and greater heart deceleration to the photo regular than to the schematic regular. The photo regular, Kagan contends, is an emergent schema whereas the schematic regular is a violation of it.

As children grow older, however, not only does their overall attention

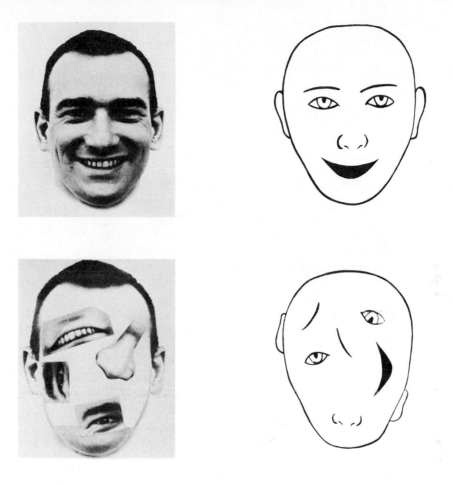

FIGURE VI–10

Examples of the regular and scrambled faces used in Kagan's research.
Courtesy Dr. Jerome Kagan.

span increase but their exploration of objects becomes progressively more systematic. Zaporozhets (1965) has documented this change of attention deployment by superimposing eye movement patterns on an outline of the stimulus being examined by children four to seven years of age (Figure VI–11). The change closely correlates with their success in recognizing observed stimuli among a set of various forms.

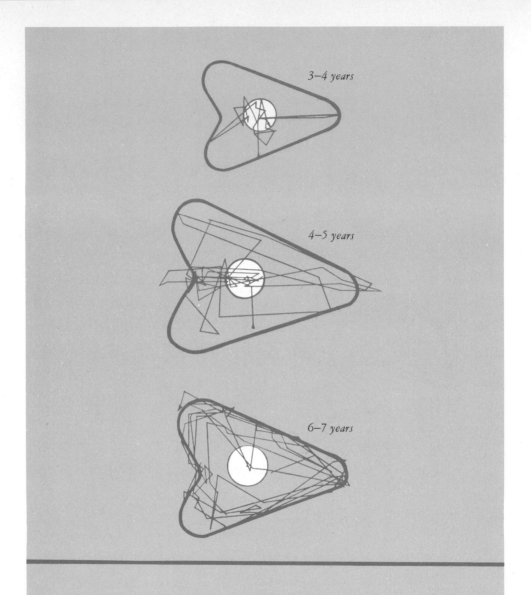

3–4 years

4–5 years

6–7 years

FIGURE VI–11

*Patterns of eye movements showing scanning of visual form at three
age levels. From A. V. Zaporozhets, The development of perception in
the preschool child. In P. H. Mussen, ed.,* European research in cognitive
development. Monographs of the Society for Research in Child Development, *1965, 30, 82-101. Copyright 1965 by the Society for Research
in Child Development, Inc. Reproduced by permission.*

Whole-part Perception

We have seen that the infant may not be able to perceive a whole pattern at once. This has led some investigators to hypothesize that the tendency to observe specific parts of a complex stimulus emerges slowly as the child matures, and that the ability to simultaneously integrate all the parts into a single whole does not appear until late childhood (Claparede, 1908; Werner, 1940).

Elkind, Krogler, and Go (1964), for example, constructed figures that emphasized parts of the whole configuration (see Figure VI–12). They

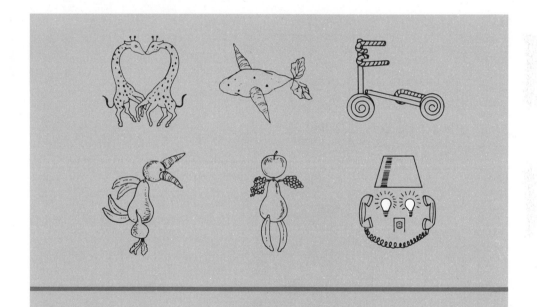

FIGURE VI–12

Sample drawings presented by Elkind et al. *in studying whole-part perception in children. Although each figure appears as a whole, its individual parts are strongly depicted. From D. Elkind, R. R. Krogler, and E. Go, Studies in perceptual development: II. Part-whole perception.* Child Development, *1964, 35, 81-90. Copyright 1964 by the Society for Research in Child Development, Inc. Reproduced by permission.*

found that very few of the youngsters (age five to nine years) responded to the stimuli only as wholes. Five- and six-year-olds responded to parts, whereas seven- to nine-year-olds responded to both parts and wholes. Thus, the stimuli per se determine, at least in part, whether young children attend to whole configurations or to details of them. It appears, however, that older children can take both into consideration.

EXTENDED DISCUSSION

HOW DOES FORM DIFFERENTIATION DEVELOP?

Even though infants can discriminate patterns, the ability to differentiate among complex forms increases with age. This is not surprising in light of some of the changes in the growing child that we have just seen—for example, youngsters increasingly scan stimuli and learn to respond to both detail and whole configurations. Precisely how differentiation comes about, however, is not agreed upon. A theoretical dispute exists between those who advocate a *distinctive features* theory and those who advocate a *prototype* explanation. The former is summarized by J. J. Gibson and E. J. Gibson, its originators: ". . . we learn to perceive in this sense; that percepts [sensory or perceptual impressions] change over time by progressive elaboration of qualities, feature, and dimensions of variation. . . . Perceptual learning, then, consists of responding to variables of physical stimulation not previously responded to" (1955, p. 34). The essential point of the prototype hypothesis, on the other hand, can be captured by supposing that individuals learn internal models or abstract representations of stimuli which gradually become more elaborated.

The Gibsons' approach is demonstrated in an experiment designed to examine, within the context of reading skill, the development of discrimination of letterlike forms (Gibson, Gibson, Pick, and Osser, 1962). Children were presented a display board with standard letter like forms, identical copies of the standards, and transformations of each standard (Figure VI–13).

They were asked to match the figures with a standard, indicating which ones were exactly like it. It was found that the mean number of errors decreased as age increased from four to eight years. But perhaps more important, some kinds of errors were made more often than others. "Break"

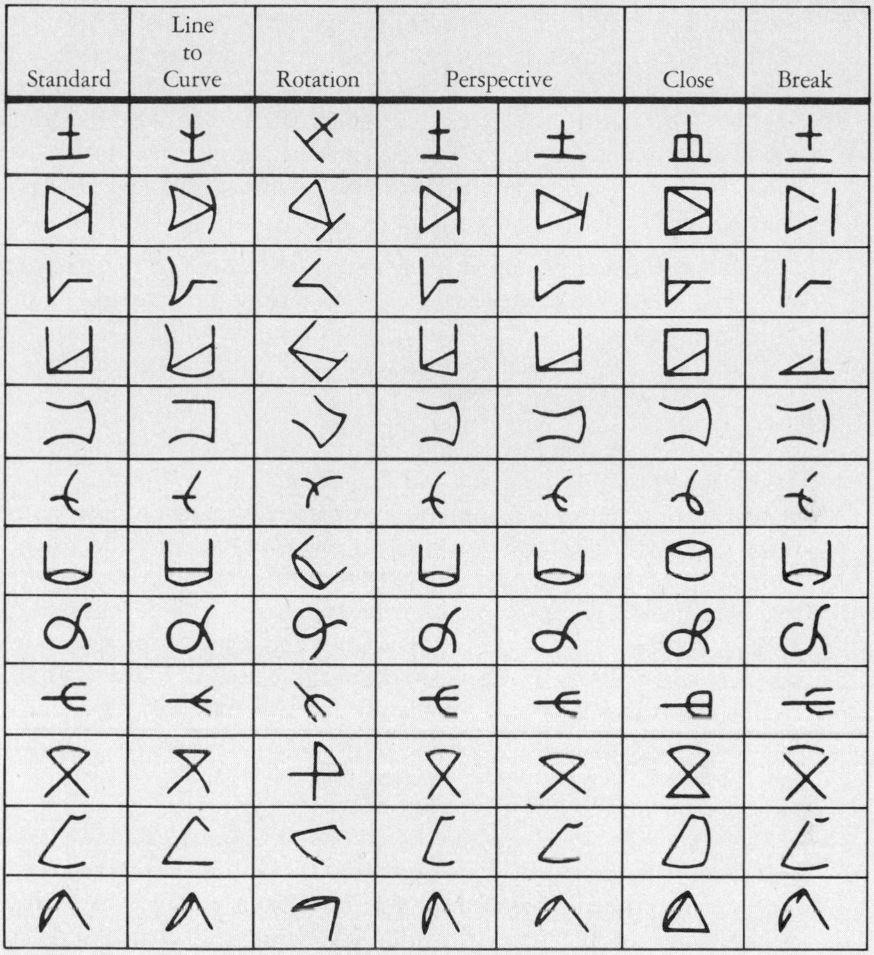

Standard	Line to Curve	Rotation	Perspective		Close	Break

FIGURE VI–13

Sample of stimuli used by Gibson, Gibson, Pick, and Osser to study the discrimination of letterlike forms. From E. J. Gibson, J. J. Gibson, A. D. Pick, and H. Osser, A developmental study of the discrimination of letter-like forms. Journal of Comparative and Physiological Psychology, *1962, 55, 897-906. Copyright 1962 by the American Psychological Association, and reproduced by permission.*

transformations, for example, were rarely chosen, even by the youngest children, as a match for the standard. "Perspective" transformation errors, however, were frequently made, although they decreased somewhat at ages seven and eight. Gibson *et al.* suggested that the inability to distinguish "perspective" transformations from standards arises because the former do not involve distinctive features which would permit them to be discriminated from the standard. "Break" transformations do, and so would be easier to distinguish.

> It is our hypothesis that it is the distinctive features of the grapheme patterns which are responded to in discrimination of letter-like forms. The improvement in such discrimination from four to eight is the result of learning to detect these invariants and of becoming more sensitive to them. [Gibson *et al.*, 1962, p. 904.]

Comparing the prototype and distinctive feature views, Pick (1965) used a subset of the standards and transformations of the original experiment. Youngsters were first trained to correctly match fifteen cards with three standards. The cards consisted of two replications and three transformations of each standard. Subjects were then assigned to either a distinctive features group or a prototype condition. The former group was given a completely new set of standards and their transformations, the *transformations being of the same type* as those used in training. If children in this group had learned distinctive features in training (e.g., the form is not slanted), presumably they would not find it difficult to handle these new forms; if they had learned only a prototype or model, the task would be very difficult.

The prototype group, on the other hand, was given the same standards again; only the transformations were new. If children had learned by prototype, they supposedly would have no difficulty in such a change inasmuch as the model of the standard would be the crucial element. All of the youngsters were then asked to match their cards and standards, and the results were compared to a control group who had received no training. Both experimental groups clearly did better than the controls. More important, those in the distinctive feature condition made fewer errors than those in the prototype group. It appeared, then, at least in this situation, that relatively little prototype learning had occurred.

And yet, other kinds of investigations give evidence supporting prototype learning. If a prototype exists, the individual has available an internal abstract model based on common aspects of a class of stimuli. It might be expected that this representation could be used, once it is evoked, to "fill in" missing parts of stimuli. Children's ability to recognize pictures of incomplete objects is, then, one way of assessing prototype learning.

Vurpillot (1962) tested this by showing children of four, seven, and eleven years of age cards depicting either a rabbit or a sheep which lacked one or more parts. Pictures of the rabbit, for example, were missing the head, ears, tail, fur, or a combination of these. When the children were requested to sort the cards into a rabbit or a sheep pile, the number of cards not placed into either category decreased with age. For the youngest group, 41 percent were not assigned; for the oldest group, 17 percent. It seemed, then, as if all the youngsters did, indeed, have some internal representation of the figures but that it was more easily evoked with older children.

A study by Gollin (1960) speaks to the question of whether younger children require more information in order to recognize incomplete pictures. He presented children aged $3\frac{1}{2}$ to 5 years and adults with pictures ranging from complete to very incomplete and trained them in recognition. Training was accomplished with intermediate or complete pictures. When asked later to identify very incomplete drawings, training on the intermediate drawings was shown to be effective for all subjects. Interestingly, though, training on complete figures was much less helpful overall, and particularly for the children. This has been interpreted (Reese and Lipsitt, 1970) as showing that the well-developed models available to adults were evoked easily under both training conditions. Children, however, with their poorly developed representations, benefited more by training with incomplete pictures because it enabled them to form more effective models—true prototypes—which they then used in the test.

It seems, then, that differentiation of form may occur by learning both distinctive features and abstract representations of stimuli. In Chapter VII we shall examine in greater detail the role that representations of the environment are thought to play in the child's increasing understanding of his world.

INTERACTION OF SENSORY SYSTEMS

In many natural situations perception involves the simultaneous use of more than one sense modality. The evidence suggests that the ability to combine this information adequately, or to reject one source appropriately in favor of another, increases markedly with age.

Gesell, Ilg, and Bullis (1949) explored the interaction of perceptual systems in infants and young children. *Eye-hand* coordination, one of the problems they studied, involves the interaction of proprioceptive and visual information in the development of manual dexterity. Although the neonate can move its eyes, it is not until about three months of age that the infant can follow a moving object across his full 180-degree visual field. Then, at four months, he can both hold and look at an object. At eight months the infant can manipulate an object with both hands. More complex eye-hand coordinations, such as eating a cookie, appear at about nine months. The one-year-old can pick up toys one at a time and hand them to another person. When we look at postural orientation, or the ability to coordinate visual information with proprioceptive cues about body position, development appears to be somewhat slower. At eighteen months the child may still be walking backward when pulling his toys. Acting out stories and other complex visual-postural maneuvers do not become sophisticated until about the fifth year of life.

Birch and Lefford (1963; 1967) have investigated children's ability to recognize the similarities and differences among geometric forms in one perceptual mode and then to transfer to another. Focusing on the interplay of the visual and haptic (touch) modes, they found that major improvements occurred through the first seven years of life. Similar findings have been obtained by Abravanel (1967). But auditory-visual integration, which is vital in many educational endeavors (such as reading) continues to develop through about the fifth grade (Birch and Belmont, 1965). During this period the visual cues appear to become increasingly *less* important, while the auditory information becomes both more salient and easier to integrate with visual cues (Rudnick, Sterritt, and Flax, 1967).

Perception of Oneself Relative to the Visual Field

All of us feel that we usually know our location in space—whether, and to what degree, our bodies are tilted or upright. This knowledge is based largely on two sensory sources, interoceptive postural cues and visual cues. Ordinarily these two sources of information coincide, but what happens if they become disparate because of a distortion in the visual field? Would we correctly rely on how our bodies feel, or compromise our judgments to align them with visual appearance?

Herman Witkin has designed an ingenious test to answer this question. The subject is seated on a specially constructed chair, in a room that is completely dark. He faces an illuminated rod and frame which can be moved independently of one another; each is seen first in a tilted (nonvertical) position. The frame remains tilted and the subject's task is to direct the experimenter in moving the rod until it appears vertical. On some trials his chair is upright, while on others it is tilted to one side. Thus:

> . . . the visual field and the subject's bodily sensations are in disagreement, each indicating a different vertical. If he reports that the rod is straight when objectively it is tipped far toward the tilt of the frame, he is relying primarily on the visual field. If, on the other hand, he adjusts it close to the true upright, he is relying mainly on body position, and is relatively independent of the visual field. When the subject sits erect, it is of course easier for him to utilize body position as a standard of reference. The degree of tilt of the rod gives us a measure of the subject's way of perceiving. [1959, pp. 3–4.]

Witkin has conducted many experiments with this apparatus, but only his developmental studies are of particular interest here. He has found, in a longitudinal study, that children of both sexes are able to overcome the influence of the visual field increasingly as they grow older.* Typical results are summarized in Figure VI–14.

The Perception of Time

Although some people are more successful than others at guessing what time it is, most adults are rather good at rough time estimations even without their watches. Such judgments probably reflect the ability to combine various sensory information such as changes in body temperature, the experience of hunger, and the like. It is relatively difficult to learn much of young children's perception of short periods of time, for they simply have not learned the "language of the clock" for communicating these perceptions to us. But Springer (1952) has provided some general information. The subjects in his study were four- to six-year-old children who had not yet been instructed in telling time. When asked what time of day various activities took place,

> . . . the youngest ones tended to use descriptive terms such as "early" or to use a sequence of activities such as "after nap." The next stages were to give an unreasonable time, then a reasonable but incorrect time, and finally the correct hour. Thus when asked what time they left school, 41 per cent of the four-year-olds gave unreasonable times, whereas 74 per cent of the six-year-olds were able to name the correct hour. [p. 323.]

---

* It is also of interest, in these longitudinal data, that a child's ability to overcome the field, relative to his age peers, remains quite stable over time.

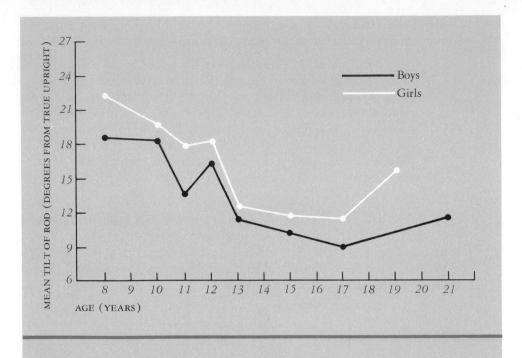

FIGURE VI—14

Age curves in Witkin's rod-and-frame experiment, showing progressive development in the direction of increasing capacity to overcome the influence of the surrounding field. Adapted from "The Perception of the Upright," by Herman A. Witkin. Copyright © 1959 by Scientific American, Inc. All rights reserved.

Piaget (1946) has argued that relatively young children confuse time with space, only later constructing the necessary abstract concept that will distinguish the two. This accomplishment involves the interaction of perception and thought (about which we will have more to say later). But it is worthwhile to digress and describe one of the intriguing Piagetian time studies. Preschool children were first shown two mechanical snails, placed at the same starting point on a table. The snails were turned on at the same moment but moved at different speeds and were permitted to run for different periods of time. When the slow snail ran for a longer period than the fast one without catching up, the children were later unable to reproduce the time sequence correctly. Asked to name the snail who had stopped first, they almost all said the slower one had—because it had not gone as far.

Some evidence is available regarding the development of longer time estimations. In one study (Cohen, 1964), subjects of a broad age range were asked to mark off the time from their birth to "now," in sections indicating how long ago yesterday, a week ago, last Christmas, a year ago, eight years ago, and so on appeared to be. It was found that "the younger the subject, the greater the distance away one week ago seemed. To the eight-year-old girl, last Christmas was [perceived as] a third of the way back toward birth. . . ." Some exemplary findings of this study are shown in Figure VI–15.

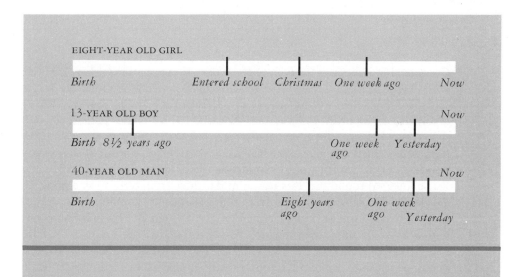

FIGURE VI–15

Some examples of the relationship between time perspective and age. Adapted from "Psychological Time," by John Cohen. Copyright ©

NATURE-NURTURE: A CENTRAL RECURRING ISSUE

Whether perception is an innate function or a process learned through experience with the environment is an ancient question. Brought to psychology from philosophical debate, the issue has remained a central one— sometimes more so, sometimes less. Current views acknowledge the contributions of both heredity and environment, but their relative roles remain an important issue for developmentalists. Many different kinds of studies have been carried out that address this issue; in writing about space perception, Epstein (1964) has categorized them into (1) deprivation studies, (2) research with newborn, naïve organisms, and (3) studies in which there is an attempt to vary environmental stimulation. Much of this work has been conducted with animals, but it has provided us with facts and fruitful hypotheses about the genesis of perception in humans.

Deprivation Studies

Considerable impetus was given to the study of deprivation by D. O. Hebb, who proposed that early experience with environmental stimulation is crucial for the development of perception. Deprivation studies involve rearing organisms from birth without sensory stimulation. Their performance is then compared with that of normally reared individuals. Several such studies have been aimed at discovering whether visual perception of distance and height is learned or innate. In support of the latter hypothesis, Lashley and Russell (1934) found that rats reared in darkness from birth to one hundred days of age were able to jump from one platform to another as accurately as those reared under normal conditions. Although their experiment met with some criticism, other research has corroborated the findings (Nealey and Edwards, 1960; Walk and Gibson, 1961), and also has shown that depth perception in chicks is not greatly impaired by early deprivation (Fantz, 1958; Kurke, 1955).

In another study designed to investigate the effect of deprivation on visual perception, two chimpanzees were reared for the first sixteen months of their lives in total darkness except for a few minutes of light each day required for their care. Subsequent tests revealed that they responded to light—their pupils constricted and followed a flashlight—but that they did not respond to objects unless they touched their bodies, nor did they blink at motion toward their faces. One of the animals, named Snark, never overcame these deficiencies and even deteriorated after months of a lighted environment. What was the cause of his visual retardation? The investigator, A. H. Riesen, noted:

> There had been no previous evidence that stimulation by light is essential for the normal growth of the primate retina or optic nerve. It was a surprise to find that, while the eyes of these chimpanzees remained sensitive to light after 16 months in darkness, the retina and optic disk in both animals did not reflect as much light as normal chimpanzee eyes do. Snark later developed a marked pallor of the optic disk in both eyes. There is other evidence suggesting that fish and amphibians, at least, need light-stimulation for normal eye development. So the physiological effects of the lack of light may be part of the explanation for Snark's loss of visual function. . . . We now have clear evidence from further experiments with chimpanzees that not merely light itself but stimulation by visual patterns is essential to normal visual development. [1965, p. 78.]

Thus, it appears that the influence of light deprivation may be attributed at least in part to impairment of physical structures. Hebb (1966), in noting the loss of retinal cells in these chimpanzees, cautions that impairment can be even more subtle. In kittens whose eyes were kept closed for two months, certain neurons (nerve cells) in the visual cortex of the brain were present as usual but did not respond to retinal excitation. It is possible that the visual system is particularly vulnerable to such physical impairment for it probably is less mature at birth than other sensory apparatus, at least in the human.

In another study (Nissen, Chow, and Semmes, 1951), a chimpanzee was subjected to tactual deprivation. His lower legs and forearms were covered with cardboard loose enough to allow joint movement but not tactual stimulation. After thirty months the cardboard was removed and his reactions were compared to those of a normally reared chimp. He was less able to locate the spot where he was pinched, and appeared not to feel a pinprick. Additionally, he required more than two thousand trials to learn to turn his head to the right or left depending on which hand was touched; the control animal took two hundred trials.

The effects of deprivation on pain perception have been demonstrated by Thompson and Melzack (1956). They raised Scottish terriers in isolation from infancy, so that the dogs were deprived of all normal stimulation. For example, while most young animals undergo a good many bumps, knocks, and scrapes while growing up, these pups had no such experience. The results, summarized by Melzack, suggest strikingly that early experience may play a vital role in the perception of pain—and the adaptive responses to which it leads—in adulthood:

> . . . when these dogs grew up they failed to respond normally to a flaming match. Some of them repeatedly poked their noses into the flame and sniffed at it as long as it was present. If they snuffed it out, they reacted similarly to a second flaming match and even to a third. Others did not sniff at the match but made no effort to get away when we touched their noses with the flame repeatedly. These dogs also endured pinpricks with little or no evidence of pain. In contrast, littermates that had been reared in a normal environment recognized potential harm so quickly that we were usually unable to touch them with the flame or pin more than once. [Melzack, 1961, p. 3.]

For obvious reasons, deprivation experiments are not carried out with human infants. But an analogous situation exists when the vision of humans who have lived in darkness for years as a result of cataracts is restored by surgery. Such patients appear to have difficulty estimating distance and identifying complex shapes. There is lack of agreement, however, over the validity of these findings (Epstein, 1964).

Studies with Newborn, Naïve Organisms

The most well known of the investigations involving newborn, naïve organisms are the studies carried out by Gibson and Walk with the visual cliff (p. 182). As these researchers note, their work with human infants does not prove conclusively that perception of depth is innate, but it does show that, if depth perception is learned, it is mastered at a very tender age. Gibson and Walk also have used the visual cliff with a variety of other species, including chicks, turtles, rats, lambs, baby goats, pigs, kittens, and dogs. Even when tested within the first twenty-four hours of life, many of these animals appear to see clearly the difference between the two sides of the cliff and refuse to go across the apparently deep end.

Studies with Environmental Variables Controlled

In the third type of research under consideration here, the experimenter controls the subject's environment from birth until the time of testing in such a way that he dictates the exact nature of the visual stimulation to which the organism is exposed. The aim is to determine whether animals that have been subjected to different visual experiences will respond differently on the same test of perception.

An example of this approach is the experiment undertaken by Hess (1956) with newborn chicks to determine whether the ability to localize and peck accurately at grain was innate or learned. Chicks which were hatched in darkness were divided into two experimental groups and one control group. The young birds in the experimental groups were fitted with hoods containing prisms which displaced the visual field seven degrees to the right or seven degrees to the left. The control chicks wore hoods that did not contain image-displacing lenses. At one day of age the pecking accuracy of these chicks was tested by allowing them to peck at a brass nail embedded in modeling clay. The accuracy of their responses was measured by the distance from the indentations left in the clay to the nail.

The experimenter reasoned that if visually guided pecking was learned, all chicks would at first make responses that miss the nail at random distances. With practice, however, chicks in all groups should finally be able to hit the target. In contrast, if the ability to peck an object accurately is innate, the first pecks of the experimental chicks should cluster about seven degrees to the left or the right of the target nail. When tested one day after birth, chicks wearing prisms missed the target by the predicted seven degrees while control chicks struck the target directly. When tested again at three or four days after birth, the chicks wearing prisms still missed the target by seven degrees. This evidence points toward the existence of some innate factors in perception. However, such evidence does not necessarily preclude the necessity of practice and experience in perceptual development.

Just as sensory deprivation has adverse effects on certain perceptions, sensory enrichment has been shown to have a positive influence. In one of the first studies of environmental enrichment, two groups of rats were raised in cages which afforded a fairly diverse visual environment, while two other groups of rats lived with little visual stimulation. Subsequently, the performance of the former groups on an "intelligence test" for rats was superior to that of the latter groups (Hymovitch, 1952). In a more recent study, researchers explored the possibility of structuring the experience of the human infant to produce maximum positive growth and development (White and Held, 1966).

The experiment, which took place at a Massachusetts hospital, provided four kinds of environments for infants. The uniform and somewhat bland surroundings of a typical hospital nursery provide a baseline against which the influence of three modified environments were tested. The first modification involved twenty extra minutes per day of handling by the nurses. Under the second modification plan, numerous forms and colors were displayed above the cribs to heighten interest and increase hand movements. Moreover, extra opportunities for head and neck movements and extra handling were provided. Under the third modification program, pacifiers were mounted on the rails of the cribs just within the infants' sight to encourage grasping (see Figure VI–16). Extra handling was also included in this program.

Some aspects of early visual motor development were extremely responsive to these attempts to encourage growth. The infants who experienced the second and third enrichment programs developed competence in reaching sooner than did infants who experienced the control and first modification conditions. Whether the accelerated development had definite long-term significance has not yet been ascertained. It is interesting to note, however, that results from enrichment studies have had a dramatic impact on social policy in the United States. For those interested in children unable to perform successfully in school, enrichment of the environment quickly came to be seen as a possible solution.

A Summary

What can be concluded from the many and various kinds of investigations that we have just sampled? First, it seems apparent that at least some forms of perception, in some organisms, have their genesis in innate mechanisms. The evidence is particularly strong with regard to distance or depth perception: rats, chicks, and many other animals judge distance and depth accurately at birth or very soon thereafter. Although we cannot say with certainty that the same is true for humans, infants less than a year old display recognition of distance and depth. Form discrimination also is present in human infants very early and at birth in several other species. Still, care must be taken in extrapolating from the latter to humans. Further, it is likely that, although innate factors may be important in some types of perceptions (or aspects of them), they may be relatively less important in others.

We also have seen that perceptual discrimination (of form and the constancies, for example) improves with age. Gibson and Gibson (1955) view this change as a process in which the child comes to respond to stimula-

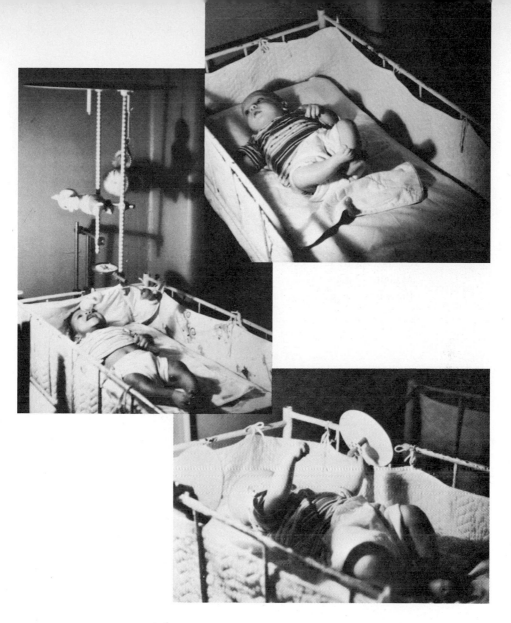

FIGURE VI–16

Three of the different environments for infants employed by White and Held: (a) the typical nursery, (b) enrichment with brightly colored objects, and (c) enrichment with pacifiers. Reprinted by permission from B. L. White and R. Held, Plasticity of sensorimotor development in the human infant, in J. F. Rosenblith and W. Allinsmith, eds., The Causes of Behavior, II, *pp. 60-70; copyright 1966 by Allyn & Bacon, Inc., Boston.*

tion that he previously had not discriminated. Undoubtedly, then, practice is important. As William James recognized long ago:

> That "practice makes perfect" is notorious in the field of motor accomplishments. But motor accomplishments depend in part on sensory discrimination. Billiard-playing, rifle-shooting, tightrope-dancing demand the most delicate appreciation of minute disparities of sensation, as well as the power to make accurately graduated muscular responses thereto. In the purely sensorial field we have the well known virtuosity displayed by the professional buyers and testers of various kinds of goods. One man will distinguish by taste between the upper and lower half of a bottle of old Madeira. Another will recognize, by feeling the flour in a barrel, whether the wheat has grown in Iowa or Tennessee. [1890, p. 509.]

VII

COGNITIVE DEVELOPMENT

DURING THE DECADES when psychologists in the United States were following the strict behavioristic approach of John B. Watson (see Chapter V), relatively little was learned about children's thought, language, and intellectual functioning. Watson recognized that such processes, with the possible exception of simple speech, were largely internal events; accordingly, he rejected them as inappropriate topics for research. Gradually, his radical approach has given way. We saw in the study of learning, for example, that behaviorally oriented psychologists have begun to utilize the concept of mediation, which assumes that influential internal processes intervene between the child's exposure to external events and his reaction to them.

The study of cognitive development, the acquisition of thought and knowledge, is now one of the most exciting and active areas of psychological research. Singularly important to this burgeoning of interest has been the work of Jean Piaget, the renowned Swiss psychologist whose theory of how children process knowledge has had enormous impact on almost every aspect of contemporary developmental psychology. This chapter is devoted to Piaget's theory and to a complementary view, set forth by Jerome Bruner, which elaborates on its psychological components. Chapters VIII and IX will detail two related areas—intelligence and language—touched on often by Piaget and Bruner.

PIAGET'S THEORY

Piaget's initial work was based primarily on observations of his own children, following a variant of the case study method. Noticing a simple bit of play behavior or a particular motor movement that suggested something about the child's thought processes, he rearranged the environment or questioned the child in order to provide support for or elaborate on the initial speculation. The method is not a particularly strong one in terms of scientific evidence, but the force of Piaget's genius and imagination has used it to generate a theory that has many compelling aspects. What is more, over the years innumerable systematic studies involving children of all ages have been conducted by both Piaget and many others to develop and test his theory.

Piaget has suggested that the child's cognitive development can be described in terms of four main periods: the *sensorimotor* period (infancy or birth to two years), the *preoperational* period (two to seven years), the period of *concrete operations* (ages seven to eleven), and the period of *formal operations* (eleven and on through adulthood).* Within each of these main periods he has provided a description of the cognitive activities which characterize the child, the processes which seem to underlie them, and, finally, the role they play in future development and adaptation.

The Sensorimotor Period

The first period of life is referred to as sensorimotor because the infant acquires motor skills in response to environmental stimuli but is not able to represent the world internally in any way. Piaget argues, though, that:

> In spite of this lack, mental development during the first 18 months of life is particularly important, for it is during this time that the child constructs

---

* The ages provided are only approximate averages and are presumed to vary with such factors as the environmental background of the child.

all the cognitive substructures that will serve as a point of departure for his later perceptive and intellectual development. . . . [Piaget and Inhelder, 1969, p. 3.]

According to Piaget, there is a continuous progression from spontaneous movements and natural reflexes to various acquired habits and then to behavior which clearly reflects intelligence. "The real problem," he states, "is not to locate the first appearance of intelligence but rather to understand the mechanism of this progression" (Piaget and Inhelder, 1969, p. 5).

What, then, is the mechanism he posits? Instead of simply and mechanically responding to external stimuli, the child adapts himself to them. He *accommodates* himself to new information from his world so that it can be *assimilated*. These dual processes can be understood by an analogy to digestion.

> When a person eats something his digestive system reacts to the substances incorporated. In order to deal with the foreign substance, the muscles of the stomach contract in various ways, certain organs release acids, and so on. Putting the matter in general terms, we may say that the person's physical structures (the stomach and related organs) *accommodated* to the environmental event (the food). In other words, the process of accommodation describes the individual's tendency to change in response to environmental demands. . . . *Assimilation* is the complementary process by which the individual deals with environmental events in terms of his current structures. In the case of digestion the acids transform the food into a form which the body can use. Thus the individual not only modifies his structures in reaction to external demands (accommodation), he also uses his structures to incorporate elements of the external world (assimilation). [Ginsburg and Opper, 1969, p. 18.]

The emphasis on the child's modification of the stimulation received from the environment reflects one of the most important characteristics of Piaget's theory: the child is both an active and an interactive organism, whose behavior can be understood only in terms of the way he adapts to the world about him.

The development of assimilation and accommodation during the sensorimotor period may, according to Piaget, be fruitfully cast into six successive substages.

Stage 1. This stage is estimated to occupy approximately the first month of life and involves merely the increasingly smooth and systematic use of natural reflexes. The infant is said to engage in the "reflex exercise" with increasing competence. During the first few days of life, for example, the sucking reflex is improved in that the nipple is more readily found when it slips out of the infant's mouth. This *functional assimilation* also gives rise to both a *generalizing assimilation* (the infant can be observed sucking either on nonnutritive objects or simply on "nothing") and a *recognitive assimilation* (the infant seems to recognize and distinguish the nipple from other objects).

Stage 2. During the second stage, from the first to approximately the fourth month of life, the child acquires his first adaptations. Among these is an adaptation of thumb-sucking. Reflexive thumb-sucking can occur even prenatally, but the Stage 1 neonate sucks his thumb only if it happens by some random action to end up in his mouth. It is not until Stage 2, however, that he acquires the ability to put his thumb in his mouth "voluntarily" and keep it there; thumb-sucking and the reflex of sucking as a nursing activity are now differentiated.

Systematic thumb-sucking is a *primary circular reaction;* "primary" because the actual content of the behavior has a biological origin and "circular" because the response is repetitive and appears to produce its own reinforcement.

Stage 3. During this stage, *secondary circular reactions* begin to appear. They are "secondary" in that they are combinations or derivatives of primary reactions developed separately at an earlier time. Shaking a rattle in order to hear the noise, for example, is a secondary circular reaction. The reaching and grasping aspects of this activity have occurred previously and have been practiced, as has the response of listening. Now they are amalgamated into the new and more complex behavioral sequence.

Occupying the period between the fourth and eighth months of life, Stage 3 shows the first transition between vision and coordinated motor response:

> The baby starts grasping and manipulating everything he sees in his immediate vicinity. For example, a subject of this age catches hold of a cord hanging from the top of his cradle, which has the effect of shaking all the rattles suspended above him. He immediately repeats the gesture a number of times. Each time the interesting result motivates the repetition. . . . Later you need only hang a new toy from the top of the cradle for the child to look for the cord, which constitutes the beginning of a differentiation between means and end. In the days that follow, when you swing an object from a pole two yards from the crib, and even when you produce unexpected and mechanical noises behind a screen, after these sights or

sounds have ceased the child will again look for and pull the magic cord. [Piaget and Inhelder, 1969, p. 10.]

Stage 4.   Examples such as the foregoing suggest at least the threshold of intelligent behavior. However, it is not until Stage 4 (between the eighth and twelfth months of life) that the acquisition of truly instrumental behavior seems to occur. Piaget finds evidence for this process by setting up problems derived from natural situations and observing the reactions of children. Here is an example in which his son Laurent had to move an obstacle in order to reach a toy:

> Until now [he was seven months and thirteen days old] Laurent has never really succeeded in setting aside the obstacle; he has simply attempted to take no notice of it. . . . For instance . . . [at six months] I present Laurent with a matchbox extending my hand laterally to make an obstacle to his prehension. Laurent tries to pass over my hand, or to the side, but he does not attempt to displace it. . . . [At seven months, ten days,] Laurent tries to grasp a new box in front of which I place my hand. . . . He sets the obstacle aside, but not intentionally; he simply tries to reach the box by sliding next to my hand and when he touches it, tries to take no notice of it. . . . Finally [at age seven months, thirteen days,] Laurent reacts quite differently almost from the beginning of the experiment. I present a box of matches above my hand, but behind it, so that he cannot reach it without setting the obstacle aside. But Laurent, after trying to take no notice of it, suddenly tries to hit my hand as though to remove or lower it; I let him do it to me and he grasps the box. . . . I recommence to bar his passage. . . . Laurent tries to reach the box, and bothered by the obstacle, he at once strikes it, definitely lowering it until the way is clear. [Piaget, 1952b, p. 217.]

Pushing the obstacle aside is now not an "accident"; rather, it is an act recognized as necessary for reaching the object. The child is behaving intentionally, successfully, and hence intelligently.

Another example is the problem of the "vanishing object." In the situation with Laurent just described, the object was visible, although a barrier blocked him from reaching it. Visibility is not essential, though; the Stage 4 child will soon locate an object hidden under a pillow. But a remarkable deficit appears when two pillows are used.

> The object is put under the red pillow and the child is allowed to retrieve it. Then, while the child watches, it is placed under the red pillow, taken out, shown to the child, and placed under the blue pillow. The question is, where will the child look for it? *At Stage 4, he looks under the red pillow.*

What does this mean? It actually represents an important failure in the child's understanding. The belief that objects continue to exist when they are invisible also requires some belief that objects are located at some point in space. When objects move they go to the point at the end of the path of movement. Therefore, we look for objects where they were last seen or at the end point of the pathway we think they followed. This strategy for recovering vanished objects is in some ways the exact opposite of what the child discovered in Stage 3, namely, to repeat the action that produced the interesting event. When the child obtains the object from under the red pillow and now looks for it there even though he has seen it put under the blue one, he is repeating the action that found him the object last time rather than looking for it where he saw it. [Baldwin, 1967, p. 213; italics added.]

The inability of the child at Stage 4 to recognize the continuous processes involved in his environment and his consequent repetition of specific acts which have been successful in the past suggest that certain cognitive processes are not yet developed. The appropriate competency appears during Stage 5 when the child is twelve to eighteen months of age.

Stage 5. During the fifth stage the child begins to search for new means to reach certain end states. Consider the situation in which some object has been placed on a rug out of the reach of the young child. What can be done? If the child pulls on a near corner of the rug he can draw the object closer until he is able to reach it directly. The discovery of such a possibility and its utilization characterize Stage 5.

Such recognition, according to Piaget, results in part from the *tertiary circular reaction.* The child discovers, as in the foregoing example, that movement of the rug also produces movement in the desired object. The basic idea may be discovered quite by accident, but the child then begins to experiment with the situation over and over again. The repetition is neither absolutely stereotyped nor simply arbitrary. Instead, the child appears to be trying out, in a more or less systematic way, variations in the newly discovered act to observe the effects they have. Such experimentation is indicated in the following example:

Jacqueline holds in her hands an object which is new to her; a round, flat box, which she turns all over, shakes, rubs against the bassinet, etc. She lets it go and tries to pick it up. But she only succeeds in touching it with her index finger, without grasping it. She nevertheless makes an attempt and presses on the edge. The box then tilts up and falls again. Jacqueline, very much interested in this fortuitous result, immediately applies herself to studying it. Hitherto it is only a question of an attempt at assimilation . . . and of the fortuitous discovery of a new result, but this discovery, instead of giving rise to a simple circular reaction, is at once extended to "experiments in order to see."

In effect, Jacqueline immediately rests the box on the ground and pushes it as far as possible (it is noteworthy that care is taken to push the box far away in order to reproduce the same conditions as in the first attempt, as though this were a necessary condition for obtaining the result). Afterward Jacqueline puts her finger on the box and presses it. But as she places her finger on the center of the box she simply displaces it and makes it slide instead of tilting it up. She amuses herself with this game and keeps it up (resumes it after intervals, etc.) for several minutes. Then, changing the point of contact, she finally again places her finger on the edge of the box, which tilts it up. She repeats this many times, varying the conditions, but keeping track of her discovery: now she only presses on the edge! [Piaget, 1952b, pp. 268–272.]

Despite the child's capacity at Stage 5 to appreciate his accidental discovery of new instrumental means, he does not yet exhibit the ability to construct these new means in a purposeful way.

Stage 6. This stage is characterized by an ability to combine various sorts of possibilities mentally to reach new solutions. The child clearly has begun to develop what Piaget refers to as *schemata*—that is, he employs miniature frameworks that allow him both to fit and to manipulate new pieces of information and hence to assimilate (and accommodate to) his environment. How does such a process work?

Piaget presents the example of a child who is given a partially opened matchbox containing a thimble. His first reaction may be one of trial-and-error efforts to open the box. But, when he fails, ". . . he presents an altogether new reaction: he stops the action and attentively examines the situation (in the course of this he slowly opens and closes his mouth, or, as another subject did, his hand, as if in imitation of the result to be obtained, that is, the enlargement of the opening), after which he suddenly slips his finger into the crack and thus succeeds in opening the box" (Piaget and Inhelder, 1969, p. 12). This is surely a major accomplishment, and surely a manifestation of intelligence. Perceptual schemes, motor movements, and their combinations are integrated internally with the end state in a way that can be characterized as effective action.

During this stage, from eighteen to twenty-four months of age, the child's performance may be seen as the integration and completion of sensorimotor coordination—the rudiments of intelligence. But whereas the insightful behavior which we have just discussed marks the completion of one sort of cognitive development, it also marks the beginning of another: *mental representation.* The road to conceptual thought is now open.

Preoperational Period

The preoperational period is characterized by the development of the ability to use symbols in an increasingly sophisticated fashion. At about the age of two the child begins to distinguish what Piaget calls *signifiers*— various symbols such as words and images—from *significates*—the actual events, objects, and actions to which the signifiers refer.

When a thing and its name are discriminated it becomes possible to manipulate the one without the other. Such "representational thought" sets the stage for symbolically discriminating between alternatives. How does this process develop? It often is suggested that it arises out of the learning of words as signifiers, but Piaget does not accept this explanation. He argues, instead, that the child begins to use motor behavior as a signifier. Many children, for example, signify the act of going to sleep by putting their heads down on a pillow or pulling a blanket over themselves. Or, as noted in an earlier example, they may use an action such as opening and closing their mouths to represent opening and closing a box. Such instances are referred to by Piaget as "imitations," implying the concept of *pretending:*

> To pretend to hit someone without distinguishing the pretense from the action is actually to hit the other. The very word *pretend* requires that the pretense represent reality but be distinguished from it. Sometimes young children lose the distinction and suddenly shift from pretending to playing for real or suddenly begin to believe their own pretense; but, if on occasion the child can genuinely pretend, he must be capable of some degree of symbolic thought. He must have some mental representation of the action he is pretending to perform which is distinguished from the action that he is really performing. [Baldwin, 1967, pp. 231–232.]

It will be recalled that two of Piaget's most basic concepts are those of accommodation and assimilation. It is, in fact, the process of accommodation of existing schema to new problems, coupled with the use of motor representations and imitations of a desired outcome, that is the basis for the development of true signifiers—or symbolization. To illustrate,

Piaget points to transitional cases in which the two-year-old child begins to symbolize an act which *he has not yet performed*. Piaget reports, for example, this observation of his daughter Lucienne:

> . . . I put the chain inside an empty matchbox (where the matches belong), then closed the box leaving an opening of 10mm. Lucienne begins by turning the whole thing over, then tries to grasp the chain through the opening. Not succeeding, she simply puts her index finger into the slit and so succeeds in getting out a small fragment of the chain; she then pulls it until she has completely solved the problem.
>
> Here begins the experiment which we want to emphasize. I put the chain back into the box and reduced the opening to 3mm. It is understood that Lucienne is not aware of the functioning of the opening and closing of the matchbox and has not seen me prepare the experiment. She only possesses the two preceding schemata: turning the box over in order to empty it of its contents, and sliding her finger into the slit to make the chain come out. It is of course this last procedure that she tries first; she puts her finger inside and gropes to reach the chain, but fails completely. A pause follows during which Lucienne manifests a very curious reaction bearing witness not only to the fact that she tries to think out the situation and to represent to herself through mental combination the operations to be performed, but also to the role played by imitation in the genesis of representations. Lucienne mimics the widening of the slit.
>
> She looks at the slit with great attention; then, several times in succession, *she opens and shuts her mouth,* at first slightly, then wider and wider! Apparently Lucienne understands the existence of a cavity subjacent to the slit and wishes to enlarge that cavity. The attempt at representation which she thus furnishes is expressed plastically, that is to say, due to inability to think out the situation in words or clear visual images she uses a simple motor indication as "signifier" or symbol. Lucienne, by opening her mouth thus expresses, or even reflects her desire to enlarge the opening of the box. This schema of imitation, with which she is familiar, constitutes for her the means of thinking out the situation. There is doubtless added to it an element of magic-phenomenalistic causality or efficacy. Just as she often uses imitation to act upon persons and make them reproduce their interesting movements, so also it is probable that the act of opening her mouth in front of the slit to be enlarged implies some underlying idea of efficacy.
>
> Soon after this phase of plastic reflection, Lucienne unhesitatingly puts her finger in the slit and, instead of trying as before to reach the chain, she pulls so as to enlarge the opening. She succeeds and grasps the chain. [Cited in Flavell, 1963, pp. 119–120, italics added.]

The use of symbolic representations or signifiers, as in the case of Lucienne, is both a major accomplishment of the preoperational period and its major characteristic. Piaget has written extensively on this period of life, and both he and many who have followed in his footsteps have reported a substantial number of case studies and experiments. It is therefore worthwhile to examine the period in somewhat greater detail.

Of considerable importance for our understanding of symbolic development is Piaget's distinction between two kinds of signifiers: symbols and signs. *Symbols* correspond in a relatively private way to the events that they represent and somewhat resemble them physically (e.g., Lucienne's opening and closing her mouth). *Signs,* on the other hand, bear no obvious resemblance to the events they represent; their meanings are arbitrary but they are shared by other members of the environment (e.g., formal language).

Piaget argues that representational thought does *not* have its beginnings in social language, but rather in private symbols which form the basis for later acquisition of language. The contribution of language to thought does, of course, enter strongly into the picture, but only in a "reflexive" manner. Language is dependent upon the usage of certain prelinguistic symbols; later, in turn, language fosters the further development of private symbols. We shall examine language development more fully in Chapter IX.

It is possible to divide the preoperational period (which encompasses approximately five years) into two broad subperiods. During the first, until the child is about four or five, he begins to represent events in more and more situations and to discover the advantages of doing so. Next, the child enters a phase of transition during which he develops the ability to engage in concrete operations of thought and reasoning.

We have noted that the preoperational child displays a fairly striking lack of understanding of certain relationships. An elaboration of the nature of these deficits may be seen clearly in the child's performance on problems of *conservation,* to which we next turn our attention.

The Conservation Problems. The concept of conservation and the manner in which children come to understand it are among the most intriguing aspects of Piaget's theory and research. The "flavor" of these problems, which mark the difference between preoperational and operational thought, can be seen through a typical investigation.

Piaget, Inhelder, and Szeminska (1960) showed four- and five-year-old children two straight sticks of equal length, placed on a table with the ends carefully aligned. When asked about the relative length of the sticks, the children judged them to be equal. However, when one of the sticks was moved forward a little it was judged to be longer than the other. Finally, when the sticks were realigned, they were again judged to be equal, and, interestingly, the children were not bothered by their inconsistency even when it was pointed out to them. Six- and seven-year-olds, on the other hand, correctly described the sticks as equal in length throughout each of the phases of the procedure.

What distinguishes the two age groups in this situation? According to Piaget's terminology, older children are able to show *conservation.* They understand, at least in this situation, that no change necessarily occurs in one or more aspects of an object or relationship simply because of changes in other, independent features or aspects.

Conservation of *length* is only one of a number of "types" of transformations in the physical universe which reveal cognitive differences in children's understanding. Studies of conservation of *amount,* for example, begin by showing the child two equal sized balls of plasticene clay. Then, while the subject watches, one of the balls is transformed in shape (e.g., rolled up like a sausage, made into a flat pancake, or divided into several pieces). Children up to about five years of age usually are unable to "see" that the quantity of plasticene has remained constant despite these changes and will identify one of the shapes as now having more clay than the other. By the age of seven or eight they understand that no change in amount occurred (Piaget and Inhelder, 1941).

In tests of conservation of *liquid quantity,* the child is presented with two identically shaped beakers of milk and adjustments are made until he agrees that each contains the same amount to drink. Then the contents of one of the beakers is poured into a third beaker, which differs in shape from the other two. The transition, which occurs entirely in the child's presence, is depicted in Figure VII–1. The preoperational child is likely to say that beakers A and C do not have the same amount of milk.

Why Does the Preoperational Child Fail to Conserve? Piaget and his associates have suggested that the preoperational child fails to conserve because he is unable to recognize the operation of certain processes in the physical world. We shall consider three of these operations. First, the preoperational child apparently fails to see the *reversibility* of certain physical operations. If an adult were asked how he knows that the amount of fluid remains the same in the example provided in Figure VII–1, he might say that if the operation were reversed (if the fluid in beaker C were poured back into beaker B), then the equality would be obvious. The preoperational child, on the other hand, does not appear to recognize this.

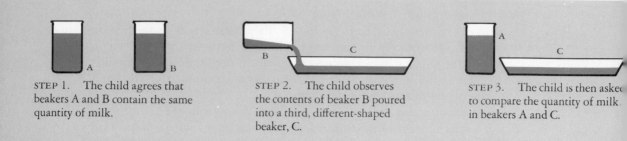

STEP 1.   The child agrees that beakers A and B contain the same quantity of milk.

STEP 2.   The child observes the contents of beaker B poured into a third, different-shaped beaker, C.

STEP 3.   The child is then asked to compare the quantity of milk in beakers A and C.

FIGURE   VII–1

A typical sequence for studying conservation of liquid quantity.

A second characteristic of the preoperational child which appears to prevent him from conserving is *centration.* This notion refers to the tendency to center or focus on a single detail of a question or problem and subsequently to be unable to shift to another detail or dimension. In the conservation of liquid, for example, the child may attend either to the height of the beaker (and thus say that the taller beaker has the greater volume) or to the width (and thus say that the wider and squatter beaker has the larger quantity of fluid). In order to solve the problem correctly, the child must *decenter*—that is, he must attend simultaneously to both the height and the width of the beakers. He then would be able to see the relationship between the changes in one of these dimensions and the compensatory changes in the other. Because the column of fluid becomes wider as it gets lower (or taller as it gets narrower) the overall quantity remains the same.

Although it is quite plausible to assume that the preoperational child tends to center upon one of the stimulus dimensions in a conservation problem, there is more than one possible interpretation of why this should occur. Inasmuch as the problems typically involve the use of relational terms (i.e., the experimenter asks: "Which one is bigger?"), it is possible that the child's responses result from his misunderstanding of the words rather than from deficiencies in logic or perception. The child may, for example, interpret the word "bigger" or "more" to mean "taller" in a particular context. Or, alternatively, the instructions may induce what Braine and Shanks (1965) have termed a phenomenal set ("looks bigger")

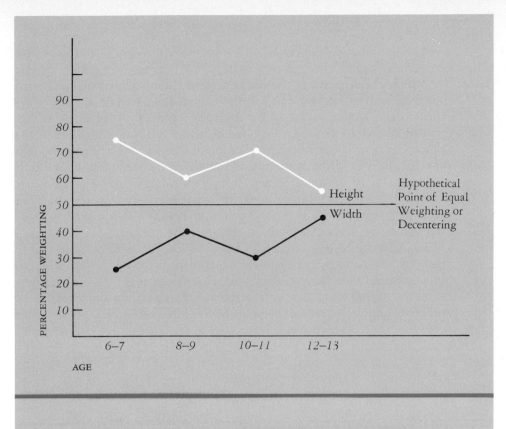

FIGURE VII−2

The relationship of decentering height and width with age. Data from Kempler, 1971.

rather than an objective set ("really is bigger"). How can one eliminate some of these competing explanatory alternatives?

In an ingenious study, Kempler (1971) presented children from four different age groups (6–7, 8–9, 10–11, and 12–13) with a series of one hundred rectangles that varied in height and width. No relational terms were involved in the question put to the child, which was simply to indicate whether a particular shape was large or small. By systematically employing all possible combinations of height and width, it was possible to determine whether the children were responding equally to height and width (which would represent the correct or fully decentered orientation) or whether they were centering more on one or the other. As seen in Figure VII–2, preoperational children decentered the least and equal weighting and coordination of height and width generally increased as a function of age.

A third characteristic of the preoperational child that prevents him from solving conservation problems appears to be that he perceives *states* rather than *transformations*. That is, he apparently attends to the series of successive conditions that are displayed in the experiment rather than the process by which the researcher changes or transforms one display into another. It is as if the nonconserving child sees a series of still pictures whereas a more advanced observer sees a moving picture. The difference is critical, for only by appreciating the transformation or continuous character of problems such as those depicted in Figure VII–1 can we be confident that the volumes must have remained the same.

To illustrate the preoperational child's tendency to perceive states rather than transformations, one Piagetian experiment involved the use of drawings to identify the perception of successive movements of a bar as it falls from the vertical to the horizontal position. Older children and adults given individual drawings such as those in Figure VII–3 in a "mixed-up" order

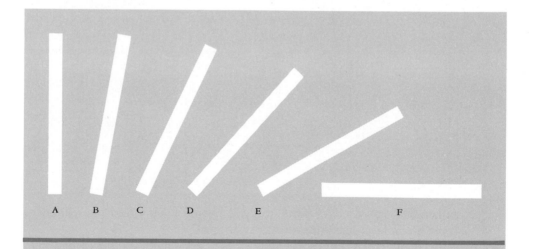

A   B   C   D   E   F

FIGURE VII–3

The "falling stick" problem, testing the ability to recognize transformations. Preoperational children, given separate illustrations (A through F) in random order, cannot arrange them correctly.

will immediately arrange them in the correct order of the transformation (i.e., A–F). In contrast, the preoperational child is unable to produce the sequence and may not even recognize it as correct when it is shown to him.

EXTENDED DISCUSSION

EXPERIMENTAL EFFORTS TO INDUCE CONSERVATION

Piaget considers that an understanding of conservation is "a necessary condition for all rational activity." To the extent that such an assertion is even partially accurate, there would be important educational advantages in speeding the acquisition of conservation. Moreover, the paradox of children contending that the amount of milk changes when an experimenter merely pours it from one glass to another has proved an irresistible challenge, especially for those interested in the development of intelligence.

According to Piaget, children below the age of six cannot learn conservation because of a cognitive immaturity that renders all relevant experience useless. The failure of early experimenters to induce conservation in young children was interpreted by some as vindication of this position (Flavell, 1963). More recent experiments, however, have met with greater success, yielding important information about the various means by which children learn.

Indirect Approaches: Teaching Logical Operations

We have seen that certain logical operations are assumed to be prerequisites for conservation mastery, whereas inability to grasp them is said to doom the young child to failure. It is not surprising, then, that the first conservation experiments were devoted to teaching nonconservers these and other relevant logical operations, in the hope that learning the basic concepts would help them solve the problems.

Experiments by Wallach and Sprott (1964), Lovell and Ogilvie (1961), Wallach, Wall, and Anderson (1967), Smedslund (1960; 1961 a, b, c),

Wohlwill and Lowe (1962), and Gruen (1965) included techniques which conformed to the Piagetian interpretation of the conservation problem. The Smedslund work is especially representative of the approach. In an early study, Smedslund (1960) tried to teach *transitivity,* a related logical operation, to five- and six-year-old children. They were told that Johnny liked dolls better than shoes, and shoes better than guns, and then asked, "Does Johnny like guns better than dolls, or does he like dolls better than guns?" The children tended to give nonlogical answers—e.g., "Johnny is a boy so Johnny likes guns better."

Later he presented nonconservers with a weight conservation problem and demonstrated that adding and then substracting an amount did not affect the weight of the original substance. The children were also shown that changing a clay ball into a cross did not affect its weight. When tested, however, the children ignored what they had seen and maintained that the ball and the cross would not weigh the same since they were different objects. Remarkably, the relevant demonstration did not help them master conservation problems. Smedslund concluded that children who are not sufficiently mentally mature do not benefit from relevant experience because they are not able to accommodate it.

The work of Irving Sigel originates from a different aspect of Piagetian theory, that of decentration. Sigel stresses that if a child is to decenter, he must be able to classify the same object on a number of different dimensions and must be able to use the technique of multiple classification. For example, answering the question "Does your brother have any brothers?" the child must define "brother" simultaneously in terms of (1) having the same parents, (2) being male, and (3) being a person other than the one in question. Thus, in a family with three male and two female children, five will have the same parents, three of these will be males, and two will be brothers of a male child. Uniform application of this multiple classification formula will yield correct answers. Roeper and Sigel (1967) therefore used elaborate and extensive decentration training techniques to teach a group of gifted four- and five-year-olds conservation. In addition to multiple classification, the children also were trained on other operations designed to induce decentering. Unlike those in Smedslund's work, many of the children in the Roeper and Sigel study subsequently solved conservation problems. Using a larger sample, Shantz and Sigel (1967) achieved similar success.

Teaching Relevant Skills

Smedslund and Sigel utilized relatively indirect approaches; other experimenters have used more direct ones. Kingsley and Hall (1967) contended that many unsuccessful training attempts "ignored the large amount of background knowledge necessary and the time needed to train children for conservation mastery." Rather than teaching logical prerequisites as Sigel had, Kingsley and Hall concentrated on teaching skills directly involved in the task. In conservation of length training, their goal was that the subject (1) know the meaning of specific terms (longer, shorter) used in the test question, (2) know how to measure length with an independent third measuring instrument, (3) know that use of a measuring stick is more accurate than visual cues, (4) know the effects of adding and subtracting length at the ends, and (5) know the effects (or lack of effects) of moving the objects. Each of the five components was taught separately, as were similar skills in a conservation of weight task. The techniques were quite successful. Later, using similar procedures, Rothenberg and Orost (1969) were able to teach conservation of number. Little generalization to other conservation tasks was evidenced in either experiment, however, leading some critics to question whether true conservation skills had been acquired.

Teaching Rules

Beilin (1965) pursued a different type of direct strategy, which he labeled "verbal rule instruction." When a child made a mistake, the experimenter presented the following rule: "Whenever we start with a length like this one (pointing) and we don't add any sticks to it or take away any sticks . . . it stays the same length even though it looks different. See, I can put them back the way they were, so they haven't really changed." While reciting the rule, the experimenter made the appropriate changes in the object so that the child would have a physical as well as a verbal representation of it. Beilin was quite successful in inducing the specific conservation but failed to produce significant generalization to related tasks.

Gelman (1969) succeeded in obtaining high levels of both specific and general conservation mastery; for this reason her methods deserve special attention. She noted the multidimensional quality of the stimuli present in conservation problems (weight, breadth, depth) and also that a child who attended to any one of them would be reinforced quite often inasmuch as the rule "whichever is taller is also bigger" is correct more often than not outside of the laboratory. The task, then, is to help the child attend to several dimensions simultaneously. In contrast with Sigel, who attempted to reach this goal through multiple-classification training, Gelman used a learning set procedure (see Chapter V, pp. 151–53). She varied irrelevant dimensions systematically and reinforced answers reflecting attention to

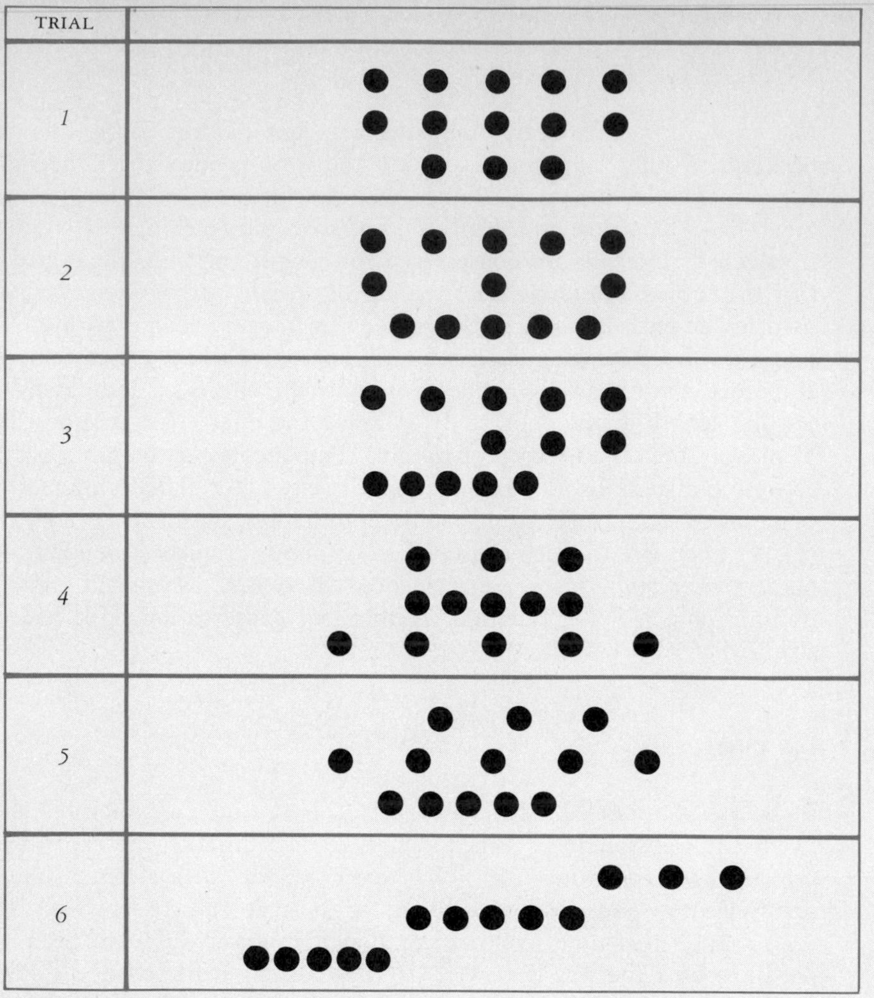

TRIAL	
1	
2	
3	
4	
5	
6	

FIGURE VII—4

Representative problems used by Gelman to induce conservation of number. The child's task is to point to the line that is different (or the two that are the same) on each trial. He is reinforced only for picking the line with 3 dots (or the two with 5 dots) and thus learns to attend only to this dimension—number—and to ignore the others. Length of the line, for example, is irrelevant; attending to it leads to reinforcement on Trial 1 but not on Trial 2, and so on. Adapted from R. Gelman, Conservation acquisition: A problem of learning to attend to relevant attributes. Journal of Experimental Child Psychology, *1969, 7, 167–187, by permission.*

the relevant variable. Figure VII–4 represents this procedure in training conservation of number. Note that the longer rows had a greater number of dots some of the time and a lesser number on other occasions so that the irrelevant dimension of length was varied. The position of the dots within each row also was varied. Thus, only by attending to the relevant variable —number—could the child obtain consistent reward.

The learning set procedure resulted in a striking degree of conservation mastery. Approximately 90 percent of subjects achieved perfect posttest scores. Impressively, more than 60 percent generalized their training to a newly presented conservation of amount problem. A related strategy has since been used by Siegler (Siegler and Liebert, 1972a,b) to teach pre- schoolers conservation of liquid quantity. Gelman's and Siegler's experi- ments conclusively answer the original question of whether four- and five- year-olds can be taught conservation skills that they will use reliably. The numerous unsuccessful and partially successful earlier studies, however, testify to the difficulty of inducing conservation in these children. To achieve experimental success required considerable persistence as well as ingenuity.

From the foregoing discussion it should be clear that the preoperational period is characterized by the child's frequent failures to think in terms of orderly operations and his inability to impose such operations upon the information available to him from the outside world. The hallmark of this period is the child's logical inconsistency. In the next period, the period of concrete operations, much of this is overcome; the child not only uses logical processes increasingly but also recognizes them, thereby developing the capacity to think consistently.

The Period of Concrete Operations

The period of concrete operations (approximately seven to eleven years of age) is characterized by the appearance of the ability to decenter, to recog- nize the nature of transformations, and, of course, to solve the so-called conservation problems. These and a variety of related intellectual phe- nomena require an understanding of the effects of certain operations in the environment and the appearance of a rudimentary grasp of logic. In fact, Piaget has elaborately detailed nine different groupings of logical classes and relations which are involved in the structure of concrete operations during this age period, although a consideration of them is beyond the intended scope of this book.* Given the large number of accomplishments of children at this age, one may reasonably ask what sorts of operations can the concrete operational child *not* perform? The answer is intriguing.

In the most general terms, he is still not able to *operate upon his operations*. Although he understands relationships among specific events in the environment, he is unable to produce formal, abstract hypotheses. He cannot imagine possible events that are not also real events, and thus cannot solve problems that involve formal abstractions. As an example, consider Archimedes' Law of Floating Bodies. This principle, which is a formal abstraction, states that an object will float in water if its density (weight per unit) is less than that of water. This law means that, if two objects are of equal volume, the heavier the object is, the more likely it will be to sink. This fact can give rise to an experimental test. Specifically, a child is given a bucket of water and several different small objects, some of which will float and some of which will sink when placed into the liquid. His job is to classify the objects in terms of whether they will float or sink, and to look for a rule that will *tie the findings together*.

The concrete operational child will say such things as an object sinks because it is iron, because it is heavy, and so on. He will be troubled, though, by the inconsistencies in such rules (i.e., a piece of wood may be heavier than a bit of rock, but the former floats while the latter sinks), and will become confused when he tries to solve the dilemmas created by them. In contrast, children who have reached the stage of formal operations appear able to abstract the appropriate statement by operating formally upon each of the operations which they have observed or tested. The phenomenon is illustrated by Piaget's description of one child who, at age twelve years, six months, comes close to a solution, saying in reference to a penny, that "it sinks because it is small, it isn't stretched enough. . . . You would have to have something larger to stay at the surface, something of the same weight and which would have a greater extension" (Inhelder and Piaget, 1958, 1958, p. 38).

As another illustration of the type of thinking displayed by the concrete operational child, we shall consider a somewhat different aspect of Piaget's research, dealing with children's understanding of morality.

Piaget and his associates (cf. Piaget, 1948) have presented children with

---

* An excellent discussion of these phenomena can be found in John Flavell's *The Developmental Psychology of Jean Piaget* (1963).

a variety of story pairs in which damage or harm has been done in both, and asked them to indicate which of the two sequences represented the "naughtier act." Such a pair of stories is shown in Table VII–1. Children at the preoperational stage regularly show a tendency to respond in an *objective* manner, by replying that naughtiness is related to the amount of damage done, rather than in a *subjective* manner, by responding to the intentions of the actor. Believing that breaking fifteen cups is worse than breaking one, regardless of intentions, children below age 7 will judge the boy in Story A of Table VII-1 to have been naughtier than the boy in Story B. Piaget and Inhelder (1969) have thus said of the preoperational child:

> Moral realism leads to objective responsibility, whereby an act is evaluated in terms of the degree to which it conforms to the law rather than with reference to whether there is malicious intent to violate the law or whether

TABLE VII–1

AN EXAMPLE OF THE STORY PAIRS USED BY PIAGET TO DETERMINE OBJECTIVE AND SUBJECTIVE MORALITY

STORY A	STORY B
John was in his room when his mother called him to dinner. John goes down, and opens the door to the dining room. But behind the door was a chair, and on the chair was a tray with fifteen cups on it. John did not know the cups were behind the door. He opens the door, the door hits the tray, bang go the fifteen cups, and they all get broken.	One day when Henry's mother was out, Henry tried to get some cookies out of the cupboard. He climbed up on a chair, but the cookie jar was still too high, and he couldn't reach it. But while he was trying to get the cookie jar, he knocked over a cup. The cup fell down and broke.

Source: Cited in Bandura and McDonald, 1963, p. 276.

the intent is good but in involuntary conflict with the law. The child, for example, is told not to lie long before he understands the social value of this order (for lack of sufficient socialization), and sometimes before he is able to distinguish intentional deception from the distortions of reality that are due to symbolic play or to simple desire. As a result veracity is external to the personality of the subject and gives rise to moral realism and objective responsibility whereby a lie appears to be serious not to the degree that it corresponds to the intent to deceive, but to the degree that it differs materially from the objective truth. One of us set up the comparison of a real lie (telling your family you got a good mark in school when you weren't called on to recite) to a simple exaggeration (telling, after being frightened by a dog, that he was as big as a horse or a cow). For young children, the first lie is not "naughty," because (1) it often happens that one gets good marks; and above all (2) "Mama believed it!" The second "lie," however, is very naughty, because nobody ever saw a dog *that* size. [p. 126.]

Not surprisingly, concrete operational children, who are capable of handling the idea of intent, responded in the subjective way, indicating, for example, that the boy in Story B has been naughtier and that a lie about grades is worse than an exaggeration about what one has seen. Further advances are made when they reach the period of formal operations to which we next turn our attention.

The Period of Formal Operations

Beginning with preadolescence, people begin to display the ability to engage in formal reasoning on an abstract level. They can draw hypotheses from their observations, imagine hypothetical as well as real events, and deduce or induce principles regarding the world around them. Efforts to solve the pendulum problem exemplify this final stage of cognitive development.

The Pendulum Problem. Inhelder and Piaget (1958) have used the following setup to explore logical thought. The subject is presented with a pendulum consisting of an object hanging from a string. He is permitted to vary the length of the string, change the weight of the suspended object, alter the height from which the pendulum is released, and push the pendulum with varying degrees of force. The problem which must be solved is a classical one in physics: to discover and state which of these factors alone or in combination will influence how quickly the pendulum swings. (In fact, length of the string is the critical variable. The shorter it is, the faster the pendulum swings.) Because the experimenter plays a nondirective role, the manner in which the problem is solved tells us much about the cognitive operations of the performer.

Children at the concrete operational period have a good deal of difficulty with the problem. In contrast, adolescents typically proceed with the three necessary steps for determining an adequate formal conclusion: they design their experiment before proceeding; observe and record systematically; and draw a logical conclusion. Inhelder and Piaget give an exemplary case of a fifteen-year-old who

> . . . after having selected 100 grams with a long string and a medium length string, then 20 grams with a long and short string, and finally 200 grams with a long and short, concludes: *"It's the length of the string that makes it go faster or slower; the weight doesn't play any role."* She discounts likewise the height of the drop and the force of her push. [1958, p. 75.]

MODES OF REPRESENTATION AND COGNITIVE GROWTH

Jerome S. Bruner has developed a theory of cognitive development which is heavily indebted to the work of Piaget. To understand how Bruner himself has proceeded, we shall survey the major aspects of his work.

Benchmarks of Intellectual Growth

According to Bruner, we may begin with the following six summary statements:

1. *Growth is characterized by increasing independence of response from the immediate nature of the stimulus.* As we already have seen in our description of Piaget's work, the very young child's behavior is often controlled by what is literally "right before his eyes." If an object is removed, covered up, or otherwise taken out of his immediate span of vision, the child will no longer respond to it. Escape from this immediate "stimulus control" clearly characterizes one aspect of the child's cognitive growth.

2. *Growth depends upon internalizing events into a "storage system" that corresponds to the environment.* It is quite clear, in many of the

examples we have seen thus far, that the child must develop some system of representing the world around him as a basis for manipulating his environment cognitively. Such a storage system does not appear full-blown; rather, it develops slowly and systematically. An adequate theory of cognitive development must describe and account for this growth.

3. *Intellectual growth involves an increasing capacity to say to oneself and to others, by means of words and symbols, what one has done or what one will do.* Bruner refers to this function as a type of self-consciousness which permits humans to go beyond mere adaptation and to engage in logical behavior.

4. *Intellectual development depends upon a systematic and contingent interaction between a tutor and a learner.* Bruner continually asserts that a child's cognitive development is fundamentally based on an interaction between the child's innate capacities and the specific information and structures which are provided by his environment. This emphasis is well characterized in the following statement:

> We take the view that cognitive growth in all its manifestations occurs as much from the outside in as from the inside out. Much of it consists in a human being's becoming linked with culturally transmitted "amplifiers" of motoric, sensory, and reflective capacities. It goes without saying that different cultures provide different "amplifiers," at different times in a child's life. One need not expect the course of cognitive growth to run parallel in different cultures, for there are bound to be different emphases, different deformations. But many of the universals of growth are also attributable to uniformities in human culture. [1966, pp. 1–2.]

5. *Teaching is vastly facilitated by the medium of language, which ends by being not only the medium for exchange but also the instrument that the learner can then use himself in bringing order into the environment.* For Bruner, as for most cognitive theorists, language serves a vital function in explaining human cognitive development. Likewise, one principal task of any cognitive theory is, in turn, to explain the development of language.

6. *Intellectual development is marked by increasing capacity to deal with several alternatives simultaneously, to attend to several sequences during the same period of time, and to allocate time and attention in a manner appropriate to these multiple demands.* These increasing abilities explain some of what Bruner has correctly described as the "great distance . . . between the one-track mind of the young child and the 10-year-old's ability to deal with an extraordinarily complex world" (1968, p. 6).

These are the benchmarks which a theory of cognitive development must take into account. How does Bruner's theory account for them? Most generally, his theory suggests that the principal achievement of the developing individual involves the manner in which he represents the world about him. Immediate experience is translated into a representational model of the world and that model in turn helps to determine further action. Bruner suggests that the world is represented in three different modes: the *enactive,* the *iconic,* and the *symbolic.*

The Enactive Mode

The enactive mode involves representation through action itself. During the sensorimotor period of intelligence, the young child appears to do just this. In an early study, Gellermann (1923) found that finger-tracing was essential for two-year-olds to learn to respond to triangularity. It is as if, in Bruner's words, "the children were translating the visual image into 'three turns' " (1966, p. 24). In explaining the phenomenon, Bruner points to Piaget's classic work on object permanence, reminding us that:

> . . . a one-year-old child, presented with a favorite toy, will not cry upon its removal unless he is holding it in his hand. Later, removal will bring tears if he has begun to move his hand out to reach it. Still later, it suffices to enrage him that it is removed when his eye has fallen on it. Finally, he will cry when the object, placed under a cover some time ago, is found to be missing when he returns to it. Objects, in short, develop an autonomy that is not dependent upon action. If at first "a rattle is to shake" and "a hole is to dig," later they are somehow picturable or conceivable without action. [1968, pp. 12–13.]

The Iconic Mode

The *iconic* mode involves the use of images to summarize and represent action. Thus, it is closely linked to perception. The child notices and stores the visible or "surface" features of objects and uses these characteristics as a basis for dealing with them representationally. If iconic representation and imagery is the principal cognitive tool of young children, then those who are high in the ability to use images should also show relatively superior school performance. Later, conceptual tasks will not be soluble simply by identifying vivid perceptual cues. For Bruner,

> It is of more than passing interest, then, that in the first two grades of primary school there is a *positive* correlation between the use of imagery

and school achievement. . . . As likely as not, the emphasis upon identifying things and attaching names to them, as well as the relatively small reliance on reasoning in most early school curricula, would account for this. By the third or fourth grade, the correlation becomes negligible. [1966, p. 27.]

Although the iconic mode obviously makes its appearance quite early in the life of the child, there is evidence that imagery becomes more sophisticated as the child grows older. This increase in sophistication is illustrated in studies which require the identification or manipulation of representations which are somehow incomplete or distorted. Very young children are not able to recognize dotted outlines as representing triangles, squares, or other forms that are familiar to them. Slightly older children succeed only by falling back on an enactive mode; faced with a difficult visual pattern, they often will "track" it with their fingers as if this action guided them to a solution (Bruner, 1966). Still older children find incomplete forms much easier to deal with. In one study, for example, children between the ages of seven and thirteen were presented with incomplete silhouettes of heads, faces, and various objects. Thir task, to sort the pictures into appropriate categories (such as boys or women), required the ability to recognize the forms as familiar patterns despite the absence of some usual information. Ability to do so increased dramatically with age (Mooney, 1957).

The Symbolic Mode

According to Bruner, symbols represent things in a remote or arbitrary way. " 'Philadelphia'," he notes, "looks no more like the city so designated than does a nonsense syllable" (1964, p. 3). This arbitrariness, of course, is symbolic representation's greatest strength, for a symbol * is by its nature manipulable far beyond actions or images. By manipulating symbols, not only can we rapidly eliminate alternatives, but we also can deduce and induce conclusions (also in abstract, symbolic form) and thus reach the greatest heights of our own cognitive capacity.

In investigating modes of representation, Bruner and his associates, like Piaget, typically have presented children of various ages with problems which they must solve. The problems are constructed in such a way that

---

* Here Bruner uses the term "symbol" much as Piaget uses the word "sign," i.e., to designate a socially shared representation of a thing that does not—or need not—resemble it in any way.

the child's answers and explanations will be likely to reveal something of the way in which he is thinking. Bruner is interested in more than merely tracing a decrease in "errors" as children grow older. Rather, he suggests: ". . . . when children give wrong answers it is not so often that they are wrong as that they are answering another question, and the job is to find out what question they are in fact answering" (1968, p. 4). Selection 5, below, illustrates his work with iconic and symbolic representation.

ON MULTIPLE ORDERING

Jerome S. Bruner and Helen J. Kenney

We are, like Inhelder and Piaget, interested in how the child reaches the point of being able to deal with logical problems, but unlike them, we believe that logical behavior grows out of and is sustained by psychological processes. . . . What seems more interesting psychologically is their hypothesis about there being some problem in reconciling a sensorimotor or perceptual mode of operating (grouping by similarity) with a symbolic mode (where one has to bear in mind not single instances, but many of them simultaneously). . . .

Our objective, then, is to learn how a child comes to deal with two aspects of a situation at a time, and we have chosen as our instrument an experiment involving the most logically "complex" of classification tasks: the matrix, a task

Reprinted from Bruner, J. S. and Kenney, H. J. On multiple ordering. In J. S. Bruner, R. R. Olver, and P. M. Greenfield, eds. *Studies in Cognitive Growth* (New York: Wiley, 1966), pp. 154–167. Copyright 1966, reproduced by permission of John Wiley & Sons, Inc.

involving the joint ordering of two ordered arrays, the so-called multiplication of classes. We have chosen this task precisely because it entails simpler logical operations, for we believe that it is more likely to reveal the underlying psychological processes that a child depends on to solve the problem (or to fail in his solution in characteristic ways). . . .

The Task

We designed a straightforward problem as our vehicle of study. It consisted of a set of nine clear-plastic beakers, to be arranged in a three-by-three matrix. The beakers varied three degrees in height and three in diameter. They were first laid out before the child on a ruled plaque of cardboard, as in Figure 1.

In order to acquaint the child with the matrix (turning now to the procedure proper), we removed first one glass, then two, and then three at a time, and asked the child to replace them. We also asked the child to tell us how the glasses in the columns and

Matrix Procedure

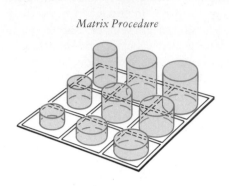

FIGURE 1

The matrix.

rows were alike and how they differed. Then we scrambled the glasses and had the child reconstruct, in effect *reproduce,* the entire arrangement by asking him to build "something like what was there before." After this we scrambled the glasses once more, but this time we placed the glass that was formerly in the southwest corner of the grid in the southeast corner (it was the shortest, thinnest glass) and asked the child again whether he could make something like what was there before, leaving the one glass where we had just put it. In short, we asked him to *transpose* the matrix, a task that could be accomplished only if the underlying rule or ordering principle of the matrix as constituted was understood.

Fifty children served as subjects, ten each of ages three, four, five, six, and seven. The procedure described was supplemented for the two younger age groups. The younger children were usually unable to handle the problems of double classification. After they had tried double classification, a comparable one-dimensional problem was given to them. Four glasses were used, varying in either height *or* diameter only. As with the other case, the task here was successively one of replacing within, then reproducing, and finally transposing the ordered one-dimensional array. A careful measure of the time needed for placing each glass in all the tasks was kept for the two youngest groups.

The gross findings can be quickly told. When asked to replace the glasses taken from the matrix, virtually all the older children (ages five, six, and seven) succeed. It is a different story with the younger ones. All manage to replace one glass correctly, but 30 percent reverse the positions when two glasses are removed, and 55 percent fail when three glasses (the diagonals of the matrix) are involved.

Just as the ability to replace items in the matrix increases with age, so too does the ability to *reproduce* the matrix in its original position after it has been scrambled. But the ability to perform this task lags behind performance on the replacement task at all ages.

Finally, the transposition task with the displaced glass proves most difficult of all. Again it is only among the oldest children that one finds as many with a perfect performance as in the reproduction task. The matter is summed up in Figure 2, where we see the lag graphically.

The data can also be described, perhaps more discriminatingly in terms of the percentage of glasses put back on the board in a correct position in each of the three tasks (Figure 3).

Our task now is to account for the difference in performance at each age

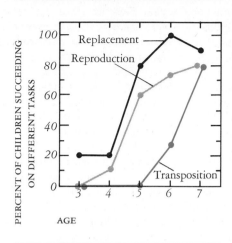

PERCENT OF CHILDREN SUCCEEDING ON DIFFERENT TASKS

AGE

FIGURE 2

Percent of children succeeding on different tasks.

glasses that are alike in either height or diameter, and the child must replace them. He usually succeeds, even at age three (seven in ten succeed). Failure in the task, rare though it is, comes from an error in matching the beaker to be replaced with the beakers around it. The child, tempted to work with a single dimension, will match the replacement beaker to the height of surrounding glasses, ignoring diameter, though it is the relevant cue. And so he fails, even though he looks steadily at the board and carries out his task with conspicuous diligence.

When he comes to replacing the three beakers in the central diagonal of the matrix, the child's task is made enormously more difficult, given his tendency to look for one-dimensional perceptual guidance. For again he uses the approach of "edge matching," plac-

—why, if you will, one type of task is so much more difficult, or why at a given age a matrix can be "dealt with" in one way but not in another, by reproduction but not by transposition, or by replacement and not by reproduction.

How Mastery is Achieved

An analysis of the three tasks—replacement, reproduction, and transposition —very quickly explains their difference in terms of "perceptual" support. In the replacement task the child fills a perceptual gap. We aid him in doing so in the first replacement task by the very nature of the task—replacing a single beaker in a "hole" in the matrix. Then two glasses are removed, two

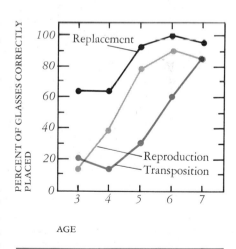

FIGURE 3

Percent of glasses correctly placed.

ing each beaker next to one that matches it in a single respect. No surprise then that there is a striking difference in the proportion of successful replacements on the two tasks, the linear and the diagonal (Figure 4). We do not know why the child prefers to be guided by the height of the beakers, but this is usually his tendency, and if one were to judge his performance on whether the matrix was in order on this dimension, the differences between the older and younger children would disappear. What is important, in any case, is that the younger children are very perceptual in their orientation, and very much given to guidance by a single visual feature of the task.

The reproduction task is more difficult. The actual matrix, with all its visual support, is destroyed and scrambled. Now it must be reproduced. Note first that virtually every child who succeeded, in fact, reproduced the matrix in its original orientation with no transposing of dimensions. It was seemingly a copying task, in which the "template" seemed to be a memory image of the original matrix. Indeed, the children appeared to be remembering rather than figuring out. When asked what they were doing, they would often tell you that they were trying to remember where the glasses had been before.

Transposition is something else. Children below six rather typically begin to perform the task by trying to take the transposed glass from its new position and returning it to "where it belongs." At the very least, success depends upon their holding in mind either some version of the verbal formula—to quote a child, "They get fat in one direction and tall in another"— or what is far less likely, matching the transposed case to one of the eight depictable versions of a three-by-three double-classification matrix. It is interesting that only the oldest group of children were able to perform the task at all well. Indeed, a comparison of the three older groups is revealing. On the reproduction task a majority of the children were able to perform perfectly. But on the transposition task none of the five-year-olds and only a small fraction of the six-year-olds succeeded. Not until the seventh year is the task well within their reach.

It is probably the same image-bound procedure that leads children to success on the reproduction procedure that produces failure in transposition. For again we see the younger children try-

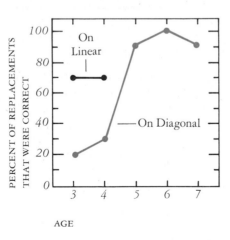

FIGURE 4

Percent of replacements that were correct.

ing to "copy" something they have in mind—an easy road to failure in transposition. Usually they will try to move the single transposed beaker to "where it belongs," i.e., its place in the original matrix. Or, when prevented from moving it, they may simply build the old matrix right around the newly positioned beaker. Another typical procedure is to handle the task by edge matching, placing one beaker at a time, matched in a single characteristic, to a beaker next to it.

Symbolic Structure in the Task

In the main, the foregoing describes how the children proceeded in these tasks and how well (or poorly) they did. What does this tell us about the organization of experience, how it related to the possible symbolic coding that makes transposition possible? We have some inklings already. For one thing, the younger children seemed to be guided by a rather nondecomposable memory image that guided their reconstruction of the matrix. . . . They put the beakers "where they had been." And, as we have already noted, this procedure failed to achieve transposition.

A second suggestion of the difficulty of younger children comes from some incidental observations. Recall that we asked each child to say how a pair of beakers were alike, and how they differed. No child had any difficulty in saying how two beakers *differed.* But often they had difficulty saying how they were similar. We were astonished that 41 percent of the three-year-olds named a *difference* in height or diameter when we asked them how two

beakers placed before them were alike. The proportion drops to half that among the four-year-olds, and is rare after that. But, throughout, the responses to the question on similarity seem somewhat slower coming than the one on difference. This suggests to us that (contrary to Inhelder and Piaget [1947]), relations of similarity are not so easily formed in early life, or if early formed, then surely not easily abstracted from the perceptual whole. This means, in effect, that the young children could not easily hold one aspect of the beakers constant on the basis of similarity, while serializing them on the basis of differences in the other. For a child who cannot do this much easily, the verbal formula: "They get fatter in one direction and taller in the other" is of no more use than a description of a sunset to a sufferer from color blindness.

Indeed, it may well be that one requires a highly differentiated discrimination of similarity *and* difference in order to be able to use a verbal rule such as that just stated. We have checked on this hypothesis as follows. Three "linguistic modes" are used by the children in describing similarities and differences. One is *dimensional,* language being used to describe two ends of a continuum, as in "fat" and "skinny," or "tall" and "short," to use two very common dimensional pairs. A second mode was *global* or undifferentiated, as when "big" and "little" were used to describe differences in either height or diameter. Finally there is *confounding,* in which one end of a continuum is described dimensionally and the other globally, as when a child says of two glasses that one is "tall" and the other "little," and of two others that one is "fat" and the other "little."

The language children use is associated with how well they carry out their tasks. For purposes of analysis we grouped all fifty children studied and examined what kind of linguistic mode they used and how they performed on the three tasks (Figure 5). Global language (associated principally with younger children) appears to diminish the quality of performance on all tasks, whether replacement, reproduction, or transposition. Confounded language has a striking association with failure on the transposition task, i.e., if a child shows confounding, he is almost sure to fail on the task. But also note well that, while dimensional language is a good prognosis of success in the transposition task, it by no means guarantees such success.

One other point about the organization of experience into a form amenable to translation into a verbal role has to do with temporal integration. Watching the two youngest groups of subjects, one gains the impression that each placement is an act unto itself. In the replacement task involving two beakers, for example, a first beaker is replaced without regard for how the

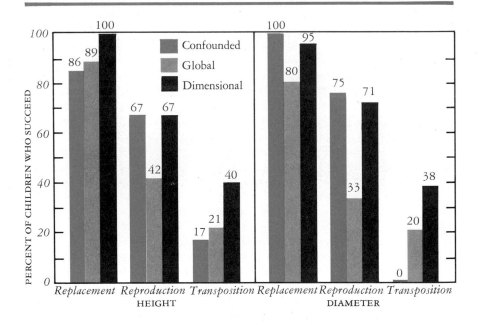

FIGURE 5

Percent of children who succeed in replacement, reproduction, and transposition using confounded, global, or dimensional language.

second has to fit in. In a nutshell, a verbal rule would be useless at this age simply because their temporal span does not match the requirements of going beyond the single placement.

To sum up matters at this point: younger children tend to be strongly guided by the perceptual nature of tasks, and by only a single perceptual feature at a time. As they grow older, they seem no less perceptual in their approach to our tasks, but they are now able to deal with several features of a task at once. But while (at age six, for example) they can reproduce complex perceptual displays, they are poorly equipped to do tasks that require a translation of a perceptual array into a verbal formulation of more general type. In a word, these are children who can do the perceptually supported replacement task but fail on reproduction and transposition. There are children who can reproduce but not transpose; and they can virtually always succeed on replacement. Finally, if a child succeeds in transposition, he will almost certainly achieve success in the other tasks. In these thirty children age five and over, there was only one who did not fit this pattern. . . .

Another way of summing up matters is to describe the nature of the performance at each age level. A convenient way of doing so is in terms of whether the arrangements made on the reproduction and transposition tasks achieved double classification, single classification (with ordering of only one variable, usually height), or apparent random ordering. The result of this analysis is presented in Figure 6. The picture is plain enough. Random ordering in response to these tasks starts high and drops to nothing by the sixth or

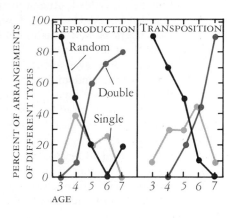

FIGURE 6

Percent of arrangements of different types.

seventh year. Single classification grows rapidly from three to four (for reproduction) and then declines, to be replaced by multiple ordering. The picture is the same for transposition, only delayed. Our supplementary observations of the two younger groups, using one-dimensional arrays, reinforces the finding that children can, by four, handle one-dimensional ordering quite well. But, and it is a big qualification, they cannot handle two dimensions, for the reasons mentioned earlier.

Time and Technique

We had noted at the outset that children were timed. The results of the analysis of solution time, while not very revealing, can at least be described briefly. The distractibility and special vagary of the three- and four-year-olds were such that the timing of their performance provided little information, save that in general very quick and very slow reactions were usually the wrong ones. If we use the three older groups, the picture is even clearer. Arrangements of the random type are usually the fastest. If we leave these out, there is a negative correlation, indeed $-.70$, between the quality of solution offered (as measured on our "scale") and the time required to reach a solution—the better the solution, the longer the time required. Time, then, can be taken as a measure of information processing.

Representation of the Task

Consider now how the children of different ages go about their task, particularly with a view toward clarifying the nature of representation. The very young children, the threes and fours, seem to "play their own game," a game consisting primarily in handling the glasses, moving them about on the grid, placing them in the center of the squares, and then looking at what they have done. When replacing glasses in the matrix, for example, they will tell you that the glasses should go where they put them because there were empty spaces for them. The relation of the replaced beakers to the component groups is not appreciated, and similarities among beakers are often attributed to the fact that pairs may be in the center of the squares or simply on the grid itself. Despite our best efforts, the task could not be grasped by our younger subjects, and they were so eager to begin manipulating the beakers, putting them here and there, that they could scarcely wait to begin.

The older children are strikingly different. In the reproduction task (at which most succeed) they uniformly produce a matrix of glasses that is positioned identically to the original display. And even those who do not reproduce the matrix exactly are obviously using the original orientation. Whatever else they may be doing, it is clear that these older children are copying an established image. They tell us that they put the glasses "where they were before." With the transposition task a further difference among the age groups appears. Before the age of six many children attempt to move the transposed glass back to "where it belongs." Failing this, they may try to rebuild the original, by edge-matching one beaker at a time to the transposed glass, working along a single row or column. The five-year-old, so well served by his imagery on the reproduction task, attempts its use again, and is thwarted by the transposition. Knowing how difficut it is to effect transformations on images, we are not surprised by his failure. But he seems to be surprised, often starting confidently and "petering" out. For the age of five seems to be a transitional stage. Imagery, where it cannot readily solve the problem as given, does allow a child to re-establish some of the constituents of the matrix, but imagery cannot handle their relation. It is this, we believe, that leads the five-year-old to start out with such confidence and end in so much confusion.

What makes the difference in the case of the successful six- and seven-year-olds? We believe there is a discontinuity in their handling of the task. The younger children treat the display as a picture or image. The older ones have translated that image into a form that can be subtly encoded into language, and have formulated a set of verbal rules that can guide them in producing transformations that include the required transposition. The two approaches are strikingly different.

We have already mentioned the child who "summed up" the matrix with the phrase, "It gets fatter going one way and taller going the other." This is a nice example, for it lays bare the striking substitutability gained by such a formulation. In the most concrete terms, there are now four ways in which which "it" can get "fatter," and once one chooses one of them, there are still two ways left for "it" to get "taller." Imagery now can serve as a check—and it does. Older children often lean back and have a look at the result of their work before being fully satisfied that the reproduction has been accomplished. In the transposition task, the transferred beaker does, of course, reduce the substitutability to two alternatives, but the crucial matter is not how *much* substitutability, but rather whether the child's representation of the task permits *any* substitution.

Here is where the cost of imagery is so high. The children who try to "copy" the original as a means of solving the transposition task end in a muddle precisely because they cannot get any match between what they place on the board and what they have in their heads. You will often see a child, relying on such imagery, try first to place a beaker by edge-matching it to one already on the board, and then moving it to where it "should" be in the light of where it had been.

We have already commented on the fact that "having" the correct dimen-

sional language helps the child toward a linguistic formulation of the display, but does not guarantee that he will be able to deal with transposition. Indeed, if the child can deal dimensionally with the language of both height *and* diameter, he is virtually sure to be able to cope with the problem. But "having" vocabulary, even organized in dimensional pairs, is not necessarily the same as using them in organizing experience or in ordering one's intellectual operations. That step, it would seem, requires further exercise. We refer to the fact that the children who fail on transposition can probably exercise the skills needed to succeed on that task—but only on simpler tasks. Analogies probably help very little, but we are reminded of the neophyte skier who can use his skis quite adequately on moderate trails, but does not yet know how to deal with steeper ones. Again, he cannot yet recognize what is demanded by the task.

To sum up, then, a study of how children represent complexly ordered arrays such as a two-dimensional one yields a variety of suggestive conclusions. One of them is that children of three and four generally go about the task with a great burst of manipulation, as if overt trial-and-error will reproduce a scrambled matrix or replace a pair or a trio of missing elements. They seem not yet able to form images or schemata that embody the ordered relation of two dimensions.

By the fifth year the child is able to develop an image of a two-dimensional array, and his efforts to reproduce it are quite effective. Once he must alter that image, however, it is apparent that he can deal with only a single dimension or grouping at a time and cannot relate these groupings to one another in a matrix. Even in the perceptually supported task of replacing beakers in the matrix, children have the most trouble with replacing the diagonal set that varies in two dimensions at once.

Finally, the six- and seven-year-olds achieve the capacity to render the matrix into a verbal or symbolic formula: one that is amenable to order-preserving transformation, including the spatial transposition we have used in this experiment. "Having" the proper language helps the child take this final step, but there is much that is still unexplained as to how the child progresses from merely having to knowing how to use. We incline to the view that what is needed for the child to take that step is organizing experience into a form that allows more complex language to be used as a tool not only for describing it but transforming it.

The young child, as we have seen, is characterized by Bruner as relying heavily on the iconic mode of representation. Although he seeks information in problem-solving situations which is based on familiarity in his environment and which can be "pointed to," he appears relatively unable to produce complex inferences or to process indirect information from "nonsensory" features of the problem. But some problems cannot be reduced to the iconic mode; they require symbolic representation.

In order to study further the development of symbolic representation, Bruner and Kenney (1966b) posed a problem to children which is, on the surface, apparently a simple one: they were presented with two vessels, each containing some liquid, and asked which glass in the pair was fuller and which was emptier. Many such combinations can be arranged, but for reasons which we shall address presently, Bruner and Kenney selected the eleven combinations shown in Figure VII–5. The results were intriguing.

Note that, when the child understands the abstract notion of proportion, the correct answer is that the glass with the greater proportion of water in it is the fuller one, and the glass that has a lesser proportion of water in it is the emptier one. This is, of course, the answer that adults will give. It is perhaps not surprising that the number of correct responses tends to increase with age from five to eleven. More interesting is the type of errors made. Here is a particularly fascinating one:

> . . . we present a pair of half-filled glasses of unequal volume. Identifying the glass of larger volume as A we often find that a child will say that A is fuller than B and then go on to say that A is emptier than B. Or he will say that both are equally full, but A is emptier. This seemed extraordinary to us, for it seemed like such a patent contradiction. [Bruner, 1968, p. 8.]

More astonishing still is the relationship of this kind of contradictory error with age. At first blush, one would expect that contradictions, like

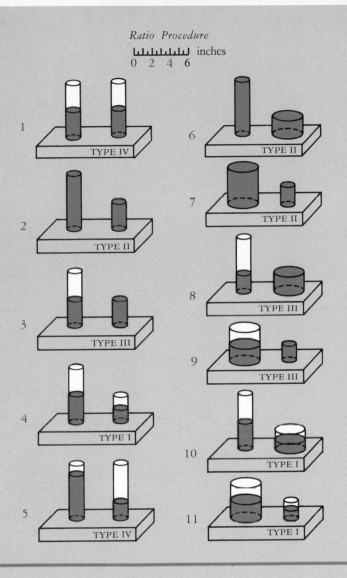

Ratio Procedure

0 2 4 6 inches

1 — TYPE IV
2 — TYPE II
3 — TYPE III
4 — TYPE I
5 — TYPE IV
6 — TYPE II
7 — TYPE II
8 — TYPE III
9 — TYPE III
10 — TYPE I
11 — TYPE I

FIGURE VII–5

Pairs of beakers presented to children by Bruner and Kenney in studying symbolic representation. Adapted from J. S. Bruner and H. J. Kenney, On multiple ordering. In J. S. Bruner, R. R. Olver, and P. M. Greenfield, eds., Studies in Cognitive Growth. *Copyright 1966, reproduced by permission of John Wiley & Sons, Inc.*

other classes of errors, would decrease in frequency with increasing age. But just the reverse is the case! When the two glasses have unequal volume, 27 percent of the errors made by five-year-olds were contradictions, whereas fully 68 percent of the errors made by seven-year-olds were contradictions (Bruner, 1968, p. 8). In fact, more generally, although the percentage of noncontradictory errors decreases with age, the percentage of contradictory errors increases with age at least through age seven. The combined data for all problems are shown in Figure VII–6.

At this point, Bruner and Kenney have no more than a surprising description of what children do. But, as we have seen earlier, Bruner argues that we must go further and attempt to understand the psychological processes that are involved in children's reasoning. He has put it this way:

> What accounts for this astonishing increase in logical contradiction—calling something fuller and then saying it is emptier, or saying that two vessels are equally full and then claiming that one is emptier? There are two alternatives. The first is that older children are less logical, less concerned with consistency—which certainly seems far-fetched in the light of what else we know about intellectual growth between the ages of 4 and 11. The other is that *logical* contradiction is not the issue at all, that it is a by-product of some other psychological process—perhaps of the way children go about defining and judging fullness and emptiness. [1968, p. 8.]

We can get some grasp of the manner in which the child is solving the problem by asking him to state the basis of his answers and to make further judgments (e.g., which glass has the higher level of water), together with analyzing the frequency of errors by problem type. For example, note that in displays 2, 6, and 7 (in Figure VII–5) both glasses are filled all the way to the top but that they hold unequal amounts. In these instances, a judgment based simply on amount is pitted against one that depends upon the relational concept of proportion. In the first case, the glass with the greater volume would be "fuller" while the glass with the lesser volume would be "emptier," although from a proportional point of view both glasses are equally full. By analyzing the nature of the particular comparison vis-à-vis the nature of the child's explanations, we can identify the psychological processes underlying various contradictions. According to Bruner and Kenney:

> What then accounts for the differences we have found between the younger and older children? We suggest that what is involved is that the children are at different points en route from the iconic to symbolic representation. The younger child differs from the older child in the number of attributes he attends to in these situations involving fullness and emptiness. It is quite clear that the younger child attends to one—the apparent amount

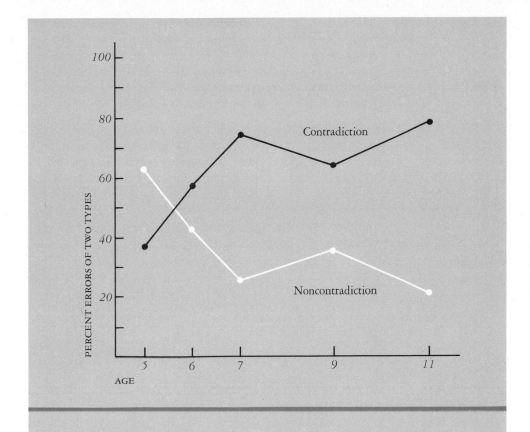

FIGURE VII–6

Percentage of errors of the contradictory and noncontradictory types. Adapted from J. S. Bruner and H. J. Kenney, On multiple ordering. In J. S. Bruner, R. R. Olver, and P. M. Greenfield, eds., Studies in Cognitive Growth. *Copyright 1966, reproduced by permission of John Wiley & Sons, Inc.*

of water; the older to two—the volume of filled space and the volume of empty space. The younger child attempts to apply a single variable to fit a contrast pair. The older child can dissociate the situation into two variables —filled space and empty space—but is not yet able to relate them to a third, the volume of the container itself. To accomplish this, the child must be able to detach himself from perceptual features in order to deal with the relationship. When the child can establish the relationship among all three terms—the amount of water, the amount of empty space, the volume of the container—he has a symbolic concept of proportion. The older child who is able to cope with several cues simultaneously is almost always the one who has some structure into which he can fit them. [1966b, pp. 180–81.]

Bruner thus explains apparent contradiction in terms of a larger consistency in psychological processes; the older child has moved from a simple solution based on perceptual judgment to a more complex one in which he is integrating several aspects of the display. But, not being able to relate several aspects of the display to a more abstract and symbolic notion, proportion itself, he superficially appears to be less logical and to enter into contradictory solutions. At a later age, correct answers are given as a true symbolic representation of proportionality emerges.

VIII

INTELLIGENCE

IN PREVIOUS CHAPTERS we traced the development of processes through which the child comes to know and adapt to his world. Now we turn to intelligence within a somewhat different context, including its meaning, measurement, and relation to other variables.

What is intelligence? Despite the vast interest by psychologists in intellectual ability and its measurement, there has been little agreement about definition. Rather, the nature of intelligence has been debated continuously and definitions of it have undergone change as new information has been acquired.

THE CONCEPT OF INTELLIGENCE

Fixed versus Fluid Models

As implied in our earlier discussion of genetics and heredity (Chapter IV), one focus of discussion about the nature of intelligent behavior has revolved around the question of whether it is innate (and therefore fixed) or learned (and therefore fluid). For the most part, the dominant view, at least until

World War II, was founded on the beliefs of fixed intelligence and predetermined development that emphasized innate factors (Hunt, 1961); each of these beliefs enjoys some empirical support. Animal research provides examples of maturation which appears relatively uninfluenced by environmental events; correlations of tested intelligence progressively increase with the degree of genetic relationship. But evidence that intelligence may be changed, sometimes dramatically, by environmental determinants also has accumulated, transforming the concept considerably.

General versus Specific Intelligence

In referring to someone as "bright" or "dull," all of us recognize a general way in which an individual deals with the world. On the other hand, we also are aware that the "bright" individual may not do everything well and that "dull" people are sometimes remarkably adept at certain tasks. In their definitions, theories, and test construction, psychologists also have recognized both the generality and specificity of intelligent behavior.

Theorists who view intelligence as a general attribute often refer to it as the ability to learn, the capacity to adjust or adapt to the environment, especially to new situations, or sometimes simply to all of the knowledge a person has acquired (Robinson and Robinson, 1965). Thus, we find intelligence defined as "an acquiring-capacity" (Woodrow, 1921, p. 207), or a "general mental adaptability to new problems and conditions of life" (Stern, 1914, p. 3). These psychologists present one view of intelligence: that it is a single, general attribute possessed to some degree by each individual.

Others, among them L. L. Thurstone (1941) and J. P. Guilford (1966), regard intelligence as consisting of a number of different attributes or capacities. According to these multifactor models of intelligence, an individual may be well endowed with one attribute, but deficient in a second. Assuming that intelligence is not general, but instead consists of a number of specific skills, these theorists have sought to discover their nature.

The procedure employed is conceptually quite simple. A group of individuals is given a large number of different tests, each of which purports to measure intelligence. It is assumed that success on some of the tests requires skill in one area, while success on other tests requires skill in other areas. For example, some tests might require skill in memory for verbal material while others might require the ability to work effectively with abstract mathematical concepts. The task of the experimenter is to discover the existence of different subgroups of tests, each of which requires a different skill to perform. To achieve that objective the experimenters employ a statistical technique called "factor analysis." Cattell (1965) has suggested that the rationale underlying this technique is similar to the rationale a jungle hunter might take in deciding whether a set of dark blobs he observes in a river is three separate rotting logs or a single alligator. To make this decision the hunter watches for movement. If the blobs move together he assumes that they are part of the same structure, an alligator. If, on the other hand, they do not move together, then they are not part of the same structure, but instead represent three different structures, three logs. Similarly, if changes in performance on one test typically are accompanied by changes in performance on a second test— i.e., they move together—one could assure that the tests are measuring the same attribute or *factor*. It remains then for the investigator to give a name to each factor based on his subjective view of the skill involved.

What are some of the factors which have been identified by the use of factor analysis? Thurstone and Thurstone (1941) concluded that there are seven primary ones: perceptual speed, word comprehension, word fluency, space, number, memory, and induction. They also acknowledged a general factor which operated in all tasks, but they believe that analysis of the several factors is more useful in assessing intellectual ability.

Applied Approach to Defining Intelligence

Since the 1920s, there has been less of an attempt to achieve a theoretical definition of intelligence and wider acceptance of a more empirical definition (Robinson and Robinson, 1965). There are several reasons for this transition. One is the failure to reach a consensus based on theoretical models of intelligence. Another is that scores on different mental tests correlate positively with each other regardless of the theory underlying their construction. A third reason for the transition stems from wider acceptance of the view that intelligence is not a concrete entity located somewhere within the individual but an idea—a hypothetical construct—that is useful in describing and predicting behavior. In this regard, the mental testing movement, to which we now turn, has been relatively successful.

THE MEASUREMENT OF INTELLIGENCE

From the beginning of the century, when test construction seriously commenced, until the late 1950s, the testing movement was characterized by expansion and public acceptance. Holtzman (1971) describes these accomplishments:

> During the past half century, the standardized mental test with nationally based norms has proven to be a highly effective instrument for selection and classification of men in the armed forces; for evaluation of educational progress within our school systems; for selective admission of college students; for selection of employees within government, business, and industry; and for clinical assessment of individuals in need of psychological services. It is estimated that within American schools alone, over 250 million standardized tests of ability are administered each year. . . . It is a rare individual indeed, especially among children and young adults, who has not been evaluated by a standardized mental test, a test that has played a significant role in determining his place in society. [p. 546.]

It is thus appropriate to consider in detail some of the principles of test construction, as well as examples of the more widely used tests.

Principles of Test Construction

Initial Item Selection. The first step in constructing any kind of psychological test is selection of appropriate items. The choice will depend upon both the purpose of the test and the theoretical persuasion of the constructor.

Norms and Standardization. Next, the test items must be administered to a representative group of individuals in order to establish normative performance. This group, the standardization sample, must be chosen carefully because its scores will be employed as a standard against which later examinees' scores will be compared. For example, if the test is being designed for children of varying ages and socioeconomic backgrounds, the standardization group should include individuals reflecting these characteristics.

Still another part of standardization procedures concerns the context within which the test is administered. When classroom tests are given in school, as in spelling or arithmetic, it is usual for individual teachers to differ widely in their selection of content, the amount of time allowed for taking the test, whether notes may be used, and so forth. Such tests are unstandardized, and do not permit direct comparisons from one classroom to another. A child who correctly answered 80 percent of the questions on Mrs. Jones' arithmetic test might very well have learned less—or more—than one who earned the same score on Mrs. Smith's test. If we are to compare many children from different parts of the country, or even different classrooms, successfully, this problem must be overcome. *Standardization of test procedures* is used for this purpose. Specifically, a standardized test is "one in which the procedure, apparatus, and scoring have been fixed so that precisely the same test can be given at different times and places" (Cronbach, 1960, p. 22). However, as Cronbach goes on to note, testing procedures cannot simply be classified as standardized or not standardized. Rather:

> Tests vary in the completeness with which they are standardized. Printing the questions and mass-producing the equipment assures uniformity in those respects, but the directions to the subject are not always worked out in complete detail. Every condition which affects performance must be specified if the test is to be regarded as truly standardized. Thus for a test of color-matching ability, one needs to use uniform color specimens, to follow uniform directions for administration and scoring, and also to use precisely the right amount and kind of illumination. If standardization of the test were fully effective, a man would earn very nearly the same score no matter who tested him or where. [1960, p. 23.]

It is sometimes felt that one of the weaknesses of psychological tests is that standardization procedures do not allow for optimal conditions under which any one individual may perform. This may be true, but if comparison with others is desired, it is more important that the test be conducted in a standard situation for all individuals than that it be conducted under optimal conditions.

Reliability. Sometime after a test has been standardized, efforts must be made to check its reliability. Reliability refers to how closely sets of scores designed to measure the same thing are related—i.e., to the consistency of the test. One common method of determining reliability is to administer a test to the same individuals on two different occasions. Another consists of administering equivalent forms of the test or items from the same form on separate occasions. In either case the two sets of scores are then correlated; the higher the correlation coefficient, the higher the reliability. Reliability, then, refers to how closely the sets of scores are related or how consistent they are.

Predictive Validity. According to many psychologists interested in measurement, questions of validity are the most important which can be asked about any psychological test. Simply, *the validity of a test is the degree to which it actually measures what it purports to measure.*

How does one determine validity? Many specific techniques are employed, but all have one feature in common: one or more independent *criterion measures* are obtained and correlated with scores from the test in question. Criterion measures are chosen on the basis of what the test is designed to measure. Anxiety exhibited in a public speaking situation, for example, might be a criterion measure for a test to evaluate self-consciousness.

The validity of intelligence tests usually is determined by employing, as criterion tasks, measures of academic achievement, such as school grades, teacher ratings, or scores on achievement tests. The reported correlations for the more widely used intelligence tests and these criterion tasks are reasonably high; for example, they fall between .40 and .75 for the Stanford-Binet intelligence test. Further, children who have been accelerated or "skipped" one or more grades do considerably better on the Stanford-Binet than do those who have shown normal progress, whereas youngsters who were held back one or more grades show considerably lower than average scores (McNemar, 1942). So the Stanford-Binet appears to measure intelligence, at least insofar as intelligence is reflected in school performance, and is thus relatively successful in predicting school achievement. Such predictive validity is largely responsible for the wide use of tests of intelligence.

TYPES OF INTELLIGENCE TESTS

In the following sections, examples will be given of a few of the most widely employed intelligence tests. All of the ones discussed are administered individually rather than in groups. Presumably this optimizes the motivation and attention of the examinee and provides opportunity for the sensitive examiner to assess subjective factors that may influence test performance. One may note that the child appears relaxed and therefore is probably functioning at a high level or one may observe that intense anxiety is interfering with performance. Such clinical judgments are not feasible on group intelligence tests. On the other hand, group tests have the undeniable advantage of providing information on many individuals quickly and often without the need of highly trained psychologists.

Tests for Children and Adults

The Binet Scales. In 1905 Alfred Binet and T. Simon, commissioned by the Minister of Public Education in Paris, devised the first successful test of intellectual ability, called the "Metrical Scale of Intelligence." Composed of thirty problems in ascending order of difficulty, its goal was to identify children who were likely to fail in school, so that they could be transferred to special classes. Systematic comparisons were thus made between normal and mentally retarded children. Later revisions of the test in 1908 and 1911 were based on the classroom observations of characteristics that teachers called "bright" and "dull" as well as a considerable amount of trial-and-error adjustment; scores obtained on them agreed strongly with teachers' ratings of intellectual ability.

Beginning with the 1908 revision, the Binet-Simon test was arranged into age levels. For example, the investigators placed all tests which normal three-year-olds could pass in the three-year level, all tests which the normal four-year-olds could pass in the four-year level, and so on up to age thirteen. This arrangement gave rise to the concept of *mental age*. A child's mental age was the age of normal children whose performance he equaled. This formula, which was simple to grasp as a complement to the youngster's chronological age, did much to popularize intelligence measurement and the mental testing movement generally.

The Stanford-Binet Tests. The Binet-Simon tests attracted much interest and translations soon appeared in many languages. Most important, however, was the work of Louis Terman at Stanford University who revised the test into the first Stanford-Binet in 1916. The Stanford-Binet was a new test in many ways; items had been changed and it had been standardized on a relatively large American population, including about one thousand children and four hundred adults. Further, Terman and his associates employed the notion of the *intelligence quotient* or IQ—the ratio of an individual's mental age to his chronological age, multiplied by 100 to avoid decimals. Thus

$$IQ = \frac{MA}{CA} \times 100$$

In conception, this new term was ingenious. If a child's mental age and chronological age were equivalent, his IQ, regardless of actual chronological age, would be 100—reflecting average performance. Further, this procedure made direct comparisons of relative retardation or acceleration possible for children of different calendar ages. If a four-year-old has a mental age of three, his IQ will be 75 ($\frac{3}{4} \times 100$), as will that of an equally retarded twelve-year-old, with a mental age of nine ($\frac{9}{12} \times 100 = 75$). The interpretation of IQ, then, is the same at different ages.

The Stanford-Binet was revised in 1937 and again in 1960, each time with the inclusion of new improvements and restandardization. The distribution of IQ scores peaks at about 100 and there are approximately as many lower scores as higher ones. Table VIII–1 shows the meaning of various scores; for example, if a child obtains a score of 112, he has done as well or better than 77 percent of the individuals in the standardization sample. The Stanford-Binet, with its various revisions, has become the standard against which new measures of intelligence are evaluated.

The present Binet Scales, like the earlier versions, consist of a large number of cognitive and motor tasks ranging from the extremely easy to the extremely difficult. The test itself may be administered to individuals ranging in age from approximately two years to adulthood but, of course, not every individual is given every question. For example, young children

TABLE VIII–1

THE MEANING OF VARIOUS IQ SCORES OBTAINED ON THE REVISED STANFORD-BINET

THE CHILD WHOSE IQ IS:	EQUALS OR EXCEEDS	THE CHILD WHOSE IQ IS:	EQUALS OR EXCEEDS
136	99 percent	98	45 percent
135	98	97	43
134	98	96	40
133	98	95	38
132	97	94	36
131	97	93	34
130	97	92	31
129	96	91	29
128	96	90	27
127	95	89	25
126	94	88	23
125	94	87	21
124	93	86	20
123	92	85	18
122	91	84	16
121	90	83	15
120	89	82	14

TABLE VIII–1 *(continued)*

THE CHILD WHOSE IQ IS:	EQUALS OR EXCEEDS	THE CHILD WHOSE IQ IS:	EQUALS OR EXCEEDS
119	88	81	12
118	86	80	11
117	85	79	10
116	84	78	9
115	82	77	8
114	80	76	8
113	79	75	6
112	77	74	6
111	75	73	5
110	73	72	4
109	71	71	4
108	69	70	3
107	66	69	3
106	64	68	3
105	62	67	2
104	60	66	2
103	57	65	2
102	55	65	2
101	52	64	1
100	50	63	1
99	48	62	1
	160		1 out of 10,000
	156		3 out of 10,000
	152		8 out of 10,000
	148		2 out of 1,000
	144		4 out of 1,000
	140		7 out of 1,000

Source: Reproduced with the permission of the publishers from *Supplementary Guide for the Revised Stanford-Binet Scale* (L) by Rudolph Pinter, Anna Dragositz, and Rose Kushner (Stanford: Stanford University Press, 1944), p. 135.

(or older retarded children), may be asked to recognize pictures of familiar objects, string beads, answer questions about everyday relationships, or fold paper into specified shapes. On the other hand, older individuals may be asked to define vocabulary words, reason through to the solution of an abstract problem, or decipher an unfamiliar code. Some of the standardized materials used in the Stanford-Binet children's scales are shown in Figure VIII–1.

FIGURE VIII—1

Some of the test materials used in administering the Stanford-Binet to children. From Introduction to Psychology *by Norman L. Munn, L. Dodge Fernald, Jr., and Peter S. Fernald, Houghton Mifflin, 1972. Used by permission of the publishers.*

The Wechsler Scales. A second set of intelligence scales, also widely used in assessment and research with children, is based on the work of David Wechsler. Although they bear many similarities to the Stanford-Binet tests, Wechsler's scales differ in several particulars. One, of especial interest, is the division of IQ into verbal and performance subtests, permitting the use of separate verbal and nonverbal performance IQs as well as a full-scale score. The original Wechsler scale, the Wechsler-Bellevue, was published in 1939 and was geared specifically to the measurement of adult intelligence for clinical use. Subsequent revisions involved a special instrument for adults (Wechsler Adult Intelligence Scale, or WAIS) and for school children (Wechsler Intelligence Scale for Children, or WISC). More recently the WPPSI (Wechsler Preschool and Primary Scale of Intelligence) has been constructed to assess children four to six years of age. All of these instruments follow a similar format, which we can examine by looking at the WISC.

The WISC consists of twelve subtests, six verbal and six performance. The last subtest of each group may be used as a supplement and/or alternate for the other five in the series. The subtests themselves are listed and described in Table VIII–2.

Infant Tests of Intelligence

Several individual tests of infant behavior have been developed in the United States during the last fifty years; examples are the Gesell Developmental Schedules, Cattell Intelligence Tests for Infants and Young Children, and the Bayley Scales of Infant Development. Performance on these tests is often labeled DQ, for developmental quotient, rather than IQ.

Gesell's test was the first specifically designed to measure mental ability in early infancy and is the most well known (Bayley, 1970). It evaluates behavior in four basic areas: motor, adaptive, language, and personal-social (Figure VIII–2). The latter scale is scored mainly from a parental interview. The child's performance is compared with norms derived from a relatively small group of middle-class children from New Haven, Connecticut, who were followed longitudinally.

The Bayley Scales of Infant Development are a recent revision of Bayley's original tests, with the addition of a broader standardization and clarification of scoring and administration (Bayley, 1970). Designed for infants two to thirty months old, they consist of Motor and Mental scales and an Infant Behavior Record. The Motor scale includes such items as holding the head up, walking, and throwing a ball. The Mental scale, designed for adaptive behavior, includes such behaviors as attending to visual and auditory stimuli, following directions, looking for a fallen toy, and imitating. The Infant Behavior Record is a rating of the child on such responses as fearfulness, happiness, endurance, responsiveness, and goal directedness.

T A B L E   V I I I – 2

THE WECHSLER INTELLIGENCE SCALE FOR CHILDREN

VERBAL SCALE	PERFORMANCE SCALE
1. *General information* A series of questions covering a wide range of information which children presumably have had an opportunity to acquire (e.g., "Who discovered America?"). Specialized knowledge is avoided.	1. *Picture completion* Picture cards from which some part (e.g., the whiskers of a cat) is missing.
2. *General comprehension* Items in which the child must explain what should be done in given circumstances, why certain practices are followed, and so on. An example: "Why is it better to build a house of brick than of wood?"	2. *Picture arrangement* Sets of picture cards are shown to the child; he must rearrange them so as to tell a story.
3. *Arithmetic* Simple, orally presented arithmetic problems, to be solved without paper or pencil.	3. *Block design* The child is given a set of blocks, with red sides, white sides, and sides that are both red and white. His job is to reproduce a pattern shown by the examiner.
4. *Similarities* Questions such as "In what way are a piano and a violin alike?"	4. *Object assembly* Cardboard puzzles which the child is to assemble.

TABLE VIII-2 *(continued)*

VERBAL SCALE	PERFORMANCE SCALE
5. *Vocabulary* Increasingly difficult words are presented orally and visually; the child is asked to tell what each means.	5. *Coding* A code-substitution test in which symbols are to be paired with digits.
6. *Digit span* Orally presented lists of digits, which are to be repeated (in order and backward).	6. *Mazes* Eight printed mazes are presented; the child must trace in pencil the correct route out.

THE RELATIONSHIP OF EARLY IQ SCORES TO LATER PERFORMANCE

Infant Tests

A question frequently asked about intelligence concerns the degree to which early tests predict scores on tests given at later times. In one study, correlations were calculated between tests given at three, six, nine, twelve, eighteen, and twenty-four months with Stanford-Binet scores obtained at five years (Anderson, 1939). As seen in Table VIII–3, the relationship was low and tended to decrease as the time span between assessments increased. The low correlation between early and later tests has been shown in many subsequent studies (Bayley, 1955; Honzik, MacFarland, and Allen, 1948; Thorndike, 1940).

Some investigators note that predictability from early assessment is higher when more global categories, rather than specific IQ scores, are considered and when clinical judgment is used along with test scores. MacRae (1955) asked examiners to assign infants to one of five categories on the basis of their subjective assessment of test performance; the categories were: superior, above average, average, below average to borderline, mental defective. Correlations with test scores obtained at 9 years 2 months were .56,

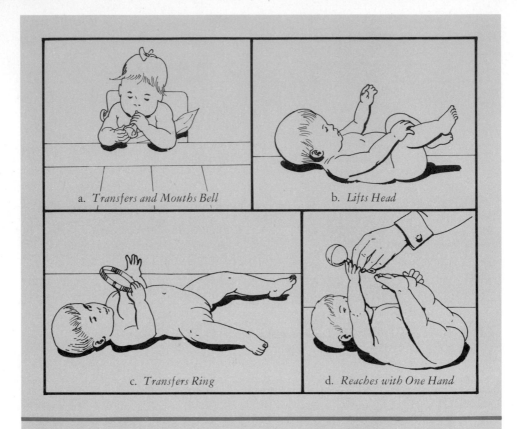

a. *Transfers and Mouths Bell*

b. *Lifts Head*

c. *Transfers Ring*

d. *Reaches with One Hand*

FIGURE VIII—2

Illustrations from the Gesell Developmental Schedules of behaviors typical at 28 weeks of age. Adapted from Arnold Gesell and Catherine S. Amatruda, Developmental Diagnosis (New York: Paul B. Hoeber, Inc.) Copyright 1941, 1947 by Arnold Gesell. By permission.

.55, and .82 when the infant tests had been given at 0 to 11 months, 12 to 23 months, and 24 to 35 months, respectively. Illingworth (1961) has pointed out that mental inferiority can be diagnosed during the first year of life; in one study employing modified Gesell tests, histories, and clinical judgment, he predicted deficiency with 75 percent accuracy as it was mea-

TABLE VIII-3

CORRELATION COEFFICIENTS BETWEEN INFANT INTELLIGENCE TESTS GIVEN AT VARIOUS AGES AND STANFORD-BINET IQ AT FIVE YEARS

AGES	NUMBER OF CHILDREN	CORRELATION COEFFICIENTS
3 mos.—5 yrs.	91	.008
6 mos.—5 yrs.	91	−.065
9 mos.—5 yrs.	91	−.001
12 mos.—5 yrs.	91	.055
18 mos.—5 yrs.	91	.231
24 mos.—5 yrs.	91	.450

Source: Adapted from Anderson, 1939.

sured independently at school age. Such success speaks well for the practical benefits of early diagnosis of problems, primarily because it makes it possible to design treatment plans or appropriately place children into adoptive homes. But the evidence is still scant that infant tests alone dependably predict future performance of those who fall into the middle or high range of intelligence scores.

We might ask why predictive power is not greater. One reason is that there is relatively little room for the display of individual differences during the early months of life (Ames, 1967), and so infants can be differentiated only in a global way. Then, too, early temperamental variations (e.g., activity level or reactivity to stimulation) may influence early achievement in a manner different than that in which they affect later performance. Another explanation for low predictability is that infant tests tap abilities other than those evaluated on later tests, placing more emphasis on sensorimotor items and less on tasks involving language and abstract problem solving. At first blush it might be expected, in the light of both Piaget's and Bruner's insistence that sensorimotor acts are the beginnings of intelligence, that early precociousness or retardation on such tasks would foretell later intelligence. Bayley suggests, though, that there is little reason to anticipate a strong relation between early simpler functions and the more complex process that develop later:

> Intelligence appears to me, rather, to be a dynamic succession of developing functions, with the more advanced and complex functions . . . depending on the prior maturing of earlier simpler ones. . . .
>
> The neonate who is precocious in the development of the simpler abilities, such as auditory acuity or pupillary reflexes, has an advantage in the slightly more complex behaviors, such as (say) turning toward a sound, or fixating an object held before his eyes. But these more complex acts also involve other functions, such as neuro-muscular coordinations, in which he may not be precocious. The bright one-month-old may be sufficiently slow in developing these later more complex functions so as to lose some or all of his earlier advantages. [Bayley, 1955, pp. 807–808.]

Tests Given Later in Time

What happens, then, when test scores obtained by older children are correlated with yet later performance? It generally has been found that: (1) the correlations are substantially higher than those for infant tests, and (2) they progressively decrease as the time interval between tests increases. Figure VIII–3 represents the correlations, from several studies, of scores obtained at maturity with those obtained at previous ages. These data clearly show that although the relationship increased progressively as time of testing approximated maturity, tests obtained during childhood substantially predict later performance.

THE CONSTANCY OF IQ

We already have noted that until relatively recently the concept of intelligence was characterized by notions of fixedness and predetermined development. An assumption inherent in this viewpoint was that intelligence does not change qualitatively but grows quantitatively in a continuous and stable fashion. But the fact that infant tests proved to have little predictive validity suggested that some qualitative change in intelligence also occurs, at least during the early years. Then, too, findings from major longitudinal studies cast doubt on the stability and continuity of growth. They showed that, although IQ scores are relatively stable for groups of examinees begin-

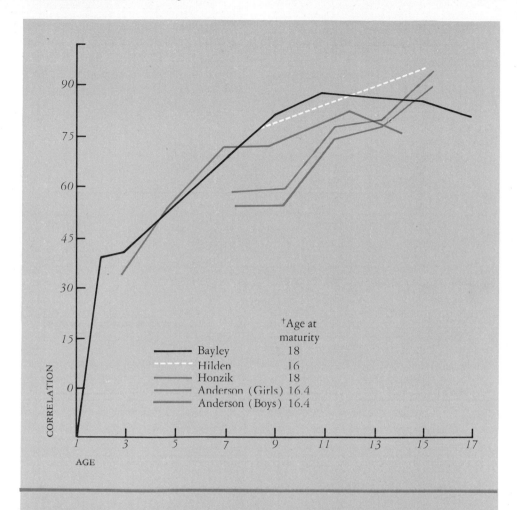

FIGURE VIII—3

Correlations between test scores obtained at various ages with those obtained at maturity. The graph lines represent data from different investigations, illustrating the substantial power of tests obtained during early childhood to predict later performance. Adapted from B. S. Bloom, Stability and Change in Human Characteristics. *Copyright 1964, reproduced by permission of John Wiley & Sons, Inc.*

ning quite early in life, large differences over time emerge for individuals.

Honzik, MacFarland, and Allen (1948) found that almost 60 percent of 252 children in the Child Guidance Study, tested several times between the ages of six and eighteen years, changed fifteen or more points. As part of the Fels study, Sontag, Baker, and Nelson (1958) administered the

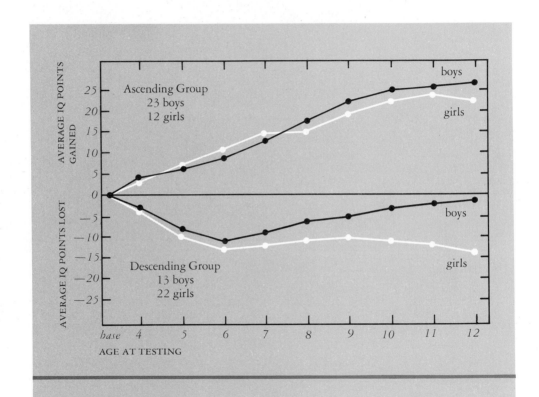

FIGURE VIII—4

Mean IQ points gained or lost by children who demonstrated the greatest increases or greatest decline. Adapted from Sontag, Baker, and Nelson, 1958. Copyright 1958 by the Society for Research in Child Development, Inc. Reproduced by permission.

Stanford-Binet several times to children between three and twelve years of age. The large majority did not obtain the same IQ scores and there was a good deal of change for some children. Figure VIII–4 shows the average gains for the thirty-five children exhibiting the most increase and the average loss for the thirty-five children displaying the greatest decline.

The early concept of intelligence was further modified by a variety of investigations which pointed to the specific influence of environmental factors. Some of these, as well as the flavor of the heated controversy which they precipitated, are discussed by L. H. Stott and R. S. Ball in Selection 6.

SELECTION 6

INFANT AND PRESCHOOL MENTAL TESTS: REVIEW AND EVALUATION

L. H. Stott and R. S. Ball

Most of, but not all, the textbook writers of the 1920's and 1930's apparently adopted the point of view . . . that both the upper limit of developmental capacity and its pattern and rate of development are predetermined by heredity. Harvey A. Carr (1926) was one notable exception. In fact, he spelled out in some detail a version of the currently widely accepted "interaction" view of mental development. He wrote,

All experiences of the individual during life are thus organized into a complex but unitary system of reaction tendencies that determine to a large extent the nature of his subsequent activity. The reactive disposition of the individual, i.e., what he does and what he can and cannot do, is a function of his native equipment, of the nature of his previous experiences and of the way in which these have been organized and evaluated. (p. 4)

Neither is the ability (intelligence) native in the sense that its development is not dependent upon environment influences. The ability is natively conditioned in that we are born with the *capacity* to develop in this manner (p 415)

The assumption that all individual, group, and racial differences of IQ are wholly determined by innate differences of constitution must be discarded because of the fact that the IQ is often altered during the course of development. (p. 417)

Perhaps the most widely known controversy to be found in the psychological literature was over this very issue. In 1932, Beth L. Wellman

Reprinted from Stott, L. H. and Ball, R. S. Infant and preschool mental tests: Review and evaluation. *Monographs of the Society for Research in Child Development*, **30**, 1965, Ser. No. 101, 9–18. Copyright 1965 by the Society for Research in Child Development, Inc. Reproduced by permission.

(1932a) of the Iowa Child Welfare Research Station published the first in a series of studies reporting marked changes in children's IQ's that were attributed to changes in environment. According to the results, the greatest gains were made by those children whose initial IQ's were below average; the average gain for them was 28 points on their fifth test. The group with average IQ's gained 22 points from their first to seventh test, while the superior group made an average gain of 12 points up to their fifth test.

Wellman's explanation for these findings was that

> Preschool attendance, at least in the laboratories of the Iowa Child Welfare Station, causes a rise in IQ, the rise being cumulative from year to year, and sustained throughout the school years when the children are in the environment provided by our University Elementary School. When the same children are home over comparable intervals they fail to gain, although maintaining their higher level. (1932a, p. 124)

At the end of her report, however, she admitted that "the question still remains whether these increased IQ's are real or inflated."

In her second report, Wellman (1932b) furnished evidence that the gains in IQ during preschool attendance were not practice effects. She reported that the same children who gained IQ points during the school session failed to make gains in a shorter period between tests during the summer vacation. Her results also indicated that during the preschool season greater gains were shown during a 7- to 8-month interval between tests than during a shorter, 5- to 6-month interval, which would be more likely to show practice effects.

In a study by Crissey (1937), the evidence indicated that children who were rated as "normal or dull-normal" on admission to an orphans' home remained normal or gained slightly in IQ, while those designated as "normal or superior-normal" showed a consistent loss. Children at all levels of ability represented who remained in an institution for the feeble-minded were also found to show a consistent loss in IQ.

During the 7 years following Wellman's initial report, a series of research papers was published by Wellman and her co-workers (Wellman, 1934; 1937; 1938; Wellman & Coffey, 1936; Crissey, 1937; Skeels & Filmore, 1937; Skeels, 1938; Skeels, Updegraff, Wellman, and Williams, 1938) which supported generally the view that the sort of environmental stimulation young children experience constitutes an important factor in their mental development.

> The concept of intelligence as fixed and unmodified, or only modified within very narrow limits, is fast being replaced by a viewpoint which conceives of intelligence in functional terms. No longer can we say that an early intelligence test rigidly classifies a child for life in terms of mental potentiality. (Crissey, 1937, p. 7)

THE CONTROVERSY. But the well ingrained idea that intelligence, as represented by the IQ, is an inherited and, therefore, a "fixed" quality that characterizes the individual for life was not so easily "replaced" by such a radically different viewpoint. Certain students of child development immediately began to look for "erroneous assumptions," flaws in methodology and statistics, and "unwarranted conclusions" in the Iowa findings. Articles extremely critical of Wellman's reports began to appear in the psychological journals. One of the most violent of these attacks was a paper entitled "The Wandering IQ: Is It Time to Settle Down?" by Simpson (1939). He assumed the role of one who is assigned the bitter task of "exposing" the devious operations of a colleague gone astray as he wrote,

> But to claim miracle working in Iowa that cannot be duplicated in other parts of the country in nursery schools, elementary schools, or high schools, that is much worse than nonsense and ought to be exposed as such, thankless as the task of exposing it may be. (p. 366)

In general, Simpson's attack apparently was based more on an emotional reaction to Wellman's point of view than upon a rational and objective evaluation of all the evidence presented. Among his personal thrusts was a charge of "statistical incompetence under the influence of wishful thinking."

Another rather strong reaction was voiced by Florence Goodenough, certainly a highly respected authority in the field of intelligence and its evaluation. It should be mentioned, at this point, that in 1928, four years prior to Wellman's initial report, an article by Goodenough appeared in which she reported an "apparent increase" in average IQ in both of two matched groups, one of which had had a year's experience in a nursery school, while the other had not. The results of the study, however, led to her conclusion that the "changes are largely, if not entirely, at-

tributable to irregular standardization of the scale at the early ages and consequently should not be regarded as an indication of actual increase in intelligence" (Goodenough, 1928, p. 368). No relation between gain in IQ and length of attendance at the nursery school was indicated. In view of her findings in this early study, it is not surprising that Goodenough was highly critical of the Wellman papers.

Dr. Goodenough continued to point out that infant tests had been shown to have no predictive value and that, because of their basic unreliability, a "regressive shift" took place in successive testings of the same groups of children. This meant that those who originally tested highest appeared, as a group, to lose in IQ because many of them, by chance, obtained IQ's that were too high; and those who originally tested at the low end of the scale appeared, as a group, to score higher at the next testing because many of their original scores were, by chance, too low. She was also concerned with an apparent lack of controls over the possibility of examiner bias in the Iowa test results. In general, Goodenough felt that little faith could be put in the results of the studies because of the lack of sufficient substantiating data.

During the following year, Goodenough and Maurer (1940) published a report of a study in which nursery-school children and non-nursery-school children were compared for changes in IQ level after 1, 2, and 3 years of nursery-school experience for the nursery-school group. Interestingly enough, their results were quite different from those of the Iowa studies. At the end of 1 year of nursery-school experience the nursery-school group and the non-nursery-school group showed precisely the same average gain in IQ—4.6 points.

This 1940 paper thus supported the idea of a hereditarily fixed potentiality as well as predetermined development, allowing no place for experience to have "any measurable effect whatever upon the mental development of children" (Goodenough and Maurer, 1940, p. 176).

These conceptions of the nature of intelligence were even more strongly emphasized in Goodenough's review (1940) in which she proposed to answer the question, "What effect, if any, is a specific environmental change likely to have upon the intellectual development of a particular group of children?"

In reviewing the Iowa studies, Goodenough "accounted" for the differential changes shown by their data in terms of such factors as inadequate control groups or control children that were not strictly comparable with respect to age, level of intelligence, and test experience, the failure to take into account and deal with "regressive effects," and other "indefensible" computational and statistical procedures.

After reviewing a number of other studies on this general problem (Kawin and Hoefer, 1931; Peterson, 1937; and Starkweather and Roberts, 1940), Goodenough reached two general conclusions, as follows:

1. It is unsafe to assume that attendance at any unspecified nursery school is likely to bring about improvement in the mental ability of the average child, for in most investigations of this matter, no evidence whatever of such an effect has been found. It appears, there-fore that ability to bring about intellectual improvement by this means is at best restricted to a few schools. The precise nature of the difference in the educational regimes of the schools that do, and of those that do not, claim to achieve these results has thus far not been made clear.

2. Analysis of the experimental studies dealing with this problem reveals many possible sources of error in the studies purporting to show a positive effect of nursery school training. Generally speaking, these studies have failed to maintain adequate control of basic variables. Their statistical techniques are also frequently of questionable validity, and in a number of instances, are certainly erroneous. (Goodenough, 1940, p. 321)

The particular Iowa studies that were, perhaps, most severely criticized because of extreme statements unjustified by the data were those of foster children. The reports were largely based upon data on the later development of a group of 154 children who were placed in adoptive homes before they were 6 months of age, and a second group of 65 who were adopted between the ages of 2 and $5\frac{1}{2}$. Certain statements that appeared in these studies were extreme, almost to the point of denying that the biological factor had any bearing at all upon later mental development. One such statement was:

. . . if there is an hereditary constitutional factor which sets the limits of mental development, these limits are extremely broad. Within these, environmental factors can operate to produce changes which for ordinary purposes may represent a shift from one extreme to another of the present distribution of intelligence among children. (Skodak, 1939, pp. 131–132)

Investigations and Discussions of Controversial Issues

Considerable discussion in the psychological literature followed the Iowa papers and the criticisms of them. The entire Thirty-ninth Yearbook of the National Society for the Study of Education (1940) consisted of discussions and research findings on the issues. Bayley (1940) reported a study in which she found that the environmental factors of attendance at nursery school, a child's health record, and his ordinal position in the family did not influence intelligence ratings. The educational level of parents, however, was found to be significantly related to intelligence ratings at later childhood ages, but was not an important factor under 18 months. Wellman (1940) considered three possible environmental effects on the child's level of intelligence as reflected in change in IQ: (1) variations in opportunity for utilizing abilities he already possesses; (2) variations in experiences that foster intellectual curiosity; and (3) variations in motivation. The child's inclination to utilize resources at hand, she felt, was determined by the nature of the group with which he associated.

Jones and Jorgensen (1940) reported finding no difference in mental growth between children who did and did not attend nursery school. In the same volume, on the other hand, a few investigators other than the Iowa group found some evidence that nursery-school experience elevated the IQ. Frandsen and Barlow (1940) noted a small average gain in IQ for an experimental group who attended a "special nursery school," although the gain was not significantly greater than that made by their matched control group.

McHugh (1943) published a monograph dealing with the relation of preschool experience to IQ changes in a group of 91 children who, after an initial Binet test, were given 30 3-hour sessions of preschool experience and then were again tested. Among McHugh's conclusions were:

1. Children do make significant mean gains in IQ score as a result of such preschool experience.

2. IQ gains from preschool experience are "adjustment gains" rather than growth in intelligence.

Another different approach to the study of environmental influences was made by Bradway (1945). A group of preschool children, selected as representative of the general population, had been given the Stanford-Binet scale. Ten years later, and with no interaction in the interim, they were re-examined on the same scale, and several environmental factors in the lives of the children who had shown the most significant changes were examined and evaluated. Environmental information was obtained by interviewing the mothers and the children without the interviewer's knowing whether the child's IQ had shown an increase or a decrease. The results are summarized as follows:

1. The mean IQ of the increase group increased 9 points, while the mean of the decrease group decreased 17 points.

2. At the initial testing, the mean IQ's of the two groups were within 6

points of each other. Ten years later, the difference between their mean IQ's was 30 points.

The factors related to these changes were:

3. The mean vocabulary score of the mothers of the increase group was significantly higher than the mean score of the mothers of the decrease group.

4. The . . . intelligence scores of the parents of the two groups also differed significantly.

The general conclusion was that the IQ changes that took place between preschool and junior high school were related to environmental factors, but the question of whether the particular factors considered in the study "operated primarily as environmental stimuli or whether they were for the most part merely related to inheritable intelligence which had not been fully realized at the time of the initial examination" could not be answered from the data.

Gesell (1940) took a position somewhat in line with Bradway's conclusions just cited. Although Gesell generally tended strongly to emphasize the biological influences in his writings, he expressed in this article an "interaction" point of view that is currently rather widely accepted. He wrote,

> In appraising growth characteristics, we must not ignore environmental influences—cultural milieu, siblings, parents, food, illness, trauma, education. But these must always be considered in relation to primary, or constitutional factors, because the latter ultimately determine the degree, and even the mode, of the reaction to so-called "environment." The organism always partici-
> pated in the creation of its environment, and the growth characteristics of the child are really the end-product expressions of an interaction between intrinsic and extrinsic determiners. Because the interaction is the crux, the distinction between these two sets of determiners should not be drawn too heavily. (p. 159)

Studies of Deprivation in Institutionalized Children

In general, the studies so far examined that have been concerned with the evaluation of specific environmental factors in relation to mental development have resulted in inconsistent and contradictory findings. Attempts to isolate and specify particular effects of experience in children reared at home have met with little success. On the other hand, comparisons of infants reared in orphanages with children reared at home, or by mothers, have rather consistently showed wide differences in rate and level of behavioral development favoring the latter group (Goldfarb, 1943; Pasamanick, 1946; Spitz, 1946; 1949).

A common feature of the particular orphanages studied was a minimum of environmental variation for the infant inmates. In a study of Rene Spitz (1949) two groups of infants were compared, one reared in a nursery by their own mothers, the other in a foundling home by an overworked nursing staff of which each nurse cared for 8 to 12 babies. The important difference in the two situations, according to Spitz, was the amount of environmental variation and stimulation, and, especially, conditions allowing for emotional interchange between the infants and those caring for them. Comparisons between the two groups were drawn in terms of developmental quotients (DQ) that represented "six sectors of personality," i.e., level of perception, mastery of bodily functions, social relations, memory and imitation, manipulative ability, and intelligence. The contrasts between the two groups over a 12-month period were striking. At age 2 to 3 months the average DQ of the mother-reared children was 95 as compared with an average of 130 for the foundling-home children. At ages 8 to 10 months the average DQ of the nursery children had risen to 110 while that of the foundling-home group had dropped to around 72. In summary Spitz wrote,

> While the children in "Nursery" developed into normal healthy toddlers, a two-year observation of "Foundling-home" showed that the emotionally starved children never learned to speak, to walk, to feed themselves. With one or two exceptions in a total of 91 children, those who survived were human wrecks who behaved either in a manner of agitated or of apathetic idiots. (Spitz, 1949, p. 149)

Spitz pointed out that in both institutions the infants received adequate food, the housing was excellent, and medical care was equally adequate.

Similar findings were reported by Goldfarb (1943). He compared the development of children who were placed in an institution during early infancy, remained there until about 3 years of age, and then were placed in foster homes, with other children who had been placed immediately in foster homes. The two groups were from much the same hereditary background.

Goldfarb concluded that prolonged residence in the institution during infancy was profoundly detrimental to the children's psychological development. The institutionalized and foster-home children showed percentages of defective speech development of 80 and 15, respectively. Comparable percentages showing mental retardation were 37.5 and 7.5; for the children showing educational difficulties the percentages were 42.5 and 15.0 respectively.

The findings of Spitz and Goldfarb quite convincingly demonstrated the retarding effects of a lack of stimulation and environmental variation upon the behavioral development of young infants. Such findings, however, are open to different interpretations of whether maturation is the sole factor in the development of mental capacity, or whether environment also is a factor of importance. Goldfarb and Spitz, in their above cited works, and Bowlby (1951), and others, assumed that the low ability to perform in an intelligence test, or the defective speech development of institutionalized children is indicative of retarded development of mental capacity. In terms of this assumption, experience in adjusting to environmental variation—coping with an ever-changing situation—is essential to the development of intellectual potentiality.

Dennis and Najarian (1957), however, disagreed with the above interpretation. They studied the development of children reared in a Lebanese foundling home in comparison with children brought to the Well Baby Clinic of the American University Hospital of Beirut, Lebanon. Their objective findings were similar to those of Spitz. The average DQ for the institution babies over the age period of from 3 to 12 months was only 63, while that of the Well Baby Clinic group was 101, a highly significant difference. In this age range, all the clinic group tested above the mean of the foundling-home group. Not one of the latter group between the ages of 3 and 12 months had a DQ above 95. In discussing the similarity between Spitz's findings and their own, Dennis and Najarian (1957) wrote:

> Spitz's data and ours agree in finding that environmental conditions can depress infant test scores after the second month of life. We disagree with Spitz in regard to the interpretation of the cause of the decline. We believe that Spitz's data, as well as ours, are satisfactorily interpreted in terms of restricted learning opportunities. We suggest that an analysis of the relationship between test items and the conditions prevailing in the Foundling Home would reveal that retardation could readily be explained in terms of restriction of learning opportunities. (pp. 10–11)

Dennis and Najarian, then, believed that the unvarying institutional environment does not necessarily interfere with the actual developmental "unfoldment" of mental potential in the child but simply hampers learning, and that life in the institution does not provide the opportunity for the child to learn to perform the tasks, or respond to the kinds of stimuli presented to him in the test situation, to nearly the same degree as does the ordinary home environment. From this point of view, the child may have possessed this capacity to learn these particular tricks, but did not have the opportunity to learn them.

This intellectual capacity to learn had been developing all along in spite of stimulus deprivation. Thus, in terms of this theory, the environmental factor is not important in the development of intelligence defined as capacity to learn.

If this latter interpretation were correct—if the retarding effects of a depriving environment were simply the absence of learned responses as a result of the lack of opportunity to learn, rather than a retardation in the development of the capacity to learn—then all that would be needed to correct the condition in a given child would be to place him in an environment rich in opportunity to learn.

In support of this possibility, Pasamanick (1946), in his study of Negro infants in a "depriving" institutional environment, found the usual, progressive behavioral retardation. However, when these infants were given more individual attention, they began to overcome the effects of deprivation.

On the other hand, further findings by Goldfarb (1947) led to the opposite conclusion. In his study of the adjustments of a group of adolescents who had spent the early months and years of their lives in an institution, Goldfarb found that the ill effects of their early environment were still with them. In discussing a particular case, he concluded that

> . . . even after years in a foster home he still demonstrated isolated, infantile impoverished character trends. His intellectual growth potential has been equally frustrated and he reacts to problems on a highly concretistic level that verifies the absence of an intelligent approach to new adjustments. (p. 449)

The investigation was begun in the hope and belief that an understanding of the factors associated with those individual variations in adjustment might help in the formation of a treatment program to counteract the effects of the privation process. The present findings are not encouraging. We have been able to do relatively little once the damage has been wrought. (p. 455)

In summary, the evidence seems generally to support the conclusion that experience in coping with a stimulating environment is a factor of importance in mental development. The assumption that mentality is "fixed" and determined in the sense that it is, somehow, derived automatically from the somatic and neural structures as they develop through the "mechanism of maturation" is hardly tenable. As Baller and Charles (1961) put it, "optimum development of both learning *capacity* and learning *achievement* demand personal involvement of the learner and interaction with a rich environment" (p. 245).

The Interaction Point of View

In view of the evidence, then, "fixed intelligence," in the sense that the rate and pattern of its development are predetermined by the genes, is no longer tenable. In another sense, however, intelligence is fixed. In this interpretation, the individual is endowed with a particular intellectual potentiality that is set by the genes, and surely it is tenable. The idea, of course, is distinct from the idea of predetermined development. There is really no inherent connection between the two concepts. There is no necessity to assume that intellectual development, within the limits set by the genetic factor, is wholly a function of maturation. The degree

to which this fixed upper limit is approached by a given individual may be largely determined by the nurture factor —by the nature of his environment and his encounters with it.

Obviously, a child's capacity to function effectively in an ever-changing environment increases with age. Intelligence tests from the beginning have been designed to measure these changes, and, in terms of test results, curves of increase in capacity have been plotted. These curves, furthermore, show a leveling off and a gradual cessation of increase as the individual approaches adulthood. Clearly, these are curves of change in capacity to learn or perform adequately in new or difficult situations and, since they do level off with adulthood and, thus, parallel generally the curves of organismic development, they undoubtedly are related to, and reflect generally the course of maturation of the neuro-effector system. It does not necessarily follow, however, that the development of the capacity thus depicted is purely maturational in nature—that it somehow arises automatically from the natural unfolding of an inherently designed anatomical structure uninfluenced by experience. On the contrary, there is increasing evidence that experience is always an important determining factor and that richness of environmental stimulation has much to do, in each case, with the extent to which mental development at any point in time has actually approached the level that the structure at its particular stage of development has made possible. The development of the intellect, like all development, comes about through the interaction of the organism (with its fixed developmental potential) and its environment (Anastasi and Foley, 1948; McCandless, 1952; Escalona and Moriarty, 1961; Hunt 1961).

As we have seen, this point of view was expressed by Harvey A. Carr back in 1926. A few years later, when the controversy over the effects of environmental change on mental development was at its height, Stoddard and Wellman (1934) proposed the following:

A theory of mental development, for which there is a small amount of supporting evidence and nothing as yet contradictory to it, may be built up along five main lines.

1. That definite limits to mental development are set by heredity, in increasing order of specificity as we go from species to race, to family, and finally to the individual.

2. That inherited mental ability, if allowed to function below its response potentialities, decreases relatively (that is, the intelligence quotient declines).

3. That inherited mental ability, in steady combination with stimulation appropriate to its needs, has the appearance of relative increase (that is, the I.Q. increases).

4. That, in certain ways, the nervous system transforms external patterns into adequate internal stimuli and drives whatever mental mechanism is present accordingly.

The mental range, for a given inheritance, runs from flabbiness to athleticism.

5. That in present day life, there are strong forces definitely subversive to mental development in individuals, in that they are substitutes for thinking, or distractions designed to discourage the process. (pp. 178–179)

The interaction theory of Stoddard and Wellman undoubtedly would be more widely accepted today than in

1934 as an explanation for IQ fluctuations and changes.

The current rather widely accepted view of mental development as a process of interaction is quite clearly expressed by Escalona and Moriarty (1961):

Certainly the authors are not alone with their assumption that intelligence must be viewed as an interaction phenomenon. With apologies to Piaget's and other developmental theories we shall crudely describe intelligence as the result of a continuous stream of transactions between the organism and the surrounding field, which field is the sum total of physical and social environmental conditions. Since the organism brings to each adaptive act certain properties, both those of intrinsic biological nature and those which are the result of the impact of previous experience upon the organism, it is correct to say that intelligence development is at all times dependent upon what the organism is like. Yet, since it requires environmental circumstances to mobilize the organism, and since the kind of transaction which develops depends on the objective content of that to which the organism must adapt, it is equally true to say that the development of intelligence depends at all times on the experience encountered by the growing child. (pp. 598–599)

Perhaps the strongest recent expositor of interaction in relation to the development of intelligence is J. McV. Hunt (1961). He marshalled the evidence in support of this point of view from research in learning, learning sets, and the effects of early experience, from the programming of electronic computers, and, especially, from the observations of Piaget on the development of logical thinking and intelligence in children. Hunt presented an extensive and systematic review of Piaget's "experiments" and stressed the fact that a basic concept in all of Piaget's theorizing on the growth of intelligence was the concept of interaction between organism and environment that involves the complementary processes of accommodation and assimilation.

> The more new things an infant has seen and the more new things he has heard, the more new things he is interested in seeing and hearing; and the more variation in reality he has coped with, the greater is his capacity for coping. Such relationships derive from the conception that change in circumstances is required during the early sensorimotor stages to force the accommodative modifications in schemata and the assimilation of these modifications that, in combination, constitute development. (Hunt, 1961, p. 262)

In his concluding chapter, Hunt pointed out some serious implications of the current, prevailing conceptions and assumptions about the nature of intelligence and how it develops in children in relation to their care and education. He wrote,

> In the light of these considerations it appears that the counsel from experts on child rearing during the third and much of the fourth decades of the twentieth century to let children be while they grow and to avoid excessive stimulation was highly unfortunate. It was suggested in the text above that perhaps the negative correlations found between intelligence test scores for the first two years and the late adolescent level of intelligence may possibly be attributable to such counsel, inasmuch as it would be those educated people at the higher levels of tested intelligence who read and can act in terms of what they read who would have been most likely to follow this advice. The problem for the management of child development is to find out how to govern the encounters that children have with their environments to foster both an optimally rapid rate of intellectual development and a satisfying life. (Hunt, 1961, pp. 362–363)

SOME CORRELATES OF INTELLIGENCE

A broad understanding of intelligence also is provided by examining the factors to which it is related. Most of the studies of the correlates of intelligence are, indeed, correlational, and as such, they allow only limited causal inferences to be drawn from them (see Chapter II). Nevertheless, they have furnished many hypotheses for further exploration.

Family Variables

Although family variables presumably are related to children's intelligence, only a few specific conclusions can be drawn from existing knowledge. It is not easy to categorize and measure the way in which parents deal with their offspring or the way in which particular attitudes might be transmitted. Further, the number of such behaviors and attitudes affecting children's performance presumably is very large, so that a vast amount of research will be required for their investigation. The following remarks, then, provide only a sample of the kinds of variables being studied and some of what is tentatively known about them.

Honzik (1967) related family variables measured when infants were twenty-one months old to test performances obtained between the ages of twenty-one months and thirty years. One of the clearer findings was the positive relation between IQ scores, particularly for the boys, and mothers' worrisomeness, tenseness, concern, and energy. The author suggests that such mothers probably are more responsive to the wants and needs of their children and do more for them. The closeness of the relationship also was important. For girls, early closeness to mother was related to test scores, but this was superseded during adolescence by the father-daughter relationship. Girls' IQs, unlike those of boys, also appeared related to parental harmony or lack of conflict.

Interesting differences relating to the sex of the child have been found in other longitudinal studies. Bayley and Schaefer (1964), for example, reported that hostility in mothers was related to high IQ scores in boys during infancy; for girls, loving, controlling maternal behavior was related to high IQ scores during infancy.

Evidence regarding the influence of methods of discipline on intelligence is ambiguous. Baldwin, Kalhorn, and Breese (1945) concluded that children of high intelligence came from democratic accepting homes, whereas those exhibiting low performance tended to come from homes categorized as rejecting and autocratic. Kent and Davis (1957) classified parents into demanding, overanxious, normal, and unconcerned and found that children of demanding families did better than those from normal families, while youngsters of unconcerned parents did less well. This finding appears consistent with the Honzig result in relating concerned, stimulating, and tense parents to high intelligence in their children. Similarly, Sontag, Baker, and Nelson (1958) found that parents of children whose IQ increased over time (see p. 264) tended to bring pressure for performance.

Socioeconomic Status, Race, and Ethnicity

In an early study, Sherman and Key (1932) tested children from several hollows in the Blue Ridge Mountains approximately one hundred miles

FIGURE VIII–5

A family from one of the isolated hollows studied by Sherman and Key. From M. Sherman and C. B. Key, The intelligence of isolated mountain children. Child Development, 3, 1932, 279–290. *Copyright 1932 by the Society for Research in Child Development, Inc. Reproduced by permission.*

from Washington, D.C. Life in this cultural setting was characterized by an extreme degree of poverty, low literacy, poor educational facilities, and isolation from other communities (Figure VIII–5). Not surprisingly, then, the children achieved less than average scores, and performance was related to the cultural level of the individual hollows.

The results of many later investigations show a clear-cut positive relationship between socioeconomic status (SES) and IQ. The procedure employed in this research consists of categorizing families on the basis of parental education, occupation, income, social standing, or a combination of these factors, and then examining the IQ scores of children who fall into different categories.

Standardization of both the Stanford-Binet and Wechsler Intelligence Scale for Children indicates that children from high status families achieve the higher IQs. For example, those whose fathers are classified as professionals obtain an average Stanford-Binet score of 115, whereas a score of 97 is achieved on the average by children whose fathers hold slightly skilled occupations (McNemar, 1942). Table VIII–4 indicates a similar relation for

TABLE VIII−4

MEAN IQ SCORES FOR THE NORMATIVE SAMPLE
ON THE WECHSLER INTELLIGENCE SCALE FOR
CHILDREN CATEGORIZED ON THE BASIS
OF FATHER'S OCCUPATION

	MEAN IQ		
OCCUPATIONAL CATEGORY	Verbal	Performance	Full Scale
Professional and semiprofessional workers	110.9	107.8	110.3
Proprietors, managers, and officials	105.9	105.3	106.2
Clerical, sales, and kindred workers	105.2	104.3	105.2
Craftsmen, foremen, and kindred workers	100.8	101.6	101.3
Operatives and kindred workers	98.9	99.5	99.1
Domestic, protective, and other service workers	97.6	96.9	97.0
Farmers and farm managers	96.8	98.6	97.4
Farm laborers and foremen, laborers	94.6	94.9	94.2

Source: Adapted from Seashore, Wesman, and Doppelt, 1950.

the WISC. It has been estimated that, in general, a fifteen- to twenty-five-point difference exists between scores of children of professionals and laborers (Eells, 1953).

Bayley and Schaefer (1964), among others, found that starting at about two years of age, measures of SES correlated more and more positively with IQ. Before that age, there was either no relationship or a negative one. This is not surprising in light of the apparent qualitative differences of infant tests. But the question remains as to how to interpret the growing correlations with age. It could reflect either the accumulative influence of the environment or the late appearance of genetically based abilities.

The great majority of studies of racial and ethnic correlates of intelligence focus on the comparison of test scores between black and white children. Because they speak to the possibility of genetic differences between racial groups, they have been hotly debated for some time.

It is by now firmly established that blacks do considerably less well on standard IQ tests than whites (Dreger and Miller, 1960; Kennedy, 1969; Shuey, 1966). The difference is in the range of fifteen to twenty points; that is, blacks score about 80–85 compared to the white average of 100. Further, the difference shows up relatively early in the lives of blacks—during pre-school years—although not before; black infants do as well as whites on the kinds of skills required by infant tests. This is particularly interesting because of the well established higher incidence of prematurity and poor medical and dietary care which often characterize the black population.

One of the reasons frequently cited for the black child's poor performance is that most IQ tests are standardized on white populations only. The black child is thus not represented in the normative sample with which he is compared. Examiners frequently make attempts to compare the black child with others of his own racial group. A score in the mid-80s usually is considered an average performance, while it is inferred from a score of 100 that the child is superior. Because this kind of extrapolation does not have a firm base, one group of investigators (Kennedy, Van De Riet, and White, 1963) established norms for 1800 black children of grades one to six in the southeastern United States. The mean IQ on the Stanford-Binet was 80.7. Children from metropolitan schools performed better than those from urban and rural communities. Figure VIII–6 shows the distribution of black scores as it compares to the distribution of the original standardization sample for this test. Note that there is considerable overlap between the two distributions whenever black and white scores are compared. This means that a percentage of black children test higher than the average white child.

It has been suggested that useful information can be gleaned about the achievement of various racial, ethnic, or social groups by an analysis of performance on different kinds of tasks (Dreger and Miller, 1960; Lesser, Fifer, and Clark, 1965). In one such analysis, first-grade children from middle- and lower-class families from Chinese, Jewish, Negro, and Puerto Rican cultural groups were studied (Lesser, Fifer, and Clark, 1965). They were administered scales which measured verbal ability, reasoning, number facility, and space conceptualization. Middle-class children obtained higher scores on all the scales, but the pattern of performance within ethnic groups differed. For example, on verbal ability the rank order among the groups was Jewish, Negro, Chinese, and Puerto Rican. On spatial ability, Chinese ranked first, followed by Jewish, Puerto Rican, and Negro, in that order.

Jensen (1969) has proposed that the relationship between intelligence

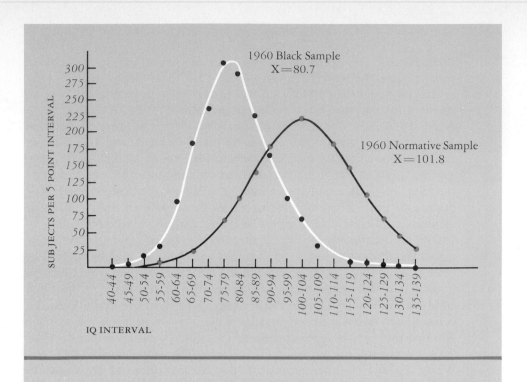

and SES can best be understood if intelligence is conceptualized into Level I (associative learning) and Level II (conceptualization) abilities. He maintains that Level I tasks are performed equally as well by lower- and middle-class children but that the latter are superior on Level II tasks. His work has created a recent storm of controversy because he favors a genetic hypothesis in explaining this differential performance.

Many studies confound the effects of race and socioeconomic status. Because a disproportionate number of blacks fall into the lower social classes, it might be expected that such variables as poverty and little education rather than characteristics unique to the black population are of crucial importance. When attempts have been made to equalize the effects of SES, blacks still usually obtain lower scores than whites. Nevertheless, it is widely argued that gross equating on measures such as occupation or income is not done very well and that it is impossible to equate more subtle but less understood factors, such as motivation. These factors have their bases in the differential socialization experiences of the white and black child and may account for a good amount of the differences in test performance between individuals of different races or cultural groups.

EXTENDED DISCUSSION

CULTURAL BIAS AND TESTING

Psychological testing has come under increasing criticism since the 1950s. One of the criticisms is a response to the consistent finding that individuals coming from cultural backgrounds other than the broad middle or upper class perform less well on tests of intelligence than those from the general population. It is asserted that conclusions about the intelligence of various minority groups are based on tests which, by the nature of their construction and administration, are biased against them.

This stance is frequently referred to as the "Chicago point of view," because much relevant writing and research was carried out at the University of Chicago. Consider the following informal description of cultural bias as it was suggested by one of the Chicago group, Kenneth Eells.

> Let us suppose for a moment that you have a friend in Australia and that you have gone to visit him in his home country. He has told you that he is to take an intelligence test that afternoon and suggests that you take it too, just for the fun of it. . . . When you first open the test booklet you say to yourself, "Well, I'm in a foreign country, but since they speak English, I shouldn't have any special difficulty with this." But soon you are in trouble. . . . You realize that because of the mutton and the kangaroo, the strange words, the local information, and the variations in word connotations your friend had an advantage over you. If he thinks this is a good measure of your intelligence you are glad that he cannot compare your score with his. . . . As a measure of your ability to get along in a certain portion of the Australian culture the test might be excellent, and

you might willingly accept your low score as an accurate reflection of your "current ability." It is the labelling of the test as an "intelligence" test, with its accompanying implication that this is somehow a measure of some basic ability or potentiality of yours, that disturbs you. . . . You wouldn't object to being told you couldn't understand Australian newspapers very well; but to be told you're not very "intelligent" implies something more serious, doesn't it? [1953, pp. 284–285.]

Eells goes on to note that the child reared on the "wrong side of the tracks" in America is in an analogous situation. He is judged on the basis of test items requiring cultural experiences different than his own. Consider, for example, a test item such as:

A symphony is to a composer as a book is to what?
paper   author   musician   man

It would surprise no one if children from the upper classes chose the correct answer, simply on the basis of experience, more often than those from the lower classes. And yet, this outcome is frequently interpreted as implying a deficiency in the lower classes in some inherent capability called intelligence.

There is no doubt that cultural background plays a part in test performance. It has long been noted that the lower test scores for children from rural or isolated towns might be due to their unfamiliarity with the material. Similarly, four-year-old lower-class black children from a large city have difficulty with words related to rural living (John and Goldstein, 1964). Vocabulary on tests—whether easy or difficult—is chosen from middle-class language. Even more subtle cultural differences exist when problem solving is considered. One test item, for example, asks what the child would do if he were sent to buy bread and the grocer had no more. The only acceptable answer is that he would go to another store. But Kagan (1972) notes that many black children living in an eastern city reply that they would go home—a reasonable answer if only one neighborhood store exists, but scored as incorrect nonetheless.

In one major study, in which eight group intelligence tests were administered in the midwest, an analysis of test items for higher and lower socioeconomic classes was made (Eells, Davis, Havighurst, *et al.,* 1951). Many items were answered differently by children of different social status; for subjects thirteen or fourteen years old this difference was as high as 85 percent of the items. The largest difference was obtained on verbal items; there was small difference on items communicated in simple vocabulary or those which were common to the social classes.

The Chicago group has argued for the use and construction of tests which eliminate aspects along which subcultures might vary. Obviously one of these aspects is the content of the items. Others are the use of language and the influence of speed (Anastasi, 1968). Several of these so-called "culture-fair" tests exist, including one constructed by the Chicago investigators themselves.

The Davis-Eells Games is based on the item analysis of the previously described midwestern study. It consists of sets of pictures depicting problem-solving situations which focus on concrete, everyday situations presumably common to all social classes. Nevertheless, it has been found that lower-class children do poorly on it also compared to upper-class subjects and that, further, it does not predict academic success.

Other culture-fair tests, though, are relatively good predictors of academic success. Raven's Progressive matrices, for example, consists of sixty designs, each having a missing section (Figure VIII–7). Examinees are required to select the missing part from several alternatives; they must abstract relationships which become increasingly more difficult. There is no time limit and instructions are simple. The Goodenough-Harris Drawing Test requires subjects merely to draw a picture of a man, woman, and themselves. It has reasonably good reliability and correlates with other intelligence tests. It should be noted, however, that both of these tests are more culture-laden than originally expected. Raven's Progressive Matrices reflect amount of education (Anastasi, 1968), while the Goodenough-Harris Drawing Test is related to the degree to which representational art exists in cultures (Dennis, 1966).

For the most part, culture-fair tests have not met the expectations of their proponents, either because they did not eliminate cultural differences or because they did not predict academic performance. It has been noted that "the search for a culture-free test, whether of intelligence, artistic ability, personal-social characteristics, or any other measurable trait is illusory . . ." (Goodenough and Harris, 1950, p. 399).

This is not to say, however, that the issue has not served the worthwhile purpose of emphasizing that differences in IQ scores among various subcultures is at least partly attributable to different experiences and not necessarily to basic abilities. There is little doubt that some injustice has resulted from poor judgment about test results. For example, it was disclosed that in California pupils with Spanish surnames constituted 28.34 percent of the educable mental retarded enrollment but only 15.22 percent of the general school population. Black children were 25.5 percent of these special classes while only 8.85 percent of the general population (Leary, 1970). Partially as a result of court order, the state is now using nonverbal tests employing the primary language used in the home and a study of the home environment—procedures which were not originally employed—to reevaluate pupils labeled retarded.

At the same time, it cannot be denied that standardized intelligence tests

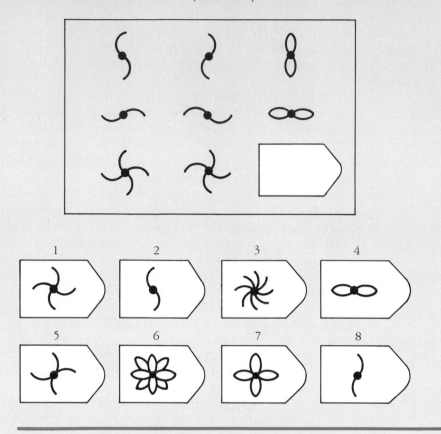

FIGURE VIII—7

Materials similar to those used in Raven's Progressive Matrices Test.

are reasonably good predictors of academic performance. Poor performance of children being raised in subcultures reflects their handicap in competing in schools or occupations defined largely by the middle-class. With this in mind, one researcher has stated, "I wish we could get it *out* of people's heads that tests are unfair to the underprivileged and get it into their heads that it is the hard facts of social circumstance and inadequate education that are unfair to them" (Dyer, 1972, p. 293).

IX

LANGUAGE

THE BEGINNING OF SPEECH is one of the most momentous events in human development. When the child is able to understand what others say, a storehouse of new information opens up to him. But language is more than a basis for new substantive learning. It is also the cornerstone for all human fellowship, playing a central role in school, home-life, and commerce. Further, just as successful and appropriate language use is closely linked to mastery of social situations, so the inability to communicate clearly can hamper, and may virtually eliminate, the ability to cope with even the simplest problems. And, as we have seen already in earlier chapters, the acquisition and modification of language is also enormously important because of its close relationship to intelligence, learning, and cognitive development.

How is language acquired? Although the question has intrigued philosophers, parents, and scientists for thousands of years, we shall see in this chapter that answers to it have not come easily. In fact, a widely accepted theory of language acquisition still has not emerged, even though much is known.

THE ROOTS AND SOUNDS OF LANGUAGE

Biological Factors

There is little doubt that human language development is made possible, at least in part, by man's biological characteristics. Man is unique among all of the species in possessing a highly developed system of communication. Although many other animals do exchange information in some systematic way, including birds' songs and the dance of the bee to signal the presence of food to other members of the hive (McNeil, 1970a), these communications are limited and virtually unmodifiable. Efforts to teach apes to talk have met with relatively little success (Kellogg and Kellogg, 1933; Hayes, 1951), although recently one team has succeeded in teaching a chimpanzee a vocabulary of about thirty words using deaf-mute signs rather than actual speech (Gardner and Gardner, 1969), and another researcher, using plastic chips as words, has successfully taught rudimentary grammar (Premack, 1970). But man remains alone as a true speaker, probably because of his unusual control of the vocal tract (the apparatus itself is present in the ape) and his innate capacity to handle complex symbols.

If children are "prepared" biologically to use language—and there appears to be no doubt that this is the case—the question remains as to the degree to which the specific patterns of language development are also biologically determined. One investigator who favors a heavily biological theory, Eric Lenneberg (1967), supports his view by pointing to two related facts: (1) certain language milestones are reached universally in a fixed sequence, and (2) these milestones are synchronized closely with motor developmental milestones which are known to be biologically determined. Lenneberg's tabular presentation of this argument, shown in Table IX–1, also serves as our first descriptive overview of language development. We will return to some further theoretical implications of Lenneberg's position later.

Preverbal Behavior

Children normally do not begin to speak meaningfully until after the first year of life, but "real" speech is preceded by less communicative vocalization. Sanger (1955) traced the development of prelinguistic behavior in

TABLE IX-1

LENNEBERG'S DESCRIPTION OF LANGUAGE
DEVELOPMENT SHOWING HOW IT IS SYNCHRONIZED
WITH MOTOR DEVELOPMENT

AT THE COMPLE-TION OF:	MOTOR DEVELOPMENT	VOCALIZATION AND LANGUAGE
12 weeks	Supports head when in prone position; weight is on elbows; hands mostly open; no grasp reflex	Markedly less crying than at 8 weeks; when talked to and nodded at, smiles, followed by squealing-gurgling sounds usually called *cooing,* which is vowel-like in character and pitch-modulated; sustains cooing for 15–20 seconds
16 weeks	Plays with a rattle placed in his hands (by shaking it and staring at it), head self-supported; tonic neck reflex subsiding.	Responds to human sounds more definitely; turns head; eyes seem to search for speaker; occasionally some chuckling sounds
20 weeks	Sits with props	The vowel-like cooing sounds begin to be interspersed with more consonantal-sounds; labial fricatives, spirants and nasals are common; acoustically, all vocalizations are very different from the sounds of the mature language of the environment

AT THE COMPLE- TION OF:	MOTOR DEVELOPMENT	VOCALIZATION AND LANGUAGE
6 months	Sitting: bends forward and uses hands for support; can bear weight when put into standing position, but cannot yet stand without holding on; reaching: uni- lateral; grasp: no thumb apposition yet; releases cube when given another	Cooing changing into bab- bling resembling one- syllable utterances; neither vowels nor consonants have very fixed recurrences; most common utterances sound somewhat like ma, mu, da, or di
8 months	Stands holding on; grasps with thumb apposition; picks up pellet with thumb and finger tips	Reduplication (or more con- tinuous repetitions) be- comes frequent; intonation patterns become distinct; utterances can signal em- phasis and emotions
10 months	Creeps efficiently; takes side- steps, holding on; pulls to standing position	Vocalizations are mixed with sound-play such as gurgling or bubble-blowing; appears to wish to imitate sounds, but the imitations are never quite successful; beginning to differentiate between words heard by making dif- ferential adjustment
12 months	Walks when held by one hand; walks on feet and hands—knees in air; mouthing of objects almost stopped; seats self on floor	Identical sound sequences are replicated with higher rela- tive frequency of occurrence and words (mamma or dadda) are emerging; defi- nite signs of understanding some words and simple commands (show me your eyes)
18 months	Grasp, prehension and release fully developed; gait stiff, propulsive and precipi- tated; sits on child's chair with only fair aim; creeps downstairs backward; has	Has a definite repertoire of words—more than three, but less than fifty; still much babbling but now of several syllables with intri- cate intonation pattern; no

AT THE COMPLE-TION OF:	MOTOR DEVELOPMENT	VOCALIZATION AND LANGUAGE
	difficulty building tower of 3 cubes	attempt at communicating information and no frustration for not being understood; words may include items such as thank you or come here, but there is little ability to join any of the lexical items into spontaneous two-item phrases; understanding is progressing rapidly
24 months	Runs, but falls in sudden turns; can quickly alternate between sitting and stance; walks stairs up or down, one foot forward only	Vocabulary of more than 50 items (some children seem to be able to name everything in environment); begins spontaneously to join vocabulary items into two-word phrases; all phrases appear to be own creations; definite increase in communicative behavior and interest in language
30 months	Jumps up into air with both feet; stands on one foot for about two seconds; takes few steps on tip-toe; jumps from chair; good hand and finger coordination; can move digits independently; manipulation of objects much improved; builds tower of six cubes	Fastest increase in vocabulary with many new additions every day; no babbling at all; utterances have communicative intent; frustrated if not understood by adults; utterances consist of at least two words, many have three or even five words; sentences and phrases have characteristic child grammar, that is, they are rarely verbatim repetitions of an adult utterance; intelligibility is not very good yet, though there is great variation among children; seems to understand everything that is said to him

TABLE IX – 1 *(continued)*

AT THE COMPLE- TION OF:	MOTOR DEVELOPMENT	VOCALIZATION AND LANGUAGE
3 years	Tiptoes three yards; runs smoothly with acceleration and deceleration; negotiates sharp and fast curves without difficulty; walks stairs by alternating feet; jumps 12 inches; can operate tricycle	Vocabulary of some 1000 words; about 80% of utterances are intelligible even to strangers; grammatical complexity of utterances is roughly that of colloquial adult langauge, although mistakes still occur
4 years	Jumps over rope; hops on right foot; catches ball in arms; walks line	Language is well-established; deviations from the adult norm tend to be more in style than in grammar

Source: Lenneberg, 1967. Copyright 1967, reproduced by permission of John Wiley & Sons, Inc.

infants at successive ages (see Table IX–2) and found that infants responded to the sound of the human voice before the age of two months. Soon after, they also stopped vocalizing to listen to adults (age two to four months), although most did not show appropriate, comprehending responses to verbal cues before eight to ten months. Conversational babbling, stimulated by the parents, occurred as early as two to four months of age, reaching a peak of eight to ten months. Vocalizing when alone also started at two to four months, but peaked in frequency at six to eight months. After the peak, infants apparently learned to call for adult attention. As they began to talk less to themselves, language became more functional—and more social.

The content of children's vocalization also shifts rapidly. For the first two or three months of life cries and grunts predominate; then, at about three months, cooing begins. These early sounds have been studied with a sophisticated device called the sound spectrograph, which provides a visual record of the physical aspects and the acoustic qualities of sound. Spectrograms show crying to be little more than the blowing of air along the vocal

TABLE IX—2

Prelinguistic Behavior

PERCENTAGE OF OBSERVATIONS AT SUCCESSIVE AGES
WHERE KINDS OF BEHAVIOR WERE NOTED

BEHAVIOR	AGE (MONTHS)						
	0–2	2–4	4–6	6–8	8–10	10–12	12+
Stimulated nonvocal							
Turns to sound	0	16	18	21	7	11	0
Stops vocalizing to listen to adult	0	10	26	29	26	6	0
Responds to voice alone	20	16	18	21	26	17	7
Appropriate response to verbal cues	0	0	0	0	19	33	53
Stimulated vocal							
Smiles or vocalizes to adult imitation	0	23	26	8	19	22	7
Conversational babbles	0	3	4	4	44	22	13
Imitates a sound	0	0	0	4	26	22	13
Appropriate sound to verbal cues	0	0	0	0	14	33	22
Spontaneous vocal							
Vocalizes when alone	0	25	18	46	11	0	13
Vocal accompaniment to grasping	0	0	9	4	33	28	13
Vocal accompaniment to nonsocial action	0	0	4	29	67	61	33
Calls for adult attention	0	0	0	8	37	33	0
Stable nonverbal sounds	0	0	0	0	4	11	67

Source: Sanger, M. D. Language learning in infancy: A review of the autistic hypothesis and an observational study of infants. Unpublished Ed. D. Thesis, Harvard University, 1955.

tract. With the exception of the opening and closing of the mouth, there is little articulation. Cooing produces a sound spectrogram which is quite different. The coo lasts about one-half second in duration—much shorter than the cry—and the articulatory organs, mainly the tongue, move during cooing. Infant cooing sometimes sounds "vowel-like" but differs from adult vowel production functionally and acoustically. The difference between the sound production of an adult speaker and a prelanguage child is illustrated in Figure IX–1. Note that even when the mother tries to imitate her own child, she makes very different sounds than does the infant.

Babbling, which typically appears after cooing, involves such productions as "uggle-uggle," "erdah-erdah," "oddle-oddle," "a-bah-bah," and "bup-bup-bup" (Shirley, 1933). Some observers, noting that the vocalizations of infants suggest the rising and falling of the voice associated with questions and declarative statements in adult speech (Miller and Ervin, 1964), have argued that infants imitate the pitch, loudness, and intonation of adults in babbling (Weir, 1962). Babbling usually continues until, or even after, true language begins to appear although for some children a short period of relative quiet precedes the onset of talking.

The cooing and babbling infant makes many more sounds than he will actually use in the production of later language. Some sounds drop out as one's "native language" is acquired. At the same time, though, single sounds are transformed into groups, called *phonemes,* which are the raw materials for language.

Phoneme Production

In a general way, phonemes correspond to the usual vowel and consonant sounds of a language. But the letters alone are not quite enough to represent the phoneme. The letter *b,* for example, is pronounced somewhat differently in *bat* than in *tab.* That the sound is recognized as *b* in both words represents part of the competence of the speaker and the listener, about which we will have more to say later.

Phonemes are basic units of speech from a physiological as well as a linguistic point of view; they start with a puff of air which passes along the windpipe until it instigates vibration in the vocal cords which produce a tone. The chest, throat, nose, and head cavity then act as resonators giving the voice its peculiar, individual quality while the tongue, lips, and teeth aid in the production of consonants and the modification of vowel sounds.

Vowel sounds begin to emerge during the first ten days of life. By one to two months of age the child has an average of 4.5 types of vowel sounds

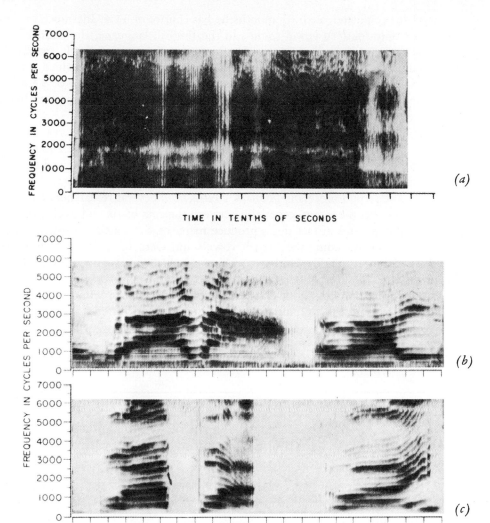

FIGURE IX–1

Some sample spectrograms of infant and mother's speech. (a) Spectrogram of a two-week-old boy crying vigorously; (b) a three-month-old boy cooing; (c) mother imitating her child after listening to a tape on which the baby's noises are recorded. From E. H. Lenneberg, Biological Foundations of Language. *Copyright 1967, reproduced by permission of John Wiley & Sons, Inc.*

at his command; at thirty months he has control of 11.4. Inasmuch as there are only fourteen vowel sounds in the English language, the child of 2½ is doing quite well in terms of mastery. Of the approximately twenty-five consonants in English, infants of one to two months produce, on the average, 2.7. But by thirty months they are up to an average of 15.8 consonant sounds and so, again, are well on their way toward mastery before age three (Chen and Irwin, 1946).

Two related but opposing processes are involved in language development during the babbling stage (Lewis, 1936; Thompson, 1962). One, *phonetic expansion,* refers to the child's expanded ability to produce more and more different sounds as he matures.

The second process is *phonetic contraction.* Several researchers have suggested that the infant, especially between the ages of six and twelve months, is able to, and in fact does, produce many of the sounds heard in human language, including the French vowels and German umlaut which are extremely difficult for English-speaking adults to master (Jespersen, 1922). As the child becomes more proficient in his native tongue, however, he ceases to produce exotic language sounds. This contraction occurs as he apparently learns to limit himself to the sounds of his own language.

EXTENDED DISCUSSION

DETERMINANTS OF EARLY SPEECH

How does speech first emerge? As with many other developmental issues, there are nature and nurture points of view here too (see Chapter I). According to the environmentalists, adults react differently to random sounds emitted by their infants, thereby increasing the frequency of some sounds and decreasing the frequency of others at an early age. From the hereditary viewpoint, on the other hand, it is argued that at least during the first half year, as a result of exercise and the spontaneous maturation of vocal apparatus, infants produce sounds which remain largely independent of environmental influences. The maturationalist further argues that early vocalizations may have little to do with the development of language (Lenneberg, 1967), whereas environmental theorists see a continuity in development (Mowrer, 1960). Before a resolution of this controversy is possible, a great deal of further data must be collected. However, some already existing research speaks to the issue and is of interest here.

Prelinguistic Vocalizations

Supporting the environmentalists' viewpoint, Rheingold, Gewirtz, and Ross (1959) showed that external social reward can influence the rate at which three-month-old infants vocalize. Their experiment lasted a total of six days; the first two days marked the baseline, during which spontaneous infant vocalizations were recorded while infants rested on their backs in their cribs. Periodically, the female experimenter leaned over the crib, keeping her face a standard fifteen inches from the infant but not giving the infant any further stimulation, nor even changing her facial expression. During the third and fourth days, which constituted the treatment period, the experimenter behaved in a similar manner except each time the infant made a sound she gave it a broad smile, made "tsk" sounds, and touched the infant's abdomen lightly with thumb and forefinger. Thus the initiation of social contact with the infant was contingent upon his vocalization. On days five and six, the extinction period, the experimenter resumed acting as she had during baseline. The adult's contingent responses brought about an increase in infant vocalization and when the reinforcing stimuli were withheld during extinction, the vocalization rate declined. But the study did not offer an entirely clear demonstration of the role of contingent social reinforcement in producing increases in infant vocalization. Whether the interaction increased vocalization, or whether the mere presence of an adult was sufficient, remained unsettled.

Weisberg (1963) therefore undertook a second investigation in which he controlled for nonsocial stimulation and the mere presence of an adult. In the social stimulation group, the experimenter rubbed the infant's chin, gave it a smile and an aspired "yeak" sound. A door chime served as the source of stimulation in the nonsocial group. The mere presence of an adult did not reliably increase vocalization over what it was when the infant was alone, nor did nonsocial stimulation affect the rate of vocalization, whether contingently or noncontingently delivered. Only contingent social stimulation served to increase the rate of infant vocalization. The reaction of adults to earlier infant vocalization thus does appear to help shape language development. But is stimulation essential?

Lenneberg (1967), taking a maturational-hereditary position, argues that language competence is biologically based and will emerge under the worst of environmental circumstances—even without parental reinforcement. In one study, Lenneberg and his associates compared vocalization in infants under three months of age born to normal parents to that of infants born to parents who were both congenitally deaf. Infants of deaf parents heard far less adult speech than infants of normal parents and were by and large unable to elicit much reaction to vocalizations from their parents. Yet extensive tapes showed little difference between the two groups in amount of vocalization and age of onset of both cooing and babbling.

The Child's First Words

O. H. Mowrer (1960) has proposed a learning account of early speech derived in part from observation of talking birds (including two parrots, a Mynah bird, two crows, two western magpies, and some Australian parakeets).

> Operationally, the first step in teaching a bird to talk is to make a "pet" of it, which is to say, tame, care for, and "baby" it in such a way as to deflect the interests and emotional attachments of the bird away from members of its own species to another species, namely *homo sapiens*. This is commonly done by isolating the bird from its own kind and making it dependent for food, water, and social attention and diversion upon its human caretakers.
>
> But there is another step involved which only a few species of birds— and apparently no mammal save man—can make. As one cares for and plays with these creatures, one makes certain characteristic noises. These may or may not be parts of conventional speech; any kind of a noise will do—be it a word or phrase, a whistled or sung fragment of a tune, a non-sense vocalization, or even a mechanical sound like the creaking of a door or the opening of a food box—anything so long as it is intimately and con-sistently associated with the trainer and his care-taking activities. As a result of the association of these sounds with basic satisfactions for the bird, they become positively conditioned, i.e., they become *good sounds;* and in the course of its own, at first largely random vocalizations, the bird will eventually make somewhat *similar* sounds. By the principle of generali-zation [see Chapter V] some of the derived satisfaction or pleasure which has become attached to the trainer's sounds will now be experienced when the bird itself makes and hears like sounds; and when this begins to happen the stage is set for the bird's learning to "talk."
>
> In terms of learning theory, what has happened is that initially neutral sounds, by virtue of their occurrence in temporal contiguity with primary reinforcements, have acquired secondary reinforcing properties. When the bird itself happens to make somewhat similar sounds, it is now secondarily

rewarded for having done so and tries to perfect these sounds so as to make them match as exactly as possible the original sounds, and thus derive from them the maximum of pleasure and comfort. [1960, pp. 79–80.]

Mowrer holds that the same process which he observed in his birds also accounted for the acquisition of speech in human infants. Words become associated with comfort and satisfaction and consequently come to sound good. When the infant accidentally emits a sound resembling a good-sounding word, he will repeat and refine it because of the pleasure associated with the word's sound. Eventually, however, the child learns that making these sounds not only comforts and reassures him but also interests and to some extent controls his mother and other adults. Thus utterances are perceived by the infant as leading to satisfaction in still another way. Credence is given to the theory by the following clinical observation.

Two years ago a young woman reported that tests had recently confirmed what she and her husband had suspected for some time, namely that their two-year-old daughter was very hard of hearing and that as a result her language development was being seriously retarded. In fact, the child had no real words and showed no interest in and refused to wear a hearing aid. The mother was convinced that the little girl had *some* hearing, as evidenced by the fact that if she were engaged in some forbidden activity and the mother shouted "No," the child, even though her back was turned to the mother, would respond.

It was apparent from these meager facts that the only sounds that were getting through to this child were "bad" sounds; and one could conjecture that the less often she heard them the better it suited her. There was, in short, no "appetite" for the vocalizations of others and consequently no desire to make similar sounds herself.

When the situation was interpreted to the mother in these terms, she quickly consented to a regime in which vocalizations would not be used for disciplinary purposes at all but would instead be associated as often and as deliberately as possible with *agreeable* experiences. Ordinarily one announces pleasant events in a soft tone of voice reserving the raised voice for warnings and condemnations. The prescribed plan thus called for a reversal of the usual situation. The mother was able to carry through, however, and very quickly the child became *interested* in words, was soon willing to tolerate a hearing aid so that she would be more clearly aware of them, and within six months was herself effectively making and using quite a number of words. [Mowrer, 1960, p. 82.]

But if words are uttered by children because they are paired in time with pleasant events, how do children learn words that invariably appear in negative, forbidding, or unpleasant situations, such as the word "No"? Mowrer holds that when the child hears only frustrating, fear-arousing words, as the two-year-old described above, language learning will be severely retarded. In normal situations, however, the infant has a great amount of experience with words uttered in many positive, rewarding contexts before negative words are introduced. By this time the child has already discovered the practical uses of language.

SEMANTICS AND THE ACQUISITION OF MEANING

Semantics is the study of the relationship of language to meaning; it recently has received a great deal of attention from developmental psychologists as well as linguists and educators. In studying semantics developmentally, the investigator is interested in how meaning is acquired.

The problem of semantics appears with the beginnings of vocabulary. Although the child usually does not utter his first words until around his first birthday (McCarthy, 1954), by the age of twenty-four months vocabulary has multiplied two hundred to three hundred times. The number of words mastered by the child continues to increase thereafter at a rapid rate (see Figure IX–2).

But how do children know what these words mean? Certainly, it may be through one or more of the learning processes discussed in Chapter V, but a more detailed analysis—a specification of exactly how meanings are learned—is required. We shall discuss two possibilities.

One is that acquiring word meaning involves the same process as forming a concept. Brown (1965) proposed such an hypothesis and illustrated it with an earlier experiment conducted by Heidbreder. Adult subjects sat in front of a memory drum—a device which presents stimuli one at a time through an aperture—as pictures appeared. After each picture came into view the experimenter called out a nonsense name; such as "Ling," "Fard," "Relk," "Pram," "Leth," "Dilt," "Stod," "Mank," and "Mulp." The subjects were told that they were to learn the name of each picture. Eventually they were to call out the appropriate name to each picture quickly enough to beat the experimenter.

The subjects viewed each of the series of pictures in Figure IX–3. Note that the pictures are different across and within series. Each nonsense word was paired with one picture per series but never with the same picture twice.

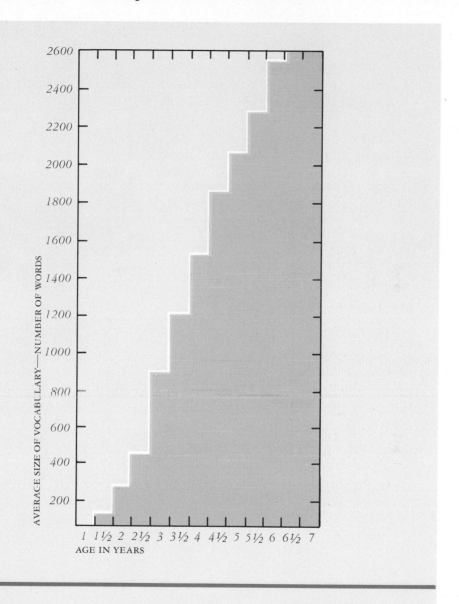

FIGURE IX–2

Size of average vocabulary of children at various ages. Data from Smith, 1926.

FIGURE IX-3

Pictures used in Heidbreder's (1946) study of concept formation. From R. W. Brown, Social Psychology *(1965), by permission.*

For example, "Pram" was the name given to the fourth figure in series I, the first figure in series II, the last figure in series III and the second figure in series IV. By now the reader might be able to guess the picture with which "Pram" is paired in series V.* So the subject could learn that "Pram" is the name for several pictures all of which share one attribute, a crossed pattern. But to have anticipated the correct use of "Pram" in series V, one must have abstracted the unique characteristic from the preceding "Pram" figures and have been able to recognize it in a new context. The ability to abstract and generalize in this way is the basis of concept formation; here the concept to be learned is the meaning for a new word (Heidbreder, 1946).

The second and perhaps the more obvious way in which word meanings are acquired is through hearing them used in various contexts. Werner and Kaplan (1952) presented children with a series of sentences in which a nonsense word such as "corplum" was embedded. Thus, for example, children might be told: " 'Corplum' may be used for support"; " 'Corplums' may be used to close off an open place"; "A 'corplum' may be long or short, thick or thin, strong or weak"; "A wet 'corplum' will not burn," and so on. After each sentence the child was asked to indicate the meaning of the word "corplum." He also was asked why he thought the word had that meaning. The children who served as subjects in this experiment ranged in age from 8½ to 13½ years of age.

The older the subject, the more likely he would be to offer a meaning that fit not only with the current sentence but also with past sentences in which the word had appeared earlier. Thus, for example, "corplum" could mean *brick* in the first sentence, but not in the context created by all the sample sentences taken together. *Stick* or *piece of wood* fits the overall context. Younger children did not always differentiate the meaning of the word from the sentence in which it occurred, and so were more likely to suggest answers such as *brick*. Learning new word meanings contextually can clearly occur, becoming easier with increasing age.

GRAMMAR

Grammar is that part of language that has to do with the production of "permissible constructions." Customarily it is divided into two parts: *syntax* or the study of how words are combined into phrases and sentences,

---

* It is the second from the last figure.

and *morphology* or the study of the formation of words. Developing an adequate theory of grammar has become one of the most intriguing issues in the study of language development.

Early Grammatical Usage

The child's first sentences, in virtually every culture, consist of the single words which, we have seen, usually occur by the first birthday. There appears to be little doubt that these communications are sentences ("Mommy!" can immediately be translated by most mothers as: "Mother, come here immediately"). The fact that a child's first words are sentences has led many theorists to suggest that the concept of a sentence is part of the human organism's inborn capacity, a linguistic universal which is not itself learned but on which grammar and speech are built through learning. McNeill (1970a) has put it this way:

> The concept of a sentence may be part of man's innate mental capacity. . . . The facts of language acquisition could not be as they are unless the concept of a sentence is available to children at the start of their learning. The concept of a sentence is the main guiding principle in a child's attempt to organize and interpret the linguistic evidence that fluent speakers make available to him. What outside observers see as distorted or "telegraphic" speech is actually a consistent effort by a child to discover how a more or less fixed concept of a sentence is expressed in the language to which he has, by accident, been exposed.
>
> Children everywhere begin with exactly the same initial hypothesis; sentences consist of single words. The entire structure of a sentence must be squeezed through this tiny space. This simplest hypothesis leads to the most peripheral of differences between children learning different languages. Only the words differ. A child exposed to English might use *hot* as a comment and a Japanese child would use *atusi,* but the difference is merely in sound, not in conceptual or linguistic structure. Not only are words sentences at the beginning, they are the same sentences in different languages. [p. 2.]

If the child naturally begins with a one-word sentence, as appears to be the case, his behavior is rapidly modified by environmental circumstances. Brown (1965) has pointed out, "By the age of thirty-six months some children are so advanced in the construction process as to produce all of the major varieties of English simple sentences up to a length of ten or eleven words" (p. 286).

This rapid change depends upon the prior development of a suitably large vocabulary. We have seen that by the age of eighteen to twenty-four months the child has mastered a vocabulary of approximately two hundred to three hundred words. By this time two-word utterances typically are found in children's speech. Extensive observations reveal that these two-word utterances are governed by some relatively simple rules and hence, at least from the child's point of view, are grammatical (Braine, 1963; Brown and Fraser, 1964; Miller and Ervin, 1964). For example, although verbalizations such as "shoe my," "hand a," "papa see" occur infrequently —if at all—sequences such as "my shoe," "a hand," and "see papa" are extremely common. From a careful examination of such utterances a rudimentary organization emerges in the form of the so-called "pivotal-open" grammar. It is supposed that the child divides his word repertoire into two classes and that one word from each class is selected for certain two-word utterances. The smaller of the two classes is called the "pivot" class while the other is called the "open" class. In the sequences "see papa," "see hand," "see shoe," *see* is a "pivot" word and all the other words fall into the "open" category.

A prominent characteristic of the pivot word *see* in the three examples above is that it occurs invariably in the first position in the utterance. Pivot words like *that* in "that car," "that blue," "that chicken"; *here* in "here chairs," "here goes," "here mum," and *two* in "two men" and "two Bobby" also occur invariably in the first position. In contrast, pivot words like *off* in "hat off," "blanket off," and "sweater off," *it* in "do it," "push it," and "buzz it," and *allgone* in "bird allgone" and "kitty allgone" occur in the second position in the sequence. Pivot words are fixed in either a first or second position whereas open words simply fill the other position. Thus, for example, the open word *blanket* may occur in "that blanket," "see blanket," "blanket off," or "blanket allgone," because its position in the sequence is not fixed.

Pivot and open words are difficult to characterize in the terms usually applied to adult grammar. Words like *bird, eyebrow,* and *kitty* are classified as open words because they all turn up in the same relationship to *allgone;* generally, but not always, they are nouns. On the other hand, *allgone* is called a pivot word because it has a fixed position in context with these and other words. Pivot words are most often pronouns, adjectives, or articles.

Pivot-open constructions usually seem to have a demonstrative quality (e.g., "see boy," "that hat") and account for about 70 percent of the verbalization of two-year-olds. From the pivot-open construction, the child progresses to pivot-open-open and similar three-word utterances (Braine, 1963; Palermo, 1970).

Children apparently begin to develop adult syntactic patterns slowly and incrementally. Features of the adult grammar are not acquired all at once, nor does every child start to produce them at the same age.

EXPLAINING SYNTACTIC DEVELOPMENT

In order to understand the genesis of more elaborate sentences from their one-word beginnings, detailed studies of the language development of a small number of children have proven extremely helpful. In one such study, Brown and his associates studied the language development of three children, "Adam," "Eve," and "Sarah," from the time they were about two years old (Brown, Cazden, and Bellugi, 1969).

> Every second week we visited each child for at least two hours and made a tape recording of everything said by the child, as well as of everything said to the child. The mother was always present and most of the speech to the child is hers. Both mother and child became very accustomed to our presence and learned to continue their usual routine with us as observers. [Brown, 1965, p. 287.]

One of the most striking aspects of the transcripts of these sessions is that the child learns speech imitatively, through a reciprocal process of interchange with the mother. Specifically, the child tends to show *imitation with reduction* of the mother's speech, whereas the mother imitates some of the child's phrases *but expands upon them*. Both types of imitations are illustrated in Table IX–3.

From interactions such as those described above, the child clearly might learn to produce correctly a fairly large number of individual sentences in their acceptable grammatical form. But there is much reason to believe that he learns more, for a catalog of sentences does not adequately represent the child's linguistic competence. To see why this is so, let us suppose for a moment that grammatically correct sentences are simply learned, stored, and delivered up on appropriate occasions like prerecorded outputs. What would be expected of the child? Miller, Galanter, and Pribram (1960) have pointed out:

> . . . there seems no alternative [within this view] but to insist that a child must hear 2^{100} sentences before he can speak and understand English. That is about 10^{30} sentences. In order to appreciate how ridiculous this condition is, recall the fact that *there are only about 3.15×10^9 seconds per century.* In short, the child would have to hear about 3×10^{20} sentences per second

TABLE IX-3

EXAMPLES OF IMITATION WITH REDUCTION (BY THE CHILD) AND IMITATION WITH EXPANSION (BY THE MOTHER) IN BROWN *ET AL.*'S STUDY

IMITATION WITH REDUCTION

Mother	*Child*
Daddy's brief case.	Daddy brief case.
Fraser will be unhappy.	Fraser unhappy
He's going out.	He go out.
No, you can't write on Mr. Cromer's shoe.	Write Cromer shoe.

IMITATION WITH EXPANSION

Child	*Mother*
Baby highchair.	Baby is in the highchair.
Mommy sandwich.	Mommy'll have a sandwich.
Pick glove.	Pick the glove up.

Source: Brown, 1965.

. . . and that is on the assumption of a childhood 100 years long with no interruptions for sleeping, eating, etc., and perfect retention of every string of twenty words after one presentation! [pp. 146–147.]

If a child's sentences are not learned verbatim, then he must somehow acquire rules for producing language. So we must turn to various theoretical explanations of how such rules are learned. Several of the most obvious ones stem from learning theory.

Skinner's Position

In the late 1950s, Skinner (1957) attempted an account of the emergence and maintenance of language, using as the basis of his speculation many of the same variables that had shaped and maintained nonverbal behavior in the laboratory through operant conditioning (see Chapter V). His account, a complex extrapolation mainly from animal research, covered several aspects of language. Here we will illustrate only its general flavor.

One facet of Skinner's theory is the notion of partially conditioned *autoclitic frames*. When a speaker has acquired responses such as "the boy's gun," "the boy's shoe," and "the boy's hat," the partial frame "the boy's _____" is presumably available and may be combined with other responses. Thus when the speaker notices a boy who has recently obtained a bicycle, he may compose a new unit "the boy's bicycle," by inserting the appropriate term in the previously acquired frame. The relational aspects of the situation determine the use of the particular frame and the specific features of the situation determine the nature of the responses fitted into it. To illustrate, Whitehurst (1972) trained two-year-old children to use partially conditioned autoclitic frames as defined by Skinner. The procedure involved teaching two subjects to label individual colors or figures with a nonsense vocabulary (e.g., "Gol" or "Tib"), and then training them to label the color and figure simultaneously, in a given order. For example, when the color red and a particular figure were presented, the correct answer would be *red car* (except that the subjects' actual responses were in the nonsense vocabulary, e.g., "Gol Tib"). Then a new figure label would be taught and simultaneously presented with the old color, red. The red stimulus, then, was retained as part of each new unit and should become a frame for learning this simple grammar. This is just what happened for both children. They soon learned to produce novel but grammatically correct descriptions of any red object for which they were taught a label, without having to hear or be rewarded for producing the particular description.

That syntax *can* be learned through reinforcing only the well-formed verbalization does not necessarily mean that children *do* in fact learn solely because they are rewarded for good grammar. In fact, they may frequently be rewarded when incorrect grammar is used. Brown and his associates (1967), in the study mentioned previously, observed:

> Once in a while an error of pronunciation was noticed and corrected. Most commonly, however, the grounds on which an utterance was approved or disapproved . . . were not strictly linguistic at all. When Eve expressed the opinion that her mother was a girl by saying "He a girl," mother answered "That's right." The child's utterance was ungrammatical but mother did not respond to the fact; instead she responded to the truth value of the proposition the child intended to express. In general the parents fit propositions to the child's utterances, however incomplete or distorted the utter-

ances, and then approved or not, according to the correspondence between proposition and reality. Thus "Her curl my hair" was approved because mother was in fact curling Eve's hair. However, Sarah's grammatically impeccable "There's the animal farmhouse" was disapproved because the building was a lighthouse and Adam's "Walt Disney comes on, on Tuesday" was disapproved because Walt Disney comes on, on some other day. It seems, then, to be truth value rather than syntactic well-formedness that chiefly governs explicit verbal reinforcement by parents. Which renders mildly paradoxical the fact that the usual product of such a training schedule is an adult whose speech is highly grammatical but not notably truthful. [Brown, Cazden, and Bellugi, 1967, pp. 57–58.]

The Role of Observational Learning

We already have seen that imitation, narrowly defined, cannot explain the child's language proficiency completely. Children produce many more sentences than they hear; more importantly, there are among them many strange syntactic structures which do not appear in adult speech. Sentences such as "Why he play little tune?" or "Why no me can't dance?", unlikely to be modeled by parents, are often produced by children (Brown, 1968). What is more, when the experimenter instructs a youngster of about three, "Adam, say what I say: Where can I put them?" the child may respond by imposing his own structure on what he hears, "Where I can put them?" (Bellugi-Klima, 1968). But whether the child must comprehend or be able to produce a particular syntactic structure before he is able to imitate it is an unsettled question. Brown, Fraser, and Bellugi (1963) found that among the three-year-olds whom they studied, the ability to imitate preceded both comprehension and production of syntactic structure.

What role, then, does observational learning play in grammatical development? Perhaps the underlying rules of grammar, its *latent structure,* are induced or abstracted from exposure to knowledgeable speakers. There are many reasons for believing that this is the case.

In the course of studying morphology, Berko (1958) has produced some intriguing evidence to show that the child does learn these rules. She employed nonsense forms and labels to determine whether young children were able to employ correctly certain language rules for which they had no formal training either in the specific situation or with the abstract rule. For example, she presented a picture of a nonsense object, such as the one shown in Figure IX—4, and said. "This is a WUG." She then showed the child

This is a wug.

Now there is another one.
There are two of them.
There are two —.

FIGURE IX–4

An example of Berko's technique for showing that children have induced certain language rules by preschool age. Adapted from Berko, 1958.

a picture of two such objects and said, "These are two _____," providing an opportunity to supply the plural form of WUG. Her subjects, preschool children, were able to perform remarkably well (i.e., by application of the rule, the plural of WUG ought to be WUGS).

Patterns of rule-regulated language in young children, of the type identified by Berko, frequently can be observed even in the casual observation of young children's language. For example, children will often "regularize" what are, in fact, irregular English forms by saying "He *doed* it" instead of "He *did* it" or "I see the sheep*s*" rather than "I see the sheep." Inasmuch as it is most unlikely that they have heard adult speakers use these particular phrases, they are presumably operating with rules which they have abstracted, incorrectly in these cases, from the language they have heard.

But we might ask how the rules displayed in Berko's study were learned. Martin Braine (1963) has attempted to explain such originality in language through the notion of "contextual generalization." According to this concept, when a child hears a new sentence such as "I walked to the store yesterday," he learns that certain phrases occur in certain positions in an English sentence. Later he can use these phrases in the correct position in new sentences. "I walked," for example, may precede any number of grammatically correct closings. The child who hears the novel sentence "I flugged" will be able to generate sentences such as "many people flug" or "Herbert flugs." Thus words and phrases learned in one context are generalized to other, novel ones.

A process similar to contextual generalization may be seen in a series of studies derived from Bandura and Walters' social learning view of imitation (see Chapter V). The first experiment (Bandura and Harris, 1967) examined the effects of observation of a model on the production of particular language constructions by second graders. The general approach involved asking second grade children to make up sentences which included a particular noun such as *table* which was presented by the experimenter, first during a base-rate period and then again after some form of intervening training. The results showed clearly that those children exposed to a combination of (1) a model who produced sentences with and without the relevant construction (for example, prepositional phrases), (2) reward to both the model and the child for producing sentences which contained the relevant construction, and (3) attention-focusing instructions soon produced many more of the relevant constructions in their sentences than did a control group.

This study clearly indicated that children's language productions may be modified rapidly through the combination of modeling and other simply controlled social learning variables. It is likely, however, that the children in the Bandura and Harris study had been exposed to, and had used the relevant constructions many times before their participation in the experiment. Therefore, the question of whether children can be shown experimentally to actually acquire new or novel language rules as a function of observational learning still remained unanswered.

Odom, Liebert, and Hill (1968) designed an experiment to determine whether children could likewise abstract and learn to use unfamiliar language rules from listening to appropriate models. The procedures were similar to those used by Bandura and Harris except that some children were exposed to modeled sentences containing unfamiliar prepositional constructions of the form article-noun-preposition (e.g., "The boy went *the house to*" or "The man was *the door at*"). Surprisingly, children of this age (most were about 8 years), when exposed to the new rule, demonstrated an increase in the frequency with which they used the *familiar* English constructions (i.e., preposition-article-noun) relative to children in a control group who saw no model and received no reward. It thus appeared that, instead of abstracting the new rule from the model's rewarded productions, the children in these conditions somehow "reordered" the unfamiliar language constructions to make them correspond to language rules with which they already were familiar. These interesting results show a remarkable cognitive strategy on the part of the child when faced with an unfamiliar situation. Unable to abstract the new rule because of their limited training, the youngsters "fell back" on a familiar one.

Liebert, Odom, Hill, and Huff (1969) repeated the essential "new-rule" treatment described above (as well as employing other procedures which need not concern us here) with three age groups—five-, eight-, and fourteen-year-olds—and found that oldest children could swiftly learn to abstract and use new rules from brief exposure to a model. From their major results, shown in Figure IX–5, it is clear that fourteen-year-olds almost immediately picked up, processed, and used the new rule *in their own sentences* after relatively brief training. The middle age group in this study (eight-year-olds) showed some use of the new rule, but the youngest subjects again failed to abstract the novel construction and tended to fall back on the new incorrect form with which they were familiar already. It is clear, then, that observational learning does play some important role in language learning, but that this input interacts with the child's understanding of grammatical forms and his ability to process information. We can appreciate further the complexity of the phenomena by turning to the theory of transformational grammar.

Transformational Grammar

There is much about children's grammar which remains unexplained by merely saying that language is learned through observation, imitation, and abstracting rules. One is that youngsters seem able to respond correctly to aspects of language that are not marked in any obvious way in speech, such as the "logical" subject of a sentence. A favorite pair of examples are sentences "John is eager to please" and "John is easy to please." Although *John* may appear, at first blush, to be the subject of both sentences, it is actually the subject only in the first. The second, "John is easy to please," actually means that it is easy for someone to please John. The question is not whether people can make the distinction—it is apparent that they can—but *how* the distinction is made. One theorist, Noam Chomsky (1968), has proposed that the answer lies in his theory of transformational grammar.

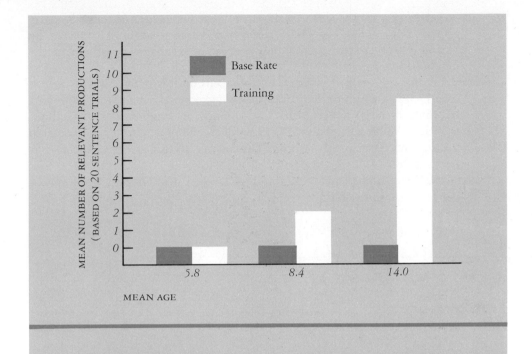

FIGURE IX–5

Mean number of new rule prepositional constructions in Liebert et al.'s experiment during base rate and training as a function of children's age. Adapted from Liebert et al., 1969. Reproduced by permission.

A transformation, for Chomsky, is a relationship between the underlying or *deep* structure of a sentence and its superficial or *surface* structure. A good illustration is the sentence, "Visiting relatives can be a nuisance." Note that this expression has two underlying possible meanings: "Relatives who visit can be a nuisance," and, "It can be a nuisance to visit relatives." We understand the sentence only when we grasp its underlying structure, which cannot be seen in the arrangement of the word string.

By turning to the development of children's interrogative sentences, those which use the "wh" words (who, what, when, where, why), we can illustrate further the ideas behind transformational grammar theory. Specifically, the view is that such sentences derive grammatically from a base or kernel string of words, usually a declarative sentence, through a series of transformations. The child "learns" the transformations, perhaps by listening to other speakers, but only because he is innately capable of noticing and applying them.

Let us begin with the sentence "John will do this." The simplest interrogative form which derives from the same kernel is "John will do what?" but this sentence is not the usual one produced by English speakers; rather, they say "What will John do?" How does one move from the kernel to the standard interrogative form? The answer offered involves the use of two transformations.

Preposing simply involves bringing the "wh" word to the beginning of the sentence, in the fashion:

1. John will do what?
2. John will do what?
3. What John will do?

Transposing involves knowing that one must exchange the order of the subject and the auxiliary verb:

1. John will do what?
2. John will do what?
3. What will John do?

This view, then, proposes a particular sequence in the development of interrogative sentences which should reflect the emergence of appropriate transformations. Such a pattern was observed by Brown and his associates (Brown, 1968) in their longitudinal study of Adam, Eve, and Sarah, that was described earlier in this chapter.

LANGUAGE IN USE

Thus far we have described language development and indicated some of the major theoretical issues in understanding this development. Ultimately, though, one of our major interests in language stems from the fact that it is functional. In this section we shall briefly overview some of the issues involved in the use of language, noting the frequent relationship between them and the theoretical matters which have been covered already.

Perhaps no purpose of language is more important than its ability to function as a tool for communication between people. We already have mentioned the various communicative roles of one-word sentences in the very young child. It is not until a bit beyond the age of two, though, that real interchange—the beginnings of conversation—emerges.

We shall begin with an excerpt (taken originally from the records of Brown and Bellugi, 1964) to provide the general feeling of what such a conversation might be like (Table IX–4). Note that certain words are missing from the child's conversation. The glaring absence of most articles, auxiliary verbs, and inflections is noticeable particularly in phrases such as "put suitcase . . . for?" "Where birdie go?" "What inere?" and "Yep, it fit." But despite the deletion of many elements, including "what," "did," "you," "it," "in," "the," from the child's sentence "Put suitcase . . . for?" the essential message can be successfully communicated. Because of the similarity between the well-trimmed telegram and the pared-down expressions used by the child, Brown and Fraser (1964) have called the speech of very young children "telegraphic."

All communication includes at least two people, so we also should pay attention to the adult's part in the conversation. The passage in Table IX–4 contains several instances in which the adult rephrases or expands something the child has said, often taking something that is ungrammatical and recasting it properly. For example, the child's question "Read da?" is recast by the adult into "Will you read it to me?" and "Put suitcase . . . for?" is expanded into "What did you put it in the suitcase for?" In expansion, then, the adult adds to the child's telegraphic message, making the utterance clearer as well as more grammatical.

McNeil (1970a; 1970b) has suggested that an adult will select an expanded sentence to fit the child's intended meaning, manufactured from both the child's utterance and the situation in which he and the child find themselves. Thus, from a transformational grammar point of view, if the child's meaning is guessed correctly, the adult is actually presenting to the child an appropriate surface structure to express the deep structure the child has in mind. Conceivably, this pattern of communication may provide a means by which children learn relationships between deep and surface structure.

Although a child's grammar has become quite sophisticated by the age of four or five, communication has not. Long ago, Piaget (1926) asked children to teach other youngsters how to use mechanical devices, such as

TYPICAL CONVERSATION BETWEEN AN ADULT AND A YOUNG CHILD

CHILD (28 MONTHS)	ADULT
What dat . . . somebody pencil	Whose pencils are they?
Floor	Floor?
Where birdie go?	
Birdie	
Birdie up dere	
Birdie	
Read dat?	
Read dat?	Will you read it to me?
What inere?	Is that a hammer, Adam?
Hammer	
Hit hammer, mommy	
No Cromer ———, mommy?	
Hurt	Poor Adam. Did you hurt yourself? What happened, Adam?
Screw (did) happen	Screw happened? You didn't even have a screw.
have screw	
———no down there . . .	
table . . . get broom	Does that one fit?
Yep, it fit	
Yep, it fit	Does it fit?
No . . . fit	
Put suitcase . . . for?	What did you put it in the suitcase for?
What dat?	That's tape. We'll use that one tomorrow.
All right 'morrow	Shall we use it tomorrow?
Yep	
Use morrow, yep	
Sure, use morrow	

a syringe. Children under six years of age did very poorly at explaining, apparently unable to see the problem from the listener's point of view; they used vague gestures and pronouns such as "this," "something," "here," "there." Even when the child receiving the instruction was blindfolded, the young speakers did not appear to grasp why their communications would be unsuccessful.

More recently, Glucksberg, Krauss, and their associates (Glucksberg, Krauss, and Weisberg, 1966; Glucksberg and Krauss, 1967; Krauss and Weinheimer, 1964) also have observed communication between children. In their experimental situation children are seated out of sight of each other, as in Figure IX–6, and asked to play a game called "stack the blocks." One child is the speaker and has the job of encoding a message to relay to another child. The second youngster, the listener, must decode the speaker's message and act on the information. In front of each player is an array of six blocks and a peg on which the blocks can be stacked. The speaker receives his blocks one by one from a dispenser and must put them on the peg in the order he receives them. The listener's blocks, however, appear in a random array on the table. The object of the game is to form two identical stacks of blocks. To accomplish this goal the speaker must verbally instruct the listener in a way that can be understood. Each block carries a design (see Figure IX–7) by which it can be identified. The designs, however, have been carefully chosen and are not ones which have readily available English names.

In the first in a series of experiments, children of approximately four and five years of age served as subjects. Results showed that the speaker child tended to use reference phrases that were private and idiosyncratic. One youngster, for example, referred to form 5 in Figure IX–7 as "a pipe, a yellow part of a pipe," a phrase that communicates much less well than such labels as a "boot," a "horse's head," or an "ax head"—which represent average adult responses. (Incidentally, the adjective "yellow" conveyed no useful information since the forms were stamped with black ink on natural redwood blocks.) Another young speaker referred to form 6 as "Mommy's hat." Apparently it resembled a particular hat belonging to that child's mother but, for the naïve listener, the message did not contain enough information to assist performance. Adults, on the other hand, tended to refer to it as "An upside down cup. It's got two triangles, one on top of the other." It is not surprising that not one of the seven pairs of children was able to complete a single game without error.

A second experiment, however, showed that children of the same age functioned much more effectively in the listener role. They now had to respond to reference phrases which had been used by adult subjects. Eight out of twelve met the criterion of two consecutive errorless games. Yet

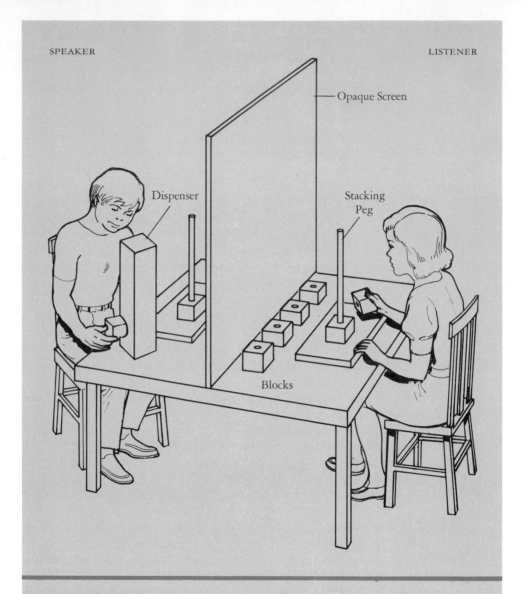

SPEAKER

LISTENER

Opaque Screen

Dispenser

Stacking
Peg

Blocks

FIGURE IX-6

The experimental task used by Glucksberg, Krauss, and their associates.

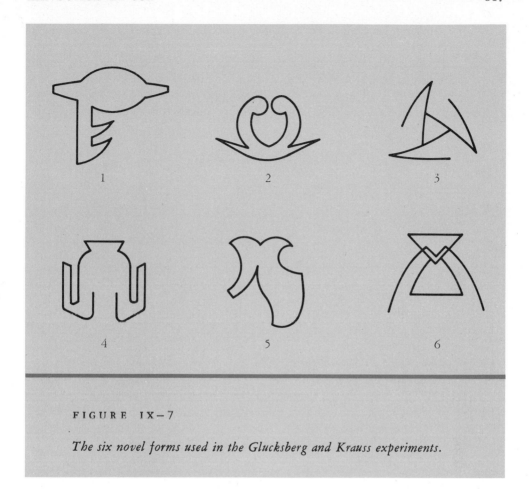

FIGURE IX–7

The six novel forms used in the Glucksberg and Krauss experiments.

a third experiment was performed to determine whether a child could understand his own idiosyncratic labels. Subjects of 4 and 5 years of age saw each of the six forms and were asked by the experimenter to "tell me what this looks like." The experimenter then played the role of speaker in the communication game, using the names that had been supplied by the child earlier. The results showed that the child's own names were adequate to guide his own actions. One young subject referred to form 4 as "Daddy's shirt" and form 6 as "another Daddy's shirt" but, in each case, selected the correct form.

Children apparently do not differ from adults on one aspect related to communication. They, as well as adults, seem to have the desire to appear knowledgeable even when they are not. Thus, for example, one young child described by Glucksberg and Krauss (1967), when instructed to pick up "this one" by another child on the opposite side of a screen that completely blocked his view, asked, "Do you mean this one?" to which the reply came, "Yes."

SOCIAL AND EMOTIONAL DEVELOPMENT:
Early Relationships with Parents and Caretakers

SO FAR OUR DISCUSSION has focused on tracing the emergence of physical, perceptual, and cognitive processes, with little mention of the behaviors involved in social and emotional development. Yet it is a truism that man is a highly socialized organism; from the moment of his birth—usually a social event in itself—he is continuously shaped by those around him. And, to some extent, each child appears to take on a unique "self" during his or her early years. The formation of a child's personality—his patterns of dealing with others and reacting to them—is thus among the most important and interesting changes that occur during the course of human development.

DEFINITIONS AND THEORETICAL VIEWPOINTS

There are many definitions of "personality," but little consensus as to what the term means. Most often, though, personality psychologists, whether theorists or researchers, have been interested in explaining the most dominant forms of interpersonal behavior which an individual displays. Perhaps the principal difference which we find among various strategies and schools of thought concerns the question of *how* to explain social and emotional development.

In a general way, theorists do agree that *socialization*—that is, all those processes by which the young come to feel and act similarly to most others in their culture—is central to this development. The family, school, church, and other institutions are agents of socialization; they influence and shape the child's behavior in a variety of ways. But the manner in which socialization takes hold and the interplay of the child's biological endowment with social experiences have given rise to a great many theories of personality. The view of Freud and his followers, for example, emphasizes internal psychological processes and conflicts. This position can be contrasted with one taken by learning theorists, who view interpersonal reactions, such as aggression and altruism, as learned social response patterns. Finally, there are those who take a structural approach to behavior; these are the so-called *trait* theorists, who seek out behavior traits which are presumed to be durable characteristics of the person. And for some, traits are thought of as real, biological attributes of the individual, like the color of his eyes.

Not surprisingly, each of these viewpoints has somewhat different implications for understanding personality and social development. The Freudian psychoanalytic approach emphasizes the importance of early emotional experiences as laying the groundwork for later aggression or passivity in adolescence and adulthood. Learning approaches emphasize the situational aspects of interpersonal behavior for both children and adults. Finally, trait approaches focus on continuity and stability in interpersonal behavior, and the development of measurement techniques to get at the underlying structure of personality. In this chapter and the two that follow we will discuss each of these views on several occasions, as they apply to the development of specific forms of social behavior.

This chapter is devoted to work describing the roots of social and emotional behavior; it provides the underpinnings for subsequent discussion of various complex behaviors that are prevalent to some degree in social settings in most cultures. We turn first to the work of Sigmund Freud, which has held great sway in the thinking of both professionals and laymen for most of the present century.

PSYCHOANALYTIC THEORY

Freud's theory is a comprehensive description of psychological development that emphasizes internal or intrapsychic events. Although few developmental psychologists today would subscribe to all of it—and many would shun most of its sweeping generalizations—Freud's views have had a tremendous impact in guiding the development of more sophisticated research and rigorous theory.

By training Sigmund Freud was a psychiatrist, concerned with trying to understand the genesis of the symptoms of his suffering patients. This attempt led him to search for missing links and transformations that had occurred earlier in development. Thus, through his career, Freud increasingly became a developmental psychologist.

Structures of Personality

Perhaps the best known aspect of Freud's theory is the idea that personality consists of three components or structures: *id, ego,* and *superego.* The id, characterized as a reservoir of primitive instincts and drives, is present at birth; it is the force that presses for immediate gratification of bodily needs and wants. The ego is the practical, rational component of personality. Freud posited that the ego begins to emerge during the first year of life, in response to the fact that the infant cannot always have his way. An example of the work of the emerging ego is the child learning other strategies for coaxing his parents into action when crying does not produce immediate results. Finally, between the third and fourth years of life the superego or "moral agent" of personality develops as the child identifies with its same-sexed parent and begins to incorporate adult standards of right and wrong.

Psychosexual Stages of Development

Freud believed that human development proceeds as a series of *universal stages* that all individuals pass through from infancy to adulthood. These stages are largely determined from the organism's innate tendency to reduce tension and achieve a pleasurable experience. Each stage is given its unique character by the development of sensitivity in a particular part of the body or erogenous zone—that is, an area which is particularly sensitive to erotic stimulation—at various times in the developmental sequence. Freud described these stages as "psychosexual" to indicate that development is the outcome of the successive focusing and reduction of tension in various erogenous zones which predominate at different times in life. Each stage is associated with a particular conflict which must be resolved before the child can move to the next stage.

There are two reasons why difficulty may be experienced in leaving one stage and going on to the next. First, present needs may be met inadequately, in which case frustration ensues and conflict remains salient in the individual's psychological makeup. Alternatively, needs may be so well satisfied that the child is unwilling to leave the stage and, as a result, the behaviors which characterize that stage may continue. Thus, either frustration or overindulgence or a combination of the two is presumed to result in some *fixation* at a particular stage of development, although chronologically the individual has already passed through it.

Freud drew an analogy between this situation and military troops on the march. As they advance, they are met by opposition or conflict. If they are successful in winning the first battle (resolving the conflict), then most of the troops (psychological energy or libido *) will be available to move on to the next battle (stage). However, the greater the difficulty in winning the battle, the more troops will be left behind on the battlefield (fixation) and the fewer will be available to go on to the next confrontation. Presumably, all individuals have some psychological investment which remains at each of the stages through which they pass; when the amount is relatively small, only vestiges of earlier patterns of behavior will remain to recur as the individual matures. On the other hand, when a substantial investment of energy has been made at an earlier stage, the individual's personality

---

* *Libido* is often described as the energy of the "sexual instincts." But in this context "sex" refers to all pleasurable actions and thoughts, not only those which are principally erotic (cf. Liebert and Spiegler, 1970).

may become dominated by those techniques of obtaining satisfaction or reducing tension which were used successfully at the earlier period.

Oral Stage. From birth through approximately the first year of life, the infant's mouth is presumed to be the prevailing source of pleasurable sensations—for example, the pleasurable sensations associated with sucking.

At the same time, he is physically and psychologically immature, so that he must be cared for by others. The child may, therefore, be characterized psychologically in terms of relations of dependence (upon the mother or other caretakers) and behavior involving chiefly acts of incorporation (taking things in). But, according to psychoanalytic theory, these behaviors are more than specific events; they represent durable or potentially durable styles of interaction with the world. Thus, Strupp (1967) points out that "the focal point of the child's personality organization at this period is not necessarily the mouth per se but the total constellation of immaturity, dependency, the wish to be mothered, the pleasure of being held, the enjoyment of human closeness and warmth" (p. 23).

It is argued within this context that individuals who become fixated at the oral stage are likely to develop an optimistic view of the world, to have relationships in adulthood which are primarily dependent in character, to be specially friendly and generous, but to expect, in turn, the world to "mother them." We can see readily how this type of theorizing, which is central to psychoanalytic theory, attempts to explain patterns of later behavior in terms of earlier experiences.

The oral stage is said to end when the child is weaned, and with weaning comes the conflict which is presumed to be crucial during this period. That is, the more difficult it is for the child to leave his mother's breast or the bottle and its accompanying pleasures, the greater will be the proportion of libido left at this stage.

Anal Stage. From about one to three years of age, the focus shifts to the anal zone, with its functions of elimination and retention. Until this time, the infant presumably has experienced few demands on him, but now there appear direct attempts by parents to interfere with the pleasure that is obtained from the excretory functions. Thus, the conflict of this stage is between these demands from society and the sensations of pleasures associated with the anus.

Various aspects of the anal period may be related to later behavior. If the child views his feces as a possession, toilet training experiences may be the foundation for a host of attitudes about possessions and valuables (Baldwin, 1967). If the bowel movement is viewed as a gift to parents, love may become associated with material possessions or bestowing gifts. Excessive cleanliness or being pedantic also are viewed as stemming from the demands of toilet training. Still other psychological features of this stage involve the development of shame, shyness (a reaction to being looked at), and impulsivity.

Toilet training, then, is the focus of resolving the conflicts of the anal stage. If parental demands are met with relative ease, the basis for self-control is established. If there is difficulty, the child may "fight back" by, for instance, deliberately defecating when and where he pleases—or, more precisely, when and where it displeases his parents. Such aggressiveness and hostility, it is reasoned, may be carried into adulthood where they take the form of excess stubbornness, willfulness, and related behavior. On the other hand, the child may react by retaining feces, thus setting the stage for the later characteristics of stinginess and stubbornness.

Phallic Stage. At about four years of age, the genital region becomes the focus of libidinal pleasure, as reflected in the young child's masturbation, curiosity, and inspection of the sexual organs. The conflict of this stage, according to Freud's theory, is the desire of the child to possess the opposite-sexed parent and fear of retaliation from the same-sexed parent. In the case of the male child, these features are particularly clear in the Oedipal complex. The young boy, in desiring his mother and thereby competing with his father, also experiences fear of his father, especially of castration at his father's hands. These fears finally are sufficiently intense and anxiety-producing so that the youngster gives up his sexual longings for his mother. This is accomplished through *identification* with the father which produces for the child the vicarious possession of the mother and, perhaps more importantly, the adoption of the father's behavior, attitudes, and values. As we shall see later, the identificatory process is extremely important in the psychoanalytic description of sex role and moral development for both sexes.

Although Freud postulated an analogous situation for the female child in the resolution of the Electra complex, certain differences prevent this theory from being quite as elegant. For the girl infant, the mother, as caretaker, is the first object of love; thus, it is necessary to explain how the female develops strivings toward the male parent. Freud suggested that the little girl, in noting the apparent difference between herself and boys in regard to sexual organs, blames her mother for the fact that she lacks a penis, which she assumes she has lost. The resulting loss of affection for the mother is accompanied by increased regard for the father. At the same time, the child also directs envy toward the father because he possesses a penis. It is clear, of course, that castration cannot be feared by the girl, but perhaps the youngster nevertheless is afraid that her mother's disapproval of her incestual desires will manifest itself in an equally threatening loss of love. In any event, she comes to identify with her mother and represses, or puts out of consciousness, longings for the male parent.

Latency and the Genital Stage. The final two stages postulated by Freud, latency and the genital stage, are of less importance to understanding the early foundations of social and emotional behavior. Not only do they occur after the age of five or six years, but Freud himself considered them insignificant to the development of the basic structure of personality (Baldwin, 1967). Latency includes the years from the resolution of phallic conflicts to puberty and, by definition, is a time during which the libido lies dormant. The latency years are described as a relatively stable and serene period during which the child acquires many cultural skills. During the last psychosexual stage, the genital stage, the libido is seen as being reactivated and directed toward heterosexual objects. Providing that strong fixations at earlier stages have not taken place, the individual is well on his way to establishing fruitful relationships with others and otherwise leading a "normal," satisfying life.

Erikson's Views

One weakness of Freudian theory is its lack of attention to the latency period, which comes just when the child begins school, his first major contact with the larger society outside his immediate family. The importance of this time was ignored by Freud and had to await the attention of other investigators. One such theorist is Erik Erikson, who is regarded as a "neo-Freudian" because he employs the framework of psychoanalytic theory but fashions it in his own direction.

Erikson accepts the notion that libidinal or emotional energy exists at birth and is at the core of human functioning. He also assumes that development passes through stages, several of which coincide with Freudian ones (Table X–1). Nevertheless, he has made some distinct deviations from Freudian theory; Maier (1969) has noted three major areas in which these differences exist.

First, Erikson places much greater emphasis on the role of the *ego,* or rational part of the personality, in man's struggle to master the environment, whereas Freud concentrated largely on the nonrational, instinctual components of the personality, which he called the *id.* Because society and

TABLE X-1

COMPARISON OF ERIKSON'S PSYCHOSOCIAL
AND FREUD'S PSYCHOSEXUAL STAGES OF DEVELOPMENT

CHRONOLOGICAL STAGES	ERIKSON'S STAGES	FREUDIAN STAGES
infancy	basic trust vs. mistrust	oral
1½–3 years (approximately)	autonomy vs. shame, doubt	anal
3–5½ years (approximately)	initiative vs. guilt	phallic
5½–12 years (approximately)	industry vs. inferiority	latency
adolescence	identity vs. role confusion	genital
young adulthood	intimacy vs. isolation	
adulthood	generativity vs. stagnation	
maturity	ego integrity vs. despair	

the changes which occur in it are important to the developing child, the psychosexual stages postulated by Freud are transformed by Erikson into psycho*social* stages. Second, the growing individual is placed within the larger social setting of the family and its cultural heritage rather than in the more restricted triangle of mother-child-father. Third, Erikson stresses the opportunity each individual has for resolving developmental crises, whereas Freud focused on the pathological outcomes of failure to resolve them adequately. "There is little," Erikson writes, "that cannot be remedied later, there is much that can be prevented from happening at all" (Erikson, 1963, p. 104).

Because of Erikson's emphasis on social context, his theory frequently appears more relevant than Freud's to the kinds of encounters that children have with their everyday world. Additionally, despite his agreement with Freud on the importance of the early years, Erikson's recognition of man as an organism continuing to develop throughout his lifetime resulted in a developmental scheme involving eight stages extending from infancy to old age. Thus, he provided both a valuable extension to psychological theory and a personal boon to all of those unalterably beyond adolescence. For our present purposes, however, discussion will focus on Erikson's interpretation of the four earlier stages of life; we will return to the later ones in Chapter XVI.

Basic Trust versus Mistrust. The foundation of development, according to Erikson, is woven around the theme of trust and hope. The newborn is seen as coming into the world experiencing a change from the warmth and regularity of the uterus. Yet he is not defenseless. Parents, particularly the mother, respond to his bodily needs, and the nature of their handling the child largely determines the establishment of attitudes of trust or mistrust. During the early months contact with the world is not only through the mouth but also through the manner in which parents embrace, talk, or smile at the infant. If a consistent and regular satisfaction of needs is received, certain expectancies about the world are set up; the child comes to trust the environment and, in doing so, becomes open to new experiences.

Autonomy versus Shame and Doubt. The major theme that next evolves, from about 1½ to three years of age, is the conflict of the child as to whether to assert or not assert his will. During this time, he rapidly acquires the physical skill to explore his world and begins to see himself as capable of manipulating some parts of it. The young child attempts to establish his autonomy, which sometimes requires a disruption of the previously established dependency upon others. But shame and doubt exist alternatively with the thrust for autonomy; they are based on the child's remaining dependency and on his fear of going beyond his capabilities. Toilet training reflects the essence of the conflicts of this stage; shame and doubt result from failure to meet parental expectations and an inability to be assertive, whereas autonomy is the outcome of self-control and assertion.

Initiative versus Guilt. Coinciding with Freud's phallic stage, Erikson postulates a conflict between initiative and guilt. The environment of the three- to five-year-old now invites—or even demands—that he assume some responsibility and master certain tasks. The child must initiate action in many spheres—action which sometimes conflicts with and intrudes upon the autonomy of others, and thus results in feelings of guilt. Like Freud, Erikson recognizes the increased interest in sex displayed by both girls and boys at this stage. But he sees the child's attraction for the opposite-sexed parent less incestually and more as the result of a reaching out to the one available representation of the opposite sex who has proven her or himself. The sense of rivalry which naturally occurs with the same-sexed parent leads to a gradual replacement of the desired parent by other love objects; a more realistic view of the inequality between himself and the same-sexed parent results in stronger relations with his peers. At the same time, the rival parent becomes the ideal toward which to strive (Maier, 1969). During this time, then, the child gradually comes to understand the roles and opportunities presented by society, and is able to overcome failure and guilt with a sense of accomplishment.

Industry versus Inferiority. Given the above outcome, the youngster is ready to grapple with the challenges that arise with entrance into the competitive world of formal schooling. This is the time of latency of sexual striving. With the Oedipal and Electra complexes settled, peers become increasingly important; the child both identifies with them and judges himself against their standards. The theme of this stage is the mastery of tasks in the face of feelings of inferiority. As the child achieves such mastery he becomes capable of facing the turbulent adolescent years which lay directly ahead.

Some Evidence on the Effects of Early Experience

We have seen that according to Freud and, to a lesser extent, Erikson, the establishment of dependency or trust occurs very early in life and focuses largely on the mother-child relationship. Freud noted the importance of the mother and her role in arousing both pleasurable and unpleasurable sensations:

> In these two relations lies the root of a mother's importance, unique, without parallel, established unalterably, for a whole lifetime as the first and strongest love-object and as the prototype of all later love-relations for both sexes. [1949, p. 45.]

Underlying this significance is the mother's role in satisfying the infant's biological needs. In fact, Freud labeled the mother-child relation "anaclitic" (literally: leaning on) to denote the child's dependency on the need for sustenance, theorizing that the infant's first love object is the mother's breast (Ainsworth, 1969). Experiences with regard to the feeding situation are, not surprisingly, considered crucial in determining later dependency.

Direct verification of such theorizing is impossible, but one indirect road is through cross-cultural comparisons of child-rearing practices. One of the most well-known studies of this type was carried out more than twenty years ago by John Whiting and Irwin Child, through reports of behavior of individuals in seventy-five primitive cultural settings.

These investigators were interested in examining child-rearing practices related to five systems of behavior which they judged prevalent around the world: oral, anal, sexual, dependence, and aggression. The first three systems were presumed to be motivated by innate drives and were obviously tied to Freudian theory; dependence and aggression were considered learned but probably universal. All of the systems were seen as disciplined through child training and as having relevance in adulthood.

The method employed in this research involved judges who analyzed conditions which were thought to produce initial satisfaction in the child before socialization commenced, ascertained the age at which socialization began, and evaluated the quality of socialization practices. Two general conclusions were reached. One pointed to the prevalence in virtually all societies of similar areas of socialization; all peoples deal with the control of excretory function and sexual impulses, and the shaping of offspring to be independent. But, conversely, a great deal of variability was discovered in the specific goals or ways in which societies carried out their socialization. This can be seen dramatically in the accounts given below of the toilet-training practices found in two different cultures. The Dahomeans were rated as being severe in their practices:

> A child is trained by the mother who, as she carries it about, senses when it is restless, so that every time it must perform its excretory functions, the mother puts it on the ground. Thus, in time, usually two years, the training process is completed. If a child does not respond to this training, and manifests enuresis at the age of four or five, soiling the mat on which it sleeps, then, at first, it is beaten. If this does not correct the habit, ashes are put in water and the mixture is poured over the head of the offending boy or girl, who is driven into the street, where all the other children clap their hands and run after the child singing,
>
> Adida go ya ya ya
"Urine everywhere."
>
> [Herskovitz, as cited by Whiting and Child, 1953, p. 75.]

In the practices of the Siriono, on the other hand, overindulgence can be seen:

> Almost no effort is made by the mother to train an infant in the habits of cleanliness until he can walk, and then they are instilled very gradually. Children who are able to walk, however, soon learn by imitation, and with the assistance of their parents, not to defecate near the hammock. When they are old enough to indicate their needs, the mother gradually leads them further and further away from the hammock to urinate and defecate, so that by the time they have reached the age of 3 they have learned not

to pollute the house. Until the age of 4 or 5, however, children are still wiped by the mother, who also cleans up the excreta and throws them away. Not until a child has reached the age of 6 does he take care of his defecation needs alone. [Holmberg, as cited by Whiting and Child, 1953, pp. 75–76.]

Similar differences are found for feeding and weaning practices. The Kwoma tribe, for example, are extremely indulgent:

Kwoma infants up to the time they are weaned are never far from their mothers. . . . Crying . . . constitutes an injunction to the mother to discover the source of the trouble. Her first response is to present the breast. If this fails to quiet him, she tries something else. . . . Thus during infancy the response to discomfort which is most strongly established is that of seeking help by crying or asking for it. [Whiting, as cited by Whiting and Child, 1953, pp. 91–92.]

In contrast, Ainu children have considerably different experiences:

Put into the hanging cradle . . . the poor little helpless creatures could not get out, and for the rest they were free to do whatever they were able. This usually meant a good deal of kicking and screaming until tired of it, followed by exhaustion, repose, and resignation. [Howard, as cited by Whiting and Child, 1953, p. 93.]

Although the investigators were interested in several other issues, we shall limit our remaining discussion to some of their hypotheses about the development of personality. Recall that from a psychoanalytic viewpoint, extreme indulgence or frustration of a particular behavior may result in fixation of the behavior. Whiting and Child extended this view, reasoning that high indulgence of a behavior would result in its positive fixation because it had been paired with reward. Behaviors that had been associated with frustration, on the other hand, would lead to negative fixation.

How did they test these hypotheses? First, societies were ranked according to how indulgent or severe their practices were for each system of behavior. Then they were ranked according to the degree that positive or negative fixations were manifested. (Positive fixations, it will be recalled, involve continuing patterns of behavior, retained from earlier stages because of the satisfaction they provided; negative fixations produce such continuing patterns because of unresolved earlier frustrations.) Finally, the two rankings for each society were compared. Positive fixation, it was reasoned, would reveal itself in the prevalence of therapeutic practices relating to a particular behavioral system. For example, positive fixation in the oral system could be seen in the ingestion or taking in of various herbs or other medicines. Negative fixation would manifest itself in the explanations employed by the society for disease; for example, explanations involving ingestion or verbal incantations would imply a negative fixation in the oral system of behavior.

Whiting and Child found some support for their hypotheses, but the complex pattern of results also makes it clear that many other factors are involved in early social and emotional development:

> The general outcome . . . was to justify the separation we made between positive fixation and negative fixation and to provide clear confirmation for the hypothesis of negative fixation. For the hypothesis of positive fixation we obtained in general only some very tentative confirmation. . . . The outcome of our tests of fixation was not uniform for the five systems of behavior we dealt with. . . . [1953, pp. 315–317.]

Evidence gathered from several other investigations likewise does not strongly support the proposed relationships derived from psychoanalytic theory. For example, regarding the relation between feeding experiences and dependency in young children, Ferguson notes:

> These studies are beset by a number of methodological problems, but it seems that the main difficulty is that the preoccupation with orality inherited from psychoanalytic theory led to a focusing on the wrong aspects of mother-infant interaction. [1970, p. 61.]

The psychoanalytic emphasis on orality to which Ferguson refers thus has given way to more systematic investigation of other dimensions of experience that play a role in early social and emotional development. Turning to an experimental approach, researchers have begun to ask some specific, intriguing questions about what is necessary for adequate development.

CONTACT COMFORT

Are bodily contact and "warmth" important for the young or does the infant only require adequate food, water, and a suitable environmental temperature? In one series of experiments, designed to answer this question, Harry Harlow and his associates substituted two types of surrogate mothers for the natural mothers of young rhesus monkeys. One surrogate was made of wire mesh, with a simple block demarked with two eyes serving as the head; the other was made of soft terrycloth and had more elaborate facial features (see Figure X–1).

In a now classic study (Harlow and Zimmerman, 1959), newborn monkeys were separated from their real mothers and placed individually in a cubicle with both a wire and cloth surrogate. Half of the infants received milk from the wire surrogates while the cloth mothers "nursed" the other half. Observations of total time spent in contact with the surrogates showed that the monkeys preferred the cloth mothers, regardless of the source of nourishment (Figure X–2). Those who received milk from the wire surrogate went to them for that purpose, but otherwise remained with the cuddly terrycloth mothers much of the time. Even with increasing age and opportunity to learn, they did not come to prefer the wire surrogate.

FIGURE   X – 1

Left, the wire and cloth "surrogate" mothers used by Harlow and his associates. Right, the infant's typical response was to run to the cloth mother when frightened, even if he had been fed only by the wire one. From H. F. Harlow and R. R. Zimmerman, Affectional responses in the infant monkey. Science, 130 (21 August 1959), 421-432, figure 1, 23. By permission of the publisher and Harry F. Harlow, University of Wisconsin Primate Laboratory.

(a)   *(b)*

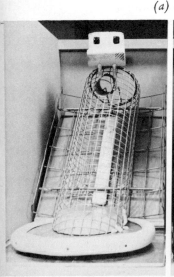

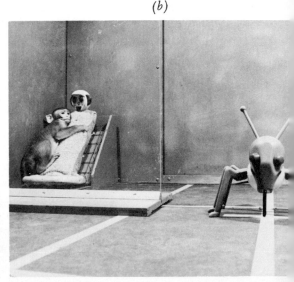

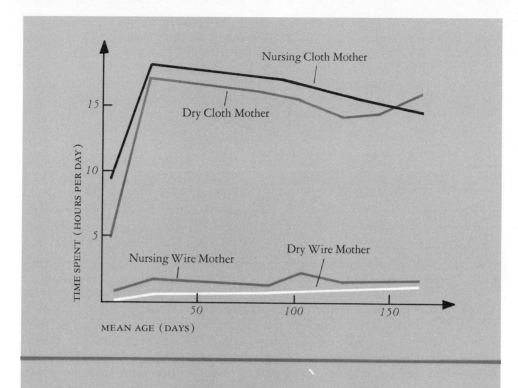

FIGURE X-2

Amount of time infant monkeys spent with their cloth and wire surro-
gate mothers. Adapted from H. F. Harlow and R. R. Zimmerman.
Affectional responses in the infant monkey. Science, 1959 130, 431–
432. By permission.

Harlow and Zimmerman also have demonstrated that the affectional
bond between the infants and the cloth mothers was based on more than
the latter's being a comfortable resting place. They observed the monkeys'
reaction to various fear stimuli, such as a moving toy bear or buglike
creature. Once again, regardless of the feeding situation, the infants displayed a preference for cloth surrogates and contact with it appeared to
reduce their fear (see Figure X–1b).

Results such as these suggest that something other than feeding gratification, most likely physical contact, contributes to the attachment between the infant and its parents. The work of a group of European investigators known as ethologists provides further description of mechanisms underlying the early dependency or attachment of the child.

THE ETHOLOGICAL APPROACH

The term ethology is derived from the Greek word *ethos,* which means habit or convention. Its roots as a scientific discipline are most clearly traceable to zoology (Eibl-Eibesfeldt, 1970). Like Harlow, the ethologists have focused their efforts on the study of animals; this strategy permits a more detailed examination of social behavior than is usually possible with humans. Like Freud, though, they have taken a strongly biological tack. Ethologists search for universal regularities in the behavior and development of a species.

A basic thesis of the ethological viewpoint is that all animals, including man, possess specieswide characteristics which are the foundations for the development of at least some social behaviors. As Freedman (1968) has noted, ". . . [this] emphasis . . . is not meant to deny that familial and cultural institutions do indeed differentially influence behavior and personality. We . . . emphasize that such institutions only support or shape man's behavior and do not create it, as it were, out of the blue" (p. 2). From this point of view, behavioral dispositions are considered to have evolved as the result of a Darwinian process of natural selection. Pressures from the environment exerted over long periods of time assure that members of a species with the most adaptable behavior are most likely to survive and, thus, pass the characteristics on to their offspring. It is argued, then, that behavioral patterns shared by all members of a species are, or were, necessary or adaptive.

The manner in which ethologists have employed the evolutionary perspective to account for human behavior can be illustrated by considering the grasping reflex of the human infant. As we saw in Chapter III, the infant will respond to a light touch on the palm by closing his fingers firmly around the object touching him. Figure X–3 are photographs of a premature infant (gestational age of seven months) hanging by its hands and then by its hands and feet to a clothesline. In an effort to account for this reflex in terms of its presumed evolutionary origins, one prominent ethologist offers the following analysis:

> The grasping reflex undoubtedly served originally the purpose of holding onto the mother's fur. This reflex is often considered a rudiment because

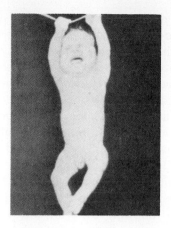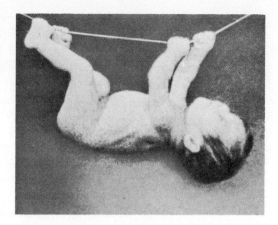

FIGURE X-3

The grasping reflex in a seven-month-old premature infant. From A. Peiper, Irenäus Eibl-Eibesfeldt, Grundrib der vergleichenden Verhaltensforschung, Ethologie. © R. Piper & Co. Verlag München 1967.

man no longer possesses fur and therefore the reflex is thought to be no longer functional. The behavior does not seem to have completely lost its function, however; one can observe how small infants sleep close to their mother's body and how they hold onto her clothing. [Eibl-Eibesfeldt, 1970, p. 400.]

Similarly, it is argued that infant behaviors such as crying or smiling reflect basic patterns that are "wired in" to all human young and form the basis of attachment. The theory is supported by a series of naturalistic investigations spanning a period of more than seventy-five years.

Early Ethological Work

In 1873, D. A. Spalding observed the tendency in young chicks to approach and follow moving objects virtually from the time they were born. His analysis of this highly reliable "following response" was that it was an innate tendency in the organism, one that was functionally advantageous for survival. At an early age, when the chick is most vulnerable, its chance for survival is increased markedly by following its mother "automatically" (without having to learn to do so) to those places where food is plentiful and danger least likely. To make his argument viable, Spalding recognized that he would have to demonstrate that the following response was not simply learned very early in life. To do so, he devised a demonstration which was ingenious for its day. Just as newborn chicks were breaking out of their shells—before they had opened their eyes—Spalding covered their heads with small hoods which were fitted around the neck by an elastic thread. In this way he prevented the chicks from learning by visual means. Nevertheless, when the chicks were finally unveiled, they followed the first moving object which crossed their field of vision.

It was not until the pioneering work of another investigator, Konrad Lorenz, that great interest in the following response appeared in psychological circles. Lorenz referred to the following behavior which was observed initially in young birds as "imprinting" (1937), a translation of his native German word "Pragung" (more literally, "stamping in"). He demonstrated imprinting by appearing in a film in which he himself served as the first object that appeared after birth in the visual field of ducklings; the film displayed baby ducklings following him as he walked through the fields (Figure X–4) or swam in a lake and flying to him as he flapped his arms from atop a small hill. Using a writing style that was both clear and vivid, Lorenz also illustrated dramatically the uniqueness of the phenomenon:

> . . . imprinting has a number of features which distinguish it fundamentally from a learning process. . . . First among the points . . . is that the object acquisition in question can only take place during a brief critical period in the life of an individual. In other words, a very specific physiological state in the young animal's development is required to accomplish it.
>
> Secondly, once the physiologically critical period is over, the animal knows the imprinted object of its innate reactions . . . as though this knowledge were innate. It cannot be forgotten! [Lorenz, 1935, cited in Sluckin, 1965, p. 8.]

opposite: FIGURE X – 4

Konrad Lorenz and ducklings demonstrating the imprinting phenomenon. From "An Adopted Mother Goose," Life, 39, No. 8, August 22, 1955, p. 74. Copyright: Thomas McEvoy, Life Magazine, © 1955 Time Inc. By permission.

This statement introduced a new concept, the *critical period,* a very short span of time in the early life of the organism during which a permanent and binding attachment to a particular object is formed. When the notion of critical period is extended somewhat, it provides a possible model for viewing human behavior. Specifically, it suggests that the absence of certain types of experiences during early development (i.e., at some hypothetical, critical period in the life of the human organism) will produce marked and nonreversible consequences for a variety of behaviors in later life.

EFFECTS OF SOCIAL DEPRIVATION

In previous chapters, we saw that restricting stimulation during the early years may impair perceptual and intellectual development. At the same time, Freud, Harlow, and the ethologists all agree that the early years are critical for normal *social* development. Their work has led to increased interest in the effects of early experience, particularly appropriate contact with other members of the species. But what happens if this contact is not available? Much of our knowledge on this matter comes from experimental work with animals.

Isolation in Dogs

In one series of studies, Scottish terriers were separated from their mothers immediately after weaning and cut off from the rest of the world by being placed into individual pens with opaque sides (Thompson and Melzack, 1956). The pups, who never saw their human caretakers either, were tested after seven to ten months. Their reactions were compared to those of control Scotties who had spent the same time living with families outside of the laboratory or, in a few cases, living free in the research facilities.

In order to examine fear reactions, the investigators exposed the dogs to strange objects such as an opening umbrella, a human skull, and a swelling balloon. The control animals did not show much excitement, but simply ran away. The experimental dogs, on the other hand, were highly agitated, whirled about, and stalked the objects purposelessly. When retested a year later in the same manner, they had become more like the controls; they were still excitable but exhibited more purposeful avoidance. However, the controls had by now developed new reactions—attacking the objects with playful snapping, biting, barking, and growling—not shown by the isolated animals.

Two other measures of social behavior, a test of dominance and a test of sociability, are also of interest. In the former the restricted dogs showed less dominance when they were placed in a situation in which they had to compete for a bone with control animals. Sociability was measured by releasing an isolated or a control animal into a large pen in which two other dogs were individually restricted to two separate corners by chicken wire. The controls spent more time staring, barking, and wagging their tails at their penned companions; the isolated dogs spent more time exploring the room itself. This lack of interest in companionship on the part of the isolated animals persisted for several years.

Isolation in Rhesus Monkeys

The Harlows (1970) isolated young rhesus monkeys at birth in a stainless steel chamber in which all light was diffused, the temperature controlled, the air flow regulated, and all environmental sounds filtered. Food and water were provided automatically and the cage was cleaned by remote control. Thus, all physical needs were met, but during the course of early development the animals saw no other living creature. After being so raised for either three, six, or twelve months, each monkey was taken from the specialized chamber and placed in its own individual cage. Thereafter, the Harlows exposed these subjects to a peer (another monkey who had also been reared in isolation) and to two otherwise similar monkeys who had been reared in open cages with others. All four individuals were then put in a special playroom, typically for half an hour a day, five days a week, for six months. The playroom was equipped with a variety of toys designed to elicit activity and play. The Harlows report:

> *Fear is the overwhelming response in all monkeys raised in isolation.* Although the animals are physically healthy, they crouch and appear terror-stricken by their new environment. Young that have been isolated for only three months soon recover. . . . But the young monkeys that had been isolated for six months adapt poorly to each other and to the controls. They cringe when approached and fail at first to join in any of the play. During six months of play sessions, they never progress beyond minimal play behavior, such as playing by themselves with toys. What little social activity they do have is exclusively with the other *isolate* in the group. When the other animals become aggressive, the isolates accept their abuse without making any effort to defend themselves. For these animals, social opportunities have come too late. . . .
>
> Monkeys that have been isolated for twelve months are very seriously affected. . . . Even primitive and simple play activity is almost non-

existent. With these isolated animals, no social play is observed and aggressive behavior is never demonstrated. Their behavior is a pitiful combination of apathy and terror as they crouch at the sides of the room, meekly accepting the attacks of the more healthy control monkeys. We have been unable to test them in the playroom beyond a ten-week period because they are in danger of being seriously injured or even killed by the others. [1970, p. 95, italics added.]

Social Deprivation in Humans

The question remains whether any similar phenomena can be found with humans—i.e., whether there are also critical periods for human development. No simple answers are available, largely because analogous experimental research is unethical. Anecdotal evidence, however, has been offered to shed some light on the problem.

As long ago as 1945, for example, Spitz described a South American orphanage in which the young appeared to show deterioration in their social behavior after their mothers left them at the age of three months. Spitz (1965) stated that "The infants remained in the Foundling Home, where they were adequately cared for in every bodily respect. Food, hygiene, medical care and so on were as good as, or even superior to, that of any other institutions we have observed." There are many similar accounts, and such deficits in general have been attributed to deprivation of maternal love.*

But maternal deprivation is a vague term that provides little information about the specific variables that underlie deficiency. Casler (1961), for example, makes a distinction between children who suffered separation from significant adults before six months of age and those to whom it did not occur until later in life. In the latter case, he warns that the problem actually is learning about rejection or the severing of an established affectional bond. In regard to children separated early in life, he concludes, "evidence is accumulating, both on the human and the animal level, that [the cause] is perceptual deprivation—the absolute or relative absence of tactile, vestibular, and other forms of stimulation" (1961, p. 49). In any event, it seems reasonable to assume that developing organisms require an optimal level of stimulation of various kinds and that a variety of social experiences can best provide them. Whether these experiences must occur at a particular time is presently not agreed upon.

---

* The reader may recall a brief description of Spitz' work earlier, in Selection 6.

SOCIAL ATTACHMENT IN HUMAN INFANCY

In light of the research considered above, it is not surprising that developmental psychologists have become increasingly interested in the formation of social attachments by humans. People can, of course, form social attachments at any age; their existence does not necessarily connote excessive dependency, helplessness, or immaturity. However, our present concern is with an attachment that develops during infancy when the organism is both helpless and immature and that presumably has important evolutionary advantage.

John Bowlby, a psychoanalyst who has been much influenced by the ethological perspective, has presented one of the most complete theoretical perspectives on human attachment, as we can see from the following review of his work:

> The keynote of Bowlby's position is that attachment behavior has biological underpinnings which can be comprehended only within an evolutionary context. He acknowledges that the human species is one in which there is a large proportion of environmentally labile behavior which enables it to cope with a wide range of environmental variation. Further, in comparison with other species, there are fewer fixed-action patterns, more plasticity for learning, and a longer period of infantile helplessness. Nevertheless, for the human species to have survived despite extreme, extended infantile vulnerability, he finds it reasonable to suppose that its young must be endowed with some relatively stable behavioral systems which, through sustaining parental care, serve to reduce risk through the long period of immautrity. Indeed, attachment behavior in the young, together with the reciprocal parental care behavior, tend to be among the most environmentally stable behavioral systems across species. [Ainsworth, 1969, p. 999.]

What are the behaviors that are most often cited as attachment behaviors? Bowlby (1958, 1969) suggests that they include clinging, sucking, crying, smiling, babbling, calling, physical approach, and following. In order to assess whether such behaviors are related, one team of researchers conducted a short-term longitudinal study of fifty-six infants, ten, fourteen, and eighteen months of age, using a variety of measures of attachment (Coates, Anderson, and Hartup, 1971). They found that both crying and orientation toward the location at which the mother was last seen were more frequent during and following separation than before separation. Significant correlations were found for all ages among visual orientation toward the mother, touching her, and moving in closer physical proximity to her. Crying, touching, and proximity to the mother also were related. Thus, it appears that these behaviors all plausibly can serve as measures of attachment.

A Developmental Study of Infant Attachment

We may ask, though, how attachment develops. In a major study, Schaffer and Emerson (1964) explored three aspects of social attachment in sixty infants: (1) age at which it occurred, (2) its intensity, and (3) the objects to which infants became attached during approximately the first eighteen months of their lives.

The investigators devised a series of situations paralleling everyday life in which the infant experiences separation—for example, being left alone in a room, being left with someone other than the mother, and being put down after being held. They reasoned that the child's immediate responses to each of these situations would provide an index of the degree to which he was attached to the adult from whom he was separated. To obtain this information they interviewed mothers four times a week up to each child's first birthday and once more at eighteen months. Parents were asked about infants' reactions during the time immediately preceding each interview.

A second, related issue involving the infant's reaction to strangers was measured directly during the home visit. At the beginning of every visit, the interviewer approached the infant in a series of steps. First, the interviewer appeared in the infant's visual range, standing still; then he successively smiled and talked to the infant without moving closer; then he approached the infant while smiling and talking, made physical contact by touching or stroking the child, offered to pick the infant up by holding out his hands; finally, he picked the infant up and sat the youngster on his knee. The specific point at which the infant began to show fear, as evidenced by whimpering, crying, lip trembling, adopting a fearful facial expression, or drawing back, thus could be assessed.

Among the major findings was that the *onset* of attachment to specific individuals occurred for most infants between the age of six and nine months, although the range varied from five months to past one year. Overall fear of strangers came about a month later than attachment (see Figure X–5). Thus, seeking proximity of certain familiar figures cannot be explained simply by the tendency to seek protection from strangers. Note, though, that there was also a tendency for children who formed attachments early to develop fear of strangers early.

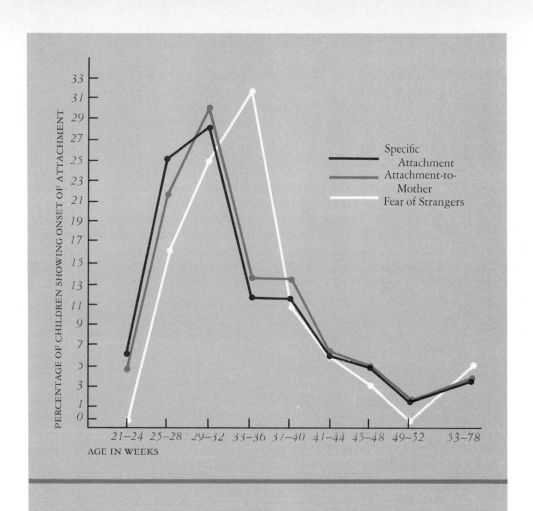

FIGURE X-5

The development of attachment in infants in the Schaffer and Emerson study. Adapted from H. R. Schaffer and P. E. Emerson. The development of social attachments in infancy. Monographs of the Society for Research in Child Development, *1964, 29, No. 3. Copyright 1964 by the Society for Research in Child Development, Inc. By permission.*

The *intensity* of attachment for specific individuals peaked between forty-one and forty-four weeks and again at seventy-eight weeks. The investigators, judging from their observations of some of the children, note that new motor skills developing between forty-four and seventy-eight weeks (e.g., crawling, sliding, walking) may have been responsible for this finding, for the children apparently were interested in the novelty of their new feats and thus were willing to leave their mothers.

The Beginnings of Separation: Exploratory Behavior

Attachment serves the infant well, for he surely would find himself in peril should he become separated from his mother before he has any skill in fending for himself. On the other hand, exploratory behavior also facilitates survival as the infant moves out from the caretaker and begins to learn about his surroundings. We are not surprised, then, that exploration gradually increases with age in a variety of species (Rheingold and Eckerman, 1970).

Ainsworth and her associates (Ainsworth and Bell, 1969; 1970; Ainsworth and Wittig, 1969) have explored the reciprocal relationship between attachment and exploration by arranging for infants to be brought individually by their mothers into an experimental room. In this room there were three chairs in a triangular arrangement; at the apex of this display stood a child's chair surrounded by toys, the mother, and another adult who was a stranger to the infant. Both the mother and the stranger behaved according to an experimental script, creating the following eight episodes:

EPISODE 1. The baby was carried into the room by the mother accompanied by an observer who subsequently left. The episode lasted three minutes.

EPISODE 2. The mother placed the baby on the floor and sat in her chair for three minutes.

EPISODE 3. The stranger entered, sat quietly for one minute, conversed with the mother for one minute, and then gradually approached the baby. After three minutes, the mother quietly left the room.

EPISODE 4. The stranger and the infant remained alone in the room for three minutes.

EPISODE 5. The mother returned and the stranger exited unobtrusively, leaving the mother and infant alone for three minutes.

EPISODE 6. The baby was left alone for three minutes.

EPISODE 7. The stranger returned and stayed with the baby for three minutes.

EPISODE 8. After the mother returned and the stranger left, the session was terminated.

The fifty-six infants in the study, aged forty-nine to fifty-six weeks, were observed from an adjoining room through a one-way vision screen. Measures of exploratory, proximity, contact-seeking, and contact-maintaining behaviors were recorded. It was found that exploratory behavior of three kinds—locomotor, manipulative, and visual—occurred most frequently when only the mother was present. In contrast, this type of activity decreased sharply when the stranger entered the room and, for the most part, remained depressed during the period when the stranger and the baby were alone. It decreased again when the mother left the room a second time and diminished still further when the stranger entered. These group data are presented graphically in Figure X–6.

Efforts to gain and maintain contact with the mother were weak during the early episodes when the parent was present, but increased in strength during the brief periods of separation. Contact-maintaining responses rose during the first reunion and increased even more sharply during the second reunion. Some of the behavior exhibited by one of the infants, Brian, is depicted in Figure X–7.

From these findings emerges a complex pattern of covariation between attachment and exploratory behavior. When the mother is present, exploration is evoked and attachment is suppressed; the mother apparently provides the infant with a "secure base" from which to observe his surroundings (Ainsworth and Wittig, 1969). In contrast, the absence of the mother reverses the processes so that curiosity is severely depressed and attachment behavior is intensified. Some infants approached the friendly stranger in each episode, several clung to her when she picked them up during Episodes 4 and 7, but proximity-seeking and contact-maintaining activity occurred far less frequently toward the stranger than toward the mother.

Given any particular setting, we might guess that certain environmental changes could induce children to leave their mothers and venture forth to explore. Rheingold and Eckerman (1970) have pursued this possibility experimentally, testing the effects of novelty on the amount of time infants spent away from their mothers. Each infant was placed beside its parent in one of two unfurnished adjoining rooms. All twenty-four infants studied were approximately ten months of age, and so could locomote by some means—toddling, creeping on hands and knees, or crawling on their stomachs. The mother sat in the so-called starting room and the infant was free to explore that room and the adjoining one, referred to as the "open field." During the first experiment, the open field remained empty for half of the infants (Group 0) and a toy was placed in it for the other half (Group 1). All the infants ventured without distress into the open field and there was no difference between the groups in time spent in it.

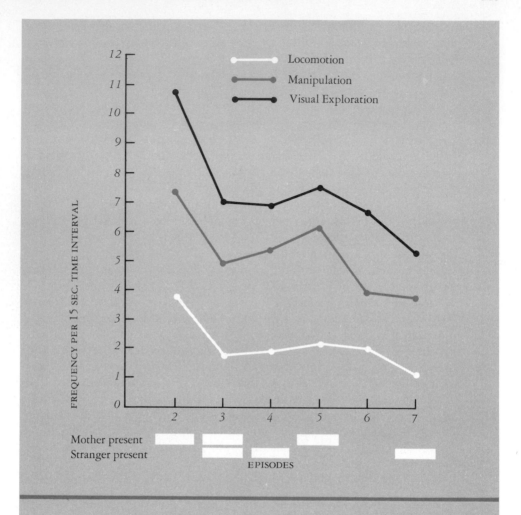

FIGURE X–6

Incidence of three kinds of exploratory behavior in the Ainsworth and Bell study. Adapted from M. D. S. Ainsworth and S. M. Bell. Attachment, exploration, and separation. Illustrated by the behavior of one-year-olds in a strange situation. Child Development, *1970, 41, 49–67. Copyright 1970 by the Society for Research in Child Development, Inc. Reproduced by permission.*

FIGURE X–7

Examples of exploratory and attachment behaviors. (a) Brian explores; (b) he turns to his mother with a cry and clings; (c) he clings when she returns again. From Ainsworth and Wittig, 1969. Courtesy Mary D. S. Ainsworth.

Interestingly, this may have been because the Group 1 children carried the toy back to the starting room, where they spent half their time playing with it.

In the second experiment, half of the original subjects in Group 1 had a toy again, while the other half of Group 1 infants had three toys arranged diagonally in the open field. Similarly, in Group 0, half of the infants now had a toy introduced into the open field while the remaining half of the infants in this group had three novel toys introduced. (The toys, then, represented a novel addition for Group 0 but not for Group 1.) Now, Group 0 infants entered the open field sooner and spent more time there than did those in Group 1. They also contacted the toy more quickly and played with it for more time. For both groups, three toys elicited more play in the open field than one toy and also induced the infants to stay there longer.

The authors conclude that the speed at which their subjects entered a new environment, how far they went, and how long they stayed were controlled by the number, location, and novelty of certain objects in the new surroundings. They also note that:

> The infant's return to the starting room and his reentry into the large room may be considered illustrative of Ainsworth's "exploration from the mother as a secure base." . . . But if the mother is considered a base, the data of our study show that the infants did not always *touch* base; on one-third of the returns, to *see* seemed sufficient. Furthermore, Ainsworth's term *secure* implies the affording of safety, and would be more appropriate here if the return to the mother were a flight from the larger environment. Of this there was no evidence. Quite the contrary; the return was often accompanied by facial and vocal expressions of pleasure and not by signs of fear or of relief from fear. [Rheingold and Eckerman, 1970, p. 82.]

So we see again that human social development is indeed complex and frequently has multiple determinants. Although fear and its reduction constitute one aspect of the attachment that individuals form with others, pleasure in another's company also plays an apparent role.

It is reasonable to assume that the motivation for dependency changes as the child becomes older. Similarly, we might expect that in the course of time there is a shift in the individuals to whom attachment or dependency is shown, as well as in the behaviors themselves. Moreover, individual experiences play a role in the development of dependency; the child who comes into the family as a first born, for example, is more likely as an adult to show dependency in times of stress (e.g., Schachter, 1959). Some of these changes are pointed out in Selection 7, a review of research by Willard W. Hartup. The author also describes the social learning approach to dependence and independence. Finally, he summarizes several childhood experiences that influence the development of dependency and cites other behaviors to which it is related.

DEPENDENCE AND INDEPENDENCE

Willard W. Hartup

Whenever the individual gives evidence that people, as people, are satisfying and rewarding, it may be said that the individual is behaving dependently.

Dependency emerges very early in life. By six months of age, most babies respond in a primitive way to the presence and attention of their mothers. The parent's presence may be calming and gratifying; her absence may elicit crying and agitation. Following these first diffuse responses, more direct modes of seeking nurturance are acquired. The older baby elicits contact and cuddling by holding up his arms and smiling; he may creep or walk, following his mother from place to place and clinging to her skirts. Another child may cry and whine. Throughout infancy and childhood manifestations of dependency such as these are tried out, practiced for a while, and subsequently given up. At

the age of four or five, the child may use intellectual or physical accomplishment to obtain parental praise or attention. Still other transformations occur on into adulthood. Thus, dependency does not refer to a small group of specific action tendencies. Rather, the term covers a wide variety of behaviors, all of which are directed toward the satisfactions derived from contact with or nurturance from other people.

Frequently, the term *independence* denotes simply the absence of dependence. Such usage places dependence and independence at opposite poles of a single behavioral continuum. High dependency is automatically low independence and vice versa. Some writers (Beller, 1955; Heathers, 1955), however, argue that dependence and independence should be conceived separately. Independence, it is suggested, should refer to behavior which is self-reliant but also self-assertive. From this standpoint, a child is independent only to the extent that: (*a*) he seeks nurturance from other people relatively infrequently, and (*b*) he manifests initiative and achievement-striving. This conceptualization of independence does not, of course, remove all overlap with the concept of dependence; independence is simply defined as something more than lack of dependence. . . .

A summary will be presented of those approaches which have most heavily influenced recent research [on dependency], psychoanalysis, on the one hand, and social learning theories, on the other.

The concept of *object relations,* usually meaning the relationship of the individual to other persons, is a central one in psychoanalysis. It is by means of such relationships that the young child obtains those gratifications needed to maintain life, but it is also postulated that the socialization of the child cannot proceed effectively in the absence of emotional bonds between the child and other persons. For example, some psychoanalytic views suggest that the internalizing of controls (i.e., the development of the superego or conscience) is contingent on the early development of a strong relationship between the child and his parents. Presumably internalization (frequently called identification) is motivated by the threat to the child posed by loss of parental love.

In addition to stressing the significance of dependency in the socialization of the child, psychoanalysis also furnishes certain hypotheses concerning the determinants of dependence. The events of infancy are believed to be paramount, primarily because the baby is so completely and necessarily dependent. It is assumed that experiences with the mother during feeding are of crucial significance and that strong manifestations of dependency in later life are traceable to oral deprivations during this period. The personality pattern called the "oral character," which is marked by excessive dependence, pas-

sivity, and depression, is presumed to be a consequence of fixations at the oral stage of development. According to the psychoanalytic view, healthy dependence in young children requires warm, affectionate, indulgent care by the mother during early infancy. The frustrations of later childhood, while they may contribute to dependency conflict and possibly increase dependence, are not presumed to be as crucial as earlier events.

Most social-learning orientations to the problem of dependence also stress the importance of early childhood. The processes which lead to the development of dependence are viewed somewhat differently from the psychoanalytic view. The following account is based on the work of Sears and his collaborators (Sears, Maccoby, and Levin, 1957; Sears, Whiting, Nowlis, and Sears, 1953), who have developed one of the more complete social-learning formulations.

Early in infancy the child acquires certain primitive techniques for obtaining help from others. These behaviors (e.g., clutching the mother, smiling at her, turning toward her) are assumed to be reinforced by the primary gratifications supplied by the mother. Most normal mothers respond nurturantly when their babies cry or behave in ways such as those mentioned; consequently, infantile supplications become part of almost every baby's response repertoire. Heathers (1955) has called these early help-seeking responses instrumental dependence. At this time, the baby does not seek his mother as an end in herself but only as a means for obtaining some basic form of gratification.

If the mother continues to be present at times when primary needs are reduced (e.g., at feeding, changing, and the like), secondary reinforcement properties are acquired by stimuli such as the sheer presence of the mother, her smile, or her voice. The child may cease to cry when the mother walks into view; the maternal smile or voice may also bring about reduction in agitation. It is assumed that a variety of stimuli associated with the mother's presence became secondary reinforcers for the child simply by repeated association with reductions in primary drives.

It is sometimes suggested that this acquisition of secondary reinforcing properties by stimuli connected with the mother's presence is the essential determinant of the dependency drive. It is postulated that, once this has occurred, the child will undergo tension when deprived of social reinforcers and will show satisfaction when they are present. Sears *et al.* (1953) suggest, however, that a dependency drive emerges only after the mother has occasionally failed to reward, or has even punished, dependent overtures in the child. According to this view, dependency acquires motivational properties as a result of a conflict induced by the mother's nonreward or punishment, a conflict between the previously acquired expectation of reward and the new-found expectation of nonreward. The events in the child's life most relevant to the development of dependence would be the nurturance of the mother (i.e., the frequency with which the mother is a source of gratification) and the frustration or punitiveness of the mother (i.e., the frequency with which she threatens the dependency relationship with the child or actually fails to reinforce it).

Walters [and Ray] (1960) take the view that anxiety is the motivational state relevant to much dependency behavior. It is suggested that dependency habits can be learned in connection with many drives—first in response to hunger, thirst, and pain, later in response to the anxiety aroused when the child's relationship with adults is threatened. In any case, reinforcements for dependency behavior center primarily in the nurturant actions of the mother. Relevant variables suggested by this theoretical approach do not differ markedly from those suggested by Sears —maternal nurturance is relevant as a factor leading to the establishment of the mother as a secondary reinforcer; maternal separation or frustration of the child is relevant as a source of anxiety; maternal reinforcement, the degree to which the mother specifically reinforces dependency responses in the child is also significant.

DEVELOPMENTAL STUDIES. As Sears, Maccoby, and Levin (1957) suggest, dependency is a form of behavior which society regards as "change-worthy." As they grow older, children are expected to alter the mode used for obtaining nurturance from others. The child is expected to give up infantile clinging and following about in favor of more "mature" forms of attention- and approval-seeking. The child also repeatedly changes the objects of his dependence. Dependence may initially be directed toward the mother, but subsequently the child directs his overtures toward other adults and peers. It is also possible that the strength of the motivation underlying dependency behavior changes over time, although most personality theories assume some continuity between the strength of dependency motivation in early childhood and in adulthood.

Three studies of preschool children demonstrate some of the changes which occur over time in mode and object of dependence. Heathers (1955) observed the frequency of two forms of dependence, *affection-seeking* and *approval-seeking* in groups of two-year-old and four-year-old children in a nursery school. The observers' records indicated whether the dependence was directed toward teachers or toward other children. It was found that dependency on teachers was significantly more frequent in the group of two-year-olds while dependency on peers was more frequent among the four-year-olds. Similarly, Marshall (1961) reports that the number of friendly contacts with nursery teachers decreases from age $2\frac{1}{2}$ to $6\frac{1}{2}$. Results such as these reflect at least one of the transfers made by young children in the object of their dependence.

Heathers also found that dependency is manifested in different ways by two-year-olds and four-year-olds. The older children showed less clinging and affection-seeking, relative to attention- or approval-seeking than the younger children. Age differences are also reported in a study of preschoolers by Gewirtz (1948). Five-year-olds sought both reassurance and positive attention more frequently than four-year-olds. The results of these two studies imply that attention- and approval-seeking are more "mature" forms of dependence than direct bids for affection made by clinging, lap-sitting, and the like.

The only longitudinal study of dependence in the literature is by Kagan and Moss (1960). These investigators obtained rating of passivity and dependence from observational data assembled when the subjects were between the ages of six and ten. Further ratings of dependence were based on interviews conducted when the subjects were between the ages of twenty and thirty. For females, those who were dependent as children tended also to be dependent as young adults. No such continuity was found, however, for males. Kagan and Moss suggest that this sex difference may be a reflection of a cultural "double standard." That is, dependency in girls and women is generally acceptable in United States culture, whereas dependency in boys is increasingly punished following the infancy and preschool period.

CHILDHOOD EXPERIENCES. The childhood experiences appearing to influence dependency behavior most heavily are parental frustration and punishment of dependence. Sears *et al.* (1954) found that when the mother is relatively punitive toward her preschool-age child and fails to respond nurturantly to the child's overtures, the frequency of dependency observed in boys is *greater,* and the incidence of dependency observed in young girls is *less,* than when amount of punishment is low. The authors employed two assumptions in interpreting this sex difference in their findings. First, they suggest that the relation between maternal punitiveness and the child's dependence is curvilinear rather than linear; that is, high dependence is associated with moderate amounts of maternal punishment while low dependence is associated with either high or low amounts of maternal punishment. Second, the authors assume that girls, being more completely "identified" with the mother, experience more severe punishment than boys. Although the maternal interviews showed that boys and girls in the sample did not differ in actual amount of punishment by the mother, the authors suggest that the mother's punishment has a greater impact on girls (due to the girl's greater identification with the mother). It is postulated, then, that all the girls in this study were relatively high on a continuum of severity of maternal punishment, at a level where less dependence would be expected with increasing amounts of punishment. On the other hand, it is postulated that boys in this sample were all relatively low on the punishment continuum, at a level where more dependence would be expected with increasing punishment.

Some additional evidence supports the hypothesis that parental frustration and punishment during childhood are associated with the frequency of dependency behavior. There is not, however, further support for the hypothesis that the relation between maternal punishment and children's dependence is curvilinear. Marshall (1961) found that parental *suppression of the child* and *interpersonal distance,* as measured by a parental attitude inventory, were positively related to number of teacher-contacts made by girls in a nursery school. Also, Whiting and Child (1953) report that greater dependency-anxiety characterizes adults in cultures where dependency is severely treated in childhood than in cultures where dependency is not severely socialized. These authors also report that anxiety about dependency was less in cultures where parents heavily indulge dependency in early childhood than where parents do not supply this form of indulgence.

Several attempts have been made to relate maternal overprotection or possessiveness to dependency in the child. Levy (1943), analyzing a group of clinical case histories found that children of extremely indulgent mothers tended to be aggressive and negative in their attempts to insure contact with the mother. On the other hand, the children of dominant overpossessive mothers tended to be passively and submissively dependent. Smith (1958) found a relation between overprotection, rated on the basis of the maternal interviews, and dependence in the child (also assessed from the mothers' reports). These data are, of course, contaminated to some extent since information about both the mother and the child was derived from the same source—the interview. Marshall (1961) also reports a positive relation between overprotection and number of contacts made by the child with his nursery-school teacher. This relation is statistically reliable, however, only for boys.

In attempting to understand the impact of overprotection on the child, some investigators have equated this pattern of maternal behavior with excessive indulgence. On the other hand, it is possible that overprotection may be frustrating to the child, particularly when maternal domination and restrictiveness are involved, and in this way contribute to the development of dependency. Also, the overprotective mother may provide relatively frequent reinforcement to the child for infantile dependency behavior. A study by Finney (1961) suggests that selective reinforcement of dependence may play an important role in developing such behavior. He reports a low, but significant, correlation (.40) between the mother's tendency to reinforce selectively the dependency and the dependency level of the child. *In any case, the literature tentatively indicates that maternal overprotection is relevant to the development of dependence in children.* [Italics added.]

Maternal rejection has also been studied as an antecedent of dependence. Sears, Maccoby, and Levin (1957), Smith (1958), and Wittenborn (1956) all report that rejection is positively related to dependency. The Wittenborn results are probably the most substantial since the other two studies used maternal interviews to obtain information about the behavior of both mother and child. Wittenborn reports a correlation of only .30 between expressions of rejection in adoptive mothers and a cluster of children's responses assumed to denote dependence. This correlation is quite low, but is statistically significant.

Relatively little empirical work has been done on the child-rearing antecedents of independence. Winterbottom (1953) reports that the mothers of high-achievement-oriented children make earlier achievement demands, more frequently reward achievement responses, and are less restrictive of independence activity than mothers of low-achievement-oriented children. McClelland [*et al.*] (1953) report inconsistent results concerning the influence of parental affection and rejection on the achievement motivation of young adults (rejection appeared to be associated with high achievement in one study, with low achievement in another). Crandall *et al.* (1960), who used observations to assess maternal affection and preschool children's achievement efforts, found no relation between these two variables. These investigators report, however, that direct reward for achievement and direct reward for approval-seeking were positively related to incidence of achievement efforts in nursery-school free play. *Thus, there is some indication that specific training for independence increases such efforts.* [Italics added.]

EXPERIMENTAL STUDIES. Experimental methods have also been used in the search for determinants of dependency behavior in children. In most instances, the independent variable has consisted of some aspect of the experimenter's behavior toward the child (such as amount of attention or approval). Criterion measures have consisted of changes in the child's dependency behavior or changes in task-performance under social reinforcement.

In an early study, Carl (1949) observed the frequency with which preschool children made dependent overtures to an experimenter who behaved "nurturantly' and "nonnurturantly" in alternate sessions. "Nurturance" consisted of being near, smiling at, and attending to the child. Differences were not found from session to session in rate of occurrence of the usual kinds of emotional dependency, although "positive interaction" (friendly conversation) was more frequent during nurturance sessions. The attention of the experimenter apparently reinforced, and thus increased casual, conversational interaction but did not affect other dependent responses.

Gewirtz (1948) used a technique similar in many ways to Carl's. The form of dependency recorded during the experimental session was attention-seeking. Preschool subjects were employed, some in a session during which attention and other social reinforcers from the experimenter were readily available (i.e., the experimenter sat near and attended to the child), others in a condition of low availability of reinforcers (i.e., the experimenter was "busy" at his own work and did not sit near the child). The results showed that the children in the low-availability condition more frequently sought the adult's attention than the children in the high-availability condition. Regardless of experimental condition, children tended to seek attention from experimenters of the opposite sex more frequently than from experimenters of the same sex.

Gewirtz and Baer (1958a) hypothesized that a period during which the child is deprived of social reinforcers would affect behavior in a manner similar to deprivation of primary reinforcers (i.e., such deprivation was expected to increase a drive for social rewards). Preschool subjects were left alone in an experimental room for twenty minutes, following which they performed a simple task and were reinforced with social approval for correct responses. Frequency of correct responses was greater following isolation than in another session which did not involve a period of being alone. A second study of social isolation effects (1958b) was conducted in which first- and second-graders were either isolated, satiated (supplied with frequent attention and approval for twenty minutes prior to the performance task), or nondeprived. The reinforcing effectiveness of the adult's approval was found to

be greatest after isolation, intermediate after nondeprivation, and least after satiation.

Hartup (1958) employed somewhat different experimental conditions in still another study of preschool children's performance under social reinforcement. One group of subjects experienced ten minutes of consistent attention and approval from the experimenter, followed by a socially reinforced task. A second group experienced five minutes of attention and approval, followed by five minutes in which the experimenter neither attended to nor approved the child. The results indicated, primarily for girls, that performance in the socially reinforced task was better following inconsistent treatment than following consistent attention and approval. The author suggests that the results may be interpreted as indication that inconsistent nurturance is frustrating or anxiety-evoking to the child. Walters (1960, 1961) has also suggested that the effects of social isolation or deprivation may be related to anxiety. This investigator has found that when anxiety is assessed or manipulated independently, social isolation does not, by itself, account for a significant portion of the variance in performance on socially reinforced tasks. Further evidence that frustration is a determinant of dependency behavior is supplied in an experiment conducted with preschool children by Beller and Haeberle (1959).

In general, the results of experimental studies of dependency are consistent with the results of the correlational studies described earlier. Specifically, frustration and inconsis-

tency in the behavior of adults toward children appear to elicit greater dependence than consistent attention and approval. At least temporarily, children strive most strongly to obtain social reinforcers when they have been deprived (or frustrated) in their efforts to obtain them. [Italics added.]

Behavioral Correlates of Dependency and Independence

Dependency appears to hold a position of pervasive importance in human personality dynamics. This is demonstrated by a large number of studies, from which some of the more significant have been selected for review in the following section.

RESPONSIVENESS TO SOCIAL REINFORCEMENT. The results of three studies show that emotional dependency is related to more general manifestations of responsiveness to social reinforcement. Using two groups of four-year-olds, Endsley (1960) found that those children who frequently sought praise from their nursery-school teachers performed at a higher-level on a socially reinforced laboratory task than low-praise-seeking children. Cairns and Lewis (1962) measured the responsiveness of male college Freshmen to the glance of an experimenter and a murmured "mmhmm" in a conditioning situation. Highly dependent subjects (as measured by the Edwards' *Personal Preference Schedule* and the *Interpersonal Check List*) showed a significantly higher level of conditioning to these social reinforcers than the low-dependent subjects. The results

showed, however, a decline in the frequency of the socially reinforced responses manifested by the low-dependency group over the 149 conditioning trials. In other words, the findings did not directly indicate that social reinforcers were more effective (or even effective at all) in producing conditioning in the highly dependent subjects.

Cairns (1961) has also studied the relation between dependency *inhibition* and responsiveness to social reinforcement. Dependency inhibition was defined in terms of reluctance to accept help from other people and was assessed by means of a five-point rating scale. The experimenter verbally reinforced "confiding" (dependency) responses during four short interview sessions with each subject (adolescent juvenile offenders). It was found that subjects who were rated low on dependency inhibition evidenced significantly more confiding responses (by the fourth interview) than subjects with high-dependency inhibition. Cairns also studied the performance of these subjects in a paired-associates task in which correct responses were reinforced socially. The effectiveness of the social reinforcers decreased over trials for subjects with high-dependency inhibition, but the investigator did not find increasing effectiveness of social rewards for subjects with low-dependency inhibition.

SUSCEPTIBILITY TO SOCIAL INFLUENCE. Various investigators have suggested that the highly dependent child should be imitative, should be open to suggestions, and should conform to group norms more readily than children who are relatively nondependent.

The basis for these hypotheses is the assumption that suggestibility, conformity, and certain other kinds of susceptibility to social influence are interpretable as forms of dependency behavior. There are comparatively few studies in this general area, but it appears that at least conformity and suggestibility may be interpreted in terms of dependency. . . .

The relation between dependency and imitative tendencies in children has not been well explored. In one study (McDavid, 1959) of preschool children, the relation between an observational measure of dependency and a laboratory measure of imitation proved to be nonsignificant.

NURTURANCE. The relation between dependency and nurturance (giving sympathy and help to others) was explored by Hartup and Keller (1960). Observations of children's free play in the nursery school indicated that frequency of nurturant behavior is positively associated with the dependency components of seeking help and seeking physical affection (relatively active expressions of dependency) but negatively associated with being near (relatively passive, indirect attention-seeking). These results suggest some commonality in underlying motivation for both dependency and its seeming opposite, nurturance.

SOCIOMETRIC STATUS. The relation of dependency to children's popularity with their peers has been examined in several studies with nursery-school children. Using a picture sociometric technique and employing white, upper-middle-class children as subjects,

Marshall and McCandless (1957) found consistently negative correlations between their measure of popularity and their measures of dependence. That is, high dependency tended to be associated with low popularity with peers. This finding was supported by a later investigation by McCandless *et al.* (1961) which was conducted with children in a racially mixed nursery school. There is some evidence (Hartup, 1959) which suggests that emotional dependence interferes generally with children's initial adjustment to the nursery school.

AGGRESSION. The relation between dependency and aggression has been thoroughly explored by Bandura and Walters (1960) in a study of delinquent adolescent boys. These investigators postulated that one of the antecedents of aggressive delinquency is frequent frustration of dependency during childhood. Using data drawn from interviews and objective tests, the investigators found that, as compared with a group of nonaggressive subjects, the aggressive delinquents showed: (*a*) less overt emotional dependency, and (*b*) greater dependency-anxiety in the form of resistance to accepting help, spending little time in the company of others, and reluctance to confiding in other people. In combination, these results indicate that conflict concerning dependency appears to be a correlate of adolescent aggression. Bandura and Walters also found from parental interviews that the delinquents had been less consistently reinforced for dependency as children, had experienced less "warmth" in their relationships with their parents, and were more frequently rejected by their parents than the control subjects.

ORALITY. As mentioned previously, psychoanalytic theory postulates a direct relation between oral frustration and dependency behavior. Presumably, indices of oral fixation and amount of emotional dependence shown by the child should be positively related. Beller (1957), correlating teachers' ratings of both dependency and independence with frequency of oral behaviors as mentioned in teachers' routine reports, found a low relation ($r = .30$) between dependence and orality in 49 subjects. This correlation rose to .51 when 16 emotionally disturbed children were eliminated from the total sample. Incidence of anal behavior (lack of bowel control, smearing, etc.) did not relate to dependence but was significantly correlated with the independence rating ($r = -.30$).

ANXIETY AND DEFENSIVENESS. Ruebush and Waite (1961) report that highly anxious boys (as determined by Sarason's *Test Anxiety Scale*) produce more *direct* oral dependency themes on the *Holtzman Inkblot Test* than low-anxious boys. This finding held only for male subjects who are relatively nondefensive; it did not hold for female subjects. These investigators also found that when anxiety is low, defensiveness is positively associated with incidence of indirect dependence in boys, but negatively associated with indirect dependency in girls. While the basis for this difference between sexes is not clear from the data of this study, the results indicate that dependency needs play a prominent role in the personality dynamics of both highly anxious and highly defensive children.

Here, then, are some of the earliest roots of social and emotional behavior, found in the child's relationships to parents and caretakers. Out of them grow other complex aspects of social interaction and personal values to which we turn in the next two chapters.

XI

THE SHAPING OF INTERPERSONAL REACTIONS

WE HAVE ALREADY CONSIDERED, to varying degrees, some important types of social behavior, such as attachment, language, and emotion. Our attention turns next to other, often more complex forms of social interaction. In this chapter we shall discuss further the emergence of interpersonal behavior in children and adolescents, while the next chapter is devoted to a somewhat different facet of personality development, involving the acquisition of self-control and achievement-related values.

SEX TYPING

A person's gender is one of the most significant determinants of interpersonal behavior. It plays a direct and important role in psychological and social development throughout the entire life span. One review has even

suggested that ". . . no other categorization is as important psychologically as the one that sorts people into male and female and dichotomizes
their characteristics as masculine or feminine" (Mischel and Mischel, 1971,
p. 357).

The significance of gender is reflected in the early age at which children
show some understanding of it. Most can recognize their sexual identity
and have knowledge of the concepts *male* and *female* by the time they
reach school (Kagan, Hosken, and Watson, 1961; Kohlberg, 1966). First-
graders will choose one toy over another (for example, a cow puzzle over
a horse puzzle or a robot over a "Frisbee") if they have been told that
members of their own sex prefer it (Liebert, McCall, and Hanratty, 1971).
And there is early recognition of appropriate sex roles. A striking example
of this was offered by a little girl, four years old, avidly watching a television program about physicians. The child's interest was so high that she
was asked: "Do you think *you* want to be a doctor when you grow up?"
The immediate reply was: "No, I can't be a doctor, *I'm a girl.* Only boys
can be doctors." Interestingly, understanding of sex roles or sex-related
behaviors does not always mean, at least in our culture, a preference for
the role society has designated.

Emergence of Sex-typed Preferences

In a number of investigations, adult men and women have been asked
questions such as:

"Have you sometimes wished you were of the opposite sex?"
"If you could be born over again, would you rather be a
    man or a woman?"
"Have you ever wished that you belonged to the opposite sex?"

Three studies (Terman, 1938; Fortune, 1946; Gallup, 1955), spanning
a period of almost twenty years, have shown a remarkably consistent pattern. While fewer than 4 percent of adult males expressed a desire ever
to be a woman, between 20 and 30 percent of the adult female population
have experienced, at some time, the desire to be a man.

These differences are not limited to adults. Brown (1957) assessed the
sex-typed preferences of kindergarteners through fifth-graders by employing the *It* Scale for Children, a test consisting of thirty-six picture cards
showing objects or people socially defined as masculine or feminine in our

culture. A child-figure, referred to as "It," is shown to subjects and used to facilitate expression of role preferences by allowing them to make a choices for "It" rather than directly. There are sixteen pictures of toys from which the subject must choose eight for "It"; half of the toys are "masculine" (e.g., a tractor, a rifle) and half are "feminine" (e.g., a doll and dishes). Another portion of the scale includes paired illustrations from which the subject must choose which one "It" would rather have or be.

Brown's findings, using this procedure, are presented in Figure XI–1. They show consistent patterns of masculine preferences by boys. Girls, on the other hand, do not show any sex-typed preference at kindergarten age, then turn sharply in the direction of masculine interests and, at the fifth grade, just as dramatically become feminine. This last change may be a result of learning that masculine preferences are considered inappropriate for them whereas feminine preferences are rewarded.

With regard to actual preferences for sex *roles* (i.e., being male or female), Brown found a parallel between children of all ages and adults; more than twice as many kindergarten girls as boys projected a preference for the parental role of the opposite sex. From the first and fifth grade the disparity becomes even greater; between three and twelve times as many girls as boys expressed a cross-sex role preference at these ages.

Sex Roles: Cross-cultural Similarities and Differences

In the majority of societies studied by sociologists and anthropologists, males are most often expected to have power, to act independently, and to be capable of decision making and assuming authority (d'Andrade, 1966). Men also are typically assigned the more physically strenuous roles, including the activities of war, commerce, and extended travel (Mussen, 1969). Not all societies, or even subcultures, show these patterns, however. Meade (1935) identified three tribes, each of which deviated from them considerably.

Among the Arapesh, both males and females are expected to behave in ways that are considered feminine in Western culture; "correct" behavior for both sexes includes cooperation and responsiveness to the needs of others. Meade contrasted the Arapesh with the Mundugumor, a tribe which would be considered uniformly masculine by our standards, with both men and women expected to be ruthless, aggressive, and unresponsive emotionally in their interpersonal relationships. In yet a third tribe, the Tchambuli, the sexes are subject to role expectations directly opposite to those of Western customs. It is the women, among the Tchambuli, who are dominant; males are expected to be emotionally dependent.

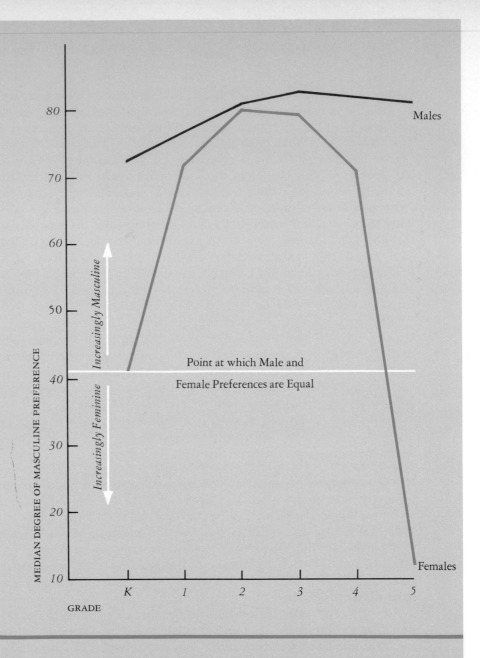

FIGURE XI–1

Degree of masculine preference by boys and girls at grades kindergarten through five. Data from Brown, 1957.

Another example of cultural influences involves sex differences in intelligence. Boys and girls often differ on various dimensions of intellectual functioning, with girls usually being more advanced than boys in various types of verbal ability such as vocabulary, spelling, and grammar (Mischel and Mischel, 1971). It appears, though, that this difference results from variations in expectancies and social training practices of parents, rather than from biologically based gender differences. Anastasi and D'Angelo (1952) found that among black children boys tend to be superior to girls on measures of verbal ability, and a study performed in England found boys to be superior to girls on four different vocabulary tests (Dunsdon and Fraser-Roberts, 1957); both results are contrary to the pattern found among white children in the United States.

Origins of Psychological Sex Differences

Biological Factors in Sex-Role Development. Although there are many important socialization differences within our own and other cultures that give rise to sex-role behavior, it is important not to forget biological factors entirely. At birth, males are typically stronger, larger, and display a better-developed musculature than do females. Females, on the other hand, have a lower mortality rate and are less susceptible to diseases both at birth and throughout the remainder of their lives (Hetherington, 1970).

Probably it is the interplay of biological and social factors which account for the development of sex differences. One writer, Eleanor Maccoby (1966), put it this way:

> . . . the sex-typed attributes of personality and temperament . . . are the product of the interweaving of differential social demands within certain biological determinants that help produce or augment differential cultural demands upon the two sexes. The biological underpinnings . . . set modal tendencies for cultural demands, and set limits to the range of variation of these demands from one cultural setting to another. Still within these limits considerable variation does occur between families, between cultures and in the nature of the behavior that a social group stereotypes as "feminine" or "masculine." [p. 50.]

We can ask, then, about the social variables that are involved in sex-typing. It is not surprising that the degree to which a child adheres to or deviates from the prescribed sex roles of his or her culture depends upon a variety of parental socialization practices.

Shaping by the Home Environment. It is clear that boys and girls are rewarded differentially for producing or imitating behavior judged appropriate for their own sex. As Bandura (1969) has cogently noted:

> Sex-role differentiation usually commences immediately after birth when the baby is named and both the infant and the nursery are given the blue or pink treatment depending upon the sex of the child. Thereafter, indoctrination into masculinity and femininity is diligently promulgated by adorning children with distinctive clothes and hair styles, selecting sex-appropriate play materials and recreational activities, promoting associations with same-sex playmates, and through nonpermissive parental reactions to deviant sex-role behavior. . . . [p. 215.]

This type of selective rewarding also appears to influence what youngsters learn, as well as what they perform. Grusec and Brinker (1972) found that five- and seven-year-old boys and girls, shown movies of male and female adults performing simple actions, are better able to remember the behavior of the performer of their own sex—apparently because they were rewarded for some sex imitation in the past. The investigators point to the following intriguing implications of their findings:

> While boys at an early age may even be equally familiar with the behaviors displayed by both their mothers and fathers, as they grow older and are exposed to more and more direct training for masculine behavior, they may come to be less familiar with the behaviors that females in our culture display. When they grow up they may be unskilled at sweeping, dusting, and making beds not just because they have not had practice in doing these things, but because they have never really concentrated too closely on how they are done. [p. 155.]

Not surprisingly, differences in the home environment—in the emphasis placed on sex-appropriate behavior—also are known to shape this aspect of personality. Minuchin (1965), for example, found that girls from home environments which emphasized individuality were less likely to display and adhere to conventional sex-role standards than were girls who came from relatively traditional backgrounds.

Consistency and Diversity in Sex-typed Behavior. Freud attempted to explain many facets of social development with a single concept: identification presumably accounted for much of a child's social and personal characteristics, including but not limited to "appropriate" sex-role behavior. According to this view, we would expect all of the various indices of masculinity/femininity to be highly related to one another for any given child, inasmuch they are all presumed to be the joint products of identification with a single adult—the youngster's same-sexed parent.

Research has shown, however, that there are marked differences depending upon the measure used. Consider, for example, the *It* Scale, described above, which appears to be a plausible index of sex-role identification. Yet the scale has been shown to be unrelated to various behavioral indicates of sex-typing as they are directly measured by raters (Mischel and Mischel, 1971).

Other work demonstrates that sex-role learning is not determined exclusively, or even predominantly, by the behavior of the same-sex parent. Rosenberg and Sutton-Smith (1968), for example, found that sex-role preferences vary as a complex interaction of the family structure; sibling affects sibling and children affect their parents' sex-role behavior just as parents influence their children. Fathers, for example, are *less* feminine in girl-girl families than in girl-boy families, and a boy with two sisters expresses more masculinity than a boy with only one (Rosenberg and Sutton-Smith, 1964).

A good summary of the various findings regarding the relationship of indices of sex-typing as they are directly measured by raters (Mischel and Mischel, 1971).

> The low intercorrelation obtained among components of sex-typed behavior gives little support to the belief that sex-typing is the result of a unitary identification process that exerts highly generalized effects. . . . The findings, instead, indicate that an individual's sex-typed behaviors may be quite specific rather than highly generalized. A young boy may, for example, be good at sports and still love art, and may like to tinker with tools and play with soldiers. Yet the same child may also be extremely dependent on his mother's attention, may like to dress his sister's dolls and may cry easily if he is hurt. [p. 365.]

The development of sex role and other sex-typed behaviors is but one of the many ways in which children are socialized. Another, moral development, also has been hypothesized to grow out of parental identification.

MORAL DEVELOPMENT

There is little doubt that most children develop, during their early years, a set of values or principles regarding correct, appropriate, or good behavior. Once the study of moral development was considered to be—at best—on the fringes of psychology, but recently it has come to the fore as a topic worthy of study and with important social implications.

The Psychoanalytic View

The traditional view of morality, favored in nineteenth-century Europe, presumed that values of the kind we call "moral" were provided by God. Then Freud, a revolutionary thinker in his time, argued that quite the reverse is true. The neonate, he argued, is naturally without concern for the welfare of others. Moral values, if they are present at all, must be cultivated after birth. Psychoanalytic theory offers a view of moral development rooted in the emergence of the *superego*. The superego—a part of each individual's personality—is said to develop as the child "takes in" the values of his parents, at about the fourth or fifth year of life. The formation process itself, intimately linked to the resolution of the Oedipal conflict (see Chapter X), is explained in terms of identification.

The implications of Freud's identification theory, as applied to moral development, are straightforward. The child's moral values either will parallel those of his parents or, if appropriate identification does not occur, the youngster will have an inadequate superego and little or no moral values. In either case, though, the critical period is presumed to be the first few years of life.

One implication of this position is the expectation that the various aspects of a child's moral behavior will be highly consistent with each other inasmuch as they are all based on the same structure of personality. One of the most important descriptive studies of moral behavior in children, conducted more than forty-five years ago (Hartshorne and May, 1928; Hartshorne, May, and Shuttleworth, 1930), was designed to address this very question.

Hartshorne and May's Research

Hartshorne and May observed thousands of children in many situations—at home, playing party games, in athletic contests—in which the child could commit transgressions such as lying, stealing, and cheating without being aware that they were detected. Contrary to their original expectations, the investigators found little consistency in the actual performance of individual children.

Suppose, for example, two children, *A* and *B,* were placed in a situation where cheating was possible and *A* cheated while *B* did not. Could we now safely predict that in another, different situation *A* would be more likely to cheat than *B?* Hartshorne and his associates found that the answer to this question was "No." *

Ironically, though, the investigation revealed a good deal of consistency in the children's responses to queries conducted in their classrooms about their moral values and opinions. But verbally expressed moral values appeared to have little to do with action; often youngsters who cheated expressed as much or more disapproval of cheating as those who did not. And it appeared that even when honesty was not "forced" by concern about detection and punishment, social factors such as approval of one's peers, rather than an inner moral code, were critical.

The entire pattern of findings of this early study anticipated much that has been learned since. We now know considerably more about consistency in children's stated moral values and the pattern of its development.

The Cognitive Approach to Moral Development

We saw in Chapter VII that Piaget suggested a sequence of stages of moral growth, roughly paralleling his general theory of cognitive development, with youngsters shifting, at about age seven, from an *objective* to a *subjective* view of morality. Another cognitive theorist, Lawrence Kohlberg, has begun to explore more completely the development of moral values within a stage theory framework. Like Piaget, he has been concerned primarily with the development of the child's moral judgments rather than his actions. The child, says Kohlberg, must be viewed as a "moral philosopher."

But what is the child's philosophy? To answer this question, Kohlberg analyzed free responses to hypothetical moral dilemmas such as the following:

> In Europe, a woman was near death from cancer. One drug might save her, a form of radium that a druggist in the same town had recently discovered. The druggist was charging $2,000, ten times what the drug cost him to make. The sick woman's husband, Heinz, went to everyone he knew to borrow the money, but he could only get together about half of what it cost. He told the druggist that his wife was dying and asked him to sell it

---

* More sophisticated later analyses of Hartshorne and May's data have shown some generality to honesty, but it is not very great (Burton, 1963).

cheaper or let him pay later. But the druggist said, "No." The husband got desperate and broke into the man's store to steal the drug for his wife. Should the husband have done that? Why? [Kohlberg, 1969, p. 379.]

A child's responses to dilemmas such as this one usually are based on one or more general aspects of the problem, such as the motives or intentions of the people involved. After eliciting responses to a large number of dilemmas from many children, Kohlberg has been able to distinguish three levels of moral thinking: *preconventional, conventional,* and *postconventional.*

The preconventional child is often well-behaved and sensitive to labels such as good and bad. But the latter are interpreted simply in terms of their physical consequences (punishment, reward, exchange of favors) or in terms of the power of those who make the rules. There is, then, no real standard of morality at the preconventional level. The conventional level is characterized by conformity to the existing social order and an implicit desire to maintain that order. Most American adults, according to Kohlberg, operate at the level of conventional morality. Finally, the postconventional level is governed by moral principles which are universal, and therefore valid independent of the authority of the groups who support them.

TABLE XI–1

KOHLBERG'S SIX STAGES OF MORAL DEVELOPMENT

PRECONVENTIONAL LEVEL

STAGE 1:

Punishment and obedience orientation. The physical consequences of an action determine whether it is good or bad. Avoiding punishment and bowing to superior power are valued positively.

STAGE 2:

Instrumental relativist orientation. Right action consists of behavior that satisfies one's own needs. Human relations are viewed in marketplace terms. Reciprocity occurs, but is seen in a pragmatic way, i.e., "you scratch my back and I'll scratch yours."

TABLE XI-1 *(continued)*

CONVENTIONAL LEVEL

STAGE 3:

Interpersonal concordance (good boy—nice girl) orientation. Good behaviors are those that please or are approved by others. There is much emphasis on conformity and being "nice."

STAGE 4:

Orientation toward authority ("law and order"). Focus is on authority or rules. It is right to do one's duty, show respect for authority, and maintain the social order.

POSTCONVENTIONAL LEVEL

STAGE 5:

Social-contract orientation. This stage has a utilitarian, legalistic tone. Correct behavior is defined in terms of standards agreed upon by society. Awareness of the relativism of personal values and the need for consensus is important.

STAGE 6:

Universal ethical principle orientation. Morality is defined as a decision of conscience. Ethical principles are self-chosen, based on abstract concepts (e.g., the Golden Rule) rather than concrete rules (e.g., the Ten Commandments).

Within each of these three levels, Kohlberg (1963; 1967) suggests, are two discernible stages, producing the full complement of six stages shown in Table XI–1.

Concrete examples of the type of moral judgments made in response to the dilemma described in the story of Heinz and his dying wife are shown in Table XI–2. The stages are *not* differentiated by what decision is made, but by the reasoning that underlies the decision.

Kohlberg finds that moral development may be either fast or slow, but that it does not skip stages. Children in Taiwan, Malaya, Mexico, and Turkey all show the same sequence. Further, this orderly pattern is not related

TABLE XI-2

THE TYPE OF MORAL REASONING EMPLOYED AT VARIOUS STAGES IN RESPONSE TO THE PROBLEM OF HEINZ

STAGE 1

Action is motivated by avoidance of punishment and "conscience" is irrational fear of punishment.

Pro —If you let your wife die, you will get in trouble. You'll be blamed for not spending the money to save her and there'll be an investigation of you and the druggist for your wife's death.

Con—You shouldn't steal the drug because you'll be caught and sent to jail if you do. If you do get away, your conscience would bother you thinking how the police would catch up with you at any minute.

STAGE 2

Action motivated by desire for reward or benefit. Possible guilt reactions are ignored and punishment viewed in a pragmatic manner. (Differentiates own fear, pleasure, or pain from punishment-consequences.)

Pro —If you do happen to get caught you could give the drug back and you wouldn't get much of a sentence. It wouldn't bother you much to serve a little jail term, if you have your wife when you get out.

Con—He may not get much of a jail term if he steals the drug, but his wife will probably die before he gets out so it won't do him much good. If his wife dies, he shouldn't blame himself, it wasn't his fault she has cancer.

STAGE 3

Action motivated by anticipation of disapproval of others, actual or imagined-hypothetical (e.g., guilt). (Differentiation of disapproval from punishment, fear, and pain.)

Pro —No one will think you're bad if you steal the drug but your family will think you're an inhuman husband if you don't. If you let

T A B L E   X I – 2   *(continued)*

your wife die, you'll never be able to look anybody in the face again.

Con—It isn't just the druggist who will think you're a criminal, everyone else will too. After you steal it, you'll feel bad thinking how you've brought dishonor on your family and yourself; you won't be able to face anyone again.

STAGE 4

Action motivated by anticipation of dishonor, i.e., institutionalized blame for failure of duty, and by guilt over concrete harm done to others. (Differentiates formal dishonor from informal disapproval. Differentiates guilt for bad consequences from disapproval.)

Pro —If you have any sense of honor, you won't let your wife die because you're afraid to do the only thing that will save her. You'll always feel guilty that you caused her death if you don't do your duty to her.

Con—You're desperate and you may not know you're doing wrong when you steal the drug. But you'll know you did wrong after you're punished and sent to jail. You'll always feel guilt for your dishonesty and lawbreaking.

STAGE 5

Concern about mainting respect of equals and of the community (assuming their respect is based on reason rather than emotions). Concern about own self-respect, i.e., to avoid judging self as irrational, inconsistent, nonpurposive. (Discriminates between institutionalized blame and community disrespect or self-disrespect.)

Pro —You'd lose other people's respect, not gain it, if you don't steal. If you let your wife die, it would be out of fear, not out of reasoning it out. So you'd just lose self-respect and probably the respect of others too.

Con—You would lose your standing and respect in the community and violate the law. You'd lose respect for yourself if you're carried away by emotion and forget the long-range point of view.

TABLE XI-2 *(continued)*

STAGE 6

Concern about self-condemnation for violating one's own principles. (Differentiates between community respect and self-respect. Differentiates between self-respect for general achieving rationality and self-respect for maintaining moral principles.)

Pro —If you don't steal the drug and let your wife die, you'd always condemn yourself for it afterward. You wouldn't be blamed and you would have lived up to the outside rule of the law but you wouldn't have lived up to your own standards of conscience.

Con—If you stole the drug, you wouldn't be blamed by other people but you'd condemn yourself because you wouldn't have lived up to your own conscience and standards of honesty.

Source: Rest, 1968.

to religious beliefs; no differences exist in the development of moral thinking among Catholics, Protestants, Jews, Buddhists, Moslems, or atheists. Thus moral thought appears to follow a universal pattern typical of all other kinds of thought; progress is characterized by increasing differentiation and integration.

Social Learning of Moral Judgments

If personality development is viewed in terms of learning (e.g., as discussed in Chapter V), it would be expected that children's moral judgments would be less age-specific and more modifiable than is suggested by Kohlberg's cognitive-stage theory. In a study designed to illustrate these points, Bandura and McDonald (1963) presented boys and girls between the ages of five and eleven with pairs of stories, similar to those used by Piaget (see p. 227). They found, consistent with the theorizing of Piaget and Kohlberg, that older children were indeed likely to make the more cognitively advanced (subjective) judgments (see Figure XI–2). However, at the

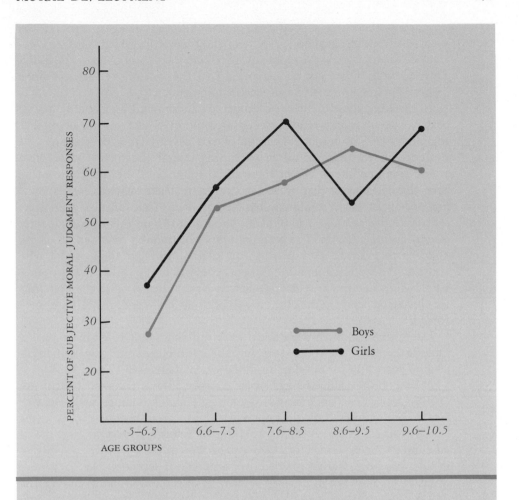

same time, there was a good deal of variability at all ages; some of the youngest children based one or more of their moral judgments on the *intentions* of the transgressor (a more advanced judgment) and some of the oldest judged, at least occasionally, according to the *amount of damage* done rather than intentions (a less advanced judgment).

In the next phase of their experiment, Bandura and McDonald showed that judgments could be altered considerably by a combination of modeling and vicarious reward. They employed several types of training, all designed to encourage children to express moral judgments based on a foundation opposite to that of their initial leanings; if they tended to make objective judgments, they were encouraged to make subjective judgments and vice-versa. One condition involved praising (reinforcing) youngsters whenever they advanced judgments opposite to those they predominantly voiced during a pretest. The other two types of training consisted of asking children to evaluate story pairs in alternation with an adult model who consistently expressed moral judgments contrary to the child's own original leanings; in one group reinforcement was given to the child for imitating this behavior, while in the other group both the child and model were reinforced.

Later, when children were asked by a different adult to evaluate twelve more story pairs, the youngsters' judgments disclosed the powerful influence of modeling for developing moral orientations (see Figure XI–3).

A later study, conducted by Cowan, Langer, Heavenrich, and Nathanson (1969), replicated Bandura and McDonald's major findings with elementary school children. Equally impressive results were obtained by Crowley (1968) using a more systematic program of reward, correction, and moral labeling by the experimenter as story pairs were presented; changes induced in this way were clearly sustained over a period of several weeks.

Le Furgy and Woloshin (1969) also have succeeded in modifying the moral judgments of young adolescents, twelve to fourteen years of age. These investigators used a form of symbolic modeling in which their subjects heard—over headsets—what were ostensibly the moral judgments of other youngsters; in fact, though, they were listening to prerecorded tapes which were consistently contrary to their own initial judgments. The effects obtained were striking and quite durable for a period of one week but, unreinforced by further experience, diminished somewhat over the course of the next one hundred days.

It appears, then, that moral judgments of children of various ages can be shaped through basic learning processes, regardless of the postulated existing stage. Similarly, with displays of aggressive behavior, learning can play a unique role.

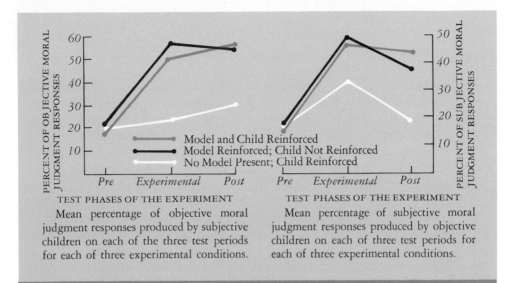

Mean percentage of objective moral judgment responses produced by subjective children on each of the three test periods for each of three experimental conditions.

Mean percentage of subjective moral judgment responses produced by objective children on each of three test periods for each of three experimental conditions.

FIGURE XI-3

Effects of modeling and reinforcement in Bandura and McDonald's study in changing the basis for moral judgment in 5 to 11-year-olds. Adapted from A. Bandura and F. J. McDonald. The influence of social reinforcement and the behavior of models in shaping children's moral judgments. Journal of Abnormal and Social Psychology, 1963, 67, 274–281. Copyright 1963 by the American Psychological Association. Reprinted by permission.

AGGRESSION

At some time or another virtually everyone aggresses, acting in a way that brings, or might bring, discomfort to someone else. We know, however, that the type of aggression that a person displays and the ability to control such action change in important ways with age and experience. The roots of these patterns and changes have long been of interest to developmental psychologists.

Frustration as a Determinant of Aggression

One view of aggression which has long held considerable sway among psychologists is the famous "frustration-aggression" hypothesis, first spelled out by John Dollard and his associates at Yale in 1939. These theorists argued that frustration, defined as any blocking of goal-directed activity, naturally leads to aggression. The original statement of this hypothesis was extremely strong: aggression was said to be *always* a consequence of frustration and frustration was said to lead *always* to some form of aggression. At first glance, this reasoning may appear intuitively rather persuasive. But there are many cases in which most people, even if severely frustrated, will refrain from showing any direct acts of aggression; the speeding driver will not assault, or even raise his voice, to the policeman who has apprehended him. And, as we shall see, factors other than frustration often lead to the occurrence of aggression.

Reward to the Aggressor as a Determinant of Aggressive Behavior

A good deal of human behavior is maintained because it has proven instrumental in securing positive outcomes from the environment. Thus, although individuals may be impelled to aggression by irritating events in the environment, alternatively, they may aggress because some incentive or reward seems to be available for acting so, or because they have learned that such rewards frequently follow aggressive behavior.

In a series of sophisticated experiments, Richard Walters and his associates (Cowan and Walters, 1963; Walters and Brown, 1963; 1964) explored the effects of rewarding aggression in a play situation upon children's subsequent aggressive behavior. For example, Walters and Brown (1963) showed that reward for behaving in an aggressive manner against a toy Bobo doll (similar to the one in Figure XI–4) could markedly influence children's aggression against other children in an interpersonal situation. The automated doll's eyes and a flower on its button hole would light up when it was punched in the stomach. The design of the study called for four groups, three of which received training and one that served as a control. Those in the experimental groups received two training sessions, separated by two days. In one experimental group *every* punch

FIGURE XI–4

The "Bobo" doll used for studying the influence of reward on aggressive behavior in the Walters' experiments. From Bandura and Walters, 1963. Courtesy Dr. Albert Bandura.

was rewarded with a colored glass marble, in the second group punching was intermittently rewarded with a marble, and in the third group the only reward was the illumination of the doll's eyes and lapel flower.

Two days later all subjects were brought into an experimental room, given some candy, and permitted to see the beginning of an exciting movie. This procedure set the stage for frustrating half of the subjects. Specifically, for these children, the projector apparently broke down halfway through the movie and, to make matters even more unpleasant, the experimenter also took away the candy which he had given them. The remaining children were permitted both to see the entire movie and to keep their candy. Thereafter all subjects were permitted to play a series of games with a naïve peer. The degree of aggressive behavior which they displayed in this situation was the primary measure of the study. The behaviors rated included butting, kneeing, elbowing, kicking, punching and pushing, and pulling by the neck and hair. Children who had been rewarded intermittently for hitting the Bobo doll two days earlier showed significantly more aggression in this game situation than did any of the remaining groups.*

In a second experiment by these same investigators (Walters and Brown, 1964) some participants were rewarded only when they hit the Bobo sharply while others were rewarded exclusively for weaker hits. Again, employing measures of aggression in physical contact games, it was found that boys rewarded for the higher magnitude of aggression were more aggressive in this new interpersonal situation than were those who had been rewarded for relatively temperate play.

The studies of Walters and Brown have several striking implications for socialization practices. Consider, for example, the father who enthusiastically encourages his son to roughneck with him in play and smash away at punching bags, praising the lad for particularly forceful assaults. In addition to building a "real boy," it may be that such training has the unintended effect of promoting aggression in other interpersonal situations. Additionally it should be noted that intermittent reinforcement, which had the greatest effect on children in Walters' experiments, is the very type that parents are likely to provide, inasmuch as they will not be present at, and certainly not attentive to, all of the child's aggressive actions.

---

* Consistent with the results of several other experiments, the apparently compelling frustration manipulation in the Walters and Brown study did not influence the children's aggression, nor did it interact with the type of training they had received.

TELEVISION AND CHILDREN'S AGGRESSIVE BEHAVIOR

What are the effects upon children of observing violent television programs? The question is one which has been posed continually since the advent of television sets as a common fixture in the American home almost two decades ago. Answers to it have ranged from statements that such programs can have an adverse effect on almost anyone to assertions that merely watching entertainment fare can do little to shape children's social behavior.

Early studies by Bandura and his associates, which have been mentioned already in our discussion of imitation (Chapter V, pp. 146–47), showed clearly that youngsters could *learn* novel aggressive responses from television and televisionlike formats. But critics (Halloran, 1964; Klapper, 1968) have pointed out that these studies did not prove that the kind of violence found on television or in movies influences the "real-life" social behavior of young observers. Since these criticisms were first advanced, a considerable body of evidence has accumulated to show that there *is* an important relationship between watching television violence and children's aggressive behavior.

Imitation of Aggression against a Human Victim

That direct imitative effects after observing aggression may occur for more than just *play* with inanimate toys is indicated by the results of several experiments. In the first (Hanratty, Liebert, Morris, and Fernandez, 1969), four- and five-year-old boys from a Sunday School kindergarten served as subjects. Half of them observed a two-and-one-half-minute color sound film in which an adult aggressed against a human clown. The behavior displayed by this symbolic model included sharp and unprovoked verbal insults to the clown, shooting at the clown with a toy machine gun, and beating the clown vigorously with a plastic mallet. Half the group saw no such film.

Thereafter, half of the subjects in each of these groups were permitted to play in a room where they found a human clown standing idly, as well as a mallet and a toy gun. The remaining children found a plastic Bobo doll rather than a human. The youngsters were left in this situation for ten minutes, during which time their aggressive responses toward the clown, plastic or human, were recorded. Not surprisingly, the brief film increased children's aggression against the inflated Bobo, with *all* the children exhibiting some aggressive action against the toy. In contrast, of those who had not observed the movie, none engaged in any sort of aggressive behavior toward the human clown. There are, of course, strong inhibitions for aggressing against a human being, even one who is attired as a clown, and there was no provocation for doing so. Nonetheless, after observation of the aggressive movie a significant number of physical assaults against the human clown did occur, including at least one swat with the mallet which was hard enough that the victim showed a red mark on her arm several hours later.

In a second experiment (Hanratty, 1969), it was again found that a film of this type, without other provocation, would lead children to physically assault a human victim. Moreover, such aggression was displayed by both boys and girls after viewing films in which either an eight-year-old boy or an adult served as a model. This finding was replicated a third and a fourth time with somewhat older boys (Hanratty, O'Neal, and Sulzer, 1972; Savitsky, Rogers, Izard, and Liebert, 1971). Under some circumstances, then, children will directly imitate filmed aggression against other people.

Still, direct imitative effects require a situation virtually identical to the one observed, and so may be less important from a social point of view than a more general disinhibition (see Chapter V). Considerable research emphasis recently has been placed on disinhibitory influences.

Disinhibitory Effects: Correlational Studies

Several correlational studies now bear directly on the possibility of a relationship between the amount of violence a child observes and the amount of aggressive behavior which he displays in naturalistic situations. Uniformly, such a relationship has been found, for both elementary (Dominick and Greenberg, 1972) and high school age youngsters (McIntyre and Teevan, 1972; McLeod, Atkin, and Chaffee, 1972). McLeod, Atkin, and Chaffee (1972), for example, examined the relationship between viewing televised violence and a variety of measures of aggressive behavior in two relatively large samples of adolescents, one in Maryland and another in Wisconsin. The outcome of these correlational studies may be summarized in the author's own words:

> Our research shows that among both boys and girls at two grade levels [junior high and senior high], the more the child watches violent television fare, the more aggressive he is likely to be as measured by a variety of self-

report measures. . . . Partialing out [total] viewing time * slightly reduces the positive correlations of violence viewing and aggressive behavior in most cases, but the basic result is the same as for the raw correlations. . . . Similarly, the partialing out of socioeconomic status and school performance does not alter the basic pattern. . . . We may conclude, then, that adolescents viewing high levels of violent content on television tend to have high levels of aggressive behavior, regardless of television viewing time, socioeconomic status or school performance. [pp. 187, 191.]

A particularly sophisticated correlational study of television and aggression was undertaken by Lefkowitz, Eron, Walder, and Huesmann (1972). Their report, based on a longitudinal study of the entire population of children of a particular age in a rural New York county, involved approximately nine hundred youngsters. Designed from the outset to relate children's aggressive behavior to various familial, social, and experimental factors which might influence it, these investigators employed a peer measurement technique of aggression, focusing exclusively upon acts which would harm or irritate other persons.

The first measures obtained in this study revealed a significant relationship, for male subjects, between the amount of television violence which they watched in the third grade and independently assessed peer ratings of aggression in the classroom at that time (Eron, 1963). This correlational finding was later replicated with a different sample—eighth-grade boys and girls in an urban city in the South.

Lefkowitz *et al.* completed the longitudinal phase of their study by obtaining data from more than four hundred of the youngsters whom they had studied ten years earlier. The measures included peer ratings of aggression at this age, self-reports of aggression in an interview, and self-reports of various aspects of television viewing. The results of this ten-year follow-up showed (but again only for boys) that amount of aggression watched in the third grade was significantly related to peer ratings of aggression at age nineteen.

Additionally, using a sophisticated approach technically referred to as a *cross-lagged panel design,* Lefkowitz *et al.* showed that their findings provide stronger evidence for a causal relationship than is usually available from correlational studies. To understand the basic logic behind this approach, consider the possibility that a relationship will appear between overt aggression and preferences for aggressive television simply because some children like to do both. This is an important "rival hypothesis" to

---

* Partialing is a statistical technique which "subtracts out" the effects of one variable in order to see if the effects of another will remain.

the notion that seeing aggressive television *causes* aggressive behavior. However, if television aggression actually produces aggressive behavior, then we would find a link between earlier television watching and later aggression but not necessarily between earlier aggression and later television watching. This is exactly what was disclosed by the Lefkowitz *et al.* data. Third-grade preferences for aggressive television predicted later aggression, but later television preferences did *not* relate to the youngsters' earlier aggressive behavior at all. It is thus reasonable to agree with the investigators' interpretation of their findings: that, for boys, ". . . on the basis of the cross-lagged correlations, the most plausible single causal hypothesis would appear to be that watching violent television in the third grade [age nine] leads to the building of aggressive habits" and ". . . that a substantial component [of overt aggressive behavior at age nineteen] can be predicted better by the amount of television violence which the child watched in the third grade than by any other causal variable measured. . . ."

Disinhibitory Effects: Experimental Laboratory Studies

At least eighteen experimental studies concerned with the instigation of aggression by observing violence were reported in the 1960s (Strauss and Poulos, 1972). Of these, sixteen (or 89 percent) provided evidence supporting the hypothesis that merely watching entertainment violence can instigate aggression. Then, in 1969–1971, under the auspices of the National Institute of Mental Health, a number of additional studies were conducted.

In one, Liebert and Baron (1972) sought to investigate the question of whether exposure to aggression, as shown in actual television fare, would disinhibit younger children in terms of their willingness to hurt another child. The investigators exposed children of both sexes and two age groups (five to six and eight to nine years) to brief excerpts taken directly from publicly broadcast television shows. For children in one group, these excerpts depicted instances of aggression (a brutal fist fight, a shooting, and the like), while for children in a second condition, exciting but nonaggressive sport events were shown. Following exposure to one of these two programs, children in both groups were provided with a series of opportunities to either *hurt* or *help* another child by pushing, respectively, either a red or a green button on a panel display. The children were told that pushing the green button would help the other child (who was not actually present during the study) to win a prize, but that pushing the red button would hurt him. In addition, they were informed that the longer they pushed either button, the more the other child would be helped or hurt.

Despite the fact that it lasted less than five minutes, children who had observed the violent television sequence pushed the red button for a significantly longer period of time than those who had observed the non-aggressive scenes.

In another study in the series, Leifer and Roberts (1972) obtained information on the subsequent willingness of children and adolescents (kindergarteners through twelfth graders) to aggress after they watched television programs which differed in the amount of violent content displayed. The programs were taken directly from the air, without editing. The children were then tested on a specially designed response hierarchy of their willingness to aggress. The child was presented with a series of real-life situations ("You're standing in line for a drink of water. A kid comes along and just pushes you out of line. What do you do?") and asked to choose between a pair of alternative responses. One of the alternatives was typically aggressive ("Push them"), while the other was not ("Go away"). (See Figure XI–5.) These investigators, too, found that the more violent programs reliably produced higher levels of aggressive responding than the less violent ones. It is of further interest that in this experiment understanding the motivations for, and consequences of, violence in a program did *not* relate to a significant degree to the aggression scores. It appears that the instigating effect of viewing is not reduced by an increased understanding of the motivations and consequences which surround it, at least for this measure and these age groups.

Leifer and Roberts also report six other studies, varying in their major purposes, in which the effects of televised aggression upon children's aggressive choices could be assessed. Three of these provide further evidence for a disinhibitory effect while none suggests a decrease in aggressiveness after exposure to aggression. The negative finding here is of some interest. Even the observation of aggression which had both bad motives and bad consequences (in programs produced by special editing) did not reduce aggression relative to a nonaggressive program.

Disinhibitory Effects: An Experimental Field Study

Laboratory studies of the sort described above provide the best source of information about basic processes and causal relationships. However, to assure generality of such findings to the more complex natural environment, such investigation can be supplemented by experimental field research. One such study was conducted by Stein and Friedrich (1972) in a relatively naturalistic situation in order to determine some of the cumulative or

"You're walking down the street. Some kid is mad at you and comes up and hits you. What do you do?"

 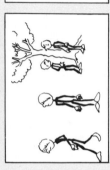

A. HIT THEM OR LEAVE THEM?

B. TELL A GROWN-UP OR CALL THEM "STUPID"?

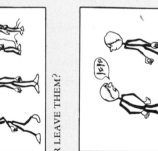 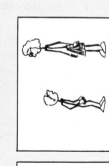

C. LEAVE THEM OR TELL A GROWN-UP?

D. LEAVE THEM OR CALL THEM "STUPID"?

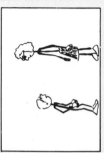

E. HIT THEM OR CALL THEM "STUPID"?

F. TELL A GROWN-UP OR HIT THEM?

FIGURE XI–5

Sample items from the response hierarchy used by Leifer and Roberts. Children were shown either slides or pictures of situations such as these. Source: Leifer and Roberts, 1972, by permission. Artist: Jurgen Wolff.

longer-range effects of observing television upon children. The subjects were ninety-seven children (fifty-two boys and forty-five girls) between $3\frac{1}{2}$ and $5\frac{1}{2}$ years of age, who were systematically exposed to television programs of differing content during the course of their participation in a summer nursery school.

This carefully designed experiment involved an initial measurement period in which the free play of children in the nursery school was observed and rated according to a variety of categories; a four-week experimental period in which children were systematically exposed either to aggressive cartoons (*Batman* and *Superman*), neutral television programming (children working on a farm and the like), or prosocial programming (episodes from the program *Mister Rogers' Neighborhood*); and a two-week postviewing period in which effects could be observed and assessed. The children were exposed to the programs for approximately twenty minutes per day three times a week for a four-week period. During this time, and during the two-week postviewing period, the children's behavior was again systematically observed in the naturalistic preschool situation.

Stein and Friedrich found that children who were initially in the upper half of the sample in interpersonal aggression subsequently showed greater interpersonal aggression if they were exposed to the aggressive programming than if they were exposed to either the neutral or prosocial programming. Thus, aggressive cartoons increased interpersonal aggression significantly for these children despite the fact that they watched television in the nursery school for less than six hours of total viewing spread over four weeks. What is more, as the investigators note:

> [The] effects occurred in naturalistic behavior that was removed both in time and environmental setting from the viewing experience. They occurred with a small amount of exposure, particularly in relation to the amount the children received at home, and they endured during the postviewing period. [p. 247.]

PROSOCIAL BEHAVIOR

Just as individuals sometimes aggress against others in selfish ways, so do they sometimes act in cooperative, helpful, and giving ways, even when these responses are more than mere gestures and are costly. Such behavior usually is considered to be in the greater interest of others and society and is thus thought of as prosocial. In this section we shall consider two classes of prosocial behavior which overlap but are not identical, describing research which helps us to understand how such actions are developed, maintained, and elicited in childhood. Our discussion begins with helping, or the rendering of personal assistance when another is in need of aid or protection.

Helping

In the late 1960s experimental social psychologists were profoundly influenced by a dramatic murder in New York, which was later described as follows:

> Several years ago, a young woman was stabbed to death in the middle of a street in a residential section of New York City. Although such murders are not entirely routine, the incident received little public attention until several weeks later when the *New York Times* disclosed another side of the case: at least 38 witnesses had observed the attack—and none had even attempted to intervene. Although the attacker took more than half an hour to kill Kitty Genevese, not one of the 38 people who watched from the safety of their own apartments came out to assist her. Not one even lifted the telephone to call the police. [Darley and Latané, 1968, p. 377.]

This surprising lack of intervention seemed inconsistent with the humanitarian and cooperative norms which our society tries to foster and raised many questions about the role of prosocial behavior in modern life. Partly as a result, much has since been learned about such behavior in adults (Darley and Latané, 1968; Latané and Rodin, 1969). For example, it has been found that adults are more likely to give assistance in an emergency if they are the only bystanders than if others are present. But an important question remains for developmental psychologists: How is a willingness to help others acquired?

Staub (1971) has hypothesized that at least two factors are critical: the ability to empathize with the needy other and possession of the knowledge or skills to help effectively. To the extent that this reasoning is correct, it should be possible to increase children's willingness to help others by training in empathy and relevant skills. With this in mind, Staub devised two procedures, role playing and "induction," to increase young children's willingness to help other children in distress. Three groups of children were used in the study, one with each of the procedures and one with a combination of both.

In the *role-playing* group, pairs of kindergarten youngsters were asked to act out situations in which one of them needed help and the other provided it. The experimenter began by describing a situation in which help was needed. The "helper" child was asked to improvise all of the helping actions which he could think of; then the experimenter described further ones, each of which was in fact acted out. Finally, the two children changed roles. The five situations which Staub used were: (1) a child had fallen off a chair in an adjoining room; (2) a child was trying to carry a chair that was too heavy for him; (3) a child was distressed because his building blocks were taken away from him by another youngster; (4) a child was standing in the path of an oncoming bicycle; and (5) a child had fallen and hurt himself. The variety of possible ways of helping, generated spontaneously by the youngsters or suggested by the experimenter, included direct intervention, verbal consolation to the victim, and calling someone else for help.

Staub's *induction* group closely followed the procedures for role playing except that the children were asked merely to describe verbally how they could provide help. Then, as in the role-playing group, the experimenter described other appropriate ways of helping and pointed out the positive consequences each of these would have for the needy child, such as an increase in positive feelings or reduction of pain and suffering. Induction, then, involved pointing out to children the consequences of their behavior for others. [It had been shown (correlationally) in previous research that children whose parents described themselves as using induction techniques tend to show somewhat more frequent prosocial acts in nursery schools than children whose parents use other socialization practices.]

In the *role playing with induction* group children were trained using both procedures. In addition to actually acting out various helping roles, the experimenter explained the positive consequences which would accrue to the needy child.

Finally, there was a control group of children who acted out a variety of scenes that were completely unrelated to helping behavior.

In order to determine the immediate effects of these treatments, each child in the experiment was taken to a room containing a variety of toys and playthings. After brief interaction with the child, the experimenter went into the adjacent room "to check on a girl who is playing there" and then announced that she (the experimenter) would have to leave for a while. Less than two minutes after the experimenter left the subject heard a loud crash coming from the adjacent room, quickly followed by about seventy seconds of severe crying and sobbing. Actually the room was empty and the distress sounds were produced by a pretaped recording.

From the subject's point of view, though, another child, alone in the next room, desperately needed help and there was no one else to provide it. What would the subject do now?

Staub categorized the children's reactions as: *active help,* if they went into the adjacent room to help; *volunteering information,* if they reported to the experimenter that something had happened in the other room; and *no help,* if they made no effort to provide direct or indirect assistance.*

The test situation described above closely followed portions of the role-playing and induction procedures used during training. It was therefore of interest to determine whether any effects obtained would generalize to situations that were somewhat different from those involved in training. So Staub created a second test in which the subject and an adult experimenter began to play a game, during which time the adult "accidentally" dropped a box of paper clips. She then expressed mild alarm ("Oh, my dear!") and began to pick up the scattered clips. The measure during this circumstance was the number of paper clips which the subject picked up, both spontaneously and with prompting (e.g., "Could you help me a little?").

Finally, there was a measure of willingness to share. Later in the sequence each child was given a bag of candy and told that there was a poor child to whom some of the candy could be donated. Thus, in sum, Staub's experiment involved a total of three measures of prosocial behavior—assisting a child in distress, assisting an adult in distress, and sharing with another child. Some of these tests were given immediately after the induction and/or role-playing treatment and others were given about one week later.

Staub's results suggested generally that role playing could be used effectively to foster prosocial behavior and that its effects were durable over a period of at least one week. The findings were therefore encouraging in that they suggested, as Staub points out in his own conclusion, "that specific training procedures, particularly role playing of specific situations, may enhance the subsequent probability of prosocial behavior" (p. 815).

However, it is of considerable interest that the effects of induction were insignificant. Indeed, inspection of Staub's results reveals that induction

---

* Of course, in such situations it is important to "debrief" the child afterward, so as to explain the situation and make sure that he or she does not leave with any negative feelings or misconceptions. Thus, Staub told his subjects ". . . that they had only heard a recording, that no one was really hurt, and that the reason they heard the recording was that [the experimenter] wanted to find out what children thought when they heard another child crying. . . . So that [the children] would have an overall pleasant experience, they engaged in additional activities, for example, making up stories about pictures of pleasant content . . . (Staub, 1971, p. 809).

actually may have made children somewhat "oppositional"; those exposed to this treatment became somewhat *less* likely to assist the adult in picking up paper clips than were children in the control group. The pressure applied by induction to "be good" apparently created some threat to the child's feeling of freedom, to which he or she responded with resistance.

Sharing

Through fate or circumstance, one person is often dependent upon another's charity; indeed, whole institutions in our society are sustained by the voluntary contributions of others. As James Bryan, an expert in the area, has written: "Most children in middle childhood will verbally, if not behaviorally, support the principle that one should aid the needy" (1970, p. 61).

In this section we shall describe some of the research which supports Bryan's summary, and ask how such apparently altruistic sharing is acquired and maintained.

Age. In general, a positive relationship between age and children's sharing has been found; older children are more likely to share or appear to be more generous (Ugurel-Semin, 1952; Handlon and Gross, 1959). In some areas, though, the relationship between age and generosity is less clear. Liebert, Fernandez, and Gill (1969) found no differences between six- to eight-year-olds and nine- to eleven-year-olds on willingness to share with another child who was described as "not well-liked and has no friends," with the younger children actually tending to be more generous than the older ones. With adult subjects the age-altruism relationship similarly may be reversed; thus, for example, young adults are proportionally more likely than older ones to be blood donors (London and Hemphill, 1965).

Reward. Perhaps the most obvious way to elicit sharing from children is to reward them directly for acts of generosity. After doing just this with four-year-old children, Fischer (1963) found that youngsters became more likely to share marbles with unknown peers if such beneficence was, in turn, directly rewarded with bubble gum. The brighter children in this study learned to share at a more rapid rate than less intelligent ones, a result consistent with correlational data showing a significant relationship between intelligence and the development of a moral code in adolescence (Havighurst and Taba, 1949).

Empathic Responses. Aronfreed and Paskal (Aronfreed, 1968) have argued that self-sacrifice may be developed because expressions of "joy" by the recipient of generous acts become conditioned to the child's own positive reactions. To illustrate this process, several rather elaborate experiments have been performed. We shall describe one of them.

Elementary school girls were asked to choose one of two levers to press for a number of successive trials; they soon learned that pressing one led to a reward—candy—60 percent of the time whereas the other only served to turn on a red light 60 percent of the time and never produced a tangible reward. Next, in one experimental group, the adult showed signs of joy whenever the red light went on and responded further by displaying warmth and affection toward the child; in a second group, the adult also showed signs of joy when the light went on but did not display affection; in a third group the adult became affectionate when the light went on but did not express joy at its appearance.

Then came the test phase of the experiment. The child and adult were seated so that the adult could see the light but the child could not. More choices between the two levers were required, but now, in all groups, the adult always displayed joy when the light lever was selected but did not attend to the child. So the subjects were faced with this alternative: Do I forsake the candy and make the adult happy or secure the candy for myself while depriving the adult of pleasure?

As Aronfreed and Paskal anticipated, being given affection together with seeing someone else's pleasure—the conditions presumed necessary to produce empathy—was most effective; those children with whom the adult had both been affectionate *and* experienced joy at the appearance of the light now pushed the "light" lever, forsaking their own gratification, more often than in either of the other groups.

The Role of Norms. We have seen that sharing may be acquired as the child learns that such behavior produces positive emotional experiences for him —that is, that sharing makes him feel good (Midlarsky and Bryan, 1967). Another possibility is that sharing in children may be fostered by a norm of reciprocity (Gouldner, 1960), as youngsters discover that their own sharing may be reciprocated, either materially or in the form of approval. Staub and Sherk (1970) explored both reciprocity and the role of need for approval in a major study of sharing by fourth-grade children.

Their measure of need for approval was Crandall, Crandall, and Katkovsky's (1965) *Children's Social Desirability Questionnaire,* which consists of a list of common but often disapproved behaviors (being disrespectful, sometimes avoiding one's duty, being angry, and the like); the fewer of these a child admits to, the higher his or her need for approval is assumed to be. Staub and Sherk asked their subjects, individually, to listen to a tape-recorded story so they could give their opinions about it. Ostensibly to make the task more enjoyable, each of these youngsters was given a small bag with nine pieces of his favorite candy. Then, under the pretense of saving time, a second child (who had been given no candy) was brought in to listen to the story, too. The experimenter then left, but watched the children from behind a one-way vision mirror. One question, then, was whether the subject would now share some of his or her candy with the other child or, perhaps, simply not eat any in the other's presence. After the story had been heard the experimenter returned and asked the children to draw a picture of something that had happened in the story; now, however, the potential sharing role was reversed. Each youngster received a piece of paper but the adult said she had only one crayon left, which she gave to the child whom she had *not* given the candy before. Again she left, now recording the amount of use and sharing of the crayon.

What can we learn of children's sharing from this complex interaction? Staub and Sherk uncovered many important facts. In the first situation, involving the candy, the amount youngsters ate and the amount they shared were highly correlated; children who ate candy in the other's presence also shared some; alternatively, those who didn't share were also least likely to eat any candy themselves as they listened to the story. The subjects, then, might be thought as broadly falling into two groups: *active* (those who ate and shared) and *inactive* (those who neither ate nor shared).

The significance of this division becomes apparent when we relate the active-inactive dimension to the measure of need for approval. The *in*active group have significantly higher scores. Why?

> The inactivity of high need-approval children may have resulted from conflict and anxiety arising out of a number of sources. For example, since the other child did not receive candy [from the experimenter] they may have thought he was not supposed to have any. Or, because they were told to listen to the story, they may have been afraid of disapproval for attending to the candy instead of listening to the story. Even the exact manner in which the candy should be divided or shared, that is, how much to give and how much to eat themselves, may have been a source of concern for children who feared disapproval, thus inhibiting action. In general, children with a strong need for approval may be inhibited and inactive in social situations, especially novel or ambiguous ones. This would limit their prosocial behavior, because helping others or sharing with others often involves initiation of action. . . . [Staub and Sherk, 1970, p. 251.]

In the crayon situation, reciprocity characterized the children's behavior. A child who had received candy from the other in the first situation was now more likely to share his crayon than was a child who had not been offered candy. Interestingly, though, reciprocity was more likely to occur if the youngsters did *not* see the other as a close friend, paralleling the findings of an earlier investigation (Floyd, 1964) in which reciprocity was also found for strangers but not for friends.

The Powerful Effects of Behavioral Example. Perhaps no other factor is more potent for eliciting sharing in children than behavioral example or modeling. In an early demonstration of this effect, Rosenhan and White (1967) asked fourth- and fifth-grade boys and girls to play a bowling game in which gift certificates, exchangeable at a local toy store, could be won. The experimenters varied a number of factors, one of which was whether the children saw an adult model donate to the "Trenton Orphans Fund" by placing some of his gift certificates in a labeled box which displayed children in ragged attire. Of those who saw this altruistic example, almost half (47.5 percent) also shared later when they were all alone; in contrast, without the instigation of a generous adult exemplar, none of the children shared. Since then, literally dozens of studies with children have shown further that exposure to sharing models can be very important in both eliciting and teaching altruistic behavior (cf., Bryan and London, 1970; Poulos and Liebert, 1972).

XII

SELF-CONTROL
AND
ACHIEVEMENT

CHILDHOOD BEHAVIOR is channeled to a large extent by numerous immediate environmental constraints: the expectations of others, parental rewards and punishments, and peer pressures. There are certain situations, however, in which the child behaves "appropriately" despite the absence of outside restrictions. He may, for example, continue to obey rules which have been enforced previously by parents, he may decide even when he is alone to ignore the gratification of immediate rewards in favor of long-range goals, or he may impose relatively high achievement standards on himself. In all of these situations the child is exhibiting *self-control*. For the purposes of our discussion, then, "self-control" will refer to behavior in which the child monitors his own actions in some way in the absence of, or in contradiction to, pressures in the immediate situation. Included in this concept are three related aspects of self-control: the ability to "resist temptation," the ability to tolerate "delay of gratification," and the imposing of standards of achievement upon oneself.

RESISTANCE TO TEMPTATION

Resistance to temptation refers to refraining from the opportunity to engage in a socially prohibited but otherwise rewarding act, such as cheating on an exam or taking cookies from a forbidden cookie jar. The desire and ability to resist tempting but prohibited activities, whether in the company of others or alone, is instilled to a large extent by early training and parental discipline; the principles involved apply to acquiring other forms of self-control as well.

Discipline and Resistance to Temptation

How does the youngster learn to restrain himself from what he wants to do but knows he should not do? This question motivated a project (Burton, Maccoby, and Allinsmith, 1961) in which the tendency of seventy four-year-olds, both boys and girls, to resist temptation was examined in light of the child-rearing methods reported by their mothers. To determine the kinds of discipline to which a child had been exposed, each mother was interviewed intensively for an average of two hours.

To assess tendencies to resist temptation, each youngster was introduced to a bean bag game, told the rules, and left to play it by himself. The object of the game, as it appeared to the child, was to hit a wire stretched behind a board on which five lights were displayed in a row. Hitting the wire presumably would turn one of the lights on and ring a bell. Actually, however, the game was completely controlled by a hidden experimenter who insured that everyone received the same score. (In this way, differences among children in the extent to which they were tempted to cheat could not be linked to differences in their scores.)

After entering the experimental laboratory the child was carefully instructed in the rules and given time to practice. Players were to throw each of the five bags over the board while standing on a foot marker placed approximately five feet from the front of the board. Each child also was allowed to select from an attractive array the toy he would choose if he were to "get enough lights on to win a prize." Children were then ostensibly left alone to play the game; in fact, however, the child's behavior was recorded by a hidden observer. Built into the situation was what might be seen as a special incentive to cheat; although only one light could be earned honestly, additional ones might be sought by stepping forward, moving the foot marker, retrieving bags incorrectly, and hitting the wire with the hand. After three minutes, the experimenter returned to supervise another round of playing for which a prize was awarded. This was done to check whether the children understood the rules, and to soothe feelings of failure among noncheaters and possible guilt among those who did cheat.

Although the interviewers obtained information about a great many child-rearing variables, we will confine our discussion to those that involve discipline. The mothers who were interviewed reported using a great variety of disciplinary techniques. Burton, Maccoby, and Allinsmith (1961) describe these methods in their summary of the manner in which the interviews were scored:

> In regard to disciplinary techniques, physical punishment included such acts as spanking, slapping and shaking. Scolding was verbal reprimand, usually with a raised voice. The mother's taking away of a toy or TV was scored deprivation of object or privilege. Isolation was primarily scored for sending [the child] to his room. The prototypical response for withdrawal of love would be, "I can't love you when you do that." Visible suffering was represented by the mother's saying . . . "You must not love me to act that way." Some mothers claimed to discipline their children by discussing why they wanted them to act in certain ways and expressed the attitude that they didn't believe in punishment. The major disciplinary techniques for these mothers was "reasoning." [pp. 699–700.]

This assortment of disciplinary measures can be classified into two categories: *psychological discipline* (reasoning, withdrawal of love, portrayal of suffering by the parent, isolation) and *physical discipline* (spanking, slapping, shaking, scolding). Psychological discipline, which at least on the surface appears to be more civilized and dignified, is often favored by many parents and psychologists.

Yet the study by Burton *et al.* indicated that the children of mothers who preferred physical discipline were more likely to refrain from cheating in the bean bag game, whereas children of mothers who tended to use reasoning were more likely to cheat. It appears that physical modes of training may be more effective when a child is young and unable to comprehend parental reasoning or subtle changes in parental mien. (Recall that these children were only four years old at the time of testing.) With the intellectual sophistication that evolves as the child develops, however, psychological techniques may become more effective. In fact, other studies with older children have found psychological discipline to play an important role in the development of self-control.

Employing Reasoning with Punishment

Parents often provide rules of conduct for their children which are specific to the situation at hand—e.g., "Don't play with your father's sunglasses because if you were to drop them they might break." Such directives, it is thought, help the child evaluate his own behavior by explaining exactly *what* activity he should avoid and *why*. To see whether this is in fact the case, Cheyne (1969), conducted an experiment with kindergarten and third-grade boys and girls to explore the effects of a combination of verbal punishment with explicit verbal directives. The children were assigned to one of three conditions:

1. Under the *punishment only* condition, children were told "That's bad" when they selected a certain toy to play with;

2. Under the *punishment plus simple rule* condition, children were told "That's bad. You should not play with that toy" when they selected a certain toy;

3. And under the *punishment plus elaborated rule* condition, children were told "That's bad. You should not play with that toy. That toy belongs to someone else."

Subsequently, when the children were left alone with the forbidden toy, those who had received the most information (those in the *punishment plus elaborated rule* condition) resisted touching and playing with it most often and for the longest periods of time. The amount of time that passed before children touched the toy is shown in Figure XII–1, which also indicates that the elaborated rule was more effective for the older children. This figure additionally suggests that the older children deviated more quickly than the younger ones when behavioral rules were presented without justification, a finding which may indicate that those old enough to benefit from a complete explanation resent not receiving one.

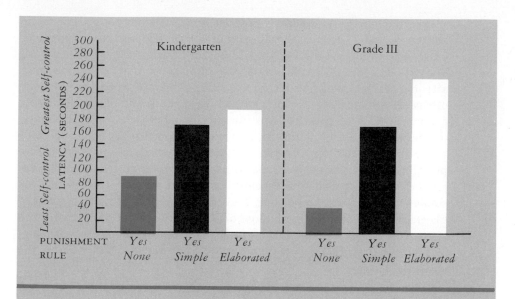

FIGURE XII—1

Amount of time (latency) before first deviation for kindergarten and third-grade boys and girls under various levels of rule structure in Cheyne's experiment. Adapted from J. A. Cheyne and R. H. Walters. Punishment and prohibition: Some origins of self-control. In New Directions in Psychology 4. *New York: Holt, Rinehart & Winston, 1970, by permission.*

Overcoming the Problem of Delayed Punishment. Long ago J. B. Watson (1924) observed: "The idea that a child's future bad behavior will be prevented by giving him a licking in the evening for something he did in the morning is ridiculous" (p. 183). As we noted in Chapter V, delay of punishment may lead the child to associate the punishment with intervening activities and not with the undesired act. To be sure, most parents probably would not administer punishment several hours after the occurrence of an offense without providing some explanation, on the assumption that by accompanying delayed punishment with a verbal explanation they provide a symbolic reinstatement of prohibited activity. But does reinstatement of this kind make any difference?

Andres (1967) conducted an experiment in which a long delay—four hours—occurred between performance of the prohibited activity (breaking a toy) and punishment (a 104 decibel buzzer). Each child was given a toy that was designed to break after a few minutes of play, and four hours after the experimental situation he was brought back to receive punishment, ostensibly for breaking it. One group of youngsters was punished without a reinstatement of the behavior. Another group saw a video recording of themselves breaking the toy before punishment occurred. A third group listened to the experimenter describe the transgression before punishment was administered, and still another was required to break a toy just before punishment. Subsequently, each child was left alone with a toy similar to the original broken one. Those who experienced no reinstatement played with the new toy much more often than did those who experienced any of the forms of reinstatement; moreover, reinstatement through film and verbal description were somewhat more effective than making the child do it again.

Rule Learning and Resistance to Temptation

Even without punishment or threat of punishment, rules of conduct may guide a child's behavior. Indeed, parents often rely heavily on such direct instruction in socializing children.

Importance of Rule Consistency. One of the questions frequently asked about rules concerns the influence of inconsistent instruction—something that occurs in the lives of most youngsters. In one study (Stouwie, 1970), two adult experimenters gave various sets of instructions to each of four groups of third graders. The four experimental treatments were:

1. Both the male and female experimenters prohibited the subject from playing with a group of toys;

2. The male experimenter prohibited the subjects from playing with the toys while the female permitted such play;

3. The male experimenter permitted and female experimenter prohibited;

4. Both the male and the female experimenters permitted the subject to play with the toys.

After the instructions were given, the children were left alone with the toys while their behavior was observed through a one-way vision screen. The children who had been permitted by both experimenters to play with the toys did so most, while those for whom playing with the toys was prohibited by both experimenters played with them least. The two inconsistent treatment conditions produced behavior of intermediate magnitude. Adult directives, then, appear to be most effective when they are not contradictory.

Vicarious Discipline. Repeatedly, we have seen that children learn a great deal about what is expected of them by society through observing the behavior and outcomes of others. That this phenomenon applies to resistance to temptation was clearly illustrated by Walters, Leat, and Mezei (1963), who brought five-year-old boys from lower-class homes individually to a room filled with attractive toys and a dictionary. Although permitted to look at the dictionary, they were directed not to play with the toys. Subsequently, the boys were divided into three groups. Those in the *model-rewarded* group saw a two-minute film in which a four-year-old boy played with the very same toys that had been available earlier in the experiment. After the boy in the movie played with the toys for a short time, his mother entered and joined in the play activity. She encouraged him, smiled, and behaved affectionately throughout the sequence. Children in the *model-punished* condition observed a movie with a different ending: the boy was scolded for playing with the toys. In this film the mother entered the room shaking her head and finger at the boy, who then dropped the toys and fled to the sofa where he held a blanket up to his face. Those in the *control* condition did not see either film.

After the two experimental groups had seen the films, subjects in all three groups were left alone with the taboo toys and the uninteresting dictionary for fifteen minutes. A hidden observer recorded their willingness to violate the experimenter's instructions by playing with the forbidden toys. Table XII–1 presents the major results of the study. That vicarious reward and punishment had differential effects on resistance to temptation is evident, with subjects exposed to a rewarded model disobeying more quickly (lower latency) and spending more time in playing with the forbidden toy than those who observed either a punished model or no model. In contrast, most boys who observed a punished model exhibited no disobedience at all.

Self-Instruction. How do rules and prohibitions come to govern a child's behavior? Considerable research suggests that a youngster begins to self-instruct quite early (e.g., Birch, 1966; Israel and O'Leary, 1973; Lovaas, 1964; Luria, 1961), and that self-instruction facilitates control of action.

TABLE XII–1

GROUP MEDIANS * OF LATENCY OF FIRST ACT OF
DISOBEDIENCE AND TIME SPENT IN DISOBEYING
(TOTAL TEST TIME = 900 SEC.)
IN THE EXPERIMENT OF WALTERS, LEAT, AND MEZEI

	MODEL-REWARDED MOVIE	MODEL-PUNISHED MOVIE	CONTROL (NO MOVIE)
Latency of first act of disobedience (sec.)	85	900	285
Time spent in disobeying (sec.)	28	0	7

Source: Adapted from Walters, Leat, and Mezei, 1963.
* The *median,* like the mean, is a measure of the central tendency of a group of scores and is defined as the score above and below which 50 percent of the scores lie (i.e., the middlemost score) when the scores are arranged in numerical order.

In investigating this possibility in regard to cheating, O'Leary (1968) directed first-grade boys to press a telegraph key in the presence of certain stimuli but not in the presence of others. Each time the key was pressed, the child received a marble, and he was told that "lots of marbles" would result in a prize. The measure of cheating was the number of times a subject pressed the lever in the presence of inappropriate stimuli, thereby violating the rules of the game outlined by the experimenter in order to obtain additional marbles. Before being left alone to play the game privately, one-half of the children were told to say to themselves, "No, it shouldn't be pressed" when pressing the key was prohibited according to the rules and to say, "Yes, it should be pressed" when it was permitted. The remaining children were not told to give themselves instructions. They were then left alone to play the game for fifteen minutes, during which time their behavior was recorded by an observer behind a one-way vision screen. Most children who were told to self-instruct did so. And self-instruction worked: those who used it cheated significantly less often than those who did not.

DELAY OF GRATIFICATION

In *Walden Two,* B. F. Skinner's novel describing an experimental utopia, the author outlines a provocative program for instilling in children the ability to shrug off unpleasantness so that it does not ruin the quality of experience unnecessarily or get in the way of constructive action. "In most cultures," says Frazier, the character who serves as guide to the reader, "the child meets up with annoyances and reverses of uncontrollable magnitude. Some are imposed in the name of discipline by persons in authority. Some, like hazings, are condoned though not authorized. Others are merely accidental. No one cares to, or is able to, prevent them" (Skinner, 1948, p. 113).

Ordinary societies, according to Skinner, teach the child to deal with such situations in a quite haphazard fashion. A few hardy children who receive unhappiness in doses they can swallow become the optimists, the contented, and the ambitious, whereas the others become the pessimists, the disgruntled, and the discouraged. In Skinner's utopia, however, all children become optimistic and ambitious because they are taught systematically to cope with frustration. Children, says Skinner, should be exposed to a deliberately designed series of situations which gradually increase in the frustration they produce. In one such situation, for example, children of three or four years of age are given lollipops which have been dipped in powdered sugar so that a single touch of the tongue can be detected. These children are then instructed that they will be allowed to eat the lollipop later in the day, provided it has not been licked at all in the meantime. In this situation, to indulge in a small immediate pleasure is to forfeit a larger delayed reward. Frazier, the guide, describes what children can learn from such an experience.

> First of all, the children are urged to examine their own behavior while looking at the lollipops. This helps them to recognize the need for self-control. Then the lollipops are concealed and the children are asked to notice any gain in happiness or any reduction in tension. Then a strong distraction is arranged—say, an interesting game. Later the children are reminded of the candy and encouraged to examine their reaction. The value of the distraction is generally obvious. . . . When the experiment is repeated a day or so later, the children all run with the lollipops to their lockers . . . a sufficient indication of the success of our training. [p. 108.]

Skinner's hypothetical training procedure raises several questions about our own nonutopian society. Do children in our society learn to delay gratification? If so, how is the ability to delay gratification taught in our culture? The answer to the first question is a definite "yes," according to more than a decade of research. In American society the ability to forego immediate pleasure is valued highly and referred to at least indirectly when we speak of the so-called "Protestant Ethic," a cluster of attitudes which emphasize self-restraint and hard work while deemphasizing pleasure and relaxation.

This is not to say, however, that children are as steadfast in the practice of self-control as those in Skinner's *Walden Two*. In many situations where alternatives are recognized, the child must make a "choice" between accepting or not accepting the frustration of delay for the sake of earning a superior outcome, and in making this decision the child probably considers the subjective values of both the immediate and delayed rewards and the probability of obtaining them (Mischel, 1958; Mischel and Metzner, 1962).

In the excerpt from *Walden Two,* for example, the delayed reward (a whole lollipop) probably would be considered superior to the immediate reward (a few licks of a lollipop) by most youngsters. But the course of action also depends on the trustworthiness of the people giving the lollipops away, which introduces an element of risk in waiting. And there is another consideration. In most life situations, attaining delayed rewards involves not only simple waiting but also engaging successfully in some required activity. Thus, the child's confidence in being able to perform this activity is undoubtedly related to his decisions. When the difference in value between the immediate and the delayed reward is slight and/or the risk of not being able to obtain the delayed reward despite the delay is great, the rational choice (and the one children presumably make) is to take the immediate reward. On the other hand, when the difference in subjective value is substantial and/or when obtaining the delayed reward is not too risky, the rational choice may be the delayed reward (Mischel and Staub, 1965).

Once the choice has been made to wait for the delayed but superior prize, a question arises as to whether the child will have the "continence of will" to go through with the plan. Although older children tend to exhibit more self-control in this respect than do younger ones (Mischel and Metzner, 1962), delaying reward can be difficult at any age.

Freud (1959) suggested that delay of gratification could be bridged by creating mental images of the desired object, thereby producing substitute satisfactions that ease the frustration of delay. Others have advanced similar notions—namely, that thinking about the delayed reward should enhance impulse control (Jones and Gerard, 1967). In accord with these hypotheses, Mischel and Ebbesen (1970) predicted that children would find waiting for a delayed reward easiest when they could see the reward for which they waited, whereas waiting would be most difficult when no rewards were in sight. This prediction flatly contradicts the principle of distraction described in the previous excerpt from *Walden Two.* As you read the actual research report, Selection 8 below, take particular note of the ingenious experimental situation.

SELECTION 8

ATTENTION IN DELAY OF GRATIFICATION

Walter Mischel and Ebbe B. Ebbesen

The concept of voluntary postponement of immediate gratification for the sake of more distant long-term gains has a central place in conceptualizations of the development of complex human behavior. Formulations stressing the role of voluntary delay of reward range from the possible origins of "psychopathy" and antisocial behavior (e.g., Mowrer and Ullmann, 1945) to characterizations of societal and cultural adaptation patterns in terms of the renunciation of immediate gratifications in favor of disciplined seeking of more substantial future gains. At the empirical level, extensive experimental work has been done on delay of reward in

Reprinted from Mischel, W., and Ebbesen, E. B. Attention in delay of gratification. *Journal of Personality and Social Psychology,* **16,** 1970, 329–337. Copyright 1970 by the American Psychological Association. Reproduced by permission. This study was supported by Research Grant M6830 from the National Institute of Health, United States Public Health Service. Grateful acknowledgment is due to Jerry Zadny for serving as an experimenter.

animals (e.g., Renner, 1967). Surprisingly, although voluntary delay behavior has been assumed to be a critical component of such concepts as "ego strength," "impulse control," and "internalization," relatively little attention has been devoted to it in empirical work on human social behavior.

One line of research has tried to apply psychoanalytic concepts concerning ego functions to motoric inhibition and impulse control (e.g., Singer, 1955). Most of the resulting empirical work has relied on highly indirect measures of delayed gratification and ego control, mainly inferred from human movement responses on the Rorschach (e.g., Spivack, Levine, and Sprigle, 1959).

In contrast, the present research is part of a larger project to investigate delay of reward with more direct behavioral measures. For example, subjects were required to choose among actual alternatives that varied in delay time and value (e.g., immediate smaller versus delayed but larger rewards) in realistic situations (e.g., Mischel, 1966). Past research in this vein has investigated the organization of self-control by exploring the relationship between various preference patterns for immediate smaller rewards or delayed larger rewards and other theoretically relevant aspects of personality functioning. The network of associations found here so far indicates, for example, significant relations between preference for delayed rewards and indexes of achievement orientation, social responsibility, age, sociocultural and rearing conditions, and intelligence (e.g., Klineberg, 1968; Mischel, 1961a, 1961b, 1961c; Mischel and Metzner, 1962). Relations have also been found with resistance to temptation (Mischel and Gilligan, 1964) and with severity of psychological disturbances (Shybut, 1968). Correlational studies were supplemented in recent years by experiments to investigate more precisely the determinants of voluntary delay of reward and similar forms of self-control in laboratory situations (e.g., Mischel and Staub, 1965; Mischel, Grusec, and Masters, 1969). As a result of both correlational and experimental studies, some of the determinants of choice preferences for delayed rewards are becoming clearer (Mischel, 1966, 1968).

Although choice preferences for immediate or delayed rewards are beginning to be understood, the psychological mechanisms through which persons manage to bridge the temporal delay of reward required for attainment of deferred gratification remain remarkably unstudied. In spite of its seemingly evident importance, little is known about the self-regulatory mechanisms during the actual delay period when the individual must engage in the waiting dictated by his choice of delayed, larger gratification. Past research has studied verbal choice preferences between rewards varying in value and in the delay time required to attain them, but just how subjects are able to wait during the temporal delay remains unknown. Given that one has chosen to wait for a larger deferred gratification, how can the delay period be managed? The mechanisms that maintain goal-directed delay seem especially important, considering the fact that the ability to sustain self-imposed delay for the sake of larger but delayed consequences appears to be a chief component of most complex higher order human behavior. A main purpose of the present research, therefore, was to investigate the psychological processes that mediate sustained waiting behavior for delayed gratification.

Freud's (1959) classic discussion of the transition from primary to secondary process is one of the few theoretical treatments of how delay of gratification may be bridged. According to the psychoanalytic formulation, ideation arises initially when there is a block or delay in the process of direct gratification discharge (Rapaport, 1967, p. 315). During such externally imposed delay, according to Freud, the child constructs a "hallucinatory image" of the physically absent need-satisfying object. Gradually, as a result of repeated association of tension reduction with goal objects, and the development of greater ego organization, the imposed delay of satisfying objects results in the substitution of hallucinatory satisfactions and other thought processes that convert "free cathexes" into "bound cathexes" (e.g., Freud, 1959; Singer, 1955). In spite of much psychoanalytic theorizing and speculation about the role of the mental representation of blocked gratifications in the development of delaying capacity, the process remains far from clear.

In their theoretical discussion of impulse control, Jones and Gerard (1967) reasoned that "time-binding," or the capacity to bridge delay of gratification, probably hinges on self-instructional processes through which the individual increases the salience of the delayed consequences or outcomes of his action. In their view, any factors (situational or within the individual) that make delayed consequences more salient should enhance impulse control and voluntary delay. Their position, while emphasizing the self-instructional aspects of attention to deferred outcomes, also implies covert self-reinforcement processes through which the subject may reinforce his own waiting behavior by vividly anticipating some of the positive consequences to which it will lead. Finally, a cognitive-developmental view might lead one to expect that young children may readily forget the delayed outcomes for which they are waiting, and hence cease to wait unless they are reminded of the relevant contingencies and rewards involved in the delay-of-gratification paradigm.

In line with all the foregoing arguments, it seems most plausible that conditions that help the individual to attend mentally to the delayed reward for which he is waiting should help him to sustain the delay. Operationally, these speculations would suggest that any cues that make the delayed gratification more salient—that help the person to make deferred consequences more psychologically vivid or immediate (e.g., by letting him look at them, by visualizing them in imagination, or by reminding him of the object for which he is waiting)—should facilitate waiting behavior. Such expectations also seem congruent with the results of earlier work on choice of immediate but smaller versus delayed but larger rewards (Maher, 1956; Mischel, 1966; Mischel and Metzner, 1962; Mischel and Staub, 1965). These earlier studies showed that an important determinant of choice preference for delayed rewards is the individual's expectation or "trust" that he will really get the delayed (but more valuable) outcome. Consequently, conditions that increase the salience or visibility of the delayed gratification may enhance the subject's willingness to wait by increasing his subjective probability that the delayed outcome will really materialize and be available after the waiting time ends.

In light of the foregoing considerations, one might expect that voluntary delay behavior is facilitated when the subject converts, as it were, the deferred or delayed object into more tangible form by making it psychologically more immediate, as by providing himself with representations or physical cues about it. The most direct way to increase the salience of the deferred outcomes and to focus attention on them would be to have them physically present and facing the subject, so that he can attend to them readily and vividly. To investigate how attention to delayed and immediate outcomes influences waiting behavior for them, a first step would be to manipulate the availability of those outcomes for attention during the delay time.

Previous research on preference for delayed rewards has been conducted mainly with subjects at least 6 years of age or older. Preliminary observations of the actual waiting behavior of nursery school children suggested, however, that the capacity to wait for long-term goals and to inhibit both immediate gratification and motoric activity seems to develop markedly at about ages 3–4. It was hoped, therefore, that research with subjects in this young age should be especially informative in revealing some of the processes that underlie the genesis of goal-directed waiting.

A first requirement was a paradigm in which such very young children would be willing to remain in an experimental room, waiting entirely alone for at least a short time without becoming upset and debilitatingly anxious. As an initial step (after the usual play periods for rapport building) each child was taught a game in which he could immediately summon the experimenter by a simple signal. This step was practiced repeatedly until the child clearly understood that he could immediately terminate his waiting period in the room simply by signaling for the experimenter, who regularly returned from outside as soon as the child signaled. After this critical procedure had been clearly established, the child was introduced to the relevant contingency. He was shown two objects (e.g., snack-food treats), one of which he clearly preferred (as determined by pretesting); to attain the preferred object he had to wait for it until the experimenter returned "by himself." The child was, however, entirely free throughout this waiting period to signal at any time for the experimenter to return; if he signaled, he could have the less preferred object at once, but would forego the more desirable one later.

To manipulate the extent to which children could attend to the reward objects while they were waiting, the rewards were removed from the experimental room in all combinations, creating four conditions with respect to the objects available for attention. In one condition, the children waited with both the immediate (less preferred) and the delayed (more preferred) reward facing them in the experimental room, so that they could attend to both outcomes. In another group neither reward was available for the subject's attention, both rewards having been removed from his sight. In the remaining two groups either the delayed reward only or the immediate reward only was left facing the child and available for attention while he waited. The dependent measure was the length of time before each child voluntarily terminated the waiting period.

In accord with the previously discussed theoretical ideas, it was predicted that conditions in which the delayed reward was present and visually available would enhance attention to it and hence increase voluntary delay time for it. It was anticipated that the condition in which the child was left without either reward would make it most difficult to bridge the delay time and therefore lead to the shortest waiting. In addition it was expected, although less confidently, that the condition in which both the delayed and immediate reward were available for attention would best facilitate waiting time. This condition might permit the subject to compare and contrast the two outcomes, possibly providing himself with persuasive arguments and self-instructions to help him delay long enough to achieve his preferred gratification. On the other hand, one might also plausibly expect maximum delay when the child could focus his attention on the delayed reward without being tempted by the immediate gratification—that is, the condition in which the delayed reward was present for attention but the immediate one was not.

Method

Subjects and Experimenters

The subjects were 16 boys and 16 girls attending the Bing Nursery School of Stanford University. Three other subjects were run but eliminated because of their failure to comprehend the instructions as described later. The children ranged in age from 3 years, 6 months, to 5 years, 8 months (with a median age of 4 years, 6 months). The procedures were conducted by two male experimenters. Eight subjects (4 males and 4 females) were assigned randomly to each of the four experimental conditions. In each condition each experimenter ran 2 males and 2 females in order to avoid systematic biasing effects from sex or experimenters.

Procedure

The procedures were designed to develop a new method for studying delay behavior experimentally with young subjects. The development of this method was one of the chief goals of the project, and the procedures therefore are described in considerable detail.

In the week prior to the start of the experiment, the two male experimenters spent a few days playing with as many children in the nursery school as they could. These nurturant sessions were designed so that the children would more readily agree to accompany the experimenters to the "surprise room" and, once there, would be at ease. After obtaining the child's consent to go to the surprise room, the experimenter escorted the child to the experimental room.

The experimental room was a small private chamber containing a table, on which lay five ⅓-inch-long pieces of pretzel and an opaque cake tin. A chair was in front of the table, and on a second chair there was an empty cardboard box. Under the cake tin on the table were five 2-inch-long pretzels and two animal cookies. On the floor near the chair with the cardboard box were four battery-operated toys. On one wall, at right angles with the table, was a one-way mirror. Apart from these objects, the room was empty. The experimenter pointed out the four toys, and before the child could begin to play with the toys, asked the child to sit in the chair which was in front of the table. He then demonstrated each toy briefly in a friendly manner, saying with enthusiasm after each demonstration that they would play with the toys later on, placing each toy in the cardboard box out of sight of the child. These references to the toys were designed to help relax the children and also to set up an expectancy that both the child and experimenter would play with the toys sometime later on in the session (thus, terminating the delay period would not mean having to terminate play in the surprise room).

The next phase required teaching the child the technique for terminating the waiting period and summoning the experimenter at will. For this purpose the experimenter said:

> Sometimes I have to go out of the room and when I do, you can bring me back. Do you see these tiny pretzels? [The experimenter pointed to the five ⅓-inch pieces of pretzel that would serve as signals.] Well, if I go out of the room and you eat one of these pretzels you can make me come back into the room. You can make me come back! Let's try it. I'll go out of the room now and shut the door. As soon as I do, you eat one of the pretzels and make me come back.

The instructions were repeated, if necessary, until the child seemed to understand them completely.

The experimenter then left the room and shut the door, observing through a small viewing hole in the door when the child ate the pretzel. As soon as the child put the pretzel in his mouth, the experimenter returned, laughing playfully and exclaiming how well the child brought him back into the room. To insure that the child learned reliably how to bring the experimenter back, this sequence was repeated four times with four of the five small pieces of pretzel, still leaving the last small piece lying next to the as yet unopened cake tin.

Next the experimenter lifted the cake tin, revealing the two sets of reward objects lying there (two cookies and five 2-inch pretzels). The experimenter asked the child which of the two rewards he liked better, and after the child chose, said:

> Oh well, you know what? In order for you to eat those _____ [naming the preferred reward] you will have to wait here in your chair and sit very still. I have to go out of the room for a while and when I come back you can eat those _____ [preferred reward] all up. You can take them off the table and eat them right up. But, you know, sometimes, I'm gone a long time and if you want to bring me back you can. Do you know how to bring me back? [All children did know how.] That's right. You eat that little piece [pointing to signal] and I have to come back. But I have to tell you something else. If you eat that and make me come back you can't have _____ [preferred reward]. You can't have them. But you can have all the _____ [naming less preferred reward]! If you sit very still in your chair until I come back *by myself,* then you can eat the _____ [preferred reward]! But if you want to make me come back all you have to do is eat that [pointing to signal] and I'll come back; but then you can't have the _____ [preferred reward]; but you can have all the _____ [less preferred].

Thus the instructions faced the child with a choice: he could either continue waiting for the more preferred reward until the experimenter returned, or he could stop waiting by bringing the experimenter back. If he stopped waiting, then he would receive the less favored (but more immediately available) reward and forego the more preferred one. The waiting contingencies were repeated once more, and then, to assess if the subject understood them, the experimenter asked three questions: "Can you tell me how to bring me back"? "What happens if you eat the pretzel"? "But what happens if you sit very still in your chair and wait for me to come back by myself?" Three children were unable to answer these questions correctly and were therefore excluded from the data a priori.

At this point the experimenter was informed of the condition in which the subject was to be placed by consulting a slip of paper concealed in the room. This method assured that the experimenter remained unaware of the subject's experimental condition until the last possible moment in the procedure. Depending on the condition and the child's choice of preferred reward, the experimenter picked up the cake tin and along with it either nothing, one of the rewards (the more preferred reward or the less preferred reward), or both. The physical arrangement was such that the rewards, if left, were directly in front of the child at about shoulder level. In all conditions the signal for summoning the experimenter was left on the table in front of the child. Thus, depending upon the condition to which the child had been assigned, he was left waiting either with both the delayed and immediate rewards, with either the delayed but more preferred or the immediate but less preferred reward, or with neither reward available for attention. Finally, in all conditions the experimenter excused himself to leave, and as he was leaving, resummarized the waiting instructions and reminded the child that "no matter what you do, whether you sit and wait for me to come back by myself or whether you bring me back. . . . No matter what you do, we're going to play with my toys when I get back" This instruction was included to stress that the child's waiting behavior would not affect his later play period in the surprise room.

Waiting time was scored from the moment the experimenter shut the door. The experimenter returned either as soon as the child signaled or after 15 minutes—the criterion time—if the child did not signal. To determine whether or not the child remembered the waiting contingencies, when the experimenter finally returned he asked the child, "What happens now?" All children answered this question correctly. Subjects were also asked why they had or had not, waited. Children who waited to criterion were allowed to eat the chosen, more preferred reward. Those who did not wait to criterion were allowed to eat the unchosen reward. Thereafter each child played with the toys for a while and then was escorted back to his nursery school playroom.

Results

In accord with the previously discussed theorizing, it was expected that as the degree of attention paid to the delayed rewards increased, the length of time which the children waited would increase. To determine whether or not this prediction was fulfilled, the mean length of time waited (in minutes) was computed for each of the four attention conditions and is depicted in Table 1. Inspection of these results revealed that unexpectedly, the children waited longest when the rewards were entirely absent—that is, in the condition in which neither the delayed nor the immediate reward was available for attention during the waiting period. Furthermore, the children waited the shortest length of time when both the delayed and the immediately rewards were facing them during the waiting session. These results were exactly opposite to the predictions.

An analysis of variance of the mean delay times (Table 2) demonstrated that the overall effect of attentional condi-

TABLE 1

MEAN MINUTES AND STANDARD DEVIATIONS
OF WAITING TIME FOR A DELAYED REWARD
AS A FUNCTION OF ATTENTION

STATISTIC	AVAILABLE FOR ATTENTION			
	No rewards	Both rewards	Delayed reward	Immediate reward
M *	11.29	1.03	4.87	5.72
SD	6.84	2.39	6.57	6.43

* M is an abbreviation for the mean or average; SD is the abbreviation for the standard deviation, a measure of variability.—ED.

tions was significant ($F = 4.42$, $df = 3/28$, $p < .025$). To determine the relative contribution of the conditions to the overall effect, orthogonal contrasts were computed (Winer, 1962). The first orthogonal contrast (C_1 in Table 2) compared the effect of having any reward present for attention with having no reward present during the delay period. This comparison yielded an F of 9.52 ($p < .005$, $df = 1/28$). Thus, children waited much longer for rewards when the rewards were absent than when any rewards were left available for attention. The second orthogonal contrast (C_2) compared mean delay times when both rewards were present with mean delay times when either the delayed or the immediate reward was available for attention. The results of this contrast suggested a slight trend toward shorter delay when both re-

wards were present for attention, rather than when only one reward was present ($F = 3.45$, $df = 1/28$, $p < .1$). The final contrast, (C_3), comparing attention to the delayed reward with attention to the immediate reward, was not statistically significant ($F < 1$).

The absolute mean waiting times were probably depressed by the low maximum waiting period used, that is, 15 minutes. Ten subjects out of the total 32 in the study waited the maximum time. Table 3 shows the number of subjects in each condition who waited the full 15 minutes. An overall frequency analysis yielded a significant chi-square ($\chi^2 = 11.07$, $p < .025$, $df = 3$). Note that not a single child waited the maximum time in the condition in which both rewards were available, whereas 6 out of 8 children waited the maximum time when neither reward was present. These results further support the findings of the parametric analysis, showing greatest delay of gratification when the reward objects were not available for attention. In summary, children who were given

TABLE 2

ANALYSIS OF VARIANCE FOR MEAN WAITING TIMES
(IN MINUTES) IN EACH ATTENTION CONDITION

SOURCE	df	MS	F
Between	3	144.2	4.42**
C_1	1	310.5	9.52***
C_2	1	112.4	3.45*
C_3	1	9.8	<1
Error	28	32.63	

* $p < .10$.   ** $p < .025$.   *** $p < .005$.

TABLE 3

NUMBER OF CHILDREN WAITING THE MAXIMUM TIME
(15 MINUTES) IN EACH ATTENTION CONDITION

SITUATION	REWARDS AVAILABLE FOR ATTENTION			
	None	Both	Delayed	Immediate
Not waiting	2	8	6	6
Waiting	6	0	2	2

the opportunity to attend to any of the rewards while they were waiting delayed less long than children who could not attend to any rewards while waiting.

Follow-Up Data

To test the stability of these findings, a partial replication was conducted in later follow-up work. In this replication, the method was altered in one major way. It was recognized that interpretation of the reported results might be somewhat hampered by the fact that the signal for terminating the delay involved eating a tiny pretzel, and that pretzels also were the rewards. Therefore, instead of the tiny pretzel, a desk bell was used as the signal to terminate the delay period in the follow-up.

Subjects of comparable age from the same nursery school were run in the two conditions that had yielded the main effects. Namely, 12 children were left waiting with neither the delayed nor immediate rewards present and 12 with both rewards present.

The findings clearly supported the previous results. The mean waiting time for the condition in which neither reward was present for attention was 8.9 minutes ($SD = 5.26$), while the mean waiting time when both rewards were visible was only 3.09 minutes ($SD = 5.59$). These means were significantly different in the same direction found previously ($t = 2.61$, $df = 22$, $p < .025$). We therefore may conclude that this attentional condition produced reliable differences in the length of time that children delayed gratification (regardless of the signal used to terminate the delay period).

Discussion

Throughout this study unexpected results emerged. A first surprise was the long duration of the waiting periods that many of these young children were able to maintain under some conditions. In pilot work, for example, some of the preschool youngsters waited for the preferred reward quietly by themselves, seated alone in a chair for periods sometimes exceeding 1 hour—an observation that is surprising, considering the widespread belief that young children are incapable of sustained delay of gratification. Moreover, throughout the entire study not a single child violated the stated contingency rule by consuming the preferred but delayed reward before the experimenter's return.

The experimental conditions exerted potent effects on the children's delay behavior, as seen in the finding that six out of eight children waited the maximum 15-minute time when they could attend to neither the immediate nor the delayed rewards, whereas the mean waiting time was about 1 minute when they could attend to both rewards. These differences between conditions suggest that it is inappropriate to conceptualize delay of gratification as if it hinged on an all-or-none "ability." Instead, most of the subjects in the present study, in spite of their young age, seemed capable of delay of gratification; the extent to which they did delay depended critically on the specific conditions of the delay period.

The initial theorizing about delay behavior led to predictions of results which were the direct opposite of the obtained findings. It was predicted that attention to the outcomes available in the choice situation while waiting would enhance delay behavior; instead it sharply reduced delay of gratification. Extensive observations of the children's behavior during the delay period provided some clues for a better understanding of the mechanisms through which they mediated their own goal-directed waiting.

One of the most striking delay strategies used by some subjects was exceedingly simple and effective. These children seemed to facilitate their waiting by converting the aversive waiting situation into a more pleasant non-waiting one. They devised elaborate self-distraction techniques through which they spent their time psychologically doing something (almost anything) other than waiting. Instead of focusing prolonged attention on the objects for which they were waiting, they avoided looking at them. Some children covered their eyes with their hands, rested their heads on their arms, and found other similar techniques for averting their eyes from the reward objects. Many seemed to try to reduce the frustration of delay of reward by generating their own diversions: they talked to themselves, sang, invented games with their hands and feet, and even tried to fall asleep while waiting —as one child successfully did. These elaborate self-distractions occurred mainly in the rewards-absent condition and almost never in the both-rewards-present condition, since in the latter group the children quickly terminated the delay period.

These observations, while obviously inconclusive, suggest that diverting one's attention away from the delayed reward (while maintaining behavior directed toward its ultimate attainment) may be a key step in bridging temporal delay of reward. That is, learning *not* to think about what one is awaiting may enhance delay of gratification, much more than does ideating about the outcomes.

These observations also seem consistent with theoretical considerations which (post hoc) could correctly predict the obtained results. Namely, from the perspective of "frustrative nonreward" theory (e.g., Amsel, 1958, 1962; Wagner, 1966), the occurrence of nonreward when reward is expected elicits a primary frustration reaction. Congruent with this formulation, when the anticipation of reward is increased, the aversive frustration effect also should be greater. Hence one might predict that cues that enhance the salience of anticipated but still unavailable (delayed) rewards should increase the aversiveness of the delay period. Presumably the greater and more vivid the anticipation of reward, the greater the frustration generated by its delay. This line of reasoning would suggest that conditions that decrease the subjects' attention to the blocked reward—and that distract him by internal or overt activity from the frustrative delay of reward—would make it less aversive for him to continue his goal-directed waiting and hence permit him to wait longer for delayed gratifications. These theoretical expectations seem closely congruent both with the obtained findings and with the more informal observations of the children's delay behavior.

The present terminology focuses on the frustrative aspects of not being able to immediately obtain the preferred reward in the delay-of-gratification paradigm. The same theoretical considerations, however, apply to the aversiveness of the waiting period and of the continuous decisional conflict (between terminating versus waiting longer). In part, attending to the rewards in the waiting paradigm may be aversive, because it increases the frustration of anticipating the attainment of a blocked reward; in part it may be frustrative, because it enhances the aversiveness of the waiting situation and accentuates the ongoing decisional conflict. All of these sources of frustration seem an integral part of the delay-of-gratification situation, and attention to them makes effective delay behavior more difficult.

It is of considerable interest that delay behavior was about the same, regardless of whether the reward in front of the child was the immediately available one or the delayed, more preferred outcome. This finding seems most clearly to contradict any Freudian theoretical expectations that a mental focus on the delayed outcome (rather than the immediate gratification) serves to bridge temporal delay of gratification by providing an internal or "hallucinatory" representation of the desired but deferred or blocked outcome.

It might also be thought that the children's waiting behavior in the present situation depends on implicit "experimenter demands." Such speculations would predict that the presence of the delayed reward should serve as a cue to the subject that waiting for the delayed outcome is expected by the experimenter. Similarly the condition in which only the immediate reward is present should cue less lengthy waiting and enhance willingness to terminate

the delay and settle for the immediate outcome. These interpretations are untenable, however, because waiting times were similar in the condition in which only the delayed reward was present and the condition in which only the immediate reward was present.

One further alternative interpretation that may be suggested is that attention to the rewards simply decreases their subjective value through some sort of habituation process, and therefore subjects wait less long. In that case one would expect the attention to the delayed reward to result in its subjective devaluation and hence predict shorter waiting when the delayed reward is present, as indeed occurred. The same reasoning, however, also would predict that the presence of the immediate reward should lead to its devaluation and hence generate longer waiting times for the more preferred and absent delayed outcome. The finding that the presence of only the immediate reward in fact led to less delay argues against such a habituation or value-reduction interpretation of the role of attention in delay behavior.

Throughout the present study it has been assumed that the content of subjects' ideation while waiting would be correlated with the attentional conditions to which they were assigned. Thus it was assumed that making reward(s) available for attention by facing the subject with them would increase the likelihood that he would actually attend to them during the delay period. While this assumption seems straightforward and parsimonious, it might conceivably be argued that subjects would actually attend mentally more to the reward objects when the rewards were not physically present than when they were facing them. In that unlikely event, however, one would again have to predict a difference in waiting time between the immediate reward only and delayed reward only conditions. Presumably subjects would then be fantasizing and thinking more about the absent outcome, which should lead to different waiting times in the immediate reward and delayed reward only attention conditions.

The lack of significant difference in waiting time when the subjects faced the immediate reward or the delayed one does seem understandable from the perspective of frustrative nonreward theory. When the subject attends to the immediate reward and is tempted to take it, he is frustrated by recalling the contingency that attainment of it now prevents his getting the preferred reward later. When the subject attends to the delayed reward, he is frustrated by the fact that he wants it now but cannot have it yet. When he attends to both objects, both of the above aversive frustrations occur, and hence delay tends to be most difficult—as was the case. In contrast, when the rewards are not visually present for attention, and therefore not made mentally salient, the subject can more easily avoid the frustration of blocked reward by engaging in various distraction maneuvers both overtly and in his thought processes.

Thus perhaps the most compelling interpretation of the findings may be in terms of the frustrativeness of delay of reward: the presence of the rewards serves to increase the magnitude of the frustration effect and hence decreases delay of gratification by making the waiting period more difficult. The overall findings tentatively suggest that learning to inhibit frustrative ideation, and to divert attention away from temptations by focusing, externally and internally, on competing and less frustrating stimuli, may be essential steps for mastery of delay of gratification. If that is true, then the attentional and cognitive processes through which people manage to transform aversive and frustrative conditions into bearable ones by generating their own frustration-reducing distractions become intriguing questions for future research on self-control. Such research should help us to understand more definitively the mechanisms underlying the present findings.

As Mischel and Ebbesen point out, children sometimes manage to change frustrating circumstances into bearable ones. These researchers observed children who talked to themselves, played games with their hands and feet, sang and fell asleep—all presumably to reduce the psychological unpleasantness of waiting (see Figure XII–2). Each of these activities serves to divert the child's attention from the goal object without interrupting behavior directed toward goal attainment.

In a follow-up study (Mischel, Ebbesen, and Raskoff, 1971) children who were distracted from thinking about the goal object waited longer for the preferred reward than did children who were not. Two kinds of

FIGURE XII–2

A preschool child waiting for delayed gratification. Courtesy Dr. Walter Mischel.

distracting events were explored: thinking "fun things" and thinking "sad thoughts." Children who were instructed to think "fun things" were able to wait, while instructions to think "sad thoughts" produced short delay times. Mischel (1971) describes the gist of the experiments on the mechanisms underlying the ability to delay reward as follows:

> The data from these experiments seem to contradict the notion that "will power" requires one to bear up and force oneself to maintain directed attention to things that are aversive, difficult, or boring. Rather than trying to maintain aversive activities such as delay of reward through "acts of will" and focused attention, effective self-control may hinge on "transforming" the difficult into the easy, the aversive into the pleasant, the boring into the interesting, while still maintaining the task-required (reward-contingent) activity.
>
> Such transformations may occur either by engaging in the appropriate overt distracting activity or changing one's own mental content and ideation

so that it functions as a covert distractor. A good way to master the difficult or aversive thus may be to think or do something pleasant while performing the necessary, task-relevant response (e.g., waiting, working). Rather than "willing" oneself to heroic bravery one needs to perform the necessary "difficult" response while engaging in another one cognitively. [p. 389.]

Social Example and Delay of Gratification

Delay of gratification may prevail as a norm in Western cultures, but is it a "universal"? Apparently not. As a case in point, Bandura and Walters (1963) have called attention to the customs of the Siriono, a primitive nomadic community of Bolivia. The Siriono observe few restrictions related to sex or aggression and few obligations toward old and infirm members of their community, whom they commonly abandon to die when the community moves on to a new location. Although the "Siriono personality" has been attributed to a chronic shortage of food, it is possible that the shortage in its turn may be due partly to lack of willingness or ability among the members of the culture to delay gratification. It is not uncommon among the Siriono for the returning hunter to enter his village empty-handed and to signal his wife to bring in his spoils, whereupon he and his family immediately eat as much of the game as they can. In fact, Siriono women have characteristically distended stomachs, which may be attributable to sporadic overeating. The other effect of eating all one's food immediately is, of course, that little is left for a time of shortage.

Or consider a county in Nova Scotia where conflicting subcultural patterns have endured side by side for a number of generations (cf. Bandura and Walters, 1963). In one, the Acadian community of Lavellée, children are supposed to control immediate impulses and to work toward distant goals. Educational and vocational achievement is stressed.

> In terms of time orientation, the main things in life are long-range goals—such as the salvation of the soul, the economic bettering of the area, the preservation and expansion of the Acadian group—even though some of these are unlikely to be achieved by any individual in his lifetime. . . . Work is a moral activity, and a man is enjoined not only to do it but also to take pride and pleasure in it under almost any circumstance. . . . Life without work would be life without meaning, and people who try only to get as much money as possible while doing as little as they can are disparaged. [Hughes, Tremblay, Rapoport, and Leighton, 1960, pp. 159–1960.]

In this community, parents spend large amounts of time with their children, in the course of which they undoubtedly transmit the adult patterns of their subculture with great efficiency. The children of Lavallée are unlikely to be swayed by the temptation to take an immediate small pleasure when it means forfeiting something worthwhile in the future.

In the same Nova Scotian county lives another group of people whose community is strikingly lacking in cohesion; fighting, drunkenness, theft, and other antisocial acts containing a component of impulse occur frequently. Adults in this subculture believe that "the best thing to do in life is to escape from ones problems as quickly as possible." They believe that work is to be avoided and that the law is to be defied. Parents transmit these beliefs to their children:

> The preference for drinking as the model recreational pattern sets the keynote for this sentiment. The drinking in turn often leads to fighting, another way of attempting to obliterate rather than solve problems. . . . So dominant is the drive for liquor that people are willing to spend exorbitant sums of money to get it from bootleggers after the Government liquor store is closed. They will also drink alcoholic substitutes such as vanilla if the need is not met with regular liquor. [Hughes, Tremblay, Rapoport, and Leighton, 1960, p. 307.]

Children growing up in this subculture are exposed to models exhibiting an overwhelming preference for little or no delay of gratification. But what would happen if a child from this settlement subculture were adopted by parents in Lavallée and a child from Lavallée were adopted by settlement parents? Would the behavior of either of these children, who come to their new surroundings with habits, beliefs, and attitudes learned in their original communities, be influenced by the new role models with whom they would have contact?

Bandura and Mischel (1965) provided a laboratory experiment which sheds light on this question, and in doing so they demonstrated the importance of modeling in the transmission of delay behavior. In the first part of the study, fourth- and fifth-grade children were given a delay-of-gratification test in which they were to make a series of fourteen choices between a small immediate reward and larger delayed outcome. For instance, they were asked to choose between a small candy bar which would be given to them immediately or a larger one which would require a week of waiting. Children who displayed either predominant preferences for immediate reward or predominant preferences for delayed reward were thus identified, and subsequently assigned to one of three conditions. In the *live modeling condition* children observed an actual adult model make a series of choices between a less valuable item which could be obtained immediately and a more valuable item which required delay.* The model consistently chose the immediate reward item in the presence of children who demonstrated a preference for the larger delayed reward, whereas the model observed by a child who preferred smaller immediate rewards always selected the delayed reward item; in both cases, he also briefly summarized a philosophy about the delay-of-reward behavior he was displaying. For example, when the choice was between a plastic chess set to be given immediately and a more expensive wooden set to be given in two weeks, the model commented, "Chess figures are chess figures. I can get much use out of the plastic ones right away" (p. 701).

In the *symbolic modeling condition,* children were exposed to the same kind of sequence except that the model's choices and comments were presented in written form. Finally, in the *no model present condition,* children serving as controls for the possible effects of mere exposure to rewards were shown the series of paired objects. All children were then given a delay-of-reward test in the model's absence; to assess the stability of any changes in behavior, they also were given a subsequent delay-of-reward test one month later. The findings are presented in Figure XII–3.

The clear result is that the child's tendency to take an immediate reward is flexible and may change as the result of seeing an adult model delay gratification. Conversely, the child's tendency to select larger delayed rewards also may change as a function of seeing an adult choose not to do so.

Having demonstrated that patterns of delay of gratification may be influenced by the observation of a model, it seems reasonable to argue that the behavior of our hypothetical child from the settlement culture in Nova Scotia would be influenced by observing the self-restraint in the behavior of the citizens of Lavallée and that, conversely, the behavior of our hypothetical child from Lavallée undoubtedly would be influenced toward less self-restraint through observation of role models in the settlement culture.

ACHIEVEMENT STANDARDS AND STRIVINGS

All people come to set standards for themselves. In general, the higher or more stringent the standard, the more effort must be expended to

---

* The prizes between which the adult model chose were suitable for adults (chess sets, magazines, and so forth) and were different from the items between which the children subsequently chose. Thus, each child was able to imitate the "principle" underlying the model's behavior but was unable to copy his specific choices.

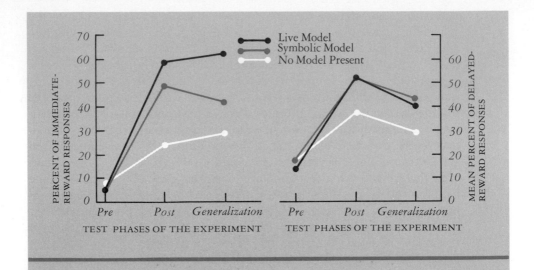

FIGURE XII-3

Mean percentage of immediate-reward choices by high-delay children (a) and delayed-reward choices of low-delay children (b) during the three phases of Bandura and Mischel's experiment. Adapted from A. Bandura and W. Mischel. Modification of self-imposed delay of reward through exposure to live and symbolic models. Journal of Personality and Social Psychology, 1965, 2, 698–705. Copyright 1965 by the American Psychological Association. Reprinted by permission.

attain it. Individuals appear to differ a great deal, though, in regard to the stringency of their self-imposed standards. Among school children, for example, some will appear pleased and delighted to receive a "B," indicating better than average mastery of academic subject matter, while others will chastise themselves for receiving the very same grade, aware that they failed to get an "A," the mark of outstanding achievement. Self-imposed standards of achievement and self-reward may be construed as reflections of underlying personality traits, such as the need to achieve; or they may be construed as responses that may be learned in their own right. Whether a child learns how high to set his own achievement standards and, if so, how this learning occurs are questions which have been studied by developmental psychologists.

Self-imposed Standards of Self-reward

One experimental situation used to study children's self-imposed standards involves three basic characteristics: (1) the child performs a task which he believes to be one of achievement or skill; (2) the child is able to administer rewards to himself so that his self-imposed criterion determines the amount and frequency of the rewards which he receives; and (3) no external socializing agent is present. A study by Liebert and Ora (1968) illustrates the manner in which children's self-imposed standards have been studied in this way, using the miniature bowling game pictured in Figure XII–4.

At the end of the three-foot runway is a panel of lights; ostensibly they indicate the score earned by rolling the ball down the alley to upset a set of pins. One of the lights—marked "5," "10," "15," or "20"—comes on after each turn. Although the apparatus is programmed to produce a fixed pattern of scores, children usually accept the game as one of skill.

Because Liebert and Ora were interested in investigating factors of training and incentive, children in their study were assigned to either the *high incentive condition,* in which each was informed that he might win one of a display of prizes ranging in price from ten cents to twelve dollars but that a large number of reward tokens would be required for the more valuable prizes, or the *low incentive condition,* in which the chance to win prizes was not mentioned. Children in the experimental groups were then given training. Those in the *modeling* condition observed an adult male bowl ten trials, rewarding himself with plastic tokens for all scores of 20 but never for lower scores. For each score of 20 he announced, "20, that's a good score. That deserves a chip"; for each score below 20 he announced, for example, "15, that's not a very good score. That doesn't deserve a chip." In the *direct training condition,* the child bowled ten trials in the training agent's presence and heard the same rules—e.g., "15, that's not a very good score. I don't think you deserve a chip for that score." Those in the *control* group received no training. Finally, each child was left alone to play the game while his behavior was surreptitiously recorded.

Children in both training groups—*modeling* and *direct*—adhered to the high achievement standard to a much greater extent than did those in the control group, but the presence of an attractive incentive tended to reduce the stringency of self-imposed standards in all cases (see Table XII–2). Thus, it appears that self-imposed standards and patterns of self-

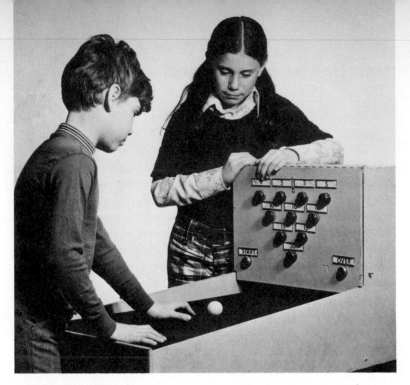

FIGURE XII-4

The bowling game used in Liebert and Ora's experiment. Photograph by Al Stopler.

reward are set in response to the specific demands of a particular situation and, potentially, are modifiable by new training and experiences.

As a further example, consider another study employing the same bowling game procedure (Liebert and Allen, 1967) which investigated the effects of combining modeling cues with the model's presentation of a rationale for his action. All children observed a model playing a bowling game in which he rewarded himself for very high scores (20) and refused to reward himself for any of the lower ones (15, 10 and 5). Half the children heard the model say: "20, that's a good score . . . that deserves a chip" or "15, that's not a very good score . . . that doesn't deserve a chip." For the other half of the subjects the model behaved in the same manner but did not offer any verbal rationale. Subsequently, all subjects were left alone to play the game. The children who heard the rule of conduct in addition to observing the model's behavior imitated the model's restraint much more when alone than did those who merely observed the model perform. Other studies subsequently have confirmed the finding that symbolic representations in the form of rules of conduct appear to

TABLE XII-2

MEAN NUMBER OF DEVIATIONS FROM THE STANDARD
PROVIDED BY THE TRAINING AGENT IN
LIEBERT AND ORA'S EXPERIMENT

SUBGROUP	CONTROL	MODELING	DIRECT TRAINING
Low incentive	7.42	0.92	0.08
High incentive	12.75	3.25	2.92

Source: Liebert and Ora, 1968.

be an effective adjunct to learning standards through observation (Liebert, Hanratty, and Hill, 1969).

In life situations, children are exposed to many models, including mother, father, teachers, and playmates, and thus may observe discrepant standards of achievement. What role might such discrepancies play in determining the child's self-imposed standards? In one study (McMains and Liebert, 1968), fourth-grade boys and girls played the bowling game mentioned previously with an adult. During the training period, the adult always imposed a stringent criterion on the child. Half of the subjects were in a *consistent training* condition in which the training agent modeled the same stringent self-reward criterion which he imposed on the child; the remaining subjects, however, were in a *discrepant training* condition in which the training agent's self-reward criterion was more lenient than the criterion he imposed on the children. Subsequently, each child was left alone to play the game; their adherence to the stringent standard initially taught them was measured (Test 1.) During the second phase of the experiment, the children looked on as a second adult played the game. The second agent exhibited either the same stringent standard that the children had been taught originally or modeled the more lenient one. Immediately thereafter a second measure of each child's own self-imposed standard was taken (Test 2).

TABLE XII-3

MEAN SELF-LENIENCY SCORES FOR
ALL SUBJECTS DURING TEST 1 IN MCMAINS
AND LIEBERT'S EXPERIMENT

CRITERION IMPOSED BY 1ST AGENT	CRITERION MODELED BY 1ST AGENT	MEAN SELF-LENIENCY SCORE
Stringent (20 only)	Stringent (20 only)	1.83 (Boys) 0.25 (Girls)
Stringent (20 only)	Lenient (20 and 15)	4.91 (Boys) 4.04 (Girls)

Source: McMains and Liebert, 1968.

The mean self-leniency scores (i.e., the average number of times subjects rewarded themselves for scores below the stringent standard) on Test 1 appear in Table XII-3; when children were taught a standard of achievement which the adult upheld himself, they imposed that standard upon themselves much more readily than when taught a standard which was not adopted by the training agent.

The data from Test 2 appear in Figure XII-5. Even though all children were taught to use the stringent standard, those who saw two adults adopt a more lenient one almost invariably ignored the rule themselves when alone. In marked contrast, children who saw two adult models behave according to the original stringent standard adopted it themselves quite readily; in fact, *all* of the girls—and most of the boys—did so. In sum, this study indicates that the achievement standards set by a child for himself are strongly influenced by the kind of behavior he observes around him; even clearly stated parental aspirations may be ignored if they are not reinforced by appropriate adult example.

Is Self-reward Reinforcing? In the studies described above, children administered rewards to themselves, contingent on their own performance. Recently investigators have begun to ask whether such self-administered conse-

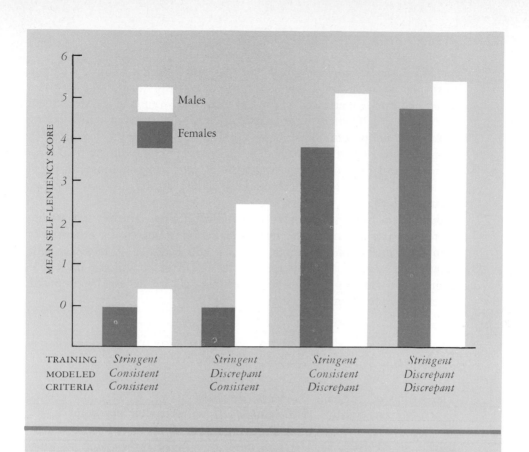

FIGURE XII–5

Mean self-reward leniency scores as a function of consistent (stringent) or discrepant (lenient) multiple modeling in McMains and Liebert's experiment. Adapted from M. J. McMains and R. M. Liebert. The influence of discrepancies between successively modeled self-reward criteria on the adoption of a self-imposed standard. Journal of Personality and Social Psychology, *1968, 8, 166–171. Copyright 1968 by the American Psychological Association. Reprinted by permission.*

quences can maintain children's behavior just as externally imposed rewards do. The answer appears to be "yes." In one study (Bandura and Perloff, 1967), for example, seven- to ten-year-old boys and girls were asked to set their own standards on a specially devised crank-turning task and to reward themselves whenever their self-imposed standards had been met. Children in another group had the same standards imposed upon them and were rewarded by an adult for meeting them; that is, these latter children experienced the usual externally imposed reinforcement procedure. Finally there were control groups who received either no reward or a lump sum "inheritance" at the outset. Results, measured in terms of actual effortful behavior, were striking: those who set their own standards and rewarded themselves were as productive as those rewarded by an adult; both groups substantially outperformed the controls (see Figure XII–6).

Subsequent studies also have shown that highly valuable self-administered rewards are more effective in maintaining one's own productivity than less valuable ones (Liebert, Spiegler, and Hall, 1970) and that self-determined reward standards are as effective in maintaining a more academic task—solving arithmetic problems—as are externally imposed criteria (Felixbrod and O'Leary, 1973).

The Achieving Child

The setting of personal standards, discussed above, is integrally related to achievement striving. Achievement-oriented behavior may occur in the arts, academics, sports, or any endeavor where level of performance competence is involved. Competence, however, can be shown only in situations in which there is a "standard of excellence" which may be applied to the performance and which is agreed upon by those concerned. For purposes of the following discussion, then, achievement behavior will be defined as any action directed at gaining approval or avoiding disapproval from oneself or from others, for competence in performance where public standards of excellence are applicable (Crandall, Katkovsky, and Preston, 1960a).

Even when they are still in nursery school, children differ in the extent of their achievement striving. While some show great persistence with tasks requiring skill and effort at this age, others do not; similarly, while some children tend to seek recognition for achievement, others seem to care little for such reward. The emergence of substantial differences in achievement striving among children of five years of age and older has been observed in a number of studies (Crandall, Preston, and Rabson, 1960; Tyler, Rafferty, and Tyler, 1962; McClelland, 1958). These studies indicate that even very young children can and do develop a personal response to achievement situations which differs from those of other children.

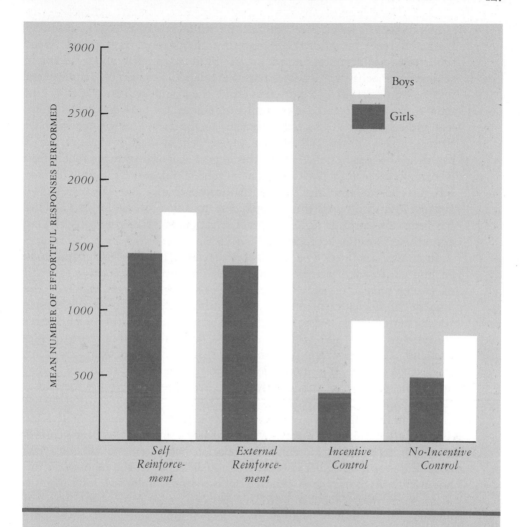

FIGURE XII-6

Number of effortful responses in all groups of Bandura and Perloff's experiment. Adapted from A. Bandura and B. Perloff, Relative efficacy of self-monitored and externally imposed reinforcement systems. Journal of Personality and Social Psychology, 1967, 7, 111–116. Copyright 1967 by the American Psychological Association. By permission.

Some theorists have conceptualized this difference as reflecting an under-lying difference in children's achievement motivation (also called "need achievement"), a concept used in an effort to predict and/or explain achievement behavior. In assessing the relative amount of achievement motivation possessed by a particular child, the examiner listens as the child tells a story about each of several ambiguous pictures set before him. The child's replies are scored according to the frequency of achievement themes in his stories; the method, developed by David McClelland, is based on the assumption that, to the degree that achievement motivation is part of the child's personality, achievement imagery will find its way into his storytelling (McClelland, Atkinson, Clark, and Lowell, 1953). Because the scoring system is applicable to any prose style, McClelland has been able to study achievement motivation in groups who lived long ago but left written accounts of their lives.

In a work entitled *The Achieving Society* (1961), McClelland took an unusual research tact; he attempted to "predict" the economic growth of twenty-three countries between 1929 and 1950 on the basis of the amount of achievement imagery appearing in their children's stories for the period 1920–1929. The achievement motive found in the children's stories correlated $+ .53$ with an index of national economic growth. Mc-Clelland concludes from this and other similar studies that children's stories reflect ". . . the motivational level of the adults at the time they are published, perhaps particularly of the adults responsible for the educa-tion of children . . ." (p. 102).

Despite this impressive economic analysis, high achievement motivation as currently measured is not always a necessary companion of high achieve-ment. Of nine studies in which the relation between these variables was observed, five indicated that children high in achievement motivation did not necessarily out-achieve children whose scores indicated low achieve-ment motivation (Crandall, 1967). It also has been found that it is not unusual for a child to spend a great deal of time and effort developing competence in one area, say physical skills, while expending a great deal less time and energy with other kinds of activities, such as artistic or intellectual pursuits (Crandall, 1961).

Parental Child-Rearing Practices and Achievement Striving

Among the questions asked by parents and educators, almost none is more frequently heard than, "What factors in child-rearing encourage and dis-courage achievement striving in youngsters?" A complex answer is suggested by a number of different correlational studies. Many parental attitudes and child-rearing practices, including independence training (Winterbottom, 1953; Feld, 1959), reward of achievement efforts (Crandall, Preston, and Rabson, 1960), and encouragement and instigation of intellectual pursuits (Crandall, Katkovsky, and Preston, 1960b), are associated with achievement striving.

Winterbottom (1953), in what is now considered a classic study, gave eight-to-ten-year-old boys the rudiments of a story (e.g., "Brothers and sisters are playing. One is a little ahead.") and asked them to elaborate on it. The frequency of achievement themes in the boys' stories was then related to the child-rearing practices to which they had been exposed, as reported by their mothers. Winterbottom's principal finding was that mothers of high achievement-oriented boys differed from other mothers in (1) fostering early independence of thought and action—e.g., encouraging the child to try things for himself, and (2) generously rewarding successful performance with affection and attention.

In a later study (Rosen and D'Andrade, 1959), a team of investigators went into private homes to observe youngsters who were either high or low in achievement motivation. Each boy was given a demanding and potentially frustrating task: to build a tower out of irregularly shaped blocks with one hand—while blindfolded. The boys' parents were asked to watch, and were permitted to give any sort of rewards they wished so long as they did not touch the blocks or provide direct assistance. Confirming Winterbottom's report, mothers of high-achieving boys were warmer and more encouraging than other mothers. The fathers of low-achieving boys also differed from others in a noticeable way: they tried to make their sons' decisions for them and became quite irritated whenever the boys had any difficulty.

The Role of Expectancies

In contrast to achievement needs, expectations of success are treated as specific to a particular kind of endeavor,—for example, sports, mathematics, or art. But the actual role of expectancies in achievement-related behavior is a question for research. Virginia Crandall and her colleagues at Fels Research Institute have made unique contributions in this area.

One important disclosure is that the degree to which a child *expects* to succeed has a major bearing on whether he actually does or not. In an Ohio junior high school, for example, it was found that students who expected to obtain good grades in mathematics and English actually got the better grades in these courses. In part, we might explain these findings by saying that the more able youngsters simply (and realistically) have higher expectancy. However, when IQ and expectancy diverged (for example, when a student with a low IQ had high expectancies or vice versa), expectation of success rather than IQ was associated with the obtained grade. In other words, to at least some degree, children who expect to succeed actually do better (Crandall, 1967). They will spend more time and effort in studying than the child who expects to fail, for whom such an investment often seems futile.

In light of the importance of expectations, it will be disquieting to many that girls' expectancy estimates are consistently lower than boys'. In a laboratory study performed at Fels Research Institute, for example, elementary school boys and girls were given six kinds of school-like tasks and each child was asked to estimate how far he or she could go before the task became too difficult. Girls tended to expect to be beaten by the task at much lower levels of difficulty than boys, despite the fact that they actually had *higher* IQs on the average (mean IQ for females 114, mean IQ for males 107).

Although girls often tend to estimate their own intellectual and academic capabilities lower than what an objective observer might expect on the basis of past performance, boys tend to behave in exactly the opposite fashion, estimating their level of competence higher than what past performance would indicate. Why should this be the case? The question has not yet been answered. It is possible that girls get less positive reward for achievement than boys, although this is probably not the sole reason for the difference. Crandall and her associates suggest that life experiences can be contradictory in the sense that situations often simultaneously provide reasons to feel competent and reasons to feel incompetent. Thus boys, they suggest, may focus on positive feedback whereas girls may be unduly sensitive to reproof and thus tend to construct biased pictures of their own capabilities (Crandall, unpublished).

Internal versus External Control

Another attitude which appears to be conducive to achievement striving is the general feeling that one has some control over the situations one encounters. Children differ in the extent to which they believe that their actions can influence the outcome of events. Some tend to assume that they are responsible for their successes and failures, others tend to attribute responsibility to outside agents, luck, fate, and other people. The extent to which children believe that the locus of responsibility for achievement is internal rather than external can be measured by the "Intellectual Achievement Responsibility Questionnaire," a thirty-four-item scale which measures responsibility for both pleasant and unpleasant consequences. (The reader may recall we mentioned this scale in Chapter II.) Each item consists of a description of an achievement-related experience which might have occurred in the child's life, followed by one alternative stating that the event occurred because of the child's own actions and another stating that the event was caused by other forces. Exemplary items from the IAR Scale are presented in Table XII–4.

TABLE XII–4

SAMPLE ITEMS FROM THE INTELLECTUAL ACHIEVEMENT
RESPONSIBILITY QUESTIONNAIRE (IAR) USED
BY CRANDALL AND HER ASSOCIATES

1. *If a teacher passes you to the next grade, would it probably be*

    _____ a. because she liked you, or

I+ _____ b. because of the work you did?

2. *When you do well on a test at school, is it more likely to be*

I+ _____ a. because you studied for it, or

    _____ b. because the test was especially easy?

3. *When you read a story and can't remember much of it, is it usually*

    _____ a. because the story wasn't well written, or

I– _____ b. because you weren't interested in the story?

4. *Suppose your parents say you are doing well in school. Is this likely to happen*

I+ _____ a. because your school work is good, or

    _____ b. because they are in a good mood?

Source: Courtesy Virginia Crandall.

In answering the questionnaire, the child is asked to pick the answer for each item "that best describes what happens to you or how you feel." It is not surprising to find that children who score high as "internalizers" on this scale tend to get better grades and do better on achievement tests than do those who score high as "externalizers" (Crandall, Katkovsky, and Crandall, 1965). Internalizers may well show greater initiative and persistence in solving difficult problems and a ready willingness to modify their behavior to achieve the desired goal, whereas externalizers may see little reason to initiate, persist, or modify their behavior inasmuch as they feel the outcome is not under their control. In some situations the IAR scale is a better predictor of achievement than are measures of achievement motivation (Crandall, Katkovsky, and Preston, 1962).

The generalized tendency to attribute control of rewards to internal or external sources was examined in eighty school children, black and white of both middle- and lower-class backgrounds (Battle and Rotter, 1963). The children were required to answer a twenty-three-item yes-or-no questionnaire and a six-item cartoon test. The results indicated that middle-class children, in general, were much more internal in their attributions than were lower-class children. Moreover, middle-class white children were most internal, whereas lower-class black children were most external. Middle-class blacks, however, held roughly the same attitudes in regard to locus of control as did middle-class whites. These results suggest that children who reasonably might perceive that opportunities are open to them—the middle-class children, whether black or white—come more easily to believe in internal control. Children who see that they have no chance to obtain material rewards may tend to defend themselves with "external" attributions of causality. Consistent with this reasoning, a report published by the U.S. Office of Education (Coleman, Campbell, Hobson, McPartland, Mood, Weinfeld, and York, 1966) showed that school achievement among children of minority groups is predicted better by belief in internal or external control of reinforcement than by any of a vast array of attitudinal, familial, and school-related variables.

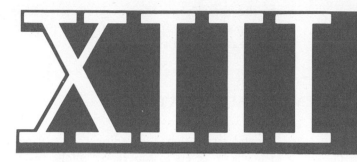

THE
INTELLECTUALLY
EXCEPTIONAL

IN CHAPTER VIII we discussed the concept of intelligence and traced the usual course and development of intellectual abilities. We also noted, in passing, that both children and adults differ reliably in their intellectual ability. Usually these differences are relatively minor, falling within a normal range of competence that creates no special problems or needs. Sometimes, though, a child differs from others so much intellectually that he is considered truly exceptional. This chapter is devoted to such intellectual exceptionality, its definition, causes, and the special demands which it may place on the individual and the society in which he lives.

Often the term "intellectually exceptional" is used as a synonym for mental retardation. We shall discuss retardation, but it is not the only type of intellectual exceptionality. The very bright and able and the very creative are also exceptions whom we are interested in identifying and who may have special needs, characteristics, or problems. They, too, will be considered as our discussion proceeds.

MENTAL RETARDATION

"Mental retardation," according to the American Association on Mental Deficiency, "refers to subaverage intellectual functioning which originates during the developmental period and is associated with impairment in adaptive behavior" (Heber, 1961, p. 3).

Note the implications of such a definition: It does not indicate any particular treatment or etiology and the inclusion of social adaptation standards takes into account the cultural setting; that is, an individual capable of adaptive behavior in a rural setting might experience much greater difficulties in the maze known as New York City. In practice, though, there is still substantial reliance on IQ scores for identifying and classifying the retarded, largely because easily administered, reliable indices of social adaptation are lacking.

Historically, terms to designate intellectually inferior individuals have fluctuated considerably. Those accepted at one time or another include "feebleminded," "moron," "imbecile," and "idiot;" even now, the phrase "mentally retarded" is being replaced by "slow learner." These changes do more than reflect linguistic fashion; they serve the beneficial purpose of helping to overcome prejudices and stereotypes that accumulate over time. It has been shown, for example, that children labeled as slow learners are judged more favorably than those termed mentally retarded (Hollinger and Jones, 1970).

Prevalence of Mental Retardation

It is often estimated that six million Americans, or 3 percent of the total population, are classified as retarded (Scheerenberger, 1964; Robinson and Robinson, 1970), but the present AAMD definition has been interpreted to include a much larger figure. Such a discrepancy is not new; Windle (1958) noted that from 1894 to the time of his article, estimates of the prevalence of mental retardation ranged from .05 percent to 13 percent. Because judgments invariably are affected by the demands of the surrounding environment, it is impossible to declare any one figure to be more correct than another. Ultimately, it might be most appropriate to limit judgments of retardation to particular settings (e.g., "His conduct is too retarded for him to function effectively in a fourth-grade classroom"). Preschool children rarely are termed retarded; the same is true for adults who are out of school and who manage to avoid encounters with police and other societal agents. However, the abstract conceptual and verbal proficiency required of school-age children often results in a large percentage of those who are at all slow being termed retarded while they are attending school (see Figure XIII–1).

Characteristics of the Retarded

As a group, mentally retarded children are slow to walk, talk, and feed themselves. They also take unusually long periods of time before they are toilet-trained. In the more severe cases, retardation extends to almost all areas of anatomical, motor, and verbal development. However, because intellectually normal children also may display one or more of these indicators, it usually is not assumed that a young child is retarded unless an extensive pattern of deficits is present.

Three or four levels of retardation typically are distinguished for descriptive purposes, with the labels varying according to time and setting (see Table XIII–1). Individuals scoring between 70 and 84 on IQ tests are termed borderline; they usually fall into lower socioeconomic ranges, rarely complete high school, usually support themselves, and are able to maintain family relationships and a family life. Unless social adaptation is incomplete, it is questionable whether they should be distinguished at all. Most other retarded individuals have IQs in the range from 50 to 69; classified as mildly or educably mentally retarded, they are rarely institutionalized and their retardation is often diagnosed as stemming from environmental causes (Stein and Susser, 1963). The educable mentally retarded usually can acquire academic skills equal to those mastered by elementary school children, but they reach this level of achievement at a later chronological age.

There are many jobs which the mildly retarded are quite capable of filling; they have become welders, miners, painters, tailors, and the like. It has been found that their out-of-school success usually depends more on social skills than on occupational ones (Telford and Sawrey, 1972). Thus, parents of these children must avoid the temptation to foster dependency, sloppiness, and other socially undesirable characteristics, "excusing" them because of intellectual deficit.

> Many jobs are sufficiently simple so that they can be rather readily mastered. If the individual has learned the value of promptness, good manners, good appearance, and dependability, he can function in a large number of jobs

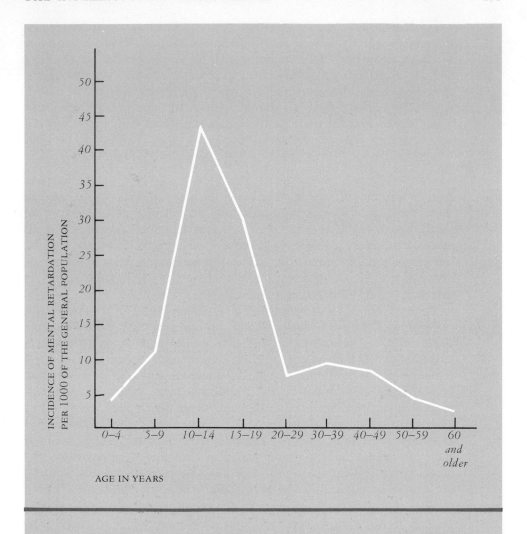

FIGURE XIII—1

Relative frequency of being labeled mentally retarded as a function of age. Note that school-age children are particularly likely to be termed retarded. Adapted and reprinted with permission from N. O'Conner and J. Tizard, The Social Problems of Mental Deficiency, *copyright 1956, Pergamon Press Ltd.*

TABLE XIII—1

TERMINOLOGY USED TO DESCRIBE
THE MENTALLY RETARDED

IQ range *	70–84	50–69	25–49	Below 25
Early labeling in the U.S.	—	moron	imbecile	idiot
AAMD and World Health Organization	border-line	mild	moderate	severe and profound
Current educational labelling (U. S.)	—	educable	trainable	custodial

* The particular IQ ranges employed for any label may vary slightly from those shown.

without too much difficulty. The social training necessary for the development of such characteristics should start early and be intensive enough so that he develops patterns of social response that will become assets rather than liabilities as he matures. Frequently the mentally retarded learn at home precisely the social behavior which will add to the burden of being mentally retarded rather than assist . . . in social adaptation. The simple social characteristics of honesty, obedience, and kindness, which are accepted as part of socialization, are often lacking in the mentally retarded *simply because they have not received the systematic training by which these are acquired.* [Telford and Sawrey, 1972, p. 245; italics added.]

In contrast to the mildly or educably retarded, the moderately or trainably retarded, with IQs ranging from 25 to 49, usually are unable to hold jobs except within sheltered workshops; they rarely marry and usually are institutionalized.

The severely and profoundly retarded—with IQs below 25—complete the categorization. Among these individuals, interpersonal communication is minimal or lacking entirely and institutionalization is virtually inevitable.

Etiology

Genetic Causes. As discussed in Chapter IV, a number of genetic abnormalities can reduce intellectual performance. A high percentage of the more severely retarded are affected by syndromes such as Down's, phenylketonuria, and Huntington's chorea.

Prenatal Causes. The developing embryo can become damaged while still in the uterine environment. Inadequate prenatal nutrition, for example, can be a cause of retardation. Kalter and Warkany (1959) demonstrated with rats that depriving females of riboflavin (vitamin B_2) resulted in significant numbers of malformed and retarded offspring. A study with humans also has provided evidence that giving vitamin supplements to women on nutritionally deficient diets during pregnancy can raise their children's IQ, measured at three years of age, by an average of four points over the offspring of women on comparable diets without the supplements. No comparable increases were observed among children of mothers judged to be eating acceptable foods (Harrell, Woodward, and Gates, 1956). While a four-point average increment might seem unimportant, it should be remembered that any individual may have been affected more (or less) than the mean, and that diets even more deficient than the ones observed might produce more striking effects.

Family Factors. In Western culture the family is a primary influence on the child's development; it is not surprising, therefore, to discover that distinct familial patterns frequently accompany retardation. The President's Task Force on Manpower Conservation (1964) found that the families of draftees rejected for intellectual deficits were characterized by poverty and poor education. Benda, Squires, Ogonik, and Wise (1963) indicated that among 205 retardates with IQs greater than 50, the majority had another retardate in the immediate family and three-quarters of the families either were separated or were not able to provide even bare necessities. Other family factors related to retardation include low achievement motivation of the parents, father's absence, lack of appropriate sex-role models, impoverished financial status, and low emphasis on education (Chilman, 1965; Robinson, 1967; Robinson and Robinson, 1970).

Social and Emotional Factors in Mental Retardation

If mental retardation is thought of as simply an intellectual disadvantage, then little attention is given to the way in which it may be intertwined with social and emotional factors. Yet it is clear that these other factors are important, as evidenced by a good deal of recent research.

Home Environment. It appears that institutionalization of retarded children results as often as not from poor home environment rather than from the lack of intelligence per se (Zigler, 1968). There is, for example, a positive relationship between the IQ scores of institutional retardates and the amount of preinstitutional deprivation which they had experienced; the relatively brighter retardate appears to be institutionalized increasingly as a function of an inadequate home environment.

It has been noted that children become increasingly autonomous from social control as they develop. Telling a seven-year-old that he has done well on a boring task may motivate him to continue, but the same praise will be ineffective with a fifteen-year-old. Given this fact, it has been hypothesized that retarded children have more frequently been neglected by adults in their early lives and therefore crave attention and praise to a greater degree than their mental age alone would predict.

To test this formulation, Zigler and Balla (1972) compared the influence of social praise on the behavior of normal and retarded children of mental ages seven, nine, and twelve, predicting that younger and retarded children, if given praise, would continue to perform a boring task for a longer time than older and normal individuals. The results confirmed their expectation; younger children performed the boring task longer than older ones and retarded children persisted more than normals. Especially striking was the finding that even the oldest retardates performed the boring task for a greater period of time than the youngest normal children (see Figure XIII–2).

Responsiveness to Incentives. Another argument advanced by Zigler and his associates is that retarded children may be motivated by different incentives than typical middle-class children. Zigler recapped an earlier investigation (Zigler and de Labry, 1962) this way:

> These investigators tested middle-class, lower-class, and retarded children *equated on MA* on a concept-switching task . . . under two conditions of reinforcement. In the first condition . . . the only reinforcement dispensed

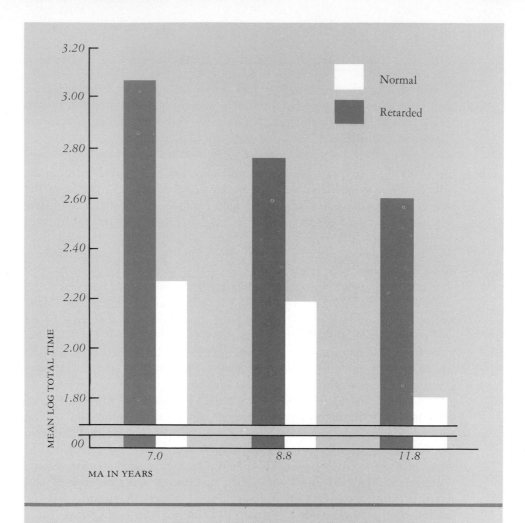

FIGURE XIII–2

Amount of time that retarded and normal children of different mental ages spent at a boring task when praised. Adapted from E. Zigler and D. Balla, Developmental cause of responsiveness to social reinforcement in normal children and institutionalized retarded children. Developmental Psychology, *1972, 6, 66–73. Copyright 1972 by the American Psychological Association. Reprinted by permission.*

was the information that the child was correct. In the second condition, the child was rewarded with a toy of his choice if he switched from one concept to another. In the "correct" condition these investigators found . . . that retardates were poorer in the concept-switching than were middle-class children. . . . [But] in the toy condition this inferiority disappeared, and retarded and lower-class children performed as well as the middle-class children. This study highlights an assumption that has been noted as erroneous by many educators; namely, that the lower-class child and the retarded child are motivated by the same incentives that motivate the typical middle-class child. [Zigler, 1968, p. 590.]

Expectancies and Self-concepts. Because retarded children almost certainly experience many frustrating and unsuccessful interactions with their environment, they may develop poor self concepts. Similarly, retardates may be more likely to "settle for" poor performance than are normal children of the same mental age (Stevenson and Zigler, 1958). The usual interpretation of this phenomenon is that retardates have a long history of failure and thus come to expect it. Indeed, Cromwell (1963) has argued that retardates are more motivated to avoid failure than to achieve success.

Social Skills and Intellectual Functioning

A question that frequently arises regarding intellectual retardation is the degree to which it constrains the development of appropriate social skills. There is a clear correlation between mental age and a variety of indices of social confidence; that is, the more retarded an individual, the poorer his social skills tend to be (Copobianco and Cole, 1960; Goulet and Barclay, 1963). It has been argued, though, that the relationship may be an artifact rather than a direct result of mental retardation. Perhaps, for example, it is not mental retardation itself, but the failure to train retarded children in more advanced social skills that gives rise to the correlation (Gunzburg, 1965).

Recently Severy and Davis (1971) have provided evidence which supports this view. They studied helping behavior of normal and retarded children under conditions in which the retarded children were "in a milieux containing models of and rewards for helping behavior" (p. 1019). There was no evidence of a deficit in helping behavior among retarded children in this situation; in fact, the older retardates actually attempted to give help more often—and succeeded in helping as often—as any of the groups of intellectually normal children.

Education of the Retarded

In the past there was considerable controversy as to whether society had a responsibility to educate its intellectually less able members, but it is now widely agreed that special education or enriched educational opportunities should be provided for the mentally retarded. Increasingly, significant sums of money are being spent in order to accomplish this end as effectively as possible.

There are four broad possibilities for education of the retarded: placement in regular public school classrooms, with some sort of special tutoring or other programs; placement in special classes within regular neighborhood schools; placement in community schools specially designated for the retarded; and placement in residential schools and residential custodial facilities. Selection for any given child will be based jointly on his intellectual ability and on the educational philosophy of the particular school district in which he resides.

Schooling for the Educable Mentally Retarded: Are Special Classes Desirable? There has long been a question as to whether children of borderline intellectual ability should be assigned to a regular classroom or be given some sort of special training. When they are assigned to regular classes, the typical procedure is to offer "social promotions" to assure that they keep up with their age peers. The reasoning behind such placement procedures is based on the premise that these children will develop greater social normalcy if they are not subject to any sort of intellectual discrimination in class assignment, and that they will be stimulated by and learn from intellectually normal peers with whom they associate. It is also argued that the negative reactions of the retarded youngster to the stigma often associated with special education should be avoided.

The problem is captured eloquently in remarks by one child who was extremely distressed after testing relegated him to a special classroom for "slow learners":

> It really don't have to be the tests, but after the tests, there shouldn't be no separation for the classes. Because, as I say again, I felt good when I was with my class, but then they went and separated us—that changed us. That changed our ideas, our thinking, the way we thought about each other and turned us to enemies toward each other—because they said I was dumb and they were smart. [Hurley, 1969, p. 48.]

But there are also disadvantages to grouping the mildly retarded with nonretarded children in regular classes. The mildly retarded can, of course, progress academically, but at a much slower rate than their peers. The discrepancy between their performance and that of others grows through junior and senior high school. Perhaps as a result of this difficulty, mildly retarded children often are isolated and rejected by normal children when they are grouped in the same class (Baldwin, 1958; Thurstone, 1959).

What, then, is the status of the controversy today? Robinson and Robinson (1965) have summarized it as follows:

> The consensus of special educators today definitely favors special class placement for the mildly retarded. This is true at least when sufficient facilities are available to make possible the homogeneous grouping of children by age and ability. [1965, p. 466.]

The Typical Class for the Educable Mentally Retarded. We saw in Table XIV–1 that the mildly retarded, with IQs between 50 and 69, also are termed educable mentally retarded (EMR). The EMR child rarely can benefit from an educational program that stresses academic accomplishments or preparation for higher education; appropriate education includes, instead, an emphasis on the development of social competence and an effort to transmit useful occupational skills (see Figure XIII–3). Reading and arithmetic, now minimal tools for getting along in our society, are also taught. As Robinson and Robinson note, "Even such a simple act as going to the movies is much more feasible and pleasant if one can learn from the newspaper the time at which the feature begins, take along enough money for ticket and popcorn, and recognize the President of the United States when he appears on the newsreel" (1965, p. 471).

Effectiveness. How effective are these special classes? The results of several studies indicate that they might not be as effective as would be hoped. Bauer (1967) studied numerous curricula that were employed in special classes and concluded that they were not programmed directly to the strengths and weaknesses of individual children, but rather were inferior copies of what was taught in normal classes. He also observed that one almost universal feature was an endless repetition, virtually guaranteed to bore children of any developmental level. Another problem with most programs designed for the retarded is that they are disconnected from the child's everyday life. Finley (1962), for example, found that retardates were better at manipulating arithmetic symbols than normals of the same mental age, but that the latter were far better in ability to solve concrete problems. Because most

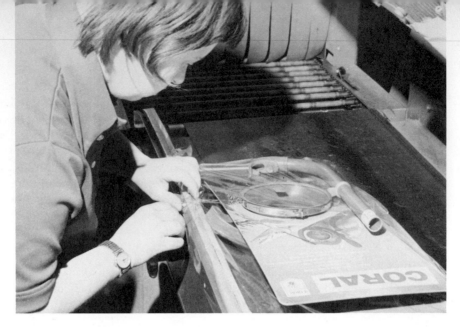

An important aspect of teaching the educable mentally retarded involves development of useful occupational skills. Courtesy Robert Sansone, Association for the Help of Retarded Children, Inc.

mentally deficient individuals need to solve practical arithmetic problems rather than theoretical ones, the classroom emphasis on manipulations of symbols appears unwise. Another study (Goldstein, Moss, and Jordan, 1965) compared the academic accomplishments of retarded children placed in regular and special classes over a four-year period and found that no substantial differences were present either in IQ test performance or in general knowledge.

Education of the Trainable Mentally Retarded. "Trainable mentally retarded" (TMR), it will be recalled, is a term usually applied to children with IQs between 25 and 49. It is important to note, though, that this is a rather wide range. At the upper end special classes, schools, or residential institutions often have succeeded in teaching these youngsters a variety of self-care skills; they may learn cooking, grooming, table-setting, and the ability to dress and feed themselves. Often, too, they are able to acquire a reasonable minimal vocabulary and sufficient skills to have some communication with others. Occupationally, they often can function in so-called "sheltered workshops," in which simple tasks are performed under the careful supervisory guidance of skillful educators and professionals.

At the lower end of this IQ range, however, the story is often discouraging. Youngsters with IQs below about 35 often have been—and frequently still are—regarded simply as custodial cases and there has been little attempt to educate them. Only quite recently have various instrumental learning procedures (e.g., reinforcement, shaping; see Chapter V) been employed with TMR children with some success.

A particularly good example of this work is that of Bijou, Birnbrauer, Kidder, and Tague (1966), who taught arithmetic, reading, and writing skills to a group of severely retarded children, including some diagnosed as brain damaged or with Down's Syndrome. Their program had three goals: (1) to institute an effective motivational system for each child; (2) to develop programmed instructional materials that would result in more cooperation and industry; (3) to program materials that would teach specific useful skills such as telling time, handling money, and reading. The first goal was accomplished by providing tokens for correct answers, cooperation, and other desired behavior. The tokens later could be traded for money, trinkets, or candy and also could be saved for more substantial benefits, such as trips.

A wide variety of prerequisite behaviors, such as sitting quietly and paying attention, was necessary before these retarded children were able to study effectively. Incompatible behaviors such as yelling and fighting had to be eliminated. The research group emphasized the importance of self-directed studying in meeting these goals, reasoning that if students could study for long periods of time—while receiving attention, praise, and tokens for their efforts—they would be less likely to be disruptive. At first the retarded children were rewarded for relatively short periods of self-directed study; gradually they were required to work for longer periods before praise and tokens were dispensed.

Recognizing that their system would not always be effective, Bijou and his associates set off a small closetlike room as a "time-out" device. When children were persistently disruptive they were removed from the classroom and placed by themselves in the time-out room for ten minutes; they were not allowed to return until they had been quiet for thirty seconds after that. The success both of this procedure and of the positive incentives that were offered is shown by the fact that the time out room was very rarely used.*

The writing program best reflects the investigators' general approach in using shaping procedures (described in detail in Chapter V). At first the

---

* The term "time-out," among those working with children's behavior problems, is an abbreviation for *time out from positive reinforcement* and refers to the fact that no one can enjoy any of the benefits of the classroom or ward while in isolation.

program capitalized on a pretraining skill—in this case, tracing letters. Later, students were presented parts of letters and required to fill in the rest. In the final step in this stage they first had to print each letter with only minimal cues, and then whole words. Next, children were requested to copy letters from a blackboard.

In summarizing their study, the investigators enthusiastically commented: "The results of this study suggest that the academic future of the majority of retarded children is much brighter than had been forecast by the theorists who assume that abilities, capacities, and traits are largely fixed" (Bijou *et al.*, 1966, p. 505).

Overworked nonprofessional employees often are the only people working with more severely retarded youngsters; it is understandable that this frequently has resulted in a situation in which the children receive little more than custodial care. But attempts are being made to train nonprofessional employees as effective teachers of the severely retarded. Such an approach, for example, was the basis of a program created to teach language to children with IQs of 35 and under (Phillips, Liebert, and Poulos, 1973). Women with high school educations were employed as aides and supplied with a "language training packet" which included (1) a simplified introduction to the use of modeling and reward as teaching techniques, (2) highly specific and detailed lesson plans, and (3) a variety of materials necessary for teaching simple language in an interesting way such as special color slides of various foods, types of clothing, and the like, and a flannel-board clown on which clothing items could be placed.

The aides worked with a trained psychologist for a week, after which they conducted classes of approximately seven children each for about two months. They first taught students to identify objects or their slide representations and then to verbalize the appropriate label. (A typical class lesson is shown in Table XIII–2.)

Employing the usual experimental approach, before and after performances of these retarded youngsters were compared with those of other children from the same wards who had been matched on the basis of IQ, sex, age, race, and behavior problems, but had not received any special training. The results were encouraging. Significant improvements in language skills were found for the trained group, with little or no corresponding changes for the untrained group. In fact, among the former, many youngsters who were previously mute or who had communicated only in grunts said their first words. At the same time these youngsters showed improvement in social behavior; behavior problems diminished or stopped, the children began actively participating in and enjoying their classes, and they began to interact more effectively with each other. It appears clear,

T A B L E X I I I – 2

A SAMPLE LESSON FROM THE PROGRAM USED
BY PHILLIPS, LIEBERT, AND POULOS (1973)

LESSON 18: COAT VERBALIZATION

Materials Needed:
Coat, slides, a variety of small candies for rewards.

Live Demonstration: COAT

1. Hold up the plate of candy in front of the class and explain how they can earn a piece. Put on the coat and say, "This is a coat." Ask the class to say "coat" several times in unison while you pass the coat around the classroom. Remind students of the characteristics that will help them to identify coat.

2. Next show the coat to each student individually and ask him to name the item. If no response, tell him the answer and ask him to repeat it after you. Students with no verbal response should be rewarded for any effort to repeat the word, such as "co." Then encourage them to say the entire word for more rewards. Make it necessary for them to improve the response each time in order to earn the reward.

3. For those students who are not verbalizing, break the word into separate parts. Start with the "k" sound; then try the "kö" and the "t" sounds. Show them how the mouth must be shaped to make each sound. Have students put their hands in front of their mouths and practice the "t' sound until they can feel the puff of air. Reward with praise and candy for improvement.

4. Flannel Clown: Hold up the clown's coat and ask, "What is this?" If anyone responds "coat" say, "Right! This is the clown's coat. Would you like to put it on the clown." If no one responds correctly, tell the class the answer and ask if someone would like to put the coat on the clown. Ask the student to say "coat" before putting it on the clown. Then hold up the other coat and repeat the above. Leave the coat on for the next day's lesson.

TABLE XIII-2 *(continued)*

Slide Demonstration: COAT

1. Introduce the slides by saying that now you are going to show the class some pictures of coats. Project the first slide and ask a good student, "What is this?" Reward a correct response with praise and a piece of candy. Ask the class to say coat in unison. If the student is incorrect or does not respond, tell the class the answer and have them repeat it after you.

2. Alternate the coat slides repeating the above until each student has had a turn.

3. Help students continuously with pronunciation, particularly emphasizing the "t" sound of coat and correcting other errors.

then, that progress can be made with youngsters of this level of intellectual ability if sufficient care is taken to develop programs which are specially suited to their needs and potentialities.

THE INTELLECTUALLY GIFTED

Interest in the gifted child in the twentieth century has gone through three distinct periods (Barbe and Frierson, 1965). First there was an emphasis, spearheaded mainly by Lewis M. Terman, on identifying and describing the gifted. Then a period ensued which largely consisted of the laying of groundwork by interested groups for special education for the gifted. Finally, the launching of Sputnik gave impetus to the provision of programs that would serve their needs.

There is no doubt that Terman, who was also responsible for developing the Stanford-Binet Intelligence Test, stands out as one of the leaders in this area. Selection 9 is a well known address in which he describes his research and findings. Terman's portrayal of the gifted may not now come as a surprise, largely as a result of the great influence his work has exerted.

Once the attitude of Americans toward the gifted was one of suspicion; they were considered strange, different, odd, if not down-right "mad." It is Terman's work which shifted this attitude in a much more favorable direction.

SELECTION 9

THE DISCOVERY AND ENCOURAGEMENT OF EXCEPTIONAL TALENT

Lewis M. Terman

I have often been asked how I happened to become interested in mental tests and gifted children. My first introduction to the scientific problems posed by intellectual differences occurred well over a half-century ago when I was a senior in psychology at Indiana University and was asked to prepare two reports for a seminar, one on mental deficiency and one on genius. Up to that time, despite the fact that I had graduated from a normal college as a Bachelor of Pedagogy and had taught school for five years, I had never so much as heard of a mental test. The reading for those two reports opened up a new world to me, the world of Galton, Binet, and their contemporaries. The following year my MA thesis on leadership among children (Terman, 1904) was based in part on tests used by Binet in his studies of suggestibility.

Then I entered Clark Unversity,

Reprinted from Terman, L. M. The discovery and encouragement of exceptional talent. *American Psychologist,* **9**, 1954, 221–230. Copyright 1954 by the American Psychological Association. Reproduced by permission.

where I spent considerable time during the first year in reading on mental tests and precocious children. Child prodigies, I soon learned, were at that time in bad repute because of the prevailing belief that they were usually psychotic or otherwise abnormal and almost sure to burn themselves out quickly or to develop postadolescent stupidity. "Early ripe, early rot" was a slogan frequently encountered. By the time I reached my last graduate year, I decided to find out for myself how precocious children differ from the mentally backward, and accordingly chose as my doctoral dissertation an experimental study of the intellectual processes of fourteen boys, seven of them picked as the brightest and seven as the dullest in a large city school (Terman, 1906). These subjects I put through a great variety of intelligence tests, some of them borrowed from Binet and others, many of them new. The tests were given individually and required a total of 40 or 50 hours for each subject. The experiment contributed little or nothing to science, but it contributed a lot to my future thinking. Besides "selling" me completely on the value of mental tests as a research method, it offered an ideal escape from the kinds of laboratory work which I disliked and in which I was more than ordinarily inept. (Edward Thorndike confessed to me once that *his* lack of mechanical skill was partly responsible for turning *him* to mental tests and to the kinds of experiments on learning that required no apparatus.)

However, it was not until I got to Stanford in 1910 that I was able to pick up with mental tests where I had left off at Clark University. By that time Binet's 1905 and 1908 scales had been published, and the first thing I undertook at Stanford was a tentative revision of his 1908 scale. This, after further revisions, was published in 1916. The standardization of the scale was based on tests of a thousand children whose IQ's ranged from 60 to 145. The contrast in intellectual performance between the dullest and the brightest of a given age so intensified my earlier interest in the gifted that I decided to launch an ambitious study of such children at the earliest opportunity.

My dream was realized in the spring of 1921 when I obtained a generous grant from the Commonwealth Fund of New York City for the purpose of locating a thousand subjects of IQ 140 or higher. More than that number were selected by Stanford-Binet tests from the kindergarten through the eighth grade, and a group mental test given in 95 high schools provided nearly 400 additional subjects. The latter, plus those I had located before 1921, brought the number close to 1,500. The average IQ was approximately 150, and 80 were 170 or higher (Terman, 1925).

The twofold purpose of the project was, first of all, to find what traits characterize children of high IQ, and secondly, to follow them for as many years as possible to see what kind of adults they might become. This meant that it was necessary to select a group representative of high-testing children in general. With the help of four field assistants, we canvassed a school population of nearly a quarter-million in the urban and semi-urban areas of California. Two careful checks on the methods used showed that not more than 10 or 12 per cent of the children who could have qualified for the group in the schools canvassed were missed. A sample of close to 90 per cent insured that whatever traits were typical of these children would be typical of high-testing children in any comparable school population.

Time does not permit me to describe the physical measurements, medical examinations, achievement tests, character and interest tests, or the trait ratings and other supplementary information obtained from parents and teachers. Nor can I here describe the comparative data we obtained for control groups of unselected children. The more important results, however, can be stated briefly: children of IQ 140 or higher are, in general, appreciably superior to unselected children in physique, health, and social adjustment; markedly superior in moral attitudes as measured either by character tests or by trait ratings; and vastly superior in their mastery of school subjects as shown by a three-hour battery of achievement tests. In fact, the typical child of the group had mastered the school subjects to a point about two grades beyond the one in which he was enrolled, some of them three or four grades beyond. Moreover, his ability as evidenced by achievement in the different school subjects is so general as to refute completely the traditional belief that gifted children are usually one-sided. I take some pride in the fact that not one of the major conclusions we drew in the early 1920's regarding the traits that are typical of gifted children has been overthrown in the three decades since then.

Results of thirty years' follow-up of these subjects by field studies in 1927–28, 1939–40, and 1951–52, and by mail follow-up at other dates, show that the incidence of mortality, ill health, insanity, and alcoholism is in each case below that for the generality of corresponding age, that the great majority are still well adjusted socially, and that the delinquency rate is but a fraction of what it is in the general population. Two forms of our difficult Concept Mastery Test, devised especially to reach into the stratosphere of adult intelligence, have been administered to all members of the group who could be visited by the field assistants, including some 950 tested in 1939–40 and more than 1,000 in 1951–52. On both tests they scored on the average about as far above the generality of adults as they had scored above the generality of children when we selected them. Moreover, as Dr. Bayley and Mrs. Oden have shown, in the twelve-year interval between the two tests, 90 per cent increased their intellectual stature as measured by this test. "Early ripe, early rot" simply does not hold for these subjects. So far, no one has developed postadolescent stupidity!

As for schooling, close to 90 per cent entered college and 70 per cent graduated. Of those graduating, 30 per cent were awarded honors and about two-thirds remained for graduate work. The educational record would have been still better but for the fact that a majority reached college age during the great depression. In their undergraduate years 40 per cent of the men and 20 per cent of the women earned half or more of their college expenses, and the total of undergraduate and graduate expenses earned amounted to $670,000, not counting stipends from scholarships and fellowships, which amounted to $350,000.

The cooperation of the subjects is indicated by the fact that we have been able to keep track of more than 98 per cent of the original group, thanks to the rapport fostered by the incomparable field and office assistants I have had from the beginning of the study to the present. I dislike to think how differently things could have gone with helpers even a little less competent.

The achievement of the group to midlife is best illustrated by the case histories of the 800 men, since only a minority of the women have gone out for professional careers (Terman, 1954). By 1950, when the men had an average age of 40 years, they had published 67 books (including 46 in the fields of science, arts, and the humanities, and 21 books of fiction). They had published more than 1,400 scientific, technical, and professional articles; over 200 short stories, novelettes, and plays; and 236 miscellaneous articles on a great variety of subjects. They had also authored more than 150 patents. The figures on publications do not include the hundreds of publications by journalists that classify as news stories, editorials, or newspaper columns; nor do they include the hundreds if not thousands of radio and TV scripts.

The 800 men include 78 who have taken a Ph.D. degree or its equivalent, 48 with a medical degree, 85 with a law degree, 74 who are teaching or have taught in a four-year college or university, 51 who have done basic research in the physical sciences or engineering, and 104 who are engineers but have done only applied research or none. Of the scientists, 47 are listed in the 1949 edition of *American Men of Science*. Nearly all of these numbers are from 10 to 20 or 30 times as large as would be found for 800 men of corresponding age picked at random in the general population, and are sufficient answer to those who belittle the significance of IQ differences.

The follow-up of these gifted subjects has proved beyond question that tests of "general intelligence," given as early as six, eight, or ten years, tell a great deal about the ability to achieve either presently or 30 years hence. Such tests do not, however, enable us to predict what direction the achievement will take, and least of all do they tell us what personality factors or what accidents of fortune will affect the fruition of exceptional ability. Granting that both interest patterns and special aptitudes play important roles in the making of a gifted scientist, mathematician, mechanic, artist, poet, or musical composer, I am convinced that to achieve greatly in almost any field, the special talents have to be backed up by a lot of Spearman's *g,* by which is meant the kind of general intelligence that requires ability to form many sharply defined concepts, to manipulate them, and to perceive subtle relationships between

them; in other words, the ability to engage in abstract thinking.

The study of Catharine Cox of the childhood traits of historical geniuses gives additional evidence regarding the role of general intelligence in exceptional achievement. That study was part of our original plan to investigate superior ability by two methods of approach: (*a*) by identifying and following living gifted subjects from childhood onward; and (*b*) by proceeding in the opposite direction and tracing the mature genius back to his childhood promise. With a second grant from the Commonwealth Fund, the latter approach got under way only a year later than the former and resulted in the magnum opus by Cox entitled *The Early Mental Traits of Three Hundred Geniuses* (1926). Her subjects represented an unbiased selection from the top 510 in Cattell's objectively compiled list of the 1,000 most eminent men of history. Cox and two able assistants then scanned some 3,000 biographies in search of information that would throw light on the early mental development of these subjects. The information thus obtained filled more than 6,000 typed pages. Next, three psychologists familiar with mental age norms read the documentary evidence on all the subjects and estimated for each the IQ that presumably would be necessary to account for the intellectual behavior recorded for given chronological ages. Average of three IQ estimates was used as the index of intelligence. In fact two IQ's were estimated for each subject, one based on the evidence to age 17, and the other on evidence to the mid-twenties. The recorded evidence on development to age

17 varied from very little to an amount that yielded about as valid an IQ as a good intelligence test would give. Examples of the latter are Goethe, John Stuart Mill, and Francis Galton. It was the documentary information on Galton, which I summarized and published in 1917 (Terman, 1917), that decided me to prepare plans for the kind of study that was carried out by Cox. The average of estimated IQ's for her 300 geniuses was 155, with many going as high as 175 and several as high as 200. Estimates below 120 occurred only when there was little biographical evidence about the early years.

It is easy to scoff at these postmortem IQ's, but as one of the three pychologists who examined the evidence and made the IQ ratings, I think the author's main conclusion is fully warranted; namely, that "the genius who achieves highest eminence is one whom intelligence tests would have identified as gifted in childhood."

Special attention was given the geniuses who had sometime or other been labeled as backward in childhood, and in every one of these cases the facts clearly contradicted the legend. One of them was Oliver Goldsmith, of whom his childhood teacher is said to have said "Never was so dull a boy." The fact is that little Oliver was writing clever verse at 7 years and at 8 was reading Ovid and Horace. Another was Sir Walter Scott, who at 7 not only read widely in poetry but was using correctly in his written prose such words as "melancholy" and "exotic." Other alleged childhood dullards included a number who disliked the usual diet of Latin and Greek but had a natural talent for science. Among these

were the celebrated German chemist Justus von Liebig, the great English anatomist John Hunter, and the naturalist Alexander von Humboldt, whose name is scattered so widely over the maps of the world.

In the cases just cited one notes a tendency for the direction of later achievement to be foreshadowed by the interests and preoccupations of childhood. I have tried to determine how frequently this was true of the 100 subjects in Cox's group whose childhood was best documented. Very marked foreshadowing was noted in the case of more than half of the group, none at all in less than a fourth. Macaulay, for example, began his career as historian at the age of 6 with what he called a "Compendium of Universal History," filling a quire of paper before he lost interest in the project. Ben Franklin before the age of 17 had displayed nearly all the traits that characterized him in middle life: scientific curiosity, religious heterodoxy, wit and buffoonery, political and business shrewdness, and ability to write. At 11 Pascal was so interested in mathematics that his father thought it best to deprive him of books on this subject until he had first mastered Latin and Greek. Pascal secretly proceeded to construct a geometry of his own and covered the ground as far as the 32nd proposition of Euclid. His father then relented. At 14 Leibnitz was writing on logic and philosophy and composing what he called "An Alphabet of Human Thought." He relates that at this age he took a walk one afternoon to consider whether he should accept the "doctrine of substantial forms."

Similar foreshadowing is disclosed by

the case histories of my gifted subjects. A recent study of the scientists and nonscientists among our 800 gifted men (Terman, 1954) showed many highly significant differences between the early interests and social attitudes of those who became physical scientists and those who majored in the social sciences, law, or the humanities. Those in medical or biological sciences usually rated on such variables somewhere between the physical scientists and the nonscientists.

What I especially want to emphasize, however, is that both the evidence on early mental development of historical geniuses and that obtained by follow-up of gifted subjects selected in childhood by mental tests point to the conclusion that capacity to achieve far beyond the average can be detected early in life by a well-constructed ability test that is heavily weighted with the *g* factor. It remains to be seen how much the prediction of future achievement can be made more specific as to field by getting, in addition, measures of ability factors that are largely independent of *g*. It would seem that a 20-year follow-up of the thousands of school children who have been given Thurstone's test of seven "primary mental abilities" would help to provide the answer. At present the factor analysts don't agree on how many "primary" mental abilities there are, nor exactly on what they are. The experts in this field are divided into two schools. The British school, represented by Thomson, Vernon, and Burt, usually stop with the identification of at most three or four group factors in addition to *g,* while some representing the American school feed the scores of 40 or 50 kinds of tests into a hopper and manage to extract from them what they believe to be a dozen or fifteen separate factors. Members of the British school are as a rule very skeptical about the realities underlying the minor group factors. There are also American psychologists, highly skilled in psychometrics, who share this skepticism. It is to be hoped that further research will give us more information than we now have about the predictive value of the group factors. Until such information is available, the scores on group factors can contribute little to vocational guidance beyond what a good test of general intelligence will provide.

I have always stressed the importance of *early* discovery of exceptional abilities. Its importance is now highlighted by the facts Harvey Lehman has disclosed in his monumental studies of the relation between age and creative achievement (Lehman, 1953). The striking thing about his age curves is how early in life the period of maximum creativity is reached. In nearly all fields of science, the best work is done between ages 25 and 35, and rarely later than 40. The peak productivity for works of lesser merit is usually reached 5 to 10 years later; this is true in some twenty fields of science, in philosophy, in most kinds of musical composition, in art, and in literature of many varieties. The lesson for us from Lehman's statistics is that the youth of high achievement potential should be well trained for his life work before too many of his most creative years have been passed.

This raises the issue of educational acceleration for the gifted. It seems that the schools are more opposed to acceleration now than they were thirty years ago. The lockstep seems to have become more and more the fashion, notwithstanding the fact that practically everyone who has investigated the subject is against it. Of my gifted group, 29 per cent managed to graduate from high school before the age of 16½ years (62 of these before 15½), but I doubt if so many would be allowed to do so now. The other 71 per cent graduated between 16½ and 18½. We have compared the accelerated with the nonaccelerated on numerous case-history variables. The two groups differed very little in childhood IQ, their health records are equally good, and as adults they are equally well adjusted socially. More of the accelerates graduated from college, and on the average nearly a year and a half earlier than the nonaccelerates; they averaged higher in college grades and more often remained for graduate work. Moreover, the accelerates on the average married .7 of a year earlier, have a trifle lower divorce rate, and score just a little higher on a test of marital happiness (Terman and Oden, 1947). So far as college records of accelerates and nonaccelerates are concerned, our data closely parallel those obtained by the late Noel Keys (1938) at the University of California and those by Pressey (1949) and his associates at Ohio State University.

The Ford Fund for the Advancement of Education has awarded annually since 1951 some 400 college scholarships to gifted students who are not over 16½ years old, are a year or even two years short of high school graduation, but show good evidence of ability to do college work. Three quarters of them are between 15½ and 16½ at the time of college entrance. A dozen colleges and univeristies accept these students and are keeping close track of their success. A summary of their records for the first year shows that they not only get higher grades than their classmates, who average about two years older, but that they are also equally well adjusted socially and participate in as many extracurricular activities (Fund for the Advancement of Education, 1953). The main problem the boys have is in finding girls to date who are not too old for them! Some of them have started a campaign to remedy the situation by urging that more of these scholarships be awarded to girls.

The facts I have given do not mean that all gifted children should be rushed through school just as rapidly as possible. If that were done, a majority with IQ of 140 could graduate from high school before the age of 15. I do believe, however, that such children should be promoted rapidly enough to permit college entrance by the age of 17 at latest, and that a majority would be better off to enter at 16. The exceptionally bright student who is kept with his age group finds little to challenge his intelligence and all too often develops habits of laziness that later wreck his college career. I could give you some choice examples of this in my gifted group. In the case of a college student who is preparing for a profession in science, medicine, law, or any field of advanced scholarship, graduation at 20 instead of the usual 22 means two years added to his professional career; or the two years saved could be used for additional training beyond the doctorate, if that were deemed preferable.

Learned and Wood (1938) have

shown by objective achievement tests in some 40 Pennsylvania colleges how little correlation there is between the student's knowledge and the number of months or years of his college attendance. They found some beginning sophomores who had acquired more knowledge than some seniors near their graduation. They found similarly low correlations between the number of course units a student had in a given field and the amount he knew in that field. Some with only one year of Latin had learned more than others with three years. And, believe it or not, they even found boys just graduating from high school who had more knowledge of science than some college seniors who had majored in science and were about to begin teaching science in high schools! The sensible thing to do, it seems, would be to quit crediting the individual high school or the individual college and begin crediting the individual student. That, essentially, is what the Ford Fund scholarships are intended to encourage.

Instruments that permit the identification of gifted subjects are available in great variety and at nearly all levels from the primary grades to the graduate schools in universities. My rough guess is that at the present time tests of achievement in the school subjects are being given in this country to children below high school at a rate of perhaps ten or twelve million a year, and to high school students another million or two. In addition, perhaps two million tests of intelligence are given annually in the elementary and high schools. The testing of college students began in a small way only 30 years ago; now almost every college in the country re-

quires applicants for admission to take some kind of aptitude test. This is usually a test of general aptitude, but subject-matter tests and tests of special aptitudes are sometimes given to supplement the tests of general aptitude.

The testing movement has also spread rapidly in other countries, especially in Britain and the Commonwealth countries. Godfrey Thomson devised what is now called the Moray House test of intelligence in 1921 to aid in selecting the more gifted 11-year-olds in the primary schools for the privilege of free secondary education. This test has been revised and is given annually to about a half million scholarship candidates. The Moray House tests now include tests of English, arithmetic, and history. In 1932, the Scottish Council for Research in Education (Scottish Council for Research in Education, 1933) arranged to give the Moray House test of intelligence (a group test) to all the 90,000 children in Scotland who were born in 1921, and actually tested some 87,000 of them. The Stanford-Binet tests have been translated and adapted for use in nearly all the countries of Europe and in several countries of Asia and Latin America. Behind the Iron Curtain, however, mental tests are now banned.

I have discussed only tests of intelligence and of school achievement. There is time to mention only a few of the kinds of personality tests that have been developed during the last thirty-five years: personality inventories, projective techniques by the dozen, attitude scales by the hundred, interest tests, tests of psychotic and predelinquent tendencies, tests of leadership, marital aptitude, masculinity-femininity, et cetera. The current output of research on personality tests probably equals or exceeds that on intelligence and achievement tests, and is even more exciting.

Along with the increasing use of tests, and perhaps largely as a result of it, there is a growing interest, both here and abroad, in improving educational methods for the gifted. Acceleration of a year or two or three, however desirable, is but a fraction of what is needed to keep the gifted child or youth working at his intellectual best. The method most often advocated is curriculum enrichment for the gifted without segregating them from the ordinary class. Under ideal conditions enrichment can accomplish much, but in these days of crowded schools, when so many teachers are overworked, underpaid, and inadequately trained, curriculum enrichment for a few gifted in a large mixed class cannot begin to solve the problem. The best survey of thought and action in this field of education is the book entitled *The Gifted Child,* written by many authors and published in 1951 (Witty, 1951). In planning for and sponsoring this book, The American Association for Gifted Children has rendered a great service to education.

But however efficient our tests may be in discovering exceptional talents, and whatever the schools may do to foster those discovered, it is the prevailing *Zeitgeist* that will decide, by the rewards it gives or withholds, what talents will come to flower. In Western Europe of the Middle Ages, the favored talents were those that served the Church by providing its priests, the architects of its cathedrals, and the painters of religious themes. A few cen-

turies later the same countries had a renaissance that included science and literature as well as the arts. Although presumably there are as many potential composers of great music as there ever were, and as many potentially great artists as in the days of Leonardo da Vinci and Michaelangelo, I am reliably informed that in this country today it is almost impossible for a composer of *serious* music to earn his living except by teaching, and that the situation is much the same, though somewhat less critical, with respect to artists.

The talents most favored by the current *Zeitgeist* are those that can contribute to science and technology. If intelligence and achievement tests don't discover the potential scientist, there is a good chance that the annual Science Talent Search will, though not until the high school years. Since Westinghouse inaugurated in 1942 this annual search for the high school seniors most likely to become creative scientists, nearly 4,000 boys and girls have been picked for honors by Science Service out of the many thousands who have competed. As a result, "Science Clubs of America" now number 15,000 with a third of a million members—a twenty-fold increase in a dozen years (Davis, 1953). As our need for more and better scientists is real and urgent, one can rejoice at what the talent search and the science clubs are accomplishing. One may regret, however, that the spirit of the times is not equally favorable to the discovery and encouragement of potential poets, prose writers, artists, statesmen, and social leaders.

But in addition to the over-all climates that reflect the *Zeitgeist,* there are localized climates that favor or hinder the encouragement of given talents in particular colleges and universities. I have in mind especially two recent investigations of the differences among colleges in the later achievement of their graduates. One by Knapp and Goodrich (1952) dealt with the undergraduate origin of 18,000 scientists who got the bachelor's degree between 1924 and 1934 and were listed in the 1944 edition of *American Men of Science*. The list of 18,000 was composed chiefly of men who had taken a PhD degree, but included a few without a PhD who were starred scientists. The IBM cards for these men were then sorted according to the college from which they obtained the bachelor's degree, and an index of productivity was computed for each college in terms of the proportion of its male graduates who were in the list of 18,000. Some of the results were surprising, not to say sensational. The institutions that were most productive of future scientists between 1924 and 1934 were not the great universities, but the small liberal arts colleges. Reed College topped the list with an index of 132 per thousand male graduates. The California Institute of Technology was second with an index of 70. Kalamazoo College was third with 66, Earlham fourth with 57, and Oberlin fifth with 56. Only a half-dozen of the great universities were in the top fifty with a productivity index of 25 or more.

The second study referred to was by Knapp and Greenbaum (1953), who rated educational institutions according to the proportion of their graduates who received certain awards at the graduate level in the six-year period from 1946 to 1951. Three kinds of awards were considered: a PhD degree, a graduate scholarship or fellowship paying at least $400 a year, or a prize at the graduate level won in open competition. The roster of awardees they compiled included 7,000 students who had graduated from 377 colleges and universities. This study differs from the former in three respects: (*a*) it deals with recent graduates, who had not had time to become distinguished but who could be regarded as good bets for the future; (*b*) these good bets were classified according to whether the major field was science, social science, or the humanities; and (*c*) data were obtained for both sexes, though what I shall report here relates only to men. In this study the great universities make a better showing than in the other, but still only a dozen of them are in the top fifty institutions in the production of men who are good bets. In the top ten, the University of Chicago is third, Princeton is eighth, and Harvard is tenth; the other seven in order of rank are Swarthmore 1, Reed 2, Oberlin 4, Haverford, 5, California Institute of Technology 6, Carleton 7, and Antioch 9. When the schools were listed separately for production of men who were good bets in science, social science, and the humanities, there were eight that rated in the top twenty on all three lists. These were Swarthmore, Reed, Chicago, Harvard, Oberlin, Antioch, Carleton, and Princeton.

The causes of these differences are not entirely clear. Scores on aptitude tests show that the intelligence of students in a given institution is by no means the sole factor, though it is an important one. Other important factors are the quality of the school's intellectual climate, the proportion of able and inspiring teachers on its faculty, and the amount of conscious effort that is made not only to discover but also to motivate the most highly gifted. The influence of motivation can hardly be exaggerated.

In this address I have twice alluded to the fact that achievement in school is influenced by many things other than the sum total of intellectual abilities. The same is true of success in life. In closing I will tell you briefly about an attempt we made a dozen years ago to identify some of the nonintellectual factors that have influenced life success among the men in my gifted group. Three judges, working independently, examined the records (to 1940) of the 730 men who were then 25 years old or older, and rated each on life success. The criterion of "success" was the extent to which a subject had made use of his superior intellectual ability, little weight being given to earned income. The 150 men rated highest for success and the 150 rated lowest were then compared on some 200 items of information obtained from childhood onward (Terman and Oden, 1947). How did the two groups differ?

During the elementary school years, the A's and C's (as we call them) were almost equally successful. The average grades were about the same, and average scores on achievement tests were only a trifle higher for the A's. Early in high school the group began to draw apart in scholarship, and by the end of high school the slump of the C's was quite marked. The slump could not be blamed on extracurricular activities, for these were almost twice as common

among the A's. Nor was much of it due to difference in intelligence. Although the A's tested on the average a little higher than the C's both in 1922 and 1940, the average score made by the C's in 1940 was high enough to permit brilliant college work, in fact was equaled by only 15 per cent of our highly selected Stanford students. Of the A's, 97 per cent entered college and 90 per cent graduated; of the C's, 68 per cent entered but only 37 per cent graduated. Of those who graduated, 52 per cent of the A's but only 14 per cent of the C's graduated with honors. The A's were also more accelerated in school; on the average they were six months younger on completing the eighth grade, 10 months younger at high school graduation, and 15 months younger at graduation from college.

The differences between the educational histories of the A's and C's reflect to some degree the differences in their family backgrounds. Half of the A fathers but only 15 per cent of the C fathers were college graduates, and twice as many of A siblings as of C siblings graduated. The estimated number of books in the A homes was nearly 50 per cent greater than in the C homes. As of 1928, when the average age of the subjects was about 16 years, more than twice as many of the C parents as of A parents had been divorced.

Interesting differences between the groups were found in the childhood data on emotional stability, social adjustments, and various traits of personality. Of the 25 traits on which each child was rated by parent and teacher in 1922 (18 years before the A and C groups were made up), the only trait on which the C's averaged as high as the A's was general health. The superiority of the A's was especially marked in four volitional traits: prudence, self-confidence, perseverance, and desire to excel. The A's also rated significantly higher in 1922 on leadership, popularity, and sensitiveness to approval or disapproval. By 1940 the difference between the groups in social adjustment and all-round mental stability had greatly increased and showed itself in many ways. By that time four-fifths of the A's had married, but only two-thirds of the C's, and the divorce rate for those who had married was twice as high for the C's as for the A's. Moreover, the A's made better marriages; their wives on the average came from better homes, were better educated, and scored higher on intelligence tests.

But the most spectacular differences between the two groups came from three sets of ratings, made in 1940, on a dozen personality traits. Each man rated himself on all the traits, was rated on them by his wife if he had a wife, and by a parent if a parent was still living. Although the three sets of ratings were made independently, they agreed unanimously on the four traits in which the A and C groups differed most widely. These were "persistence in the accomplishment of ends," "integration toward goals, as contrasted with drifting," "self-confidence," and "freedom from inferiority feelings." For each trait three critical ratios were computed showing, respectively, the reliability of the A-C differences in average of self-ratings, ratings by wives, and ratings by parents. The average of the three critical ratios was 5.5 for perseverance, 5.6 for integration toward goals, 3.7 for self-confidence, and 3.1

for freedom from inferiority feelings. These closely parallel the traits that Cox found to be especially characteristic of the 100 leading geniuses in her group whom she rated on many aspects of personality; their three outstanding traits she defined as "persistence of motive and effort," "confidence in their abilities," and "strength or force of character."

There was one trait on which only the parents of our A and C men were asked to rate them; that trait was designated "common sense." As judged by parents, the A's are again reliably superior, the A-C difference in average rating having a critical ratio of 3.9. We are still wondering what self-ratings by the subjects and ratings of them by their wives on common sense would have shown if we had been impudent enough to ask for them!

Everything considered, there is nothing in which our A and C groups present a greater contrast than in drive to achieve and in all-round mental and social adjustment. Our data do not support the theory of Lange-Eichbaum (1932) that great achievement usually stems from emotional tensions that border on the abnormal. In our gifted group, success is associated with stability rather than instability, with absence rather than with presence of disturbing conflicts—in short with well-balanced temperament and with freedom from excessive frustrations. The Lange-Eichbaum theory may explain a Hitler, but hardly a Churchill; the junior senator from Wisconsin,* pos-

---

* The reference is to Joseph McCarthy. —ED.

sibly, but not a Jefferson or a Washington.

At any rate, we have seen that intellect and achievement are far from perfectly correlated. To identify the internal and external factors that help or hinder the fruition of exceptional talent, and to measure the extent of their influences, are surely among the major problems of our time. These problems are not new; their existence has been recognized by countless men from Plato to Francis Galton. What is new is the general awareness of them caused by the manpower shortage of scientists, engineers, moral leaders, statesmen, scholars, and teachers that the country must have if it is to survive in a threatened world. These problems are now being investigated on a scale never before approached, and by a new generation of workers in several related fields. Within a couple of decades vastly more should be known than we know today about our resources of potential genius, the environmental circumstances that favor its expression, the emotional compulsions that give it dynamic quality, and the personality distortions that can make it dangerous.

Education of the Gifted

One of the issues raised by Terman that is still relevant today concerns school acceleration as a method of educating the gifted. In essence, acceleration involves some kind of early admission that moves the child through formal education more rapidly than average. The youngster may be allowed to start kindergarten earlier or skip grades. Critics of such an approach consistently have voiced the fear that acceleration is detrimental because a child is forced to interact with physically and socially more mature peers. As Terman noted, however, facts do not support this view, although obviously it is possible that acceleration can be harmful in some individual cases. Nevertheless, many educators argue that curriculum enrichment and special placement are better alternatives.

Enrichment. Enrichment procedures ensure that the gifted student will be maintained at average age-grade level while being exposed to experiences beyond the usual. He may be given special work or opportunity for additional studies, and generally will be encouraged to work with initiative and independence. At the present, enrichment is a popular notion with educators. It requires little obvious organizational change within a school system—and it is inexpensive. Nevertheless, it has its drawbacks. The effort, talent, and time required for teachers to plan a systematic program for individual children is considerable. Further, teachers are sometimes left to their own resources to identify gifted students, a procedure that is less than adequate.

For example, in one study it was found that 70 percent of the youngsters selected as bright by kindergarten teachers had a mean IQ of only 102.5, while 68 percent of those with IQs of 116 or above were not identified (Kirk, 1972). Similar errors occur for students in higher grades, perhaps because extremely high intelligence is often manifested in ways which teachers consider behavior problems. Many years ago Leta Hollingworth, a pioneer in the study of the gifted, recorded this example:

> The foolish teacher who hates to be corrected by a child is unsuited to these children. [I can] illustrate the difficulty from recent conversation with a ten-year-old boy of I.Q. 165. This boy was referred to us as a school problem: "Not interested in the school work. Very impudent. A liar." The following is a fragment of conversation with this boy:
>
> What seems to be your main problem in school?
>
> Several of them.
>
> Name one.
>
> Well, I will name the teachers. Oh, boy! It is bad enough when the pupils make mistakes, but when the teachers make mistakes, oh, boy!
>
> Mention a few mistakes the teachers made.
>
> For instance, I was sitting in 5A and the teacher was teaching 5B. She was telling those children that the Germans discovered printing, that Gutenberg was the first discoverer of it, mind you. After a few minutes I couldn't stand it. I am not supposed to recite in that class, you see, but I got up. I said, "No; the Chinese invented, not discovered printing, before the time of Gutenberg—while the Germans were still barbarians."
>
> Then the teacher said, "Sit down. You are entirely too fresh." Later on, she gave me a raking over before the whole class. Oh, boy! What teaching!
>
> It seemed to me that one should begin at once in this case about suffering fools gladly. So I said, "Ned, that teacher is foolish, but one of the very first things to learn in the world is to suffer fools gladly." The child was so filled with resentment that he heard only the word "suffer."
>
> "Yes, that's it. That's what I say! Make 'em suffer. Roll a rock on 'em."
>
> Before we finished the conversation, Ned was straightened out on the subject of who was to do the suffering. He agreed to do it himself. [1942, pp. 424–425.]

Special Grouping. The most blatantly different education for the gifted involves specially designed classes or programs. Children may be kept in their neighborhood schools where they attend classes only with other gifted students, or they actually may attend different schools. The curriculum is advanced and/or emphasizes the development of initiative and intellective skills.

A modification of this procedure allows the student to participate in the usual classes part of the day and in special classes for the remainder of the time.

Resistance to Special Programs: Equality of Education. It is apparent that some sort of special education is desirable for the gifted. In the final analysis, though, commitment to such programs may depend on societal attitudes toward them, and in general, the commitment to special education for the gifted has not been strong. Among twenty-seven school districts chosen from a national sample because of their model programs for exceptional children, a total of only five programs for the gifted are reported (Martinson, 1971). Although Americans have a philosophical bent toward facilitating the growth of each individual, the strong belief in equal opportunities sometimes leads to providing the same treatments to people who differ in needs. Then, too, the gifted often do not appear, superficially at least, to require special help, and concern has been precluded by fear that those already privileged would be given even more privilege. DeHaan and Havighurst note these attitudes succinctly:

> [We] find various aspects of the "equality" theory working against special programs for the gifted. The stubborn equalitarianism in American public opinion says: "Treat everybody alike. Give every child a good chance, and every child an equal chance. That is the responsibility of the public schools. It is up to the child and his parents to make much or little out of what is offered to him." These sentiments sound good to American ears.
>
> Taxpayers who have children are likely to feel that their children should get everything other people's children get. Therefore they tend to look askance at a program that spends more money on a few "gifted" children than is spent on their own "average" children.
>
> Also people tend to accept the idea of spending public money on the handicapped but not on the gifted. The handicapped "deserve a break," as it were. . . . So runs the reasoning of the average taxpayer. But the gifted child has an initial advantage. Why should he be given more help in school than the average child when he can learn so much more easily? [1957, p. 23.]

Effectiveness of Special Programs. Overall, there has been little precise evaluation of special education for the gifted. The evidence regarding the effects of special classes is not clear, although it tends to show positive results (McCandless, 1967). In California, for example, academic achievement of 929 gifted elementary and secondary students was compared on the basis of whether or not they participated in special education procedures (Martinson, 1961) and it was found that acceleration, enrichment, and special classes all resulted in better performance.

Defining Giftedness: A Continuing Issue. It is obvious that before any child can be placed in special programs, he must be identified as potentially able to profit from such placement. As with other exceptional individuals, defining giftedness remains a problem. For example, in one recent survey of schools in the United States, 57.5 percent reported that they had *no* gifted students, despite the fact that most researchers in the field agree that the gifted make up 2 to 3 percent of the population. Although this may mirror indifference or hostility toward recognizing the needs of the exceptionally able (Martinson, 1971), it also may reflect confusion as to how to define giftedness.

Performance on intelligence tests most often determines who will or will not be labeled gifted. Perhaps the most commonly used cutoff is an IQ of 130. There is, however, a growing tendency to widen this criterion to include special talents and, more often, creativity. In one recent survey, a congressional inquiry into the educational needs of the gifted, experts favored multiple means for identification, including individual intelligence tests and measures of achievement, talent, and creativity (Marland, 1971). It is to the topic of the creative child that we now turn.

CREATIVITY

We have seen that IQ scores are relatively good predictors of a variety of behaviors labeled intelligent or adaptive. One may wonder, though, whether there isn't something else, beyond intellective skills as usually measured, which contributes to the production of great ideas and significant accomplishments—in other words, to creativity.

Relationship between School Performance and Life Accomplishments

One strategy for trying to understand creativity is through a comparison of "average" and very successful people in various occupations, such as art, scientific research, mathematics, and writing. Are those who have made the most significant adult contributions the ones with higher intelligence? Did they have the better grades in school?

To answer these questions, researchers at the Institute for Personality Assessment and Research, University of California at Berkeley, have compared creative and less creative people. In one study (Helson and Crutchfield, 1970) involving mathematicians, the index of creativity was nominations by other mathematicians for significant accomplishment in mathematics research. The highly creative scholars were compared with others, matched for age (they were all in their late thirties), who had doctorates from universities of equally high standing. The men in the two groups were approximately equivalent in terms of the amount of time which they spent on their work yet, by agreement of their peers, they differed markedly in terms of the quality of their products. It came as a surprise, then, that the two groups were entirely comparable in terms of IQ as usually measured; at this range of ability, intelligence was unrelated to creativity.

The Helson and Crutchfield findings are not unusual or anomalous. Those who are creatively accomplished as adults are often unidentifiable by school grades. D. W. MacKinnon, speaking of creative individuals as they have been studied in many investigations, has written that, "As students, they were, in general, not distinguished for the grades they received, and in none of the samples did their high school grade-point average show any significant correlation with their subsequently achieved and recognized creativeness" (1968, p. 103).

Similar findings emerge from many other reports. A scientist's later standing in his field is not related to his undergraduate grades, even in his own science major (Harmon, 1963). Nor are grades as a graduate student relevant. Mednick (1963), for example, asked psychology professors to rate their graduate students in terms of creativity—the level of imaginativeness and potential of their research efforts—and found that this index of creativity was unrelated to intelligence. More striking, creativity was not even related to the grades which the subjects were receiving—from the same professors for their graduate course work in psychology. Thus, *at least within certain ranges,* creative accomplishment seems to involve something other than, or in addition to, high intelligence. It is important to note, though, that creativity and IQ are unrelated only among individuals with a relatively high level of intellectual ability; we do not usually find exceptionally creative individuals below the normal range.

Defining and Measuring Creativity

Studies described in the previous section suggest that we may fruitfully speak of creativity as distinct from intelligence, and perhaps can measure and foster it relatively early in life. To do so, we must face again the hard problems of definition and measurement. Psychologists have devised many ways by which they attempt to measure creativity; usually pictures, words, or stories are presented to the individual, who is then asked to generate a product of some kind which is then judged for creativity (see Figure XIII–4).

One way to define creativity, proposed by Jackson and Messick (1968), involves judging a person's products in terms of four criteria: novelty, appropriateness, transcendence of constraints, and coalescence of meaning. It is perhaps obvious that a creative product must be *novel* in the sense of being unusual, but more is also required. If we asked a nine-year-old: "How much is 2 + 2?" and he replied "17" we would be obliged to call the response unusual, but hardly creative. Thus, we add the criterion of *appropriateness.* In practice, though, appropriateness is not always easy to agree on. An artist dismissed as merely unusual and vulgar by one generation may be hailed for true creativity by the next.

The third criterion, *transcendence of constraints,* refers to combining elements in a way that at once defies tradition and yields a new perspective. The production of innovative scientific theories illustrates this quality. James Watson, one of the Nobel Laureates who uncovered the structure of the DNA molecule, wrote of his own insight:

> It came while I was drawing. . . . Suddenly I realized the potentially profound implications of a DNA structure in which the adenine residue formed hydrogen bonds similar to those found in crystals of pure adenine. . . . As the clock went past midnight I was becoming more and more pleased. There had been far too many days when Francis [Crick, Watson's colleague] and I worried that the DNA structure might turn out to be superficially very dull, suggesting nothing about either its replication or its function in controlling cell biochemistry. But now, to my delight and amazement, the answer was turning out to be profoundly interesting. For over two hours I happily lay awake with pairs of adenine residues whirling in front of my closed eyes. Only for brief moments did the fear shoot through me that an idea this good could be wrong. [1968, pp. 116–118.]

The final criterion suggested by Jackson and Messick, *coalescence of meaning,* is also reflected in Watson's account. The term suggests that creative products do not divulge themselves fully at first glance. The implications of a scientific innovation and the subtleties of great art both require, and reward, careful and repeated inspection.

Jackson and Messick's model helps us to understand further what we are trying to "get at" as creativity, but we still need a definition sufficiently precise to suggest measurement techniques. The search was begun in the work of J. P. Guilford and his associates. Their distinction between convergent and divergent cognitive operations has direct implications for measuring and understanding creativity. Guilford himself has described it this way:

> In view of the active nature of creative performances, the production aspects or steps are most conspicuous and probably most crucial. . . . With some productive-thinking factors, and the tests that measure them, thinking must at some time converge toward one right answer. . . . With other productive-thinking factors and their tests, thinking need not come out with a unique answer; in fact, going off in different directions contributes to a better score in such tests. This type of thinking and these factors come under the heading of "divergent" thinking. It is in divergent thinking that we find the most obvious indications of creativity. [1957, pp. 111–112.]

The Guilford group has researched quite extensively various dimensions of divergent thinking, in children, adolescents, and adults, in search of measures that can be discriminated from convergent thinking and from general intelligence as usually reflected in IQ. The principal research technique, factor analysis, is sufficiently complex that a variety of technical disputes exist regarding some interpretations of the work (see earlier mention of this method, p. 249). Yet Wallach (1970) is on firm ground in stating that the significant outcome has been to identify *ideational fluency* —a person's ability to generate a plentiful number of ideas that are appropriate to a task constraint—as a measurable characteristic which is cohesive but readily distinguishable from measures of convergent thinking.

Wallach's Studies

The work of Michael Wallach and his associates stands at the fore in determining (1) whether children differ from one another in a consistent way in ideational fluency that can be readily measured, and (2) whether such measures can be used to predict later creative accomplishments.

After reviewing a variety of sources of evidence, Wallach and Kogan (1965) began by devising a number of tasks to measure ideational fluency in children. One, an "alternative uses" test, involved asking youngsters to name as many uses as they could for a number of common objects, such as a shoe or a cork. Another required the subjects to point out all of the similarities they could think of between a pair of objects—for example, a train and a tractor or a potato and a carrot. A third involved naming as many concrete instances as possible of an abstract category such as round

FIGURE XIII—4

Examples of the tasks given to individuals to test creativity, and judgments of the projects.

Children are asked what these lines mean to them. Adapted from M. A. Wallach and N. Kogan, Modes of Thinking in Young Children, *page 36, figure 3. New York: Holt, Rinehart & Winston, 1965. By permission of author and publisher.*

A Usual Answer:
Mountains

An Unusual Answer:
Squashed piece of paper.

Children are given colored materials and asked to make mosaics (similar to Hall, 1958).

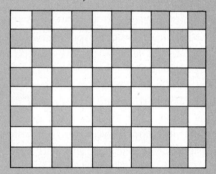 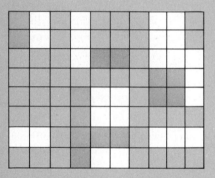

Children are asked to tell a story about a picture of a man working late or early in an office. Adapted from Getzels and Jackson, 1962.

There's ambitious Bob, down at the office at 6:30 in the morning. Every morning it's the same. He's trying to show his boss how energetic he is. Now, thinks Bob, maybe the boss will give me a raise for all my extra work. The trouble is that Bob has been doing this for the last three years, and the boss still hasn't given him a raise. He'll come in at 9:00, not even noticing that Bob has been there so long, and poor Bob won't get his raise.

Judged Less Creative

This man has just broken into this office of a new cereal company. He is a private eye employed by a competitor firm to find out the formula that makes the cereal bend, sag, and sway. After a thorough search of the office he comes upon what he thinks is the current formula. He is now copying it. It turns out that it is the wrong formula and the competitor's factory blows up. Poetic justice!

Judged Creative

FIGURE XIII–4 *(continued)*

Children are asked to draw a picture around the theme "playing tag in the school yard." Adapted from J. W. Getzels and P. W. Jackson, Creativity and Intelligence. *Copyright 1962, reproduced by permission of John Wiley & Sons, Inc.*

Judged Less Creative   *Judged Creative*

things or things that make noise. Finally, in addition to these three verbal measures, children were asked to generate ideas when presented with visual arrays; for example, they were asked to identify all of the meanings they could think of for abstract patterns or abstract line drawings.

Participants in the first study were 151 fifth-grade children, both boys and girls. The investigators note that at least two types of measures could be derived from their results, the actual number of responses produced by a child and the number that are original. Interestingly, the two measures are very highly correlated. In other words, the rank ordering of the children is very similar regardless of whether performance is assessed by the total number of ideas produced or simply the number that are unique. The Wallach-Kogan findings show clearly that the various procedures are internally reliable or consistent.

> Children who tended to generate larger numbers of ideas—or larger numbers of original ideas—in response to one of these procedures tended also

to do this for the rest of the tasks. It did not matter, for example, whether the requests for ideas were framed in visual or verbal terms. On the other hand, children who generated smaller numbers of ideas—or smaller numbers of unique ideas—for one of the tasks were comparably low in their standing for each of the remaining tasks. [Wallach, 1971, p. 8.]

The next question was to determine whether these individual differences among children reflected anything more than differences in intelligence. To do so, WISC IQ scores for each child were obtained. It was found that IQ was *not* related to the creativity measure. Whether a child produced a large number of ideas, or unique ideas, simply was not predictable from the traditional measure of intelligence. This important pattern of results has since been replicated many times with younger boys (Ward, 1968), additional samples of elementary school children (Pankove and Kogan, 1968), and with college freshmen (Wallach and Wing, 1969).

Originally, Wallach and his associates felt that sound, independent measures of creativity could be obtained only if the tasks were presented in a relaxed, permissive atmosphere with no time constraints. The argument was that presenting the measurement procedures as tests, administered under pressure in a group setting, might very well mask the demonstration of creativity. Certainly the presence of such constraints is inconsistent with what we usually have in mind when thinking about creative people and creative products. But, despite the plausibility of the argument, it now appears that creativity, as a characteristic independent of intelligence, can be successfully measured in a "testing" environment. To be sure, such circumstances lower the absolute level of creativity (such as the actual number of imaginative responses which a child will produce), but the creative child will maintain his position relative to others (Wallach, 1971).

An adequate measure and definition of creativity is just the beginning of the exploration. We next want to know whether creativity measures are related to, or will predict, real-life accomplishments. The answer, on the basis of a growing body of evidence, appears to be *yes.*

Dewing (1970) obtained IQ scores and several measures of creativity, including ideational fluency for almost four hundred seventh-grade boys and girls. With IQ held constant, it was clear that the creativity measures were related significantly to meaningful accomplishments such as writing highly original compositions or being judged by teachers to have been the "motivating force" behind major class projects, such as the production of a magazine.

Wallach and Wing (1969), in an extensive and particularly well-designed investigation, likewise found clear relationships between measures of ideational fluency and creative products among a sample of about five hundred college students. Looking at attainments such as prizes in art and science contests, political leadership, roles in major dramatic productions, and awards in the fine arts, they found that while differences in intelligence test scores failed to predict any kind of *nonacademic* attainment, ideational fluency did predict accomplishments in many areas (see Figure XIII–5).

Fostering Creativity

The discovery that creativity can be identified as a characteristic that predicts accomplishment leads us to the practical question of whether it is possible to train for creativity. Evidence in this area is limited, but there are two sources to which we can turn for some preliminary information.

Family Variables. One of the places where we can look for answers is in the retrospective accounts of creative persons; from these we can determine something of the background, home life, and pressures (or lack of them) which are associated with later accomplishment. Using this strategy, Mac-Kinnon (1962) has reported that his sample of creative architects often received extraordinary respect from their parents, who expressed confidence in their ability to do what was appropriate. These same parents granted much freedom of exploration and decision, believing that their children would act independently, reasonably, and responsibly. At the same time, strong emotional parental ties were frequently absent. It was not only that closeness was lacking but that the overdependency and fear of rejection which often characterize parent-child relationships were not experienced. Fathers were models of effective behavior in their careers while mothers were active women with autonomous careers and interests. Further, one or both parents frequently were of artistic skill and temperament.

As children, many of the architects showed early interest in painting and drawing; this was rewarded and encouraged primarily by the mother but was allowed to develop without undue pressures. There also was little parental pressure in regard to a particular career, even when parents were themselves architects.

Reports of shyness, isolation, aloneness, and little adolescent dating were frequent. MacKinnon suggests that this may have been related to the high incidence of moving or perhaps to unusual introversion or sensitivity. In either case, the apparent isolation may have fostered an awareness of inner life and interests in imaginal, symbolic processes.

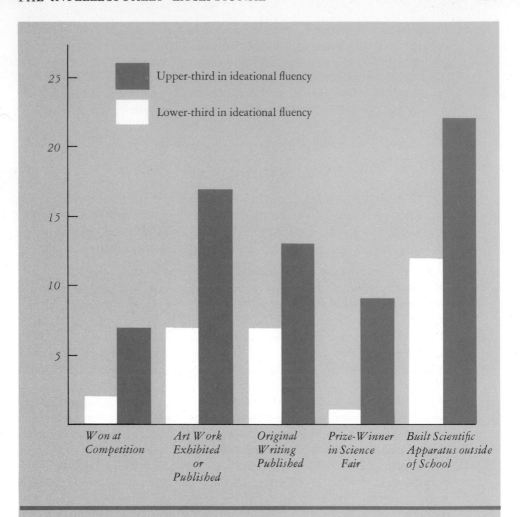

FIGURE XIII—5

Differences in productivity of college students high and low in ideational influency (a measure of creativity) in Wallach and Wing's research. Adapted from M. A. Wallach and C. W. Wing, The Talented Student: A Validation of the Creativity-Intelligence Distinction. *New York: Holt, Rinehart & Winston, 1969, by permission.*

Discipline and religious training appeared to contribute to the development of marked personal autonomy. Within the family explicit rules and standards existed; discipline was predictable and consistent and there was relatively little corporal punishment. Religious practices varied considerably, with two-thirds of the families practicing only perfunctory or no formal religion. However, emphasis was placed on the development of one's own code of ethics, with integrity, pride, joy in work, intellectual and cultural endeavors, success, ambition, and doing the right thing being highly valued.

Training for Creativity. We can look to experimental studies for evidence that creativity can be fostered by training. The evidence tentatively suggests that this is possible. In a relatively early study, for example, Anderson and Anderson (1963) trained groups of sixth-grade boys to think of unusual uses for familiar objects by pointing out the unique properties of each object and then rewarding them for offering interesting possibilities. As hoped for, some generalization effects were observed. The boys were now able to generate more novel uses for other familiar objects that had not been included in the training series.

Another demonstration of the possibility of training in ideational fluency is found in a study by Yonge (1966). The criterion task was recognizing that an electrical switch could be employed as a pendulum—a distinctly novel use—to attach two strings which were hung from a ceiling in such a way that merely stretching one's arms would not succeed in tying them together. Without training, the subjects were unable to envision the possibility of using the switch in the string problem. When experience in novel use was provided, such as by showing the subjects that the switch could be used as a straightedge ruler to draw designs or as a holder for a piece of cardboard, many subjects were able to generate for themselves the possibility of using the switch as a pendulum.

These studies are only demonstrations that under certain circumstances one can successfully train for creativity; there is no guarantee that an extension of these procedures will be effective. But the research on the creativity-intelligence distinction has provided a clear step toward possible changes in both our educational curricula and in measurement practices, suggesting that we have placed too great an emphasis on IQ alone.

Such a shift has already begun. Reese and Parnes (1970), for example, have developed programmed materials—a sequence of twenty-eight booklets designed to teach the principles of creative problem solving—for stimulating creativity in junior high school students. Their experimental evaluation of the program in six schools showed it to be highly effective (eg., in producing greater flexibility and originality as measured by standard tests). Most interestingly, significant increments in creativity occurred relative to a control group even when the program was delivered in "do-it-yourself" form without a classroom instructor.

XIV

THE SOCIALLY DISADVANTAGED

RECENT YEARS HAVE WITNESSED increasing public concern with the plight of the socially disadvantaged. Psychologists, long interested in possible differences between individuals of varied social and economic backgrounds, have played a significant role in translating this concern into practical knowledge. Developmentalists have particular interest in trying to understand the relationship between development and factors unique to the disadvantaged. They also are increasingly involved in various remedial efforts. In this chapter, after first briefly identifying the socially disadvantaged, we shall explore factors that presumably are relevant to their development and then describe some ongoing programs designed for underprivileged children.

WHO ARE THE SOCIALLY DISADVANTAGED?

How can the socially disadvantaged be characterized? First and foremost, they are economically poor. The disadvantaged child is a product of poverty —or more accurately, is caught up in the self-perpetuating cycle of poverty and failure. Intricately involved in this cycle is a host of factors that play a part in preventing the poor from moving into the mainstream of society. They live in crowded, inadequate housing, suffer high rates of illness and malnutrition, experience family instability, and are surrounded by delinquency and crime.

The disadvantaged also are more likely to belong to certain ethnic groups than others. Havighurst (1970) found that among the approximately 32 million individuals whose family incomes were below the poverty line, approximately 20 million were English-speaking Caucasians, 8 million were blacks, 3 million were of Spanish descent, and 500,000 were American Indians. Although these figures show clearly that the majority of the poor are native-born whites, they also show that minority groups are more frequently represented than their percentage in the total population would indicate. Blacks, for example, constitute approximately 11 percent of the United States citizenry, but 25 percent of those with very low incomes. Many of the disadvantaged, then, are exposed to prejudices commonly inflicted upon minority groups. Perhaps more important, their background —in terms of language, customs, and attitudes—subtly prepares them for life different from that of the middle class.

At the same time, the disadvantaged are also unsuccessful in school. Havighurst (1964) examined twenty-one Chicago school districts representing a wide range of incomes and educational levels in order to contrast the achievement test performance of middle- and lower-class children. He found that the performance of sixth-grade students in the seven districts with the highest average socioeconomic status (SES) ranged from at grade level to one year above grade level on reading and mathematics tests; in the seven lowest SES districts, the test scores clustered around one year below grade level. Similar differences have been found on more specialized achievement tests probing knowledge in science, writing, and social studies.

The Coleman Report, a recent extensive survey by the Office of Education, shows that black first graders are already behind their white peers one full grade level, with the difference being most pronounced in the South (Coleman, 1966). Moreover, an increasing gap between blacks and whites as they advance to higher grades frequently has been noted in the literature (Coleman, 1966; Hess, 1970). As shown in Table XIV–1, whereas third graders in Harlem perform about a year under grade level, by eighth grade they are two years behind. It is not surprising, then, that the rate for dropping out of school for black youngsters in California is twice that for whites, and that at least 50 percent of American Indians do not complete high school (Nimnicht, 1970).

At least partly because of the resulting lack of formal education and vocational training, the poor continue to be underemployed or unemployed.

TABLE XIV-1

GRADE-LEVEL ACADEMIC ACHIEVEMENT OF THIRD-,
SIXTH-, AND EIGHTH-GRADE CHILDREN IN HARLEM
COMPARED TO THAT OF STUDENTS FROM
NEW YORK CITY AND THE REST OF THE NATION

	READING COMPREHENSION			WORD KNOWLEDGE			ARITHMETIC		
GRADE	Harlem	NYC	USA	Harlem	NYC	USA	Harlem	NYC	USA
3	2.5	3.6	3.7	2.7	3.6	3.7	–	–	–
6	4.1	6.1	6.2	4.1	6.1	6.2	5.0	6.4	6.5
8	6.0	8.1	8.5	6.0	8.1	8.5	5.8	8.1	8.5

Source: Hess, 1970.

Twice as many nonwhites as white workers in all age groups are unemployed, and the rate for nonwhite teenagers is two-and-one-half that for white adolescents (Birch and Gussow, 1970). This situation naturally precludes a rise from poverty—and completes the cycle of poverty, school failure, and unemployment (see Figure XIV-1).

FAMILY STRUCTURE

A number of factors militate against the stability of lower-class families. Poverty itself is doubtless one important factor; individuals with inadequate incomes are harassed constantly by financial worries and tensions that strain marital bonds. In addition, the disadvantaged frequently are powerless to change the factors that affect their livelihood. The amount paid in welfare checks, for example, depends on prevailing political climates and broad economic trends but is not affected by the financial emergencies faced by an individual family. Poverty-stricken families are unlikely to save any substantial sum of money, so when an operation is required or a robbery

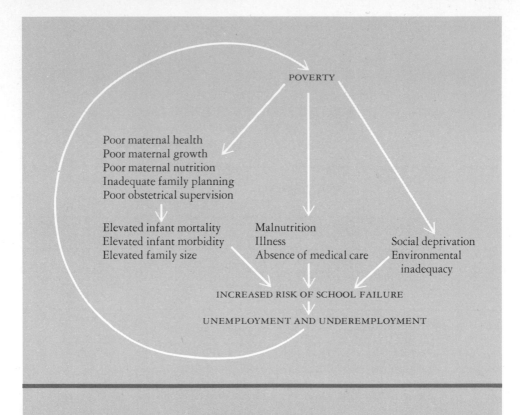

FIGURE XIV-1

The cycle of poverty, school failure, and unemployment experienced by the disadvantaged. Adapted from H. G. Birch and J. D. Gussow, Disadvantaged Children: Health, Nutrition and School Failure. *New York: Grune & Stratton, 1970. By permission.*

or fire depletes the family's possessions, there is no reserve to fall back on. Finally, under the present welfare structure it is sometimes easier for a mother to obtain financial aid when no man is present in the home.

For a variety of reasons, then, family stability is lower among the poor. Rainwater (1972) points out that among blacks, particularly urban blacks, many women are heads of their households for a good portion of their lives—and were themselves reared in families headed by women (see Table

XIV–2). He notes: "The relevant effective status for many Negro women is that of 'having been married' rather than 'being married'; having the right to be called 'Mrs.' rather than currently being 'Mrs. Someone in Particular' " (p. 117). Among poor whites there is a similar disruption of family structure.

The effects of such disruption are difficult to ascertain. It is reasonable to assume that children, particularly boys, growing up in the absence of a father are deprived of a relevant model for behavior. But poor families, especially black ones, tend to live in extended families—that is, within a circle of relatives—rather than in the restricted unit of parents and off-spring. Support and models thus are potentially available from several sources. Further, Herzog and Lewis (1971) note that clear and conclusive findings are lacking on the influence of father absence on such specific areas as poor school achievement, delinquency, and sex identity and that its impact may be dwarfed by other factors.

Child neglect, though, is associated with low socioeconomic status, a one-parent family structure, and a large number of children. In an attempt to elucidate factors which might distinguish adequate mothers from neglect-ful ones, Giovannoni and Billingsley (1971) related interview data from

TABLE XIV–2

PROPORTION OF FAMILIES HEADED BY FEMALES ACCORDING TO RACE, INCOME, AND RURAL-URBAN CATEGORIES

	RURAL	URBAN	TOTAL
Negroes			
under $3000	18%	47%	36%
$3000 and over	5%	8%	7%
Whites			
under $3000	12%	38%	22%
$3000 and over	2%	4%	3%

Source: U. S. Census: 1960, PC (1) D. U. S. Volume, Table 225; State Volume, Table 140.

186 *low-income* black, Caucasian, and Spanish-speaking mothers to previous judgments of their adequacy as parents. They concluded that gross indicators of past family breakdown and structure did not distinguish neglectful mothers but current situational stress did.

> The neglectful mothers were much more likely to have more children, to be without a husband, to have experienced recent marital disruption, to be poorer, and to be without necessary resources for caring for their children. . . . [There was also] impoverishment of relationships with extended kin among neglectful parents, while adequate mothers enjoyed frequent and rewarding contacts with relatives. . . . This is not to suggest that poverty is an invariant concomitant of neglect. Rather, the implication is that poverty exposes parents to the increased likelihood of additional stress that may have deleterious effects upon their capacities to care adequately for their children. [pp. 332–333.]

CHILD-REARING PRACTICES

In Western society children spend most of their early childhood in the company of one or both parents. Child-rearing practices are likely, then, to exercise great influence on subsequent development. To the extent that families of different SES vary in their modes of interaction, their children might be expected to develop in somewhat different directions and perhaps at different rates as well.

It has been suggested that differences among socioeconomic classes in regard to child-rearing practices may be partially explained by differential job experiences. Kohn (1963), for example, notes that one of the chief differences between the occupations of the lower and middle classes is the way they foster either self-direction or compliance. The lower-class occupations place more emphasis on manipulation of concrete things than on abstraction, ideas, and interpersonal relations; they are also more likely to be supervised and routinized, and to depend upon group efforts rather than individual initiative. As parents, lower-class adults may carry these experiences over to the way in which they control their youngsters.

Although extrapolation from this formulation should not be oversimplified, certain findings are not incongruent with it. Bronfenbrenner (1958) found that lower-class mothers more frequently punish failures of self-control such as toilet mishaps, are more likely than middle-class mothers to rely on physical punishment, are more concerned with appearances, and expect less independent activity from their children.

Kamii and Radin (1967) studied two groups of black mothers; one was receiving public assistance while the other consisted of upper-middle-class wives. To provide the most natural setting possible, the investigation was conducted within the homes of the subjects. On the surface, the purpose of the experiment was to determine how well each mother could teach a task to her child. Before entering into the task, however, the experimenter posed a long series of questions to the mother, completely excluding the child from the conversation. The youngster naturally became restless; how the mothers handled his complaints was the focus of the study.

Middle- and lower-class mothers differed substantially in how they responded to their youngsters. The latter initiated fewer verbal interactions and more often relied on commands without explanations. They also were less likely to react with affection to complaints or offer praise for good behavior. The two groups, however, did not differ significantly in the frequency with which they made negative comments about their children's bad behavior.

Although it is not possible at present to trace directly the antecedents of social class differences in child-rearing, it is reasonable to assume that a variety of experiences of the lower class fosters certain patterns of dealing with offspring. These, in turn, may have an impact on children that perpetuates a certain life style.

EXPECTANCY AND SELF-CONCEPT

Behavior frequently conforms to the expectations set for it by others. Thus, if an individual were hired for a factory job but few in the plant thought him capable of performing the work, he might be likely to fail. A number of factors could be involved: coworkers might not help because "he couldn't learn it anyway," or, alternatively, they might be excessively alert for mistakes, exchanging "I told you so" glances whenever they find them.

Brophy and Good (1970) have provided telling information on the different ways that teachers interact with children for whom high and low success is expected. After asking teachers to rank their first graders' level of achievement, the investigators selected the six highest and six lowest in each class for observation. Pupil-teacher interactions were carefully observed and records were kept of the frequency of various teacher and student behaviors, such as hand raising, providing correct answers, giving praise, and giving criticism. With those pupils for whom they held high expectations, teachers were more likely to praise correct answers, less likely to criticize wrong answers, more likely to follow wrong answers with a restatement of the problem (giving the child a second chance), and more likely to provide some kind of feedback after each answer. It seems reasonable to expect that the effect of such teacher behavior would be to improve future performance of those thought to be higher achievers and, conversely, to depress the relative standing of those from whom little was expected. Because achievement expectancy is usually low for the disadvantaged, teacher behavior will work against them. Although little research of this type has been performed in other settings, the phenomenon also may operate in occupational and social situations.

Aside from being influenced by expectations of others, performance also may be shaped by self-expectancy. We have already seen (Chapter XII) that children who expect to succeed tend to do so, and that expectations regarding one's control over situations is related to school achievement. What else do we know relevant to the disadvantaged child's expectations of his own performance?

Despite the "melting pot" nature of the United States, it remains a country of many distinct and often antagonistic ethnic and social groups. If a group is disliked or looked down upon by much of society, its members might have a relatively unfavorable image of themselves. For stereotyping to have a negative effect, the individual must first be aware that he is a member of the despised group. Available evidence indicates that this awareness occurs early, usually before the age of four, and that the tendency is more pronounced among minority group members (Vaughn, 1964). Consistent with this analysis, Wylie (1963) found that in estimating their ability blacks were more modest than whites, and individuals of lower socioeconomic status more modest than those of higher status.

Low self-esteem may then lead to poorer performance that, in turn, perpetuates low self-esteem. Rosenberg (1965) found that students who did not achieve high grades in school typically had relatively low self-images and low occupational expectations. In addition, they frequently described themselves as withdrawn, overly sensitive, and suspicious—qualities not likely to lead to experiences of success that might improve their self-concepts.

LANGUAGE OF THE SOCIALLY DISADVANTAGED

Comparison of the language of middle- and lower-class youngsters frequently has resulted in conclusions that the lower-class child is considerably deficient in many aspects of language development, such as sentence length, vocabulary, grammer, and syntax. Because language not only serves a communicative function but also is intricately involved in thinking, there is much interest in this finding.

One investigator, Bernstein, recorded group conversations among lower- and middle-class British adolescents. He found that lower-class individuals used longer phrases and hesitated less between phrases, almost as if they were stringing together a set of prefabricated ideas. Middle-class youngsters employed a great number of uncommon adjectives and adverbs, more unusual sentence constructions, and fewer diffuse pronouns such as *they* and *we* (Bernstein, 1962a; 1962b). Bernstein thus distinguished between *restricted* and *elaborate* language codes and argued that reliance upon the former by lower-class children limits their learning of conceptual skills. In restricted language there is a dependence upon a relatively small number of words and phrases so that another individual will be able to predict fairly accurately what will be said and how it will be phrased on the basis of the situation. There is also little attempt to communicate fine nuances of ideas or feelings. Middle-class speakers are capable of using a restricted code, but additionally possess an elaborated structure with which they can express themselves more precisely. Relying implicitly on the theory that the way people talk influences the way they think, Bernstein contends that, lacking an elaborated code, lower-class youngsters have difficulty developing and applying abstract ideas. He also predicts that their power of analysis will be handicapped by their language.

Bernstein's theory has not gone uncriticized. Robinson (1965) argues that impoverished individuals are able to speak either in elaborated or restricted codes, but do not feel compelled to use more formal language in experimental situations. To test this hypothesis, he instructed twelve- and thirteen-year-old English children to write two letters, one to a friend and the other to a school administrator. There were few differences between the middle- and lower-class letters written to the administrator; however, letters written by lower-class children to friends contained more restricted language. Robinson concluded that the difference resided in the type of speech used in everyday life rather than in any inability to use elaborated language.

Labov, Cohen, Robins, and Lewis (1968) studied the language of lower-class blacks in the United States. Observing adolescent residents of Harlem, they noted discrepancies between standard English and black English. Among these are differences in use of the verb "to be," nonstandard use of verb forms, double negatives, and unusual use of pronouns. Labov *et al.* argue that these features do not indicate inferiority of the black language but merely *difference*. Language of the lower class follows consistent rules and someone competent in the language clearly can discern what is meant by each statement. Motivational and attitudinal factors rather than language, they argue, are responsible for discrepancies in academic performance between lower-class blacks and middle-class whites.

To illustrate their point, the investigators refer to the division of black youths into club members and nonmembers. The values espoused by club members are deviant from the conventional morality at virtually every point (e.g., fighting, stealing, use of drugs and alcohol). The statements of individuals not belonging to clubs are more closely congruent with middle-class standards. In examining scores on a reading achievement test, Labov's group found that approximately one-third of the nonmembers achieved at grade level or above, whereas not one of the club members did so. Labov *et al.* also note a richness in lower-class black language that does not manifest itself in the school setting, but rather in out-of-class verbal activity such as ritual toasts. These toasts adopt the form of epic poems and reflect experiences common to group members. Great value is placed on club members who are able to generate clever and rhythmic poems that are in accordance with group norms.

Thus it is increasingly apparent that lower socioeconomic status blacks have developed a language that differs in several respects from Standard English, but is rich in its own right. However, it remains unclear if this language is well adapted to the type of conceptual precision that is required in school situations. It is also difficult to assess the extent to which lower-class language aids or hinders cognitive development; the fact that lower-class members use uncommon adjectives and adverbs less often than middle-class individuals may be more directly related to their vocabulary and usage than to thought processes.

COGNITIVE GROWTH AND MOTHER-CHILD INTERACTION

We noted earlier in this chapter that the way in which youngsters are handled by parents may vary across socioeconomic class. Robert Hess and Virginia Shipman (1968) have looked at child-parent interaction with the specific intent of determining if and how it might be related to cognitive growth. They assume that information processing strategies are learned through experience with others, that a significant part of each child's early learning is accomplished through communication with his mother, that methods of discipline emphasizing reasons rather than obedience are most conducive to cognitive development, and that communication between mother and child is partially a function of social class. With regard to the last two points, Hess and Shipman note that lower-class mothers more frequently resort to telling the child *what* to do rather than telling him *why* he should do it; they reason further that this disciplinary form is unlikely to teach children exactly what they should do and when. Control is external rather than internal and learning is depressed.

Consider the two different maternal communications strategies illustrated in the following responses that mothers gave when asked how they would prepare their child to go to school: "First of all, I would take him to see his new school, we would talk about the building, and after seeing the school I would tell him that he would meet new children who would be his friends; he would work and play with them. I would explain to him that the teacher would be his friend, would help him and guide him in school, and that he should do as she tells him to" (Hess and Shipman, 1968, p. 96). This mother has provided numerous reasons that the child could use in deciding that school probably will be a pleasant and rewarding experience. While telling him that he should obey the teacher, the mother also has given him several reasons why this is a good idea.

Contrast her statements with those given by another mother: "Well, I would tell him he going to school and he have to sit down and mind the teacher and be a good boy, and I show him how when they give him milk, you know, how he's supposed to take his straw and do, and not put nothing on the floor when he get through" (Hess and Shipman, 1968, p. 96). Not only does this mother concentrate on a relatively minor aspect of the school experience, but she also does little to give the child reason to look forward (or not look forward) to school. He has no basis on which to form any expectation and can only carry out a set of instructions for which he has not been given a rationale.

Selection 10, below, illustrates further the methods that Hess and Shipman have used, the kinds of topics they have explored, and the results they have obtained. Their data present an effective argument for the importance of mother-child communication patterns in cognitive development, an aspect of child rearing that is critical regardless of social class.

SELECTION 10

EARLY EXPERIENCE AND THE SOCIALIZATION OF COGNITIVE MODES IN CHILDREN

Robert D. Hess and Virginia C. Shipman

The Problem

One of the questions arising from the contemporary concern with the education of culturally disadvantaged children is how we should conceptualize the effects of such deprivation upon the cognitive faculties of the child. The outcome is well known: children from deprived backgrounds score well below middle-class children on standard individual and group measures of intelligence (a gap that increases with age); they come to school without the skills necessary for coping with first grade curricula; their language development, both written and spoken, is relatively poor; auditory and visual discrimination skills are not well developed; in scholastic achievement they are retarded an average of 2 years by grade 6 and almost 3 years by grade 8; they are more

likely to drop out of school before completing a secondary education; and even when they have adequate ability are less likely to go to college (Deutsch, 1963; Deutsch and Brown, 1964; Eells, Davis, Havighurst, Herrick, and Tyler, 1951; John, 1963; Kennedy, Van de Riet, and White, 1963; Lesser, 1964).

For many years the central theoretical issues in this field dealt with the origin of these effects, argued in terms of the relative contribution of genetic as compared with environmental factors. Current interest in the effects of cultural deprivation ignores this classic debate; the more basic problem is to understand how cultural experience is translated into cognitive behavior and academic achievement (Bernstein, 1961; Hess, 1964).

The focus of concern is no longer upon the question of whether social and cultural disadvantage depress academic ability, but has shifted to a study of the mechanisms of exchange that mediate between the individual and his environment. The thrust of research and theory is toward conceptualizing social class as a discrete array of experiences and patterns of experience that can be examined in relation to the effects they have upon the emerging cognitive equipment of the young child. In short, the question this paper presents is this: what *is* cultural deprivation, and how does it act to shape and

Reprinted from Hess, R. D., and Shipman, V. C. Early experience and the socialization of cognitive modes in children. *Child Development,* **36**, 1965, 869–888. Copyright 1965 by the American Psychological Association. Reproduced by permission. This research was supported by the Research Division of the Children's Bureau, Social Security Administration; Department of Health, Education, and Welfare; Ford Foundation for the Advancement of Learning; and grants-in-aid from the Social Science Research Committee of the Division of Social Sciences, University of Chicago. Project staff members who made specific contributions to the analysis of data are Jere Brophy, Dina Feitelson, Roberta Meyer, and Ellis Olim.

depress the resources of the human mind?

The arguments we wish to present here are these: first, that the behavior which leads to social, educational, and economic poverty is socialized in early childhood—that is, it is learned; second, that the central quality involved in the effects of cultural deprivation is a lack of cognitive meaning in the mother-child communication system; and, third, that the growth of cognitive processes is fostered in family control systems which offer and permit a wide range of alternatives of action and thought and that such growth is constricted by systems of control which offer predetermined solutions and few alternatives for consideration and choice.

In this paper we will argue that the structure of the social system and the structure of the family shape communication and language and that language shapes thought and cognitive styles of problem-solving. In the deprived-family context this means that the nature of the control system which relates parent to child restricts the number and kind of alternatives for action and thought that are opened to the child; such constriction precludes a tendency for the child to reflect, to consider and choose among alternatives for speech and action. It develops modes for dealing with stimuli and with problems which are impulsive rather than reflective, which deal with the immediate rather than the future, and which are disconnected rather than sequential.

This position draws from the work of Basil Bernstein (1961) of the University of London. In his view, language structures and conditions what the child learns and how he learns, setting limits within which future learning may take place. He identifies two forms of communication codes or styles of verbal behavior: *restricted* and *elaborated*. Restricted codes are stereotyped, limited, and condensed, lacking in specificity and the exactness needed for precise conceptualization and differentiation. Sentences are short, simple, often unfinished; there is little use of subordinate clauses for elaborating the content of the sentence; it is a language of implicit meaning, easily understood and commonly shared. It is the language form often used in impersonal situations when the intent is to promote solidarity or reduce tension. Restricted codes are nonspecific clichés, statements, or observations about events made in general terms that will be readily understood. The basic quality of this mode is to limit the range and detail of concept and information involved.

Elaborated codes, however, are those in which communication is individualized and the message is specific to a particular situation, topic, and person. It is more particular, more differentiated, and more precise. It permits expression of a wider and more complex range of thought, tending toward discrimination among cognitive and affective content.

The effects of early experience with these codes are not only upon the communication modes and cognitive structure—they also establish potential patterns of relation with the external world. It is one of the dynamic features of Bernstein's work that he views language as social behavior. As such, language is used by participants of a social network to elaborate and express social and other interpersonal relations and, in turn, is shaped and determined by these relations.

The interlacing of social interaction and language is illustrated by the distinction between two types of family control. One is oriented toward control by *status* appeal or ascribed role norms. The second is oriented toward *persons.* Families differ in the degree to which they utilize each of these types of regulatory appeal. In status- (position-) oriented families, behavior tends to be regulated in terms of role expectations. There is little opportunity for the unique characteristics of the child to influence the decision-making process or the interaction between parent and child. In these families, the internal or personal states of the children are not influential as a basis for decision. Norms of behavior are stressed with such imperatives as, "You must do this because I say so," or "Girls don't act like that," or other statements which rely on the status of the participants or a behavior norm for justification (Bernstein, 1964).

In the family, as in other social structures, control is exercised in part through status appeals. The feature that distinguishes among families is the extent to which the status-based control maneuvers are modified by orientation toward persons. In a person-oriented appeal system, the unique characteristics of the child modify status demands and are taken into account in interaction. The decisions of this type of family are individualized and less frequently related to status or role ascriptions. Behavior is justified in terms of feelings, preference, personal and unique reactions, and subjective states. This philosophy not only permits but demands an elaborated linguistic code and a wide range of linguistic and behavioral alternatives in interpersonal interaction. Status-oriented families may be regulated by less individuated commands, messages, and responses. Indeed, by its nature, the status-oriented family will rely more heavily on a restricted code. The verbal exchange is inherent in the structure—regulates it and is regulated by it.

These distinctions may be clarified by two examples of mother-child communication using these two types of code. Assume that the emotional climate of two homes is approximately the same; the significant difference between them is in style of communication employed. A child is playing noisily in the kitchen with an assortment of pots and pans when the telephone rings. In one home the mother says, "Be quiet," or "Shut up," or issues any one of several other short, preemptory commands. In the other home the mother says, "Would you keep quiet a minute? I want to talk on the phone." The question our study poses is this: what inner response is elicited in the child, what is the effect upon his developing cognitive network of concepts and meaning in each of these two situations? In one instance the child is asked for a simple mental response. He is asked to attend to an uncomplicated message and to make a conditioned response (to comply); he is not called upon to reflect or to make mental discriminations. In the other example the child is required to follow two or three ideas. He is asked to relate his behavior to a time dimension; he must think of his behavior in relation to its effect upon another person. He must perform a more complicated task to follow the communication of his mother in that his relationship to her is mediated in part through concepts and shared ideas; his mind is stimulated or exercised (in an elementary fashion) by a more elaborate and complex verbal communication initiated by the mother. As objects of these two divergent communication styles, repeated in various ways, in similar situations and circumstances during the preschool years, these two imaginary children would be expected to develop significantly different verbal facility and cognitive equipment by the time they enter the public-school system.

A person-oriented family allows the child to achieve the behavior rules (role requirements) by presenting them in a specific context for the child and by emphasizing the consequences of alternative actions. Status-oriented families present the rules in an assigned manner, where compliance is the *only* rule-following possibility. In these situations the role of power in the interaction is more obvious, and, indeed, coercion and defiance are likely interactional possibilities. From another perspective, status-oriented families use a more rigid learning and teaching model in which compliance, rather than rationale, is stressed.

A central dimension through which we look at maternal behavior is to inquire what responses are elicited and permitted by styles of communication and interaction. There are two axes of the child's behavior in which we have a particular interest. One of these is represented by an *assertive, initiatory* approach to learning, as contrasted with

a *passive, compliant* mode of engagement; the other deals with the tendency to reach solutions impulsively or hastily as distinguished from a tendency to *reflect,* to compare alternatives, and to choose among available options.

These styles of cognitive behavior are related, in our hypotheses, to the dimensions of maternal linguistic codes and types of family control systems. A status-oriented statement, for example, tends to offer a set of regulations and rules for conduct and interaction that is based on arbitrary decisions rather than upon logical consequences which result from selection of one or another alternatives. Elaborated and person-oriented statements lend themselves more easily to styles of cognitive approach that involve reflection and reflective comparison. Status-oriented statements tend to be restrictive of thought. Take our simple example of the two children and the telephone. The verbal categoric command to "Be quiet" cuts off thought and offers little opportunity to relate the information conveyed in the command to the context in which it occurred. The more elaborated message, "Would you be quiet a minute? I want to talk on the phone" gives the child a rationale for relating his behavior to a wider set of considerations. In effect, he has been given a *why* for his mother's request and, by this example, possibly becomes more likely to *ask* why in another situation. It may be through this type of verbal interaction that the child learns to look for action sequences in his own and others' behavior. Perhaps through these more intent-oriented statements the child comes to see the world as others see it and learns to take the role of others in viewing himself and his actions. The child comes to see the world as a set of possibilities from which he can make a personal selection. He learns to role play with an element of personal flexibility, not by role-conforming rigidity.

Research Plan

For our project a research group of 163 Negro mothers and their 4-year-old children was selected from four different social status levels: Group A came from college-educated professional, executive, and managerial occupational levels; Group B came from skilled blue-collar occupational levels, with not more than high-school education; Group C came from unskilled or semiskilled occupational levels, with predominantly elementary-school education; Group D from unskilled or semiskilled occupational levels, with fathers absent and families supported by public assistance.

These mothers were interviewed twice in their homes and brought to the university for testing and for an interaction session between mother and child in which the mother was taught three simple tasks by the staff member and then asked to teach these tasks to the child.

One of these tasks was to sort or group a number of plastic toys by color and by function; a second task was to sort eight blocks by two characteristics simultaneously; the third task required the mother and child to work together to copy five designs on a toy called an Etch-a-Sketch. A description of various aspects of the project and some preliminary results have been presented in several papers (Brophy, Hess, and Shipman, 1965; Jackson, Hess, and

Shipman, 1965; Meyer, Shipman, and Hess, 1964; Olim, Hess, and Shipman, 1965; Shipman and Hess, 1965).

Results

The data in this paper are organized to show social-status differences among the four groups in the dimensions of behavior described above to indicate something of the maternal teaching styles that are emerging and to offer examples of relations between maternal and child behavior that are congruent with the general lines of argument we have laid out.

Social-Status Differences

VERBAL CODES: RESTRICTED *versus* ELABORATED. One of the most striking and obvious differences between the environments provided by the mothers of the research group was in their patterns of language use. In our testing sessions, the most obvious social-class variations were in the total amount of verbal output in response to questions and tasks asking for verbal response. For example, as Table 1 shows, mothers from the middle-class gave protocols that were consistently longer in language productivity than did mothers from the other three groups.

Taking three different types of questions that called for free response on the part of the mothers and counting the number of lines of typescript of the protocols, the tally for middle-class mothers was approximately 82 contrasted with an average of roughly 49 for mothers from the three other groups.

These differences in verbal products

TABLE 1

MEAN NUMBER OF TYPED LINES IN THREE DATA-GATHERING SITUATIONS

	UPPER MIDDLE N = 40	UPPER LOWER N = 40	LOWER LOWER N = 36	ADC N = 36
School situations	34.68	22.80	18.86	18.64
Mastery situations	28.45	18.70	15.94	17.75
CAT card	18.72	9.62	12.39	12.24
Total	81.85	51.12	47.19	48.63

indicate the extent to which the maternal environments of children in different social-class groups tend to be mediated by verbal cue and thus offer (or fail to offer) opportunities for labeling, for identifying objects and feelings and adult models who can demonstrate the usefulness of language as a tool for dealing with interpersonal interaction and for ordering stimuli in the environment.

In addition to this gross disparity in verbal output there were differences in the quality of language used by mothers in the various status groups. One approach to the analysis of language used by these mothers was an examination of their responses to the following task: They were shown the Lion Card of the Children's Apperception Test and asked to tell their child a story relating to the card. This card is a picture of a lion sitting on a chair holding a pipe in his hand. Beside him is a cane.

In the corner is a mouse peering out of a hole. The lion appears to be deep in thought. These protocols were the source of language samples which were summarized in nine scales (Table 2), two of which we wish to describe here.

The first scale dealt with the mother's tendency to use abstract words. The index derived was a proportion of abstract noun and verbal types to total number of noun and verb types. Words were defined as abstract when the name of the object is thought of apart from the cases in which it is actually realized. For example, in the sentence, "The lion is an *animal*," "animal" is an abstract word. However, in the sentence, "This animal in the picture is sitting on his throne," "animal" is not an abstract noun.

In our research group, middle-class mothers achieved an abstraction score of 5.6; the score for skilled work levels was 4.9; the score for the unskilled

T A B L E   2

SOCIAL STATUS DIFFERENCES IN LANGUAGE USAGE
(SCORES ARE THE MEANS FOR EACH GROUP)

	SOCIAL STATUS			
SCALE	Upper Middle N = 40	Upper Lower N = 42	Lower Lower N = 40	ADC N = 41
Mean sentence length [a]	11.39	8.74	9.66	8.23
Adjective range [b]	31.99	28.32	28.37	30.49
Adverb range [c]	11.14	9.40	8.70	8.20
Verb elaboration [d]	.59	.52	.47	.44
Complex verb preference [e]	63.25	59.12	50.85	51.73
Syntactic structure elaboration [f]	8.89	6.90	8.07	6.46
Stimulus utilization	5.82	4.81	4.87	5.36
Introduced content	3.75	2.62	2.45	2.34
Abstraction [g]	5.60	4.89	3.71	1.75

[a] Average number of words per sentence.
[b] Proportion of uncommon adjective types to total nouns, expressed as a percentage.
[c] Proportion of uncommon adverb types to total verbs, adjectives, and adverbs, expressed as a percentage.
[d] Average number of complex verb types per sentence.
[e] Proportion of complex verb types to all verb types, simple and complex.
[f] Average number of weighted complex syntactic structures per 100 words.
[g] Proportion of abstract nouns and verbs (excluding repetitions) to total nouns and verbs (excluding repetitions), expressed as a percentage.

group was 3.7; for recipients of Aid to Dependent Children (ADC), 1.8.

The second scale dealt with the mothers' tendency to use complex syntactic structures such as coordinate and subordinate clauses, unusual infinitive phrases (e.g., "To drive well, you must be alert"), infinitive clauses (e.g., "What to do next was the lion's problem"), and participial phrases (e.g., "Continuing the story, the lion . . ."). The index of structural elaboration derived was a proportion of these complex syntactic structures, weighted in accordance with their complexity and with the degree to which they are strung together to form still more complicated structures (e.g., clauses within clauses), to the total number of sentences.

In the research group, mothers from the middle class had a structure elaboration index of 8.89; the score for ADC mothers was 6.46. The use of complex grammatical forms and elaboration of these forms into complex clauses and sentences provides a highly elaborated code with which to manipulate the environment symbolically. This type of code encourages the child to recognize the possibilities and subtleties

inherent in language not only for communication but also for carrying on high-level cognitive procedures.

CONTROL SYSTEMS: PERSON VERSUS STATUS ORIENTATION. Our data on the mothers' use of status- as contrasted with person-oriented statements comes from maternal responses to questions inquiring what the mother would do in order to deal with several different hypothetical situations at school in which the child had broken the rules of the school, had failed to achieve, or had been wronged by a teacher or classmate. The results of this tally are shown in Table 3.

TABLE 3

PERSON-ORIENTED AND STATUS-ORIENTED UNITS ON SCHOOL SITUATION PROTOCOLS (MOTHER)

A. MEAN NUMBER

Social Class	Person-Oriented	Status-Oriented	P/S Ratio	N
Upper middle	9.52 (1–19)	7.50 (0–19)	1.27	40
Upper lower	6.20 (0–20)	7.32 (2–17)	0.85	40
Lower lower	4.66 (0–15)	7.34 (2–17)	0.63	35
ADC	3.59 (0–16)	8.15 (3–29)	0.44	34

B. MEAN PER CENT

Social Class	Person-Oriented	Status-Oriented	N
Upper middle	36.92	27.78	40
Upper lower	31.65	36.92	40
Lower lower	26.43	40.69	35
ADC	20.85	51.09	34

As is clear from these means, the greatest differences between status groups is in the tendency to utilize person-oriented statements. These differences are even greater if seen as a ratio of person-to-status type responses.

The orientation of the mothers to these different types of control is seen not only in prohibitive or reparative situations but in their instructions to their children in preparing them for new experiences. The data on this point come from answers to the question: "Suppose your child were starting to school tomorrow for the first time. What would you tell him? How would you prepare him for school?"

One mother, who was person-oriented and used elaborated verbal codes, replied as follows:

"First of all, I would remind her that she was going to school to learn, that her teacher would take my place, and that she would be expected to follow instructions. Also that her time was to be spent mostly in the classroom with other children, and that any questions or any problems that she might have she could consult with her teacher for assistance."

"Anything else?"

"No, anything else would probably be confusing for her at her particular age."

In terms of promoting educability, what did this mother do in her response? First, she was informative; she presented the school situation as comparable to one already familiar to the child; second, she offered reassurance and support to help the child deal with anxiety; third, she described the school situation as one that involves a personal relationship between the child and the teacher; and, fourth, she presented the classroom situation as one in which the child was to learn.

A second mother responded as follows to this question:

"Well, John, it's time to go to school now. You must know how to behave. The first day at school you should be a good boy and should do just what the teacher tells you to do."

In contrast to the first mother, what did this mother do? First, she defined the role of the child as passive and compliant; second, the central issues she presented were those dealing with authority and the institution, rather than with learning; third, the relationship and roles she portrayed were sketched in terms of status and role expectations rather than in personal terms; and, fourth, her message was general, restricted, and vague, lacking information about how to deal with the problems of school except by passive compliance.

A more detailed analysis of the mothers' responses to this question grouped their statements as *imperative* or *instructive* (Table 4). An imperative statement was defined as an unqualified injunction or command, such as, "Mind the teacher and do what she tells you to do," or "The first thing you have to do is be on time," or "Be nice and do not fight.' An instructive statement offers information or commands which carry a rationale or justification for the rule to be observed. Examples: "If you are tardy or if you stay away from school, your marks will go down"; or "I would tell him about the importance of minding the teacher. The teacher needs his full cooperation. She will have so many children that she won't be able to pamper any youngster."

TABLE 4

INFORMATION MOTHERS WOULD GIVE TO CHILD
ON HIS FIRST DAY AT SCHOOL

Social Status	Imperative	Instructive	Support	Preparation	Other	N
			% of Total Statements			
Upper middle	14.9	8.7	30.2	8.6	37.6	39
Upper lower	48.2	4.6	13.8	3.8	29.6	41
Lower lower	44.4	1.7	13.1	1.2	39.6	36
ADC	46.6	3.2	17.1	1.3	31.8	37
			% of Mothers Using Category			
Upper middle	48.7	38.5	76.9	33.3	87.2	—
Upper lower	85.4	17.1	39.0	19.5	70.7	—
Lower lower	75.0	5.6	36.1	8.3	77.8	—
ADC	86.5	16.2	43.2	8.1	86.5	—

STATUS DIFFERENCES IN CONCEPT UTILIZATION. One of the measures of cognitive style used with both mothers and children in the research group was the S's mode of classificatory behavior. For the adult version (Kagan, Moss, and Sigel, 1963), S is required to make 12 consecutive sorts of MAPS* figures placed in a prearranged random order on a large cardboard. After each sort

* MAPS is an abbreviation for Make A Picture Story, and, as the name implies, involves asking the examinee to make a story from a series of pictures that may be related in various ways.—ED.

she was asked to give her reason for putting certain figures together. This task was intended to reveal her typical or preferred manner of grouping stimuli and the level of abstraction that she uses in perceiving and ordering objects in the environment. Responses fell into four categories: descriptive part-whole, descriptive global, relational-contextual, and categorical-inferential. A descriptive response is a direct reference to physical attributes present in the stimuli, such as size, shape, or posture. Examples: "They're all children," or "They are all lying down," or "They are all men." The subject may also

TABLE 5

MEAN RESPONSES TO ADULT SIGEL SORTING TASK (MAPS)

	SOCIAL STATUS			
CATEGORY	Upper Middle N = 40	Upper Lower N = 42	Lower Lower N = 39	ADC N = 41
Total descriptive	3.18	2.19	2.18	2.59
Descriptive part-whole	1.65	1.33	1.31	1.49
Descriptive global	1.52	0.86	0.87	1.10
Relational-contextual	5.52	6.79	7.38	6.73
Categorical-inferential	3.30	3.00	2.23	2.66

choose to use only a part of the figure —"They both have hats on." In a relational-contextual response, any one stimulus gets its meaning from a relation with other stimuli. Examples: "Doctor and nurse," or "Wife is cooking dinner for her husband," or "This guy looks like he shot this other guy." In categorical-inferential responses, sorts are based on nonobservable characteristics of the stimulus for which each stimulus is an independent representative of the total class. Examples: "All of these people work for a living" or "These are all handicapped people."

As may be seen in Table 5, relational responses were most frequently offered; categorical-inferential were next most common, and descriptive most infrequent. The distribution of responses of our status groups showed that the middle-class group was higher on descriptive and categorical; low-status groups were higher on relational. The greater use of relational categories by the working-class mothers is especially significant. Response times for relational sorts are usually shorter, indicating less reflection and evaluating of alternative hypotheses. Such responses also indicate relatively low attention to external stimuli details (Kagan, 1964). Relational responses are often subjective, reflecting a tendency to relate objects to personal concerns in contrast with the descriptive and categorical responses which tend to be objective and detached, more general, and more abstract. Categorical responses, in particular, represent thought processes that are more orderly and complex in organizing stimuli, suggesting more efficient strategies of information processing.

The most striking finding from the data obtained from the children's Sigel Sorting Task was the decreasing use of the cognitive style dimensions and increasing nonverbal responses with decrease in social-status level. As may be seen in the tables showing children's performance on the Sigel Sorting Task (Tables 6 and 7), although most upper middle-class children and a majority of the upper lower-class children use relational and descriptive global responses, there is no extensive use of any of the other cognitive style dimensions by the two lower lower-class

groups. In looking at particular categories one may note the relative absence of descriptive part-whole responses for other than the middle-class group and the large rise in nonverbal responses below the middle-class level. These results would seem to reflect the relatively undeveloped verbal and conceptual ability of children from homes with restricted range of verbal and conceptual content.

Relational and descriptive global responses have been considered the most immature and would be hypothesized to occur most frequently in preschool children. Relational responses are often subjective, using idiosyncratic and irrelevant cues; descriptive global re-

TABLE 6

CHILDREN'S RESPONSES TO SIGEL SORTING TASK (MEANS)

	SOCIAL STATUS			
CATEGORY	Upper Middle N = 40	Upper Lower N = 42	Lower Lower N = 39	ADC N = 41
Descriptive part-whole	2.25	0.71	0.20	0.34
Descriptive global	2.80	2.29	1.51	0.98
Relational-contextual	3.18	2.31	1.18	1.02
Categorical-inferential	2.02	1.36	1.18	0.61
Nonscorable verbal responses	5.75	6.31	6.64	7.24
Nonverbal	3.00	6.41	7.08	8.76
No sort	1.00	0.62	2.21	1.05

TABLE 7

PERCENTAGE OF FOUR-YEAR-OLD CHILDREN
RESPONDING IN EACH OF THE CATEGORIES

| | SOCIAL STATUS | | | |
CATEGORY	Upper Middle N = 40	Upper Lower N = 42	Lower Lower N = 39	ADC N = 41
Descriptive part-whole	40.0	28.6	18.0	14.6
Descriptive global	70.0	54.8	53.8	31.7
Total descriptive	80.0	66.7	59.0	39.0
Relational-contextual	77.5	66.7	41.0	43.9
Categorical-inferential	52.5	45.2	30.8	24.4
Nonscorable verbal	85.0	88.1	92.3	85.4
Nonverbal	52.5	66.7	82.0	87.8
No sort	12.5	7.1	25.6	19.5

sponses, often referring to sex and occupational roles, are somewhat more dependent upon experience. On the other hand, descriptive part-whole responses have been shown to increase with age and would be expected to be used less frequently. However, these descriptive part-whole responses, which are correlated with favorable prognostic signs for educability (such as attentiveness, control and learning ability), were almost totally absent from all but the upper middle-class group. Kagan (1964) has described two fundamental cognitive dispositions involved in producing such analytic concepts: the tendency to reflect over alternative solutions that are simultaneously available and the tendency to analyze a visual stimulus into component parts. Both behaviors require a delayed discrimination response. One may describe the impairment noted for culturally disadvantaged children as arising from differences in opportunities for developing these reflective attitudes.

The mothers' use of relational responses was significantly correlated with their children's use of nonscorable and nonverbal responses on the Sigel task and with poor performance on the 8-Block and Etch-a-Sketch tasks. The mothers' inability or disinclination to take an abstract attitude on the Sigel task was correlated with ineffectual teaching on the 8-Block task and inability to plan and control the Etch-a-Sketch situation. Since relational responses have been found (Kagan, Moss, and Sigel, 1963) to be correlated with impulsivity, tendencies for nonverbal rather than verbal teaching, mother-domination, and limited sequencing and discrimination might be expected and would be predicted to result in limited categorizing ability and impaired verbal skills in the child.

Analysis of Maternal Teaching Styles

These differences among the status groups and among mothers within the groups appear in slightly different form in the teaching sessions in which the mothers and children engaged. There were large differences among the status groups in the ability of the mothers to teach and the children to learn. This is illustrated by the performance scores on the sorting tasks.

Let us describe the interaction between the mother and child in one of the structured teaching situations. The wide range of individual differences in linguistic and interactional styles of these mothers may be illustrated by excerpts from recordings. The task of the mother is to teach the child how to group or sort a small number of toys.

The first mother outlines the task for the child, gives sufficient help and explanation to permit the child to proceed on her own. She says:

"All right, Susan, this board is the place where we put the little toys; first of all you're supposed to learn how to place them according to color. Can you do that? The things that are all the same color you put in one section; in the second section you put another group of colors, and in the third section you put the last group of colors.

Can you do that? Or would you like to see me do it first?"

Child: "I want to do it."

This mother has given explicit information about the task and what is expected of the child; she has offered support and help of various kinds; and she has made it clear that she impelled the child to perform.

A second mother's style offers less clarity and precision. She says in introducing the same task:

"Now, I'll take them all off the board; now you put them all back on the board. What are these?"

Child: "A truck."

"All right, just put them right here; put the other one right here; all right put the other one there."

This mother must rely more on nonverbal communication in her commands; she does not define the task for the child; the child is not provided with ideas or information that she can grasp in attempting to solve the problem; neither is she told what to expect or what the task is, even in general terms.

A third mother is even less explicit. She introduces the task as follows:

"I've got some chairs and cars, do you want to play the game?" Child does not respond. Mother continues: "O.K. What's this?"

Child: "A wagon?"

Mother: "Hm?"

Child: "A wagon?"

Mother: "This is not a wagon. What's this?"

The conversation continues with this sort of exchange for several pages. Here again, the child is not provided with the essential information he needs to solve or to understand the problem. There is clearly some impelling on the part of the mother for the child to perform, but the child has not been told what he is to do. There were marked social-class differences in the ability of the children to learn from their mothers in the teaching sessions.

Each teaching session was concluded with an assessment by a staff member of the extent to which the child had learned the concepts taught by the mother. His achievement was scored in two ways: first, the ability to correctly place or sort the objects and, second, the ability to verbalize the principle on which the sorting or grouping was made.

Children from middle-class homes were well above children from working-class homes in performance on these sorting tasks, particularly in offering verbal explanations as to the basis for making the sort (Tables 8 and 9). Over 60 per cent of middle-class children placed the objects correctly on all tasks; the performance of working-class children ranged as low as 29 per cent correct. Approximately 40 per cent of these middle-class children who

TABLE 8

DIFFERENCES AMONG STATUS GROUPS IN
CHILDREN'S PERFORMANCE IN TEACHING SITUATIONS
(TOY SORT TASK)

SOCIAL STATUS	PLACED CORRECTLY (%)	VERBALIZED CORRECTLY (%)		N
A. Identity sort (cars, spoons, chairs):				
Upper middle	61.5	28.2	45.8 [a]	39
Upper lower	65.0	20.0	30.8	40
Lower lower	68.4	29.0	42.3	38
ADC	66.7	30.8	46.2	39
B. Color sort (red, green, yellow):				
Upper middle	69.2	28.2	40.7 [a]	39
Upper lower	67.5	15.0	22.2	40
Lower lower	57.9	13.2	22.7	38
ADC	33.3	5.1	15.4	39

[a] Percent of those who placed object correctly.

TABLE 9

DIFFERENCES AMONG STATUS GROUPS IN
CHILDREN'S PERFORMANCE IN TEACHING SITUATIONS
(8-BLOCK TASK)

SOCIAL STATUS	PLACED CORRECTLY (%)	ONE-DIMENSION VERBALIZED (%)		BOTH VERBALIZED (%)		N
A. Short O:						
Upper middle	75.0	57.5	57.5 [a]	25.0	33.3 [a]	40
Upper lower	51.2	39.0	43.2	2.4	4.8	41
Lower lower	50.0	29.0	33.3	15.8	31.6	38
ADC	43.6	20.5	22.2	2.6	5.9	39
B. Tall X:						
Upper middle	60.0	62.5	64.1 [a]	27.5	45.8 [a]	40
Upper lower	48.8	39.0	42.1	17.1	35.0	41
Lower lower	34.2	23.7	26.5	7.9	23.1	38
ADC	28.2	18.0	20.0	0.0	0.0	39

[a] Percent of those who placed object correctly.

were successful were able to verbalize the sorting principle; working-class children were less able to explain the sorting principle, ranging downward from the middle-class level to one task on which no child was able to verbalize correctly the basis of his sorting behavior. These differences clearly paralleled the relative abilities and teaching skills of the mothers from differing social-status groups.

The difference among the four status levels was apparent not only on these sorting and verbal skills but also in the mother's ability to regulate her own behavior and her child's in performing tasks which require planning or care rather than verbal or conceptual skill. These differences were revealed by the mother-child performance on the Etch-a-Sketch task. An Etch-a-Sketch toy is a small, flat box with a screen on which lines can be drawn by a device within the box. The marker is controlled by two knobs: one for horizontal movement, one for vertical. The mother is assigned one knob, the child the other. The mother is shown several designs which are to be reproduced. Together they attempt to copy the design models. The mother decides when their product is a satisfactory copy of the original. The products are scored by measuring deviations from the original designs.

These sessions were recorded, and the nonverbal interaction was described by an observer. Some of the most relevant results were these: middle-class mothers and children performed better on the task (14.6 points) than mothers and children from the other groups (9.2; 8.3; 9.5; [Table 10]). Mothers of the three lower-status groups were relatively persistent, rejecting more complete figures than the middle-class mothers; mothers from the middle class praised the child's efforts more than did other mothers but gave just as much criticism; the child's cooperation as rated by the observer was as good or better in low-status groups as in middle-class pairs (Table 11), there was little difference between the groups in affect expressed to the child by the mother (Brophy et al., 1965).

In these data, as in other not presented here, the mothers of the four status groups differed relatively little, on the average, in the affective elements of their interaction with their children. The gross differences appeared in the verbal and cognitive environments that they presented.

Against this background . . . return for a moment to the problem

TABLE 10

PERFORMANCE ON ETCH-A-SKETCH TASK (MEANS)

	SOCIAL STATUS			
	Upper Middle N = 40	Upper Lower N = 42	Lower N = 40	ADC N = 41
Total score (range 0–40)	14.6	9.2	8.3	9.5
Average number of attempts	12.7	17.2	12.2	15.1
Complete figures rejected	2.3	3.6	3.5	3.4
Child's total score	5.9	4.0	3.4	4.0
Child's contribution to total score (per cent)	40.4	43.5	41.0	42.1

of the meaning, or, perhaps more correctly, the lack of meaning in cultural deprivation. One of the features of the behavior of the working-class mothers and children is a tendency to act without taking sufficient time for reflection and planning. In a sense one might call this impulsive behavior—not by acting out unconscious or forbidden impulses, but in a type of activity in which a particular act seems not to be related to the act that preceded it or to its consequences. In this sense it lacks meaning; it is not sufficiently related to the context in which it occurs, to the motivations of the participants, or to the goals of the task. This behavior may be verbal or motor;

it shows itself in several ways. On the Etch-a-Sketch task, for example, the mother may silently watch a child make an error and then punish him. Another mother will anticipate the error, will warn the child that he is about to reach a decision point; she will prepare him by verbal and nonverbal cues to be careful, to look ahead, and to avoid the mistake. He is encouraged to reflect, to anticipate the consequences of his action, and in this way to avoid error. A problem-solving approach requires reflection and the ability to weigh decisions, to choose among alternatives. The effect of restricted speech and of status orientation is to foreclose the need for reflective weighing of alter-

TABLE 11 [a]

MOTHER-CHILD INTERACTION ON ETCH-A-SKETCH TASK (MEANS)

	SOCIAL STATUS			
	Upper Middle N = 40	Upper Lower N = 41	Lower Lower N = 39	ADC N = 39
Praises child	4.6	6.9	7.2	7.5
Criticizes child	6.4	5.5	6.4	5.9
Overall acceptance of child	2.2	3.2	3.4	3.6
Child's cooperation	5.6	5.3	4.5	5.1
Level of affection shown to child	4.8	5.4	5.2	5.8

[a] Ratings made by observer; low number indicates more of the quality rated.

natives and consequences; the use of an elaborated code, with its orientation to persons and to consequences (including future), tends to produce cognitive styles more easily adapted to problem-solving and reflection.

The objective of our study is to discover how teaching styles of the mothers induce and shape learning styles and information-processing strategies in the children. The picture that is beginning to emerge is that the meaning of deprivation is a deprivation of meaning—a cognitive environment in which behavior is controlled by status rules rather than by attention to the individual characteristics of a specific situation and one in which behavior is not mediated by verbal cues or by teaching that relates events to one another and the present to the future. This environment produces a child who relates to authority rather than to rationale, who, although often compliant, is not reflective in his behavior, and for whom the consequences of an act are largely considered in terms of immediate punishment or reward rather than future effects and long-range goals.

When the data are more complete, a more detailed analysis of the findings will enable us to examine the effect of maternal cognitive environments in terms of individual mother-child transactions, rather than in the gross categories of social class. This analysis will not only help us to understand how social-class environment is mediated through the interaction between mother and child but will give more precise information about the effects of individual maternal environments on the cognitive growth of the young child.

COMPENSATORY EDUCATION FOR THE DISADVANTAGED

Although the schools are obviously not a panacea, they have been, and continue to be, considered a powerful instrument for social improvement.

> It is evident from various analyses that the gap between the "haves" and the "have nots" and between the "less equal" and the "more equal" has been broadening in our affluent society. . . . In the war on poverty and in the civil rights struggle, the role of education has become central—both *de jure* through federal legislation and *de facto* as the schools have been asked (perhaps forced) to reaffirm their traditional function of providing equal and appropriate educational opportunities for all children and youth. [Frazier, 1968, p. 2.]

The schools are currently attempting to fulfill this role by both restructuring the old and adding innovative programs.

Changes in Organization of the Traditional School. One of the major ways in which schools are being reorganized is through grouping of students. Interestingly, this involves both the bringing together of students who share the same academic needs and the elimination of homogeneous classes. The latter is frequently a demand of minority groups and is aimed at social integration. At the same time, there is an increase in reorganization of staff, such as in team teaching, and in the addition of social workers and teacher-aides.

Curriculum and Method Changes. Changes in curriculum and method include an increase in flexibility, individualized programming, self-instructional materials, and emphasis on activities to overcome presumed deficits of the disadvantaged, such as in language and reading.

Extensions of School Programs. Many new types of programs have been instituted for the school-age child, ranging from extra tutoring after school to enrichment experiences such as visiting museums or attending camps. Underlying this approach is the assumption that the disadvantaged child can benefit both by additional academic practice and a widening of his horizons. Frequently there is an attempt to include parents in the planning or implementing of these programs. Perhaps the most dramatic extension of schooling, however, is to be found in the recent emphasis on early education, as reflected in preschooling.

Early Educational Intervention

Although schooling for very young children has been known in the United States for more than a century, it had been confined largely to the middle and upper classes until the mid-1960s. Project Head Start, inaugurated in 1965 with federal funds, radically changed this state of affairs. Its thrust clearly was to eliminate the disparity which existed between lower- and middle-class children in intellectual achievement. From its conception Head Start was designed to prepare the disadvantaged child for school by not only offering preschool experience but also by providing health care and better nutritional standards and encouraging families to participate in the well-being of the child.

The rationale for preschooling per se grew from a convergence of sources: psychological theory that early experience is critical for future learning, investigations demonstrating that enriched environments raised

the performance of animals on a variety of tasks, and the increasing awareness of the interaction of heredity and environment. Palmer has commented
on the marriage of politics and science that underlies preschool intervention:

> While behavioral scientists were beginning to speak their private thoughts
> aloud, the awkward American concern for relating politics with humanity
> was seeking something new to assuage our guilt and to provide a rallying
> cry for votes to support the Great Society. The rallying point became pov-
> erty and its truly iniquitous effects, and what aspect of poverty is better
> suited to attract the American voter than the disadvantaged child? From
> Harvard was heard [that] under proper conditions and instructions the
> child could be taught any task at any age. Regardless of the dearth of data
> to solidly support that hypothesis, society was handed a touchstone where
> political action and the frustrated drives of scientists, educators, and legis-
> lators could be joined at last. [1969, p. 26.]

In 1967 the federal government extended its funding to the Follow
Through Program, aimed at slightly older children, and to Parent Child
Centers designed to involve parents of youngsters under three years of age.
Meanwhile, demands for extensive support for day care services for em-
ployed mothers promise an even greater mushrooming of programs for
the young.

EXTENDED DISCUSSION

A SURVEY OF COMPENSATORY PROGRAMS
FOR DISADVANTAGED PRESCHOOLERS

Even at the present time, it is impossible to survey all of the many compensatory education programs designed for preschoolers. Our approach,
therefore, will be to describe several that represent different facets of the
early education movement. More specifically, we will consider programs
that vary with regard to amount of structure, underlying theoretical base,
and the child's age.

Home Intervention for Children under Three Years. Like many home intervention programs, that of Karnes, Teska, Hodgins, and Badger (1970) provided direct instruction in effective teaching methods to mothers of one- to three-year-olds. Mothers attended weekly two-hour meetings during which staff members related particular teaching methods thought to be effective and discussed problems that parents had encountered with their children. Staff members also paid monthly visits to the children's homes to observe how the procedures were being implemented. During the home training, children were given toys that would foster verbal interactions between them and their parents. Picture scrapbooks in which children could identify objects with which they were familiar proved particularly helpful.

The basic approach of the investigators is embodied in four teaching principles stressed to the parents:

1. If you have a good working relationship with your child you can become an effective teacher. A good relationship is based on mutual respect.

2. Be positive in your approach. Acknowledge the child's success in each new task, even when the child simply tries to do as he is instructed. Minimize mistakes, show the right way immediately, have the child attempt the task again, and praise him.

3. Break the task into separate steps. Teach one step at a time, starting with the simplest. Do not proceed to the next step until the child is successful with the first.

4. If the child does not attend or try to do as instructed (and you are absolutely sure he can do what is asked), put the toys away until later. Do not scold, beg, or bribe. The time together should be fun for both of you. [Karnes *et al.*, 1970, p. 929.]

Of the twenty families who started, fifteen completed the two-year program. The high level of motivation reflected in this fact may have been enhanced by small stipends that were given to the mothers and by the children's fondness for toys which had been made available by the project. The youngsters themselves showed large and striking superiority in IQ scores, both compared to a control group of the same age who had not been exposed to the program and compared to the scores obtained by older siblings when they had been the same age. There were additional indications of intellectual growth as measured by the ITPA, a test of language development. At present, however, no data are available concerning the durability over time of the gains.

Day Care Intervention for the Very Young. One of the first educationally oriented day care centers for disadvantaged children between six months and three years of age was begun by Caldwell and her associates. Children attend five days per week, six to nine hours each day. Emphasis was placed on a wide range of goals, including helping the child to "become maximally aware of the world around him, eager to participate in it, and confident that what he does will have some impact on it" (Caldwell and Richmond, 1964, p. 485). The program also encompassed many more specific aims, such as improving social skills, teaching toleration of delays in rewards, and communicating knowledge that will later be useful in school. Children's progress in meeting these goals was accompanied by significant increases in their IQS (Caldwell, 1968).

More recently Caldwell has developed a comprehensive program providing educational and day care service to children from six months of age to the end of childhood. Predicated on the belief that early childhood education will not have a significant impact until it is part of public education, the program is partially supported by the public schools of Little Rock, Arkansas, and housed in one of them—the Kramer School (Caldwell, 1972). Youngsters may spend most or a portion of the day at the school, depending upon their need for day care. In the early childhood section, children are grouped according to developmental level—babies, toddlers, threes, fours, and fives. There is one adult for every four or five youngsters three years of age or younger. Figure XIV-2 shows one kind of activity, aimed primarily at motor development, engaged in by two-year-olds. Although it is too soon to assess the overall impact of the Kramer School, it is among the more innovative and exciting programs.

An Eclectic Approach for Four- to Six-year-olds. One of the first preschool programs, Gray and Klaus's Early Training Project (1970), involved poor black youngsters between four and six years of age who attended summer school for several years and with whom contact was continued on a weekly basis during the year. Spending half days at the center, youngsters worked in small groups of four or five to one teacher. Activities focused on two areas, one of which was attitudes toward achievement; it involved training such aspects as delay of gratification and persistence. The other, aptitude toward achievement, was designed to foster perceptual, cognitive, and language skills. In general, there was considerable emphasis on shaping desirable behavior with reinforcement, using both concrete rewards and social approval such as hugging. Home visits were also provided in order to encourage families to motivate their children.

Intelligence and achievement tests were administered to the students at the end of first, second, and fourth grades. The results, which were compared to performance of control youngsters from both the same locale and a distant city who did not participate in the program, are encouraging. On the intelligence tests, the experimental subjects remained superior, even three years after training ended. Achievement tests administered in the year following training also reflected benefits of having participated in the program, but these gains were not apparent three years after the program's end. Of additional interest, the younger brothers and sisters—at least those born in the years immediately following the births of the experimental subjects—also benefited from the program. Preschool training programs thus may have something of a snowball effect, benefiting even those to encourage families to motivate their children.

FIGURE XIV–2

Scene from the Kramer School, depicting the development of motor skills in two-year-old children. Courtesy Dr. Bettye M. Caldwell.

The Piagetian Approach for Four- to Six-year-olds. The Ypsilanti Perry Preschool Project was intended to assess the long-term effects of a two-year preschool program on economically disadvantaged black children. Five "waves" of children attended the daily preschool program between 1962 and 1967; each was exposed to a Piagetian curriculum designed to foster cognitive growth. A high level of verbal stimulation, participation in sociodramatic plays, and the learning of concepts through active interaction with the environment characterized the curriculum. In addition, parents were encouraged to apply similar methods in their instruction of their children; weekly home visits by project personnel and group meetings of parents were used to accomplish this goal.

Weikart (1972) lists several conclusions concerning the long-term effectiveness of the preschool program. Children who were experimental participants did better in first and second grade on IQ tests, but the difference disappeared by third grade. On the achievement test measure, experimentally trained children were significantly superior in first and third grades, though not in second. In all three grades, teachers rated the social-emotional status of experimental participants more positively than that of nonparticipants.

A Structured Approach for Four- to Six-year-olds. Carl Bereiter and Siegfried Engelmann have developed one of the more structured preschool programs for the disadvantaged (Bereiter and Engelmann, 1966). A typical Bereiter-Engelmann classroom consists of fifteen four- and five-year-olds and three teachers. The school day is two-and-one-half hours; language, reading, and arithmetic are taught for twenty minutes every day. Most of the remaining time is structured in small group sessions concentrating on music, writing, and vocabulary building.

Because Bereiter and Engelmann assign to inadequate language development an extremely important role in the inferior classroom performance of disadvantaged children, much emphasis is given to language training. The curriculum underscores learning the kinds of words and phrases that are likely to be used by elementary school teachers. Oral presentation of material is rapid, with frequent opportunity for responses from the children both as a group and individually; feedback is directed at specific rather than global aspects of the child's performance. Thus, a Bereiter-Engelmann teacher would be likely to say, "That answer was good because it referred to what we talked about before" rather than stopping at "That was a good answer." The program also encourages children to speak loudly and clearly, a somewhat unusual approach inasmuch as most teachers of disadvantaged children spend considerable time trying to quiet their class.

However, Bereiter and Engelmann have argued that disadvantaged children often fail to receive appropriate feedback because they mumble and are hard to understand.

The Bereiter-Engelmann approach makes frequent use of pattern drills, especially in identifying and labeling objects. The following passage represents the kind of pattern used:

> Teacher: "This is a spoon. Is this a spoon?"
> Class (in unison). "Yes."
> Teacher: "What is this?"
> Class (in unison): "A spoon."
> Teacher: "Is this a knife?"
> Leroy: "No, it is a spoon."
> Teacher: "That's right Leroy. It is a fork."
> Leroy: "No, it's a spoon."
> Teacher: "Oh, I guess that you're right."

As in this passage, teachers frequently err and praise students for correcting them. This serves the dual purpose of keeping the class on its collective toes and communicating the message that knowledge is power: students who try hard and pay attention can succeed where even the teacher has failed.

Children who have participated in the two-year preschool program have shown impressive IQ gains. Bereiter (1972) also reports that kindergarten graduates of the program display second-grade levels of proficiency in reading and arithmetic and that they compile better attendance records in regular classrooms than children not exposed to preschool training. This may indicate improvement in the attitude of the youngsters toward school. Perhaps most important, there is indication that the classroom superiority of participants in the program may last through the fourth grade.

Some Issues in Preschool Education

Structured versus Unstructured Curricula. Preschool curricula vary greatly in the amount of structure they impose on classroom activities. Some, usually those explicitly aimed at aiding the child's social and emotional development, leave the teachers the task of selecting what activities to engage in. Others prescribe specific methods and content. Evaluating one unstructured program, Alpern (1966) found that there were no differences in readiness, attitudes, or communications skills between children who had attended it and those who had not been exposed to preschool. In addition, a comparison between two relatively structured programs—those of Karnes and of Bereiter and Engelmann—and one unstructured traditional nursery school approach found first- and second-grade students who had attended the structured programs achieving at a higher level than their peers who attended the unstructured one. It appears, then, that some degree of structure is desirable in preschool programs for disadvantaged students.

Comparisons of Relatively Structured Curricula. The foregoing statements should not be interpreted to mean that the more structure, the better the program. Programs that are termed moderately structured—those of Weikart and of Gray and Klaus—do not appear to be significantly inferior to highly structured efforts. Weikart (1972) reports a comparison among his own cognitively oriented curriculum, a language training curriculum based on Bereiter and Engelmann's work, and a more traditional approach. Somewhat to the investigator's surprise, in the first year of training children in all three groups showed substantial gains. Even into the third year, no differences were apparent between the Weikart and Bereiter-Engelmann programs. Similarly, Karnes, Hodgins, Teska, and Kirk (1969) found no substantial differences in IQ scores between the less structured Karnes program and the more structured Bereiter-Engelmann approach.

The reasons for similar impact of programs initiated from quite different theoretical positions may stem from similarity in actual content areas stressed; Karnes, Gray-Klaus (1970), and Bereiter-Engelmann programs all emphasize use of language and proficiency in labeling familiar objects. There seems to be general agreement that no one curriculum and no one theoretical stance has been shown more productive than any other (Weikart, 1972; Bereiter, 1972).

Importance of Teacher and Curriculum. Weikart (1971) attributes the lesser effectiveness of unstructured curricula to their failure to provide sufficient guidance to teachers. "The curriculum," he says, "is for the teacher not the child." He emphasizes that curricula are most effective in focusing teachers' energy on procedures that will help children learn. The danger of not having effective curricula is that teachers might otherwise diffuse their energies on relatively unrewarding tasks.

Weikart also notes, however, that many observed differences in program effectiveness may be due to demoralization of teachers who realize at some point that their class is only a control group. To the extent that this consideration is an important one, differences between groups using a particular curriculum and those in control groups must be interpreted cautiously.

Experimental Control and Future Applications

The preschool projects reported in the previous section have been among the most successful efforts in the field. All have been characterized by close working relationships between the main investigators, teachers, and other project personnel. Results of less closely supervised efforts have been far less encouraging. An initial evaluation of the Headstart program (Westinghouse Learning Corporation, 1969), for example, found that effects of preschool training were small and transitory. This casts a somewhat disturbing shadow over future mass-enrollment compensatory programs. There will never be a sufficient number of research investigators to supervise all projects. Unless curricula are developed that allow teachers to educate preschoolers effectively without extensive supervision, the accomplishments cited above will have been somewhat empty ones. One of the most immediately important tasks for investigators in the preschool area, therefore, is to design curricula that can be implemented without constant overviewing and to investigate the effectiveness of a variety of such curricula given various degrees of supervision.

XV

BEHAVIOR PROBLEMS OF CHILDHOOD

IN THIS CHAPTER we turn to behavior problems in development. Rather than attempting an exhaustive treatment of the subject, however, we have selected from among the major types of problems which children experience. As in earlier chapters, our interest goes beyond mere description, for we also are concerned with how these problems can be dealt with and overcome.

PREVALENCE OF CHILDREN'S BEHAVIOR PROBLEMS: AN OVERVIEW

Behavior disorders in childhood are known only to the extent that they come to the attention of various societal institutions and agents. The middle-class child whose parent immediately takes him to a psychological clinic upon the first display of a temper tantrum will make his way into the actuarial records, whereas the extremely troubled child of a very poor rural family may never be counted. Despite these difficulties, though, it is possible to obtain at least some general information about the incidence and prevalence of a variety of behavior disorders in childhood. One tactic, which provides a "bird's eye" view of the problem, is to examine admission rates for psychological and psychiatric services according to youngsters' sex and age.

Such a strategy was used by Rosen, Bahn, and Kramer (1964). Some of their findings are shown in Figure XV–1, from which it can be seen that boys are much more likely than girls, through most of childhood, to be judged as requiring psychological or psychiatric help, and that there are two distinct peaks (consistent for the sexes) at which difficulties appear to be most frequent.

A longitudinal study by MacFarlane, Allen, and Honzik (1954) helps round out the picture provided by the above cross-sectional study. Examining behavior problems of normal children between the ages of twenty-one months and fourteen years, MacFarlane and his associates found five different developmental trends. These trends, as well as a behavioral example of each, are shown in Table XV–1.

The relative frequency of various difficulties in childhood appears to be rather constant across Western cultures. Anthony (1970), for example, has brought together information collected in Buffalo, New York, and Edinburgh, Scotland, to compare the prevalence of behavior symptoms in childhood. Some of the findings, presented in Table XV–2, illustrate both the relative prevalence of a number of fairly common problems and also the consistency between two distinct cultures.

Classification of Behavior Disorders

"Abnormal" behavior once was regarded as a substantial departure from normalcy, so that a child was thought to be mentally ill or mentally well in the same way that a stick is either broken or not. Today this view largely has been rejected. Instead, behavior problems in childhood are assumed to fall on a continuum with all other childhood behaviors, ranging from those which are pleasing to everyone to those which are extremely disturbing (cf. Ross, 1974). Thus, the child with a "psychological" problem simply

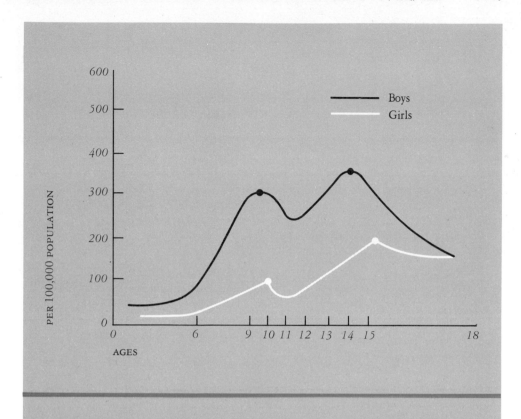

The clinic termination rate for boys and girls, showing a higher incidence of treatment for boys than for girls and two distinct age peaks. (Rosen, Bahn, and Kramer actually used termination rate rather than admission rate as their index. However, because the number of admissions and terminations will average out to the same percentage in a nonresidential facility, the terms may be used interchangeably for our purposes.) Adapted from B. M. Rosen, A. K. Bahn, and M. Kramer, Demographic and diagnostic characteristics of psychiatric outpatients in the U.S.A., 1961. American Journal of Orthopsychiatry, *1964, 24, 455–467. Copyright © 1964, the American Orthopsychiatric Association, Inc. Reproduced by permission.*

T A B L E   X V – 1

FIVE DEVELOPMENTAL TRENDS IN EXPRESSION OF
BEHAVIORAL DISORDERS, AND EXAMPLES OF EACH

TYPE OF TREND	BEHAVIORAL ITEM
I. Symptoms declining with age	Enuresis,* encopresis,* speech problems, fears, thumbsucking, overeating, temper tantrums, destructiveness
II. Symptoms increasing with age	Nail biting
III. Symptoms declining and then increasing with age	Restless sleep, disturbing dreams, timidity, irritability, attention-seeking, dependence, jealousy, food finickiness (boys), somberness
IV. Symptoms increasing and then declining with age	Poor appetite, lying
V. Symptoms unrelated to age	Oversensitivity

Source: MacFarlane, Allen, and Honzik, 1954.
* Enuresis and encopresis refer to bladder and bowel incontinence, respectively.
A more complete description of each will be found on p. 520.

presents more extreme forms of behaviors which any child may show. Still, severity must be taken into account. It is traditional that the most severe disturbances are referred to as *psychoses* while the relatively less profound difficulties are referred to as *neuroses*.

NEUROTIC REACTIONS IN CHILDHOOD

The relatively more mild problems of childhood encompass a wide range of difficulties. Some, like bedwetting, appear to be sufficiently isolated to be considered categories in themselves; others, like refusal to go to school,

TABLE XV–2

PREVALENCE OF BEHAVIOR SYMPTOMS FOR
CHILDHOOD POPULATIONS IN TWO DIFFERENT CULTURES

AREA	STAM-MERING	ENURESIS	TICS	TEMPER TAN-TRUMS	THUMB SUCKING	NAIL BITING
Buffalo, USA	4%	17%	12%	80%	10%	27%
Edinburgh, U.K.	4%	14%	18%	82%	12%	34%

Source: Lapouse and Monk, and Wolff. In Anthony, 1970.

fear of going near harmless dogs, and timidity in interacting with others, may occur quite separately but seem to fall into the more general category of fears and phobias; yet others, like hitting, kicking, biting, and yelling often appear together and thus may be put into a single descriptive diagnostic category (i.e., aggressive behavior).

Excessive Aggression

Aggression toward others, if excessive, is one type of behavior which may be a problem in childhood. It is impossible, of course, to describe its frequency clinically, inasmuch as a host of social factors determines whether any one response or any one child will be considered too aggressive. But a great deal is known about the antecedents of aggression. As we saw earlier (Chapter XI), aggressive behavior is fostered by direct reward and exposure to live and symbolic aggressive models, but can be reduced dramatically when positive consequences are curtailed.

A particularly dramatic example of this latter point is found in a study by Patterson, Littman, and Bricker (1967). They observed thirty-six nursery school children for nine months, noting the occurrence and consequences of more than 2500 aggressive responses among the youngsters. Their findings, consistent with a learning approach, were straightforward: when an aggressive response was successful (for example, when the victim gave in to the antagonist's demand), the same aggressive response usually would be repeated against the same victim on a subsequent occasion. In sharp contrast, if retaliation followed such a response the aggressor usually would take another approach in the future or select a different victim.

Problems Associated with Elimination

In our culture it is expected that control of the eliminative functions be achieved during the first few years of life. *Enuresis,* or bedwetting, usually is not considered a clinical problem until the child is at least three years old; often parents do not report the problem until school age is reached (Millon, 1969).

Enuresis is fairly frequent, occurring in about 15 percent of all children referred to mental health clinics; it is more than twice as frequent among males as among females (Tapia, Jekel, and Domke, 1960; Millon, 1969). The reported incidence declines quite rapidly with age, though; the ratio of enuretics to non-enuretics is 1 to 35 at age fourteen (Lovibond, 1964). Although in part it may be traced to constitutional difficulties, enuresis is most often considered a problem in learning (i.e., the child simply has not learned to awaken before wetting occurs); we shall see later that to a considerable extent it is subject to treatment from this viewpoint.

Encopresis, a much rarer problem, refers to inappropriate defecation. It usually occurs when the child is awake, and frequently alternates with periods of constipation (Millon, 1969). Most studies of encopresis have been simply case reports. In one of the few more extensive investigations (Anthony, 1957), it was found that encopretic children fall into two general classes: those for whom original bowel-training had been successful and then deteriorated, and those who had never been successfully trained. The youngsters in the two groups differed in an interesting way. The former typically had been subjected to quite coercive toilet-training practices from which they were now apparently rebelling, whereas the latter had experienced a generally neglectful upbringing. In both instances, it appears that teaching parents to toilet train (or retrain) their children can alleviate the problem (Barrett, 1969; Conger, 1970).

Anxieties and Phobias

Anxiety is usually thought of as a fairly severe feeling of discomfort, either associated unrealistically with anticipated present or future circumstances or not directly traceable to any particular situation or event. Closely related to anxieties are phobias, profound and unrealistic fears of particular events, objects, people, or circumstances. It is not surprising, then, that traditional views of abnormal behavior link phobic or avoidant reactions in childhood to an underlying base of uninterpreted feelings of anxiety.

The antecedents of anxiety and phobic reactions appear to be found both in specific situations and in characteristics of early upbringing. Recall, for example, that Watson and Rayner conditioned fear in a young boy by creating an extremely traumatic experience in the laboratory (see Chapter V).

Trauma, which literally means wound, was found in one early study (Langford, 1937) to be associated with the first attack of acute anxiety in sixteen out of twenty children who suffered from this type of neurotic reaction. The specific traumatizing experiences included tonsillectomies given under ether, a death in the family, and, in two cases, witnessing violent deaths. At a less extreme level, children often have specific fears or phobias of particular animals, things, and situations.

Common Fears in Childhood. In a classic study, Jersild and Holmes (1935) disclosed a number of fears common to childhood, revealing that some of them (e.g., of noise, strangers, shadows, and unexpected movements) decreased during the first six years of life, while others actually increased over the same period. In the latter group were fears of dreams, animals, and threats of danger. Some of these patterns are shown in Figure XV–2. It should be noted, though, that many common fears of childhood do not reach highly serious levels and that almost all of those shown in the figure show a decline by later childhood or the early teen years.

School Phobias. Few types of neurotic disorders in childhood have been studied more extensively than so-called "school phobias." The school phobic child is simply one who refuses to go to, or to remain in, school. For at least some children the problem can be conceptualized as an unwillingness to leave the parents, thereby relating it to earlier forms of attachment to one's mother (see Chapter X). In fact, there is reason to believe that overprotection by parents is associated with the development of such phobic reactions. Eisenberg (1958) has argued that school phobic children and their mothers simply have developed a mutually dependent relationship in which separation is difficult or disturbing. To the extent that this is the case, beginning school merely represents the first occasion which demands separation. Eisenberg supported this contention through his study of eleven preschool children (six boys and five girls) with separation problems. Observation of the mothers and their offspring at the beginning of nursery school atten-

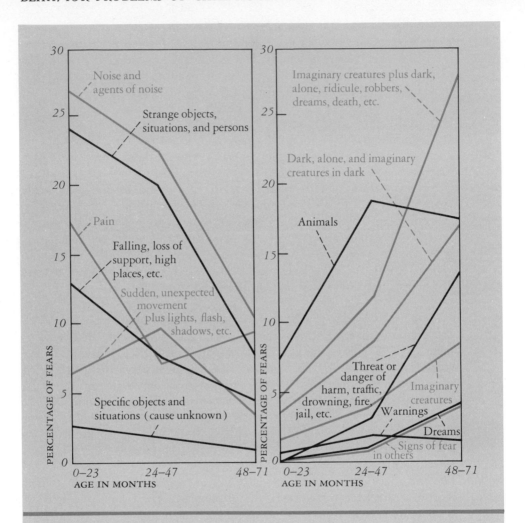

FIGURE XV-2

*Relative frequency of fears in children during the first six years of life,
as observed by parents or teachers or reported by the youngsters themselves. (Starred items represent two or more categories, some of which
are depicted separately.) Adapted from Jersild, A. T. and Holmes,
F. B., Children's fears.* Child Development Monograph, *1935, No. 20.
Teachers College, Columbia University Bureau of Publications, by permission.*

dance showed that the mother made at least as much contribution as the child to the separation problem.

> During the first days a typical child would remain close to mother and then begin to oscillate toward and away from the attractions of the play area. As the child began to look less at mother and move away from her, she would take a seat closer to the child and occasionally use a pretext of wiping his nose or checking his toilet needs for intruding into the child's activity. Separation was as difficult for mother as for the child. Similar resistance to separation was shown by the mother when she was required to move to an adjacent room as part of the program for reducing the mutual separation anxiety. [Hetherington and Martin, 1972, p. 59.]

Psychosomatic Disorders

Psychosomatic disorders are real physical illnesses that are either caused or markedly influenced by psychological factors. A variety of such difficulties are known to occur in childhood: asthma, rheumatoid arthritis, ulcerative colitus, and peptic ulcers (Hetherington and Martin, 1972). The interactions between parents and children suffering from these disorders has been found to differ rather markedly from the interactions that characterize parent-child pairs in which the youngster suffers from a physical illness not based on psychological factors (such as congenital heart disease or polio). In one study (Garner and Wenar, 1959) it was found that youngsters with psychosomatic disorders typically have a relationship with their mothers in which there is little personal closeness; rather, the mothers tend to be easily irritated and angered, and the children themselves also are rated as high on anger. There is, further, a keen sense of competition between the mother and the child, with an effort by the parent to exert a good deal of domination. Just as this pattern distinguishes between children who are psychosomatically troubled and those who are only physically ill, it also distinguishes the former group from youngsters who are psychotic. The severely psychotic child's mother does not try to dominate or compete with him; rather, she is rated high on "obliviousness," often seeming to be insensitive to the child and impervious to the consequences of his bizarre behavior (Wenar, Handlon, and Garner, 1960).

Asthma. The physical basis for asthmatic attack is constriction of the bronchial ducts which supply air to the lungs, resulting in difficulty in breathing and a wheezing sound when the victim exhales. More than half of all asthmatic children seem to suffer from clear-cut physical difficulty, such as whooping cough, bronchitis, pneumonia, or specific allergies (Rees, 1964). The remaining cases, though, appear to be based on either psychological factors or a mixture of psychological and physical ones. Evidence suggesting the importance of family patterns in the etiology of psychologically induced asthma is found in the fact that some asthmatic children improve markedly when removed from their homes and placed in hospitals (e.g., Long, Lamont, Whipple, Bandler, Blom, Burgin, and Jessner, 1958; Purcell, Brady, Chai, Muser, Molk, Gorden, and Means, 1969). Because one possible reason for this dramatic change is the elimination of particular kinds of dust and other potential allergens in their own households, Long and his associates (1958) controlled for this factor by spraying the hospital rooms of their subjects with dust from their respective homes. Despite the fact that many of these children previously had shown skin sensitivity to house dust, none of them developed asthmatic symptoms in the hospital as a result of exposure to the dust. Other investigations (e.g., Gerard, 1946; Mohr, Tausend, Selesnick, and Augenbraun, 1963) have suggested that one specific family pattern associated with psychosomatic asthma is overprotectiveness on the part of the child's mother.

CHILDHOOD PSYCHOSES

There are many definitions of psychoses; they vary widely and are often used inconsistently. For our purposes, however, childhood psychoses will refer to the entire range of very severe disturbances in behavior among the young. The major categories, as they generally appear in the literature, are childhood schizophrenia and early infantile autism. Sometimes the two diagnoses are considered to be quite separate and distinct, while at other times they are employed interchangeably.

Childhood Schizophrenia

Most broadly, schizophrenia is characterized by a defective interaction with outer reality, but the definition usually does not end there. Lauretta Bender, a prominent worker in the area, views childhood schizophrenia as a total psychobiological disorder of all the basic behavior functions. The implications of this broad definition are captured well in the observations of Goldfarb (1970), who notes:

> The daily rhythmic pattern of physiological responses is also disordered. Sleeping, eating, and elimination rhythms are abnormal. Growth abnormali-

ties are to be seen; so that children are too obese or too thin, or too tall or too short. Menstruation in girls and puberty in boys may start at an abnormally young or abnormally advanced age. . . . Incoordination, developmental delay in coordination, and motor insecurity are noteworthy. [p. 771.]

The incidence of childhood schizophrenia is not high. For example, fewer than 3 percent of children seen in outpatient psychiatric clinics and mental hospital services are diagnosed as psychotic (Kessler, 1966), and this figure is, of course, a good deal higher than one would find in the population at large.

Early Infantile Autism

In 1943 Leo Kanner described eleven psychotic children whose behavioral patterns during development appeared unique. Unlike most schizophrenic children, they had not withdrawn from the social environment; rather, they had never interacted with it at all, being "alone" from the start. More recently, another investigator, Bernard Rimland (1964), has argued that a specific syndrome of early infantile autism does indeed exist, encompassing about 10 percent of all psychotic children. According to Rimland, aside from the earlier onset of the disorder, autistic children differ in several important ways from schizophrenic children. Some are listed below.

1. Autistic children are described as unusually attractive and healthy.

2. The abnormal EEGs (electroencephalographs) frequently reported in schizophrenic youngsters seldom appear in the autistic.

3. Autistic children have a need for sameness in their environment; they become extremely upset over changes viewed as quite ordinary by most people, such as a variation in the daily schedule.

4. These youngsters display severe language deficiencies and unusual language patterns. They may, for example, repeat exactly the words spoken by another (echolalia), or they may incorrectly use pronouns (pronoun reversal), rarely using "I" or "me" but referring to themselves as "you" or "he."

5. The families of autistic children are different in that there is a *low* incidence of familial mental dysfunction and the parents are well-educated and with high IQs.

6. The "aloneness" of autistic youngsters is striking.

Their pathology is soon evidenced . . . by their avoidance of another's eye and by a lack of visual or auditory response to others. They are deaf and blind to peole. In retrospect one can detect the first signs of psychopathology in infancy. There was no social smile, no evidence of pleasure in the mother's company. One mother complained, "He didn't look at me when I fed him in my arms," and other typical complaints include, "He was never cuddley," or "He never noticed when I came into or left his room." There was no physical reaching out: the autistic child did not get set to be lifted into his parent's arms. There was no particular reaction to strangers either. Usually, these children were regarded as especially good babies, because their demands were few: they were content to be left alone and did not make the normal fuss at bedtime or other moments of separation. . . . There is no imitation of gestures (e.g., waving bye-bye) or sounds and also the baby remained uninterested in social games like peek-a-book and patty-cake. [Kessler, 1966, p. 265.]

In an attempt to categorize the "truly" autistic child, Rimland (1971) has requested parents to complete a specially devised scale describing eighty aspects of their troubled children's characteristics and behavior (see Table XV–3). Thus far his data provide some support for the existence of a very

TABLE XV – 3

SAMPLE ITEMS FROM RIMLAND'S CHECKLIST
DESIGNED TO COMPARE AUTISTIC AND
NON-AUTISTIC PSYCHOTIC CHILDREN

ITEM	*Autistic**		*Nonautistic**
	Speaking (N = 65)	*Mute (N = 53)*	*(N = 230)*
21. Did you ever suspect the child was very nearly deaf?			
_____1 Yes	77	94	54
_____2 No	23	6	46
	100	100	100

TABLE XV-3 (continued)

ITEM	Autistic*		Nonautistic*
	Speaking (N = 65)	Mute (N = 53)	(N = 230)
29. (Age 2-5) Is he cuddly?			
____1 Definitely, likes to cling to adults	2	2	20
____2 Above average (likes to be held)	8	8	18
____3 No, rather stiff and awkward to hold	90	88	56
____4 Don't know	0	2	6
	100	100	100
33. (Age 3-5) How skillful is the child in doing fine work with his fingers or playing with small objects?			
____1 Exceptionally skillful	71	75	33
____2 Average for age	6	9	23
____3 A little awkward, or very awkward	15	8	33
____4 Don't know	8	8	11
	100	100	100
40. (Age 3-5) How interested is the child in mechanical objects such as the stove or vacuum cleaner?			
____1 Little or no interest	19	9	23
____2 Average interest	4	0	21
____3 Fascinated by certain mechanical things	77	92	56
	100	100	100

TABLE XV-3 *(continued)*

ITEM	Autistic*		Nonautistic*
	Speaking (N = 65)	*Mute (N = 53)*	*(N = 230)*
45. (Age 3–5) Does child get very upset if certain things he is used to are changed (like furniture or toy arrangement, or certain doors which must be left open or shut)?			
_____1 No	4	2	29
_____2 Yes, definitely	87	86	41
_____3 Slightly true	9	12	30
	100	100	100
71. (Age 3–5) Does the child typically say "Yes" by repeating the same question he has been asked? (Example: You ask "Shall we go for a walk, Honey?" and he indicates he does want to by saying "Shall we go for a walk, Honey?" or "Shall we go for a walk?")			
_____1 Yes, definitely, does not say "yes" directly	94	12†	22
_____2 No, would say "Yes" or "OK" or similar answer	0	3	8
_____3 Not sure	4	6	8
_____4 Too little speech to say	2	79	62
	100	100	100

Source: Rimland, B. The differentiation of childhood psychoses: An analysis of checklists for 2,218 psychotic children. *Journal of Autism and Childhood Schizophrenia,* **1**, 1971, 161–174. By permission.
* All values are expressed as percentages.
† A speech item not applicable to the mute group.

specific autistic syndrome. Rimland believes that autism has its basis in damage to the reticular area of the brain; he advises, though, that the most effective treatment presently available involves systematic behavioral manipulation.

The work of O. Ivaar Lovaas and his associates is based upon this approach. Their treatment program attempts to overcome gross behavioral deficiencies through positive or negative reinforcement and imitation (Lovaas, 1968). For example, self-destructive action, common to autistic youngsters, is reduced by isolating the children; echolalic speech is similarly decreased by nonattention; and normal speech is very gradually shaped by food rewards for the imitation of the experimenter's verbalizations (see Figure XV–3). Realizing both that social reinforcement is typically the

FIGURE XV–3

The use of positive reinforcement—food and praise—by Lovaas and his associates in the shaping of appropriate social behavior in autistic children. Photograph by Allan Grant, by permission.

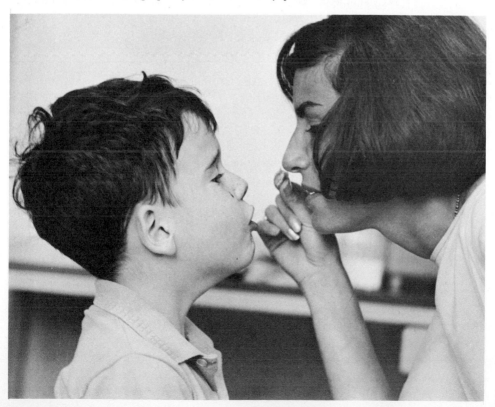

cornerstone for building and modifying behavior in the natural environment and that autistic children appear unresponsive to such reinforcement, Lovaas and his associates make a concerted effort to establish the importance of social rewards by pairing them with tangible ones. Thus, for example, when food reinforcement is presented for a particular act, it is paired with the word "good." Later praise alone may become a reinforcer. (For a discussion of the ethical and practical considerations in the use of tangible rewards in treating behavioral problems, see O'Leary, Poulos, and Devine, 1972).

Given all we know about the effectiveness of these learning procedures in other situations (see, for example, Chapter V), it is not surprising that Lovaas and his associates have enjoyed considerable success in teaching rudimentary language and social skills to autistic children. What is more, there is also evidence that the effects of such training pervade other aspects of the autistic child's life:

> While it is evident that the children acquire new behaviors within our treatment situation, we must consider how well these behaviors stand up on the outside. To test for the amount of generalization, we have devised an extremely simple procedure where the children are placed in a situation completely different from the one in which the training has taken place. Essentially, the child is placed in a room where he has never been before, the room being furnished in typical playroom manner. He is then observed in three somewhat different situations. First, when he is alone within that room; secondly, when an unfamiliar adult is present in the room, attending to the child but without initiating any behavior; and third, where the adult initiates a set of prescribed interactions, such as "What is your name?" "Please come and sit with me," "Let's do some drawing," etc. Several behaviors of the child are then recorded on our free-play measuring apparatus. These behaviors include self-stimulatory behaviors, tantrums, eye-to-face contact, physical contact, appropriate play behavior, echolalic and bizarre speech, grammatically correct speech related to the immediate context, etc. Over time, we observe changes in the children's behavior; for example, the emergence of appropriate play behavior and the suppression of self-stimulation, the emergence of physical contact and eye-to-face contact with the attending adult, etc. This procedure also allows us to assess the kinds of behaviors, including levels of social interaction, that the children manifested prior to treatment. . . .

> In almost every aspect of training, we have observed response generalization. This is particularly true in the language training area, where the children are acquiring concept or sentence forms. It is also true, when one works

with a specific response such as echolalia or self-destruction, that rather large changes are occurring in a number of behaviors not specifically manipulated in the experimental situation. [Lovaas, 1968, pp. 118–119.]

CHILDHOOD BEHAVIOR AND LATER PROBLEMS

One question regarding childhood disorders that has been of continued general interest is whether or not the appearance of abnormalcy or problem behavior in later years can be predicted from its presence during the earlier years of life. Obviously, the issue is not only of theoretical importance; it also has practical implications for the treatment of children displaying some sort of psychological dysfunction. If behavior disorders merely disappear or are markedly reduced by the time adulthood is reached, they would be of less concern than if they were highly predictive of later problems. What, then, is known about this issue?

To begin with, it seems there has been a tendency to overinterpret the importance of certain childhood problems. The point is well illustrated by examining one of what Anthony (1970) has referred to as the "fashionable trends" which sometimes have been involved in defining abnormal.

One such trend has been traced by Kanner (1960), following the history of the meaning attributed to children's nail-biting over a twenty-five-year period.

> In 1908, nail biting was regarded as a "stigma of degeneration"; in 1912 it was seen as "an exquisite psychopathic symptom"; in 1931 it was described as "a sign of an unresolved Oedipus complex." Following this, a survey indicated that 66% of school children had been nail-biters at some time or another, which led Kanner to remark that it was "hardly realistic to assume that two-thirds of our youth are degenerate, exquisitely psychopathic or walking around with an unresolved Oedipus complex." [Anthony, 1970, p. 668, citing Kanner, 1960, p. 18.]

For the most part, children who display annoying behaviors such as nail-biting, nose-picking, "nervousness," and masturbation grow up to be well-adjusted and productive adults. Fears, irritability, and "nervousness" in childhood fail to predict most adult disorders, and minor sexual deviations in childhood do not relate to deviant adult sex behavior (Robins, 1966). Further, children judged to be shy, withdrawn, or inhibited are no more likely to become neurotic later than are their matched controls

(Kohlberg, La Crosse, and Ricks, 1972; Robins, 1966). In fact, Kohlberg and his associates have noted that youngsters brought to guidance clinics for emotional problems without accompanying antisocial behavior or other complications are likely to be almost as well, when they reach adulthood, as those from a random sample of the population.

Years ago Wickman (1928) compared teachers' and clinicians' views of maladaptive behavior among children. The teachers, he found, viewed hyperaggressive and similar antisocial behavior as considerably "sicker" than social withdrawal and shyness; the clinicians took the opposite view. Through the past few decades the "mental health view" that withdrawal is the more serious psychological problem has been promulgated widely, even though, as we have seen, it does not predict later difficulties. What, then, about antisocial and aggressive behavior?

In a major longitudinal study, Robins (1966) followed more than five hundred children, seen in a guidance clinic in the 1920s and 1930s, into adulthood. The results were clear: antisocial behavior in childhood—physical aggression, truancy, vandalism, theft, illicit sexual activity—was by far the best early behavior predictor of later problems. Fully 37 percent of those with serious episodes of antisocial behavior during childhood became sociopathic adults—i.e., they repeatedly failed to conform to social norms in many areas of life, whereas *no* child without this history was later judged sociopathic. Youngsters with an early history of antisocial behavior were also two-and-a-half times more likely than controls to have an adult criminal record. Nor is the predictiveness of early antisocial behavior limited to criminality. Antisocial children were 50 percent more likely than controls to be mentally ill adults, and also more likely to become psychotics or alcoholics. Even more impressive, the frequency of antisocial symptoms in childhood bears an almost linear relationship to later difficulties. A child had a 15 percent chance of being a well adult if he had six antisocial symptoms and only a 5 percent chance of being well if he had ten or more. The predictability of adult maladjustment from antisocial behavior in childhood has been confirmed further by Field (1969).

Closely related to antisocial behavior as reported by parents and teachers is the occurrence of early problems in peer relations. Children who "broke down" as adults were, as youngsters, more disturbing to their peers than those who did not. This difference, Kohlberg and his associates have pointed out, "occurred in spite of rigorous matching for age, IQ, sex, social class, and childhood rearing conditions" (1972, p. 1257). Indeed, Mednick and Schulsinger (1967) have reported that among children with schizophrenic mothers early peer relations predicted whether the youngsters themselves would later become psychotic whereas psychiatric ratings did not.

TRADITIONAL TREATMENT OF CHILDHOOD DISORDERS

Today there is a great deal of concern about children with behavior problems, but this is a relatively new state of affairs. Indeed, it appears that the term "emotional disturbances" was not applied to children until 1932 (Despert, 1965); before then youngsters exhibiting troubled behavior were thought of in terms of moralistic labels such as "possessed, wicked, guilty, insubordinate, incorrigible," and so on. Such views naturally determined the kind of treatment children with behavior problems received; in ancient Greece and Rome they might be left to die, in nineteenth-century London they were imprisoned (O'Leary and O'Leary, 1972).

In the 1930s all of this began to change. The psychiatric movement, largely inspired by the writings of Sigmund Freud, gave rise to the appearance of a number of child psychiatric clinics that provided treatment based on traditional psychoanalytic and counseling views of psychotherapy. The focus of these efforts usually was global; the purpose of treatment, it was argued, was to help the child see or "work through" his difficulties. In psychoanalytically oriented therapy, for example, emphasis is placed on the relationship between child and therapist, and on broad categories such as anxiety and anxiety defense, rather than on particulars:

> The child psychoanalyst sees her patients three, four or five times a week. This promotes an intense relationship and continuity of the flow of materials; it also makes it unnecessary for the patient to remain long alone with the anxiety which may be aroused by treatment. He can look forward to seeing his therapist next day, and so has less need to erect defenses against his anxiety. [Kessler, 1966, p. 377.]

There is even less systematic direction in nondirective play therapy. Axline, whose use of this approach is widely known, lists the following eight basic principles:

1. The therapist must develop a warm, friendly relationship with the child.

2. The therapist accepts the child exactly as he is.

3. The therapist establishes a feeling of permissiveness in the relationship.

4. The therapist is alert to recognize the feelings and to reflect the feelings back to the child so that he gains insight into his behavior.

5. The therapist maintains a deep respect for the child's ability to solve his own problems.

6. The child leads the way; the therapist follows.

7. The therapist does not attempt to hurry the therapy along.

8. The therapist establishes only those limitations that are necessary to anchor the therapy to the world of reality and to make the child aware of his responsibility in the relationship. [1947, p. 75.]

Is the Traditional Approach Effective?

In 1952, Hans J. Eysenck, a British psychologist and researcher, published an article entitled "The effects of psychotherapy: An evaluation." Dealing with the question of whether or not various types of psychological treatments were actually helpful in treating adult psychological disorders, Eysenck asked about the rate of improvement among those who received treatment. At first blush, the results seemed reasonably promising; approximately two-thirds of those who received treatment showed measurable improvement. However, it is possible, as Eysenck realized, that improvement might occur even if there had been no therapy; a variety of natural experiences in a person's life and the transient nature of certain types of psychological disorders might conspire to produce improvement in some cases. So Eysenck made a comparable study of persons who sought or apparently needed psychotherapy but were unable to receive it. Strikingly, he found that among this group, too, approximately two-thirds showed improvement —despite their receiving no formal therapy whatsoever. It is not surprising, then, that the Eysenck paper stirred a great deal of controversy.

Five years later, E. E. Levitt conducted a similar analysis assessing the effects of psychotherapy with children. Examining results of seventeen different studies involving thousands of youngsters, Levitt was forced to state:

> . . . the results, and the conclusions of this paper are markedly similar to those of Eysenck's study. Two-thirds of the patients examined at close of therapy and about three-quarters seen in follow-up have improved. *Approximately the same percentages of improvements are found for comparable groups of untreated children.* [1957, p. 194; italics added.]

The findings described above are quite reliable; Levitt reported a further analysis of twenty-two other "outcome" studies of psychotherapy with children, abstracting his new findings this way: "It must still be concluded that there does not seem to be a sound basis for the contention that psychotherapy facilitates recovery from emotional illness in children" (Levitt, 1963, p. 45). And the pattern has continued. More recently, for example, a two-year follow-up of children with a variety of disturbances revealed that 63 percent of those who had been seen in a clinic improved, but so had 61 percent of matched control children who had not been seen in a clinic at all (Shepherd, Oppenheim, and Mitchell, 1966).*

SOME NEWER APPROACHES

If the traditional approaches are ineffective—or at least no more effective than natural processes that occur with the passage of time—what kind of intervention is possible for children with behavior problems? Many researchers have begun to ask this question. The answer varies, of course, with the type of problem involved, but there have been a number of significant advances in recent years. A few examples will give the flavor of what seems to be the wave of the future.

Project Re-ED

Project Re-ED is a new treatment approach for helping children so seriously disturbed that they cannot remain in a regular school setting. The objectives of the program are to provide a total "re-education" (both academically and socially) in a brief, high-impact, residential program that is feasible economically for most families and communities. Re-ED has taken an educational approach, using specially trained teachers instead of therapists, who work with the children twenty-four hours a day for approximately six months.

To meet the needs of the school approach, a new professional was created: the teacher-counselor. Recruited from the ranks of effective classroom teachers, they were carefully chosen for the special qualities that are needed for the many roles they assume at Re-ED—that of teacher, mental health professional, recreational leader, professional counselor, and parent substitute.

---

* It would be misleading, of course, to conclude from these reports that children with behavior problems do not need treatment "since they get better anyway." Rather, the relatively more mild problems pass with time while more serious one are not corrected either by waiting *or* by traditional forms of intervention.

Two teacher-counselors (TCs) and a liaison teacher are assigned to each group of eight children. Together they set specific individual goals, plan programs, and evaluate each child's progress. The TCs live, work, and sleep with the children; responsibilities are divided between them. One TC concentrates on the in-school teaching aspects of the program, providing needed academic skills; the other handles the counseling, recreational, and group functions that help children acquire social and personal skills such as learning how to kick a football or how to share with others. An important strength of the program is that nonschool hours are supervised by a sensitive and competent person. This makes it possible to meet the Re-ED goal of constructively using all hours of the day to facilitate both learning and emotional adjustment.

The liaison-teacher's job is to find a "better fit" between the child and his environment. The liaison makes contact with the home and school before the child's enrollment, maintains contact while the child is in the program, and plans optimal conditions for the child's return. He also monitors the child's home weekend visits. Then, after the child returns to his family, the liaison serves as a consultant to both the parents and the classroom teacher, suggesting techniques to cope with any problems. He may, for example, try to alter parental expectations, teach them behavior management, or arrange to hire a tutor.

Justification for the Re-ED program can be found at several levels. First, the need for such services is great; Nicholas Hobbs (1966), the project's innovator and director, points out that there are approximately 1.5 million children with emotional problems sufficiently profound to prevent their functioning adequately in normal family or school settings. Second, the cost is relatively low: the Re-ED per day cost is about one-third of in-patient psychiatric care in a state facility. Most important, though, is that Re-ED seems to work.

An extensive evaluation was part of the original design of the Re-ED project (Weinstein, 1969; 1971). Based on data collected on each child prior to his enrollment, at discharge, and again at six and eighteen months after return home, Re-ED has been shown to produce a substantial and durable gain; all Re-ED children were in regular schools eighteen months after discharge and only one had a "special class" placement. A matched control group of disturbed children who remained in regular schools showed no improvement and, in fact, became somewhat worse over the six-month period.* Because these results convincingly show that improvement in Re-ED children was not due simply to the passage of time, it is

---

* Note that such a finding is not necessarily inconsistent with the high average improvement rate reported for youngsters in other studies (cf. p. 535, note).

not surprising that the program is now a model for special school facilities in several states.

A Computer-aided System for Psychotic Children

Project Re-ED is for children with problems of no more than moderate severity, children who probably would receive the label of "neurotic" in many diagnostic centers. Let us turn now to innovations in the treatment of severely disturbed psychotic children. One, developed by Kenneth Colby (1968), takes advantage of computer technology to increase the language productivity of schizophrenic and autistic children. Colby argues:

> Conventional psychotherapeutic and conditioning methods are slow, involve daily sessions lasting maybe hours, and require human effort on the part of therapists, as well as children. A computer-aided method would be a worthwhile alternative if it could yield equal or better results in a shorter time and with less effort costs to the participants [1968, p. 652.]

The apparatus which was developed appears, from the child's point of view, to be a screen similar to a television set with a bank of keys below it. The keys, when struck, produce a variety of displays on the screen, including English letters, numbers, logical and mathematical symbols, words, phrases, and pictures of objects. When normal children are brought into a room and told that the apparatus is a machine for children to play with, they almost inevitably start typing; disturbed children, even though they sometimes must be shown how it works, also find it enormously appealing.

In practice, a child is brought in for a session lasting between thirty and forty minutes, while an adult (whom Colby calls a "sitter") stays in the room. Primarily, though, the child's interaction is with the device; the adult is not supposed to interfere with or correct the child during his play or to change the pace of learning.

The device is in fact programmed for a variety of different games, of which Colby has described eleven. To appreciate their flavor, purpose, and variety, we will describe two.

Game 1. The simplest program, Game 1, is used for every child. Each time the youngster strikes a key, its symbol appears on the screen while a voice produces the appropriate corresponding sound. If, for example, the "A" key is struck, then the letter A appears on the screen and a voice says "A."

> The symbol alternates between a large and small representation. The voice is that of an adult man or woman who speaks clearly but not professionally. At times the recordings are those of children's voices. . . . The idea of this

game is to acquaint the child with letters and numbers in their spoken and written forms. He learns that an action on his part produces a visible and audible response from the machine. [p. 643.]

Game 10. This game, one of the more sophisticated ones in the system, is described as follows:

A drawing of a small star appears on the screen. A child can move the drawing around by means of a light pen or by verbal command. In the latter case, a listener in the adjoining room moves the star with a light pen. Initially, simple commands are used by the sitter as illustrations—"up," "down," and "around," "dance back and forth," etc. Again the intent is to show a child that objects can be controlled by speech and to encourage verbalization, first of words and then of phrases. [p. 644.]

Colby reports ten cases of highly disturbed children who were "treated" with this device; of these, eight showed marked improvement. One of the successful cases, described below, is instructive:

N. was a nine-year-old "schizophrenic" boy who rarely had been heard to speak intelligibly. He was very frightened in the first two sessions, but by session 3 he began to play with the machine. He held his hands over his ears whenever the voice spoke. He hummed, gazed at the ceiling, and often smiled to himself.

By session 5 he began to vocalize, but no clear words appeared. He laughed a lot at the symbols on the screen. His first imitated word was "slash," in session 7. When the computer system broke down and several people were in the room he used, he refused to enter the room.

In sessions 10–15 he uttered several imitated words and pronounced many of the letters. He continued to laugh and chuckle at some secret joke. Often he attempted to disguise his pronunciation of a letter which previously he had been heard to say clearly. In session 12 he said "I don't want to," showing both his reluctance and an ability to speak sentences. The staff felt he was able to talk but was refusing to do so and was enjoying the struggle to get him to talk. [pp. 645–646.]

Behavior Modification

Of all the innovative approaches that have appeared since Levitt's review of the inefficacy of traditional approaches to children's behavior problems, perhaps none is more widely talked about than the so-called "behavior modification" programs. The term means both more and less than it implies.

It surely does not mean *simply* an effort to change the way in which youngsters act; therapists, teachers, and parents have used all kinds of techniques in an effort to modify maladaptive behavior long before the term was invented. Rather, behavior modification refers to a particular approach to the treatment of psychological problems.

EXTENDED DISCUSSION

ASSUMPTIONS UNDERLYING BEHAVIOR MODIFICATION AND THEIR IMPLICATIONS FOR TREATMENT

Behavior modification, sometimes referred to as behavior therapy, is an approach that has grown almost exclusively out of psychology rather than psychiatry. As such, it is based upon a different set of assumptions than the traditional therapy approaches. These assumptions, in turn, dictate, at least in part, the manner in which treatment is carried out. Perhaps the most significant assumptions have to do with the etiology and interpretation of psychological problems. We can best understand them by first stating what they are not.

Abnormal or maladaptive behavior is most usually considered within the context of a "disease model" (Ullmann and Krasner, 1965). In medicine, the patient's complaints or atypical physical characteristics are considered symptoms of a disease. The first step in a therapeutic plan is to diagnose the disease on the basis of the symptoms; then it is possible to prescribe treatment. The physician has a large number of sources, within his personal experience and in books, to which he can turn for the preferred treatment.

The main ancestral stream of traditional therapy is to be found in medicine. Indeed, the language that is familiar to us, such as "mental illness," and the reference to behaviorally troubled individuals as "patients," attests to the influence of the medical model. Much of the responsibility for this can be attributed to Freud and his conceptualization of personality structure and psychotherapy (Munroe, 1955), and, in fact, Freud was always emphatic about the difference between symptoms and their causes (Ford and Urban, 1963). He once noted:

> In the eyes of the general public the symptoms are the essence of a disease, and to them a cure means the removal of the symptoms. In medicine, how-

ever, we feel it important to differentiate between symptoms and diseases, and state that the disappearance of the symptoms is by no means the same as the cure of the disease. [Freud, 1960, p. 367.]

Various authors (Ford and Urban, 1963; Mowrer, 1964) have emphasized that Freud's concept of symptom formation revolved around his conflict theory; psychological or behavioral problems represented conflict among instinctual demands (id), conscious thoughtful regulation (ego), and self-evaluative thoughts (superego). The conflict was postulated to be unconscious, and treatment was designed to bring it into consciousness. This procedure, it was suggested, would result in removal of the symptom, or at least would allow the patient to understand the symptom and better control it (London, 1964). Thus, the focus of treatment for all those therapists who follow Freud rests on the underlying difficulty, conflict, or cause.

The model followed by behavior therapists is very much in opposition to the medical model. Emphasizing the role of learning principles, they consider atypical or maladaptive behaviors as learned behaviors that are in themselves the problem. Neurotic behavior, for example, is defined as a habit of unadaptive behavior acquired by normal learning processes in a normal organism (Wolpe, 1958); the failure of a neurotic behavior to extinguish readily leads to the inaccurate assumption that some more basic pathology must underlie it. But for behavior modifiers, the "symptom" *is* the neurosis; once it is removed, the individual is presumably free of the difficulty. The focus of therapy is thus very directly on behavior itself—a fact singled out frequently by critics.

It has been suggested, in this regard, that a symptom-oriented therapy that ignores deep inner causes will not be effective in the long run because new symptoms of the underlying problem will appear. Investigations into this possibility have been carried out by a number of researchers, many of whom are behavior modifiers. In general, they show that new symptoms do *not* occur (e.g., Eysenck, 1960; Lazarus, 1963; Wolpe, 1958). Compellingly, the same conclusion has been reached by Weitzman (1967), a psychoanalytically oriented therapist.

Behavior Modification as a Technique

At the technique level, most behavior modification approaches are characterized by direct observation, systematic manipulation, and repeated assessment (cf., Lovitt, 1970).

Direct Observation. Many types of therapy rely on standardized tests of personality or adjustment, or on projective tests to assess the difficulties of individuals seeking help. The behavior modification approach to assessment is quite different, as a result of the assumption that specific learning contingencies rather than more general personality problems underlie abnormal behavior. Even when particular behavior patterns occur together, as in the case of autism, the specifics are presumed to be critical information for the therapist to begin treatment. Thus, there is considerable reliance on direct observation, and, as necessary, quite individualized assessment of the actual behavior of each youngster for whom treatment is suggested or requested. As Lovitt explains:

> Behavior modifiers agree that before a behavior can be measured, much less changed, it must be directly recorded. If, for example, the target behavior is tantrums, the outbursts are recorded directly; an indirect approach such as an interview or a standardized adjustment test is not scheduled. If the target behavior is reading, direct measurement on various reading components would be obtained instead of using a standardized reading or achievement test to determine skills. [1970, pp. 87–88.]

Systematic Manipulation. In part it is obvious that a child's behavior can be altered successfully only if something is done with (or to) him; in this sense, of course, manipulation is involved in all types of therapy. We have seen, though, that in traditional therapies the intervention is global or nondirective. The behavior modification approach, in contrast, usually is characterized by a very specific, detailed, and systematic plan for intervention, generally with an eye to altering particular consequences for behaving in certain ways.

Repeated Assessment. Behavior modification is an almost uniquely pragmatic endeavor; a manipulation is tried and an immediate effort is made to determine whether the desired changes are being attained. If they are not, the plan usually will be changed; i.e., a different manipulation will be introduced, and then it too will be assessed. Thus repeated assessment, based on regular direct evaluation, is typical of the approach.

These are the general principles of behavior modification, usually carried out against one or more of the more general principles of learning. A more concrete notion of how the approach works can be seen through examples.

A Classical Conditioning Approach to Enuresis. Earlier we pointed out that the difficulty of the enuretic child, viewed in learning terms, is that he has not learned to awaken before bedwetting occurs. Presumably this is because internal stimulation (i.e., bladder tension) does not serve to rouse him from sleep so that he can go to the lavatory. Many years ago, Mowrer and Mowrer (1938) related the problem to classical conditioning; they reasoned that the desired response could be produced by pairing the ringing of a fairly loud bell (a UCS, or unconditioned stimulus, which inevitably would awaken the child) with bladder stimulation (the CS, or conditioned stimulus). Waking up—an unconditioned response (UCR) to the bell—should then become a conditioned response to the bladder tension alone, permitting the child to reach the toilet in time.

The Mowrers attempted to treat enuretic youngsters accordingly. The children slept on a specially prepared pad made of two pieces of bronze screening separated by a heavy layer of cotton. When urination occurred it invariably would seep through the fabric, close an electrical circuit, and cause the bell to ring. After repeated pairings, bladder tension alone would be expected to waken the child. Thirty children were treated by the Mowrers in this way, for a maximum period of two months, and bedwetting was successfully eliminated in every case. Additionally,

> Personality changes, when they occurred . . . have uniformly been in a favorable direction. In no case has there been any evidence of "symptom substitution." Our results, therefore, do not support the assumption, sometimes made, that any attempt to deal directly with the problem of enuresis will necessarily result in the child's developing "something worse." [Mowrer and Mowrer, 1938, p. 451.]

The apparatus devised by the Mowrers has been used successfully ever since; it is now available commercially from a number of stores and mail-order houses and is widely prescribed in the treatment of enuresis.

An Operant Conditioning Approach to a Studying Problem. A study by Hall, Lund, and Jackson (1968) illustrates the use of operant conditioning in behavior modification with a quite different type of problem—increasing good study habits in elementary school children. One of their participants, Robbie, reportedly disrupted classroom activities frequently and studied very little. To confirm this description and provide a more precise measure of the problem, Hall and his associates began by obtaining a base line of Robbie's ongoing rate of studying; their findings are presented in the first block of Figure XV–4.

As can be seen, Robbie was studying only about 25 percent of the time, spending the other 75 percent in such activities as "snapping rubber bands, playing with toys from his pocket, talking and laughing with peers, slowly drinking the half-pint of milk served earlier in the morning, and subsequently playing with the empty carton" (Hall *et al.,* 1968, p. 3). Robbie's teacher responded to this minor mischief by attending to him, urging him to work and put away his toys, and so on.

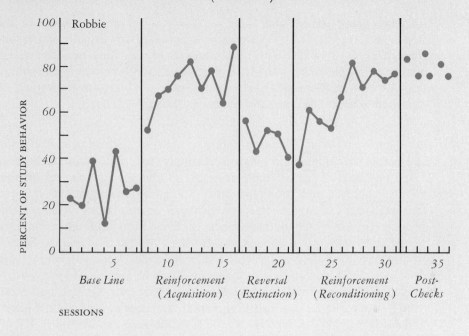

FIGURE XV—4

A record of study behavior for Robbie. Adapted from R. V. Hall, D. Lund, and D. Jackson, Effects of teacher attention on study behavior. Journal of Applied Behavior Analysis, *1968, 1. By permission.*

After the assessment of the problem had been made, the learning phase of the treatment was initiated. Whenever Robbie studied for one minute an observer signaled his teacher, who promptly rewarded him with her attention. At the same time, failure to study and the pursuit of other activities (which previously had resulted in teacher attention) were ignored. The findings, shown in the second block of Figure XV–4, were striking. Robbie was soon studying more than 70 percent of the time. But was the change really due to a shift in the contingencies which earned Robbie teacher attention? To be certain, a reversal or extinction phase was introduced; Robbie's teacher stopped providing reward for his new industriousness. As expected, his studying rate began to drop. Finally, teacher attention for studying was reinstated; again his studying rose to a rate of between 70 and

80 percent, and continued to hold at that level for the remainder of the school year (see the last two blocks of Figure XV–4). Equally important, the quality of Robbie's work also improved during this period; for example, he completed his written assignments, missed few words on spelling tests, and so on. Similar procedures are now used in a wide variety of classroom settings (O'Leary and O'Leary, 1972).

A Modeling Approach to Extreme Isolation. Recent behavior modification approaches to children's problems increasingly have come to use techniques based on observational or imitative learning. One of the great advantages of this approach lies in its potential for group treatment. If children can learn new forms of desirable behavior merely from watching appropriate examples, then mass media such as films and television programs potentially may become a tool for the child psychotherapist. Several studies now have shown that this rather ambitious tactic can work; children's fears of dogs have been reduced markedly by exposure to appropriate modeling films (e.g., Bandura and Menlove, 1968; Hill, Liebert, and Mott, 1968), as has the fear of receiving dental treatment (Herskovitz, Liebert, and Adelson, 1971). A typical viewing situation is shown in Figure XV–5.

Here we shall consider treatment of a somewhat different problem. Interested in extreme forms of social isolation among nursery school children, O'Connor (1969) selected thirteen children who almost never engaged in social interaction with their peers; these children, observed initially by both their teachers and other highly trained individuals, differed very sharply from an arbitrarily selected group of "normal" children in the same situation. Six of the youngsters were then assigned to a modeling treatment condition while the remainder served as controls.

The carefully designed modeling treatment was deceptively simple; the children simply saw a film, presented to them on a large television console.

> The film portrayed a sequence of 11 scenes in which children interacted in a nursery school setting. In each of these episodes, a child is shown first observing the interaction of others and then joining in the social activities, with reinforcing consequences ensuing. The other children, for example, offer him play material, talk to him, smile and generally respond in a positive manner to his advances into the activity. The scenes were graduated on a dimension of threat in terms of the vigor of the social activity and the size of the group. The initial scenes involve very calm activities such as sharing a book or toy while two children are seated at a table. In the terminal scenes, as many as six children are shown gleefully tossing play equipment around the room. [O'Connor, 1969, p. 18.]

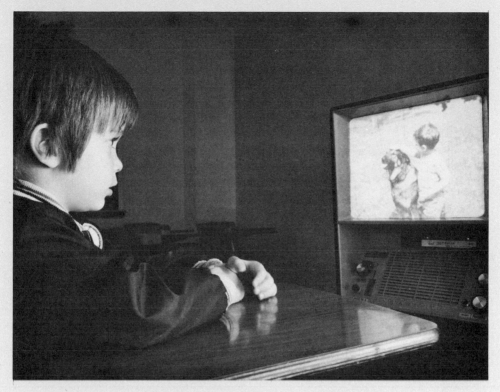

FIGURE XV–5

A child viewing the film produced by Hill, Liebert, and Mott (1968) to reduce children's fear of dogs.

Children in the control group saw a television film about dolphins that was not designed to teach social interaction.

The effects of one treatment session upon the previously isolated children were dramatic; they were now willing and able to engage in as many (or more) appropriate social interactions as were children not isolated in the first place (see Figure XV–6 posttest). A follow-up at the end of the school year revealed that all but one of the children in the modeling condition had continued their new habits of social interaction; * control children, on the other hand, tended still to be rated as extreme isolates by their teachers.

---

* And this one child, O'Connor points out, saw the film with an unsynchronized sound track, as a result of a mechanical failure.

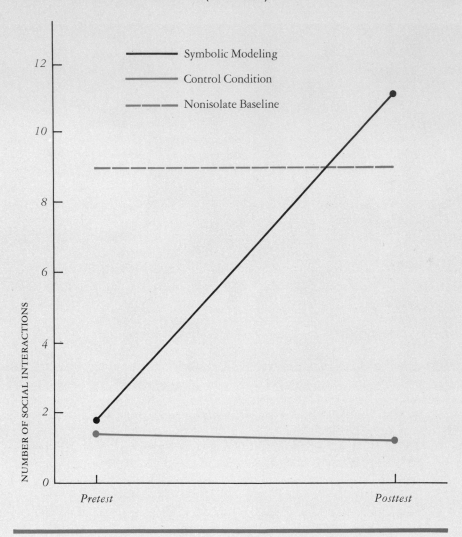

NUMBER OF SOCIAL INTERACTIONS

Symbolic Modeling
Control Condition
Nonisolate Baseline

Pretest   *Posttest*

FIGURE XV–6

Mean number of social interactions displayed by children in the modeling and control conditions, before and after the experimental sessions. The dotted line represents the level of interactions manifested by 26 nonisolate children who were observed at the pretest phase of the study. Adapted from R. D. O'Connor, Modification of social withdrawal through symbolic modeling. Journal of Applied Behavior Analysis, *1969, 2. By permission.*

Combining Professional Resources

Perhaps the most important innovation of all those that have been introduced in recent years is the tendency for real collaboration among workers of various persuasions and talents, each bringing some special facet of ability and expertise to the treatment. As one example, we shall consider the "Five-Two" program developed by Drabman, Spitalnik, Hagamen, and Van Witsen (1973).

The goal of the program devised by Drabman and his associates is to change the traditional function of the children's psychiatric hospital from a long-term "put away" place that provides only custodial care to one that integrates the best features of the patient's home, a special school, and the hospital. The program is called the "Five-Two Plan" because the children gradually go from full hospitalization to five days at home and only two days in the hospital.

How does the program work? Consider the case of Randy, an eight-year-old boy who was diagnosed as "childhood schizophrenia, autistic type." Randy had never spoken and was described by his parents as entirely out of control. He lacked toilet training and would spend hours tearing paper and throwing it around the house. Sometimes he would combine these two distressing practices—by tearing paper into shreds and then, using his feces as glue, decorating the walls of the house with the torn paper.

A portion of the program involved operant conditioning adopted for use in behavior modification; Randy's parents were taught some of the specific techniques as he gradually reached the "five-two" stage of therapy. For toilet training a step-by-step shaping procedure (see pp. 133–34) was used at home until the youngster was able to sit on the toilet; material rewards were then made contingent upon appropriate urination or defecation. Randy, who had been almost completely enuretic, learned to urinate appropriately more than 90 percent of the time and to defecate appropriately more than 30 percent of the time. Careful use of punishment when Randy reached for paper—and praise when he stopped—eliminated entirely his paper tearing and fecal smearing. And, in addition to decreasing negative behavior, his parents used social and material reinforcements for increasing positive behaviors: the youngster learned to play with toys as other children do and to help his mother by setting the table.

As part of the integrated approach of the program, Randy spent six hours each day at a special school for emotionally disturbed children. His teachers, also trained in behavior modification, continued the toilet training and other home programs—in addition to teaching appropriate school behavior. Though much of the early school program had to concentrate on reducing negative behaviors and establishing a situation conducive to learning, Randy learned to print some letters of the alphabet and to say "more" and "Hi" appropriately.

It is clear, then, that the role played by the school is vital in maintaining and extending the program begun in the home. The interaction is completed by having parents praise schoolwork and continue school lessons. The hospital plays an important role in separating the parents and child enough to provide rest for the parents, thus allowing them to live more normal lives without institutionalizing their child completely. Additionally, the hospital staff is responsible for diagnosis, planning the optimal combination of home and institutional living, and coordinating the entire program. Not only has the integrated approach of hospital, home, and school worked with severe cases like Randy, but it also has been applied successfully with less serious problem children.

XVI

THE ROAD
TO MATURITY

ALTHOUGH INFANCY AND CHILDHOOD are times of rapid change and growth, the interests of developmental psychologists go much beyond these years; development is seen to proceed through the whole life span. Covering the entire metamorphosis of human life in detail is beyond the intended scope of this book, but it is appropriate to close by turning briefly to maturity—the culmination of many of the processes that have been discussed thus far.

We can speak of maturity on many different levels. The adolescent, for example, is recognized as a person who has reached physical maturity and usually has achieved an important measure of autonomy and responsibility toward others. But the adolescent does not arrive at the static place of "adulthood"; a variety of biological, psychological, and social experiences still abound as the bases for further development. Young and middle adulthood is ideally marked, according to Erikson, by the establishment of intimate relationships, productivity, and passing on to the next generation the knowledge and wisdom one has accumulated (see Chapter X, pp. 326–27). In a somewhat different vein, Havighurst (1953) describes these years in terms of developmental tasks that all individuals face, including establishing and maintaining family life, economic independence, and social responsibility. Table XVI–1 shows a summary of these tasks, as well as those that Havighurst accords to the very last years of the life span. We can speak of maturity at any time of life—recognizing that the individual is changing, though perhaps not as rapidly as he once did, and continuing to develop as a unique being.

In this chapter, we shall focus on only two periods of later development —adolescence and the last years of life. Both frequently are seen as particularly stressful times, requiring a considerable adjustment. Studying them serves to help complete our understanding of the entire developmental process.

ADOLESCENCE: THE TRANSITION FROM CHILDHOOD TO ADULTHOOD

We noted at the outset, in Chapter I, that only in the past hundred years or so has our society come to recognize childhood as a formative period of life, distinguishable from adulthood. Adolescence is most often seen as a time of transition in which the developing child is specifically invited or permitted to try out adult roles in a more tentative or protected way than will be expected of him later. There are no clear boundary years to define adolescence; generally, though, the period may be said to begin with puberty, the onset of physical maturation (twelve to fourteen years of age), and to terminate when the individual assumes adultlike responsibilities such as marriage, full-time employment, or a serious commitment to career training, usually between the ages of eighteen and twenty in our culture.

The problems associated with adolescence have been widely studied by workers with diverse interests—anthropologists, sociologists, and psychologists. As might be expected, it is viewed somewhat differently from these perspectives.

Views of Adolescence

The Psychoanalytic View: Adolescence as a "Necessary Upheaval." Speaking from a psychoanalytic approach, Anna Freud provides this view of adolescence

> [Some] deplore the adolescent upset. . . . As analysts, who assess personalities from the structural point of view, we think otherwise. We know that

TABLE XVI-1

HAVIGHURST'S DEVELOPMENTAL TASKS OF ADULTHOOD

TASKS OF EARLY ADULTHOOD	TASKS OF MIDDLE AGE	TASKS OF LATER MATURITY
1. Selecting a mate.	1. Achieving adult civic and social responsibility.	1. Adjusting to decreasing physical strength and health.
2. Learning to live with a marriage partner.	2. Establishing and maintaining an economic standard of living.	2. Adjustment to retirement and reduced income.
3. Starting a family	3. Developing adult leisure-time activities.	3. Adjusting to death of spouse.
4. Rearing children.	4. Assisting teenage children to become responsible and happy adults.	4. Establishing an explicit affiliation with one's age group.
5. Managing a home.	5. Relating oneself to one's spouse as a person.	5. Meeting social and civic obligations.
6. Getting started in an occupation.	6. Accepting and adjusting to the physiological changes of middle age.	6. Establishing satisfactory physical living arrangements.
7. Taking on civic responsibility.	7. Adjusting to aging parents.	
8. Finding a congenial social group.		

Source: Copyright 1953 by Longmans, Green, and Co., Inc. From the book *Human Development* by Robert J. Havighurst. Reprinted by permission of the Davis McKay Co., Inc.

the character structure of a child at the end of the latency period represents the outcome of long drawn-out conflicts between id and ego forces. The inner balance achieved . . . is preliminary only and precarious. . . . [I]t has to be abandoned to allow adult sexuality to be integrated into the individual personality. The so-called adolescent upheavals are no more than the external indications that such internal adjustments are in progress.

. . . We all know individual children who as late as the age of fourteen, fifteen, or sixteen show no such outer evidence of inner unrest. . . . They are, perhaps more than any others, in need of therapeutic help to remove the inner restrictions and clear the path for normal development, however "upsetting" the latter may prove to be. [1972, pp. 317–318.]

The Sociological-Anthropological View: Adolescence as a Social Category. Others view adolescence simply as a social category, very much influenced by cultural factors. Anthropologists have long noted that cultures differ in encouraging children to engage in or witness adult activities; if such encouragement is extensive, adolescent upset is minimized. Cultures also differ in the amount of support they provide during the adolescent transition; some clearly demark the entrance into adulthood by ritual, such as puberty rites, that make it easier for the child to assume the adult role. This kind of support is not extensively available in our culture, although adolescents may themselves provide rites of passage by engaging in particular activities. A number of years ago, for example, when alcohol consumption was more important and the use of marijuana and similar drugs less important than today in adolescent cultures, one major study (Maddox and McCall, 1964) reported:

> . . . teen-agers in this study perceive most adults as drinkers. Moreover, particularly among boys, the teen-ager who plays or prefers to play adult roles is more likely than others both to use alcohol and to identify himself as a drinker. . . . An important aspect of the drinking behavior of the high-school student is the status-conferral possibilities of the act of drinking where the society makes adulthood a valued status and institutionalizes drinking as one aspect of what it means to be an adult. [p. 81.]

The Social-Learning View. Bandura (1964), speaking for the social learning view, argues that the frequently given storm and stress description of adolescence is largely exaggerated. He notes, for example, that although teenagers may indeed be faddish in dress, so are adult women who sack, trapeze, and chemise themselves following a fashion show in Paris. According to Bandura, overinterpretation of adolescent faddish nonconformity is one reason for popular versions of adolescence as a period of great upheaval; mass media sensationalism, generalizations from deviant youth, and self-fulfilling prophecy are others. He does not view adolescence as completely problem-free, however; rather, he sees it merely as one more developmental period with behavioral characteristics related to and consistent with past behavior and training.

In general, the majority of individuals probably move into the adult years with relative comfort. It cannot be denied, nevertheless, that dramatic change and adjustment occurs, that the adjustment is not always satisfactorily met, and that it is often reached only with difficulty. In this section, then, we shall look at some areas that are widely considered particularly critical to the transition of the adolescent years.

Physical Maturation

Some of the adolescent's concern about himself certainly stems from the physical changes that he experiences. As noted in Chapter III, there is, at this time, both a general growth spurt of tissues such as muscle and bone and sharply accelerated maturation of the reproductive system. Some physical changes are sufficiently gradual to be almost unnoticeable; others, such as growth in height, breast development, or the appearance of whiskers, are extremely apparent. The adolescent, therefore, must adjust not only to the new self he is becoming but also to the reactions others display to his new image.

Obviously, the amount of adjustment required will depend somewhat on the rate and course of physical development, which varies across individuals. Figure XVI–1, for example, shows photographs of two adolescent boys and two adolescent girls of the same chronological age. Note how, in each case, one is clearly large and physically mature while the other still looks like a young child.

There is also a regular difference between the sexes in physical maturity, with girls advancing more rapidly than boys up through adolescence, so that, for a given age, they are almost inevitably more mature than their male counterparts. Girls show their maximum growth rate when they are approximately 12½ years of age, whereas the maximum growth rate for boys occurs on the average over two years later. Girls also reach full bodily maturity and stop growing several years before boys. The pattern of sex differences in body size as a function of age is illustrated in Figure XVI–2,

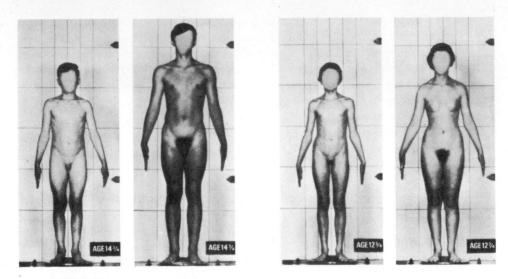

F I G U R E   X V I – 1

Photographs of adolescents of the same age, illustrating differences in rates of maturation. From J. M. Tanner, in P. H. Mussen, Carmichael's Manual of Child Psychology, *3rd ed., Vol. I. Copyright 1970, reproduced by permission of John Wiley & Sons, Inc. and Dr. James M. Tanner.*

which shows the difference in the heights of males and females at various ages. Note that between the ages of eleven and thirteen, girls are actually taller than boys, although by adulthood males are taller than females by an average of more than four inches.

Social Correlates of Differences in Rate of Maturing. The differences in rate of physical maturation displayed by adolescents may, in turn, have social and personal consequences. In the elementary school years, the very early-maturing girl will feel somewhat out of place; she is "embarrassingly" larger than her peers and may experience a menstrual flow while her age-mates are still ignorant of the process. It is not surprising, then, that sixth-grade girls evaluate their prepuberal female classmates more positively than puberal ones. But soon the differentiation reverses; in junior high it is the mature postpuberal girl who is the most popular (Faust, 1960).

For boys, the situation is more clear-cut: early-maturing males enjoy a number of advantages in social position with their peers (e.g., Eichorn,

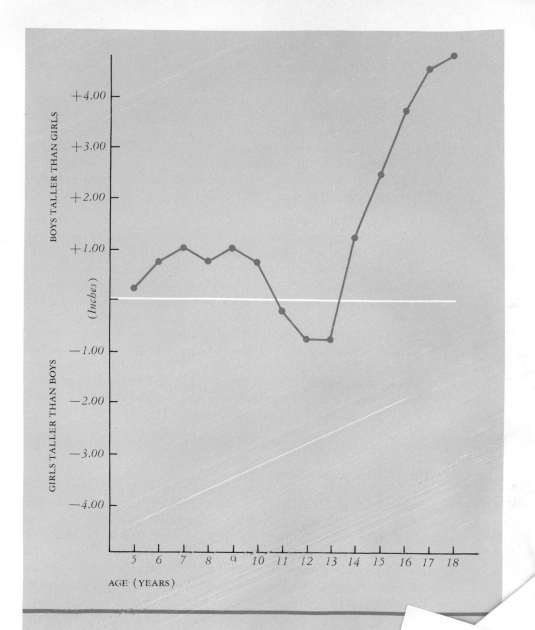

FIGURE XVI–2

Differences in height between boys and girls at various ages
E. H. Watson *and* G. H. Lowrey, Growth and Development
Chicago: Year Book Medical Publishers, Inc., 1962, p

1963). The larger and stronger boy, with his increased physical capacities and more adultlike appearance, is more likely to be elected an officer of his class, to have his name appear in the school newspaper, and, not surprisingly, to excel athletically (Jones, 1958). Although these advantages tend to diminish as physical differences disappear, at age thirty-three some social differences favoring the early-maturing boys—such as better occupational adjustment—are still present (Jones, 1957).

What factors account for the advantages which accrue to early-maturing boys? Eichorn puts it this way:

> Is it simply that they are destined to come into the world "trailing clouds of glory"? Although rate of maturing is to some extent genetically determined . . . even sexual behavior in man and other primates appears to be more dependent on experiential than on somatic factors. Many of the behavioral differences between early- and late-maturers may reasonably be interpreted as functions of differential experience. The early- and late-maturing differ not only in superficial characteristics but also in actual physical abilities. . . . Adults and peers may react first to the physical appearance of the early-maturer and give him tasks and privileges ordinarily reserved for older individuals. Often he is able to meet the challenge, and in so doing confirms their impression, increases his own skill, and derives personal satisfaction. If he was also larger than his age mates before puberty, this circular process may have been recurring for some time. [1963, pp. 50–51.]

Cognitive Change in Adolescence

According to David Elkind (1967), a leading interpreter of Piaget, the major task of adolescence involves the conquest of thought through the emergence of formal operations. (Recall that, as we saw in Chapter VII, this stage of mental operations allows the child to begin to conceptualize in terms of possible alternative propositions; he becomes better able to examine his own thoughts, as well as those of others.) But, Elkind notes, the adolescent fails to distinguish between what he and others think *about.* Because he is concerned primarily with himself, he believes that others too are preoccupied with his appearance and behavior. Elkind refers to this as *adolescent egocentrism* and notes two consequences: an imaginary audience and a personal fable.

The *imaginary audience* refers to the adolescent's belief that he is being ~erved by others. It in turn plays a role in determining certain behaviors ~elings—for example, in the self-consciousness, loudness, and faddish ~t frequently characterize adolescents. The *personal fable,* on the other hand, involves a belief on the part of the adolescent in the uniqueness of his feelings, and in his immortality. Thus, Elkind points out, we see lengthy diaries depicting with great drama the special experiences and frustrations of young people which they presumably regard as of universal importance.

In his attempt to understand and treat adolescent problems, Elkind attributes much adolescent behavior to the imaginary audience and the personal fable:

> The imaginary audience . . . seems often to play a role in middle-class delinquency. . . . As a case in point, one young man took $1,000 from a golf tournament purse, hid the money, and then promptly revealed himself. It turned out that much of the motivation for this act was derived from the anticipated response of "the audience" to the guttiness of his action. In a similar vein, many young girls become pregnant because, in part at least, their personal fable convinces them that pregnancy will happen to others but never to them. . . . [Elkind, 1967, pp. 1031–1032.]

Achieving Identity

Earlier we had occasion to note the work of Erikson in describing development as a series of psychosocial stages through which each individual passes. One of Erikson's greatest contributions has been to focus on the adolescent's struggle to establish an identity. So critical is this crisis that Erikson labels the adolescent stage as the period of identity versus role confusion (Chapter X, pp. 326–27). The basis of the struggle lies not only in societal demands regarding impending adulthood but also in the physical changes rapidly taking place. Previous trust in physical being and bodily functions is now seriously questioned and can be reestablished only by a reevaluation of the self (Maier, 1969). The adolescent seeks to discover who he is and what he will become. He searches for a sameness within himself and a reflection of this constancy in others.

How does the adolescent achieve this vital identity? Erikson sug first of all, that our culture allows a moratorium or period which the rapidly developing child has the opportunit tegrated into society. A certain amount of experimentati that the adolescent may indeed "try on" various commitm much as one tries on new garments before selecting the ing on" is manifested in many ways: endless examin the self, vocations, ideologies; a rich fantasy life i a variety of roles; identification with particular individuals, frequently involving a herolike worship. Erikson writes:

> The danger of this stage is role confusion. Where this is based on a strong previous doubt as to one's sexual identity, delinquent and outright psychotic episodes are not uncommon. If diagnosed and treated correctly, these incidents do not have the same fatal significance which they have at other ages. In most instances, however, it is the inability to settle on an occupational identity which disturbs individual young people. To keep themselves together they temporarily overidentify, to the point of apparent complete loss of identity, with the heroes of cliques and crowds. This initiates the stage of "falling in love," which is by no means entirely, or even primarily, a sexual matter—except where the mores demand it. To a considerable extent adolescent love is an attempt to arrive at a definition of one's identity by projecting one's diffused ego image on another and by seeing it thus reflected and gradually clarified. This is why so much of young love is conversation. [Erikson, 1963, p. 262.]

Changing Social Relations: Orientation away from Family. According to Erikson's analysis, one of the potentially troublesome areas in adolescence is the change that occurs in social relationships. The problem arises from the fact that the child, who was predominantly a member of a family, now is becoming the adolescent, who is both a member of family and of peer group.

Bowerman and Kinch (1969) studied the relative orientation toward family or peers in 686 fourth to tenth graders in a middle-class school. The youngsters completed questionnaires that permitted conclusions about (1) the extent to which they identified with either family or peers, (2) the group with which they preferred to associate, and (3) the group whose values and norms they considered most like their own.

To assess *identification,* subjects were asked whether family or friends understood them better and whether they would rather become the kind of persons their parents are or the kind their friends presumably would be. For *association orientation,* they were asked which group they most enjoyed doing things with, and which one they would rather spend time with. For the *norm orientation,* subjects were queried as to whose ideas were most like theirs with respect to decisions of right and wrong, things that are fun to do, the importance of school, and what they would do if ne group wanted them to do something of which the other did not approve.

e youngsters were allowed to choose family, friends, or a neutral re- indicating that they felt the same about the two groups. For each of the three types of orientation, subjects were categorized as neutral if there were an equal number of family and peer choices or if choices were neutral; as family-oriented if there were more family than peer choices; and as peer-oriented if the choices were predominantly of friends. A combined orientation rating was made from the three separate orientation ratings.

As Table XVI–2 shows, there was a dramatic shift in all aspects of orientation with age; 87.1 percent of fourth graders but only 31.6 percent of tenth graders expressed a family orientation on the combined score. There was, on the other hand, an increase not only in peer orientation but in the percentage of individuals showing orientation equally toward family and friends. The greatest shift was in association—reflecting the adolescent's preference to spend time with his age-mates. Interestingly, 51.9 percent of tenth graders still identified most closely with family.

In discussing the transition of social relationship, Bowerman and Kinch observed:

> . . . the nature of family interaction is affected by the decreasing participation and interest of the child in family activities as he becomes more involved in peer assoication; by the decline of the family as the primary source of affection with increasing attachment to peers; and by the weakening of authority and control of the parents as the child grows in independence and as norms and values of parents must compete for acceptance with those of peers. These are among the reasons why this transitional period is one of potential increase in parent-child conflict, due not only to the striving of the child to achieve status in two important primary groups with conflicting or competing interests, but also to the difficulties which parents as well as children experience in reacting to the changing situational and interactional characteristics of interpersonal relationships. [p. 137.]

Conflict is not inevitable, however; its occurrence depends upon a multiplicity of factors. Other data collected by Bowerman and Kinch suggested that family-peer orientation was affected by the adolescents' opinions as to how well they got along with their family, how their families treated them, whether they received attention from the family, and whether personal problems were discussed in the family. Adolescents also perceive family life as happier when parents discuss family problems and when they respect the opinions of their offspring than when these factors are absent (Slocum, 1958).

The Struggle for Autonomy. One of the focal points of parent-adolescent conflict, when it does occur, is the struggle on the part of young people for autonomy and independence. We have noted before (Chapter X) that de-

TABLE XVI-2

PERCENTAGE OF FOURTH THROUGH TENTH GRADERS DEMONSTRATING FAMILY, PEER, OR NEUTRAL ORIENTATIONS

ORIENTATION TOWARD	GRADE IN SCHOOL			
	4th	6th	8th	10th
Combined Orientation				
Family	87.1	80.2	41.7	31.6
Neutral	6.9	11.2	18.3	20.2
Peer	5.9	8.6	40.0	48.1
Normative Orientation				
Family	82.2	69.8	33.0	30.4
Neutral	5.9	12.1	14.8	19.0
Peer	11.9	18.1	52.2	50.6
Association Orientation				
Family	75.2	62.1	20.9	15.2
Neutral	15.8	25.0	39.1	29.1
Peer	8.9	12.9	40.0	55.7
Identification				
Family	81.2	77.6	57.4	51.9
Neutral	13.8	18.1	24.3	21.5
Peer	5.0	4.3	18.2	26.6

Source: Adapted from Bowerman and Kinch, 1969.

pendence and independence do not exist as polar opposites; children may become independent in one area or in relation to some individuals but may increase their dependence in other areas or in relation to other people. Complete independence is not possible and has been described, in a memorable phrase, as "an unnamed form of insanity" (Dewey, 1920). Nevertheless, the adolescent's pressing desire to run his own life—to decide what he will wear, where he will go, what activities he will engage in, what values he will adopt—frequently runs counter to the established role of authority to which parents are accustomed.

Some parents tend, perhaps simply out of habit, not to want to relinquish decision-making power. Others recognize the need for autonomy for their offspring but are concerned with the speed and circumstances under which it occurs (Campbell, 1969). In either case, variation can be found in how parents deal with the development of autonomy.

In one investigation, adolescents in grades seven through twelve were requested to rate the behavior of their parents (Elder, 1962). From their answers, seven descriptive categories emerged, ranging from the autocratic parent who allowed no expression of views or self-regulation of behavior by the adolescent, to the ignoring parent who took no role in directing his children.

The students also were asked whether they thought their mothers' and fathers' ideas, rules, or principles were good and reasonable or wrong and unreasonable. As Table XVI–3 shows, children from democratic homes

TABLE XVI–3

PERCENTAGE OF ADOLESCENTS PERCEIVING THEIR PARENTS AS "FAIR" ACCORDING TO THE PARENTS' CHILD-REARING POLICIES

ADOLESCENT'S PERCEPTION OF:	ADOLESCENTS WITH PARENTS WHO ARE:		
	Auto-cratic	Demo-cratic	Permis-sive
Mother	55.1	85.5	80.4
Father	50.7	85.1	74.6

Source: Adapted from Elder, 1962.

were most satisfied with the policies of their parents whereas those of autocratic parents were least satisfied. Interestingly, though, at least three-fifths of the students expressed a favorable disposition toward their parents' policies regardless of the extent to which they were allowed self-regulation.

Changing Peer Relationships: The Culture of Youth. We have seen that peers become increasingly important to the adolescent. The influence that teenagers have on each other has been strongly documented by James S. Coleman from reports by youths from ten high schools in the Midwest that varied in size and description (1960; 1961). Coleman concluded that adolescent groupings in high school form nothing short of a subculture quite distinct from adult society:

> Industrial society has spawned a peculiar phenomenon, most evident in America but emerging also in other Western societies: adolescent subcultures, with values and activities quite distinct from those of the adult society —subcultures whose members have most of their important associations within and few with adult society. Industrialization, and the rapidity of change itself, has taken out of the hands of the parent the task of training his child, made the parent's skills obsolescent, and put him out of touch with the times—unable to understand, much less inculcate, the standards of a social order which has changed since he was young. [1960, p. 337.]

Coleman's work has led many to view adults and adolescents as existing in antagonistic, impenetrable spheres. Others argue that the distance between the generations is not nearly so severe, that adolescents choose friends who have similar values, consider their parents important, show concern about parental disapproval, and conform to parental or peer wishes depending upon the immediate issue at hand (Douvan and Adelson, 1966; Epperson, 1964; Rosen, 1955). There is also evidence (Costanzo and Shaw, 1966) that the influence of peers is high during early adolescence but then decreases. All in all, the issue about which we most need to know is not the relative strength of peer influence but the functions that youth culture might actually serve in reducing problems during adolescence (e.g., Ausubel, 1954; Campbell, 1969; Eisenstadt, 1956; Matza, 1961). Some of them are listed below.

1. In a complex society, the family, with a relatively simple structure of control going from parents to children, cannot provide adequate experience that is relevant to other relationships. Operating within a peer group allows the adolescent to experiment with a greater variety of other situations, thereby preparing him to assume roles of responsibility and authority.

2. The peer group serves both as a standard against which to measure one's accomplishments and as a same-aged group that judges more objectively than family. In this sense, it provides independent status to the adolescent.

3. It provides opportunity for practicing and discussing alternative roles, behaviors, and identities.

4. It sometimes protects adolescents from coercion that adults might impose.

5. Since all adolescents share some of the same experiences, the peer group gives support during transition and decision making concerning social, academic, and occupational matters.

6. It also may lessen the burdens adults would have to bear if they assumed complete responsibility for their offspring.

7. Finally, the peer group actually may decrease the likelihood of deviancy by providing institutionalized forms of behaviors that otherwise might be labeled delinquent.

Antisocial Behavior in Adolescence: Juvenile Delinquency

Juvenile delinquency, like other behavioral problems in development (see Chapter XV), is more fruitfully thought of in psychological or sociological terms than in terms of the medical perspective of "illness." Thus, for example, Kuhlen and Thompson (1970) say:

> there is no simple explanation for juvenile delinquency because it is merely one of many possible forms of adjustment—classified as maladjustment on the basis of the prevailing social-cultural codes. Since delinquent acts are responses of a kind that reduce (at least temporarily) the individual's needs (and so in a sense "adjust"), such behavior patterns tend to recur again and again. [p. 565.]

Characteristics of Delinquents: The Healy and Bronner Study. Although much of our knowledge of human development is fairly recent, occasionally we find that an older study, through the imagination and foresight of the investigators, has provided knowledge that still is pertinent. Such a case exists in the study of juvenile delinquency; a classic investigation by William Healy and Augusta Bronner (1936) has provided unique information on some of the characteristics of juvenile delinquents.

These investigators began with a sample of 133 families, each of which had at least one delinquent youngster. Among this group they found 105 delinquents who had a nondelinquent sibling (in eight cases, a twin) with whom a comparison could be made which held at least socioeconomic and certain family factors constant.

Healy and Bronner found some remarkable differences in the physical health and general developmental history of delinquents as compared with nondelinquents. Some of their findings are found in Table XVI–4, from which it can be seen that there is a uniform and striking pattern of poor physical health among the delinquents compared to the nondelinquents both through development and at the time of the study. It is not possible, of course, to determine directly any causal relationships from such

T A B L E   X V I – 4

CONTRASTS BETWEEN 105 DELINQUENTS AND THEIR
NONDELINQUENT CONTROLS FROM THE SAME FAMILIES

	NUMBER OF CASES	
CHARACTERISTIC	Delinquents	Controls
Developmental History (100)		
Much worried pregnancy	10	3
Very sickly pregnancy	13	6
Premature birth	2	1
Very difficult delivery	12	5
Much underweight in early childhood	12	5
Very early bottle fed	10	8
Very late breast fed	7	4
Very difficult weaning	2	0
Cross fussy babyhood	14	5
Difficult sphincter training	31	13
Many illnesses or severe illness	28	8
Diseases of central nervous system	5	3
Otitis media	3	6
Severe head injury	5	0
Encephalitis	2	1
History of distinctly good health	44	75

TABLE XVI-4 *(continued)*

CHARACTERISTIC	NUMBER OF CASES	
	Delinquents	Controls
Physical Conditions at Time of Study		
Weight deviates (more than 10% under or 20% over)	11	10
Very premature sexual development	4	0
Retarded sexual development	5	1
Defective vision—more than slight	17	6
Slight strabismus	3	2
Marked strabismus	0	1
Otitis media	1	5
Moderately defective hearing	1	3
Markedly enlarged or diseased tonsils	20	12
Nasal obstruction	6	2
At least some badly carious teeth	27	19
Endocrine disorder	4	0
Phimosis	4	1
Very poor posture	3	0
Miscellaneous liabilities	7	3

Source: Healy and Bronner, 1936.

data. A poor medical history might provide frustrations and impediments in a youngster's life which in turn might lead to delinquent behavior. On the other hand, certain kinds of difficult behavior might be linked to physical defects through some genetic factor.

Perhaps one of the most fascinating outcomes of the Healy and Bronner study is the *lack* of differences between delinquents and nondelinquents in intellectual ability. The authors point out:

> . . . the great amount of carefully conducted and intensive psychological testing done in this study resulted, quite unexpectedly, in establishing no signs of differentiation between the mental equipment of the delinquents and the controls in our series. . . . About 60% of the delinquents were out-and-out truants, with evasions of attendance running as high as one year

in one case. The scholarship record was, of course, affected by this but not to the extent that might be surmised. Definitely poor scholarship was registered for only 34% of the delinquents, as against 18% of the controls. So by no means are all delinquents found to be recorded to be poor students. [cited in Kuhlen and Thompson, 1970, p. 570.]

But if delinquents in the study were surprisingly like nondelinquents on measures of intellectual ability, they were just as surprisingly different on another dimension: hyperactivity. Healy and Bronner found that almost half—fully forty-six—of the delinquent youngsters in their study exhibited hyperactivity, "overrestlessness," and the like, whereas not one of the control youngsters from the same family and matched for age could be so characterized. Additionally, they experienced greater feelings of rejection, insecurity, inadequacy, unhappiness, and guilt.

The investigators also sought information as to exactly how delinquent tendencies and behaviors had been acquired. The research was remarkably prescient for its day. In their evaluation of movies, for example, it was learned that a large percentage of the delinquents (much larger than was true for the controls) attended the movies excessively, several times a week or more often if they were able to, and sometimes stayed to see a performance over and over again. Indeed, a few of the delinquents actually stated that they had patterned their own criminal behavior after material that they had seen in gang and crime motion pictures. Equally important, Healy and Bronner report that what we would now think of as the "social-learning history" of delinquents conspired to produce much of their antisocial behavior. They had been, in the investigators' terms, "loaded with ideas of delinquency." Healy and Bronner described it this way:

> This particular educative process generally began with information received from youthful comrades. . . . Some said they had learned about delinquency from a mixture of sources, for example, the communications of delinquent companions, perhaps even observations of them in delinquency, plus ideas derived from detective or crime stories and the movies. Some had given really planful thought to possible delinquent exploits—a couple of youthful burglars told of making studies and sketches of the places they entered. Reinforcement of ideas already entertained frequently assailed the individual to further contact with delinquent companions—some gave accounts of much talk about delinquency in detention homes or other institutions. Or further observations of opportunities or of actual delinquencies perpetrated, or further reading or movies gave new suggestions. [cited in Kuhlen and Thompson, 1970, p. 572.]

There is no doubt that the opportunities for being educated in crime have increased markedly in the past few decades with the advent of various forms of mass media entertainment and communications describing such activities in great detail. Whether or not these changes are a causal factor, juvenile delinquency has been increasing in the United States for many years (see Figure XVI–3). It is noteworthy that the rise is associated with particular segments of the juvenile population: the rate of increase is higher for girls than for boys, is higher in urban areas, and is higher in minority than in majority groups (Hurlock, 1967).

Increased Delinquency among the Affluent. Although the likelihood of delinquency by middle- or upper-class adolescents is lower than for those in the lower classes, delinquency has increased substantially among affluent youth in recent years. It is not difficult to hypothesize factors underlying such behavior among the poor, but explanations are not as immediately obvious in the case of the adolescent who, superficially at least, appears to be growing up in comfortable circumstances.

One investigator (Pine, 1966) has offered several hypotheses to account for the phenomenon. He notes, first of all, that the period of adolescence has been extended, particularly for the college-going middle and upper class, from the midteens to at least age twenty-one or twenty-two. The tacking on of additional years to the transition period, Pine suggests, produces an "existential vacuum" for the young; without meaning or purpose, there is an increase in rebellious behavior. And, ironically, the adolescent must at the same time contend with the tremendous pressures of his elders and society to achieve during the high school and college years. Pine also suggests that changes in middle-class values—particularly with regard to delay of gratification and the work ethic—may contribute to a lessening of discipline and decreased self-control of impulses; with a reduction of both external and internal restrictions, increased delinquency is not a surprising outcome. Finally, Pine notes that successful social mobility is itself a basis for some types of delinquency inasmuch as the adolescent may feel insecure about being accepted in a new environment, he may temporarily lose his identity, and a contempt for traditional institutions and beliefs may result.

Middle-class delinquency also has been explained in terms of family dynamics. Elkind (1967), for example, argues that adolescents who frequently get into trouble are reacting to parental exploitation. This may involve the parents' attempts to bolster their own self-esteem through their children's achievement, their tendency to take advantage of the adolescent

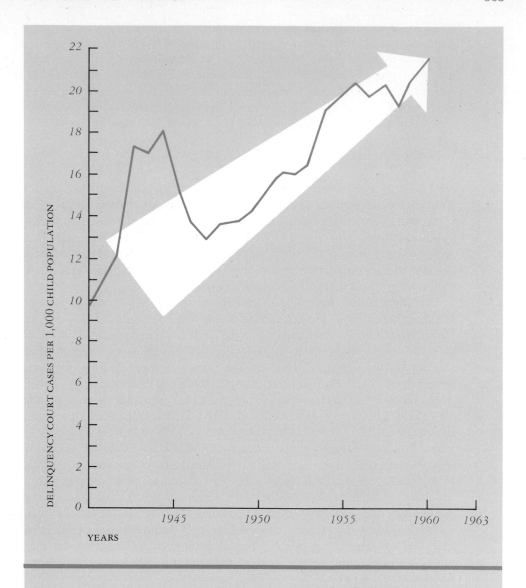

FIGURE XVI-3

The rise in juvenile delinquency in recent years. Adapted from Beck, 1965.

through "slave labor," or their reaping of vicarious satisfaction through the behavoir of their offspring:

> . . . exploitation is illustrated by a case in which a sexually frustrated mother encouraged her daughter to act out sexually. When the daughter returned from a date, the mother would demand a kiss-by-kiss description of the affair and end by calling the girl a tramp. When I saw the girl, who was being adjudicated for sexual vagrancy, she told me, "I have the name so I might as well play the role." When she left my office, her mother, who had been waiting outside, teasingly asked her how far she had gotten with the "cute psychologist." [Elkind, 1967, pp. 312–313.]

Although Elkind recognizes that adolescents may be exploitative of parents, he feels that parents can often be blamed for delinquency. He comments, then, that middle-class acting out is not antisocial so much as it is *antifamilial*.

EXTENDED DISCUSSION

ADOLESCENTS AND THE USE DRUGS

The increase in the use of drugs in the United States is one of the most striking social changes to occur during the 1960s, and there is excellent reason to believe that young people are the primary users of them. Much concern is expressed about drug use, including the threat of possible physical damage, psychological addiction or dependency, and concommitant increases in crime. The complicated issues surrounding drug use are not easy to resolve; in fact, we are just beginning to understand some of the presumably more simple facts, such as who uses drugs and under what circumstances.

Knowledge is limited for several reasons. To begin with, it is not adequate to speak of "drugs" as an entity, for the many different kinds of drugs that are consumed differ dramatically in composition and effects. (See Table XVI–5.) What is more, any one drug may vary in potency depending upon its dosage, quality, and even individual reactions to it. Then, too, it is difficult to obtain information about drug use because

(text continues on page 574)

TABLE XVI-5
COMPARISON CHART OF MAJOR SUBSTANCES USED FOR MIND-ALTERATION

OFFICIAL NAME	SLANG NAME(S)	USUAL SINGLE ADULT DOSE	DURATION OF ACTION (hours)	METHOD OF TAKING	LEGITIMATE MEDICAL USES (present and projected)	Psychological Dependence	POTENTIAL FOR Tolerance (leading to increased dosage)	Physical Dependence	Overall Abuse and Toxicity (2)
Alcohol Whiskey, gin, beer, wine	Booze Hooch Suds	1½ oz. gin or whisky 12 oz. beer	2-4	Swallowing liquid	Rare. Sometimes used as a sedative (for tension).	High	Yes	Yes	High
Caffeine Coffee, tea, Coca-Cola, No-Doz, APC	Java	1-2 cups 1 bottle 5 mg.	2-4	Swallowing liquid	Mild stimulant. Treatment of some forms of coma.	Moderate	Yes	No	Very Minimal
Nicotine (and coal tar) Cigarettes, cigars	Fags, Nails	1-2 cigarettes	1-2	Smoking (inhalation)	None (used as an insecticide).	High	Yes	No	High
Sedatives Alcohol— see above Barbiturates Amytal Nembutal Seconal Phenobarbital Doriden (Glutethimide) Chloral hydrate Miltown, Equanil (Meprobamate)	Downers Barbs Blue Devils Yellow jackets, Dolls Red devils Phennies Goofers	50-100 mg. 500 mg. 500 mg. 400 mg.	4	Swallowing pills or capsules	Treatment of insomnia and tension. Induction of anesthesia.	High	Yes	Yes	High
Stimulants Caffeine—see above Nicotine—see above Amphetamines Benzedrine Methedrine Dexedrine Preludin Cocaine	Uppers Pep Pills, Wake-ups Bennies, cartwheels Crystal, speed, Meth Dexies or Xmas trees (spanules) Coke, snow	2.5-5.0 mg. Variable	4	Swallowing pills, capsules or injecting in vein. Sniffing or injecting.	Treatment of obesity, narcolepsy, fatigue, depression. Anesthesia of the eye and throat.	High	Yes	No	High

REASONS DRUG IS SOUGHT (DRUG EFFECTS AND SOCIAL FACTORS)	SHORT TERM EFFECTS (PYSCHO-LOGICAL, PHARMACOLOGICAL, SOCIAL) (3)	LONG TERM EFFECTS (PSYCHO-LOGICAL, PHARMACOLOGICAL, SOCIAL)	FORM OF LEGAL REGULATION AND CONTROL (4)
To relax. To escape from tensions, problems and inhibitions. To get "high" (euphoria). Seeking manhood or rebelling (particularly those under 21). Social custom and conformity. Massive advertising and promotion. Ready availability.	CNS(6) depressant. Relaxation (sedation). Euphoria. Drowsiness. Impaired judgment, reaction time, coordination and emotional control. Frequent aggressive behavior and driving accidents.	Diversion of energy and money from more creative and productive pursuits. Habituation. Possible obesity with chronic excessive use. Irreversible damage to brain and liver, addiction with severe withdrawal illness. (D.T.s) with heavy use. Many deaths.	Available and advertised without limitation in many forms with only minimal regulation by age (21, or 18), hours of sale, location, taxation, ban on bootlegging and driving laws. Some "black market" for those under age and those evading taxes. Minimal penalties.
For a "pick-up" or stimulation. "Taking a Break." Social custom and low cost. Advertising. Ready availability.	CNS(6) stimulant. Increase alertness. Reduction of fatigue.	Sometimes, insomnia, restlessness, or gastric irritation. Habituation.	Available and advertised without limit with no regulation for children or adults.
For a "pick-up" or stimulation. "Taking a Break." Social custom. Advertising. Ready availability.	CNS stimulant. Relaxation (or distraction) from the process of smoking.	Lung (and other) cancer, heart and blood vessel disease, cough, etc. Higher infant mortality. Many deaths. Habituation. Diversion of energy and money. Air pollution. Fire.	Available and advertised without limit with only minimal regulation by age, taxation, and labeling of packages.
To relax or sleep. To get "high" (euphoria). Widely prescribed by physicians, both for specific and nonspecific complaints. General climate encouraging taking pills for everything.	CNS depressants. Sleep induction. Relaxation (sedation). Sometimes euphoria. Drowsiness. Impaired judgment, reaction time, coordination and emotional control. Relief of anxiety-tension. Muscle relaxation.	Irritability, weight loss, addiction with severe withdrawal illness (like D.T.s). Diversion of energy and money. Habituation, addiction.	Available in large amounts by ordinary medical prescription which can be repeatedly refilled or can be obtained from more than one physician. Widely advertised & "detailed" to M.D.s & pharmacists. Other manufacture, sale or possession prohibited under federal drug abuse & similar state (dangerous) drug laws. Moderate penalties. Widespread illicit traffic.
For stimulation and relief of fatigue. To get "high" (euphoria). General climate encouraging taking pills for everything.	CNS stimulants. Increased alertness, reduction of fatigue, loss of appetite, insomnia, often euphoria.	Restlessness, irritability, weight loss, toxic psychosis (mainly paranoid). Diversion of energy and money. Habituation. Extreme irritability, toxic psychosis.	Amphetamines, same as Sedatives above. Cocaine, same as Narcotics below.

T A B L E   X V I – 5   *(continued)*

COMPARISON CHART OF MAJOR SUBSTANCES USED FOR MIND-ALTERATION

OFFICIAL NAME	SLANG NAME(S)	USUAL SINGLE ADULT DOSE	DURATION OF ACTION (hours)	METHOD OF TAKING	LEGITIMATE MEDICAL USES (present and projected)	Psychological Dependence	POTENTIAL FOR Tolerance (leading to increased dosage)	Physical Dependence	Overall Abuse and Toxicity (2)
Tranquilizers									
Librium (Chlordiazepoxide)		5-10 mg.	4-6	Swallowing pills or capsules	Treatment of anxiety, tension, alcoholism, neurosis, psychosis, psychosomatic disorders and vomiting.	Minimal	No	No	Minimal
Phenothiazines									
Thorazine		10-25 mg.							
Compazine		10 mg.							
Stelazine		2 mg.							
Reserpine (Rauwolfia)		1 mg.							
Marijuana Cannabis Sativa (5)	Pot, grass, tea, weed, stuff, hash, joint, reefers	Variable—1 cigarette or pipe, or 1 drink or cake (India)	4	Smoking (inhalation) Swallowing	Treatment of depression, tension, loss of appetite, and high blood pressure.	Moderate	No	No	Minimal to Moderate
Narcotics (opiates, analgesics)									
Opium	Op	10-12 "pipes" (Asia)	4	Smoking (inhalation) Injecting in muscle or vein.	Treatment of severe pain, diarrhea, and cough.	High	Yes	Yes	High
Heroin	Horse, H, Smack, Shit, Junk	Variable— bag or paper w. 5-10% heroin							
Morphine		15 mg.							
Codeine		30 mg.							
Percodan		1 tablet							
Demerol		50-100 mg.							
Methadone	Dolly								
Cough syrups (Cheracol, Hycodan Romilar, etc.)		2-4 oz. (for euphoria)		Swallowing					
Hallucinogens	Acid, sugar cubes, trip	150 micrograms	10-12	Swallowing liquid, capsule, pill (or sugar cube)	Experimental study of mind and brain function. Enhancement of creativity and problem solving. Treatment of alcoholism, mental illness, and the dying person. (Chemical warfare)	Minimal	Yes (rare)	No	Moderate
LSD									
Psilocybin	Mushrooms	25 mg.	6-8						
S.T.P.		5 mg.							
D.M.T.				Smoking					
Mescaline (Peyote)	Cactus	350 mg.	12-14	Chewing plant					
Antidepressants				Swallowing pills or capsules	Treatment of moderate to severe depression.	Minimal	No	No	Minimal
Ritalin		10 mg.	4-6						
Dibenzapines (Tofranil, Elavil)		25 mg., 10 mg.							
MAO inhibitors (Nardil, Parnate)		15 mg., 10 mg.							

REASONS DRUG IS SOUGHT (DRUG EFFECTS AND SOCIAL FACTORS)	SHORT TERM EFFECTS (PYSCHOLOGICAL, PHARMACOLOGICAL, SOCIAL) (3)	LONG TERM EFFECTS (PSYCHOLOGICAL, PHARMACOLOGICAL, SOCIAL)	FORM OF LEGAL REGULATION AND CONTROL (4)
Medical (including psychiatric) treatment of anxiety or tension states, alcoholism, psychoses, and other disorders.	Selective CNS depressants. Relaxation, relief of anxiety-tension. Suppression of hallucinations or delusions, improved functioning.	Sometime drowsiness, dryness of mouth, blurring of vision, skin rash, tremor. Occasionally jaundice, agranulocytosis, or death.	Same as Sedatives above, except not usually included under the special federal or state drug laws. Negligible illicit traffic.
To get "high" (euphoria). As an escape. To relax. To socialize. To conform to various subcultures which sanction its use. For rebellion. Attraction of behavior labeled as deviant. Availability.	Relaxation, euphoria, increased appetite, some alteration of time perception, possible impairment of judgment and coordination. Mixed CNS depressant-stimulant.	Usually none. Possible diversion of energy and money. Habituation. Occasional accute panic reactions.	Unavailable (although permissible) for ordinary medical prescription. Possession, sale, and cultivation prohibited by state and federal narcotic or marijuana laws. Severe penalties. Widespread illicit traffic.
To get "high" (euphoria). As an escape. To avoid withdrawal symptoms. As a substitute for aggressive and sexual drives which cause anxiety. To conform to various sub-cultures which sanction use. For rebellion.	CNS depressants. Sedation, euphoria, relief of pain, impaired intellectual functioning and coordination.	Constipation, loss of appetite and weight, temporary impotency or sterility. Habituation, addiction with unpleasant and painful withdrawal illness.	Available (except heroin) by special (narcotics) medical prescriptions. Some available by ordinary prescription or over-the-counter. Other manufacture, sale, or possession prohibited under state and federal narcotics laws. Severe penalties. Extensive illicit traffic.
Curiosity created by recent widespread publicity. Seeking for meaning and consciousness—expansion. Rebellion. Attraction of behavior recently labeled as deviant. Availability.	Production of visual imagery, increased sensory awareness, anxiety, nausea, impaired coordination; sometimes consciousness-expansion.	Usually none. Sometimes precipitates or intensifies an already existing psychosis: more commonly can produce a panic reaction.	Available only to a few medical researchers (or to members of the Native American Church). Other manufacture, sale, or possession prohibited by state dangerous drug or federal drug abuse laws. Moderate penalties. Extensive illicit traffic.
Medical (including psychiatric) treatment of depression.	Relief of depression (elevation of mood), stimulation.	Basically the same as Tranquilizers above.	Same as Tranquilizers above.

TABLE XVI–5 (*continued*)
COMPARISON CHART OF MAJOR SUBSTANCES USED FOR MIND-ALTERATION

OFFICIAL NAME	SLANG NAME(S)	USUAL SINGLE ADULT DOSE	DURATION OF ACTION (hours)	METHOD OF TAKING	LEGITIMATE MEDICAL USES (present and projected)	Psychological Dependence	POTENTIAL FOR Tolerance (leading to increased dosage)	Physical Dependence	Overall Abuse and Toxicity (2)
Miscellaneous									
Glue, gasoline & solvents		Variable	2	Inhalation	None except for antihistamines used for allergy and amyl nitrite for fainting.	Minimal to Moderate	Not known	No	Moderate to High
Amyl nitrite		1-2 amputes							
Antihistaminics		25-50 mg.							
Nutmeg		Variable		Swallowing					
Nonprescription "sedatives" (Compoz)									
Catnip									
Nitrous Oxide									

Source: Fort, 1969. Copyright by Joel Fort, M.D., founder-leader, the National Center for Solving Special Social & Health Problems, FORT HELP, San Francisco; lecturer, University of California, Berkeley; author, *The Pleasure Seekers: the Drug Crisis, Youth & Society* (Grove, 1970) and *Alcohol: Our Biggest Drug Problem* (McGraw-Hill, 1973); former Consultant on Drug Abuse, World Health Organization.

[1] The term "habituation" has sometimes been used to refer to the combination of tolerance and an abstinence otherwise specifically harmful to society.

[2] Drug Abuse (Dependency) properly means: (excessive, often compulsive) use of a drug to an extent that it damages an individual's health or social or vocational adjustment; or is otherwise specifically harmful to society.

individuals may elect not to share the experiences they have had with illegal substances. Research done in the laboratory provides us with some data but obviously is limited to that setting. Finally, insufficient time has elapsed to permit careful study of the long-term effects of drug use. It is not possible here to survey what we do know about illegal drugs even briefly, but a quick look at some information on marijuana, one of the more widely used drugs, permits us a partial view of drugs in relation to youth and the concerns of society.

Use and Effects of Marijuana

Marijuana refers to the dried leaves, stems, and flowering tops of the hemp plant which grows wild in many temperate climates. It is a relatively weak form of cannabis; charas and hashish, made from resin exuded by the tops of the female plants, are the most potent forms.

REASONS DRUG IS SOUGHT (DRUG EFFECTS AND SOCIAL FACTORS)	SHORT TERM EFFECTS (PYSCHO-LOGICAL, PHARMACOLOGICAL, SOCIAL) (3)	LONG TERM EFFECTS (PSYCHO-LOGICAL, PHARMACOLOGICAL, SOCIAL)	FORM OF LEGAL REGULATION AND CONTROL (4)
Curiosity. To get "high" (euphoria). Thrill seeking. Ready availability.	When used for mind-alteration generally produces a "high" (euphoria) with impaired co-ordination and judgment.	Variable—some of the substances can seriously damage the liver or kidney and some produce hallucinations.	Generally easily available. Some require prescriptions. In several states glue banned for those under 21.

[3] Always to be considered in evaluating the effects of these drugs is the amount consumed, purity, frequency, time interval since ingestion, food in the stomach, combinations with other drugs, and most importantly, the personality or character of the individual taking it and the setting or context in which it is taken. The determinations made in this chart are based upon the evidence with human use of these drugs rather than upon isolated artificial experimental situations, animal research, or political (propagandistic) statements.

[4] Only scattered, inadequate health, educational or rehabilitation programs (usually prison hospitals) exist for narcotic addicts and alcoholics (usually out-patient clinics) with nothing for the others except sometimes prison.

[5] Hashish or Charas is a more concentrated form of the active ingredient THC (Tetrahydrocannabinol) and is consumed in smaller doses analogous to vodka beer ratios.
[6] CNS is The Central Nervous System.

Cannabis has been used by man for medical reasons for about five thousand years to reduce pain or as an anticonvulsant, muscle relaxant, and sedative; however, it is not currently used in the United States for such purposes. Recognition of its psychoactive effects go far back into history, which records its use in the Hindu culture as an aid to meditation. With the exception of alcohol, cannabis may be the most widely taken psychoactive drug in the world (Nowlis, 1969).

The effects of marijuana depend upon factors already mentioned as important in all drug taking. At the dosages most often used, short-term effects may include overestimates of time, interference with immediate memory, feelings of euphoria, hilarity, disconnected ideas, and spatial distortion. Regardless of dosage, though, variation in individual reactions is found: some report little effect while others actually note hallucinations. The experience is not always positive either; dizziness, nausea, anxiety, and paranoid reactions may occur (*Marijuana and Health,* 1971).

Who are the marijuana users? (Users refers to the range from those merely experimenting out of curiosity to those using the drug daily.) One researcher (Goode, 1970) points out that we would be mistaken either to stereotype these individuals as unkempt hippies or to think that they are no different than anyone else. Rather, marijuana users can be defined along some dimensions.

First, they are more likely to be young; for example, two studies independenlty conducted in New York City show that most users are in their late teens or early twenties (Goode, 1970). There is reason to believe that increases are occurring among high school and even junior high school students, and we might anticipate an extension into the older-age categories if marijuana use is not a fad of youth.

Men are more likely than women to be involved in all aspects of the drug culture—from tasting, to using, to selling. Irrespective of sex, however, the chances are that users are urban dwellers or people who live near the urban environment, and that they are college youth. In fact, the rise in percentage of users in colleges is striking; in 1966–1967, it was estimated that approximately 6 percent of college students were users, but more recent evidence suggests that the figure is now closer to 25 percent.

Related to this fact, perhaps, is the finding that social class is higher for marijuana smokers than for nonusers, regardless of whether income, education, or occupation is employed as the index of class status. This is probably a recent reversal from a few years ago when the average marijuana user came from the ghetto, and the pattern is quite different from that of heroin use, which is still largely an urban slum problem.

Society's direct concern over marijuana use involves the possibility of development of psychotic reaction and/or dependence, the enactment of crimes as a result of drug influence, and the possibility of progression to other, perhaps more harmful drugs. Evidence suggests that immediate reactions to marijuana in the usual dosage leads to neither psychotic episodes nor to crime. The issue of dependence is less clear, although marijuana is not addictive and does not lead to a need for increased levels. Nevertheless, there are several worldwide reports of its chronic, heavy consumption resulting in decreased conventional motivation and a rise in social indifference (*Marijuana and Health,* 1971). The problem in interpretating these data, however, is the problem of correlation: perhaps individuals who are poorly motivated are especially attracted to the drug.

A similar interpretation problem exists when progression to other drugs is investigated. For example, Blum (1969) found in one student survey that marijuana was associated with the use of other illicit drugs. This fact, though, does not establish a causal link; as he notes, it may point to a *general disposition* to use psychoactive drugs as a means to alter states of consciousness, biological cycles, and social relations. Indeed, analysis of Blum's data showed just that result. Consistent with a hypothesis of drug proneness is the finding that the more marijuana is used, the greater is the likelihood of other drug use (see Table XVI–6). One investigator who observed this fact commented:

> By smoking marijuana, one does not automatically hurl oneself into an LSD miasma. But by smoking marijuana regularly, one makes friends who also smoke. By making friends who smoke, one's attitudes about not only marijuana use, but also the use of the hallucinogens may change as well. The more that one smokes, the more likely it is that one will make friends who approve of LSD use, and who offer opportunities for the use of the LSD-type drugs. We must think of this process in dynamic, as well as in dimensionalist, terms. [Goode, 1970, p. 190.]

Why Do Adolescents Use Drugs?

There is probably no one reason why the adolescent uses drugs, just as there is no one reason for adult consumption of alcohol and tranquilizers. We can attempt, though, to understand the various factors underlying drug use, so that we can effectively deal with a phenomenon that is not going

TABLE XVI–6

PERCENTAGE OF INDIVIDUALS VARYING IN MARIJUANA USE WHO REPORT INVOLVEMENT WITH OTHER DRUGS

MARIJUANA USE	EVER TRIED AT LEAST THREE DRUGS ASIDE FROM MARIJUANA	EVER TOOK LSD AT LEAST ONCE
Daily	92	82
3 to 6 times per week	69	71
1 or 2 times per week	29	49
1 to 4 times monthly	19	25
Less than monthly	9	22

Source: Table 8–2 of *The Marijuana Smokers,* by Erich Goode, © 1970 by Basic Books, Inc., Publishers, N.Y. By Permission.

to suddenly disappear from our culture. In her book, *Drugs on the College Campus* (1969), Helen Nowlis discusses several factors associated with drug consumption that can be applied to many of those who use drugs.

She points out that throughout the ages man has employed drugs to escape misery—and that misery can exist among the apparently successful just as it does among the economically depressed. For the student, misery may involve the anxiety of being enmeshed in an achieving society, the inability to find an identity, and the lack of meaningful experiences in an environment that is increasingly becoming secular and depersonalized. Temporarily, at least, drugs provide the opportunity simply to escape and drop out from facing these problems. But the escape is not, in all cases, just getting away; rather, it is putting one's self into a situation in which one draws into a personal inner world, frequently sharing the experiences with others. In a related way, many marijuana users point to the drug's mind-expanding effects as a positive experience in their lives.

Adolescence as a Crossroad: Vocational Choice

Despite the adolescent's lack of experience, he must make decisions about his future occupation. Because a large number of hours of most days of many years are devoted to work, this selection is of considerable importance. Obviously, choosing one's work is not an irrevocable decision; many individuals change jobs several times throughout their lives. Nevertheless, the path that is first chosen always has some implications for the future.

Ideally, each of us should have the opportunity to be occupied in a vocation that suits our talents, interests, and personality. It is, in fact, not a simple matter, even for adults, to assess themselves adequately, to be aware of the wide range of vocations and how to prepare for them, and then to make a realistic "best" choice. For the adolescent, the task is even more difficult and, unfortunately, the ideal is perhaps seldom achieved.

We may ask, then, what factors, for good or bad, determine vocational choice? It is possible to conceptualize them broadly into several categories.

Society's Needs and Rewards. In a very broad sense, society sets the limits within which any young person can realistically choose his vocation. Today there is considerably less opportunity in the United States in agriculture than in technical areas, compared to a century ago. Similarly, the demand for semiskilled and unskilled workers is decreasing. While these changes are particularly relevant for those adolescents of the lower socioeconomic levels who may lack the training, aspiration, or opportunity for other kinds of work, more recent events also have resulted in poor job prospects for many young Ph.D.s and those preparing for careers in teaching.

Aside from changing demands, other social determinants come into play (Blau, Gustad, Jessor, Parnes, and Wilcock, 1968). An individual must meet the functional requirements of any job; simply, he must be trained for any one particular opening. He also must fulfill nonfunctional requirements, such as age, race, and sex. Finally, the amount of reward given by a society—in terms of financial return, prestige, or freedom—determines which adolescents will enter certain vocations.

Sex. Vocational choice is often considered a more crucial decision for the male than for the female. It is tied closely to his sex-role identity as breadwinner and eventually defines not only his own social status but also that of his family. Girls, on the other hand, presumably can be or are less concerned with this issue because being "only a housewife" requires little formal preparation and frequently hardly any real decision. Females who do enter the job market are not expected by others or by themselves to have the higher prestige jobs or to define themselves as individuals by their work. Until recently their vocational goals often reflected helping roles such as secretary, teacher, nurse, or stewardess (Witty, 1961). In the long run, of course, failures by young females to seriously consider their occupational goals is damaging to those who, by talent and interest, should be engaged in a vocation suitable to them. One would hope that the women's liberation movement will be successful in changing this state of affairs.

Social Class and Parental Attitudes. That vocational aspiration of adolescents is clearly related to their socioeconomic background is demonstrated by the results of one study in which youths from a small midwestern city listed their preferred future occupations (Hollingshead, 1949). Over three-quarters of those categorized in Class I and II, the higher social strata, chose business and professional vocations, whereas only 7 percent of Class V youth did so (see Figure XVI–4).

Although it is possible that adolescents of varying social classes hold different values in regard to occupations, other reasons probably exist for this finding. Children often follow in their parents' vocations simply because they know about them, because they identify with their parents, or because they are rewarded for doing so. Some lower SES youths may be

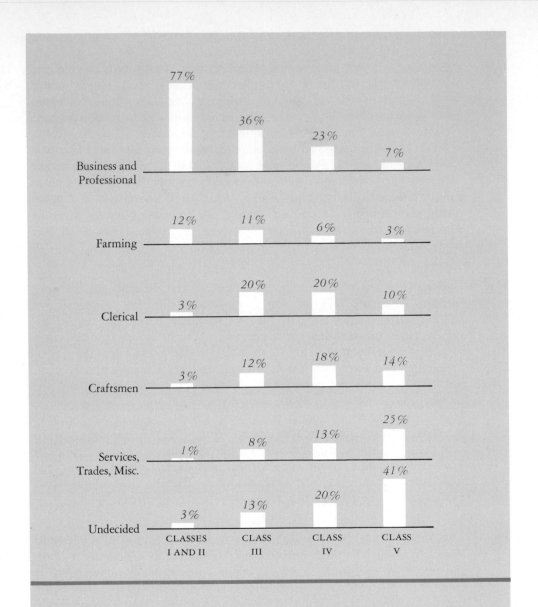

FIGURE XVI-4

Percentage of adolescents of different socioeconomic class selecting various occupational aspirations. Adapted from Karl C. Garrison, Psychology of Adolescence, 5th ed., p. 418, © 1956. Reprinted by permission of Prentice-Hall, Inc., Englewood Cliffs, New Jersey.

discouraged from upward job mobility because it is threatening to the older generation, but, for the most part, parents of *all* classes, including the poor, have high aspirations for their offspring. So the problem may be more that lower SES adolescents simply lack the information about how to enter certain vocations, or they may consider aspiring to them unrealistic. In any event, parental attitude is an important influence on adolescent vocational strivings regardless of social class. One study, for example, has shown that working-class boys whose parents encourage mobility are more likely to move in this direction than are those who do not have such support (Simpson, 1962).

Love and Marriage

Until recently, remarkably little was known about attitudes toward love and marriage or how they changed developmentally or with experience. Some of the first systematic research addressed to this question has been conducted by Knox and Sporakowski (1968). They argue that attitudes about love can be thought of as arranged on a continuum, with one extreme being romantic love and the other extreme being conjugal love. Romantic love, as they define it, is characterized by perceiving love as a mysterious, strange, and incomprehensible force; a romantic attitude toward love typically includes the notion that one falls in love at first sight, that love alone should be the criterion for marriage, that true love is eternal and comes only once, and the like. Included also is an extreme feeling of urgency associated with love and an emphasis upon the feeling of excitement, thrills, and palpitations of the heart that are associated with it. This last characteristic, often associated with the views of adolescents, is referred to by Knox and Sporakowski as "cardiac respiratory" love.

The opposite of romantic love, according to these investigators, is conjugal love. Characterized by a realistic orientation, this is the sort of love that one would expect to exist between two people whose relationship is primarily calm, solid, and comforting. The contrast can be seen best by examining a scale devised by Knox and Sporakowski and shown in Table XVI–7. Each of the twenty-nine items is given an answer between 1 and 5 (see the table); note that the lower the number the more romantic the response is presumed to be.

With this distinction in mind, it becomes possible to obtain some information on attitudes toward love among individuals over a variety of ages, backgrounds, and so on, and to compare these to the experience of marriage. In one study, for example, Knox and Sporakowski (1968) ad-

TABLE XVI-7

ATTITUDES TOWARD LOVE

Please read each statement carefully and circle the number which you believe most adequately represents your opinion.

1. Strongly agree (definitely yes)   4. Mildly disagree (probably not)
2. Mildly agree (I believe so)   5. Strongly disagree (definitely not)
3. Undecided (not sure)

	SA	MA	U	MD	SD
1. When you are really in love, you just aren't interested in anyone else.	1	2	3	4	5
2. Love doesn't make sense. It just is.	1	2	3	4	5
3. When you fall head-over-heels-in-love, it's sure to be the real thing.	1	2	3	4	5
4. Love isn't anything you can really study; it is too highly emotional to be subject to scientific observation.	1	2	3	4	5
5. To be in love with someone without marriage is a tragedy.	1	2	3	4	5
6. When love hits, you know it.	1	2	3	4	5
7. Common interests are really unimportant; as long as each of you is truly in love, you will adjust.	1	2	3	4	5
8. It doesn't matter if you marry after you have known your partner for only a short time as long as you know you are in love.	1	2	3	4	5
9. As long as two people love each other, the religious differences they have really do not matter.	1	2	3	4	5
10. You can love someone even though you do not like any of that person's friends.	1	2	3	4	5

TABLE XVI-7 *(continued)*

	SA	MA	U	MD	SD
11. When you are in love, you are usually in a daze.	1	2	3	4	5
12. Love at first sight is often the deepest and most enduring type of love.	1	2	3	4	5
13. Usually there are only one or two people in the world whom you could really love and could really be happy with.	1	2	3	4	5
14. Regardless of other factors, if you truly love another person, that is enough to marry that person.	1	2	3	4	5
15. It is necessary to be in love with the one you marry to be happy.	1	2	3	4	5
16. When you are separated from the love partner, the rest of the world seems dull and unsatisfying.	1	2	3	4	5
17. Parents should not advise their children whom to date; they have forgotten what it is like to be in love.	1	2	3	4	5
18. Love is regarded as a primary motive for marriage, which is good.	1	2	3	4	5
19. When you love a person, you think of marrying that person.	1	2	3	4	5
20. Somewhere there is an ideal mate for most people. The problem is just finding that one.	1	2	3	4	5
21. Jealousy usually varies directly with love; that is, the more in love you are, the greater the tendency for you to become jealous.	1	2	3	4	5
22. Love is best described as an exciting thing rather than a calm thing.	1	2	3	4	5
23. There are probably only a few people that any one person can fall in love with.	1	2	3	4	5

TABLE XVI–7 *(continued)*

	SA	MA	U	MD	SD
24. When you are in love, your judgment is usually not too clear.	1	2	3	4	5
25. Love often comes but once in a lifetime.	1	2	3	4	5
26. You can't make yourself love someone; it just comes or it doesn't.	1	2	3	4	5
27. Differences in social class and religion are of small importance in selecting a marriage partner as compared with love.	1	2	3	4	5
28. Day dreaming usually comes along with being in love.	1	2	3	4	5
29. When you are in love, you don't have to ask yourself a bunch of questions about love; you will just know that you are in love.	1	2	3	4	5

Source: Knox, D. H., and Sporakowski, M. J., Atttiudes of college students toward love, *Journal of Marriage and the Family,* 1968, 638–642.

ministered their scale to one hundred male and one hundred female college students between the ages of eighteen and twenty-two, all of whom were single. Results indicated some striking relationships. For example, males were somewhat *more* romantic than females in their attitudes toward love at this age. Why should this be the case? Knox and Sporakowski suggest that the views of females are less romantic and more practical because they have somewhat more at stake in the relationship. Another interesting finding is that despite the stereotype of the adolescent as being swamped with the notion of romantic love, in a relative way both males and females were more conjugal than romantic in their views toward love.

Knox and Sporakowski also divided their sample according to the age of the respondents; freshman, sophomores, juniors and seniors all participated in the study. Again, a clear relationship was found: in this case, perhaps unsurprisingly, the older the student, the less romantic and more conjugal was his or her attitude toward love. As the authors note, the increased seriousness of the dating relationship probably is closely related to this phenomenon:

> As the senior year approaches, many students begin to select a date in terms of a future mate rather than for a "romantic evening." Consequently, the criterion shifts from: "Can he (or she) dance?" to: "Does he (or she) have life goals that are consistent with mine?" [1968, p. 641.]

More recently, Knox (1970) administered the attitudinal scale to people older and younger than the college students in the original sample. Specifically, the second study included one hundred high school seniors, one hundred people who were married less than five years, and one hundred who were married more than twenty years. Interestingly, a clear difference was found between the attitudes of the high school seniors and of those who were married less than five years, with the high school seniors showing a "romantic" orientation while a more "realistic" orientation was found among the young married adults. A clear difference also was found when comparisons were made between individuals married less than five years and those married more than twenty years. Contrary to many views, individuals married twenty years were *not* less romantic than those married five years or less; they were more romantic. It appears, then, that the growing years of marriage brought individuals increasingly to the view that a mystical "one true love" view was correct. In fact, the views of high school students and of persons married over twenty years did not differ from one another, but both were significantly more romantic than those of young marrieds of less than five years.

REACHING FULL MATURITY

The later years of life obviously are a continuation of much of what has gone before. But they also frequently, sometimes inevitably, bring dramatic change—decline in physical functioning and appearance, retirement from long-held occupations, and death of peers and families. We shall look briefly at some of these changes, at some factors that may be involved in adjustment to them, and finally, at the reactions of the aged as they approach death.

Biological Aspects

There is a general biological decline in all humans between the ages of thirty and ninety years, but great differences exist in the rate and degree of the decrements peculiar to individual organ systems. The basal metabolism rate, for example, declines less than 20 percent between ages thirty and ninety, but maximum breathing capacity is reduced to less than one-half of its former level. Adding to this variability are large individual differences among those over sixty-five; physicians often encounter eighty-year-olds whose physiological capacities resemble those of men twenty years younger (Shock, 1968).

Psychologists have been particularly interested in the effects of aging on various sensory systems. Here again, markedly different patterns are found among the various capacities studied. Visual acuity, as indicated by the smallest letter that could be read from a particular distance, appears quite constant until age fifty-five, after which a rather sharp decline is observed. In contrast, auditory sensitivity starts to decline much earlier; the decrement is already quite pronounced by the time many individuals reach age sixty. The pattern for the sense of taste more closely resembles that of vision than that of audition; relative constancy into the late fifties, followed by a steep decline in sensitivity to sweet, salty, bitter, and sour substances appears the rule (Corso, 1971).

Health

Not surprisingly, increasing age brings an increasing number of long-term chronic illnesses, with arteriosclerosis being most common. By age sixty-five more than one-half of all Americans have some form of heart disease, and an almost equal number is afflicted with arthritis. The rate of acute or short-term diseases, though, is lower for those over sixty-five years than for members of any other age group. In the course of living, it seems, individuals build up a large number of immunities that lower their susceptibility to many diseases (Estes, 1969). However, when older people do succumb to an illness, their activities are restricted for a greater number of days.

Self-evaluations of Health Among the Elderly. Although there is a general rise in the number of chronic ailments suffered with increasing age, there appears to be no direct relation between age and self-evaluation of health —e.g., as many eighty-year-olds as sixty-five-year-olds rate their health as good or fair. Apparently, age norms are considered in making the evaluation; combinations of infirmities that might lead individuals of age sixty-five to declare their health poor result in very different conclusions in those over eighty (Shanas, 1968). Older people also are relatively optimistic. When Shanas (1968) interviewed 2500 senior citizens concerning their own estimate of their health, 52 percent stated that they were in good health, 30 percent said their health was fair, and only 18 percent indicated that they were in poor health. Fully 75 percent considered their own health better than that of their contemporaries.

Medicare. Prior to the passage of federal medicare legislation, many opponents had predicted that large numbers of elderly citizens possessing only minor complaints, but desiring the time and comfort of physicians, would flood existing medical facilities. However, Palmore and Jeffers (1971) interviewed individuals over sixty-five in 1960 and 1968, before and after the passage of the medicare bill, and found this not to be the case. In the period 1960–1968, no increase in number of visits to physicians was evident. This actually ran counter to the trend that might have been expected under unchanged circumstances, inasmuch as the individuals were eight years older and presumably would be suffering from at least an equal number of ills. Whatever the reason, medicare does not seem to have fulfilled the dire prophecies made by its opponents.

Sexual Attitudes and Behavior

One of the many beliefs regarding sexual behavior is that the later years of life are sexless. Several recent studies have shown this view to be a myth. To be sure, there are anatomical and physiological changes in the reproductive system that can be interpreted as decline. Masters and Johnson (1966), among others, found a lessening of sexual responsiveness with age in their sample of men aged fifty-one to eighty-nine and women between forty and seventy-eight. In males, particularly those over sixty, erection was not attained as quickly and ejaculation was of less duration and force; in females duration of orgasm was decreased, and both the size of the vagina and the amount of lubrication resulting from stimulation was reduced. The latter two changes, which may result in painful intercourse, are the result of a decrease in the hormone estrogen that occurs after menopause.

But the changes described above do not mean that interest and participation in sexual activity are necessarily lost. One investigation, for example, showed that of 149 men and women between the ages of sixty and ninety-three who were living with their spouses, fully 54 percent still engaged in sexual relations (Newman and Nichols, 1960). Studying individuals from the time they were sixty-seven years until the time they were seventy-seven, another team of investigators (Pfeiffer, Verwoerdt, and Wang,

1969) has reported no decline in interest in sex in their subjects. There is high agreement that interest in sex, as well as capacity and performance in the later years, depends crucially on regularity of sexual activity for both sexes (Rubin, 1968) and is correlated with that of the earlier years (Masters and Johnson, 1966).

We might ask, then, about the factors which influence somewhat earlier sexual behavior. Masters and Johnson (1966) attribute decrements in males' responsiveness to:

1. Monotony associated with a long-standing sexual relationship which may involve lack of interest on the part of the female partner, loss of attractiveness of the female, and failure of the relationship to develop further.

2. Male preoccupation with careers.

3. Physical or mental fatigue.

4. Excessive alcohol consumption, particularly in men in their late forties and early fifties.

5. Physical and mental dysfunction of either partner, occurring increasingly with age.

6. Fear of failure.

For women, the menopause, which occurs at about the age of forty-nine, serves to clearly mark off the aging of the reproductive system. It seems, though, that menopause in itself may not be crucial to sexual activities. In one survey of women's attitudes (Neugarten, 1963, 1967), 65 percent voiced the opinion that menopause had no effect on their sexual relations. On the other hand, although perhaps only 10 to 15 percent of all females seek medical care for problems involving climacteric changes (Rubin, 1968), many believe that menopause has a negative effect on appearance and almost none think that it has a positive influence (see Table XVI–8). Moreover, in a society that is youth-oriented and that largely equates sex with youth, it is almost inevitable that women have concerns about lessening physical attractiveness.

Intelligence

Intelligence, as measured by IQ scores, is maintained, and sometimes increases, into early and middle adulthood. We turn now to further evidence concerning IQ changes that correlate with age, this time examining performance of the elderly.

TABLE XVI–8

WOMEN'S SELF-REPORTS ON THE EFFECTS OF MENOPAUSE

HOW MENOPAUSE AFFECTS A WOMEN'S APPEARANCE

negative changes	50%
no effect	43
positive changes	1
no response	6

HOW MENOPAUSE AFFECTS A WOMEN'S SEXUAL RELATIONS

sexual relations more important	18%
no effect	65
sexual relations less important	17

Source: Based on Neugarten, 1967.

Green (1969) conducted a cross-sectional study of change in IQ scores among Puerto Rican citizens between ages twenty-five and sixty-four and noted the same kind of pattern that had led other investigators to conclude that after adolescence there is a steady decrease in intelligence (e.g. Bromley, 1966). However, Green also observed that the older subjects, on the average, had received fewer years of education and hypothesized that reduced educational experience rather than age was responsible for the results. When he adjusted the analysis so that educational level was equated for all age groups, he found that full-scale IQ scores increased until age forty and thereafter remained constant. When verbal and nonverbal sections were examined separately, it was found that verbal intelligence steadily increased from ages twenty-five to sixty-four, while nonverbal intelligence was constant from twenty-five to forty, after which it showed some decline. At least for those under sixty-four, age per se does not appear to be associated with any overall decline in intelligence.

Extending this research, Blum, Jarvik, and Clark (1970) reported trends in IQ change among individuals between ages sixty-five and eighty-five. Using a longtitudinal design, they found that there was a small decline in intelligence test scores between sixty-five and seventy-three and a much steeper decline between seventy-three and eighty-five. They also discovered that the rate of change for different parts of the intellignce test was not constant. On tests of pure information, such as the vocabulary section, no decline was observed through age eighty-five, whereas on tests requiring speed or perceptual-spatial reasoning, the decline was already sharp between ages sixty-five and seventy-three.

A number of investigators have hypothesized that the largest decrements in IQ are exhibited by those close to death. In keeping with this theory, Blum *et al.* found that IQ decrements between ages sixty-five and seventy-three were smaller for those who lived to the age of eighty-five than for those who died before then. Adding support, Reimanis and Green (1971) tested residents of a Veteran's Administration hospital at mean age fifty-eight and again ten years later, and found that IQ scores of those who died within one year of the second testing declined significantly further between the two tests than the scores of those who lived longer.

Citing these findings and others of a similar nature, Riegel and Riegel (1972) postulated a "predeath drop." According to their formulation, the intelligence of most individuals, at least until age seventy, remains constant. They presented evidence that before this age almost all of the observed decline in average intelligence was accounted for by sharp drops among those destined not to survive the next five years. In the over seventy category, even long-term survivors exhibited some declines, but the decrements among nonsurvivors were much greater. Riegel and Riegel therefore proposed that declines in the average intelligence of aging individuals resulted from increasing numbers of individuals experiencing "terminal drops" in performance rather than from all of the aged experiencing steady declines.

The Effects of Changes in Circumstances

Not all of the changes in the lives of those over sixty-five are products of biological and intellectual aging. The organization of society produces other important alterations, notably in the areas of economics, living circumstances, and social roles. These changes, in turn, have broad implications both for the ways that older citizens live and for their morale.

Changes in Economic Circumstances. Kreps (1969) indicated that in 1967 approximately one-half of older families had incomes below $4,000. In relative terms, the incomes of single individuals were even lower; one-half had incomes below $1,500. The gap between older and younger families increased during the 1960s. By 1967, three of ten older families had incomes below the poverty line, compared to one of nine younger families (McCamman, Kreps, Schulz, Brewster, and Sheppard, 1969).

Several factors can be identified that militate against the economic well-being of elderly Americans. Primary among them is decreased participation in the labor force. In 1950 an estimated 60 percent of those over sixty-five were working, but the current figure is closer to 30 percent. Retirement is often involuntary; an increasing number of corporations have adopted mandatory retirement policy, usually at age sixty-five. Interestingly, this policy has not been implemented at the very highest levels, as demonstrated by the large percentage of elderly Supreme Court Justices and senators. The capable performance of individuals in their seventies and eighties in these positions suggests that mandatory retirement policies stem more from a national difficulty in supplying sufficient numbers of jobs to accommodate all who wish to work than from any incapability of those over sixty-five to perform in their previous occupation.

Back (1969) refers to retirement as both a privilege and an obligation. In 1948, only 13 percent of those over sixty-five received social security benefits; the 1975 figure is estimated to be 90 percent. Such support makes retirement, at least at a modest economic level, a possibility for millions who would otherwise need to continue working regardless of their preferences. At the same time, those who would rather continue working are placed in a difficult position by the very benefits that were designed to help them. As Back notes:

> From being the provision of aid at a time when the worker was unable to work, the benefits have become a basis for the definition of this disability; i.e., whenever a worker can have full benefits, he should then retire. The shift in emphasis has become widespread, and has resulted in the age of 65 becoming an almost inviolable borderline between work and retirement. Even legislation against job discrimination because of age does not apply to individuals over this age. [1969, p. 103.]

Morale in Retirement. Another issue raised by mandatory retirement is more subtle but no less real. It concerns the decrement in status that occurs when an individual who has been employed in a respected occupation for a number of years no longer occupies that role. As might be expected, in the first year after retirement a greater percentage of blue- than white-collar retirees express a high degree of satisfaction with their circumstances (Stokes and Maddox, 1967). The blue-collar worker may have fallen less far in status and the leisure of retirement may seem a welcome substitute for the drudgery of their previous occupations. Over time, however, the pattern reverses; white-collar workers retired more than three years appear more contented than their blue-collar counterparts. Stokes and Maddox hypothesized that this is because of the white collar workers' greater number of outside interests and nonwork activities suited to old age.

Having obtained a general measure of morale, Kutner, Fanshel, Togo, and Langner (1970) found that men experienced a far greater decrement in morale between the ages of sixty-five and sixty-nine than women. Again, this can be explained in terms of role change; most men are employed before they are sixty-five and not afterward, whereas many women continue in the same homemaker role that they occupied when they were younger.

Kutner and his associates also found that—independent of income—elderly citizens who worked indicated higher morale than those who did not. This held true for those earning less than $25 per week, for those earning between $25 and $50, and for those whose incomes exceeded $50 per week. Even though poor health and other indisposing factors may have contributed to the lower morale of those who were not employed, the evidence is nevertheless suggestive that, for those over sixty-five, continuing in some employed capacity may entail rewards above and beyond financial gains.

Although employment may be related to high morale independent of income, the direct contribution of economic well-being should not be ignored. In the Kutner sample, virtually one-half of those rated well-to-do, compared to less than one-fourth of those rated low in socioeconomic status, reported a high degree of contentment. There is also a differential impact of health according to economic well-being. For those of low socioeconomic status, health was significantly related to morale; for those who were wealthier this relationship was not present.

Living Circumstances of the Elderly

Rosow (1967) examined the relation between living circumstances and friendship patterns among twelve hundred aged residents of Cleveland. He was especially interested in the effects on those over sixty-five of having few or many age peers living in close proximity. The study's most basic finding was that the greater the concentration of old people, the more friends each resident made. This result was in direct opposition to theories of social integration that stress the importance of older individuals living among younger ones. The density of senior citizens residing in the immediate area was particularly important to working-class individuals; whereas those of higher socioeconomic status were likely to have friends outside of the neighborhood, former blue-collar workers depended almost exclusively on those who lived nearby for extrafamilial companionship. The same tendency applied also to those older than seventy-five; they too drew very heavily on their age peers in the immediate neighborhood for friendship.

The individuals sampled exhibited a wide range of attitudes concerning their social lives. Rosow identified four basic themes that seemed common to fairly large groups within the population. He labeled "cosmopolitan" the approximately 30 percent who had little contact with their neighbors and appeared content with the arrangement. The 20 percent who visited infrequently and desired more interpersonal stimulation were termed "isolated." The label "sociable" was applied to the 23 percent who indicated a high degree of social contact and who were satisfied with their social lives, while the description "insatiable" was reserved for the 10 percent having a high level of contact and desiring more.

In this context, the growth of neighborhoods having high concentrations of older individuals seem a reasonable attempt by those over sixty-five to seek out others among whom friendship possibilities are great. This interpretation is also supported by Rosow's observation that concentration of age peers is particularly important not only to working-class members and those over seventy-five but also to the maritally unattached and to women in general. Finally, friends tend to be similar in social class and marital status, and more often than not are of the same sex.

The End of Life

A central fact of human aging is that with each year after age thirty it becomes increasingly likely that death will occur (see Figure XVI–5). Not only does death become more probable between ages thirty and ninety, but the rate of increase of its probability also accelerates. The basic trend is present for whites and blacks and for males and females. Nevertheless, there are differences in the life expectancies of these different groups. A white male born in 1964 would be expected to live sixty-eight years, while his female counterpart would have a life expectancy of seventy-five (Goldman, 1968).

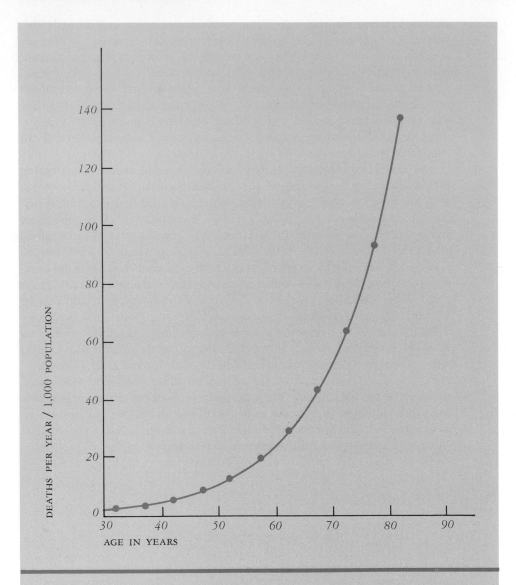

FIGURE XVI—5

Probability of death as a function of age. Adapted from Shock, 1968. By permission of the American Psychiatric Association.

Goldman distinguishes two causes of death: extrinsic and intrinsic. Extrinsic causes are the most commonly cited immediate ones; the category includes a number of specific maladies such as cancer, accidents, injuries, and malnutrition. There is, however, an additional category of general factors that also make death more likely. Many cells do not reproduce, and even those that do often reproduce at decreasing rates as aging occurs. The strength of bones and the elasticity of blood vessels also decrease. There is also an overall decline in resiliency; injuries take longer to heal, illness are more difficult to shake off, and physical problems that once would have caused little distress assume major proportions. This parallels the decrements in reserve capacities of many bodily systems. Evidence for the importance of these intrinsic factors has led some experts to conclude that further substantial progress in increasing life spans may depend on finding ways to slow down the overall developmental cycles (Goldman, 1968).

As a specific category, heart disease is the most frequently cited cause of death. Other common factors include cancer, strokes, vascular ailments other than heart disease, and accidents. Together, these factors account for approximately 80 percent of all deaths. It must be realized, however, that the more general trends listed under intrinsic causes are not cited in the present classification system.

Psychological Aspects. Erikson (1972), in his eight stages of man formulation, contrasts ego integrity and despair as two basic stances toward aging. He postulates that these stages are universal; this is reflected in his memorable statement: "A wise Indian, a true gentleman, and a mature peasant share and recognize in one another the final stage of integrity." Those who ascend to this stage are said to possess an overall sense of world order, an acceptance of their lives as necessary and inevitable, "a comradeship with the ordering ways of distant times and different pursuits," and a general serenity in the face of death. In contrast, despair entails disgust over many small details, disappointment that there is too little time to attempt an alternative path to dignity, and a fear of dying (Erikson, 1972, p. 28).

In Erikson's view, an individual's attitude toward old age is not independent of his earlier life, but rather a logical and necessary continuation of it. This view is supported by the findings of Templer, Ruff, and Franks (1971), who correlated a number of variables with a measure of death anxiety. They found that mothers and fathers within families tended to hold similar views, and that there was a significant correlation between the degree of fear expressed by adolescents and the degree indicated by their same-sex parent. In contrast, no significant correlation was found between age and death anxiety. The finding indicates that fear of death is as great in young as in old people and suggests that parents in some way communicate their views to their children and thereby influence them. Individual attitudes toward death, too, may vary considerably depending upon a host of past and present factors.

Frances C. Jeffers and Adriaan Verwoerdt describe, in Selection 11, how the aged face death—what it means to them, how they react emotionally to its prospect, and what coping mechanisms they employ.

SELECTION 11

HOW THE OLD FACE DEATH

Frances C. Jeffers and Adriaan Verwoerdt

Professional persons working with older individuals are concerned that adjustment to the later years of life be as healthy and satisfying as possible, whatever the future may hold for such individuals or however long that future may be. Whatever the circumstances, at this phase of the life-span there can be no avoidance of the fact of death. To its approach the older person must either make some type of adjustment or he must build up defenses which shield him to some extent from facing the necessity that he, too, must die. According to Feifel (1965), "the adaptation of the older person to dying and to death may well be a crucial aspect of the aging process." To the extent that one

agrees with this statement, the aging person's awareness of death, its personal meaning to him, and the effects of these on behavior, all become important factors in understanding and managing the problems of late life.

The realization of the inevitability of death, and thus of the extinction of the individual personality, is seen by many therapists as the ultimate threat to a human being. Koestenbaum (1964), speaking from an existential point of view, interprets death anxiety as a dread of seeing the world itself disappear. Our modern culture has attempted to alleviate such anxiety by taboos on the topic of death, by increasing the impersonality of memorial services, and by disguising cemeteries as ordinary parks (Mitford, 1963; Riley, 1968). But from those persons on "the shady side of the hill" of life, death can scarcely be hidden. A realistic acceptance of death as the "appropriate" end of life may well be the hallmark of emotional maturity (Weisman and

Reprinted from Jeffers, F. C. and Verwoedt, A. How the old face death. In E. W. Busse, and E. Pfeiffer, eds. *Behavior and Adaptation in Late Life.* Boston: Little, Brown, and Company, 1969, p. 163–181. Copyright 1969, reproduced by permission of Little, Brown, and Company.

Hackett, 1961). If awareness and acceptance of death are characteristics of the emotional maturity of elderly persons, one may also ask to what extent they occur in younger persons and what the effects may be of such factors as age, physical illness, and personality adjustment. At the present time, some research evidence is beginning to accumulate, but much work remains to be done. Kastenbaum (1966a), in chairing a Gerontological Society symposium in 1965, outlined some of the difficulties and challenges of "death research."

Several problems of research methodology exist in the area of personal attitudes toward death and dying, awareness of death, and means of coping with death anxiety. First, in reading the literature it becomes clear that there are difficulties with regard to the conceptualization of death and in arriving at operational definitions suitable for research purposes. Second, authors tend to utilize diverse subject groups, methods, questionnaires, and/or interview schedules, so that it is difficult to compare findings from different studies. Third, some of the research methods utilized to date (direct questioning, death attitude scales, sentence completions, projective techniques, and so on) may be inadequate to measure accurately and fully the degrees of death awareness and the meanings death has for different individuals. In addition, such data are generally obtained at only one point in time. Data obtained from serial interviews over a prolonged period of time might shed additional light on the "deeper" significance of death to the personality. Thus far, reports on this type of ma-

terial are not available except tangentially (e.g., Lindemann's [1944] reports on the effects of grief and bereavement).

Awareness of Death

Awareness of external events, inner physiological processes, or subjective experiences is not an "all-or-none" phenomenon, but rather it can be manifested in varying degrees of consciousness. It follows that awareness of death may be revealed indirectly through the existence of ideas that are related to death. Thus it may be that frequently awareness of one's own death occurs on a preconscious level.

A special instance of preconscious awareness of impending death was described by Verwoerdt and Elmore, who studied 30 hospitalized patients (age range 24 to 74) with fatal illness (Verwoerdt and Elmore, 1967). The data suggested a relationship between actual temporal distance to death, hopelessness, and decreased expectation of futurity. None of the patients could know, or alleged to know, exactly how long they still had to live. Nor was this interval before death known to the investigators at the time of the study; it was obtained instead from a follow-up study one year later. Patients who were closer to death expressed more hopelessness and evidenced a greater reduction of expectation of futurity. This same finding was reported by Lieberman (1965) in his study of 22 older persons a year or less distant from death. In illness, especially in fatal illness, the patient may well be aware of the rate of decline in his physical status. By "monitoring" these internal physiological changes, he may be able to "estimate" the rate of his decline from the present to a terminal point (Glaser and Strauss, 1965). It is possible that to some extent similar mechanisms may also be activated by the much slower biological changes which occur as a result of the aging process.

Studies of comparison on death awareness between younger and older persons in the general population are few and far between. Investigators appear to be primarily concerned with one group or with the other, in descriptive rather than in comparative studies. J. Riley reported, in a study of 1,500 adults, that most persons 61 years and older said they think at least occasionally, and 45 percent said they think often, about the uncertainty of their own life or of the death of someone close to them. Such thoughts were somewhat more widespread among people over age 60 than among the younger persons in his sample (Riley, 1968).

In a Duke study (1966) of frequency of death thoughts among 140 elderly noninstitutionalized persons (60 to 94 years old), it was found that 49 percent of them reported being reminded of death at least once a day, if only by reading the obituaries; 20 percent admitted to death thoughts about once a week, 25 percent less than once a week, while 5 percent denied they ever thought about it; and 1 percent were undecided (Jeffers and Verwoerdt, 1966). It was reported by 7 percent of the subjects that they had thoughts related to death constantly on their minds. Several factors differentiated these subjects from the "deniers." The latter tended to believe that such awareness would affect enjoyment of life;

they were more active, less "disengaged," and had higher "morale"; their subjective health assessment was higher, although there was no difference with regard to objective health ratings; they had higher IQ scores, and their occupations were primarily in the nonmanual categories. Finally, these subjects were younger than those who always had death thoughts on their mind.

Hence, those who shut out thoughts of death presumably felt more distant from it by reason of being chronologically younger and by considering themselves to be in better health. But it is interesting to note that when the two groups were given a sentence completion test in which they were asked to speak directly about personal meanings of death, they differed very little in type of emotional reaction: The incidence of positive (nonthreatened, accepting) reactions in each group was about 50 percent, with neutral or negative reactions making up the other 50 percent.

Richardson and Freeman (1968) found that thoughts of death were more common among those in poor than in good health. This is in keeping with the above-mentioned finding at Duke of an inverse relationship between favorable self-health evaluations and frequency of death thoughts, and with the findings reported by Shrut (1958) and by Rhudick and Dibner (1961). The latter two investigators, using death references from TAT stories, found additionally that neurotic patients showed much more death concern than did psychotic patients. This phenomenon is also mentioned by May (1950), who states that whenever *concern* about death arises, it is to be assumed that a neurotic element may be present.

Summarizing these findings, current research evidence suggests that *frequency of death thoughts* may be higher in older age groups and also in conditions of physical illness. *Concerns about death* tend to occur in individuals with neurotic conflicts rather than in either normal or psychotic individuals.

Personal Meanings of Death

Closely linked with awareness of death is the meaning of death to the individual. Doubtless the significance of death for the person has a great number of determinants, both personal and sociocultural. "The meaning of death" is not to be equated with the actual experience of the event of dying, but is taken to signify the subjective anticipations, interpretations, inferences, or projections of personal feelings onto the fact of death. It is likely that there are as many meanings of death as there are human beings capable of reflection. In spite of such an infinite variety of meanings—with their subtle differences and nuances—a certain degree of classification would seem desirable even on an arbitrary basis. Several possible categories emerge from a scrutiny of the data obtained from sentence completion tests in the Duke study referred to above (Jeffers and Verwoerdt, 1966). The elderly subjects were asked to complete the following phrases:

1. When a man dies, _____
2. Death is _____
3. I feel that when I die, I _____

It appeared that for the most part the responses could be categorized under one or another of the following headings:

1. *Continuation or cessation of life.* The greater part of the subjects expressed firm religious convictions (it must be remebered that North Carolina lies within the "Bible belt"), as for example: "When a man dies, he lives again," "Death is passing from this life into another world," or, "I feel that when I die, I think my spirit or soul will carry on." The end of life on this earth is seen by these persons as a stepping-stone to another life. Another thought expressed was that, "When a man dies, he will keep living on in the minds and hearts of those still here." There were some persons, on the other hand, who thought of death primarily as extinction of the personality and loss of identity. One "ceases to exist," "he's dead all over," "he's soon forgotten." Or, "It's very final." Thus, death was seen as "inevitable" or—more positively—as rest and release: "I will be out of all my troubles," "I'll leave behind me the troubles and worries of life."

2. *Death as the enemy.* Only infrequently was death viewed as an enemy disrupting life patterns and relationships, e.g., "Death is a cruel master." However, more subjects expressed fear of the dependency, disability, or pain which they associated with the act of dying.

3. *Reunion or isolation.* Many persons expressed reunion beliefs, as, for example, "I am going to meet the ones who have gone ahead of me." For some, death involved departure from a known existence and separation from loved ones here with sadness but without the element of decreased self-esteem: "I wouldn't be afraid to die but I dread to leave my children and loved ones."

4. *Reward or punishment.* Most of the subjects viewed death as a transition to a better state of being, a reward for a life well lived: "I will go to heaven, and into the joys of the Lord." This was in keeping with the firm religious beliefs of the study panel members as a whole. Only seldom were there direct expressions that death meant punishment: "He's at rest if he lived right and he's gone if he didn't."

5. *The anticipated or the unknown.* Several subjects expressed uncertainty or curiosity, as follows: "I can't say," or, "I don't know what death is—tell me—what is it?" Or, "I wonder what it is going to be like—who knows?— sort of like going to Egypt." The anticipation of death as an event made familiar through religious rituals was observed in such responses as, "Death is going to my long home," and, "My spirit will go back to God."

In a similar manner Feifel (1965) categorized the two dominant outlooks of 40 disabled World War I veterans. One group visualized death as the dissolution of bodily life and the doorway to a new life; the other group, with a "philosophic resignation," looked on death as "the end."

Emotional Reactions to Death Awareness

Typically, the older subjects studied at Duke seemed to experience feelings which were appropriate to the particular ideas about death which they had expressed; for example, it was commonly observed that beliefs in reunion after death were associated with feelings of happy expectation (Jeffers and Verwoerdt, 1966). Those few subjects who felt threatened by the sentence completion test tended to view death as being cruel or as punishment: "Those questions are very tough, I tell you, they shook me up." There was also some evidence of ambivalent feelings. Several persons stated, for example, "Heaven may be my home, but I'm not homesick yet."

Notably absent were any expressions of angry protest or rage in response to the disruptive or cruel aspects of death. The death-defying mood portrayed by poet Dylan Thomas ("Rage, rage, against the dying of the light') is perhaps more characteristic of the attitude of younger persons.

A number of investigators are in agreement that only a relatively small proportion of older persons—only 10 percent or less in several studies—express fear of death (Feifel, 1955; Jeffers, Nichols, and Eisdorfer, 1961; Swenson, 1961). In the National Institute of Mental Health sample of healthy older persons, overt fear of death was present in 30 percent of the subjects (Birren, Butler, Greenhouse, Sokoloff, and Yarrow, 1963). In a sentence completion test conducted by Kogan and Shelton (1962), 200 individuals, aged 49 to 92, thought that death was more frightening to "people in general" than to old people. They also felt that old people were comparatively less likely to regard death as one of their greatest fears but rather thought of it as an escape or as inevitable. Kogan and Wallach (1961) found, in comparing older persons with college students, that the responses to the concept of death, utilizing the semantic differential, were less negative among the older subjects than they were among the younger subjects.

In another study at Duke University, only 10 percent of the elderly community subjects answered the question

"Are you afraid to die?" in the affirmative (Jeffers, Nichols, and Eisdorfer, 1961). Thirty-five percent of the subjects denied being afraid, while 55 percent were hesitant or ambivalent in their answers. The responses admitting fear of death tended to be devoid of religious references; the finding that these particular subjects showed less belief in life after death confirms that in Swenson's (1961) study. In addition, it was found at Duke that those persons who admitted fear of death gave fewer responses on the Rorschach test, had fewer leisure activities, and lower IQ scores. J. Riley (1968) reported a similar relationship between negative views of death and lower educational level in his sample of 1,500 adults. Finally, the Duke subjects who expressed fear of death had a higher incidence of feelings of rejection and depression. Rhudick and Dibner (1961) suggest that death concern may not necessarily manifest itself as overt anxiety but may be accompanied by somatizing and withdrawal tendencies.

Butler (1968) points out that even though many older persons may not show any obvious fear of death, one cannot conclude that the problem of death does not exist for them. Rather, one may need to study the person at a particular stage of his adaptation to the reality of death. As one of the elderly volunteers at Duke put it, "No, I'm not afraid to die—it seems to me to be a perfectly normal process. But you never know how you will feel when it comes to a showdown. I might get panicky."

In summary, it appears from the expressions of older persons that death is feared much less than prolonged illness, dependency, or pain, which may bring the several threats of rejection and isolation, as well as loss of social role, self-determination, and dignity as an individual. To some of the elderly ill who are cared for in their own homes, life may still seem worth living, but even here regret is often expressed for "the bother I am to those I love." Glaser and Strauss (1968) point out that terminal geriatric patients often decide to stay in the hospital in order not to be a burden to their families. Experience in nursing homes suggests that, except for an occasional geriatric patient who clings tenaciously to life, death is seen by most of them as preferable to continued illness or chronic disability. These patients may have already become "socially dead"—according to Kalish's concept—in their own eyes as well as to others, and thus they view their impending death as timely and welcome (Glaser and Strauss, 1968; Kalish, 1966). Kastenbaum (1966b) quotes staff reports in a geriatric hospital to the effect that, among older persons who were dying, most of their references to death were positively valued, such as calm waiting for death or a desire for the end of all suffering.

There has been such a wide disparity between findings on the one hand of lack of fear of death in older persons and, on the other hand, the assumption of some clinicians of the universality of this fear that Kastenbaum, in taking note of the difference in opinion, has challenged the use of this concept altogether in the study of aging (Kastenbaum, 1966a; Kastenbaum and Aisenberg, 1972).

Coping with the Prospect of Death

It has become a truism that individual variations in adaptive behavior may exist to a greater degree among the elderly than in other age groups because their relative longevity may provide a greater quantity and variety of life experiences. Thus their coping behavior vis-à-vis death may be varied as well. Muriel Spark (1964) has written an absorbing piece of fiction, *Memento Mori*, in which she deals in some detail with the varied behaviors of several older persons in response to anonymous phone calls of four words only, "Remember you must die."

Certain coping techniques or defense mechanisms may be adaptive for one person but maladaptive for another. Whether or not a particular defense is adaptive or not depends further on quantitative factors. Some of the determinants for the type of mechanism utilized may be: (1) the temporal factor: chronological age and distance from death; both of these were found to be of importance in the Duke geriatric studies (Jeffers and Verwoerdt, 1966); (2) physical and mental health; (3) the influence of varying frames of reference such as religious orientation and socioeconomic and occupational status; (4) community attitudes; (5) family and personal experiences with death; (6) attitudes of persons currently in the immediate environment; and (7) the individual's own psychological integrity and maturity. A major determinant of the adjustment is probably how the individual has adjusted to changes and crises in his past life. Payne (1967) cites—as an additional determinant to a person's acceptance of his death—the nature of his emotional commitments during his lifetime to people and to productive endeavors. Wahl (1958) hypothesizes that the well-loved child is more likely to re-

tain an unconscious proclivity toward infantile omnipotence which he is able to put into use in handling the death anxiety, as he has had confidence to face new situations in the past.

In most instances of successful adaptation, an interlocking of several coexisting adaptive approaches may be utilized. By functioning simultaneously, one adaptational technique fosters, or even potentiates, another one.

To many persons is given the ability to cross into old age and to face death with a conscious, though perhaps unverbalized, feeling of satisfaction with past achievements and a sense of contentment with life as they have lived it. A decreased energy level may reconcile them to rest from struggle and facilitate a philosophical attitude toward closure. Wahl (1958) quotes Spinoza as having said that the adult who sees death as completion of a pattern and who has spent his time, unfettered by fear, in living richly and productively, can accept the thought that his self will one day cease to be.

Mastery and adaptation to the prospect of death may—in addition to the predominantly intrapsyschic processes of synthesis and integrity—be achieved in other ways, as through the anchorage point of mature religious beliefs or the securities and satisfactions derived from social relationships.

Feifel's (1965) reports and others have confirmed that for many older persons a belief in life after death or a trust in religious support serves as a bolster against the threat of death. The study of the geriatrics panel in North Carolina revealed that there was almost universal belief in a life after death, with only 2 percent of the number of 254 denying such a belief outright

(Jeffers, Nichols, and Eisdorfer, 1961). Twenty-one percent compromised by saying they were "not sure" of such after-life, but 77 percent wished to be counted among those who were sure, with almost as many variations as individuals in imagining what it might be like. On the other hand, for a few in the Duke panel and also for some persons in Feifel's studies strong belief in religion and in an after-life can be threatening if the person fears retribution at death for his sins. As Choron (1963) notes, belief in "immortality" may generate its own kind of death-fear.

One of the most satisfying adaptations to the ending of life is a close but nonambivalent relationship with children and grandchildren. This satisfies not only the mutual affectional needs but bestows on the older person the reminder of continuity of life and tangible evidence of his own ongoing contribution to mankind. The grandparents can participate, often without overstrained responsibility, in the pleasures of learning, wonder, and companionship of a new generation.

Planning by a person around whatever inheritance he may have to leave to his family and friends is often a tangible mark of his acceptance of the ultimate closure of his life, however near or distant that closure may be. Judging sheerly by the more probable proximity to the end, it would seem logical that, the older a person is, the more time he would have had for preparation and getting his affairs in proper shape for his death. For some persons, however, intervening variables—denial, hostility, fear, or disturbed reactions of family members—may operate to arouse resistance to such plan-

ning. Occasionally one can observe the superstitious fear that being prepared for death might actually hasten its coming. In a study at Duke (1965) on the extent of concern and planning for chronic illness, for example, the elderly persons studied expressed relatively little concern and little actual planning for such an eventuality. Many gave the impression that they did not wish to consider such a possibility (Heyman and Jeffers, 1965).

In a current study at Duke, based on the Rosow Death-Awareness Scale, the older panel members appeared to be more practical with regard to such financial matters as keeping up their life insurance for funeral costs, making wills, and signing their homes over to their children. One 90-year-old woman had purchased her cemetery lot and her tombstone, and had even paid in advance for engraving the date of death after her name. More involvement in planning might well be expected by those who also indicated more awareness of death; Rosow found this correlation among the 100 community respondents in his study (Rosow and Chellam, 1966). However, resistance to giving away a few of the most valued keepsakes before death is a hopeful sign, indicating a wish to live as fully as possible until the last; often such treasures are assigned to the appropriate recipients, who will get them "later." These preparations signify a realistic acceptance of personal death and the desire to "set one's house in order" well in advance. But such planning for separation from life is too often upsetting to the older person's family and friends and is viewed as morbid preoccupation with death.

The taboo in Western culture on

open discussion of death presents peculiar difficulties both for those who work or live with older persons and for the older persons themselves (Fulton, 1965). Yet the one who is threatened by the prospect of his death has great need to communicate with someone about the problem. Often his own family members are unable to speak with him about this; the prospect of his death and his awareness of it disturbs them too greatly because of their own emotional involvement with him. The finding of J. Riley (1968) indicates that older persons may be more comfortable discussing the problems associated with death with clergymen or with doctors. But even some of those associated with the medical profession—doctors, nurses, social workers—admit to uneasiness when faced with the care of dying patients or with older persons who seek to discuss their death. As Verwoerdt (1966) has pointed out, the physician "sides with health against illness and with life against death." Thus he and others concerned must come to terms with their own anxieties in order to communicate with empathy and to provide supportive therapy for the older person who is threatened by the prospect of dying (Group for the Advancement of Psychiatry, 1967; Quint, 1967; Saunders, 1960).

In general, in those instances when the outcome of facing the threat of death has been unsuccessful or maladaptive for the aged person, it may be expected that he has automatically repeated old defenses, that his repertoire of coping techniques is only a limited one, that a few defenses are used rigidly and excessively, and/or that innovative techniques tend to be absent. The essence of maladaptive behavior is

that it aggravates the very problem against which it is directed or creates new problems which require additional problem-solving techniques. Keeping in mind the importance of qualitative and quantitative factors, as well as the existence of the individual uniqueness of personality and interindividual variability, it may be well to review various types of coping with the prospect of personal death which have been observed by the present authors as well as by others.

Denial, which is aimed at avoiding clear awareness of a painful threat, has been considered by many psychiatrists to be a major mechanism for palliating fear of death. Attitudes of denial may manifest themselves in a great variety of ways. For example, an older person may acknowledge that "Death is inevitable," but in the privacy of his mind may add, "For me, however, it's only probable," or, "Only in the distant future," or even, "Inevitable—except for me." However, persistent denial is difficult to maintain, for the aged are surrounded by death's signposts: the sickness and death of contemporaries, as well as their own decreasing capacities. "Blinders" need to be powerful indeed to block out such ever-present and increasing stimuli. Other defenses which also serve the purpose of exclusion from awareness include suppression, rationalization, and externalization. Frequently these mechanisms occur in clusters rather than singly.

In another group of defenses, the goal of the coping behavior is not so much to exclude the threat from conscious awareness, but rather retreat from the source of anxiety. These defenses include such mechanisms as regression, withdrawal, "disengagement," or even surrender, as in certain cases of suicide. It is well known that direct death-seeking behavior occurs in old age. In fact, the rate of actual suicide increases sharply with advancing age, especially among men, and unsuccessful suicide attempts are of greater significance in old age than in younger years. . . . Furthermore, attention should be given to what might be called occult or slow suicide in old age, due to depression, loss of appetite, or lowered vitality. No statistics are available on this point, but the impression of physicians and attendants in hospitals and homes for the aged is that death occurs much more rapidly when there is no will to live.

In cases of withdrawal and disengagement there is a move away from people. This defensive pattern may be aimed at protecting the individual against the painful loss, through death, of significant others. In the void of social isolation, the stage is set for hypochondriacal preoccupation with the bodily self. At the same time, hypochondriasis may imply a call for closeness, inasmuch as the physical complaints represent a wish for attention or support.

Among the less socially acceptable mechanisms employed against death fears is that of withdrawal and/or escape by way of alcohol and drugs. Because of social disapproval and the need to hide such behavior, it cannot be ascertained to what extent this mechanism is utilized by older persons, but clinical experinece and occasional newspaper stories suggest that it is not uncommon.

A third category of coping behavior is characterized by its emphasis on attempts at mastery and resolution. Included here are defenses such as intellectualization, counterphobic mechanisms, hyperactivity, sublimation, and acceptance.

Butler (1968) cites counterphobic behavior as a defensive maneuver when old persons adopt greatly inappropriate dress and behavior in their effort to appear young: "One sees older people who cannot bear to look at themselves in a mirror and whose drawings show signs of dissolution despite intact cognitive and psychologic functions."

Hyperactivity may be observed in certain vigorous older persons and may be vented on hobbies, restless travels, or civic enterprises; it is often accompanied by loquaciousness. This could be interpreted as an almost frenetic hold onto some phase of life which promises an opportunity for continued usefulness and a sense of past achievement, or it may be an anodyne to despair. On the other hand, losing oneself in activity adaptively can be observed in artists, musicians, or professional persons who continue to be absorbed in creative activity, thus keeping death at arm's length, often physically as well as psychologically.

Another important mechanism utilized—for better or worse—by the aged as they face the end of their existence is that of the life review. Butler (1964) postulates this as "a universal normal experience, intensifying in the aged, and occurring irrespective of environmental conditions." He views such life review as a primary factor in reminiscence and discusses its contribution to certain disturbances in later life, as well as its probable role in the evolution of more positive characteristics of old people, such as candor, serenity, and wisdom. When an individual cannot dodge the fact that time on this earth is running out for him, the nearness of death brings with it almost inevitably, if not a total life review, at least a recall of some of the major events and relationships in his past life. Perhaps this is related to the old belief that a drowning man's life flashes before his eyes before he goes down for the last time.

Thus it is not abnormal that the later years become for many persons a time for introspection and looking back, for creativity in the writing of an autobiography (or for compilation of material toward an autobiography which may actually never be written), for endless recitals of reminiscences often enjoyed only by the central figure himself, or—more unhappily still—for lapses into melancholia and depression triggered by unhappy memories of losses or of regret over misspent years or wrongs done for which it is now too late to atone (McMahon and Rhudick, 1967). Depression, for example, tends to predispose the older person toward a sensitization for previous unhappy experience, so that eventually a bleak perspective emerges. Finally, there are those tragic instances when the review and stocktaking lead to the discovery that one "missed the boat" and that it is now too late to repair previous mistakes. Particularly painful may be the awareness that large or significant areas of human experience had been avoided, that life had not been fully lived.

For those who cannot face the mirror of themselves, and the burden of their memories, the life review may be difficult if not shattering. The reminiscences of such persons appear repetitious, shot through with conscious or unconscious misrepresentations, without apparent purpose except to escape the present by filling time. Or they appear to be mere monologues with disturbing themes of old guilt or bitterness, obviating communication with others. Or should they be listened to carefully in an attempt to understand them as the older individual's efforts to establish a final identity in his own eyes as well as in that of the listener?

At the time of crisis when an individual comes to full realization of the foreshortening of his life-span and the approach of death, the self seeks to renew and establish itself before it may be lost. Robert Fulton (1965) puts it succinctly: "Death asks us for our identity." It is as if Charon, the boatman from Greek mythology, or St. Peter at the gate of heaven, were asking the mortal to present his passport.

From an existential point of view ("The essence of life is its mortality"), Koestenbaum (1964) argues that only through awareness of death can a man achieve integrity. Under such pressure man will attempt to find the meaning and fulfillment of his life. "The vitality of death lies in the fact that it makes almost impossible the repression of unpleasant but important realities . . . and one is able to see all events in life from the perspective of his total existence."

Viewed in this way, the constructive and therapeutic aspects of the self-review—whether it be by spoken or silent reminiscing—are apparent when the individual can develop a satisfying pattern and meaning out of the conglomerate of events in his past life. Coming to terms with himself—his failures and achievements, his griefs and satisfactions—he seeks to integrate a new identity with a new acceptance of his own humanness, not judging himself too harshly for his limitations. This new crystallization of his self-awareness may affect his relationships with others and may bring increased tolerance, mellowness, and affection as he sees others in a different light as well. The factors that favor constructive reorganization of the personality through life review may include flexibility, resilience, and self-awareness; the reevaluation of the past may facilitate the person's "serene and dignified acceptance of death" (Butler, 1964). This in turn may facilitate a better acceptance also of whatever life may bring before the final curtain.

Postscript

We have seen that those near death are preoccupied with it. The preoccupation, though, need not be morbid; many aged individuals appear to have well integrated philosophies of life and death and are willing to discuss them (Lieberman and Coplan, 1970). The views range from despair to wisdom and strength. In the latter category are the remarks of an elderly man who stated, shortly before dying: ". . . death is unavoidable. One hour is a blessed thing. . . . The thing I like about myself is that I am all together in one piece. . . . The future is to look ahead for better things to come. Think more about the future. The past is gone" (p. 77).

There is, we think, no better summary statement of the goal of human development reaching full cycle.

ABRAVANEL, E. Developmental changes in the intersensory patterning of space. *Proceedings of the 75th Annual Convention of the American Psychological Association,* 1967, **2,** 161–162.

AINSWORTH, M. D. S. The development of infant-child interaction among the Ganda. Paper read at Tavistock Study Group on Mother-Infant Interaction, London, 1961.

AINSWORTH, M. D. S. Object relations, dependency, and attachment: A theoretical review of the infant-mother relationship. *Child Development,* 1969, **40,** 969–1025.

AINSWORTH, M. D. S., & BELL, S. M. Some contemporary patterns of mother-infant interaction in the feeding situation. In J. A. Ambrose, ed., *Stimulation in early infancy.* London: Academic Press, 1969.

AINSWORTH, M. D. S., & BELL, S. M. Attachment, exploration, and separation: Illustrated by the behavior of one-year-olds in a strange situation. *Child Development,* 1970, **41,** 49–67.

AINSWORTH, M. D. S. & WITTIG, B. A. Attachment and exploratory behavior of one-year-olds in a strange situation. In B. M. Foss, ed., *Determinants of infant behavior.* London: Methuen, 1969, pp. 111–136.

ALPERN, G. D. The failure of a nursery school enrichment program for culturally disadvantaged children. *American Journal of Orthopsychiatry,* 1966, **36,** 244–245.

AMBROSE, J. A. The development of smiling response in early infancy. In B. M. Foss, ed., *Determinants of infant behavior.* New York: Wiley, 1961.

AMERICAN PSYCHIATRIC ASSOCIATION. *Diagnostic and statistical manual: Mental disorders* (DSM–I). Washington: American Psychiatric Association, 1952; special printing, 1965.

AMES, E. W., & SILFEN, C. K. Methodological issues in the study of age differences in infants' attention to stimuli varying in movement and complexity. Paper presented at the meeting of the Society for Research in Child Development, Minneapolis, Minnesota, 1965.

AMES, L. B. Predictive value of infant behavior examination. In J. Hellmuth, ed., *Exceptional infant.* New York: Brunner/Mazel, 1967, pp. 207–239.

AMSEL, A. The role of frustrative nonreward in noncontinuous reward situations. *Psychological Bulletin,* 1958, **55,** 102–119.

AMSEL, A. Frustrative nonreward in partial reinforcement and discrimination learning. *Psychological Review,* 1962, **69,** 306–328.

ANASTASI, A. Heredity, environment, and the question "How?" *Psychological Review,* 1958, **65,** 197–208.

ANASTASI, A. *Psychological testing.* New York: Macmillan, 1968.

ANASTASI, A., & D'ANGELO, R. A comparison of Negro and white preschool children in language development and Goodenough Draw-a-Man IQ. *Journal of Genetic Psychology,* 1952, **81,** 147–165.

ANASTASI, A. & FOLEY, J. P. A proposed reorientation in the heredity-environment controversy. *Psychological Review,* 1948, **55,** 239–249.

ANDERSON, L. D. The predictive value of infant tests in relation to intelligence at 5 years. *Child Development,* 1939, **10,** 202–212.

ANDERSON, R. C., & ANDERSON, R. M. Transfer of originality training. *Journal of Educational Psychology,* 1963, **54,** 300–304.

ANDRES, D. H. Modification of delay-of-punishment effects through cognitive restructuring. Unpublished doctoral thesis, University of Waterloo, 1967.

ANDRÉ-THOMAS. Ontogénèse de la vie psychoaffective et de la douleur. *Encéphale,* 1954, **43,** 289–311.

ANTHONY, E. J. An experimental approach to the psychopathology of childhood: Encopresis. *British Journal of Medical Psychology,* 1957, **30,** 146–175.

ANTHONY, E. J. The behavior disorders of childhood. In P. H. Mussen, ed., *Carmichael's manual of child psychology.* New York: Wiley, 1970, pp. 667–764.

ARIÈS, P. *Centuries of childhood,* trans. R. Baldick. New York: Knopf, 1962.

ARONFREED, J. *Conduct and conscience.* New York: Academic Press, 1968.

AUSUBEL, D. P. *Theory and problems of adolescent development.* New York: Grune & Stratton, 1954.

AXLINE, V. M. *Play therapy.* Boston: Houghton Mifflin, 1947.

BABBILL, F. C. (trans.). *Plutarch's Moralia,* Vol. I, Cambridge: Harvard University Press, 1927.

BABSON, S., KANGAS, J., YOUNG, N., & BRAMHALL, J. Growth and development of twins of dissimilar size at birth. *Pediatrics,* 1964, **33,** 327–333.

BACK, K. W. The ambiguity of retirement. In E. W. Busse and E. Pfeiffer, eds., *Behavior and adaptation in later life.* Boston: Little, Brown, 1969.

BAER, D. M., PETERSON, R. F., & SHERMAN, J. A. The development of imitation by reinforcing behavioral similarity to a model. *Journal of the Experimental Analysis of Behavior,* 1967, **10,** 405–416.

BAER, D. M. & SHERMAN, J. A. Reinforcement control of generalized imitation in young children. *Journal of Experimental Child Psychology,* 1964, **1,** 37–49.

BALDWIN, A. L. *Theories of child development.* New York: Wiley, 1967.

BALDWIN, A. L., KALHORN, J., & BRESSE, F. H. Patterns of parent behavior. *Psychological Monographs,* 1945, **58,** No. 3.

BALDWIN, W. K. The social position of the educable mentally retarded child in the regular grades in the public schools. *Exceptional Children,* 1958, **25,** 106–108.

BALLER, W. R. & CHARLES, D. C. *The psychology of human growth and development.* New York: Holt, Rinehart & Winston, 1961.

BANDURA, A. The stormy decade: Fact or

fiction? *Psychology in the Schools,* 1964, 1, 224–231.

BANDURA, A. Influence of models' reinforcement contingencies on the acquisition of imitative responses. *Journal of Personality and Social Psychology,* 1965, 1, 589–595.

BANDURA, A. A social learning interpretation of psychological dysfunctions. In P. London, & D. Rosenhan, eds., *Foundations of abnormal psychology.* New York: Holt, Rinehart & Winston, 1968, pp. 293–344.

BANDURA, A. Social-learning theory of identificatory processes. In D. A. Goslin, ed., *Handbook of socialization theory and research.* Chicago: Rand McNally, 1969, pp. 213–262.

BANDURA, A., & HARRIS, M. B. Modification of syntactic style. *Journal of Experimental Child Psychology,* 1967, 4, 341–352.

BANDURA, A., & McDONALD, F. J. The influence of social reinforcement and the behavior of models in shaping children's moral judgments. *Journal of Abnormal and Social Psychology,* 1963, 67, 274–281.

BANDURA, A., & MENLOVE, F. L. Factors determining vicarious extinction of avoidance behavior through symbolic modeling. *Journal of Personality and Social Psychology,* 1968, 8, 99–108.

BANDURA, A., & MISCHEL, W. Modification of self-imposed delay of reward through exposure to live and symbolic models. *Journal of Personality and Social Psychology,* 1965, 2, 698–705.

BANDURA, A., & PERLOFF, B. Relative efficacy of self-monitored and externally imposed reinforcement systems. *Journal of Personality and Social Psychology,* 1967, 7, 111–116.

BANDURA, A., & WALTERS, R. H. *Adolescent aggression.* New York: Ronald Press, 1960.

BANDURA, A., & WALTERS, R. H. *Social learning and personality development.* New York: Holt, Rinehart & Winston, 1963.

BARBE, W. B., & FRIERSON, E. C. Teaching the gifted: A new frame of reference. In W. B. Barbe, ed., *Psychology and education of the gifted: Selected readings.* New York: Appleton-Century-Crofts, 1965, pp. 321–324.

BARRETT, B. H. Behavior modification in the home: Parents adapt laboratory-developed tactics to bowel-train a 5½ year-old. *Psychotherapy: Theory, Research, and Practice,* 1969, 6, 172–176.

BATTLE, E., & ROTTER, J. Children's feelings of personal control as related to social class and ethnic group. *Journal of Personality,* 1963, 31, 482–490.

BAUER, E. E. Suggested curriculum for educable mentally retarded children. Unpublished paper, Indiana University, 1967.

BAYLEY, N. Factors influencing the growth of intelligence. *39th Yearbook of the National Society of the Study of Education,* 1940, Part II, 49–79.

BAYLEY, N. Some increasing parent-child similarities during the growth of children. *Journal of Educational Psychology,* 1954, 45, 19.

BAYLEY, N. On the growth of intelligence. *American Psychologist,* 1955, 10, 805–818.

BAYLEY, N. Research in child development: A longitudinal perspective. *Merrill-Palmer Quarterly of Behavior and Development,* 1965, 11, 184–190.

BAYLEY, N. Development of mental abilities. In P. H. Mussen, ed., *Carmichael's manual of child psychology.* New York: Wiley, 1970, **1**, 1163–1209.

BAYLEY, N., & SCHAEFER, E. S. Correlations and maternal and child behaviors with the development of mental abilities: Data from the Berkeley Growth Study. *Monographs of the Society for Research in Child Development,* 1964, **29** (6, Whole No. 97).

BECK, B. M. Innovations in combating juvenile delinquency. *Children,* 1965, **12**, 69–74.

BEILIN, H. Learning and operational convergence in logical thought development. *Journal of Experimental Child Psychology,* 1965, **2**, 317–339.

BELL, R. Q. Relations between behavior manifestations in the human neonate. *Child Development,* 1960, **31**, 463–477.

BELLER, E. K. Dependency and independence in young children. *Journal of Genetic Psychology,* 1955, **87**, 23–25.

BELLER, E. K. Dependency and autonomous achievement striving related to orality and anality in early childhood. *Child Development,* 1957, **29**, 387–315.

BELLER, E. K., & HAEBERLE, A. W. Motivation and conflict in relation to phantasy responses of young children. Paper read at meetings of Society for Research in Child Development, 1959.

BELLUGI-KLIMA, U. Linguistic mechanisms underlying child speech. In E. M. Zale, ed., *Proceedings of the Conference on Language and Language Behavior.* New York: Appleton-Century-Crofts, 1968.

BENDA, C. E., SQUIRES, N. D., OGONIK, N. J., & WISE, R. Personality factors in mild mental retardation: Part I. Family background and sociocultural patterns. *American Journal of Mental Deficiency,* 1963, **68**, 24–40.

BEREITER, C. An academic preschool for disadvantaged children: Conclusions from evaluation studies. In J. C. Stanley, ed., *Preschool programs for the disadvantaged.* Baltimore: Johns Hopkins University Press, 1972, pp. 1–21.

BEREITER, C., & ENGELMANN, S. *Teaching disadvantaged children in the preschool.* Englewood Cliffs, N. J.: Prentice-Hall, Inc., 1966.

BERKO, J. The child's learning of English morphology. *Word,* 1958, **14**, 150–177.

BERLYNE, D. E. Children's reasoning and thinking. In P. H. Mussen, ed., *Carmichael's manual of child psychology.* New York: Wiley, 1970, **1**, 939–981.

BERNARD, G., & SONTAG, L. W. Foetal reactivity to tonal stimulation: A preliminary report. *Journal of Genetic Psychology,* 1947, **70**, 205–210.

BERNSTEIN, B. Social class and linguistic development: A theory of social learning. In A. H. Halsey, J. Floud, and C. A. Anderson, eds., *Education, economy, and society.* New York: The Free Press, 1961.

BERNSTEIN, B. Linguistic codes, hesitation phenomena and intelligence. *Language and Speech,* 1962a, **5**, 31–46.

BERNSTEIN, B. Social class, linguistic codes and grammatical elements. *Language and Speech,* 1962b, **5**, 221–240.

BERNSTEIN, B. Family-role systems, communication, and socialization. Paper presented at Conference on Development of Cross-National Research on the Education of Children and Adolescents, University of Chicago, February 1964.

BIJOU, S. W. Patterns of reinforcement and resistance to extinction in young children. *Child Development,* 1957, **28**, 47–54.

BIJOU, S. W., BIRNBRAUER, J. S., KIDDER, J. D., & TAGUE, C. Programmed instruction as an approach to teaching reading, writing, and arithmetic to retarded children. *Psychological Record,* 1966, **16,** 505–522.

BIRCH, D. Verbal control of nonverbal behavior. *Journal of Experimental Child Psychology,* 1966, **4,** 66–275.

BIRCH, H. G., & BELMONT, L. Auditory-visual integration, intelligence and reading ability in school children. *Perceptual and Motor Skills,* 1965, **20,** 295–305.

BIRCH, H. G., & GUSSOW, J. D. *Disadvantaged children: Health, nutrition and school failure.* New York: Grune & Stratton, 1970.

BIRCH, H. G., & LEFFORD, A. Intersensory development in children. *Monographs of the Society for Research in Child Development,* 1963, **28,** Whole No. 89.

BIRCH, H. G., & LEFFORD, A. Visual differentiation, intersensory integration and voluntary motor control. *Monographs of the Society for Research in Child Development,* 1967, **32,** Serial No. 110.

BIRNS, B. Individual differences in human neonates' responses to stimulation. *Child Development,* 1965, **36,** 249–256.

BIRREN, J. E., BUTLER, R. N., GREEN-HOUSE, S. W., SOKOLOFF, L., & YARROW, M., eds., *Human aging: A biological and behavioral study.* Public Health Service Publication No. 986. Washington, D.C.: U.S. Government Printing Office, 1963.

BIRREN, J. E., BUTLER, R. N., GREEN-HOUSE, S. W., SOKOLOFF, L., & YARROW, M. R. Interdisciplinary relationships: Interrelations of physiological, psychological, and psychiatric findings in healthy elderly men. In Birren, Butler, Greenhouse, Sokoloff, and Yarrow, 1963, pp. 283–305.

BLAU, P. M., GUSTAD, J. W., JESSOR, R., PARNES, H. S., & WILCOCK, R. C. Occupational choice: A conceptual framework. In D. G. Zytowski, ed., *Vocational behavior: Readings in theory and research.* New York: Holt, Rinehart, & Winston, 1968, pp. 358–370.

BLAUVELT, H., & MCKENNA, J. Capacity of the human newborn for mother-infant interaction, II: The temporal dimensions of a neonate response. *Psychiatric Research Report,* 1960, **13,** 128–147.

BLOOM, B. S. *Stability and change in human characteristics.* New York: Wiley, 1964.

BLUM, J. E., JARVIK, L. F., & CLARK, E. T. Rate of change on selective tests of intelligence: A twenty year longitudinal study. *Journal of Gerontology,* 1970, **25,** 171–176.

BLUM, R. H., & ASSOCIATES. *Students and drugs.* San Francisco: Jossey-Bass, 1969, **2.**

BORSTELMANN, L. J. Sex of experimenter and sex-typed behavior of young children. *Child Development,* 1961, **32,** 519–526.

BOWDITCH, H. P. Comparative rate of growth in the two sexes. *Boston Medical and Surgical Journal,* 1872, **10,** 434–435.

BOWER, G., & TRABASSO, T. Concept identification. In R. C. Atkinson, ed., *Studies in mathematical psychology.* Stanford: Stanford University Press, 1964, pp. 32–94.

BOWER, T. G. R. Slant perception and shape constancy in infants. *Science,* 1966a, **151,** 832–834.

BOWER, T. G. R. The visual world of infants. *Scientific American,* 1966b, **215,** 80–92.

BOWERMAN, C. E., & KINCH, J. W. Changes in family and peer orientation of children between the fourth and tenth grades. In M. Gold and E. Douvan, eds., *Adolescent development.* Boston: Allyn and Bacon, 1969, pp. 137–141.

BOWLBY, J. *Maternal care and mental health.* Geneva: World Health Organization, 1951.

BOWLBY, J. The nature of the child's tie to his mother. *International Journal of Psychoanalysis,* 1958, **39,** 1–24.

BOWLBY, J. *Attachment and loss,* Vol. I: *Attachment.* London: Hogarth; New York: Basic Books, 1969.

BRACKBILL, Y., & KOLTSOVA, M. M. Conditioning and learning. In Y. Brackbill, ed., *Infancy and early childhood.* New York: Free Press, 1967, pp. 207–286.

BRADWAY, K. P. An experimental study of the factors associated with Stanford-Binet IQ changes from the preschool to the junior high school. *Journal of Genetic Psychology,* 1945, **66,** 107–128.

BRAINE, M. D. S. & SHANKS, B. L. The development of conservation of size. *Journal of Verbal Learning and Verbal Behavior,* 1965, **4,** 227–242.

BRAINE, M. D. S. The ontogeny of English phrase structure: The first phase. *Language,* 1963, **39,** 1–13.

BRIDGER, W. H. Sensory habituation and discrimination in the human neonate. *American Journal of Psychiatry,* 1961, **117,** 991–996.

BROGDEN, W. J., & CULLER, E. Experimental extinction of higher-order responses. *American Journal of Psychology,* 1935, **47,** 663–669.

BROMLEY, D. B. *The psychology of human aging.* Baltimore: Penguin Books, 1966.

BRONFENBRENNER, U. Socialization and social class through time and space. In E. E. Maccoby, T. M. Newcomb, and E. L. Hartley, eds., *Readings in social psychology.* New York: Holt, 1958.

BRONSHTEIN, A. I., ANTONOVA, T. G., KAMENETSKAYA, A. G., LUPPOVA, N. N., & SYTOVA, V. A. On the development of the functions of analyzers in infants and some animals at the early stage of ontogenesis. In *Problems of evolution of physiological functions.* OTS Report No. 50–61066. (Translation obtainable from United States Department of Commerce.) Moscow: Academy of Science, 1958.

BROPHY, J. E., & GOOD, T. L. Teachers' communication of differential expectations for children's classroom performance: Some behavioral data. *Journal of Educational Psychology,* 1970, **61,** 365–374.

BROPHY, J., HESS, R. D., & SHIPMAN, V. Effects of social class and level of aspiration on performance in a structured mother-child interaction. Paper presented at Biennial Meeting of Social Research and Child Development, Minneapolis, Minnesota, March 1965.

BROWN, D. G. Masculinity-feminity development in children. *Journal of Consulting Psychology,* 1957, **21,** 197–202.

BROWN, R. *Social psychology.* New York: The Free Press, 1965.

BROWN, R. The development of Wh questions in child speech. *Journal of Verbal Learning and Behavior,* 1968, **7,** 279–290.

BROWN, R., & BELLUGI, U. Three processes in the child's acquisition of syntax. *Harvard Educational Review,* 1964, **34,** 133–151.

BROWN, R., CAZDEN, C. B., & BELLUGI, U. The child's grammar from I to III. Paper read at 1967 Minnesota Symposium on Child Psychology. Minneapoils, 1967.

BROWN, R., CAZDEN, C. B., & BELLUGI-KLIMA, U. The child's grammar from I to III. In J. P. Hill, ed., *Minnesota symposia on child psychology*. Minneapolis: The University of Minnesota Press, 1969, **2,** 28–73.

BROWN, R., FRASER, C., & BELLUGI, U. Control of grammar in imitation, comprehension, and production. *Journal of Verbal Learning and Verbal Behavior,* 1963, **2,** 121–135.

BROWN, R., FRASER, C. The acquisition of syntax. In U. Bellugi and R. Brown, eds., The acquisition of language. *Monographs of the Society for Research in Child Development,* 1964, **29,** (1 Whole No. 92), 43–78.

BRUNER, J. S. The course of cognitive growth. *American Psychologist,* 1964, **19,** 1–15.

BRUNER, J. S. On cognitive growth, I and II. In J. S. Bruner, R. R. Olver, & P. M. Greenfield, eds., *Studies in Cognitive Growth.* New York: Wiley, 1966, pp. 1–67.

BRUNER, J. S. *Toward a theory of instruction.* New York: Norton, 1968.

BRUNER, J. S., & KENNEY, H. J. On multiple ordering. In J. S. Bruner, R R. Olver, & P. M. Greenfield, eds., *Studies in Cognitive Growth* New York: Wiley, 1966a, pp. 154–167.

BRUNER, J. S., & KENNEY, H. J. On relational concepts. In J. S. Bruner, R. R. Olver, & P. M. Greenfield, eds., *Studies in Cognitive Growth.* New York: Wiley, 1966b, pp. 168–182.

BRUNSWIK, E. Zur Entwicklung der Albedowahrnehmung. *Zeitschrift für Psychologie,* 1929, **109,** 40–115.

BRYAN, J. H. Children's reactions to helpers: Their money isn't where their mouths are. In J. Macaulay & L. Berkowitz, eds., *Altruism and helping behavior.*

New York: Academic Press, 1970, pp. 61–73.

BRYAN, J. H., & LONDON, P. Altruistic behavior by children. *Psychological Bulletin,* 1970, **73,** 200–211.

BUNCH, C. C. Age variations in auditory acuity. *Archives of Otolaryngology,* 1929, **9,** 625–636.

BURT, C. The genetic determination of differences in intelligence: A study of monozygotic twins reared together and apart. *British Journal of Psychology,* 1966, **57,** 137–153.

BURTON, R. V. Generality of honesty reconsidered. *Psychological Review,* 1963, **70,** 481–499.

BURTON, R. V., MACCOBY, F., & ALLINSMITH, W. Antecedents of resistance to temptation in four-year-old children. *Child Development,* 1961, **32,** 689–710.

BUTLER, R. N. The Life Review: An Interpretation of Reminiscence in the Aged. In R. Kastenbaum, ed., *New thoughts on old age.* New York: Springer, 1964.

BUTLER, R. N. Toward a psychiatry of the life-cycle. In A. Simon and L. J. Epstein, eds., *Aging in modern society.* Psychiatric Research Report No. 23. Washington, D.C.: American Psychiatric Association, 1968.

CAIRNS, R. B. The influence of dependency inhibition on the effectiveness of social reinforcement. *Journal of Personality,* 1961, **29,** 466–488.

CAIRNS, R. B., & LEWIS, M. Dependency and the reinforcement value of a verbal stimulus. Journal of *Consulting Psychology,* 1962, **26,** 1–8.

CALDWELL, B. M. The fourth dimension in early childhood education. In R. D. Hess and R. M. Bear, eds, *Early education.* Chicago: Aldine Publishing Co., 1968, pp. 71–82.

CALDWELL, B. M. Kramer School—something for everybody. In S. J. Braun and E. P. Edwards, eds., *History and theory of early childhood education.* Worthington, Ohio: Charles A. Jones, 1972.

CALDWELL, B. M., & RICHMOND, J. B. The impact of theories of child development. *Children,* 1962, **9,** 73–78.

CALDWELL, B. M., & RICHMOND, J. B. Programmed day care for the very young child: A preliminary report. *Journal of Marriage and Family,* 1964, **26,** 481–488.

CAMPBELL, E. Q. Adolescent socialization. In D. A. Goslin, ed., *Handbook of socialization theory and research.* Chicago: Rand McNally, 1969, pp. 821–859.

CAPUTO, D. V., & MANDELL, W. Consequences of low birth weight. *Developmental Psychology,* 1970, **3,** 363–383.

CARL, J. An experimental study of the effect of nurturance on preschool children. Unpublished doctor's dissertation, State University of Iowa, 1949.

CARLSON, V. R. Size-constancy judgments and perceptual compromise. *Journal of Experimental Psychology,* 1962, **63,** 68–73.

CARMICHAEL, L. Onset and early development of behavior. In P. H. Mussen, ed., *Carmichael's manual of child psychology* (3rd. ed.). New York: Wiley, 1970, Vol. I, pp. 447–563.

CARR, H. A. *Psychology: A study of mental activity.* New York: Longmans Green, 1926.

CARTER, C. O. The genetics of common malformations. In *Congenital malformations: Papers and discussions presented at the second international conference on congenital malformations.* New York: The International Medical Congress, 1964, pp. 306–313.

CASLER, L. Maternal deprivation: A critical review of the literature. *Monographs of the Society for Research in Child Development,* 1961, **26,** No. 2.

CATTELL, R. B. *The scientific analysis of personality.* Baltimore: Penguin Books, 1965.

CHEN, H. P., & IRWIN, O. C. Infant speech vowel and consonant types. *Journal of Speech Disorders,* 1946, **11,** 27–29.

CHEYNE, J. A. Behavioral and physiological reactions to punishment: Attention, anxiety and the timing of punishment hypothesis. Paper presented at the Biennial Meeting of the Society for Research in Child Development, Santa Monica, 1969.

CHEYNE, J. A., & WALTERS, R. H. Punishment and prohibition: some origins of self-control. In *New Directions in Psychology 4,* New York: Holt, Rinehart, & Winston, 1970, pp. 279–366.

CHILMAN, C. S. Child-rearing and family relationship patterns of the very poor. *Welfare in Review,* 1965, 9–19.

CHOMSKY, N. *Language and Mind.* New York: Harcourt, Brace, Janovich, 1968.

CHORON, J. *Death and western thought.* New York: Collier-Macmillan, 1963.

CHURCHILL, J. A. The relationship between intelligence and birth weight in twins. *Neurology,* 1965, **15,** 341–347.

CLAPAREDE, E. Exemple de perception syncretique chez un enfant. *Archives de Psychologie,* 1908, **7,** 195–198.

COATES, B., ANDERSON, E. P., & HARTUP, W. W. Interrelations in the attachment behavior of human infants. *Developmental Psychology,* 1972, **6,** 218–230.

COATES, B., & HARTUP, W. W. Age and verbalization in observational learning. *Developmental Psychology,* 1969, **1,** 556–562.

COHEN, J. Psychological time. *Scientific American,* 1964, **211,** 116–124.

COLBY, K. M. Computer-aided language development in nonspeaking children. *Archives of General Psychiatry,* 1968, **19,** 641–651.

COLEMAN, J. C. *Abnormal psychology and modern life.* Fairlawn, N.J.: Scott, Foresman and Co., 1964.

COLEMAN, J. S. The adolescent subculture and academic achievement. *The American Journal of Sociology,* 1960, **65,** 337–347.

COLEMAN, J. S. *The Adolescent Society.* New York: The Free Press, 1961.

COLEMAN, J. S., CAMPBELL, E. Q., HOBSON, C. J., McPARTLAND, J., MOOD, A. M., WEINFELD, F. D., & YORK, R. L. *Equality of educational opportunity.* Report from Office of Education. Washington, D.C.: U.S. Government Printing Office, 1966.

CONGER, J. C. The treatment of encopresis by the management of social consequences. *Behavior Therapy,* 1970, **1,** 386–390.

COPOBIANCO, R. J., & COLE, D. A. Social behavior of mentally retarded children. *American Journal of Mental Deficiency,* 1960, **64,** 638–651.

CORSO, J. F. Sensory processes and age effects in normal adults. *Journal of Gerontology,* 1971, **26,** 90–105.

COSTANZO, P. R., & SHAW, M. E. Conformity as a function of age level. *Child Development,* 1966, **37,** 967–975.

COWAN, P. A., LANGER, J., HEAVENRICH, J., & NATHANSON, M. Social learning and Piaget's cognitive theory of moral development. *Journal of Personality and Social Psychology,* 1969, **11,** 261–274.

COWAN, P. A., & WALTERS, R. H. Studies of reinforcement of aggression, Part I: Effects of scheduling. *Child Development,* 1963, **34,** 543–552.

COX, C. C. The early mental traits of three hundred geniuses. In L. M. Terman, ed., *Genetic studies of genius.* Stanford: Stanford University Press, 1926, **2.**

CRANDALL, V. Parents as identification models and reinforcers of children's achievement behavior. Progress report, NIMH Grant M-2238, January 1961.

CRANDALL, V. Achievement behavior in young children. In *The Young Child: Reviews of Research.* Washington, D.C.: National Association for the Education of Young Children, 1967.

CRANDALL, V. Sex differences in expectancy of intellectual and academic reinforcement. Unpublished paper.

CRANDALL, V., KATKOVSKY, W., & CRANDALL, V. J. Children's beliefs in their own control of reinforcements in intellectual-academic achievement situations. *Child Development,* 1965, **36,** 91–109.

CRANDALL, V., KATKOVSKY, W., & PRESTON, A. A conceptual formulation for some research on children's achievement development. *Child Development,* 1960a, **31,** 787–797.

CRANDALL, V., KATKOVSKY, W., & PRESTON, A. Parent behavior and children's achievement development. Paper read at the meeting of *American Psychological Association,* Chicago, 1960b.

CRANDALL, V., KATKOVSKY, W., & PRESTON, A. Motivational ability determinants of young children's intellectual achievement behaviors. *Child Development,* 1962, **33,** 643–661.

CRANDALL, V., PRESTON, A., & RABSON, A. Maternal reactions and the development of independence and achievement behavior in young children. *Child Development*, 1960, **31**, 243–251.

CRANDALL, V. C., CRANDALL, V. J., & KATKOVSKY, W. A children's social desirability questionnaire. *Journal of Consulting Psychology*, 1965, **29**, 27–36.

CRISSEY, O. L. Mental development as related to institutional residence and educational achievement. *University of Iowa Studies on Child Welfare*, 1937, **13**, No. 1.

CROMWELL, R. L. A social learning approach to mental retardation. In N. R. Ellis, ed., *Handbook of mental deficiency*. New York: McGraw-Hill, 1963, pp. 41–91.

CRONBACH, L. J. *Essentials of psychological testing*. 2nd ed. New York: Harper & Row, 1960.

CROWLEY, P. M. Effect of training upon objectivity of moral judgment in grade-school children. *Journal of Personality and Social Psychology*, 1968, **8**, 228–232.

D'ANDRADE, R. G. Sex differences and cultural institutions. In E. E. Maccoby, ed., *The development of sex differences*. Stanford: Stanford University Press, 1966, pp. 174–204.

DARLEY, J. M., & LATANÉ, B. Bystander intervention in emergencies: Diffusion of responsibility. *Journal of Personality and Social Psychology*, 1968, **8**, 377–383.

DASHKOVSKAYA, V. S. First conditioned reactions in newly born children in normal state and in certain pathological states. *Zh. vyssh, nervn. Deiatel.*, 1953, **13**(2), 247–259.

DAVIDSON, E. S., & LIEBERT, R. M. Effects of prior commitment on children's evaluation and imitation of a peer model's perceptual judgments. *Perceptual and Motor Skills*, 1972, **35**, 825–826.

DAVIS, B. D. Prospects for genetic intervention in man. *Science*, 1970, **170**, 1279–1283.

DAVIS, K. Final note on a case of extreme isolation. *American Journal of Sociology*, 1947, **57** 432–457.

DAVIS, W. Communicating science. *Journal of Atomic Scientists*, 1953, 337–340.

DAVISON, G. C., & NEALE, J. M. *Abnormal psychology: An experimental-clinical approach*. New York: John Wiley, 1974.

DAYTON, G. O., JR., JONES, M. H., AIU, P. RAWSON, R. H. STEELE, B. & ROSE, M. Developmental study of coordinated eye movements in the human infant: I. Visual acuity in the newborn human: A study based on induced optokinetic nystagmus recorded by electro-oculography. *Archives of Ophthalmology*, 1964, **71**, 865–870.

DEARBORN, W. F., & ROTHNEY, J. W. M. *Predicting the child's development*. Cambridge: Sci-Art, 1941.

DEHAAN, R. F., & HAVIGHURST, R. J. *Educating gifted children*. Chicago: University of Chicago Press, 1957.

DE HIRSH, K., JANSKY, J., & LANGFORD, W. S. Comparisons between prematurely and maturely born children at three age levels. *American Journal of Orthopsychiatry*, 1966, **36**, 616–628.

DENNIS, W. Goodenough scores, art experience, and modernization. *Journal of Social Psychology*, 1966, **68**, 211–228.

DENNIS, W., & NAJARIAN, P. Infant development under environmental handicap. *Psychological Monographs*, 1957, **71**, No. 7 (Whole No. 436).

DESPERT, J. L. *The emotionally disturbed child—then and now*. New York: Vantage, 1965.

DEUTSCH, M. The disadvantaged child and the learning process. In A. H. Passow, ed., *Education in depressed areas*.

New York: Columbia University Teachers College, 1963, pp. 163–180.

DEUTSCH, M., & BROWN, B. Social influences in Negro-white intelligence differences. *Journal of Social Issues,* 1964, **20** (2), 24–35.

DEWEY, J. *Reconstruction in philosophy.* New York: Holt and Co., 1920.

DEWING, K. The reliability and validity of selected tests of creative thinking in a sample of seventh-grade Western Australian children. *British Journal of Educational Psychology,* 1970, **40**, 35–42.

DOMINICK, J. R., & GREENBERG, B. S. Attitudes toward violence: The interaction of television exposure, family attitudes, and social class. In G. A. Comstock and E. A. Rubinstein, eds., *Television and social behavior,* Vol. III. *Television and adolescent aggressiveness.* Washington, D.C.: U.S. Government Printing Office, 1972, pp. 314–335.

DOUVAN, E., & ADELSON, J. *The adolescent experience.* New York: Wiley, 1966.

DRABMAN, R., SPITALNIK, R., HAGAMEN, M. B., & VAN WITSEN, B. The "five-two" plan: An integrated approach to treating severely disturbed chldiren. *Hospital and Community Psychiatry,* 1973, **24**, 33–36.

DREGER, R. M. MILLER, K. S. Comparative psychological studies on Negroes and whites in the United States. *Psychological Bulletin,* 1960, **57**, 361–402.

DRILLIEN, C. M. The incidence of mental and physical handicaps in school-age chilren of very low birthweight. *Pediatrics,* 1961, **17**, 452–464.

DUNFORD, R. E. The genetic development of cutaneous localization. *Journal of Genetic Psychology,* 1930, **37**, 499–513.

DUNSDON, M. I., & FRASER-ROBERTS, J. A. A study of the performance of 2,000 children on four vocabulary tests. *British Journal of Statistical Psychology,* 1957, **10**, 1–16.

DYER, H. S. Is testing a menace to education? In J. O. Whittaker, ed., *Recent discoveries in psychology.* Philadelphia: W. B. Saunders, 1972, pp. 292–296.

EDWARDS, C. D., & WILLIAMS, J. E. Generalization between evaluative words associated with racial figures in preschool children. *Journal of Experimental Research in Personality,* 1970, **4**, 144–155.

EELLS, K. Some implications for school practice of the Chicago studies of cultural bias in intelligence tests. *Harvard Educational Review,* 1953, **23**, 284–297.

EELLS, K., DAVIS, A., HAVIGHURST, R. J., HERRICK, V. E., & TYLER, R. W. *Intelligence and cultural differences.* Chicago: University of Chicago Press, 1951.

EIBL-EIBESFELDT, I. *Ethology: The biology of behavior.* New York: Holt, Rinehart, & Winston, 1970.

EICHORN, D. H. Biological correlates of behavior. In H. W. Stevenson, ed., *Child psychology.* Chicago: The University of Chicago Press, 1963, **1**, 4–61.

EIMAS, P. D. A developmental study of hypothesis behavior and focusing. *Journal of Experimental Child Psychology,* 1969, **8**, 160–172.

EISENBERG, L. School phobia: A study in the communication of anxiety. *American Journal of Psychiatry,* 1958, **114**, 712–718.

EISENSTADT, S. N. *From generation to generation.* New York: The Free Press, 1956.

ELDER, G. H. Structural variations in the child rearing relationship. *Sociometry,* 1962, **25**, 241–262.

ELKIND, D. Egocentrism in adolescence.

Child Development, 1967, **38,** 1025–1034.

ELKIND, D. KROGLER, R. R., & GO, E. Studies in perceptual development: II. Part-whole perception. *Child Development,* 1964, **35,** 81–90.

ENDSLEY, R. C. Dependency and performance by preschool children on a socially-reinforced task. Unpublished master's thesis, State University of Iowa, 1960.

ENGEN, T., LIPSITT, L. P., & KAYE, H. Olfactory responses and adaptation in the human neonate. *Journal of Comparative and Physioloical Psycholoy,* 1963, **56,** 73–77.

ENGLISH, H. B., & ENGLISH, A. C. *A comprehensive dictionary of psychological and psychoanalytical terms.* New York: Longman's, 1958.

EPPERSON, D. C. A reassessment of indices of parental influence in "the adolescent society." *American Sociological Review,* 1964, **29,** 93–96.

EPSTEIN, W. Experimental investigations of the genesis of visual space perception. *Psychological Bulletin,* 1964, **61,** 115–128.

ERIKSON, E. H. *Childhood and society.* New York: Norton, 1963.

ERIKSON, E. H. Eight ages of man. In C. S. Lavatelli and F. Stendler, eds., *Readings in child behavior and child development.* New York: Harcourt, Brace, Jovanovich, 1972.

ERLENMEYER-KIMLING, L., & JARVIK, L. F. Genetics and intelligence: A review. *Science,* 1963, **142,** 1477–1479.

ERON, L. D. Relationship of TV viewing habits and aggressive behavior in children. *Journal of Abnormal and Social Psychology,* 1963, **67,** 193–196.

ERVIN, S. M. Imitation and structural changes in children's language. In E. H.

Lenneberg, ed., *New directions in the study of language.* Cambridge, Mass.: M.I.T. Press, 1964.

ESCALONA, S. K., & MORIARTY, A. Prediction of school age intelligence from infant tests. *Child Development,* 1961, **32,** 597–605.

ESTES, E. H. Health experience in the elderly. In E. W. Busse and E. Pfeiffer, eds., *Behavior and adaptation in later life.* Boston: Little, Brown, 1969.

ESTES, W. K. An experimental study of punishment. *Psychological Monographs,* 1944, **57** (3, Whole No. 263).

EVANS, W. F. *Anatomy and physiology.* Englewood Cliffs: Prentice-Hall, 1971.

EYSENCK, H. J. The effects of psychotherapy: An evaluation. *Journal of Consulting Psychology,* 1952, **16,** 319–324.

EYSENCK, H. J. The inheritance of extraversion-introversion. *Acta Psychologica,* 1956, **12,** 95–110.

EYSENCK, H. J., ed. *Behavior therapy and the neuroses.* London: Pergamon Press, 1960.

FANTZ, R. L. Depth discrimination in dark-hatched chicks. *Perceptual and Motor Skills,* 1958a, **8,** 47–50.

FANTZ, R. L. Pattern vision in young infants. *Psychological Record,* 1958b, **8,** 43–47.

FANTZ, R. L. The origin of form perception. *Scientific American,* 1961, **204,** 66–72.

FANTZ, R. L. Ontogeny of perception. In A. M. Schrier, H. F. Harlow, & F. Stollnitz, eds, *Behavior of nonhuman primates.* New York: Academic Press, 1965, pp. 365–403.

FANTZ, R. L. Studying visual perception and the effects of visual exposure in early infancy. In D. Gelfand, ed., *Social learn-*

ing in childhood. Belmont, California: Books/Cole Publishing Co., 1969, pp. 46–56.

FAUST, M. S. Developmental maturity as a determinant in prestige of adolescent girls. *Child Development,* 1960, **31,** 173–184.

FEIFEL, H. Attitudes toward death. In H. Feifel, ed., *The meaning of death.* New York: McGraw-Hill, 1965.

FELD, S. Need achievement and test anxiety in children and maternal attitudes and behaviors toward independent accomplishments: A longitudinal study. Paper read at the meeting of American Psychological Association, Cincinnati, 1959.

FELIXBROD, J. J., & O'LEARY, K. D. Effects of reinforcement on children's academic behavior as a function of self-determined and externally imposed contingencies. *Journal of Applied Behavior Analysis,* 1973, **6,** 241–250.

FERGUSON, L. R. Dependency motivation in socialization. In R. A. Hoppe, G. A. Milton, & E. C. Simmel, eds., *Early experiences and the processes of socialization.* New York: Academic Press, 1970, pp. 59–79.

FIELD, H. Prediction of character disorder and psychotic outcome from childhood behavior. Unpublished thesis. New York: Teacher's College, Columbia University, 1969.

FINLEY, C. J. Arithmetic achievement in mentally retarded children: The effect of presenting the problem in different contexts. *American Journal of Mental Deficiency,* 1962, **67,** 281–286.

FINNEY, J. C. Some maternal influences on children's personality and character, *Genetic Psychology Monographs,* 1961, **63,** 199–278.

FISCHER, W. F. Sharing in preschool children as a function of amount and type of reinforcement. *Genetic Psychology Monographs,* 1963, **68,** 215–245.

FITZGERALD, H. E., & PORGES, S. W. A decade of infant conditioning and learning research. *Merrill-Palmer Quarterly,* 1971, **17,** 79–117.

FLAVELL, J. H. *The developmental psychology of Jean Piaget.* New York: Van Nostrand, 1963.

FLAVELL, J. H., BEACH, D. R., & CHINSKY, J. M. Spontaneous verbal rehearsal in a memory task as a function of age. *Child Development,* 1966, **37,** 283–299.

FLOYD, J. M. K. Effects of amount of reward and friendship status of the other on the frequency of sharing in children. Unpublished doctoral thesis, University of Minnesota, 1964.

FORBES, H. S., & FORBES, H. B. Total sense reaction: Hearing. *Journal of Comparative Psychology,* 1927, **7,** 353–356.

FORD, D., & URBAN, H. *Systems of psychotherapy.* New York: Wiley, 1963.

FORGUS, R. *Perception.* New York: McGraw-Hill, 1966.

FORT, J. Comparison chart of major substances used for mind-alteration. In H. H. Nowlis, ed., *Drugs on the college campus.* New York: Doubleday, 1969.

Fortune Survey. *Fortune,* August 1946.

FRANDSEN, A., & BARLOW, F. P. Influence of the nursery school on mental growth. *39th Yearbook of the National Society for the Study of Education,* 1940, Part II, 143–148.

FRAZIER, A., ed. *Educating the children of the poor.* Washington, D.C.: Association for Supervision and Curriculum Development, NEA, 1968.

FREEDMAN, D. G. Personality development in infancy: A biological approach.

In S. L. Washburn and P. C. Jay, eds., *Perspectives on human evolution.* New York: Holt, Rinehart & Winston, 1968, **1,** 258–287.

FREEDMAN, D. G., & KELLER, B. Inheritance of behavior in infants. *Science,* 1963, **140,** 196–198.

FREUD, A. Adolescence. In J. F. Rosenblith, W. Alinsmith, and J. P. Williams, eds., *The causes of behavior.* Boston: Allyn and Bacon, 1972, pp. 317–323.

FREUD, S. *An outline of psycho-analysis.* Translated and newly edited by J. Strachey. New York: Norton, 1949.

FREUD, S. Formulations regarding the two principles in mental functioning. In *Collected Papers,* Vol. 4. New York: Basic Books, 1959, **4.** (Originally published in 1911.)

FREUD, S. *A general introduction to psychoanalysis.* New York: Washington Square Press, 1960.

FULLER, J. L., & THOMPSON, W. R. *Behavior Genetics.* New York: Wiley, 1960.

FULTON, R. *Death and identity.* New York: Wiley, 1965.

Fund for the Advancement of Education. *Bridging the gap between school and college.* New York: The Fund for the Advancement of Education, 1953.

GALLUP, G. *Gallup poll.* Princeton: Audience Research, Inc., June 1955.

GARDNER, E. J. *Principles of genetics.* New York: Wiley, 1968.

GARDNER, R. A., & GARDNER, B. T. Teaching sign language to a chimpanzee. *Science,* 1969, **165,** 664–672.

GARNER, A. M., & WENAR, G. *The mother-child interaction in psychosomatic disorders.* Urbana: University of Illinois Press, 1959.

GARRISON, K. C. *Psychology of adolescence.* 5th ed. Englewood Cliffs, N.J.: Prentice-Hall, Inc., 1956.

GELLERMANN, L. W. Form discrimination in chimpanzees and two-year-old children: I. Form (triangularity) *per se. Journal of Genetic Psychology,* 1933, **42,** 3–27.

GELMAN, R. Conservation acquisition: A problem of learning to attend to relevant attributes. *Journal of Experimental Child Psychology,* 1969, **7,** 167–187.

GERARD, M. W. Bronchial asthma in children. *Nervous Child,* 1946, **5,** 327–331.

GESELL, A. Maturation and infant behavior pattern. *Psychological Review,* 1929.

GESELL, A. The stability of mental-growth careers. *39th Yearbook of the National Society for the Study of Education,* 1940, Part II, 149–159.

GESELL, A. *Youth: The years from ten to sixteen.* New York: Harper & Row, 1956.

GESELL, A., & AMATRUDA, C. S. *Developmental diagnosis.* Paul B. Hoeber, Inc., 1941, 1947.

GESELL, A., & AMES, L. B. The development of handedness. *Journal of Genetic Psychology,* 1947, **70,** 155–175.

GESELL, A., HALVERSON, H. M., THOMSON, H., ILG, F. L., CASTNER, B. M., AMES, L. B., & AMATRUDA, C. S. *The first five years of life: A guide to the study of the preschool child.* New York: Harper & Row, 1940.

GESELL, A., & ILG, F. L. *Infant and child in the culture of today.* New York: Harper & Row, 1943.

GESELL, A., & ILG, F. L. *The child from five to ten.* New York: Harper & Row, 1946.

GESELL, A., ILG, F., & BULLIS, G. *Vision:*

Its development in infant and child. New York: Hoeber, 1949.

GESELL, A., & THOMPSON, H. Learning and growth in identical twins. *Genetic Psychology Monographs,* 1929, **6,** 1–124.

GETZELS, J. W., & JACKSON, P. W. *Creativity and intelligence.* New York: Wiley, 1962.

GEWIRTZ, J. L. Succorance in young children. Unpublished doctor's dissertation, State University of Iowa, 1948.

GEWIRTZ, J. L. A learning analysis of the effects of normal stimulation, privation, and deprivation on the acquisition of social motivation and attachment. In B. M. Foss, ed., *Determinants of infant behavior.* New York: Wiley, 1961.

GEWIRTZ, J. L., & BAER, D. M. Deprivation of social reinforcers as drive conditions, *Journal of Abnormal Social Psychology,* 1958a, **57,** 165–172.

GEWIRTZ, J. L., & BAER, D. M. The effects of brief social deprivation on behaviors for a social reinforcer. *Journal of Abnormal Social Psychology,* 1958b, **56,** 49–56.

GHOLSON, B., LEVINE, M., & PHILLIPS, S. Hypotheses, strategies, and stereotypes in discrimination learning. *Journal of Experimental Child Psychology,* 1972, **13,** 423–446.

GIBSON, E. J., GIBSON, J. J., PICK, A. D., & OSSER, H. A developmental study of the discrimination of letter-like forms. *Journal of Comparative and Physiological Psychology,* 1962, **55,** 897–906.

GIBSON, E. J., & WALK, R. D. The "visual cliff." *Scientific American,* 1960, **202,** 64–71.

GIBSON, J. J. *The perception of the visual world.* Boston: Houghton-Mifflin, 1950.

GIBSON, J. J., & GIBSON, E. J. Perceptual learning: Differentiation or enrichment? *Psychological Review,* 1055, **62,** 33–40.

GINSBURG, H., & OPPER, S. *Piaget's theory of intellectual development: An introduction.* Englewood Cliffs, N.J.: Prentice-Hall, Inc., 1969.

GIOVANNONI, J. M., & BILLINGSLEY, A. Child neglect among the poor: A study of parental adequacy in families of three ethnic groups. In S. Chess and A. Thomas, eds., *Annual progress in child psychiatry and child development.* New York: Brunner/Mazel, 1971, pp. 323–334.

GLASER, B. G., & STRAUSS, A. L. *Awareness of dying.* Chicago: Aldine, 1965.

GLASER, B. G., & STRAUSS, A. L. *Time for dying.* Chicago: Aldine, 1968.

GLINER, C. R. Tactual discrimination thresholds for shape and texture in young children. *Journal of Experimental Child Psychology,* 1967, **5,** 536–547.

GLUCKSBERG, S., & KRAUSS, R. M. What do people say after they have learned to talk? Studies of the development of referential communication. *Merrill-Palmer Quarterly,* 1967, **13,** 309–316.

GLUCKSBERG, S., KRAUSS, R. M., & WEISBERG, R. Referential communication in nursery school children: Method and some preliminary findings. *Journal of Experimental Child Psychology,* 1966, **3,** 333–342.

GOLDFARB, W. Infant rearing and problem behavior. *American Journal of Orthopsychiatry,* 1943, **13,** 249–265.

GOLDFARB, W. Variations in adolescent adjustment of institutionally reared children. *American Journal of Orthopsychiatry,* 1947, **17,** 449–457.

GOLDFARB, W. Childhood psychosis. In P. H. Mussen, ed., *Carmichael's manual of child psychology.* New York: Wiley, 1970, pp. 765–830.

GOLDMAN, G. Clinical Perspectives. In A. Simon and L. J. Epstein, eds., *Aging in modern society.* Washington, D.C.: American Psychiatric Association, 1968.

GOLDSTEIN, H., MOSS, J. W., & JORDAN, L. J. The efficacy of special class training on the development of mentally retarded children. Cooperative Research Project No. 619. Washington, D.C.: U.S. Office of Education, 1965.

GOLLIN, E. S. Developmental studies of visual recognition of incomplete objects. *Perceptual and Motor Skills,* 1960, **11,** 289–298.

GOODE, E. *The marijuana smokers.* New York: Basic Books, 1970.

GOODENOUGH, F. L. A preliminary report on the effects of nursery school training upon intelligence test scores of young children, *27th Yearbook of the National Society for the Study of Education,* 1928, 361–369.

GOODENOUGH, F. L. New evidence on environmental influence on intelligence. *39th Yearbook of the National Society for the Study of Education,* 1940, Part I, 307–365.

GOODENOUGH, F. L., & HARRIS, D. B. Studies in the psychology of children's drawings: II. 1928–1949. *Psychological Bulletin,* 1950, **47,** 369–433.

GOODENOUGH, F. L., & MAURER, K. M. The mental development of nursery school children compared with that of non-nursery school children. *39th Yearbook of the National Society for the Study of Education,* 1940, Part II, 161–178.

GORMAN, J. J., COGAN, D. G., & GELLIS, S. S. A device for testing visual acuity in infants. *Sight-Saving Review,* 1959, **29,** 80–84.

GOTTESMAN, I. I. Heritability of personality. *Psychological Monographs,* 1963, **77,** 1–21.

GOTTESMAN, I. I. Genetic variance in adaptive personality traits. *Journal of Child Psychology, Psychiatry, and Allied Disciplines,* 1966, **7,** 199–208.

GOULDNER, A. The norm of reciprocity: A preliminary statement. *American Sociological Review,* 1960, **25,** 161–178.

GOULET, L. R., & BARCLAY, A. The Vineland Social Maturity Scale: Utility in assessment of Binet MA. *American Journal of Mental Deficiency,* 1963, **67,** 916–921.

GRAY, S. W., & KLAUS, R. A. The early training project: A seventh-year report. *Child Development,* 1970, **41,** 909–924.

GREEN, R. Age-intelligence relationship between ages sixteen and sixty-four: A rising trend. *Developmental Psychology,* 1969, **1,** 618–627.

Group for the Advancement of Psychiatry. *Death and dying: Attitudes of patient and doctor.* New York: Mental Health Materials Centers, 1967.

GRUEN, G. E. Experiences affecting conservation. *Child Development,* 1965, **36,** 963–979.

GRUSEC, J. E., & BRINKER, D. B. Reinforcement for imitation as a social learning determinant with implications for sex-role development. *Journal of Personality and Social Psychology,* 1972, **21,** 149–158.

GUILFORD, J. P. Creative abilities in the arts. *Psychological Review,* 1957, **64,** 110–118.

GUILFORD, J. P. Intelligence: 1965 model. *American Psychologist,* 1966, **21,** 20–26.

GUNZBURG, H. C. A "finishing school" for the mentally subnormal. *Medical Officer,* 1965, **114,** 99–102.

HALL, R. V., LUND, D., & JACKSON, D. Effects of teacher attention on study behavior. *Journal of Applied Behavior Analysis*, 1968, **1**, 1–12.

HALL, W. B. The development of a technique for assessing esthetic predispositions and its application to a sample of professional research scientists. Unpublished paper presented at the annual convention of the Western Psychological Association, 1958.

HALL, W. S. The first 500 days of a child's life. *Child Study Monthly*, 1896–97, **2**, 330–342, 394–407, 458–473, 522–537, 586–608.

HALLORAN, J. D. Television and violence. *The Twentieth Century*, 1964, **174**, 61–72.

HALVERSON, H. M. An experimental study of prehension in infants by means of systematic cinema records. *Genetic Psychology Monographs*, 1931, **10**, 107–286.

HALVERSON, H. M. Complications of the early grasping reactions. *Genetic Psychology Monographs*, 1936, **47**, 47–63.

HAMMOND, W. H. The constancy of physical types as determined by factorial analysis. *Human Biology*, 1957, **29**, 40–61.

HANDLON, J. & GROSS, P. The development of sharing behavior. *Journal of Abnormal and Social Psychology*, 1959, **59**, 425–428.

HANRATTY, M. A. Imitation of film-mediated aggression against live and inanimate victims. Unpublished master's thesis. Vanderbilt University, 1969.

HANRATTY, M. A., LIEBERT, R. M., MORRIS, L. W., & FERNANDEZ, L. E. Imitation of film-mediated aggression against live and inanimate victims. *Proceedings of the 77th Annual Convention of the American Psychological Association*, 1969, **4**, 457–458 (Summary).

HANRATTY, M. A., O'NEAL, E., & SULZER, J. L. The effect of frustration upon imitation of aggression. *Journal of Personality and Social Psychology*, 1972, **21**, 30–34.

HARLOW, H. F. The nature of love. *American Psychologist*, 1958, **13**, 673–685.

HARLOW, H. F. *Learning to love.* San Francisco: Albion Publishing, 1971.

HARLOW, H. F., & HARLOW, M. K. Learning to think. *Scientific American*, 1949, **181**, 36–39.

HARLOW, H. F., & HARLOW, M. K. The young monkeys. In P. Cramer, ed., *Readings in developmental psychology today.* Del Mar, California: CRM Books, 1970, pp. 58–63.

HARLOW, H. F., & ZIMMERMAN, R. R. Affectional responses in the infant monkey. *Science*, 1959, **130**, 431–432.

HARMON, L. R. The development of a criterion of scientific competence. In C. W. Taylor and F. Barron, eds., *Scientific creativity: Its recognition and development.* New York: Wiley, 1963.

HARRELL, R. F., WOODWARD, E., & GATES, A. I. The influence of vitamin supplementation of the diets of pregnant and lactating women on the intelligence of their offspring. *Metabolism*, 1956, **5**, 552–561.

HARTSHORNE, H., & MAY, M. A. *Studies in the nature of character,* Vol. I: *Studies in deceit.* New York: Macmillan, 1928.

HARTSHORNE, H., MAY, M. A., & SHUTTLEWORTH, F. K. *Studies in the nature of character,* Vol. III: *Studies in the organization of character.* New York: Macmillan, 1930.

HARTUP, W. W. Nurturance and nurturance-withdrawal in relation to the dependency behavior of young children. *Child Development,* 1958, **29,** 191–201.

HARTUP, W. W. An evaluation of the Highberger Early-Adjustment-to-School Scale, *Child Development,* 1959, **30,** 421–432.

HARTUP, W. W. Dependence and independence. In H. W. Stevenson, ed., *Child psychology: The sixty-second yearbook of the National Society for the Study of Education.* Chicago: University of Chicago Press, 1963, pp. 333–363.

HARTUP, W. W., & KELLER, E. D. Nurturance in preschool children and its relation to dependency, *Child Development,* 1960, **31,** 681–689.

HAVIGHURST, R. J. *Human development and education.* New York: Longmans Green, 1953.

HAVIGHURST, R. J. *The public schools of Chicago.* Chicago: The Board of Eucation of the City of Chicago, 1964.

HAVIGHURST, R. J. Minority subcultures and the law of effect. In F. F. Korten, S. W. Cook, and J I. Lacey, eds., *Psychology and the problem of society.* Washington, D.C.: American Psychological Association, 1970, pp. 275–288.

HAVIGHURST, R. J., & TABA, H., eds. *Adolescent character and personality.* New York: Wiley, 1949.

HAYES, C. *The ape in our house.* New York: Harper & Row, 1951.

HEALY, W., & BRONNER, A. F. *New light on delinquency and its treatment.* New Haven: Yale University Press, 1936.

HEATHERS, G. Acquiring dependence and independence: A theoretical orientation. *Journal of Genetic Psychology,* 1955a, **207,** 277–91.

HEATHERS, G. Emotional dependence and independence in nursery-school play. *Journal of Genetic Psychology,* 1955b, **207,** 37–58.

HEBB, D. *A textbook of psychology.* Philadelphia: W. B. Saunders Co., 1966.

HEBER, R. F. A manual on terminology and classification in mental retardation. *American Journal of Mental Deficiency,* 1959, **64,** Monograph Supplement (Rev. Ed., 1961).

HEIDBREDER, E. The attainment of concepts: Terminology and methodology. *Journal of Genetic Psychology,* 1946, **35,** 173–189.

HELSON, R., & CRUTCHFIELD, R. S. Mathematicians: The creative researcher and the average Ph.D. *Journal of Consulting and Clinical Psychology,* 1970, **34,** 250–257.

HERSKOVITZ, A., LIEBERT, R. M., & ADELSON, R. A motion picture as a substitute for experience in health delivery environment. *Journal of the Biological Photographic Association,* October 1971, pp. 193–195.

HERZOG, E., & LEWIS, H. Children in poor families: Myths and realities. In S. Chess and A. Thomas, eds., *Annual progress in child psychiatry and child development.* New York: Brunner/Mazel, 1971, pp. 307–322.

HESS, E. H. Space perception in the chick. *Scientific American,* 1956, **195,** 71–80.

HESS, E. H. Imprinting. *Science,* 1959, **130,** 133–141.

HESS, R. D. Educability and rehabilitation: The future of the welfare class. *Marriage and Family Living,* 1964, **26,** 422–429.

HESS, R. D. Social class and ethnic influences on socialization. In P. H. Mussen, ed., *Carmichael's manual of child psychol-*

ogy. New York: Wiley, 1970, **2,** 457–557.

HESS, R. D., & SHIPMAN, V. C. Early experience and the socialiaztion of cognitive modes in children. *Child Development,* 1965, **36,** 869–888.

HESS, R. D., & SHIPMAN, V. C. Maternal attitudes toward the school and the role of the pupil: Some social class comparisons. In A. H. Passow, ed., *Developing programs for the educationally disadvantaged.* New York: Teachers College, Columbia University, 1968.

HESTON, L. L. Psychiatric disorders in foster home reared children of schizophrenic mothers. *British Journal of Psychiatry,* 1966, **112,** 819–825.

HETHERINGTON, E. M. Sex typing, dependency, and aggression. In T. D. Spencer and N. Kass, eds., *Perspectives in child psychology: Research and review.* New York: McGraw-Hill, 1970, pp. 193–231.

HETHERINGTON, E. M., & MARTIN, B. Family interaction and psychopathology in children. In H. C. Quay and J. S. Werry, eds., *Psychopathological disorders of childhood.* New York: Wiley, 1972, pp. 30–82.

HEYMAN, D. K., & JEFFERS, F. C. Observations on the extent of concern and planning by the aged for possible chronic illness. *Journal of the American Geriatric Society,* 1965, **13,** 152–159.

HILGARD, E. R., & BOWER, G. H. *Theories of learning.* New York: Appleton-Century-Crofts, 1966.

HILL, J. H., LIEBERT, R. M., & MOTT, D. E. W. Vicarious extinction of avoidance behavior through films: An initial test. *Psychological Reports,* 1968, **22,** 192.

HOBBS, N. Helping disturbed children: Ecological and psychological strategies.

American Psychologist, 1966, **21,** 1105–1115.

HOLLINGER, C. S., & JONES, R. L. Community attitudes toward slow learners and mental retardates: What's in a name? *Mental Retardation,* 1970, **8,** 19–23.

HOLLINGSHEAD, A. B. *Elmtown's youth: The impact of social classes on youth.* New York: Wiley, 1949.

HOLLINGWORTH, L. S. *Children above 180 IQ.* New York: World Book Co., 1942, pp. 300–302.

HOLTZMAN, W. H. The changing world of mental measurement and its social significance. *American Psychologist,* 1971, **26,** 546–553.

HONZIG, M. P. Environmental correlates of mental growth: Prediction from the family setting at 21 months. *Child Development,* 1967, **38,** 337–364.

HONZIK, M. P., MACFARLAND, J. W., & ALLEN, L. The stability of mental test performance between 2 and 18 years. *Journal of Experimental Education,* 1948, **17,** 309–324.

HUGHES, C. C., TREMBLAY, M., RAPOPORT, R. N., & LEIGHTON, A. H. *People of cove and woodlot: Communities from the viewpoint of social psychiatry.* New York: Basic Books, 1960.

HUNT, J. McV. *Intelligence and experience.* New York: The Ronald Press, 1961.

HUNTER, I. M. L. Tactile-kinaesthetic perception of straightness in blind and sighted humans. *Quarterly Journal of Experimental Psychology,* 1954, **6,** 149–154.

HURLEY, R. *Poverty and mental retardation.* New York: Random House, 1969.

HURLOCK, E. B. *Adolescent development.* New York: McGraw-Hill, 1967.

HYMOVITCH, B. The effects of experimental variations on problem solving in the rat. *Journal of Comparative and Physiological Psychology,* 1952, **45,** 313–321.

ILLINGWORTH, R. S. Predictive value of developmental tests in the 1st year. *Journal of Child Psychology and Psychiatry,* 1961, **2,** 210–215.

INGALLS, R. P., & DICKERSON, D. J. Development of hypothesis behavior in human concept identification. *Developmental Psychology,* 1969, **1,** 707–716.

INHELDER, B., & PIAGET, J. *The growth of logical thinking from childhood to adolescence.* New York: Basic Books, 1958.

ISRAEL, A. C., & O'LEARY, K. D. Developing correspondence between children's words and deeds. *Child Development,* 1973, **44,** 575–581.

JACKSON, C. M. Some aspects of form and growth. In W. J. Robbins, S. Brody, A. F. Hogan, C. M. Jackson, & C. W. Greed, eds., *Growth.* New Haven: Yale University Press, 1929, p. 118.

JACKSON, D. *The etiology of schizophrenia.* New York: Basic Books, 1960.

JACKSON, J. D., HESS, R. D., & SHIPMAN, V. Communication styles in teachers: An experiment. Paper presented at American Education and Research Association, Chicago, February 1965.

JACKSON, P. W., & MESSICK, D. Creativity. In P. London and D. Rosenhan, eds., *Foundations of abnormal psychology.* New York: Holt, Rinehart, & Winston, 1968, pp. 226–250.

JAMES, W. *Principles of psychology.* New York: Holt, 1890.

JEFFERS, F. C., NICHOLS, C. R., & EISDORFER, C. Attitudes of older persons toward death: A preliminary study. *Journal of Gerontology,* 1961, **16,** 53–56.

JEFFERS, F. C., & VERWOERDT, A. Factors associated with frequency of death thoughts in elderly community volunteers.

Proceedings of the 7th International Congress of Gerontology, Vienna, 1966, **6,** 149–152.

JENSEN, A. R. How much can we boost I.Q. and scholastic achievement? *Harvard Educational Review,* 1969, **39,** 1–123.

JERSILD, A. T., & HOLMES, F. B. *Children's fears.* New York: Bureau of Publications, Teacher's College, Columbia University, 1935.

JESPERSON, J. O. *Language: Its nature, development, and origin.* London: Allen and Unwin, 1922.

JOHN, V. The intellectual development of slum children: Some preliminary findings. *American Journal of Orthopsychiatry,* 1963, **33,** 813–822.

JOHN, V. P., & GOLDSTEIN, L. S. The social context of language acquisition. *Merrill-Palmer Quarterly,* 1964, **10,** 265–275.

JONCICH, G. M. *Psychology and the science of education.* New York: Columbia University Press, 1962.

JONES, F., & GERARD, H. B. *Foundations of social psychology.* New York: Wiley, 1967.

JONES, H. E., & JORGENSEN, A. P. Mental growth as related to nursery-school attendance. *39th Yearbook of the National Society for the Study of Education,* 1940, Part II, 207–222.

JONES, M. C. A laboratory study of fear: The case of Peter. *Pedagogical Seminar,* 1924, **31,** 308–315.

JONES, M. C. The later careers of boys who were early- or late-maturing. *Child Development,* 1957, **28,** 113–128.

JONES, M. C. A study of socialization patterns at the high-school level. *Journal of Genetic Psychology,* 1958, **90,** 87–111.

KAGAN, J. Information processing in the

child: Significance of analytic and reflective attitudes. *Psychological Monographs,* 1964, **78**, No. 1 (Whole No. 578).

KAGAN, J. The growth of the "face schema": Theoretical significance and methodological issues. In J. Hellmuth, ed., *Exceptional infant.* New York: Brunner/Mazel, 1967, **1**, 337–348.

KAGAN, J. The concept of intelligence. *The Humanist,* January/February, 1972, **32**, 7–8.

KAGAN, J., HOSKEN, B., & WATSON, S. The child's symbolic conceptualization of the parents. *Child Development,* 1961, **32**, 625–636.

KAGAN, J., & MOSS, H. A. The stability of passive and dependent behavior from childhood through adulthood. *Child Development,* 1960, **31**, 577–591.

KAGAN, J. MOSS, H. A., & SIGEL, I. E. Psychological significance of styles of conceptualization. *Monographs of the Society for Research in Child Development,* 1963, **28**, No. 2.

KALISH, R. A. A continuum of subjectively perceived death. *Gerontologist,* 1966, **6**, 73–76.

KALLMANN, F. J. *The genetics of schizophrenia.* Locust Valley, N.Y.: J. J. Augustin, Publisher, 1938.

KALTER, H., & WARKANY, J. Experimental production of congenital malformation in mammals by metabolic procedures. *Physiological Review,* 1959, **39**, 69–115.

KAMII, C. K., & RADIN, N. L. Class differences in the socialization practices of Negro mothers. *Journal of Marriage and Family,* 1967, **29**, 302–310.

KANNER, L. Autistic disturbances of affective contact. *Nervous Child,* 1943, **2**, 217–250.

KANNER, L. Do behavior symptoms always indicate psychopathology? *Journal of Child Psychology and Psychiatry,* 1960, **1**, 17–25.

KARLSSON, J. L. *The biologic basis of schizophrenia.* Springfield, Ill.: Charles C. Thomas, Publisher, 1966.

KARNES, M. B., HODGINS, A. S., TESKA, J., & KIRK, S. *Investigation of classroom and at-home intervention. Research and development program on preschool disadvantaged children: final report.* Vol. I. University of Illinois, Urbana: Institute for Research on Exceptional Children, May 1969.

KARNES, M. B., TESKA, J. A., HODGINS, A. S., & BADGER, E. D. Educational intervention at home by mother of disadvantaged infants *Child Development,* 1970, **41**, 925–935.

KASTENBAUM, R. Death as a research problem in social gerontology: An overview. *Gerontologist,* 1966a, **6**, 67–69.

KASTENBAUM, R. The mental life of dying geriatric patients. *Proceedings of the 7th International Congress of Gerontology,* Vienna, 1966b, **6**, 153–159.

KASTENBAUM, R., & AISENBERG, R. B. *The psychology of death.* New York: Springer, 1972.

KATKOVSKY, W., CRANDALL, V. C., & GOOD, S. Parental antecedents of children's beliefs in internal-external control of reinforcements in intellectual achievement situations. *Child Develpoment,* 1967, **38**, 765–776.

KAWIN, E. & HOEFER, C. *A comparative study of a nursery school versus a non-nursery school group.* Chicago: University of Chicago Press, 1931.

KELLOGG, W. N., & KELLOGG, L. A. *The ape and the child: A study of environmental influence upon early behavior.* New York: McGraw-Hill, 1933.

KEMPLER, B. Stimulus correlates of area

judgments: A psychophysical developmental study. *Developmental Psychology,* 1971, **4,** 158–163.

KENDLER, H. H. *Basic psychology.* (2nd ed.) New York: Appleton-Century-Crofts, 1968.

KENDLER, H. H., & KENDLER, T. S. Vertical and horizontal processes in problem-solving. *Psychological Review,* 1962, **69,** 1–16.

KENDLER, T. S. Development of mediating responses in children. In J. C. Wright and J. Kagan, eds., *Basic cognitive processes in children.* Monographs of the Society for Research in Child Development, 1963, **28,** 33–51.

KENDLER, T. S., KENDLER, H. H., & LEARNARD, B. Mediated responses to size and brightness as a function of age. *American Journal of Psychology,* 1962, **75,** 571–586.

KENNEDY, W. A. A follow-up normative study of Negro intelligence and achievement. *Monographs of the Society for Research in Child Development,* 1969, **34,** Serial No. 126.

KENNEDY, W. A., VAN DE RIET, V., & WHITE, J. C., JR. A normative sample of intelligence and achievement of Negro elementary school children in the southeastern United States. *Monographs of the Society for Research in Child Development,* 1963, **28,** No. 6.

KENT, N., & DAVIS, D. R. Discipline in the home and intellectual development. *British Journal of Medical Psychology,* 1957, **30,** 27–33.

KESSEN, W. Research in the psychological development of infants: An overview. *Merrill-Palmer Quarterly,* 1963, **9,** 83–94.

KESSEN, W. *The child.* New York: Wiley, 1965.

KESSEN, W., & LEUTZENDORFF, A. M.

The effect of non-nutritive sucking on movement in the human newborn. *Journal of Comparative and Physiological Psychology,* 1963, **56,** 69–72.

KESSEN, W., SALAPATEK, P., & HAITH, M. M. The ocular orientation of newborn infants to visual contours. Paper presented at the meeting of the Psychonomic Society, Chicago, October 1965.

KESSEN, W., WILLIAMS, E. J., & WILLIAMS, J. P. Selection and test of response measures in the study of the human newborn. *Child Development,* 1961, **32,** 7–24.

KESSLER, J. W. *Psychopathology of childhood.* Englewood Cliffs, N.J.: Prentice-Hall, Inc., 1966.

KETY, S. S., ROSENTHAL, D., WENDER, P. H., & SCHULSINGER, F. The types and prevalence of mental illness in the biological and adoptive families of adopted schizophrenics. In Rosenthal and Kety, eds., 1968, pp. 345–362. [See p. 644.]

KEYS, N. The underage student in high school and college. *University of California Public Education,* 1938, **7,** 145–272.

KINGSLEY, R. C., & HALL, V. Training conservation through the use of learning sets. *Child Development,* 1967, **38,** 111–126.

KIRK, S. A. *Educating exceptional children.* 2nd ed. Boston: Houghton-Mifflin, 1972.

KLAPPER, J. T. The impact of viewing "aggression": Studies and problems of extrapolation. In O. N. Larsen, ed., *Violence and the mass media.* New York: Harper & Row, 1968.

KLINEBERG, S. L. Future time perspective and the preference for delayed reward. *Journal of Personality and Social Psychology,* 1968, **8,** 253–257.

KNAPP, P. Symposium: expression of

emotions in man. Annual meeting, American Association for the Advancement of Science, 1960.

KNAPP, R. H., & GOODRICH, H. B. *Origins of American scientists.* Chicago: University of Chicago Press, 1952.

KNAPP, R. H., & GREENBAUM, J. J. *The younger American scholar: His collegiate origins.* Chicago: University of Chicago Press, 1953.

KNOBLOCH, H., & PASAMANICK, B. Seasonal variations in the births of the mentally deficient. *American Journal of Public Health,* 1958, **48,** 1201–1208.

KNOX, D. H. Conceptions of love at three developmental levels. *The Family Coordinator,* 1970, **19,** 151–157.

KNOX, D. H., & SPORAKOWSKI, M. J. Attitudes of college students toward love. *Journal of Marriage and the Family,* 1968, **30,** 638–642.

KOESTENBAUM, P. The vitality of death. *Journal of Existentialism,* 1964, **5,** 139–166.

KOGAN, N., & SHELTON, F. C. Images of "old people" and "people in general" in an older sample. *Journal of Genetic Psychology,* 1962, **100,** 3–21.

KOGAN, N., & WALLACH, M. A. Age changes in values and attitudes. *Journal of Gerontology,* 1961, **16,** 272–280.

KOHLBERG, L. The development of children's orientations toward a moral order: I. Sequence in the development of moral thought. *Vita Humana,* 1963, **6,** 11–33.

KOHLBERG, L. A cognitive-developmental analysis of children's sex-role concepts and attitudes. In E. E. Maccoby, ed., *The development of sex differences.* Stanford: Stanford University Press, 1966, pp. 82–173.

KOHLBERG, L. Moral and religious education and the public schools: A developmental view. In T. Sizer, ed., *Religion and public education.* Boston: Houghton-Mifflin, 1967.

KOHLBERG, L. Stage and sequence: The cognitive-developmental approach to socialization. In D. A. Goslin, ed., *Handbook of socialization theory and research.* Chicago: Rand McNally, 1969, pp. 347–480.

KOHLBERG, L., LA CROSSE, J., & RICKS, D. The predictability of adult mental health from childhood behavior. In B. Wolman, ed., *Manual of child psychopathology.* New York: McGraw-Hill, 1972, pp. 1217–1283.

KOHN, M. L. Social class and parent-child relationships: An interpretation. *American Journal of Sociology,* 1963, **68,** 471–480.

KORSLUND, M. K., & EPPRIGHT, E. S. Taste sensitivity and eating behavior of preschool children. *Journal of Home Economics,* 1967, **59,** 168–170.

KRAUSS, R. M., & WEINHEIMER, S. Changes in reference phrases as a function of frequency of usage in social interaction: A preliminary study. *Psychonomic Science,* 1964, **1,** 343–346.

KREPS, J. M. Economics of retirement. In E. W. Busse and E. Pfeiffer, eds., *Behavior and adaptation in later life.* Boston: Little, Brown, 1969.

KUHLEN, R. G. & THOMPSON, G. G. *Psychological studies of human development.* New York: Appleton-Century-Crofts, 1970.

KURKE, M. The role of motor experience in the visual discrimination of depth in the chick. *Journal of Genetic Psychology,* 1955, **86,** 191–196.

KUTNER, B., FANSHEL, D., TOGO, A., & LANGNER, T. S. Factors related to adjustment in old age. In R. G. Kuhlen and G. G. Thompson, eds., *Psychological studies of human development.* New York: Appleton-Century-Crofts, 1970, pp. 583–595.

LABOV, W., COHEN, P., ROBINS, C., & LEWIS, J. *A study of the non-standard English of Negro and Puerto Rican speakers in New York City.* 2 vols. Final Report, U.S. Office of Education Cooperative Research Project No. 3288. New York: Columbia University, 1968. (Mimeographed.)

LANDRETH, C. *Early childhood: Behavior and learning.* New York: Knopf, 1967.

LANGE-EICHBAUM, W. *The problem of genius.* New York: Macmillan, 1932.

LANGER, J. *Theories of development.* New York: Holt, Rinehart, & Winston, 1969.

LANGFORD, W. Anxiety attacks in children. *American Journal of Orthopsychiatry,* 1937, **7,** 210–219.

LASHLEY, K. S., & RUSSELL, J. T. The mechanism of vision: XI. A preliminary test of innate organization. *Journal of Genetic Psychology,* 1934, **45,** 136–144.

LATANÉ, B., & RODIN, J. A lady in distress: Inhibiting effects of friends and strangers on bystander intervention. *Journal of Experimental Social Psychology,* 1969, **5,** 189–203.

LAZARUS, A. The result of behavior therapy in 126 cases of severe neuroses. *Behavior Research and Therapy,* 1963, **1,** 69–79.

LEARNED, W. S., & WOOD, B. D. The student and his knowledge. *Carnegie Foundation Advanced Teaching Bulletin,* 1938, No. 29.

LEARY, M. E. Children who are tested in an alien language: Mentally retarded? *The New Republic,* 1970, **162,** 17–18.

LEFKOWITZ, M. M., ERON, L. D., WALDER, L. O., & HUESMANN, L. R. Television violence and child aggression: A followup study. In G. A. Comstock and E. A. Rubinstein, eds., *Television and social behavior,* Vol. III: *Television and adolescent aggressiveness.* Washington, D.C.: U. S. Government Printing Office, 1972, pp. 35–135.

LE FURGY, W. G., & WOLOSHIN, G. W. Immediate and long-term effects of experimentally induced social influence in the modification of adolescents' moral judgments. *Journal of Personality and Social Psychology,* 1969, **12,** 104–110.

LEHMAN, H. C. *Age and achievement.* Princeton: Princeton University Press, 1953.

LEIFER, A. D., & ROBERTS, D. F. Children's responses to television violence. In J. P. Murray, E. A. Rubinstein, and G. A. Comstock, eds., *Television and social behavior,* Vol. II: *Television and social learning.* Washington, D.C.: U.S. Government Printing Office, 1972, pp. 43–180.

LENNEBERG, E. H. *Biological foundations of language.* New York: Wiley, 1967.

LENNOX, W. G., GIBBS, E. L., & GIBBS, F. A. Inheritance of cerebral dysrhythmia and epilepsy. *Archives of Neurological Psychiatry,* 1940, **44,** 1155.

LERNER, I. M. *Heredity, evolution and society.* San Francisco: W. H. Freeman and Co., 1968.

LESSER, G. Mental abilities of children in different social and cultural groups. New York: Cooperative Research Project No. 1635, 1964.

LESSER, G. H., FIFER, G., & CLARK, D. H. Mental abilities of children from different social-class and cultural groups. *Monographs of the Society for Research in Child Development,* 1965, **30,** (4, Whole No. 102).

LEVENTHAL, A. S., & LIPSITT, L. P. Adaptation, pitch discrimination, and sound localization in the neonate. *Child Development,* 1964, **35,** 759–767.

LEVINE, M. Mediating processes at the outset of discrimination learning. *Psychological Review,* 1963, **70,** 254–276.

LEVINE, M. Hypothesis behavior by humans during discrimination learning. *Journal of Experimental Psychology,* 1966, **71,** 331–338.

LEVINE, S. Infantile experience and resistance to psychological stress. *Science,* 1957, **126,** 405.

LEVITT, E. E. The results of psychotherapy with children: An evaluation. *Journal of Consulting Psychology,* 1957, **21,** 189–196.

LEVITT, E. E. Psychotherapy with children: A further evaluation. *Behavior Research and Therapy,* 1963, **1,** 45–51.

LEVY, D. *Maternal overprotection.* New York: Columbia University Press, 1943.

LEWIS, M. M. *Infant speech: A study of the beginnings of language.* New York: Harcourt, Brace, 1936.

LIEBERMAN, M. A. Psychological correlates of impending death: Some preliminary observations. *Journal of Gerontology,* 1965, **20,** 182–190.

LIEBERMAN, M. A., & COPLAN, A. S. Distance from death as a variable in the study of aging. *Developmental Psychology,* 1970, **2,** 71–84.

LIEBERT, R. M. Television and social learning: Some relationships between viewing violence and behaving aggressively. In J. P. Murray, E. A. Rubinstein, and G. A. Comstock, eds., *Television and social behavior,* Vol. II: *Television and social learning.* Washington, D.C.: U.S. Government Printing Office, 1972, pp. 1–43.

LIEBERT, R. M., & ALLEN, M. K. The effects of rule structure and reward magnitude on the acquisition and adoption of self-reward criteria. *Psychological Reports,* 1967, **21,** 445–452.

LIEBERT, R. M., & ALLEN, M. K. Effects of a model's experience on children's imitation. *Psychonomic Science,* 1969, **4,** 198.

LIEBERT, R. M. & BARON, R. A. Some immediate effects of televised violence on children's behavior. *Developmental Psychology,* 1972, **6,** 469–475.

LIEBERT, R. M., & FERNANDEZ, L. E. Effects of vicarious consequences on imitative performance. *Child Development,* 1970, **41,** 847–852.

LIEBERT, R. M., FERNANDEZ, L. E., & GILL, L. Effects of a "friendless" model on imitation and prosocial behavior. *Psychonomic Science,* 1969, **16,** 81–82.

LIEBERT, R. M., HANRATTY, M., & HILL, J. H. Effects of rule structure and training method on the adoption of a self-imposed standard. *Child Development,* 1969, **40,** 93–101.

LIEBERT, R. M., McCALL, R. B. & HANRATTY, M. A. Effects of sex-typed information on children's toy preferences. *Journal of Genetic Psychology,* 1971, **119,** 133–136.

LIEBERT, R. M., ODOM, R. D., & POULOS, R. W. *Language development in the mentally retarded.* Final Report, Project No. RD–2952–S–69, Social and Rehabilitation Service, Department of Health, Education, and Welfare, 1971.

LIEBERT, R. M., ODOM, R. D., HILL, J., & HUFF, R. Effects of age and rule familiarity on the production of modeled language constructions. *Developmental Psychology,* 1969, **1,** 108–112.

LIEBERT, R. M., & ORA, J. P. Children's adoption of self-reward patterns: Incentive level and method of transmission. *Child Development,* 1968, **39,** 537–544.

LIEBERT, R. M., SOBOL, M. P., & COPEMANN, C. D. Effects of vicarious consequences and race of model upon imitative performance by black children. *Developmental Psychology,* 1972, **6,** 453–456.

LIEBERT, R. M., & SPIEGLER, M. D. *Personality: An introduction to theory and research.* Homewood, Ill.: The Dorsey Press, 1970.

LIEBERT, R. M., SPIEGLER, M. D. & HALL, M. Effects of the value of contingent self-administered and noncontingent externally imposed reward on children's behavioral productivity. *Psychonomic Science,* 1970, **18,** 245–246.

LINDEMANN, E. Symptomatology and management of acute grief. *American Journal of Psychiatry,* 1944, **101,** 141–148.

LIPSITT, L. P., ENGEN, T., & KAYE, H. Developmental changes in the olfactory threshold of the neonate. *Child Development,* 1963, **34,** 371–376.

LIPSITT, L. P., & LEVY, N. Electrotactual threshold in the neonate. *Child Development,* 1959, **30,** 547–554.

LONDON, P. *The modes and morals of psychotherapy.* New York: Holt, Rinehart & Winston, Inc., 1964.

LONDON, P., & HEMPHILL, B. M. The motivations of blood donors. *Transfusion,* 1965, **5,** 559–568.

LONG, R. T., LAMONT, J. H., WHIPPLE, B., BANDLER, L., BLOM, G. E., BURGIN, L., & JESSNER, L. A psychosomatic study of allergic and emotional factors in children with asthma. *American Journal of Psychiatry,* 1958, **114,** 890–899.

LORENZ, K. The companion in the bird's world. *Auk,* 1937, **54,** 245–273.

LOVAAS, O. I. Cue properties of words: The control of operant responding by rate and content of verbal operants. *Child Development,* 1964, **35,** 245–256.

LOVAAS, O. I. Some studies on the treatment of childhood schizophrenia. In J. M. Shlien, ed., *Research in psychotherapy: Proceedings of the third conference.* Washington, D.C.: American Psychological Association, 1968, pp. 103–121.

LOVAAS, O. I., BERBERICH, J. P., PERLOFF, B. F. & SCHAEFFER, B. Acquisition of imitative speech by schizophrenic children. *Science,* 1966, **151,** 705–707.

LOVELL, K., & OGILVIE, E. The growth of the concept of volume in junior school children. *Journal of Child Psychology and Psychiatry,* 1961, **2,** 118–126.

LOVIBOND, S. H. *Conditioning and enuresis.* New York: Macmillan, 1964.

LOVITT, T. Behavior modification: The current scene. *Exceptional Children,* 1970, **37,** 85–91.

LOWENSTEIN, W. R. Biological transducers. *Scientific American,* 1960, **203,** 98–104.

LUBCHENCO, L. O., HORNER, F. A., REED, L. H., HIX, I. E., METCALF, D., COHIG, R. ELLIOTT, H. C. & BOURG, M. Sequelae of premature birth. *American Journal of Diseases of Children,* 1963, **106,** 101–115.

LUNDIN, R. W. *Personality.* New York: Macmillan, 1961.

LURIA, A. R. The genesis of voluntary movements. In N. O'Connor, ed., *Recent Soviet psychology.* New York: Liverwright, 1961, pp. 273–289.

McCALL, R. B. Intelligence quotient pattern over age: Comparisons among siblings and parent-child pairs. *Science,* 1970, **170,** 644–648.

McCAMMAN, D., KREPS, J. M., SCHULZ, J. H., BREWSTER, A. W., & SHEPPARD, H. L. Economics of aging: Toward a full share in abundance. Prepared for the Special Committee on Aging, U.S. Senate, 91st Congress, 1st session, March 1969.

McCANDLESS, B. R. Environment and intelligence. *American Journal of Mental Deficiency,* 1952, **56,** 674–691.

McCANDLESS, B. R. *Children.* 2nd ed. New York: Holt, Rinehart & Winston, 1967.

McCANDLESS, B. R., BILOUS, C. B., & BENNETT, H. L. Peer popularity and dependence on adults in preschool-age socialization. *Child Development,* 1961, **32,** 511–518.

McCARTHY, D. Language development in children. In L. Carmichael, ed., *Manual of child psychology.* 2nd ed. New York: Wiley, 1954, pp. 492–630.

McCARTNEY, W. *Olfaction and odours.* New York: Springer-Verlag, 1968.

McCLEARN, G. E. The inheritance of behavior. In L. Postman, ed., *Psychology in the making.* New York: Knopf, 1963, pp. 144–252.

McCLELLAND, D. C. The importance of early learning in the formation of motives. In J. Atkinson, ed., *Motives in fantasy, action and society.* Princeton: Van Nostrand, 1958.

McCLELLAND, D. C. *The achieving society.* Princeton, N.J.: Van Nostrand, 1961.

McCLELLAND, D. C., ATKINSON, I. W., CLARK, R., & LOWELL, E. *The achievement motive.* New York: Appleton-Century-Crofts, 1953.

MACCOBY, E. E. Sex differences in intellectual functioning. In E. E. Maccoby, ed., *The Development of Sex Differences.* Stanford: Stanford University Press, 1966, pp. 25–55.

McDAVID, J. W. Imitative behavior in preschool children. *Psychological Monographs,* 1959, **73** (Whole No. 486).

MACFARLANE, J. W., ALLEN, L., & HONZIK, M. P. *A developmental study of the behavior problems of normal children.* Berkeley: University of California Press, 1954.

McGRAW, M. G. *Growth: A study of Johnny and Jimmy.* New York: Appleton-Century, 1935.

McHUGH, G. Changes in IQ at the public school kindergarten level. *Psychological Monographs,* 1943, **55,** No. 2.

McINTYRE, J. J., & TEEVAN, J. J. Television violence and deviant behavior. In G. A. Comstock and E. A. Rubinstein, eds., *Television and social behavior,* Vol. III: *Television and adolescent agressiveness.* Washington, D.C.: U.S. Government Printing Office, 1972, pp. 202–317.

MACKINNON, D. W. The nature and nurture of creative talent. *American Psychologist,* 1962, **17,** 484–495.

MACKINNON, D. W. Selecting students with creative potential. In P. Heist, ed., *The creative college student: An unmet challenge.* San Francisco: Jossey-Bass, 1968.

McLEOD, J. M., ATKIN, C. K., & CHAFFEE, S. H. Adolescents, parents and television use: Adolescent self-report measures from Maryland and Wisconsin samples. In G. A. Comstock and E. A. Rubinstein, eds., *Television and social behavior,* Vol. III: *Television and adolescent aggressiveness.* Washington, D.C.:

U.S. Government Printing Office, 1972, pp. 173–238.

McMahon, A. W., Jr., & Rhudick, P. J. Reminiscing in the aged: An adaptational response. In S. Levin and R. J. Kahana, eds., *Psychodynamic studies on aging: Creativity, reminiscing, and dying.* New York: International Universities Press, 1967.

McMains, M. J., & Liebert, R. M. The influence of discrepancies between successively modeled self-reward criteria on the adoption of a self-imposed standard. *Journal of Personality and Social Psychology,* 1968, **8,** 166–171.

McNeil, E. B. *The concept of human development.* Belmont, California: Wadsworth Publishing Co., 1966.

McNeill, D. *The acquisition of language.* New York: Harper & Row, 1970a.

McNeill, D. The development of language. In P. Mussen, ed., *Carmichael's Manual of Child Psychology.* New York: Wiley, 1970b, pp. 1061–1161.

McNemar, Q. *The revision of the Stanford-Binet Scale: An analysis of the standardization data.* Boston: Houghton Mifflin, 1942.

MacRae, J. M. Retests of children given mental tests as infants. *Journal of Genetic Psychology,* 1955, **87,** 111–119.

Maddox, G. L., & McCall, B. C. *Drinking among teen-agers.* New Brunswick, N.J.: Rutgers Center of Alcohol Studies, 1964.

Mahrer, A. R. The role of expectancy in delayed reinforcement. *Journal of Experimental Psychology,* 1956, **52,** 101–105.

Maier, H. W. *Three theories of child development.* New York: Harper & Row, 1969.

Marihuana and health. Department of Health, Education and Welfare, Washington, D.C.: U.S. Government Printing Office, 1971.

Marland, S. P. *Education of the gifted and talented.* Vol. I: *Report to the Congress of the United States by the U.S. Commissioner of Education.* August 1971.

Marquis, D. P. Can conditioned responses be established in the newborn infant? *Journal of Genetic Psychology,* 1931, **39,** 479–492.

Marshall, H. R. Relations between home experiences and children's use of language in play interactions with peers. *Psychological Monographs,* 1961, **75** (Whole No. 509).

Marshall, H. R., & McCandless, B. R. Relationships between dependence on adults and social acceptance by peers. *Child Development,* 1957, **28,** 413–419.

Martinson, R. A. *Educational programs for gifted children.* Sacramento: California State Department of Public Instruction, 1961.

Martinson, R. A. Analysis of problems and priorities: Advocate survey and statistical sources. Appendix B. In Marland, 1971, pp. B1–B35.

Masters, W. H., & Johnson, V. E. *Human sexual response.* Boston: Little, Brown, 1966.

Mateer, F. *Child behavior: A critical and experimental study of young children by the method of conditioned reflexes.* Boston: R. G. Badger, 1918.

Matza, D. Subterranean traditions of youth. *The Annals of the American Academy of Political and Social Sciences,* 1961, **338,** 102–118.

May, R. *The meaning of anxiety.* New York: Ronald Press, 1950.

Meade, M. *Sex and temperament in*

three primitive societies. New York: Morrow, 1935.

MEDNICK, M. T. Research creativity in psychology graduate students. *Journal of Consulting Psychology,* 1963, **23,** 827–830.

MEDNICK, S. A., & SCHULSINGER, F. Some premorbid characteristics related to breakdown in children with schizophrenic mothers. Paper presented at the Conference on Transmission of Schizophrenia. Dorado Beach, Puerto Rico, 1967.

MELZACK, R. The perception of pain. *Scientific American,* February 1961.

MENDEL, G. Experiments in plant-hybridization, 1865. Reprinted in J. A. Peters, ed., *Classic papers in genetics.* Englewood Cliffs, N.J.: Prentice-Hall, Inc., 1959, pp. 1–20.

MEYER, R., SHIPMAN, V., & HESS, R. D. Family structure and social class in the socialization of curiosity in urban preschool children. Paper presented at APA meeting, Los Angeles, September 1964.

MIDLARKSY, E., & BRYAN, J. H. Training charity in children. *Journal of Personality and Social Psychology,* 1967, **5,** 408–415.

MILLER, G. A., GALANTER, E., & PRIBRAM, K. H. *Plans and the structure of behavior.* New York: Holt, 1960.

MILLER, N. E., & DOLLARD, J. *Social learning and imitation.* New Haven: Yale University Press, 1941, 1953.

MILLER, W., & ERVIN, S. The development of grammar in child language. In U. Bellugi and R. Brown, eds., The acquisition of language. *Monographs of the Society for Research in Child Development,* 1964, **29** (1, Whole No. 92), 9–34.

MILLON, T. *Modern psychopathology: A biosocial approach to maladaptive learning and functioning.* Philadelphia: Saunders, 1969.

MINUCHIN, P. Sex-role concepts and sex-typing in childhood as a function of school and home environments. *Child Development,* 1965, **36,** 1033–1048.

MISCHEL, W. Preference for delayed reinforcement: An experimental study of a cultural observation. *Journal of Abnormal and Social Psychology,* 1958, **56,** 57–61.

MISCHEL, W. Delay of gratification, need for achievement, and acquiescence in another culture. *Journal of Abnormal and Social Psychology,* 1961a, **62,** 543–552.

MISCHEL, W. Father-absence and delay of gratification: Cross-cultural comparisons. *Journal of Abnormal and Social Psychology,* 1961b, **62,** 116–124.

MISCHEL, W. Preference for delayed reinforcement and social responsibility. *Journal of Abnormal and Social Psychology,* 1961c, **62,** 1–7.

MISCHEL, W. Theory and research on the antecedents of self-imposed delay of reward. In B. A. Maher, ed., *Progress in experimental personality research.* New York: Academic Press, 1966, **3,** 85–132.

MISCHEL, W. *Personality and assessment.* New York: Wiley, 1968.

MISCHEL, W. *Introduction to personality.* New York: Holt, Rinehart, & Winston, 1971.

MISCHEL, W., & EBBESEN, E. Attention to delay of gratification. *Journal of Personality and Social Psychology,* 1970, **16,** 329–337.

MISCHEL, W., EBBESEN, E., & RASKOFF, A. Cognitive and attentional mechanisms in delay of gratification. Unpublished manuscript, Stanford University, 1971.

MISCHEL, W., & GILLIGAN, C. F. Delay of gratification, motivation for the prohibited gratification, and responses to temptation. *Journal of Abnormal and Social Psychology,* 1964, **69,** 411–417.

MISCHEL, W., GRUSEC, J., & MASTERS, J. C. Effects of expected delay time on the subjective value of rewards and punishments. *Journal of Personality and Social Psychology,* 1969, **11,** 363–373.

MISCHEL, W., & LIEBERT, R. M. Effects of discrepancies between observed and imposed reward criteria on their acquisition and transmission. *Journal of Personality and Social Psychology,* 1966, **3,** 45–53.

MISCHEL, W., & METZNER, R. Preference for delayed reward as a function of age, intelligence, and length of delay interval. *Journal of Abnormal and Social Psychology,* 1962, **64,** 425–431.

MISCHEL, W., & MISCHEL, H. The nature and development of psychological sex differences. In G. S. Lesser, ed., *Psychology and educational practice.* Glenview, Ill.: Scott, Foresman, 1971, pp. 357–379.

MISCHEL, W., & STAUB, E. Effects of expectancy on waiting and working for larger rewards. *Journal of Personality and Social Psychology,* 1965, **2,** 625–633.

MITFORD, J. *The American way of death.* London: Hutchinson, 1963.

MOHR, G. J., TAUS, H., SELESNICK, S. & AUGENBRAUN, B. Studies of eczema and asthma in the pre-school child. *Journal of American Academic Child Psychiatry,* 1963, **2,** 271–291.

MOORE, K. C. The mental development of a child. *Psychological Review Monographs Supplement,* 1896, **3.**

MOWRER, O. H. *Learning theory and the symbolic processes.* New York: Wiley, 1960.

MOWRER, O. H. Freudianism, behavior therapy and "self-disclosure." *Behavior Research and Therapy,* 1964, **1**(4), 321–337.

MOWRER, O. H., & MOWRER, W. M. Enuresis: A method for its study and treatment. *American Journal of Orthopsychiatry,* 1938, **8,** 436–447.

MOWRER, O. H., & ULLMAN, A. D. Time as a determinant in integrative learning. *Psychological Review,* 1945, **52,** 61–90.

MUNN, N. L. *Psychology: The fundamentals of human adjustment.* Boston: Houghton Mifflin, 1946.

MUNROE, R. *Schools of psychoanalytic thought.* New York: Holt, Rinehart, & Winston, 1955.

MUSSEN, P. H. Early sex-role development. In D. A. Goslin, ed., *Handbook of socialization theory and research.* Chicago: Rand McNally, 1969, pp. 707–731.

NEALE, J. M., & LIEBERT, R. M. Reinforcement therapy using aides and patients as behavioral technicians: A case report of a mute psychotic. *Perceptual and Motor Skills,* 1969, **28,** 835–839.

NEALEY, S. M., & EDWARDS, B. J. "Depth perception" in rats without pattern vision experience. *Journal of Comparative Physiological Psychology,* 1960, **53,** 468–469.

NELSON, M. M., ASLING, C. W., & EVANS, H. M. Production of multiple congenital abnormalities in young by pteroylglutamic acid deficiency during gestation. *Journal of Nutrition,* 1952, **48,** 61–80.

NEUGARTEN, B. L. A new look at menopause. *Psychology Today,* December 1967.

NEUGARTEN, B. L., WOOD, V. KRAINES, R. J., & LOOMIS, B. Women's attitudes toward the menopause. *Vita Humana,* 1963, **6,** 140–151.

NEWBERRY, H. Studies in fetal behavior, IV: The measurement of three types of fetal activity. *Journal of Comparative Psychology,* 1941, **32,** 521–530.

NEWMAN, G., & NICHOLS, C. R. Sexual activities and attitudes in older persons. *Journal of the American Medical Association,* 1960, **173,** 33–35.

NEWMAN, H. H., FREEMAN, F. N., & HOLZINGER, K. J. *Twins: A study of heredity and environment.* Chicago: University of Chicago Press, 1937.

NIMNICHT, G. P. A model program for young children that responds to the child. Paper prepared for Conference on Conceptualization of Preschool Curricula, The City University of New York, May 1970.

NISSEN, H. W., CHOW, K. L., & SEMMES, J. Effects of restricted opportunity for tactile, kinaesthetic and manipulative experience on the behavior of a chimpanzee. *American Journal of Psychology,* 1951, **64,** 485–507.

NOWLIS, H. H. *Drugs on the college campus.* New York: Doubleday, 1969.

NUNNALLY, J. C., DUCHNOWSKI, A. J., & PARKER, R. K. Association of neutral objects with rewards: Effects on verbal evaluation, reward expectancy, and selective attention. *Journal of Personality and Social Psychology,* 1965, **1,** 270–274.

NUNNALLY, J. C., STEVENS, D. A., & HALL, G. F. Association of neutral objects with rewards: Effect on verbal evaluation and eye movements. *Journal of Experimental Child Psychology,* 1965, **2,** 44–57.

O'CONNER, N., & TIZARD, J. *The social problems of mental deficiency.* New York: Pergamon Press, 1956.

O'CONNOR, R. D. Modification of social withdrawal through symbolic modeling. *Journal of Applied Behavior Analysis,* 1969, **2,** 15–22.

ODOM, R. D., & COON, R. C. The development of hypothesis testing. *Journal of Experimental Child Psychology,* 1966, **4,** 285–291.

ODOM, R. D., LIEBERT, R. M., & HILL, J. H. The effects of modeling cues, reward, and attentional set on the production of grammatical and ungrammatical syntactic constructions. *Journal of Experimental Child Psychology,* 1968, **6,** 131–140.

O'LEARY, K. D. The effects of self-instruction on immoral behavior. *Journal of Experimental Child Psychology,* 1968, **6,** 297–301.

O'LEARY, K. D., & O'LEARY, S. G. *Classroom management.* New York: Pergamon Press, 1972.

O'LEARY, K. D., POULOS, R. W., & DEVINE, V. T. Tangible reinforcers: Bonuses or bribes? *Journal of Consulting and Clinical Psychology,* 1972, **38,** 1–8.

OLIM, E. G., HESS, R. D., & SHIPMAN, V. Relationship between mothers' language styles and cognitive styles of urban preschool children. Paper presented at Biennial Meeting of Social Research and Child Development, Minneapolis, Minnesota, March 1965.

PALERMO, D. S. Language acquisition. In H. Reese and L. Lipsitt, eds., *Experimental child psychology.* New York: Academic Press, 1970.

PALMER, F. H. Inferences to the socialization of the child from animal studies: A view from the bridge. In D. A. Goslin, ed., *Handbook of socialization theory and research.* Chicago: Rand McNally, 1969, pp. 25–55.

PALMORE, E., & JEFFERS, F. C. Health care in a longitudinal panel before and after medicare. *Journal of Gerontology,* 1971, **26,** 532–536.

PANKOVE, E., & KOGAN, N. Creative

ability and risk-taking in elementary school children. *Journal of Personality,* 1968, **36,** 420–439.

PAPOUŠEK, H. A physiological view of early ontogenesis of so-called voluntary movements. In P. Sobotka, ed., *Functional and metabolic development of the central nervous system.* Prague: State Pedagogic Publishers, 1961.

PARKE, R. D. Nurturance, nurturance withdrawal, and resistance to deviation. *Child Development,* 1967, **38,** 1101–1110.

PARKE, R. D. Effectiveness of punishment as an interaction of intensity, timing, agent nurturance and cognitive structuring. *Child Development,* 1969, **40,** 213–235.

PARKE, R. D. The role of punishment in the socialization process. In R. A. Hoppe, G. A. Milton, & E. C. Simmel, eds., *Early experiences and the processes of socialization.* New York: Academic Press, 1970, pp. 81–108.

PARKE, R. D., ed. *Recent trends in social learning theory.* New York: Academic Press, 1972.

PARKER, R. K., & NUNNALLY, J. C. Association of neutral objects with rewards: Effects of reward schedules on reward expectancy, verbal evaluation, and selective attention. *Journal of Experimental Child Psychology,* 1966, **3,** 324–332.

PARTENAN, J., BRUUN, K., & MARK-KANEN, T. *Inheritance of drinking behavior.* Helsinki: Finnish Foundation for Alcohol Studies, 1966.

PASAMANICK, B. A comparative study of the behavior development of Negro infants. *Journal of Genetic Psychology,* 1946, **69,** 3–44.

PASAMANICK, B., ROGERS, M. E., & LILIENFELD, A. M. Pregnancy experience and the development of behavior disorder in children. *American Journal of Psychiatry,* 1956, **112,** 613–618.

PATTERSON, G. R., LITTMAN, R. A., & BRICKER, W. Assertive behavior in children: A step toward a theory of aggression. *Monographs of the Society for Research in Child Development,* 1967, **32**(5).

PAVLOV, I. P. *Conditioned reflexes.* New York: Liveright, 1927.

PAYNE, E. C., JR. The physician and his patient who is dying. In S. Levin and R. J. Kahana, eds., *Psychodynamic studies on aging: Creativity, reminiscing, and dying* New York: International Universities Press, 1967.

PEIPER, A. Sinnesempfindungen des Kindes vor seiner. *Geburt. Wschr. Kinderheilk.,* 1925, **29,** 236–241.

PEIPER, A. *Die Eigenart der Kindlichen Hirntatigkeit* (2nd. ed.). Leipzig: Thieme, 1956.

PEREZ, B. *Les trois premières années de l'enfant de trois à sept ans.* Paris: Ballière et Cie, 1878.

PESTALOZZI, J. H. *Sammtlich Werke.* Liegnitz: Seyffarth, 1889–1902.

PETERSON, I. J. A preliminary study of the effects of previous nursery school attendance upon the first-year children entering kindergartens. *Studies in preschool Education,* Iowa City: University of Iowa, 1937, pp. 197–248.

PFEIFFER, E., VERWOERDT, A., & WANG, H. S. The natural history of sexual behavior in a biologically advantaged group of aged individuals. *Journal of Gerontology,* 1969, **24,** 193–199.

PHILLIPS, S., LIEBERT, R. M., & POULOS, R. W. Employing paraprofessional teachers in a group language training program for severely and profoundly retarded children. *Perceptual and Motor Skills,* 1973, **36,** 607–616.

PIAGET, J. *The language and thought of the child.* New York: Harcourt, Brace, 1926.

PIAGET, J. *The moral judgment of the child.* Glencoe, Ill.: Free Press, 1948.

PIAGET, J. *The child's concept of number.* New York: Norton, 1952a.

PIAGET, J. *The origins of intelligence in children.* New York: International Universities Press, 1952b.

PIAGET, J. *The child's conception of movement and speed.* New York: Basic Books, 1969; London: Routledge and Kegan Paul, 1969, and JEAN PIAGET, *Le Développement de la notion du temps chez l'enfant* (Paris: Presses Universitaires de France, 1946).

PIAGET, J., & INHELDER, B. *Le développement des quantités chez l'enfant.* Neuchâtel: Delachaux and Niestle, 1941.

PIAGET, J., & INHELDER, B. *The psychology of the child.* New York: Basic Books, 1969.

PIAGET, J., INHELDER, B., & SZEMINSKA, A. *The child's conception of geometry.* London: Routledge & Kegan Paul, 1960.

PICK, A. D. Improvement of visual and tactual form discrimination. *Journal of Experimental Psychology,* 1965, **69,** 331–339.

PICK, H. L. Research on taste in the Soviet Union. In M. R. Kare and B. P. Halpern, eds., *Physiological and behavioral aspects of taste.* Chicago: University of Chicago Press, 1961.

PICK, H. L., & PICK, A. D. Sensory and perceptual development. In P. H. Mussen, ed., *Carmichael's manual of child psychology.* New York: Wiley, 1970, **1,** 773–847.

PINE, G. J. The affluent delinquent. *Phi Delta Kappan,* 1966, **48** (4), 138–143.

PINTER, R., DRAGOSITZ, A., & KUSHNER, R. *Supplementary Guide for the Revised Guide for the Revised Stanford-Binet Scale* (Form L). Stanford: Stanford University Press.

PORTER, W. T. The relative growth of individual school boys. *American Journal of Physiology,* 1922, **61,** 311–325; also *Boston Medical and Surgical Journal,* 1923, **188,** 639–644.

POULOS, R. W. & LIEBERT, R. M. Influence of modeling, exhortative verbalization, and surveillance on children's sharing. *Developmental Psychology,* 1972, **6,** 402–408.

PRATT, K. C. The neonate. In L. Carmichael, ed., *Manual of child psychology.* 2nd ed. New York: Wiley, 1954, pp. 215–291.

PRECHTL, H. F. R. The directed head turning response and allied movements of the human baby. *Behavior,* 1958, **13,** 212–242.

PRECHTL, H. F. R. The mother-child interaction in babies with minimal brain damage. In B. M. Foss, ed., *Determinants of infant behavior.* New York: Wiley, 1963, Vol. II, pp. 53–66.

PREMACK, D. A functional analysis of language. *Journal of the Experimental Analysis of Behavior,* 1970, **14,** 107–125.

President's Task Force on Manpower Conservation. *One-third of a nation.* Washington D.C.: U.S. Government Printing Office, 1964.

PRESSEY, S. L. *Educational acceleration: Appraisals and basic problems.* Columbus: Ohio State University Press, 1949.

PREYER, W. *Die Seele des Kindes.* Leipzig: Grieben, 1882.

PURCELL, K., BRADY, K., CHAI, H., MUSER, J., MOLK, L., GORDEN, N., & MEANS, J. The effect on asthma in children of experimental separation from the family. *Psychosomatic Medicine,* 1969, **31**, 144–164.

QUINT, J. C. *The nurse and the dying patient.* New York: Macmillan, 1967.

RAINWATER, L. Crucible of identity: The Negro lower-class family. In C. S. Lavatelli and F. Stendler, eds., *Readings in child behavior and development.* New York: Harcourt, Brace, Javanovich, 1972, pp. 112–126.

RAPAPORT, D. The structure of psychoanalytic theory: A systematizing attempt. In S. Koch, ed., *Psychology: A study of a science,* Vol. III. New York: McGraw-Hill, 1959.

RAPAPORT, D. On the psychoanalytic theory of thinking. In M. M. Gill, ed., *The collected papers of David Rapaport.* New York: Basic Books, 1967.

REES, L. The importance of psychological, allergic and infective factors in childhood asthma. *Journal of Psychosomatic Research,* 1964, **7**, 253–262.

REESE, H. W., & LIPSITT, L. *Experimental child psychology.* New York: Academic Press, 1970.

REESE, H. W., & PARNES, S. J. Programming creative behavior. *Child Development,* 1970, **41**, 413–423.

REIMANIS, G., & GREEN, R. Imminence of death and intellectual decrement in the aging. *Developmental Psychology,* 1971, **5**, 270–272.

RENNER, K. E. Temporal integration: An incentive approach to conflict resolution. In B. A. Maher, ed., *Progress in experimental personality research.* New York: Academic Press, 1967, **4**, 127–177.

RENNINGER, C. A., & WILLIAMS, J. E. Black-white color connotations and racial awareness in preschool children. *Perceptual and Motor Skills,* 1966, **22**, 771–785.

RENSHAW, S. The errors of cutaneous localization and the effect of practice on the localization movement in children and adults. *Journal of Genetic Psychology,* 1930, **28**, 223–238.

REST, J. Developmental hierarchy in preference and comprehension of moral judgment. Unpublished doctoral dissertation, University of Chicago, 1968.

RHEINGOLD, H. L. The modification of social responsiveness in institutional babies. *Monographs of the Society for Research in Child Development,* 1956, **21**(2).

RHEINGOLD, H. L. The measurement of maternal care. *Child Development,* 1960, **31**, 565–575.

RHEINGOLD, H. L., & ECKERMAN, C. O. The infant separates himself from his mother. *Science,* 1970, **168**, 78–83.

RHEINGOLD, H. L., GEWIRTZ, J. L., & ROSS, H. W. Social conditioning of vocalizations in the infant. *Journal of Comparative and Physiological Psychology,* 1959, **52**, 68–73.

RHUDICK, P. J., & DIBNER, A. S. Age, personality and health correlates of death concerns in normal aged individuals. *Journal of Gerontology,* 1961, **16**, 44–49.

RICHARDSON, A. H., & FREEMAN, H. E. Behavior, attitudes and disengagement among the very old. Unpublished manuscript quoted in M. W. Riley and A. Foner, eds., *An inventory of research findings,* Vol. I: *Aging and society.* New York: Russell Sage Foundation, 1968.

RICHMOND, J. B., & LUSTMAN, S. L. Autonomic function in the neonate, I: Implications for psychosomatic theory.

Psychosomatic Medicine, 1955, **17,** 269–275.

RIEGEL, K. F., & RIEGEL, R. M. Development, drop, and death. *Developmental Psychology,* 1972, **6,** 306–319.

RIESEN, A. H. Arrested vision. In R. S. Daniel, ed., *Contemporary readings in general psychology.* Boston: Houghton-Mifflin, 1965, pp. 76–79.

RILEY, J. Attitudes toward death. Unpublished manuscript quoted in M. W. Riley and A. Foner, eds., *An inventory of research findings,* Vol. I: *Aging and society.* New York: Russell Sage Foundation, 1968.

RIMLAND, B. *Infantile autism: The syndrome and its implications for a neural theory of behavior.* New York: Appleton-Century-Crofts, 1964.

RIMLAND, B. The differentiation of childhood psychoses: An analysis of checklists for 2,218 psychotic children. *Journal of Autism and Childhood Schizophrenia,* 1971, **1,** 161–174.

ROBERTSON, J., & BOWLBY, J. Responses of young children to separation from their mothers. *Courrier de la centre internationale de l'enfance,* 1952, **2,** 131–142.

ROBINS, L. N. *Deviant children grown up: A sociological and psychiatric study of sociopathic personality.* Baltimore: Williams and Wilkins, 1966.

ROBINSON, H. B. *Social-cultural deprivation as a form of child abuse.* Governor's Council on Child Abuse. Raleigh: North Carolina State Board of Health, 1967.

ROBINSON, H. B., & ROBINSON, N. M. *The mentally retarded child: A psychological approach.* New York: McGraw-Hill, 1965.

ROBINSON, H. B., & ROBINSON, N. M. Mental retardation. In P. H. Mussen, ed.,

Carmichael's Manual of Child Psychology. New York: Wiley, 1970, **2,** 615–658.

ROBINSON, N. M., & ROBINSON, H. B. A follow-up study of children of low birthweight and control children at school age. *Pediatrics,* 1965, **35,** 425–433.

ROBINSON, W. P. The elaborated code in working class language. *Language and Speech,* 1965, **8,** 243–252.

ROEPER, A., & SIGEL, I. Finding the clue to children's thought processes. In W. W. Hartup and N. L. Smothergill, *The young child.* Washington, D.C.: National Association for Education of Young Children, 1967.

ROSEKRANS, M. A. Imitation in children as a function of perceived similarity to a social model and vicarious reinforcement. *Journal of Personality and Social Psychology,* 1967, **7,** 307–315.

ROSEN, B. C. The reference group approach to the parental factor in attitude and behavior formation. *Social Forces,* 1955, **34,** 137–144.

ROSEN, B. C., & D'ANDRADE, R. The psychological origins of achievement motivation. *Sociometry,* 1959, **22,** 185–218.

ROSEN, B. M., BAHN, A. K., & KRAMER, M. Demographic and diagnostic characteristics of psychiatric clinic outpatients in the U.S.A., 1961. *American Journal of Orthopsychiatry,* 1964, **24,** 455–467.

ROSENBERG, B. G., & SUTTON-SMITH, B. Ordinal position and sex-role identification. *Genetic Psychology Monographs,* 1964, **70,** 297–328.

ROSENBERG, B. G., & SUTTON-SMITH, B. Family interaction effects on masculinity-femininity. *Journal of Personality and Social Psychology,* 1968, **8,** 117–120.

ROSENBERG, M. *Society and the adolescent self-image.* Princeton, N.J.: Princeton University Press, 1965.

ROSENHAN, D., & WHITE, G. M. Observation and rehearsal as determinants of prosocial behavior. *Journal of Personality and Social Psychology,* 1967, **5,** 424–431.

ROSENTHAL, D. *Genetic theory and abnormal behavior.* New York: McGraw-Hill, 1970.

ROSENTHAL, D., & KETY, S. S., eds. *The transmission of schizophrenia.* London: Pergamon Press, 1968.

ROSOW, I., & CHELLAM, G. An awareness-of-death scale. In *Proceedings of the 7th International Congress of Gerontology,* Vienna, 1966, **6,** 163–165.

ROSOW, I. *Social integration of the aged.* New York: The Free Press, 1967.

ROSS, A. O. *Behavior disorders of children.* New York: General Learning Press, 1971.

ROSS, A. O. *Psychological disorders of children: A behavioral approach to theory, research, and therapy.* New York: McGraw-Hill, 1974.

ROTTER, J. B. *Social learning and clinical psychology.* Englewood Cliffs, N.J.: Prentice-Hall, 1954.

ROTTER, J. B., CHANCE, J. E., & PHARES, E. J. *Applications of a social learning theory of personality.* New York: Holt, Rinehart, & Winston, Inc., 1972.

RUBIN, I. Sex and aging man and woman. In C. E. Vincent, ed., *Human sexuality in medical education and practice.* Springfield, Ill.: Charles C. Thomas, 1968, pp. 517–531.

RUCH, F. L., & ZIMBARDO, P. G. *Psychology and life.* 8th ed. Glenview, Ill.: Scott Foresman, 1971.

RUDNICK, M., STERRITT, G. M., & FLAX, M. Auditory and visual rhythm perception and reading ability. *Child Development,* 1967, **38,** 581–588.

RUEBUSH, B. K., & WAITE, R. R. Oral dependency in anxious and defensive children, *Merrill-Palmer Quarterly,* 1961, **7,** 181–190.

SAINT-ANNE DARGASSIES, S. Part V: Neurological maturation of the premature infant of 28 to 41 weeks gestational age. In F. Falkner, ed., *Human development.* Philadelphia: W. B. Saunders, 1966, pp. 306–326.

SALAPATEK, P., & KESSEN, W. Visual scanning of triangles by the human newborn. *Journal of Experimental Child Psychology,* 1966, **3,** 155–167.

SANGER, M. D. Language learning in infancy: A review of the autistic hypothesis and an observational study of infants. Unpublished Ed.D. Thesis, Harvard University, 1955.

SAUNDERS, C. *Care of the dying.* London: Macmillan, 1960.

SAVITSKY, J. C., ROGERS, R. W., IZARD, C. E., & LIEBERT, R. M. The role of frustration and anger in the imitation of filmed aggression against a human victim. *Psychological Reports,* 1971, **29,** 807–810.

SCARR, S. Social introversion-extroversion as a heritable response. *Child Development,* 1969, **40,** 823–832.

SCHACHTER, S. *The psychology of affiliation.* Stanford: Stanford University Press, 1959.

SCHAEFER, E. S., BELL, R. Q., & BAYLEY, N. Development of a maternal behavior research instrument. *Journal of Genetic Psychology,* 1959, **95,** 83–104.

SCHAEFER, W. S., & BAYLEY, N. Maternal behavior, child behavior and their intercorrelations from infancy through adolescence. *Monographs of the Society for Research in Child Development,* 1963, **28,** 1–27.

SCHAFFER, H. R., & CALLENDER, W. M. Psychological effects of hospitalization in infancy. *Pediatrics,* 1959, **24,** 528–539.

SCHAFFER, H. R., & EMERSON, P. E. The development of social attachments in infancy. *Monographs of the Society for Research in Child Development,* 1964, **29,** No. 3.

SCHAIE, C. W. A general model for the study of developmental problems: Symposium on research methods in developmental psychology. *American Psychologist,* 1964, **19,** 537.

SCHEERENBERGER, R. C. Mental retardation: Definition, classification, and prevalence. *Mental Retardation Abstract,* 1964, **1,** 432–441.

SCHMEIDLER, G. The relation of fetal activity and the activity of the mother. *Child Development,* 1941, **12,** 63–68.

SCHNEIRLA, T. C. An evolutionary and developmental theory of biphasic processes underlying approach and withdrawal. In M. R. Jones, ed., *Nebraska symposium on motivation,* 1959. Lincoln: University of Nebraska Press, 1959.

Scottish Council for Research in Education. *The intelligence of Scottish children.* London: University of London Press, 1933.

SEARS, R. R., MACCOBY, E. E., & LEVIN, H. *Patterns of child rearing.* Evanston, Ill.: Row Peterson, 1957.

SEARS, R. R., WHITING, J. W. M., NOWLIS, V., & SEARS, P. S. Some child-rearing antecedents of dependency and aggression in young children, *Genetic Psychology Monographs,* 1953, **47,** 135–234.

SEASHORE, H. G., WESMAN, A. G., & DOPPELT, J. E. The standardization of the Wechsler Intelligence Scale for Children. *Journal of Consulting Psychology,* 1950, **14,** 99–110.

SEVERY, L. J., & DAVIS, K. E. Helping behavior among normal and retarded children. *Child Development,* 1971, **42,** 1017–1031.

SHANAS, E. The aged report on their health problems. In A. Simon and L. J. Epstein, eds., *Aging in modern society.* Washington, D.C.: American Psychiatric Association, 1968.

SHANTZ, C., & SIGEL, I. Logical operations and concepts of conservation in children. Report to Office of Education, U.S. Department of Health, Education & Welfare, June 1967.

SHEPHERD, M., OPPENHEIM, A. N., & MITCHELL, S. Childhood behavior disorders and the child guidance clinic: An epidemiological study. *Journal of Psychology and Psychiatry,* 1966, **7,** 39–52.

SHERMAN, M., & KEY, C. B. The intelligence of isolated mountain children. *Child Development,* 1932, **3,** 279–290.

SHERMAN, M., & SHERMAN, J. C. Sensorimotor responses in infants. *Journal of Comparative Psychology,* 1925, **5,** 53–68.

SHIELDS, J. *Monozygotic twins brought up apart and brought up together.* London: Oxford University Press, 1962.

SHINN, M. W. *The development of the senses in the first three years of life.* Berkeley: University of California Publications in Education, 1907.

SHIPMAN, V., & HESS, R. D. Social class and sex differences in the utilization of language and the consequences for cognitive development. Paper presented at Midwest Psychological Association, Chicago, April 1965.

SHIRLEY, M. M. The first two years: A study of twenty-five babies. *Intellectual development.* Institute of Child Welfare Monograph Series No. 7. Minneapolis:

University of Minnesota Press, 1933, 1961.

SHOCK, N. W. Biologic concepts of aging. In A. Simon and L. J. Epstein, eds., *Aging in modern society.* Washington, D.C.: American Psychiatric Association, 1968, pp. 1–25.

SHRUT, S. D. Attitudes toward old age and death. *Mental Hygiene,* 1958, **42,** 259–266.

SHUEY, A. M. *The testing of Negro intelligence.* 2d ed. Lynchburg, Va.: Bell, 1966.

SHYBUT, J. Delay of gratification and severity of psychological disturbance among hospitalized psychiatric patients. *Journal of Consulting and Clinical Psychology,* 1968, **32,** 462–468.

SIDMAN, M. *Tactics of scientific research.* New York: Basic Books, 1960.

SIEGLER, R. S., & LIEBERT, R. M. Effects of presenting relevant rules and complete feedback on the conservation of liquid quantity task. *Developmental Psychology,* 1972a, **7,** 133–138.

SIEGLER, R. S., & LIEBERT, R. M. Learning of liquid quantity relationships as a function of rules and feedback, number of training problems, and age of subject. *Proceedings of the 80th Annual Convention of the American Psychological Association,* 1972b, **7,** 117–118.

SIMPSON, B. R. The wandering IQ: Is it time to settle down? *Journal of Psychology,* 1939, **7,** 351–367.

SIMPSON, R. L. Parental influence, anticipatory socialization, and social mobility. *American Sociological Review,* 1962, **27,** 517–522.

SINGER, J. L. Delayed gratification and ego development: Implications for clinical and experimental research. *Journal of*

Consulting Psychology, 1955, **19,** 259–266.

SINNOT, E. W., DUNN, L. C., & DOBZHANSKY, T. *Principles of genetics.* New York: McGraw-Hill, 1958.

SKEELS, H. M. Mental development of children in foster homes. *Journal of Consulting Psychology,* 1938, **2,** 33–43.

SKEELS, H. M., & FILMORE, E. A. Mental development of children from underprivileged homes. *Journal of Genetic Psychology,* 1937, **50,** 427–439.

SKEELS, H. M., UPDEGRAFF, R., WELLMAN, B. L., & WILLIAMS, H. M. A study of environmental stimulation: An orphanage preschool project. *University of Iowa Studies in Child Welfare,* 1938, **15,** No. 4.

SKINNER, B. F. *Walden two.* London: MacMillan, 1948.

SKINNER, B. F. *Science and human behavior.* New York: Macmillan, 1953.

SKINNER, B. F. *Verbal behavior.* New York: Appleton-Century-Crofts, 1957.

SKINNER, B. F. *The technology of teaching.* New York: Appleton-Century-Crofts, 1968.

SKODAK, M. Children in foster homes: A study of mental development. *University of Iowa Studies in Child Welfare,* 1939, **16,** No. 1.

SKODAK, M., & SKEELS, H. M. A final follow-up study of 100 adopted children. *Journal of Genetic Psychology,* 1949, **75,** 85–125.

SLATER, E. A review of earlier evidence on genetic factors in schizophrenia. In Rosenthal and Kety, eds., 1968, pp. 15–26. [See p. 644.]

SLOBIN, D. I., & WELSH, C. A. Elicited imitation as a research tool in developmental psycholinguistics. In C. A. Ferguson and D. I. Slobin, eds., *Readings on child language acquisition*. New York: Holt, Rinehart, & Winston, in press.

SLOCUM, W. C. Some factors associated with happiness in unbroken homes. *Family Life Coordination*, 1958, **6,** 35–39.

SLUCKIN, W. *Imprinting and early learning*. Chicago: Aldine Publishing Company, 1965.

SMEDSLUND, J. Transitivity of preference patterns as seen by pre-school children. *Scandinavian Journal of Psychology*, 1960, **1,** 49–54.

SMEDSLUND, J. The acquisition of conservation of substance and weight in children: II. External reinforcement of conservation of weight and of the operations of addition and subtraction. *Scandinavian Journal of Psychology*, 1961a, **2,** 71–84.

SMEDSLUND, J. The acquisition of conservation of substance and weight in children: IV. Attempt at extinction of the visual components of the weight concept. *Scandinavian Journal of Psychology*, 1961b, **2,** 153–155.

SMEDSLUND, J. The acquisition of conservation of substance and weight in children. *Scandinavian Journal of Psychology*, 1961c, **2,** 11–20.

SMITH, D. H. A speaker's model project to enhance pupil's self-esteem. *Journal of Negro Education*, 1967, **36,** 177–180.

SMITH, H. T. A comparison of interview and observation measures of mother behavior. *Journal of Abnormal Social Psychology*, 1958, **57,** 278–282.

SMITH, M. S. An investigation of the development of the sentence and the extent of vocabulary in young children. *University of Iowa Studies in Child Welfare*, 1926, **3,** No. 5.

SMITH, R. T. A comparison of socioenvironmental factors in monozygotic and dizygotic twins, testing an assumption. In S. G. Vandenberg, ed., *Methods and goals in human behavior genetics*. New York: Academic Press, Inc., 1965.

SOLOMON, R. L. Punishment. *American Psycholoist*, 1964, **19,** 239–253.

SONTAG, L. W. Effect of fetal activity on the nutritional state of the infant at birth. *American Journal of Diseases of Children*, 1940, **60,** 621–630.

SONTAG, L. W., BAKER, C. T., & NELSON, V. L. Mental growth and personality development: A longitudinal study. *Monographs for Society for Research in Child Development*, 1958, **23,** No. 68.

SONTAG, L. W., REYNOLDS, E. L., & TORBET, V. Status of infant at birth as related to basal metabolism of mothers in pregnancy. *American Journal of Obstetrics and Gynecology*, 1944, **48,** 208–214.

SONTAG, L. W., & WALLACE, R. F. The effect of cigarette smoking during pregnancy upon the fetal heart rate. *American Journal of Obstetrics and Gynecology*, 1935, pp. 3–8.

SPARK, M. *Memento mori*. (Time Reading Program No. 17.) Chicago: Time-Life Books, 1964.

SPITZ, R. A. Hospitalism: A follow-up report. *Psychoanalytic Studies of Children*, 1946, **2,** 113–117.

SPITZ, R. A. The role of ecological factors in emotional development in infancy. *Child Development*, 1949, **20,** 145–155.

SPITZ, R. A. *A genetic field theory of ego formation: Its implications for pathology*. New York: International University Press, 1959.

SPITZ, R. A. *The first year of life*. New York: International Universities Press, 1965.

SPIVACK, G. LEVINE, M., & SPRIGLE, H. Intelligence test performance and the delay function of the ego. *Journal of Consulting Psychology,* 1959, **23,** 428–431.

SPOCK, B. M. *The common sense book of baby and child care.* New York: Duell, Sloan, and Pearce, 1946.

SPRINGER, D. Development in young children of an understanding of time and the clocks. *Journal of Genetic Psychology,* 1952, **80,** 83–96.

STAATS, A. W., & STAATS, C. K. Attitudes established by classical conditioning. *Journal of Abnormal and Social Psychology,* 1958, **57,** 37–40.

STAMBAK, M. Contribution à l'étude du développement moteur chez le nourrisson. *Enfance,* 1956, **9**(4), 49–59.

STAPLES, F. R. The responses of infants to color. *Journal of Experimental Psychology,* 1937, **15,** 119–141.

STARKWEATHER, E., & ROBERTS, K. IQ changes occurring during nursery attendance at the Merrill-Palmer School. *39th Yearbook of the National Society for the Study of Education,* 1940, Part II, 315–336.

STAUB, E. The use of role playing and induction in children's learning of helping and sharing behavior. *Child Development,* 1971, **42,** 805–816.

STAUB, E., & SHERK, L. Need for approval, children's sharing behavior, and reciprocity in sharing. *Child Development,* 1970, **41,** 243–252.

STECHLER, G., BRADFORD, S., & LEVY, L. Attention in the newborn: Effect on motility and skin potential. *Science,* 1966, **151,** 1246–1248.

STEIN, A. H., & FRIEDRICH, L. K. Television content and young children's behavior. In J. P. Murray, E. A. Rubinstein, and G. A. Comstock, eds., *Television and social behavior,* Vol. II: *Television and social learning.* Washington, D.C.: U.S.

Government Printing Office, 1972, pp. 202–317.

STEIN, Z., & SUSSER, M. The social distribution of mental retardation. *American Journal of Mental Deficiency,* 1963, **67,** 811–821.

STEINSCHNEIDER, A. Developmental psychophysiology. In Y. Brackbill, ed., *Infancy and early childhood.* New York: Free Press, 1967, pp. 3–47.

STERN, L. W. The psychological methods of testing intelligence. Trans. G. M. Whipple. *Educational Psychology Monographs,* 1914, No. 13.

STEVENSON, H. W. Developmental psychology. In D. Sills, ed., *International encyclopedia of the social sciences.* New York: Macmillan, 1968.

STEVENSON, H. W. Learning in children. In P. H. Mussen, ed., *Carmichael's manual of child development.* New York: Wiley, 1970, **1,** 849–938.

STEVENSON, H. W., & ZIGLER, E. Probability learning in children. *Journal of Experimental Psychology,* 1958, **56,** 185–192.

STODDARD, G. D., & WELLMAN, B. L. *Child psychology.* New York: Macmillan, 1934.

STOKES, R. G., & MADDOX, G. L. Some social factors in retirement adaptation. *Journal of Gerontology,* 1967, **22,** 329–333.

STOTT, L. H., & BALL, R. S. Infant and preschool mental tests: Review and evaluation. *Monographs of the Society for Research in Child Development,* 1965, **30** (No. 3).

STOUWIE, R. J. The effects of inconsistent verbal instructions and experimenter personality characteristics upon children's resistance-to-temptation behavior. *Disserta-*

tion Abstracts International, July 1970, **31** (1–B), 427.

STRAUSS, G. D., & POULOS, R. W. TV and social learning: A summary of the experimental effects of observing filmed aggression. In J. P. Murray, E. A. Rubinstein, and G. A. Comstock, eds., *Television and social behavior,* Vol. II: *Television and social learning.* Washington, D.C.: U.S. Government Printing Office, 1972, pp. 35–40.

STRUPP, H. H. *An introduction to Freud and modern psychoanalysis.* Woodbury, N.Y.: Barron's Educational Series, 1967.

SWENSON, W. M. Attitudes toward death in an aged population. *Gerontology,* 1961, **16**, 49–52.

SYDOW, VON G., & RINNE, A. Very unequal identical twins, *Acta Paediatricia,* 1958, **47**, 163–171.

TANNER, J. M. The regulation of human growth. *Child Development,* 1963, **34**, 816–847.

TANNER, J. M. Physical growth. In P. H. Mussen, ed., *Carmichael's manual of child psychology* (3rd. ed.). New York: Wiley, 1970, Vol. I, pp. 77–155.

TANNER, J. M., TAYLOR, G. R., & the Editors of Time-Life Books. *Growth.* New York: Time-Life Books, 1969.

TAPIA, F., JEKEL, J., & DOMKE, H. Enuresis: An emotional symptom? *Journal of Nervous and Mental Disease,* 1960, **130,** 61–66.

TATE, B. G., & BAROFF, G. S. Aversive control of self-injurious behavior in a psychotic boy. *Behavior Research and Therapy,* 1966, **4,** 281–287.

TELFORD, C. W., & SAWREY, J. M. *The exceptional individual.* Englewood Cliffs, N.J.: Prentice-Hall, Inc., 1972.

TEMPLER, D. I., RUFF, C. F., & FRANKS,

C. M. Death anxiety: Age, sex, and parental resemblance in diverse populations. *Developmental Psychology,* 1971, **4,** 108.

TERMAN, L. M. A preliminary study in the psychology and pedagogy of leadership. *Pedagogical Seminar,* 1904, **11,** 413–451.

TERMAN, L. M. Genius and stupidity: A study of some of the intellectual processes of seven "bright" and seven "dull" boys. *Pedagogical Seminar,* 1906, **13,** 307–373.

TERMAN, L. M. The intelligence quotient of Francis Galton in childhood. *American Journal of Psychology,* 1917, **28,** 209–215.

TERMAN, L. M. Mental and physical traits of a thousand gifted children. In L. M. Terman, ed., *Genetic studies of genius.* Stanford: Stanford University Press, 1925, **1.**

TERMAN, L. M. *Psychological factors in marital happiness.* New York: McGraw-Hill, 1938.

TERMAN, L. M. The discovery and encouragement of exceptional talent. *American Psychologist,* 1954a, **9,** 221–230.

TERMAN, L. M. Scientists and nonscientists in a group of 800 gifted men. *Psychological Monographs,* 1954b, **68,** 1–44.

TERMAN, L. M., & ODEN, M. H. The gifted child grows up. In L. M. Terman, ed., *Genetic studies of genius.* Stanford: Stanford University Press, 1947, **4.**

THOMAS, A., CHESS, S., & BIRCH, H. G. The origin of personality. *Scientific American,* 1970, **223,** 102–109.

THOMAS, A., CHESS, S., BIRCH, H., & HERTZIG, M. E. A longitudinal study of primary reaction patterns in children. *Comprehensive Psychiatry,* 1960, **1,** 103–112.

THOMPSON, G. G. *Child psychology.* 2nd ed. Boston: Houghton-Mifflin, 1962.

THOMPSON, W. R. The inheritance and development of intelligence. *Research Publications of the Association for Research in Nervous and Mental Diseases,* 1954, **33,** 209–331.

THOMPSON, W. R., & MELZACK, R. Early environment. *Scientific American,* 1956, **114,** 38–42.

THORNDIKE, E. L. Animal intelligence: An experimental study of the associative process in animals. *Psychological Review Monograph Supplement,* 1898, **2** (4, Whole No. 8).

THORNDIKE, E. L. *The elements of psychology.* New York: Seiler, 1905.

THURSTONE, L. L., & THURSTONE, T. G. Factorial studies of intelligence. *Psychometric Monograph,* 1941, No. 2.

THURSTONE, T. G. *An evaluation of educated mentally handicapped children in special classes and in regular classes.* U.S. Office of Education, Cooperative Research Project, Project No. OE–SAE–6452. University of North Carolina, 1959.

TIEDEMANN, D. Die vier erste Jahre meiner Kinder. *Journal général d'instruction publique,* April 1863.

TYLER, F. B., RAFFERTY, J., & TYLER, B. Relationships among motivations of parents and their children. *Journal of Genetic Psychology,* 1962, **101,** 69–81.

UGUREL-SEMIN, R. Moral behavior and moral judgment of children. *Journal of Abnormal and Social Psychology,* 1952, **47,** 463–474.

ULLMANN, L., & KRASNER, L., eds. *Case studies in behavior modification.* New York: Holt, Rinehart, & Winston, 1965.

UPDEGRAFF, R. The visual perception of distance in young children and adults: A comparative study. *University of Iowa Studies of Child Welfare,* 1930, **4** (No. 40).

VANDENBERG, S. G. Contributions to twin research in psychology. *Psychological Bulletin,* 1966, **66,** 327–352.

VANDENBERG, S. G. Hereditary factors in normal personality traits (as measured by inventories). In J. Wortis, ed., *Recent advances in biological psychiatry,* Vol. 9. New York: Pelnum, 1967.

VAUGHN, G. M. Ethnic awareness in relation to minority group membership. *Journal of Genetic Psychology,* 1964, **105,** 119–130.

VERWOERDT, A. *Communication with the fatally ill.* Springfield, Ill.: Thomas, 1966.

VERWOERDT, A., & ELMORE, J. L. Psychological reactions in fatal illness: I. The prospect of impending death. *Journal of the American Geriatric Society,* 1967, **15,** 9–19.

VURPILLOT, E. Détails caractéristiques et reconnaissance de formes familières. *Psychologie Française,* 1962, **7,** 147–155.

WAGNER, A. R. Frustration and punishment. In R. N. Haber, ed., *Research on motivation.* New York: Holt, Rinehart & Winston, 1966, pp. 229–239.

WAHL, C. W. The fear of death. *Bulletin of the Menninger Clinic,* 1958, **22,** 214–223.

WALK, R. D., & GIBSON, E. J. A comparative and analytical study of visual depth perception. *Psychological Monographs,* 1961, **75,** (15, Whole No. 519).

WALLACH, L., & SPROTT, R. L. Inducing number conservation in children. *Child Development,* 1964, **35,** 1057–1071.

WALLACH, L., WALL, A. J., & ANDERSON, L. Number conservation: The role of reversibility, addition-subtraction, and misleading perceptual cues. *Child Development,* 1967, **38,** 425–442.

WALLACH, M. A. Creativity. In P. H.

Mussen, ed., *Carmichael's manual of child psychology.* 3rd edition. New York: Wiley, 1970, 1211–1272.

WALLACH, M. A. *The intelligence/creativity distinction.* New York: General Learning Press, 1971.

WALLACH, M. A., & KOGAN, N. *Modes of thinking in young children: A study of the creativity-intelligence distinction.* New York: Holt, Rinehart, & Winston, 1965.

WALLACH, M. A., & WING, C. W. *The talented student: A validation of the creativity-intelligence distinction.* New York: Holt, Rinehart, & Winston, 1969.

WALTERS, R. H. Anxiety and social reinforcement. Paper read at American Psychological Association meetings, 1961.

WALTERS, R. H., & BROWN, M. Studies of reinforcement of aggression, Part III: Transfer of responses to an interpersonal situation. *Child Development,* 1963, **34,** 563–572.

WALTERS, R. H., & BROWN, M. A test of the high-magnitude theory of aggression. *Journal of Experimental Child Psychology,* 1964, **1,** 376–387.

WALTERS, R. H., LEAT, M., & MEZEI, H. Response inhibition and disinhibition through empathetic learning. *Canadian Journal of Psychology,* 1963, **17,** 235–243.

WALTERS, R. H., & RAY, E. Anxiety, social isolation, and reinforcer effectiveness. *Journal of Personality,* 1960, **28,** 354–367.

WARD, W. C. Creativity in young children. *Child Development,* 1968, **39,** 737–754.

WATSON, E. H., & LOWREY, G. H. *Growth and development of children.* Chicago: Year Book Publishers, 1954, 1962.

WATSON, J. B. *Behavior: An introduction to comparative psychology.* New York: Holt, 1914.

WATSON, J. B. *Behaviorism.* New York: Norton, 1924.

WATSON, J. B. *Psychological care of infant and child.* London: Allen and Unwin, 1928.

WATSON, J. B. *Behaviorism.* Chicago: University of Chicago Press, Rev. ed., 1958.

WATSON, J. B., & RAYNER, R. Conditioned emotional reactions. *Journal of Experimental Psychology,* 1920, **3,** 1.

WATSON, J. D. *The double helix.* New York: The New American Library, 1968.

WATSON, J. D. & CRICK, F. H. C. Molecular structure of nucleic acids: A structure for deoxyribose nucleic acid. *Nature,* 1953, **171,** 737–738.

WEIKART, D. P. Early childhood special education for intellectually subnormal and/or culturally different children. Paper prepared for the National Institute in Early Childhood Development, Washington, D.C., October 1971.

WEIKART, D. P. Relationship of curriculim, teaching, and learning in preschool education. In J. C. Stanley, ed., *Preschool programs for the disadvantaged.* Baltimore: Johns Hopkins University Press, 1972, pp. 22–66.

WEINSTEIN, L. Project Re-ED schools for emotionally disturbed children: Effectiveness as viewed by referring agencies, parents, and teachers. *Exceptional Children,* 1969, **35,** 703–711.

WEINSTEIN, L. The evaluation research: The effectiveness of the Re-ED intervention. Unpublished manuscript, George Peabody College for Teachers, 1971.

WEIR, R. H. *Language in the crib.* The Hague: Mouton, 1962.

WEISBERG, P. Social and nonsocial conditioning of infant vocalizations. *Child Development,* 1963, **34,** 377–388.

WEISMAN, A. D., & HACKETT, T. P. Predilection to death: Death and dying as psychiatric problem. *Psychosomatic Medicine,* 1961, **23,** 232–256.

WEITZMAN, B. Behavior therapy and psychotherapy. *Psychological Review,* 1967, **74**(4), 300–317.

WELLMAN, B. L. Some new bases for interpretation of the IQ. *Journal of Genetic Psychology,* 1932a, **41,** 116–126.

WELLMAN, B. L. The effects of preschool attendance upon the IQ. *Journal of Experimental Education,* 1932b, **1,** 48–49.

WELLMAN, B. L. Growth in intelligence under different school environments. *Journal of Experimental Education,* 1934, **3,** 59–83.

WELLMAN, B. L. Mental growth from the preschool to college. *Journal of Experimental Education,* 1937, **6,** 127–138.

WELLMAN, B. L. The intelligence of preschool children as measured by the Merrill-Palmer scale of performance tests. *University of Iowa Studies on Child Welfare,* 1938, **15,** No. 3.

WELLMAN, B. L. The meaning of environment. *39th Yearbook of the National Society for the Study of Education,* 1940, Part 1, 21–40.

WELLMAN, B. L., & COFFEY, H. S. The role of cultural status in intelligence changes for preschool children. *Journal of Experimental Education,* 1936, **5,** 191–202.

WENAR, C., HANDLON, N. W., & GARNER, A. M. Patterns of mothering in psychosomatic disorders and severe emotional disturbances. *Merrill-Palmer Quarterly,* 1960, **6,** (3).

WERNER, H. *Comparative psychology of mental development.* Chicago: Follet, 1948.

WERNER, H., & KAPLAN, E. The acquisition of word meaning: A developmental study. *Monographs of the Society for Research in Child Development,* 1952, **15,** No. 51.

Westinghouse Learning Corporation. *The impact of Head Start: An evaluation of the effects of Head Start experience on children's cognitive and effective development.* Preliminary draft of April 1969. Westinghouse Learning Corporation: Ohio University.

WHITE, B., & HELD, R. Plasticity of sensorimotor development in the human infant. In J. F. Rosenblith and W. Allinsmith, eds., *The causes of behavior.* 2nd ed. Boston: Allyn and Bacon, 1966, pp. 60–71.

WHITEHURST, G. Production of novel and grammatical utterances by young children. *Journal of Experimental Child Psychology,* 1972, **13,** 502–515.

WHITING, J. W. M. Fourth presentation. In J. M. Tanner and B. Inhelder, eds., *Discussions on child development:* II. London: Tavistock, 1954.

WHITING, J. W. M., & CHILD, I. L. *Child training and personality: A cross-cultural study.* New Haven: Yale University Press, 1953.

WICKMAN, E. K. *Children's behavior and teacher's attitudes.* New York: Commonwealth Fund, 1928.

WIENER, G. Scholastic achievement at age 12–13 of prematurely born infants. *Journal of Special Education,* 1968, **2,** 237–250.

WIENER, G., RIDER, R. V., OPPEL, W. C., FISCHER, L. K., & HARPER, P. A. Correlates of low birthweight: Psychological status of 6–7 years of age. *Pediatrics,* 1965, **35,** 434–444.

WILLERMAN, L., & CHURCHILL, J. A. Intelligence and birthweight in identical twins. *Child Development,* 1967, **38,** 623–629.

WILLIAMS, R. J. *The human frontier.* New York: Harcourt, Brace & World, 1946.

WILSON, W. H., & NUNNALLY, J. C. A naturalistic investigation of acquired meaning in children. *Psychonomic Science,* 1971, **23,** 149–150.

WINDLE, W. F., ed. *Neurological and psychological deficits of asphyxia neonatorum.* Springfield, Ill.: Charles C. Thomas, 1958.

WINER, B. J. *Statistical principles in experimental design.* New York: McGraw-Hill, 1962.

WINTERBOTTOM, M. R. The relation of childhood training in independence to achievement motivation. Unpublished doctoral dissertation, University of Michigan, 1953.

WITKIN, H. A. The perception of the upright. *Scientific American,* February 1959 (offprint).

WITTENBORN, J. R. A study of adoptive children: III, Relationship between some aspects of development and some aspects of environment for adoptive children. *Psychological Monographs,* 1956, **70,** No. 410.

WITTY, P., ed. *The gifted child.* Boston: Heath, 1951.

WITTY, P. A study of pupil's interests, grades 9, 10, 11, 12. *Education,* 1961, **82,** 169–174.

WOHLWILL, J. F. Developmental studies of perception. *Psychological Bulletin,* 1960, **57,** 249–288.

WOHLWILL, J. F., & LOWE, R. C. Experimental analysis of the development of the conservation of number. *Child Development,* 1962, **33,** 153–167.

WOLFF, P. H. *The developmental psychologies of Jean Piaget and psychoanalysis.* New York: International University Press, 1960.

WOLFF, P. H. The causes, controls, and organization of behavior in the neonate. *Psychological Issues,* 1966, **5**(1), Monograph 17, 1–105.

WOLPE, J. *Psychotherapy by reciprocal inhibition.* Stanford: Stanford University Press, 1958.

WOODROW, H. Intelligence and its measurement: A symposium. *Journal of Educational Psychology,* 1921, **12,** 207–210.

WYLIE, R. C. Children's estimates of their schoolwork ability, as a function of sex, race, and socioeconomic level. *Journal of Personality,* 1963, **31,** 203–224.

YONGE, G. D. Structure of experience and functional fixedness. *Journal of Educational Psychology,* 1966, **57,** 115–120.

ZAPOROZHETS, A. V. The development of perception in the preschool child. In P. H. Mussen, ed., *European research in cognitive development: Monographs of the Society for Research in Child Development,* 1965, **30** (2, Whole No. 100), 82–101.

ZIGLER, E. Motivational and emotional factors in the behavior of the retarded. *Connecticut Medicine,* August 1968, pp. 584–592.

ZIGLER, E., & BALLA, D. Developmental cause of responsiveness to social reinforcement in normal children and institutionalized retarded children. *Developmental Psychology,* 1972, **6,** 66–73.

AUTHOR INDEX

AUTHOR INDEX

Abravanel, E., 196
Adelson, J., 562
Adelson, R., 544
Ainsworth, M. D. S., 71–72, 328, 341, 344–47
Aisenberg, R. B., 601
Aiu, P., 178
Allen, L., 259, 264, 516, 518
Allen, M. K., 141, 422
Allinsmith, W., 205, 394, 395
Alpern, G. D., 512
Amatruda, C. S., 83, 260
Ambrose, J. A., 71
Ames, E. W., 188
Ames, L. B., 81, 82–84, 261
Amsel, A., 413
Anastasi, A., 8, 274, 283, 363
Anderson, E. P., 341
Anderson, L. D., 227, 259, 261
Anderson, R. C., 473
Anderson, R. M., 473
Andres, D. H., 398
André-Thomas, 67
Anthony, E. J., 516, 519, 520, 531
Antonova, T. G., 68
Apgar, V., 58
Aries, P., 3
Aronfreed, J., 138, 390
Asling, C. W., 55
Atkin, C. K., 380
Atkinson, I. W., 428
Augenbraun, B., 524
Ausubel, D. P., 562
Axline, V. M., 533

Babson, S., 60
Back, K. W., 591

Badger, E. D., 507
Baer, D. M., 143–45, 355
Bahn, A. K., 516–17
Baker, C. T., 264, 276
Baldwin, A. L., 276, 323, 325
Baldwin, W. K., 24, 212, 214, 443
Ball, R. S., 265
Balla, D., 439, 440
Baller, W. R., 273
Bandler, L., 524
Bandura, A., 106, 145–49, 227, 309, 357, 364, 372–75, 377, 417, 418, 420, 425, 527, 544, 552
Barbe, W. B., 448
Barclay, A., 441
Barlow, F. P., 269
Baroff, G. S., 44–45
Baron, R. A., 382
Barrett, B. H., 520
Battle, E., 432
Bauer, E. E., 443
Bayley, N., 23, 29, 66–67, 87, 97–98, 111, 257, 259, 261, 262, 269, 276, 278, 451
Beach, D. R., 156
Beck, B. M., 568
Beilin, H., 223
Bell, R. Q., 65–67
Bell, S. M., 344, 346
Beller, E. K., 349, 355, 358
Bellugi, U. (See Bellugi-Klima)
Bellugi-Klima, U., 22, 304, 307, 313, 314
Belmont, L., 196
Benda, C. E., 438
Bender, L., 524
Berberich, J. P., 19
Bereiter, C., 510–12
Berko, J., 307, 308

657

SUBJECT INDEX

SUBJECT INDEX